O9-AIG-873

**Revision Guide, Documentation at a
Glance, and a list of Common Errors
boxes appear in the rear inside cover.**

Writing in the World Projects

Writing in the World projects are self-contained writing projects on the **Penguin Handbook Companion Website**. Projects contain complete information about the rhetorical situation as well as files of all documents necessary to complete the project.

Clean Up Towering Pines (or Not)!
A Newspaper Editorial

You have been invited to write a guest editorial for the *Hammond Courier* to persuade others in your community to support your plan for Towering Pines, a local wilderness preserve.

Homelessness in Portland: A Reflective Essay

The City Council is considering passing an ordinance that some residents believe is an attempt to get homeless people off the streets and out of sight. In this context, you have decided to interview two homeless men you often see outside the University bookstore, and write a reflective essay based on your interviews.

Visit Big Bend! A Persuasive Brochure

You work for an advertising firm in Alpine, Texas, that has been hired to produce a persuasive brochure on the Big Bend region for vacationing retirees.

Help a Neighbor Learn to Read:
An Informational Home Page

A volunteer for Literacy Memphis, which provides instruction in basic reading skills to adults, you have been asked to design and write a home page that will encourage other community members to volunteer as tutors.

Assessing the "Most Feared Man in Hollywood": An Academic Review

Harry Knowles is the founder and chief writer for *Ain't It Cool News,* a popular Web site for movie reviews and Hollywood gossip. Knowles is a controversial figure who has been called the "most feared man in Hollywood." You have been asked to review his work as a movie critic for *College Review*, an academic journal that publishes work by undergraduates.

**Get your assignments online at
www.ablongman.com/faigley.**

THE
Penguin
Handbook

The Penguin Handbook–

A handbook students *want* to use.

In *The Penguin Handbook,* Lester Faigley rethinks the way handbooks present information and ideas with a reference that is tailored for today's visually and technologically-oriented students. To create this text, he drew on student feedback and a wealth of classroom experience to design a handbook that would give students the information they need in a format that they would actually use. Addressing the changing nature of today's students as well as today's writing assignments, this text offers unique features such as "At-a-glance" documentation pages which help students visually understand how to cite sources, and "Common Errors" boxes for grammar and style which help students identify the building blocks necessary for academic writing. Additional visuals throughout the text help students with everything from how to construct a descriptive paragraph, to understanding how visual information can be used in a paper, presentation, or Web site.

Looking at Writing in a New Way

Finally, there is a handbook that offers students relevant, useful images that bring the text to life *and* illustrate the concepts being discussed.

A stunning full color design includes **photographs that accompany everyday topics such as writing paragraphs, freewriting, and writing to inform or reflect.**

42

Narration or Process

Narrative paragraphs tell a story for a reason. Organized by time, narratives explain a series of events in the order they occur. This approach is useful when the temporal order of ideas or events is essential to their logic, such as how-to writing.

The ascent goes easier than they expected. In two hours they reach the yak pastures where they will make the high camp. The view from the high camp is spectacular, with Dhaulagiri in clouds above them and the three sunlit summits of Nilgiri across the valley, with snow plumes blowing from their tops. Jim and Lester drop their packs at the campsite and continue walking to scout the route above the camp that they will follow in the darkness of early morning the next day. They find a steep path that parallels a fern-lined gorge, now rich in fall color. It is the lushest forest they have seen in Nepal. They congratulate each other on their decision to attempt the climb to the Dhaulagiri icefall, unaware that they will soon experience the mountain's furious weather, even on its lower slopes.

Verbs establish the sequence of events to orient the reader in time.

Narrative paragraphs often include description to orient the reader in space.

18

Point of View in Verbal Texts

At the most basic level, point of view means selecting among first person (I, we), second person (you), and third person (he, she, it) when you write about your subject. Using *I* puts the relationship between writer and reader in the foreground. Using *you* emphasizes the writer or the teller of the story in fiction. Using *he, she,* or *it* keeps the focus more on the subject and diminishes the prominence of the writer.

Point of view is also determined by how you locate yourself in relation to your subject. Whether you write in first or third person, you can write about a subject from close, firsthand experience or you can place yourself at a distance from your subject, giving the sense of being an impartial observer offering an overview.

You can write about the Grand Canyon as if you were looking out from the window of an airplane.

The Grand Canyon is 218 miles long, from 4 to 18 miles wide, and over a mile deep in some places. From the sky the contrast between the north and south rims of the Grand Canyon is striking. The north rim is above 9,000 feet and covered by a thick forest; the south rim is about 1,200 feet lower than the north rim and has much less vegetation. The bottom of the canyon is the northernmost extension of the Sonoran Desert, where several different species of cacti, thistle, and other desert plants are found.

You can write about the Grand Canyon from the bottom.

On a late afternoon in August with the temperature well over 100°, we paddled our kayaks into Elves Chasm after getting pounded most of the day by some of the biggest rapids in the Grand Canyon—Granite, Hermit, Crystal, Serpentine, and Waltenberg—taking our casualties in turbulent swims when rolls failed. The cool trickle from the waterfall brought relief to the scorching canyon. The droplets glistened on the intense green moss and ferns like thousands of gems.

Chapters on Words and Images, Critical Reading and Viewing, and Design address issues of visual rhetoric and literacy that students are beginning to confront with increasing frequency.

Rethinking the Way Handbooks Present Information

Presenting information tailored to the needs of today's students means more than just using visuals — it means presenting information in ways that are more visually accessible.

"At-a-Glance" documentation pages help students better understand the process of citation, and illustrate more citation models more clearly, than any other handbook on the market!

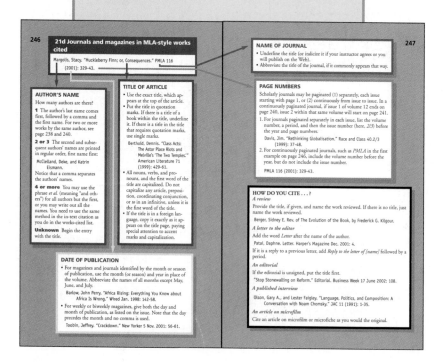

246   21d Journals and magazines in MLA-style works cited

Margolis, Stacy. "Huckleberry Finn; or, Consequences." PMLA 116 (2001): 329-43.

AUTHOR'S NAME

How many authors are there?

1 The author's last name comes first, followed by a comma and the first name. For two or more works by the same author, see page 238 and 240.

2 or 3 The second and subsequent authors' names are printed in regular order, first name first:

McClelland, Deke, and Katrin Eismann.

Notice that a comma separates the authors' names.

4 or more You may use the phrase *et al.* (meaning "and others") for all authors but the first, or you may write out all the names. You need to use the same method in the in-text citation as you do in the works-cited list.

Unknown Begin the entry with the title.

TITLE OF ARTICLE

- Use the exact title, which appears at the top of the article.
- Put the title in quotation marks. If there is a title of a book within the title, underline it. If there is a title in the title that requires quotation marks, use single marks.

  Berthold, Dennis. "Class Acts: The Astor Place Riots and Melville's 'The Two Temples.'" American Literature 71 (1999): 429-61.

- All nouns, verbs, and pronouns, and the first word of the title are capitalized. Do not capitalize any article, preposition, coordinating conjunction, or in an infinitive, unless it is the first word of the title.
- If the title is in a foreign language, copy it exactly as it appears on the title page, paying special attention to accent marks and capitalization.

NAME OF JOURNAL

- Underline the title (or italicize it if your instructor agrees or you will publish on the Web).
- Abbreviate the title of the journal, if it commonly appears that way.

247

PAGE NUMBERS

Scholarly journals may be paginated (1) separately, each issue starting with page 1, or (2) continuously from issue to issue. In a continuously paginated journal, if issue 1 of volume 12 ends on page 240, issue 2 within that same volume will start on page 241.

1. For journals paginated separately in each issue, list the volume number, a period, and then the issue number (here, 2/3) before the year and page numbers.

   Davis, Jim. "Rethinking Globalisation." Race and Class 40.2/3 (1999): 37-48.

2. For continuously paginated journals, such as *PMLA* in the first example on page 246, include the volume number before the year, but do not include the issue number.

   PMLA 116 (2001): 329-43.

HOW DO YOU CITE . . . ?

A review

Provide the title, if given, and name the work reviewed. If there is no title, just name the work reviewed.

Berger, Sidney E. Rev. of The Evolution of the Book, by Frederick G. Kilgour.

A letter to the editor

Add the word *Letter* after the name of the author.

Patai, Daphne. Letter. Harper's Magazine Dec. 2001: 4.

If it is a reply to a previous letter, add *Reply to the letter of [name]* followed by a period.

An editorial

If the editorial is unsigned, put the title first.

"Stop Stonewalling on Reform." Editorial. Business Week 17 June 2002: 108.

A published interview

Olson, Gary A., and Lester Faigley. "Language, Politics, and Composition: A Conversation with Noam Chomsky." JAC 11 (1991): 1-35.

An article on microfilm

Cite an article on microfilm or microfiche as you would the original.

DATE OF PUBLICATION

- For magazines and journals identified by the month or season of publication, use the month (or season) and year in place of the volume. Abbreviate the names of all months except May, June, and July.

  Barlow, John Perry. "Africa Rising: Everything You Know about Africa Is Wrong." Wired Jan. 1998: 142-58.

- For weekly or biweekly magazines, give both the day and month of publication, as listed on the issue. Note that the day precedes the month and no comma is used.

  Toobin, Jeffrey. "Crackdown." New Yorker 5 Nov. 2001: 56-61.

Helping Students Find the Information They Need

Special features ensure that students find what they need – in a format they can quickly apply to their work.

Practical, accessible coverage of grammar and style issues includes the use of 40 "Common Errors" boxes. A key at the back of the book makes it easy to find topics quickly.

frag 33 Fragments, Run-ons, and Comma Splices

The university's enrollment rose unexpectedly during the fall semester. Because the percentage of students who accepted offers of admission was much higher than previous years and fewer students than usual dropped out or transferred.

Such fragments compel a reader to stop and reread. When a sentence starts with *because*, we expect to find a main clause later. Instead, the *because* clause refers back to the previous sentence. The writer no doubt knew that the fragment gave reasons why enrollment rose, but a reader must stop to determine the connection.

Common Errors

Recognizing fragments

If you can spot fragments, you can fix them. Grammar checkers can find some of them, but they miss many fragments and identify other sentences wrongly as fragments. Ask these questions when you are checking for sentence fragments.

1. **Does the sentence have a subject?** Except for commands, sentences need subjects:

   Jane spent every cent of credit she had available. And then applied for more cards.

2. **Does the sentence have a complete verb?** Sentences require complete verbs. Verbs that end in *-ing* must have an auxiliary verb to be complete.

   Ralph keeps changing majors. He trying to figure out what he really wants to do after college.

3. **If the sentence begins with a subordinate clause, is there a main clause in the same sentence?**

   Even though Seattle is cloudy much of the year, no American city more beautiful when the sun shines. Which is one reason people continue to move there.

Remember:

1. A sentence must have a subject and complete verb.
2. A subordinate clause cannot stand alone as a sentence.

For step-by-step discussion, examples, and practice of this common error, go to www.ablongman.com/faigley/000

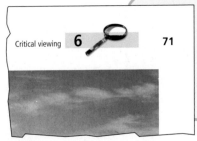

Critical viewing **6** **71**

Photographic icons are used in tandem with a keyword for each chapter to offer yet another way to locate needed material.

Writing for College and Beyond

The *Penguin* handbooks offer a unique blend of coverage of **academic and real-world approaches** to writing and communication. While academic writing is emphasized throughout, the texts also include coverage of written genres that are used more typically outside the classroom.

7e A REFLECTIVE MAGAZINE ARTICLE

Sylvia Herrera wanted to write an article for a college magazine produced by Mexican American students. She decided to write a review of the Bob Bullock Texas State History Museum in Austin, Texas. To make the review more appealing to her audience, she wrote it as a personal reflection about her first visit to the museum.

Whose Story?
Sylvia Herrera

When the Bob Bullock Texas State History museum opened in March 2001, it advertised itself as "The Story of Texas." It still calls itself the story of Texas in letters chiseled into the top of the building, on its Web site, on signs directing visitors to the museum, and even on the refrigerator magnets you can buy in the gift shop. When I first saw the slogan, I wondered how there could be "the" story of Texas, since Texas has been culturally diverse throughout its history as a part of Mexico that became a separate nation and later a state. Shortly Texas will have no one group as a majority. I grew up in the Rio Grande Valley, where the great majority of the population, like me, is Mexican American. How was this new museum going to present *my* story? I had to go and find out.

When I first walked into the lobby, I noticed the large mosaic on the floor but I couldn't figure out what it depicted. I just saw a campfire and a bunch of wiggly figures. Someone next to me told their kids that they'd be able to see the entire mosaic from the third floor. I decided to wait and do the same.

The first exhibit I saw was the "It Ain't Braggin' if it's True" (one of my

friends told me I had to see the shrine to Lance Armstrong and the rhinestone car). The name of the exhibit didn't make much sense to me though; aren't all museum exhibits, especially ones about history, supposed to be true? The big banner in the middle of the room didn't help much either. It simply said "Vision" and had a quote about how only those with great vision can see opportunity where others see empty space. Maybe those who have this type of vision get the braggin' rights?

Texas was never a big empty space. The Spaniards and later the

Part Two addresses three different purposes for writing: writing to reflect, to inform, and to persuade. Essays for each purpose are discussed, as well as genres such as the reflective magazine article, the brochure, and the resume.

Writing in the World

Stereotypical images

Most Americans now realize that overtly racist images are offensive. The notable exception is representations of American Indians. Currently over eighty college sports team (along with a few professional teams) have American Indian mascots. These mascots have long been controversial. Most were adopted in the early decades of the twentieth century when European Americans enjoyed putting on paint and feathers and "playing Indian." Supporters of the mascots claim that they honor American Indians. Critics argue that the mascots perpetuate stereotypes of American Indians as primitive, wild, and bellicose. Furthermore, fans of schools that compete with those that have Indian mascots often shout derogatory slogans and create derogatory images of American Indians.

Subtle stereotyping comes through the media. Based on images in the news media, many Americans think that women in Islamic countries cover their faces in public, but this practice is typical only in Saudi Arabia and the most conservative sectors of Islamic society. The majority of men in Islamic countries do not have long beards. Again, the issue is accuracy. Some people in Holland still wear wooden shoes, but wooden shoes do not represent everyday Dutch footwear.

Sign over a service station in New Mexico

"Writing in the World" boxes offer tips on writing contexts, with answers to questions such as: 'When, where, and why do various rules of usage apply?' or 'What is the norm in the professional world?'

Reference for Using Computers

Whether conducting research on the Internet, creating visuals for papers and oral presentations, or designing documents and Web pages, *The Penguin Handbook* provides help on any issue one is likely to encounter when writing with computers in today's academic environment and beyond.

 Start a working bibliography **17**   209

Computer Strategies

Organize your bookmarks and save them on a disk

Bookmarks on Netscape and Favorites on Explorer allow you to return quickly to Web sites you have visited. But when you do research and frequently add new bookmarks, you'll soon have a long list that makes it hard to find the particular Web site you want to return to. At this point you need to organize your bookmarks into folders:

1. Open the Bookmarks menu and select Edit Bookmarks. You'll see a list of your bookmarks.
2. Open the File menu and select New Folder.
3. Name the folder and drag the bookmarks into it.

You can also save your bookmark file on a disk by using the Save As command on the File menu. Then you can take your bookmarks with you and use them on more than one computer. This is very handy if you do some of your work in a campus computer lab and some at home. You also can have more than one list of bookmarks, but you can see only one list at a time.

"Computer Strategies" boxes give suggestions for working effectively on the computer while writing, revising, editing, and conducting research on the Web.

---

166   **14**   Steps in Creating a Web Site

Customizing a page

With the basic elements of her page now assembled, Rachel can concentrate on improving the look of her page. She changes the gray background to white by following these steps:

1. Select **Page Properties** from the **Format** menu, which shows another dialog box.
2. Select **Use Custom Colors**.
3. Select a color (Rachel chooses **Black on Off-White** from the list).

Next she makes the links into a bulleted list. She highlights the list, then clicks on the **bullet list** icon on the **Formatting** toolbar (see Figure 14.4). Rachel wants to put her email address at the bottom of her page. She first clicks on the **horizontal line** icon, which puts a line at the bottom of her page. Then she includes her email address.

Figure 14.4. Formatting a bulleted list in Composer

Giving your page a title

Finally Rachel has one last, important step—giving her page a title. The **Page Title** is different from both the filename and the heading on the page. The page title shows up on the frame on the top of the page. Giving your page an accurate title helps people remember what's on the page when they have bookmarked it. To give your page a title, follow these steps:

1. Select **Page Properties** from the **Format** menu.
2. Type the name of your page in the **Title** box.
3. Click OK.

Comprehensive coverage of technology throughout includes Part 4, "Writing for the Web," with three chapters of practical, step-by-step instructions for building Web sites using web editors and HTML.

The Penguin Handbooks Companion Website

Integrated with URLs throughout each text, this innovative Web site offers interactive exercises and activities that relate directly to the material presented.

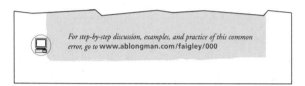

For step-by-step discussion, examples, and practice of this common error, go to **www.ablongman.com/faigley/000**

Common Errors Workbooks – "Common Errors" boxes in the text offer quick advice on the problems that students see most often. Within each box, a URL directs students to the Web site's interactive exercises – giving students practice and immediate feedback in key areas of grammar and usage.

ESL Workbooks– The Web site also offers students with ESL issues special interactive workbooks that focus on the problems they encounter most frequently.

Model Student Papers with Audio Commentary– Throughout the text, model student papers are accompanied by URLs where students can go to listen to audio commentaries on each paper by the author.

Writing in the World Projects & Worksheets– These projects offer students all the tools and source materials they need to complete a variety of writing assignments. Interactive worksheets help walk them through the writing process for each project.

About the Author

Lester Faigley holds the Robert Adger Law
and Thos. H. Law Professorship in Humanities at
the University of Texas at Austin. He has taught college writing courses
for 32 years and was the founding director of both the Division of
Rhetoric and Composition and the Concentration in Technology, Literacy,
and Culture at Texas. He served as the 1996 Chair of the Conference on
College Composition and Communication. Faigley has published three
previous books with Longman, including *The Longman Guide to the
Web*, *Good Reasons* (now in its second edition), and *Good Reasons with
Contemporary Arguments*. His academic books include *Fragments of
Rationality* (Pittsburgh, 1992), which received the MLA Mina P.
Shaughnessy Prize and the CCCC Outstanding Book Award.

In 1980 a federal grant allowed him to get on ARPANET, the original
Internet in the Department of Defense, at a time when the users
numbered under a thousand and most were doing secret military
research. He has been immersed in technology ever since, except for
a few days a year when he goes to places that don't have microwave
towers, Internet access, or even trails. An avid hiker and kayaker,
he recently traveled to the Arctic National Wildlife Refuge where he
hiked through the Brooks Range then paddled 130 miles down the
Sheenjek River.

THE
Penguin
Handbook

Lester Faigley
University of Texas at Austin

PEARSON
Longman

New York   San Francisco   Boston
London   Toronto   Sydney   Tokyo   Singapore   Madrid
Mexico City   Munich   Paris   Cape Town   Hong Kong   Montreal

Senior Vice President and Publisher: Joseph Opiela
Acquisitions Editor: Lynn M. Huddon
Development Director: Janet Lanphier
Development Editor: Leslie Taggart
Senior Supplements Editor: Donna Campion
Media Supplements Editor: Nancy Garcia
Marketing Manager: Christopher Bennem
Senior Production Manager: Bob Ginsberg
Project Coordination, Text Design, and Electronic Page Makeup:
    Pre-Press Company, Inc.
Cover Design Manager: Wendy Ann Fredericks
Cover Designer: Kay Petronio
Cover Photos: ©Artville
Senior Manufacturing Manager: Dennis J. Para
Printer and Binder: RR Donnelley & Sons Company
Cover Printer: Phoenix Color Corporation

For permission to use copyrighted material, grateful acknowledgment is made to the
copyright holders on pp. 861–862, which are hereby made part of this copyright page.

Library of Congress Cataloging-in-Publication Data

Faigley, Lester, 1947-
    The Penguin handbook/Lester Faigley.
        p. cm.
    Includes index.
    ISBN 0-321-21628-8 — ISBN 0-321-21627-X (pbk.)
    1. English language—Rhetoric—Handbooks, manuals, etc. 2. English language—
Grammar—Handbooks, manuals, etc. 3. Report writing—Handbooks, manuals,
etc. I. Title.

PE1408 .F25 2003b
808'.042—dc21   2002034111

Copyright © 2003 by Pearson Education, Inc.

All rights reserved. No part of this publication may be reproduced, stored in a retrieval system, or transmitted, in any form or by any means, electronic, mechanical, photocopying, recording, or otherwise, without the prior written permission of
the publisher. Printed in the United States.

Please visit our Web site at http://www. ablongman.com/faigley

ISBN 0-321-21628-8 (hardcover)

ISBN 0-321-21627-X (paperback)

2345678910—DOC—050403

Contents

Preface

Veteran writing teachers know that two tools are indispensable for student writers—a good dictionary and a good handbook. Indeed, nearly everyone who writes regularly depends on a dictionary, and a great many writers find their college handbooks valuable long after their college years. After thirty years of teaching college writing, I'm convinced that any motivated student can make significant strides in improving as a writer by learning to use a dictionary and a handbook effectively. Furthermore, after many years of consulting in the workplace and serving as a writing program administrator, I'm convinced that these habits benefit students enormously after college, in their careers and public life.

Too many students, however, use neither a dictionary nor a handbook to good advantage. The key to using a dictionary is learning to look beyond spelling to the etymology and various meanings of a word. Effective use of a handbook requires more skills because handbooks have diverse kinds of information. Students need to become familiar with the types of information in a handbook, and they need to learn how to find what they need. Unfortunately, handbooks are often difficult for students to use. Most handbooks are comprehensive and accurate, but they suffer from the forest/trees problem. Students often cannot find what is most important amidst the mass of information. Unless they become proficient with using the index, students may seldom open their handbooks.

The *Penguin Handbook* attempts a different approach to the concept of a handbook. It is designed to be browsed in addition to being accessed with its table of contents and index. Writing teachers know from experience, confirmed by numerous surveys, that students typically make the same kinds of errors. These frequent errors are highlighted in Common Errors boxes that offer simple, robust principles for dealing with the errors. Furthermore, each Common Error box links to the book's Web site for additional examples and opportunities for practice in avoiding the error.

The documentation sections of handbooks present students with a similar forest/trees problem. Nothing in college writing seems more mysterious to students than documentation, largely because handbooks typically value thoroughness over everything else and present long lists of examples, each seemingly different. *The Penguin Handbook* takes a different approach, focusing on the core examples and introducing students to the logic of each major system of documentation, emphasizing what is similar. The less frequent examples are referenced in relation to the major types, and no handbook has more of these examples, including the various styles used in the sciences.

Every handbook now talks about computers and the Internet, but in general they have not acknowledged that even low-cost computers allow students to perform the tasks that required entire production teams just a few years ago. Writing is a visual medium, but until recently most writers have had so few choices that this aspect of writing has been neglected. *The Penguin Handbook* emphasizes how verbal and visual communication are alike and how they differ. It explains many of the design tools offered on a word processing program and gives practical instruction on creating Web pages and visuals for paper and oral presentations.

Finally, *The Penguin Handbook* stresses the relationship of the writing students do in college to the writing (and increasingly, the multimedia presentations) they will do after college. While an emphasis on the process of academic writing and research is maintained throughout, the book and its Web site also include coverage of nonfiction genres—brochures, personal Web sites, magazine articles, memos, letters, résumés, and reports—that are more typical outside the classroom.

I chose not to rely on many professional examples or use many professional images, but instead I have used to a large extent student examples, my writing, and my images. The examples you see in *The Penguin Handbook* represent what college writers can reasonably expect to achieve. And I've tried to suggest that writing can even be fun. I hope you will enjoy browsing *The Penguin Handbook*.

CONTENTS

The Penguin Handbook is innovative but does not discard any of the essential elements and the breadth of coverage found in traditional handbooks. Its ten parts give a comprehensive introduction and reference to writing in college and beyond.

Part 1, Composing in the Digital Era. *The Penguin Handbook* begins with the writing process, starting with how to think about the rhetorical situation of a piece of writing, and then moving to the acts of planning and drafting, composing paragraphs, rewriting, editing, and proofreading. Basic strategies for prewriting (analyzing an assignment, finding a topic, asking questions, freewriting, brainstorming, and making idea maps) are given in Chapter 3, and in Chapter 4 seven common paragraph strategies (description, narration, comparison and contrast, definition, examples and illustrations, cause and effect, classification and division) are discussed along with more general paragraph topics such as explicit and implicit topic sentences. Writing exercises throughout ask students to consider realistic rhetorical situations to decide how they would analyze audience, purpose, and situation and how writing processes would aid them in writing various types of nonfiction.

Several elements of Part 1 are unique. The Introduction, "Writing for Different Purposes in Different Media," shows students the importance of writing in the everyday life of a college-educated professional. Chapter 2, on verbal and visual texts, examines how communicating with words and communicating with images differ while acting to fulfill similar purposes nevertheless. In Chapter 4 sample paragraphs by the author on a single subject are paralleled by a series of images taken by the author to demonstrate how words and images can reinforce each other.

Part 2, Writing in College and Beyond.   Chapter 6 covers both critical reading and critical viewing, in line with the emphasis throughout on the need to think critically about visual culture. Chapters 7, 8, and 9 include ten nonfiction genres in the context of three different purposes for writing: writing to reflect, writing to inform, and writing to persuade. In addition to academic essays, these chapters include the genres of the reflective magazine article; the personal Web site; the brochure; the business genres of the memo, letter, and report; and the résumé and accompanying letter of application. Each genre is illustrated with a topical, well-written example. Throughout, exercises ask students to apply the ideas they are learning to their own pieces of writing.

Part 3, Visual Rhetoric.   Part 3 offers both design principles and instruction in creating graphics, tables, and charts. Practical advice is given on how best to use visuals in texts, including details on the appropriate file formats and the manipulations possible in image editors. The part ends with a chapter on how to use visuals in making effective oral presentations.

Part 4, Writing for the Web.   Increasingly student writing is finding its way to the Web. Some students now independently maintain portfolios of their work on the Web. Three chapters—"Web Basics," "Steps in Creating a Web Site," and "Building a Multipage Site"—demystify all the most important aspects and processes of Web design.

Part 5, Researching.   Part 5 is organized by chapters that follow the process of research: "Planning Your Research," "Finding Sources," "Evaluating Sources," "Avoiding Plagiarism When Using Sources," and "Writing the Research Project." Chapter 16 examines the strengths and weaknesses of Web resources and the advantages and disadvantages of library sources—a parallel emphasis that continues throughout this part. Chapters 17 and 18 discuss finding and evaluating different types of source material; research profiles demonstrate using different strategies to conduct searches of diverse subjects. Chapter 19 covers the purpose of documenting sources, explains intellectual property, and describes how to avoid plagiarism. Exercises ask students to practice the skills that will help them avoid plagiarism: identifying source material that needs to be cited, integrating sources into writing, and revising to ensure that source material is used correctly. Chapter 20 traces the development of a student research paper with concrete examples.

Part 6, Documenting.   All major documentation styles are discussed in depth—MLA, APA, CMS (Chicago), and CSE (Council of Science Editors, formerly "CBE"). Unique to *The Penguin Handbook* is a new method of presentation that groups elements logically and offers at-a-glance visual explanations. Full-length student papers are included for MLA and APA documentation, and example pages are supplied for CMS. In addition an entire chapter is devoted to writing about literature, complete with a sample student literary analysis.

Part 7, Effective Style and Language.   Part 7 contains three chapters that teach how to achieve a concise, effective style, emphasizing a few robust principles that can take students a long way toward this goal. The remaining three chapters supply sound advice about using effective words, inclusive language, and accurate spelling. Exercises in Parts 7–10 draw on material from diverse sources and disciplines in order to give students a wide range of experience in working with material written at the college level. Exercises are often given as connected discourse rather than discrete sentences to allow for realistic practice.

Part 8, Understanding Grammar. Students are given the terms that they need at the beginning of Part 8 and then they are guided through key principles of grammar. All sentence and grammar terms are introduced in the first chapter of this part rather than scattering this critical information. The six chapters make information easy to access in other ways; in many cases, the student will need to consult only the Common Errors box to figure out how to solve a grammatical problem.

Part 9, Understanding Punctuation and Mechanics. Part 9 gives detailed coverage of punctuation and mechanics—from commas in Chapter 38 to abbreviations, acronyms, and numbers in Chapter 46. Thorny writing problems are highlighted—such as using commas with nonrestrictive modifiers—and in the process implicit lessons in stylistic options are given as an added bonus.

Part 10, If English Is Not Your First Language. Part 10 identifies the most pervasive problems for ESL students in mainstream classrooms, including issues involving count and noncount nouns and the articles used with them, verb combinations, English sentence structure, and idiomatic structures. Second-language writers are referred throughout to an online tutorial designed by an ESL expert for more extended review and practice of discrete skills. Exercises focus on typical problems of writers using English as a nonnative language.

Writing Essay Examinations is an appendix that describes how to prepare for an essay exam and how to write a successful response, including advice on analyzing the verbs used in the question and sample essay exam questions from across the disciplines.

SUPPLEMENTS

Accompanying *The Penguin Handbook* is a large array of supplements for both instructors and students, including:

- The Companion Website to accompany *The Penguin Handbook* (at http://www.ablongman.com/faigley/). References to this useful, consistently relevant Web site can be found throughout the handbook; URLs are provided throughout that link directly to specific pages within the Companion Website. This site presents a variety of learning experiences to help students become better writers:

  Writing in the World Projects, self-contained projects that include complete information about the rhetorical situation and all the source materials needed to complete the projects

  Writing in the World Worksheets that provide specific guidance to students in more than twenty-five different aspects of writing, revising, and research

  Common Errors Workbook & Common ESL Errors Workbook, which offer step-by-step explanations, numerous examples, and practice, with immediate feedback in those areas of grammar and usage where writers need the most help

  Student Writing Samples that reprint the student papers from the handbook with audio commentary by Lester Faigley

  Additional teaching resources are also available on this site for Instructors.

- *The Penguin Handbook Interactive CD-ROM* offers the entire text of the handbook, supplemented with video and audio clips, Web links, and exercises. In addition to the CD-ROM, students and instructors will receive access to the *Longman CompSolutions* Web site, where they will find all the resources of Longman's best multimedia solutions for composition in one, easy-to-use place. This site includes: *The Longman Writer's Warehouse for Composition, The Longman ExerciseZone,* the *Avoiding Plagiarism* interactive tutorial, *ContentSelect,* and an online reference library.

- An *Instructor's Resource Manual,* by Eric Lupfer and Victoria Davis, offers guidance to new and experienced teachers for using the handbook and its ancillary package to the best advantage.

- A separate *Answer Key* is also available to instructors for the exercises contained in *The Penguin Handbook.*

ACKNOWLEDGMENTS

When once asked what it is like to write a handbook, I replied that it's like walking across Europe and Asia. The journey is long and lonesome. Without a great deal of help along the way, I could not have completed it. Acquisitions editor Lynn Huddon has supported the project from the beginning and shaped it in many ways. My guide and mentor has been Leslie Taggart, the development editor who encouraged me to think in new ways, taught me how to bring my ideas to fruition, and contributed many innovative ideas on her own. She's the best. Others at Longman who have contributed their wisdom and experience are Joseph Opiela, editor-in-chief; Janet Lanphier, development manager; Christopher Bennem, marketing manager; Nancy Garcia, media supplements editor; Donna Campion, senior supplements editor; Wendy Ann Fredericks, designer; and Bob Ginsberg, senior production manager. Elsa van Bergen, assisted by Robin Gordon at Pre-Press, has skillfully guided the production and been a joy to work with. My copy editor, Carol Noble, has been not only meticulous but also sensitive to the goals of the book. Thanks go also to proofreaders Jenifer Cooke, Genevieve Coyne, and Vernon Nahrgang.

I am especially grateful to four people at Texas who worked closely with me in writing several sections of the book. Sue Mendelsohn made major contributions to the style, grammar, mechanics, and writing about literature chapters, bringing a fresh perspective to many traditional topics. Madison Searle is largely responsible for the ESL chapters, and Ellen Crowell and Victoria Davis did fine work on the documentation chapters; Victoria in particular proved that the spreads would work. Sue and Victoria guided the writing of the exercises, assisted by Alex Barron, Ellen Crowell, Kelly Kessler, Casey McKittrick, Kyre Osborn, Paula Smith, and George Waddington. Ian Faigley and Lois Kim assisted in preparing the manuscript for production. I thank the students whose work is represented, especially Grace Bernhardt. Eric Lupfer, Madison Searle, and Kathryn Riley have been extraordinary in creating the Companion Website. Professor Julie Allen at Sonoma State University was generous in providing me with pictures of Portland's MAX light rail, which appear in the Introduction.

Over the years I've learned and continue to learn from colleagues around the country. I am fortunate to have the benefit of advice from a splendid group of reviewers, who were not only perceptive in their suggestions but could imagine a handbook that breaks new ground. They are James E. Allen, College of DuPage; Thomas Amorose, Seattle Pacific University; Susan H. Aylworth, California State University, Chico; Susan L. Booker, Hampden-Sydney College; Robert I. Carr, III, Wayne State University; Angela Clark-Oates, Southwest Texas State University; Sara Cutting, Kent State University; Rebecca Damron, Oklahoma State University; Jane Detweiler, University of Nevada, Reno; Debra L. Druesedow, Kent State University; Chris Fosen, California State University at Chico; Gabrielle Gautreaux, University of New Orleans; Casey Gilson, Broward Community College; Margaret Graham, Iowa State University; Susan Gunn, St. Edward's University; Mary Hadley, Georgia Southern University; Jay Halpern, Southern Connecticut University, Sacred Heart University; Dr. Bradley A. Hammer, Duke University; Michael Hogan, Southeast Missouri State University; Alex M. Joncas, Estrella Mountain Community College; Colin K. Keeney, University of Wyoming; Marshall Kitchens, Oakland University; Jeff Koloze, Lorain County Community College; Mary Kramer, University of Massachusetts, Lowell; Robert Lamm, Arkansas State University; Sonya Lancaster, University of Kansas; Lisa Langstraat, University of Southern Mississippi; Delma McLeod-Porter, McNeese State University; Mada J. Morgan, Southern Oregon University; Matthew S. Novak, California Polytechnic State University; Ruth Oleson, Illinois Central College; Laura Ross, Seminole Community College; Caroll Shreeve, Weber State University; William H. Thelin, University of Akron; Mary Trachsel, University of Iowa; Mary Vroman Battle, The University of Memphis; Matt Willen, Elizabethtown College; and Joanna Wolfe, University of Louisville.

I'd also like to thank the members of several focus groups who gave us valuable suggestions and insights as we began development of *The Penguin Handbook:* Deborah Adelman, College of DuPage; Linda Adler-Kassner, Eastern Michigan University; Margrethe Ahlschwede, University of Tennessee at Marti; John Beard, Coastal Carolina University; Cynthia A. Cochran, Illinois College; Joseph Colavito, Northwestern State University;

Bill Condon, Washington State University; Angela Crow, Georgia Southern University; Joel English, Old Dominion University; Joe Essid, University of Richmond; Maureen Fitzpatrick, Johnson County Community College; Sherri Gradin, Portland State University; Lynne Graft, Saginaw Valley State University; Susanmarie Harrington, Indiana University-Purdue University, Indianapolis; Judith Kilborn, St. Cloud State University; Lisa Langstraat, University of Southern Mississippi; Janice Neuleib, Illinois State University; Rich Rice, Ball State University; Susan Romano, University of Texas, San Antonio; Connie Rothwell, University of North Carolina, Charlotte; Mary Trachsel, University of Iowa; Karen Uehling, Boise State University; Patricia Webb, Arizona State University.

A group of students from Irvine Valley College, coordinated by Professors Dale Larson and Lewis Long, also participated enthusiastically in discussions about what is useful in a handbook. Thanks go to Kevin Chau, Annie Cody, Mike Esfahani, Yuniar Estell, Maribel Garcia, Chelsea Halim, Kathy Held, Ginger Hughes, Nicole Michaelian, Scott Morgan, Jeanette Morton, Anthony Vu Nguyen, Vanessa Radley, Son Tran, Raymond Tsang, and Meredith Winsor for sharing their ideas about content and design with us.

I thank my kayaking, climbing, and trekking companion of thirty years, Jim Witte (who appears in Chapter 4), for getting me to some of the greatest places on earth, and, more important, getting me back. My greatest debt of gratitude is to my wife, Linda, whose enduring support and encouragement has allowed me to complete this journey with good humor intact.

—LESTER FAIGLEY

Composing in the Digital Era 1

Introduction

Writing for Different Purposes in Different Media

Learning how to write well is a critical part of your college education. Many surveys that ask college graduates what they most value about their education report that they rank writing and communication skills far above anything else they learned. If you write well, you will become more confident and more successful in whatever you do.

In your lifetime, digital technologies have profoundly changed what it means to write well. With a personal computer and powerful software, individuals today can publish high-quality documents with visuals, create sophisticated multimedia presentations, and produce Web sites that tens of millions of people around the world can view. Nevertheless, the new literacies made possible by digital technologies haven't replaced the old literacies of pencil, pen, printing press, and paper. New technologies have simply added more choices, raising the ante for being an effective communicator in the digital era. Let's look at an example of what a college-educated professional does in a typical day.

A DAY IN THE LIFE OF A COLLEGE-EDUCATED PROFESSIONAL

Catherine Chandler, a transportation engineer for the city of Portland, Oregon, begins her day by getting up and looking into her nearly empty refrigerator, finding only a carton of yogurt to take for her lunch. On a pad beside the fridge, she jots down a few items to pick up on the way home. She finishes reading the newspaper on the bus and pulls out her personal digital assistant (PDA) to check her schedule for the day.

When she gets to work, she logs on to her computer, checks for messages, and responds to the most urgent ones. The big project on her desk is a proposal to build a south-north light rail line from the Clackamas town center south of Portland through the downtown area to the Kenton business district north of Portland. This proposal will be presented to the Tri-County Metropolitan Service District of Oregon (Tri-Met), which was created by the Oregon legislature in 1969 to take over Portland's ailing transit system. Tri-Met built light rail lines running east and west of Portland and is now considering a north-south corridor line. Chandler's task is to project the effects of the new line on expected traffic congestion, and include her research and conclusions in the proposal.

She begins by examining population growth, which increased in the Portland metropolitan area from 1.1 million people in 1975 to 1.6 million in 1995, a 45% increase. She projects that when the system is completed around 2010, it will carry 42,000 riders a day. As a consequence, 2,200 fewer parking spaces will be needed in downtown Portland, and commuters in cars will spend 4,400 fewer hours stuck in rush-hour traffic. Chandler makes presentation software slides that illustrate each of these statistical projections. She will use these as visuals during her presentation before the Tri-Met board, and she will later import the graphics into the printed report.

In the afternoon, Chandler meets with the planning team to discuss strategies for presenting the proposal to the Tri-Met board. The proposal is extraordinarily complicated because it must take into account many factors beyond providing transportation. The new system must reduce traffic congestion and traffic infiltration into neighborhoods, promote desirable land-use patterns, avoid negative environmental impacts, run efficiently, and pay for itself in the long run.

The meeting focuses on potential objections to the project. Opponents will probably argue that the proposed south-north light rail line will not relieve congestion because many people will still drive and much commuting is from suburb to suburb. They will maintain that an all-bus system is more

flexible and more economical. Probably they will claim that the benefits of any new jobs created will be offset by increased taxes. The team will have to be prepared to address both these objections and any others that might be raised by the board. Chandler knows her projections about numbers of riders are likely to be questioned, and she makes a note to herself to research how accurate past predictions have been. After the meeting Chandler writes a memo to her supervisor, summarizing the discussion and the status of the proposal.

Her last task of the day is to write a letter of recommendation for a former student intern who is now interviewing for jobs. Chandler thinks about the special qualities the intern possesses and how she might best represent them, then writes the letter in a single draft.

When she gets home from work after stopping at the grocery store, Chandler checks her personal email and visits Web sites associated with her favorite activity, fly fishing. In Oregon, a dam on the Sandy River was recently scheduled for breaching, but a second dam remains unbreached on a section of the river with a viable salmon fishery. Breaching the second dam would add spawning habitat for the salmon and enhance that fishery.

On a discussion board on one of the Web sites, she finds a posting urging readers to ask their Congressional representatives to vote to breach the remaining dam. Aware that economic arguments often carry more weight than environmental ones (in this case, based on building the numbers of salmon), Chandler posts a message advising those who write letters to stress the economic importance of sport fishing to the region. She then browses airline Web sites to check for low fares for an upcoming vacation.

After Chandler turns off her computer, she writes an entry in her journal as her last act of the day. She has been keeping a journal for many years

and often finds it invaluable just for remembering what she was doing on a particular day.

Chandler's day is typical of those of many college-educated people. She would not describe herself as a professional writer, yet writing is a large part of her professional and personal life. Chandler lives in an information economy. Her primary product on the job is information presented in several forms—reports, memos, letters, visuals, and oral presentations. But even off the job Chandler deals in information. She uses the information resources of the Internet not only to remain current and participate in her favorite political cause—the restoration of salmon runs in the Pacific Northwest—but for a variety of other uses, such as making airline reservations.

THE COMPLEX WRITING DEMANDS OF THE DIGITAL ERA

Catherine Chandler's day represents the complexity of writing in a digital era. People who can write effectively are far more successful in their professional and civic lives than those who can't. In large companies and organizations, often the only way others know you is by what you write. Likewise, if you expect to be able to influence decisions that affect you and your community, you most often have to communicate in writing. Let's look at what is demanded of you.

- **Writers today use a variety of writing technologies.** People do not throw away their pencils and ballpoint pens when they buy a laptop computer. Each writing tool is well suited to particular uses; it's hard to top a pencil for jotting down a grocery list as you walk out the door in the morning.

- **Writers today do many different kinds of writing:** letters, reports, memos, newsletters, evaluations, articles, charts, Web sites, computer-assisted presentations, press releases, brochures, proposals, résumés, agendas, users' manuals, analyses, summaries, and email. Each kind of writing has its own special set of demands.

- **Writers today have multiple purposes.** An email may convey both business strategies and personal news. A proposal may have as its unacknowledged purpose the request for a new job or wider responsibilities. Even a simple memo often conveys many unstated messages, such as the attitude of the writer toward her coworkers.

- **Writers today have multiple audiences.** Often documents are read by readers who have different interests. The speed of digital media allows many points of view to be expressed simultaneously. Skilled writers in the digital era know they must negotiate among these many points of view.

- **Writers today often work in teams.** They communicate with colleagues to achieve a common goal, so the ability to collaborate effectively may be an unanticipated need in writing effectively.

- **Writers today know that it is critical to emphasize what is important.** They understand that readers face an overdose of information, have little patience, and want to know quickly what is at stake.

- **Writers today recognize that an active and personal style free from errors is often most effective.** Readers in general prefer a personal and accessible style.

- **Writers today communicate visually as well as verbally.** Computers and digital media give writers the ability to use pictures and graphics in addition to text. Knowing how to communicate visually is important to your success in the digital era.

Chapter 1

The Rhetorical Situation

Communicating in the World

Roberto de Nobili

In May 1605, a Portuguese ship arrived at the colony of Goa on the west coast of India, the administrative center for Portuguese trade in the East. On the ship was a young Italian aristocrat, Roberto de Nobili, who had abandoned his inherited title and wealth to become a Jesuit missionary. He found the wealth of Goa dazzling, but it did not take long for de Nobili to discover that the spiritual mission of the Jesuits had failed. After nearly a hundred years of occupation, almost all the converts to Christianity were either the servants of the Portuguese or under their direct control.

Roberto de Nobili quickly learned Tamil, the language spoken in much of southern India. His talents made him the ideal candidate for an attempt to convert people in India living in the interior. He was sent to Madurai, a provincial capital in southern India, where his predecessor had failed to make a single convert in eleven years. Over time de Nobili came to understand why the record of success had been so poor. The Portuguese ignored the basic values of the local people such as the prohibition on eating beef; consequently, the people in India regarded the Portuguese as subhuman beings beneath the lowest caste.

(continued next page)

De Nobili decided that he needed to take a different approach. He wore the clothing of a Hindu holy man, ate one meal a day of herbs and rice, observed local customs, and preached in Tamil. Gradually, de Nobili drew many visitors and became the first European to learn Sanskrit, giving him access to Hindu religious texts. With this knowledge he could draw parallels between certain Hindu and Christian beliefs. He gained widespread acceptance among the upper castes of Hindu society. Even though his dream of converting much of India to Christianity did not come to pass, de Nobili taught us how people from vastly different cultural backgrounds might engage in dialogue.

1a THE RHETORICAL TRIANGLE

The lessons that Roberto de Nobili learned still apply today. He recognized that the message alone is inadequate for effective communication. If de Nobili were to convince anyone in southern India to convert to Christianity, he would first have to convince them that he was a person worth listening to. De Nobili realized that to gain respect he would have to respect the values of the community.

All too often, as was the case with de Nobili, we become aware of how communication works only when communication breaks down. De Nobili understood that communication is more than the message—that the speaker and the audience are also essential components of communication. These components are often represented with a triangle.

The rhetorical triangle (Figure 1.1) depicts two important points about any kind of communication. First, all three elements—speaker, subject, and audience—are necessary for an act of communication to occur. Even if you are talking to or writing to yourself, you still have an audience. Second, the three elements are in a dynamic relationship, which the example of Roberto de Nobili illustrates. De Nobili had to change his dress, his eating habits, his language, and indeed, his entire way of living in order to convince his audience that he was a person of good will with their best in-

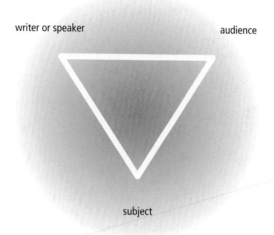

writer or speaker   audience

subject

Figure 1.1. **The rhetorical triangle**

terests in mind. Few people ever go to these extremes to communicate, but every one of us makes adjustments depending on our audience (think of how you talk to small children). Similarly, just as speakers adjust to audiences, audiences continually adjust to speakers (think of how your attitude toward speakers changes when they are able to laugh at themselves).

Persuasive appeals

The ancient Greeks recognized that the dynamic nature of the rhetorical triangle is the key to understanding how an audience is persuaded. The most important teacher of rhetoric in ancient Greece, Aristotle (384-323 BCE), defined rhetoric as the art of finding the best available means of persuasion in any situation. He set out three primary tactics of persuasion: appeals based on the trustworthiness of the speaker (*ethos*); appeals to the emotions and deepest-held values of the audience (*pathos*); and appeals to logic, reasoning, and evidence (*logos*). These appeals likewise can be represented using the rhetorical triangle (Figure 1.2, page 10).

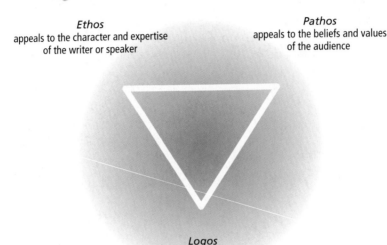

Ethos
appeals to the character and expertise
of the writer or speaker

Pathos
appeals to the beliefs and values
of the audience

Logos
appeals based on logic, reasoning, and
evidence concerning the subject

Figure 1.2. Persuasive appeals

Let's take a practical example of persuasion. Imagine that you drive every day on Lakeside Boulevard, a divided four-lane highway with a narrow grass median in the middle. You've read in the newspaper about numerous accidents on Lakeside Boulevard, many of them fatal. You yourself have witnessed two horrible accidents, when cars and trucks skidded across the median and collided head-on with traffic in the opposite lanes. You want your city council to vote to erect a concrete barrier that will prevent these frequent head-on collisions. One approach would be to use logic and evidence, documenting that Lakeside Boulevard has far more fatal accidents per mile than other streets in your city (logos). Another would be to invite an expert on traffic safety to speak to the city council (ethos). A third way would be to appeal to the council about the unnecessary loss of life caused by the unsafe street (pathos). Often you will use all of these appeals to gain support of an audience.

The larger context

The rhetorical triangle is useful for understanding how an act of communication works at a particular time. What is missing, however, is a sense of how the participants happened to be talking about that particular subject at that time in that place. Roberto de Nobili did not arrive in southern India by accident. He was part of an expanding Portuguese empire that extended from Macao off the coast of China, across south Asia and Africa, to Brazil in South America. De Nobili was also a priest who represented the Roman Catholic Church. Likewise, the people of the higher castes in southern India, whom de Nobili was attempting to convert, were not vegetarians because they had suddenly decided to stop eating meat; they were following a centuries-old Hindu religious tradition of not taking the lives of animals.

We do not think much about long-standing cultural traditions when we talk to people who live in our own culture, but we often become aware of the historical dimensions of particular subjects for particular audiences. For example, you might know that certain species of sharks are becoming increasingly rare. Large coastal sharks are vulnerable to overfishing because they grow slowly and have a slow reproductive rate. Nonetheless, it's much harder to convince a general audience that sharks need protection than it is to argue for the protection of a cuddly species like the panda. Most people have seen too many movies like *Jaws* and read too many accounts of shark attacks to think of sharks in the same way they think of pandas.

Any act of communicating is never quite the neutral situation that a simple rhetorical triangle implies. Speaker, subject, and audience each bring histories to a particular rhetorical situation (Figure 1.3, page 12). People who know how to communicate effectively use those histories to their advantage. They understand that many people have spoken and written about the subject before them and that they are entering an ongoing conversation.

The writing situation

When the rhetorical situation changes from speaking to writing, it becomes more complex. It might seem that we can simply substitute "writer" for

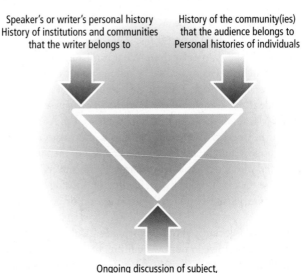

Speaker's or writer's personal history
History of institutions and communities
that the writer belongs to

History of the community(ies)
that the audience belongs to
Personal histories of individuals

Ongoing discussion of subject,
often going back many years

Figure 1.3. Social and historical contexts of the rhetorical situation

"speaker" and "readers" for "audience" in the rhetorical triangle, but it's not that simple. While every healthy person above infancy can speak and listen, people can read and write only if they are taught. Writing requires a system of representation, in which symbols stand for sounds or words. Writing requires an instrument for writing, even if it is only your finger making letters in the sand at the beach. More important, writing changes the dynamics of the rhetorical triangle because usually writer and reader are separated by time and space. Writing changes the nature of the audience and the nature of the speaker in more ways than merely substituting written words for those spoken.

EXERCISE 1.1 Read the following passages and decide which appeal (to logic, to credibility and trustworthiness, to emotions and values) is being addressed.

1. I wanted the perfect meal.

    I also wanted—to be absolutely frank—Col. Walter E. Kurtz, Lord Jim, Lawrence of Arabia, Kim Philby, the Consul, Fowler, Tony Po, B. Traven, Christopher Walken . . . I wanted to find—no, wanted to be—one of those debauched heroes and villains out of Graham Greene, Joseph Conrad, Francis Coppola, and Micheal Cimino. I wanted to wander the world in a dirty seersucker suit, getting into trouble.

    —Anthony Bourdain, *A Cook's Tour,* 2001

2. Whenever any group can vote in a bloc, and decide the outcome of elections, and it *fails* to do this, then that group is politically sick. Immigrants once made Tammany Hall the most powerful single force in American politics. In 1880, New York City's first Irish Catholic Mayor was elected and by 1960 America had its first Irish Catholic President. America's black man, voting as a bloc, could wield an even more powerful bloc.

    —Malcolm X, *The Autobiography of Malcolm X,* 1965

3. In times of crisis, we must all decide again and again whom we love.

    —Frank O'Hara, "To the Film Industry in Crisis," *Meditations in an Emergency,* 1957

4. When in the course of human events, it becomes necessary for one people to dissolve the political bands which have connected them with one another, and to assume among the powers of the earth, the separate and equal station which the Laws of Nature and of Nature's God entitle them, a decent respect to the opinions of mankind requires that they should declare the causes which impel them to the separation.

    —Thomas Jefferson, *Declaration of Independence,* 1776

5. I do not deeply distrust my country. She is not dead, but in my time she sleepeth, and the spirit of our fathers flames no more, but lies hid beneath the ashes.

    —Margaret Fuller, *Writings,* 1941

1b | A WRITER'S AUDIENCE

On occasion you may write to a person who is close enough to talk to. For example, in a large lecture class you might write a note to the person sitting beside you. Other times, even though the person isn't present, you know the person so well that writing seems almost like speaking, such as when you send email to a member of your family. You know your family member shares much in common with you and will pick up on your tone and meaning when you write "Aunt Sally made her mystery meatloaf once again."

At other times your audience may consist of many individuals whose knowledge is relatively uniform and similar to yours. If you write an article for a journal in your major field, you can assume that your readers are familiar with the terms and concepts in that field even though your readers are different as individuals. When you can easily characterize the knowledge and attitudes of your audience, the audience can be called a **simple** audience.

Frequently, however, the issue of audience is much more complicated when you write. When an accountant writes a financial analysis for a bank, different people—officers of the bank, other employees, shareholders, government regulatory officials, financial analysts, and potential investors—might read that analysis for different reasons. This kind of complex audience—people with different backgrounds who read the same document for different reasons—is called a **multiple** audience. When you write for multiple audiences, you need to consider differing levels of knowledge about your subject, as well as differing attitudes toward both you and the topic you are writing about.

Critical to what you write is your audience's knowledge of your subject. If you know that your readers will be unfamiliar with your subject, you should provide background information and connect your new information to what your readers already know. Another critical factor is the level of expertise of your audience. If you are writing for an audience of experts in a field, you can use the technical language of that field. If you are unsure how much your audience knows, you may need to explain technical terms. For example, a newspaper article about the options for connecting to the

Internet from home should explain key concepts such as kilobits per second, the measure of connection speed. If your audience knows nothing about your subject, then you may have to convince them that they should be interested.

Thinking more about your audience

1. Who is most likely to read what you write?
2. Is there a broader, secondary audience who might read what you write?
3. How much does your audience know about your subject? Are there any key terms or concepts that you will need to explain?
4. How interested is your audience likely to be? If they are unfamiliar or lack interest, how can you get them interested?
5. What is their attitude likely to be toward your subject? If they hold attitudes different from yours, how can you get them to consider your views?
6. What would motivate your audience to want to read what you write?

EXERCISE 1.2 Suppose you are a freelance writer who has lined up several assignments for a variety of publications. Your topics and the publications are listed. Analyze your intended audience: How much information will they most likely have about your subject (much, none, some); what is their attitude likely to be (positive, negative, neutral); what is their interest level most likely to be (low, moderate, high). In a few cases, you might need to do some research into the readership for the publication.

1. A chapter about the Vietnam War for a high school textbook
2. An article evaluating health care plans for *Modern Maturity*
3. A profile of a prominent Republican senator for *Mother Jones*
4. A feature on women's rights in the Middle East for Oprah Winfrey's magazine, *O*
5. An article about the importance of emissions-control features for engines in *Car and Driver*

1c | A WRITER'S ETHOS

Your college newspaper may print guest editorials by fellow students and others connected with the school on the editorial pages. When you glance through its columns, you make quick decisions about what to read. When you read an editorial, you form an opinion about how much the writer seems to know about the subject. And if the writer urges you to do something— such as vote for a candidate or initiative—you decide whether the writer has your best interests in mind before you act.

This short example illustrates two key principles about a writer's ethos. Writers must convince their readers that the writers

- Are knowledgeable about the subject
- Have their readers' needs in mind

If a writer fails on either count, readers either stop reading or do not believe that what they have read has any relevance to them.

Thinking more about your credibility

1. How can you convince your audience that you are knowledgeable about your subject? Do you need to report first-hand experience? Do you need to do research?
2. How can you convince your audience that you have their interests in mind? What can you write that will demonstrate that you are aware of the needs and beliefs of your audience?
3. What strategies can you use that will enhance your credibility? Should you cite experts on your subject? Can you find research or statistics that show you've done your homework? Can you acknowledge opposing positions, indicating that you've taken a balanced view on your subject?
4. Does the appearance of your writing give you credibility?
5. Is your writing free of spelling mistakes and other errors?

Some writers begin with credibility because of who they are. If you wonder what foods compose a balanced meal for your dog, you probably would take seriously the advice of a veterinarian. If you want to develop a powerful backhand in tennis, you might read carefully advice from Venus Williams in a tennis magazine. Most writers, however, do not begin with an established ethos. They have to convince their readers to keep reading by demonstrating knowledge of their subject and concern with their readers' needs. No matter how much you know about a subject or how good your ideas are, your ethos as a writer will be destroyed by sloppy, error-filled writing. Perhaps people should not make strong negative judgments on the basis of a few mistakes, but in the workplace and in public life, they often do.

EXERCISE 1.3 Evaluate the following passages, as well as the example(s) of appeals to ethos you found in Exercise 1.1, for their appeals to credibility. What sort of ethos does the author present? How might this affect his or her presentation of the topic?

1. Topic: Colonialism

> In Moulmein, in Lower Burma, I was hated by large numbers of people—the only time in my life that I have been important enough for this to happen to me. I was sub-divisional police officer of the town, and in an aimless, petty kind of way anti-European feeling was very bitter.
>
> —George Orwell, "Shooting an Elephant," 1936

2. Seattle, Chief of the Suquamish, Treaty Oration, 1854: originally published in the *Seattle Sunday Star, 29 Oct. 1887.*

> Yonder sky that has wept tears of compassion upon my people for centuries untold, and which to us appears changeless and eternal, may change. Today is fair. Tomorrow it may be overcast with clouds. My words are like the stars that never change. Whatever Seattle says, the great chief at Washington can rely upon with as much certainty as he can upon the return of the sun or the seasons. The white chief says that Big Chief at Washington sends us greetings of friendship and goodwill. This is kind of him for we

know he has little need of our friendship in return. His people are many. They are like the grass that covers vast prairies. My people are few. They resemble the scattering trees of a storm-swept plain. The great, and I presume good, White Chief sends us word that he wishes to buy land but is willing to allow us enough to live comfortably. This indeed appears just, even generous, for the Red Man no longer has rights that he need respect, and the offer may be wise, also, as we are no longer in need of an extensive country.

3. Topic: The impeachment of President Nixon

We will not have Richard Nixon to kick around much longer—which is not especially "sorrowful news" to a lot of people, except that the purging of the cheap little bastard is going to have to take place here in Washington and will take up the rest of our summer.

—Hunter S. Thompson, "The Scum Also Rises," 1974

1d A WRITER'S PURPOSE

The starting point for effective writing is determining in advance what you want to accomplish. You may want to reflect on your experience or the experience of others. You may want to inform your readers about a subject. Or you may want to change your readers' attitudes about a subject or persuade them to take action. Your purpose will determine the tone and presentation of your message. You will find more about these purposes in Chapters 7, 8, and 9.

To give one example, imagine that you are invited to contribute a guest editorial to your college newspaper. Your purpose is to convince your readers that state government should provide parents with choices among public and private schools. Your position is that the tax dollars that now automatically go to public schools should go to private schools if parents so choose.

First, you have to establish your ethos by doing your homework. You discover evidence that the sophomore-to-senior dropout rate in private schools is less than half the rate of public schools. Furthermore, students from private schools attend college at nearly twice the rate of public school graduates. You argue that one of the reasons private schools are more successful is that they spend more money on instruction and less on administration. And you feel that school choice speaks to the American desire for personal freedom.

But you know from the outset that not everyone on your campus will agree with you. Many of the faculty and other students will feel strongly that public money should not be given to private schools. You can anticipate that critics of the public funding of private schools will raise the objection that because many students in private schools come from more affluent families, it's no surprise that they do better. You will have to deal with that objection. Anticipating points of view different from yours and stating them in a way that is recognizable to those who hold those different viewpoints is a means to building your ethos. Even though you know from the outset that you will not convince everyone, if you can get your readers to consider your position seriously you will have succeeded.

Purposes for writing

Reflective

- Personal letters and personal email maintain relationships and family ties.
- Memoirs re-create lived experiences and reflect on their significance.
- Personal responses offer the writer's feelings about people, places, and experiences.
- Travel narratives describe the experiences of individuals in unfamiliar places.

Informative

- Business letters inform clients, customers, and employees of products and policies.

(continued next page)

- Profiles of people tell stories of individual lives.
- Newspaper and magazine articles report events, sports, entertainment, and other topics.
- Brochures inform people about organizations and services.
- Businesses and government organizations produce reports that provide background information and describe activities.
- Reports of experiments, case studies, surveys, and observations present new knowledge.
- Histories and analyses of many kinds of activity, from public policy to works of art, help us make sense of the world we live in.

Persuasive

- Letters of application and résumés try to convince an employer or institution to interview and perhaps hire the applicant.
- Advertisements seek to persuade consumers to purchase products and services.
- Reviews make evaluative judgments based on criteria.
- Position arguments make a claim about a controversial issue.
- Proposal arguments recommend a course of action in response to a recognizable problem.

Chapter 2
Words and Images

2a | VERBAL VERSUS VISUAL MEDIA

Knowing when to use images and when to use words requires you to think about them as media—as different means of conveying information, ideas, and emotions. Language is extremely well adapted for describing things that fall into a linear order. Because we perceive time as linear, language allows us from a very young age to tell stories and recall lived experience. It's also possible to tell stories with images, and indeed, with the invention of movies and later television in the twentieth century, images have become the preferred medium. But it's less easy to put together a video story, say of your last vacation, no matter how user-friendly the editing features on your camcorder are, than it is simply to tell someone the story of your vacation. You just have to remember where you went and what you did.

Even when you are describing a place, you have to decide what to tell about first. Suppose someone asks you how your house is laid out. You might begin by saying that when you walk through the front door, an entryway leads to the living room. The dining room is on the right and the kitchen is adjacent. On the left is a hallway that connects to two bedrooms on the right, a bedroom on the left, and a bathroom at the end. The directions sound complicated. But if you draw a floor plan, you can show at once how the house is arranged.

Spoken language requires you to put words in a **sequence**; visual design requires you to arrange objects in **space**. Increasingly, the verbal and the visual are used in combination. We've come to expect certain verbal information such as statistical trends to be displayed as charts, for example, but we depend on the verbal to explain the significance of the trend. Understanding the principles that underlie verbal and visual structure helps you to use each effectively.

Communicating in the World

Communicating in multimedia

For the past few hundred years in Western culture, people typically communicated using one medium at a time. The more highly valued the communication, the more likely they would use only one medium. The most valued writing, such as great literature, academic books and articles, and legal contracts, was characterized by dense pages of print with no illustration. Great art was limited to a few materials—oil on canvas or chiseled stone. Great music likewise was performed on orchestral instruments by formally dressed musicians.

With the development of mass media, people have increasingly been exposed to communication that involves more than one medium. For example, in the nineteenth century magazines were illustrated with drawings; in the twentieth century they used photographs as well. Silent films relied on written words to accompany images; later, when sound was added to films, it became possible to combine images, music, and dialogue.

Recent developments in personal computers and software have made it possible for individuals to create multimedia texts that formerly required production staffs. Today, word processing programs not only permit you to control type styles and size but also allow you to insert pictures, add tables and other graphics, and print in color and prepare sophisticated visuals for oral presentations. The problem today is not whether you can add images and graphics but when to add them and for what effects. Just as for other rhetorical situations, it finally comes down to what you hope to accomplish—your purpose for communicating.

Figure 2.1. Newspaper Rock, Utah. People were communicating by using images long before recorded history.

Figure 2.2. Around 3500 BCE, the early Sumerians, who lived along the Tigris and Euphrates Rivers and who created the first cities, began recording legal and business transactions using a sophisticated writing system that combined abstract symbols with pictograms.

Organization is the path the writer creates for readers to follow. Even in a reference book like this one, in which readers consult particular chapters and sections according to their needs, there still is a path from beginning to end. Sentences, paragraphs, sections, and chapters are the writer's materials in constructing the pathway. The various subjects the writer treats are the places along the pathway. If the trail is well marked and the places identified, the reader can follow without getting lost and can revisit particular places.

Mapping of ideas

Some kinds of writing demand particular kinds of organization. A short memo in an office typically begins with an announcement of the subject. But in other kinds of writing, the organization is not so predictable. How you begin and how you take the reader along a pathway depends on what you are trying to achieve. Thinking about your purpose often helps you to map out the organization.

Titles, headings, and paragraphs

Titles and headings combine verbal and visual indicators of levels of importance and major divisions in subject matter. Paragraphs give visual cues to the progression of ideas in verbal texts. Other visual indicators such as boldface and italics provide emphasis at the level of words and phrases. Print, after all, is a visual as well as a verbal medium.

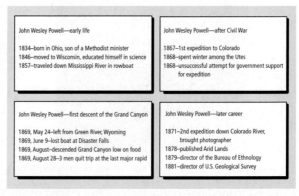

John Wesley Powell—early life

1834–born in Ohio, son of a Methodist minister
1846–moved to Wisconsin, educated himself in science
1857–traveled down Mississippi River in rowboat

John Wesley Powell—after Civil War

1867–1st expedition to Colorado
1868–spent winter among the Utes
1868–unsuccessful attempt for government support
for expedition

John Wesley Powell—first descent of the Grand Canyon

1869, May 24–left from Green River, Wyoming
1869, June 9–lost boat at Disaster Falls
1869, August–descended Grand Canyon low on food
1869, August 28–3 men quit trip at the last major rapid

John Wesley Powell—later career

1871–2nd expedition down Colorado River,
brought photographer
1878–published Arid Lands
1879–director of the Bureau of Ethnology
1881–director of U.S. Geological Survey

Figure 2.3. Notecards are a traditional method for mapping ideas.

Organization is often called *composition* by photographers, artists, and designers. The materials for photographers and artists are objects placed in space.

Both of the pictures below are of the same subject. Which do you find more appealing, the image on the left or the one on the right?

Static versus dynamic

The image on the left is a typical snapshot. The person is placed at the exact center and the horizon is about at the midpoint. Putting the subject in the exact center is typical of people who take snapshots without thinking about how they are composed. The effect is static because the focus is on the object.

The image on the right moves the person away from the center and places him in relation to a large rock illuminated by the setting sun. Instead of focusing on the man, we now see him in relation to objects on the beach and the sea and sky behind.

If the picture is divided into thirds horizontally and vertically, we can see that the prominent rock and the man are placed at the intersections of these imaginary lines. This principle of organization is known as the "rule of thirds." While there is no beginning and ending in a photograph, principles of organization still apply.

At the most basic level, point of view means selecting among first person (I, we), second person (you), and third person (he, she, it) when you write about your subject. Using *I* emphasizes the writer or the teller of the story in fiction. Using *you* puts the relationship between writer and reader in the foreground. Using *he, she,* or *it* keeps the focus more on the subject and diminishes the prominence of the writer.

Point of view is also determined by how you locate yourself in relation to your subject. Whether you write in first or third person, you can write about a subject from close, firsthand experience or you can place yourself at a distance from your subject, giving the sense of being an impartial observer offering an overview.

You can write about the Grand Canyon as if you were looking out from the window of an airplane.

The Grand Canyon is 218 miles long, from 4 to 18 miles wide, and over a mile deep in some places. From the sky the contrast between the north and south rims of the Grand Canyon is striking. The north rim is above 9,000 feet and covered by a thick forest; the south rim is about 1,200 feet lower than the north rim and has much less vegetation. The bottom of the canyon is the northernmost extension of the Sonoran Desert, where several different species of cacti, thistle, and other desert plants are found.

You can write about the Grand Canyon from the bottom.

On a late afternoon in August with the temperature well over 100°, we paddled our kayaks into Elves Chasm after getting pounded most of the day by some of the biggest rapids in the Grand Canyon—Granite, Hermit, Crystal, Serpentine, and Waltenberg—taking our casualties in turbulent swims when rolls failed. The cool trickle from the waterfall brought relief to the scorching canyon. The droplets glistened on the intense green moss and ferns like thousands of gems.

Where we choose to stand when we take a photograph makes all the difference in how the audience sees the subject. The photographer gives the audience a vantage point to take in the subject by allowing the audience to see what the photographer sees, creating an effect comparable to the use of *I* in writing. But photographers can also diminish the immediacy of a photograph by placing subjects at a distance or photographing them in stereotypical ways.

Three views of a bullpen

The bullpen is the part of a baseball park where relief pitchers warm up and wait their turn to pitch. What difference does point of view make in how we see the bullpen?

Photographers also create a *you* relationship with their subjects. Photographing people at close range creates a sense of interaction between subject and photographer.

When you write, maintain focus on one subject at a time. You achieve focus by what you choose to include and what you choose either to leave out or to postpone until later.

When you write about a complex subject, often you think about many things at once and try to get them all into your prose.

Our era is not unique as a time of uncertainty. In the past the Four Horsemen of the Apocalypse—war, disease, famine, and death—represented uncertainty. Today much of the risk is produced by humans. Science and technology are both the cause of and the solution to our problems. In the past spirits or demons took the blame for catastrophes; today the blame circles back on us. The media tell us that things go wrong because we choose the wrong lifestyle or the wrong partner or the wrong kind of food or the wrong occupation, and it's our responsibility to fix what is wrong.

When you write about a complex subject, sort the issues and present them one at a time.

Our era is not unique as a time of uncertainty. The Four Horsemen of the Apocalypse—war, disease, famine, and death—have been the daily reality for most humans in times before modernity and for many living now. There are two major differences between uncertainty today and in the past.

First is the degree to which risk is produced by humans. Science and technology are both the cause of and the solution to our present risks. Every new technology brings associated risks; trains brought the risk of train wrecks, airplanes brought plane crashes, automobiles brought traffic accidents and smog, nuclear power brought radiation leaks, the Internet brought rapidly spreading computer viruses.

Second is the absence of traditions to account for risks. In the past spirits or demons took the blame for catastrophes. Today the blame circles back on us. We chose the wrong lifestyle or the wrong partner or the wrong kind of food or the wrong occupation. When things go wrong, it is the individual's responsibility to seek counseling, to retrain herself, to pull himself up by his bootstraps.

Just as in writing, make the subject of your images clear to the viewer. Beginning photographers tend to see only what is at the center of the viewfinder. More experienced photographers pay attention to the edges of the frame because they know the frame is critical to how the viewer sees the subject.

What's the subject of this picture? The soccer players? The spectators? The two kids playing behind the spectators?

If the subject is soccer, then change the frame to one that focuses on the action.

Most of the time you should aim for simplicity in images.

When your subject is complex, you can still achieve simplicity by paying close attention to point of view and frame.

Readers will plow through pages of boring writing if they have a strong purpose for reading, such as a financial report for a company they plan to invest in. Most of the time, however, you have to create and hold readers' interest if you expect them to finish what you write. When you create interest, you also build your credibility as a writer.

Details make writing lively.

Lamesa is typical of the hard towns of west Texas, which you quickly learn to associate with the smell of sulfur. Coming into town you pass the lots of the oil field suppliers surrounded by chain-link fences with red dirt blown over the lower third. Inside are rusted oil tanks, mutated steel skeletons of derrick parts, and squat buildings with plank porches lined with orange and blue oil drums—model railroad buildings blown up to full scale. On the small lots in between are shabby motels and windowless liquor stores with names like "Pinkies" on art deco signs above.

Dialogue brings people to life.

When we reached the pass, we stood for a moment and looked again at Glacier Peak and, far below us, the curving white line of the Suiattle. Park said, "When you create a mine, there are two things you can't avoid: a hole in the ground and a dump for waste rock. Those are two things you can't avoid."

　　Brower said, "Except by not doing it at all."

　　　　　　　　　　—John McPhee, *Conversations with the Archdruid*

Humor rewards readers and can make points memorable.

Large, naked, raw carrots are acceptable as food only to those who live in hutches eagerly awaiting Easter.

Inhabitants of underdeveloped nations and victims of natural disasters are the only people who have ever been happy to see soybeans.

　　　　　　　　　　—Fran Lebowitz, *Metropolitan Life*

Interest in visual texts is created by composition and subject matter. Some subjects possess inherent interest, but the photographer or artist must build on that interest. Kittens and puppies are cute, but viewers' interest fades quickly if the images are predictable.

Even potentially interesting subjects can be rendered boring if they are photographed in stereotypical ways.

Children often express a spontaneity lacking in adults, which provides visual interest.

Lines

Lines create interest in photographs. Strong diagonal lines can create dynamic photographs. Curved lines can produce graceful images.

EXERCISE 2.1 Think about the dingbats (the icons and symbols) that come with the font sets in a computer. Look at the following symbols and write out what each one is typically used to represent. Are there any that you don't know? Compare your answers with your classmates' answers. Do the meanings seem universal, or are meanings dependent on cultural factors?

1. 🕯 *light*
2. ⏳ *time*
3. 🕉
4. ☠ *death*
5. Ⓟ *park*

6. ☪ *muslim*
7. ✌ *peace*
8. ☑ *check*
9. 🗣 *speak*
10. ⓘ *info*

2b WHERE IMAGES WORK BEST

"A picture is worth a thousand words" is an old cliché. We could just as easily turn around the cliché to say that certain words such as *justice, truth,* and *faith* are worth a thousand pictures. It's not that images are necessarily more powerful than words but that images and words are different media. Our eyes and brains are able to take in a great deal of visual information and sort that information for relevance. People have little difficulty distinguishing familiar faces in a crowd or recognizing familiar patterns.

For example, we've now become accustomed to deciding whether we'll need to wear a sweater outside tomorrow by looking at the colors on a weather map. But even then, we depend on words to tell us whether the forecast is for today or tomorrow, and what each color signifies. Visuals are typically used in combination with text. Visuals work well when they

- Deliver spatial information, especially about spatial relationships
- Represent statistical relationships
- Produce a strong immediate impact, even shock value
- Emphasize further a main point you've made in words

In the digital era how you choose to incorporate visual elements in your communications contributes a great deal to the construction of your ethos as a writer. Just as grammar, punctuation, and spelling errors can damage your ethos, so too can elementary mistakes in visual presentation, such as placing dark text on a dark background, making it unreadable. Your awareness of how to signal important elements visually and incorporate effective graphics enhances your credibility.

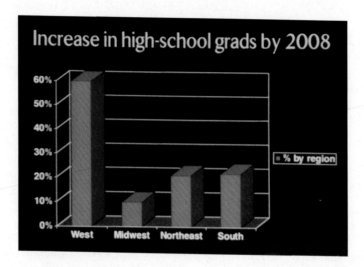

EXERCISE 2.2 Which of the following would be best represented by a visual? Which would be best represented by text? Which would benefit from both kinds of representation?

1. The definition of plagiarism
2. The increase in cases of plagiarism on college campuses each year since the Internet became readily available to students
3. Other possible causes for the rise in plagiarism cases
4. A proposal for an advertising campaign alerting students to the possible penalties for plagiarism
5. Instructions for kindergarten-age children for making a peanut butter and jelly sandwich
6. A complaint to your city's tenant council about the maintenance of your apartment complex

7. An agreement with your landlord dividing up responsibilities for maintenance of your apartment complex
8. An evaluation of NASCAR drivers
9. A comparison of the fighting styles of two martial arts masters
10. A description of renovations that should be made to the student gymnasium

2c WHERE WORDS WORK BEST

Words can do many things that images cannot. Written words work best when they

- Communicate abstract ideas
- Record information
- Report information
- Persuade using elaborated reasoning
- Communicate online using minimal bandwidth
- Adapt to specific users' needs (Words can be converted from oral to written language for those who are hearing impaired, or from written to oral for those who are visually impaired.)

If you've ever visited a Web site that opens with a glitzy Flash screen that takes forever to load and then discovered there was no significant content behind the opening screen, you know the problem of style without substance. While more of our communication in the digital era will take advantage of the multimedia capabilities of new technologies, these technologies will not replace the need for effective writing.

EXERCISE 2.3 Find an example of words and visuals used effectively to convey a message. This can be an advertisement, a poster announcing a public service, a brochure, an article in a periodical, a page in a textbook or other book, a manual, a work of art, a flyer for a concert or show, a Web site, or anything else that appeals to you to use. Describe the work accomplished by the visuals and the text both separately and in combination with one another. Why is the example you've chosen effective?

Chapter 3
Planning and Drafting

Good architects begin by asking who will use a building and what they will use it for. Good writers ask similar questions: Who is likely to read what I write? Why should they be interested in reading what I have to say? What am I trying to accomplish? How do I anticipate that readers will be influenced by what I write? Will they know something they didn't know before? Will they think about something familiar in a different way or at least acknowledge that other viewpoints exist? Will they consider taking some action based on what I have written?

Even if you are writing a diary only for yourself, you still ask these questions in some form. If, for example, you are writing a journal during a trip you take, you might record where exactly you went, how long it took to get there, and how much money you spent. Or you might concentrate on describing in detail what you saw and whom you met. Or you might focus on your reactions to particular places and people. Thinking about how people will use a building guides a successful architect in drawing blueprints and in supervising construction. Thinking about how you want readers to respond helps you make a global plan about what to write and helps you carry out that plan, revising it when necessary.

3a ESTABLISH YOUR GOALS

When you are writing for a college class, your instructor is generally your primary audience and your goal is to convince the instructor that you are an effective writer. Nevertheless, your instructor is aware that the goal of your course is to prepare you for other kinds of writing you will do in college and later in life. Likely you will be asked to think about audiences besides your instructor, including members of your class, your college community, and others beyond the campus.

Your instructor will give you specific suggestions about how to think about your audience and topic. Two ways to make your task simpler are to

- Be sure you are responding to the assignment appropriately
- Select a topic that both fits the assignment and appeals to you enough to make you want to write about it

Look carefully at your assignment

When your instructor gives you a writing assignment, look closely at what you are asked to do. Often the assignment will contain key words such as *analyze, compare and contrast, define, describe, evaluate,* or *propose* that will assist you in determining what direction to take.

- **Analyze:** Find connections among a set of facts, events, or readings, and make them meaningful.
- **Compare and contrast:** Examine how two or more things are alike and how they differ.
- **Define:** Make a claim about how something should be defined, according to features that you set out.
- **Describe:** Observe carefully and select details that create a dominant impression.
- **Evaluate:** Argue that something is good, bad, best, or worst in its class, according to criteria that you set out.
- **Propose:** Identify a particular problem and explain why your solution is the best one.

A specific audience might be mentioned in the assignment. If you are writing for a specific audience, what will those readers know about your topic? What will they likely have read about your topic? What attitudes are they likely to have about your topic?

Find a topic you care about

If you do not have an assigned topic, a good way to find one is to list possible topics to write about. It's hard to write about something that doesn't interest you, so start by writing down things that do interest you. If your assignment gives you a wide range of options, you might write more than one list, starting with your personal interests. Think also about campus topics, community topics, and national topics that intrigue you. Your lists might resemble these:

Personal

1. Benefits of weight training
2. Wordplay in Marx brothers movies
3. History of hairstyles

Campus

1. Pros and cons of charging computer fees
2. Should my university have a foreign language requirement?
3. Affirmative action admissions policies

Community

1. Helmet laws for people who ride bicycles and motorcycles
2. Bilingual education programs
3. More bike lanes to encourage more people to ride bicycles
4. Better public transportation

Nation/World

1. Advertising aimed at preschool children
2. Censorship of the Internet
3. Genetically altered crops
4. Setting aside the laws that govern police searches, in the effort to stop terrorism

Often you will find that, before you can begin writing, you need to clarify and narrow your topic. You may have to analyze exactly what you mean by a phrase like "censorship of the Internet," for example—do you mean censorship of Web sites, or of everything that goes over the Internet, including private email?

After you make a list or lists, you should review it:

- Put a checkmark beside the topics that look most interesting or the ones that mean the most to you.
- Put a question mark beside the topics that you don't know very much about. If you choose one of these issues, you probably will have to do research.
- Select two or three topics that look the most promising.

EXERCISE 3.1 Make a list of topics you care about. Add to your list by taking a survey of topics your friends, classmates, and family members care about. Hold on to this list for future exercises.

EXERCISE 3.2 A student generated the following list for his research paper on the history of the horror movie. Choose a topic for the paper from the list. Then organize the list into categories that the student could deal with in a paper. Eliminate any dead-end topics or redundancies.

> *Nosferatu* (1922)
> Bela Lugosi *Dracula* (1931)
> Boris Karloff *Frankenstein* (1931)
> Christopher Lee as Dracula in the 1960s
> monster movies
> *Creature from the Black Lagoon* (1956)
> werewolves
> slasher films
> women
> Wes Craven *Scream* (1996)
> Hammer Films and Christopher Lee
> blood vs. suspense
> Stephen King
> mutants, aliens, robots in the 1950s
> irony and independent film
> demons/possession

what was scary then/now? (1920s to late 1990s and beyond)
special effects
cult movies
Friday the 13th (1980)
cannibalism
Jamie Lee Curtis
The Exorcist (1973)
Carrie (1976)
weird trilogies they made in the 1960s
Vincent Price as Dr. Phibes in in the 1970s
teenagers in the woods
The Blair Witch Project (1999)
silent movies with haunted castles
Edgar Allan Poe popular in the 1970s

3b   EXPLORE YOUR TOPIC

Once you have identified a potential topic, the next step is to figure out what you already know about that topic and what you need to find out. Experienced writers use many strategies for exploring what they already know about a topic and how interesting it really is to them. Here are a few.

Ask questions

These classic reporter's questions will assist you in thinking through a topic:

1. *Who* is doing it?
2. *What* is happening or at issue?
3. *When* is it happening?
4. *Where* is it happening?
5. *How* is it happening?
6. *Why* is it happening?

Freewrite

Another method you can use to find out how much you know about a topic is to **freewrite**: Write as quickly as you can without stopping for a set time, usually five or ten minutes. The goal of freewriting is to get as much down as possible. Don't stop to correct mistakes. Let your ideas flow wherever they take you, even if they take you well outside the boundaries of your topic. The constant flow of words should generate ideas—some useful, some not.

If you get stuck, write the same sentence over again, or write about how hungry you are, or how difficult freewriting is, until thoughts on your selected topic reappear. After you've finished, read what you have written and single out any key ideas.

Freewrite on problem geese

Didn't even think about the problem until I took my nephew to the park. Don't think I even knew what a Canada goose looks like. Boy did I find out fast. They scared the be-jabbers out of Andy before I could lock the car. BIG GREEN POOP EVERYWHERE. We got it all over our shoes. What a mess!!!! Then mom told me they were rounding up the geese and gassing them. Incredible!!! Never thought there could be a legal massacre of wild animals bigger than roaches in western Washington. Short piece on tv that geese are a problem all across the country. Showed some golfer on a green trying to putt through goose poop. Funny except I remember how yucky it was to clean off our shoes.

Ideas to Use

1. Canada geese can make parks unusable.
2. Killing geese is an extreme solution.
3. Geese are a problem in many parts of the country.

You may want to use a key word or idea as a starting point for a second freewrite. After two or three rounds you will discover how much you already know about your topic and possible directions for developing it.

Computer Strategies

Computers and freewriting

Computers are good tools for freewriting because you won't tire as quickly as you would when writing by hand, and you can write faster. If you find you cannot stop yourself from going back to reread what you have written, darken the monitor screen so you cannot see what you are typing. Using a computer also allows you to cut and paste phrases or sentences later on.

Brainstorm

An alternative method of discovery is to **brainstorm**. The end result of brainstorming is usually a list—sometimes of questions, sometimes of statements. You might come up with a list of observations and questions, such as these for problem geese:

- Geese make parks unusable.
- Where did Canada geese come from all of a sudden?
- How can geese be discouraged?
- Why did local government decide to kill geese?
- Do geese carry diseases?
- How widespread is the problem?

Writing in the World

Storyboarding

Filmmakers, multimedia designers, and Web designers all use story-boarding as a primary tool for planning. Storyboards are a series of rough sketches of successive screen contents. In film, video, and animation, the sketches represent the script, something like a comic book without speech bubbles. Storyboards for Web sites also include the links that are required from one page to others.

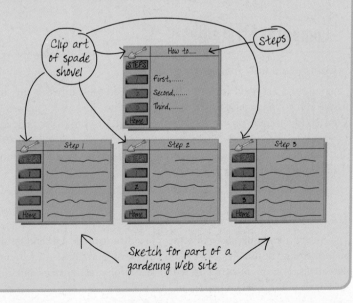

Sketch for part of a gardening Web site

Computer Strategies

Researching online

Online subject directories such as Yahoo divide big subjects into subtopics. They can help you narrow the focus of a big subject down to a topic that is manageable (see Chapter 17). Likewise, your library's online resources often divide big subjects into more manageable segments. For example, if you type "genome" in a subject search in your library's online catalog, you will get several more specific subtopics.

SUBJECT INDEX Search Results

(Records 1 - 10) For Brief Records, click on number.

YOUR SEARCH: GENOME has no exact match. The next entry is:

1 Genome mapping. --1 item(s)

2 Genomes --20 item(s)

3 Genomes--Computer programs. --1 item(s)

4 Genomes--Congresses. --7 item(s)

5 Genomes--Data processing. --4 item(s)

6 Genomes--Data processing--Congresses. --1 item(s)

7 Genomes--Data processing--Periodicals. --2 item(s)

8 Genomes--Nomenclature--Congresses. --1 item(s)

9 Genomes--Periodicals. --5 item(s)

10 Genomes--Research--International cooperation. --2 item(s)

Make an idea map

Still another strategy for exploring how much you know about a potential topic is to make an **idea map**. Idea maps are useful because they let you see everything at once, and you can begin to make connections among the different aspects of an issue—definitions, causes, effects, proposed solutions, and your personal experience. A good way to get started is to write down ideas on sticky notes. Then you can move the sticky notes around until you figure out which ideas fit together.

Let's go back to the topic of problem geese. If you decided to write on this topic, you would need to find out more. Since the topic is quite current,

newspaper sources are important. Your library has tools that can help you to find recent articles in newspapers from around the country. Figure 3.1 shows what your idea map on problem geese might look like.

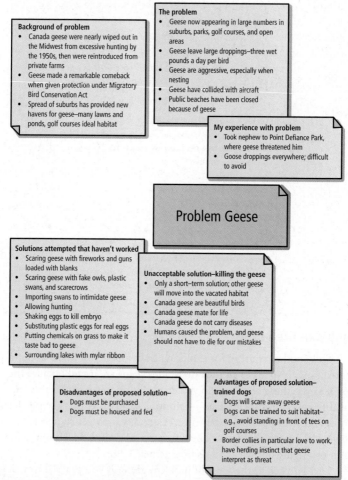

Background of problem
- Canada geese were nearly wiped out in the Midwest from excessive hunting by the 1950s, then were reintroduced from private farms
- Geese made a remarkable comeback when given protection under Migratory Bird Conservation Act
- Spread of suburbs has provided new havens for geese–many lawns and ponds, golf courses ideal habitat

The problem
- Geese now appearing in large numbers in suburbs, parks, golf courses, and open areas
- Geese leave large droppings–three wet pounds a day per bird
- Geese are aggressive, especially when nesting
- Geese have collided with aircraft
- Public beaches have been closed because of geese

My experience with problem
- Took nephew to Point Defiance Park, where geese threatened him
- Goose droppings everywhere; difficult to avoid

Problem Geese

Solutions attempted that haven't worked
- Scaring geese with fireworks and guns loaded with blanks
- Scaring geese with fake owls, plastic swans, and scarecrows
- Importing swans to intimidate geese
- Allowing hunting
- Shaking eggs to kill embryo
- Substituting plastic eggs for real eggs
- Putting chemicals on grass to make it taste bad to geese
- Surrounding lakes with mylar ribbon

Unacceptable solution–killing the geese
- Only a short–term solution; other geese will move into the vacated habitat
- Canada geese are beautiful birds
- Canada geese mate for life
- Canada geese do not carry diseases
- Humans caused the problem, and geese should not have to die for our mistakes

Disadvantages of proposed solution–
- Dogs must be purchased
- Dogs must be housed and fed

Advantages of proposed solution– trained dogs
- Dogs will scare away geese
- Dogs can be trained to suit habitat– e.g., avoid standing in front of tees on golf courses
- Border collies in particular love to work, have herding instinct that geese interpret as threat

Figure 3.1. Idea map on problem geese

Annotating texts and taking reading notes

Most of the writing you do in college will be linked to texts you are reading. When you sit down to write your paper after reading extensively, good reading notes are like a gift. Whether you write in the margins (of your own books or photocopies) or make notes separately on notebook paper is your preference. What you focus on when you annotate and take notes on texts depends on your purpose in reading. Sometimes you will want to annotate in a general way; it is always useful to highlight key points and write key words and phrases in the margins when you read. Other times, when you are reading after you have formulated a thesis, your notes will be more specific.

No matter whether your purpose in reading is to remember, to explore ideas, or to find evidence for a particular argument, "talking" to a text by writing questions and comments about it will help you feel at home with it. What would you say to the author if he or she were on the other side of the table from you? Answering her or him by writing responses can bring that text to life. It can also help you realize that the author is, like you, a person with a point of view.

Keeping a journal

Freewriting and idea mapping can help you to discover what you know about a topic at a given time. Keeping a journal, by contrast, allows you to keep a record of ideas you come up with over time, perhaps even over many years. Whether its lifespan is long or short, a journal gives you a chance to see how your ideas grow and shift. A journal can be a sourcebook for essay ideas. Or it can be written simply for its own sake—for the satisfaction of recording your experiences and observations, and exploring your thoughts. Writers (and people who do not call themselves writers) keep many different kinds of journals—diaries, accounts of travel, dream journals, reading journals, nature journals, and so on. Some journals are meant to stay private; others are written with publication in mind. Your teacher may ask for a particular type of journal, but even if the topic or kind of writing is assigned, usually you have more freedom in a journal than in formal kinds of writing to try out ideas or writing styles. A journal is a good place to be bold and experiment.

Talking and listening

People often have the impression that writers are hermits who reject the company of others in favor of lives of seclusion. We are led to believe that ideas come to writers only when they are locked in their musty studies or leaning dreamily against the trunk of a tree at the edge of an empty meadow. Some writers and some literary traditions have encouraged this stereotype. Thoreau built his little cabin in the woods and announced to the world that he had found "no companion so companionable as solitude."

Anyone who has written knows that writing requires concentration, and solitude has its role, but many ideas come from conversation, and all ideas are born from other ideas. When we talk, we discover. A more realistic picture of the productive writer, then, is a person engaged in a community where ideas are discussed. Your writing class is a writing community. To make the community as useful as possible, it is important to ask your peers for specific and genuine feedback on your drafts and to pay close attention to your classmates' writing as well.

If any of your class communication is done through email or online discussion, you already have a head start on your assigned writing. Emails and online discussions can be used the way journals and freewrites are—as material for essays. When you are planning your essay, you may find that you already have a wealth of written material to draw from.

EXERCISE 3.3 Read the following passage and freewrite for ten minutes. When you are done, look over what you wrote and pick out two or three topics that would be worth pursuing in a paper.

That in the beginning when the world was young there were a great many thoughts but no such thing as a truth. Man made the truths himself and each truth was a composite of a great many vague thoughts. All about in the world were the truths and they were all beautiful.

The old man had listed hundreds of the truths in his book. I will not try to tell you of all of them. There was the truth of virginity and the truth of passion, the truth of wealth and of poverty, of thrift and of profligacy, of carelessness and abandon. Hundreds and hundreds were the truths and they were all beautiful.

And then the people came along. Each as he appeared snatched up one of the truths and some who were quite strong snatched up a dozen of them.

It was the truths that made the people grotesques. The old man had quite an elaborate theory concerning the matter. It was his notion that the moment one of the people took one of the truths to himself, called it his truth, and tried to live his life by it, he became a grotesque and the truth he embraced became a falsehood.

—Sherwood Anderson, "The Book of the Grotesque," *Winesburg, Ohio*, 1919

3c | WRITE A WORKING THESIS

Narrow your topic

So far the planning process has involved reaching for ideas, expanding and broadening your thoughts, and recording ideas from written sources and conversations. It may seem odd, then, that the next stage of thinking, after you have decided on a topic, is *narrowing* your topic so that you focus on a particular aspect of it. But having a narrow focus is the key to writing a strong essay. Choosing a focus or central idea does not mean that the idea cannot change as you write drafts; your focus probably will change somewhat. Having a strong focus, however, will give you direction as you begin to write a draft.

Narrowing your focus means doing two things: (1) selecting a manageable part of your overall topic, and (2) deciding on your purpose in writing about that specific topic. One student, for example, decided she wanted to write about immigration to the United States. She still had many choices to make to narrow her topic: Would she focus on legal or illegal immigration? Would she write about the effects of immigration on the U.S. economy or about the struggles of immigrants when they arrive in the United States? Should she limit her discussion to one state or region, or make an argument about national immigration law? She decided she was most interested in the plight of undocumented workers in her hometown.

This topic was specific and manageable. Now she had to decide on her purpose in writing. Her approach would be different depending on what she wanted her essay to do: Did she want mainly to *describe* a particular family's situation? To *analyze* or *evaluate* proposed programs that would help families to gain legal status? To *convince* readers of a point of view, or *call them to action*? It is easy to see that even with her topic narrowed, she could still go in many directions.

Formulate your thesis

Your thesis states your main idea. Much of the writing that you will do in college and later in your career will have an explicit thesis, usually stated near the beginning. The thesis announces your topic and indicates what points you want to make about that topic.

Your thesis should be closely tied to your purpose—to reflect on your own experience, to explain some aspect of your topic, or to argue for a position or course of action.

A REFLECTIVE THESIS	My experiences of watching wildlife over a long time have taught me that they spend much of their time competing with other members of their own species for territory and food.
AN INFORMATIVE THESIS	The spread of the suburbs has created new habitats for wild animals that can adapt to living near people, such as coyotes and Canada geese.
A PERSUASIVE THESIS	Even if their first efforts were unsuccessful, communities should continue to develop methods for discouraging Canada geese instead of killing them.

Evaluate your working thesis

Ask yourself these questions about your working thesis.

1. Is it specific?
2. Is it manageable in the length and time you have?
3. Is it interesting to your intended readers?

Consider the following examples.

Example 1

Eating disorders remain a serious problem on college campuses.

Specific? The thesis is too broad. Exactly who suffers from eating disorders? Is the problem the same for men and women?

Manageable? Because the thesis is not limited to a particular aspect of eating disorders, it cannot be researched adequately.

Interesting? The topic is potentially interesting, but most people know that many college students suffer from eating disorders. If you chose this topic, what could you tell your readers that they don't know already?

Revised thesis

Glamorous images of ultrathin people in the fashion industry, the movie industry, and other media are a contributing cause of eating disorders on college campuses because they influence young people to believe they are fat when in fact their weight is normal.

Example 2

The United States entered World War II when the Japanese bombed Pearl Harbor on December 7, 1941.

Specific? The thesis is too narrow. It states a commonly acknowledged fact.

Manageable? A known fact is stated in the thesis, so there is nothing to research. The general topic of the attack on Pearl Harbor is too large for essay-length treatment.

Interesting? The attack on Pearl Harbor remains interesting to Americans (witness a recent Hollywood film that deals with the subject), but there is no topic to work from.

Revised thesis

Although combat between the United States and Japan began at Pearl Harbor, the unofficial war began when President Roosevelt froze Japanese assets in the United States in July 1940 and later declared a commercial embargo.

These examples suggest that the key to writing an effective thesis is finding a topic that is neither too vast nor too narrow, and one that is not obvious. You may have to adjust your working thesis more than once as you plan and begin drafting.

EXERCISE 3.4 Look at the following theses. What kind (reflective, informative, persuasive) is each?

1. Reading Sylvia Plath's poem "Daddy" awakened me to the depth of complexity possible in the father-daughter relationship.
2. Critics should recognize that the field of trauma studies could not exist without the works of Sylvia Plath.
3. Sylvia Plath's relationship with poet Ted Hughes affected her later work deeply.
4. No-kill animal shelters are finding creative ways to persuade people to adopt older pets.
5. My experience with Sylvester, a cat so old he was museum-quality, has given me a great fondness for elderly pets.
6. The city should fine anyone who willfully abandons a pet.
7. Lawmakers need to see that school vouchers will be the death of public schools.
8. My parents, going against their friends' advice, sent me to a public school in the inner city. Their decision made a huge impact on how I, as an adult, feel about education.
9. The voucher issue has set off a heated debate in both major political parties.
10. The school voucher program has worked wonders for many at-risk kids.

EXERCISE 3.5 Write two summaries of the following passage. In the first summary, provide just the key points, as they appear. When you are done with this summary, rank the ideas in the order of their importance. For your second summary, focus on the top two ideas from your ranking and give more detail from the passage about these ideas. At the end of the second summary, explain why you decided this idea or these ideas were the most important. Finally, rewrite this explanation as one sentence. This is a thesis.

When two people talk, they don't just fall into physical and aural harmony. They also engage in what is called motor mimicry. If you show people pictures of a smiling face or a frowning face, they'll smile or frown back, although perhaps only in muscular changes so fleeting that they can only be captured with electronic sensors. If I hit my thumb with a hammer, most people watching will grimace: they'll mimic my emotional state. This is what is meant, in the technical sense, by empathy. We imitate each other's emotions as a way of expressing support and caring and, even more basically, as a way of communicating with each other.

—Malcolm Gladwell, *The Tipping Point: How Little Things Can Make a Big Difference*, 2000

EXERCISE 3.6 Here are several assignments and the thesis statement that a student has decided to use for that assignment. Evaluate these thesis statements according to their level of specificity, manageability, and interest. Then, rewrite each one to make them meet all three of the requirements.

1. Design a three-panel brochure intended to educate teenage boys about the responsibilities of fatherhood.

   Thesis: Think before having a baby. They are really expensive.

2. Write a three- to five-page paper for a child development class. The papers from this class will be published on a child-advocacy Web site.

   Thesis: Many formerly accepted methods of discipline are now considered child abuse.

3. Write a 10- to 15-page research paper on a revolutionary break-through in urban transportation to enter in a contest. Your paper will be evaluated by a panel of graduate students majoring in city planning.

   Thesis: Washington, D.C., has a great subway system called the Metro.

4. Write a 200- to 300-word article for a magazine geared toward 8- to 12-year-olds.

   Thesis: It's never too early to start thinking about a career.

5. Write a one-page paper for your ethics class. You will use this paper to start class discussion.

   Thesis: Reading employees' email is a violation of privacy.

3d | PLAN A STRATEGY

People who write frequently on the job or who make their living by writing have many different ways of producing a successful piece of writing. Some may plan extensively in advance, either individually or as a team, specifying exactly what will go in each section. **Advance planners** don't start writing until they know what will go into each part. They believe that detailed planning cuts down on the need for rewriting.

Other writers find that putting ideas into words often changes the ideas and generates new ones. These writers know that writing drafts is a way of discovering their subject, and they count on one or two or more rewrites to get their document into shape. **Deep revisers** trust that the structure of what they write will evolve during the process of writing, and they realize that they can make major changes if necessary. No matter what their style of composing, successful writers are aware of what they will need to do to complete a writing task, and they have strategies for when they get stuck or encounter the unexpected. Even more important, they have a good sense of the writing situation. (See Chapter 1.)

Consider making an outline

At some point in school you may have been required to produce a formal outline to submit along with a paper. A formal outline typically begins with the thesis statement, which anchors the entire outline. Each numbered or lettered item clearly supports the thesis, and the relationship among the items is clear from the outline hierarchy. The following outline shows how the levels are related to each other: Roman numerals indicate the highest level; next come capital letters, then numbers, and finally lowercase letters. The rule to remember when deciding whether you need to use the next level down is that each level must have at least two items—a "1." needs a "2."; an "a." needs a "b." Such outlines can be helpful for revising because they force you to look carefully at the organization, but few writers plan in such detail before beginning.

Following is a formal outline for a paper on problem geese.

Thesis statement: The goose problem in Tacoma can be solved with dog patrols instead of killing the geese.

I. Canada geese have become a nuisance in urban and suburban parks and green spaces.
   A. Geese are aggressive.
   B. Geese make parks unusable because of their droppings.
II. The problem with Canada geese was created by people.
   A. Canada geese were hunted almost to extinction in 1950s.
   B. A surviving flock was captured and raised on farms.
   C. Geese stopped migrating and learned to live in urban parks and suburbs, leading to a population explosion.
III. Many unsuccessful attempts have been made to discourage problem geese.
   A. Hunting is an ineffective means of controlling urban geese.
   B. Several methods have been attempted to scare away geese.
      1. Fireworks and guns
      2. Flags, scarecrows, fake owls, plastic swans
      3. Real swans
   C. Several other approaches have been tried.
      1. Spraying eggs with oil
      2. Substituting plastic eggs for real eggs
      3. Spraying grass to make geese leave
      4. Putting red mylar tape around ponds
   D. In frustration communities have started killing geese.
IV. Geese are a nuisance, not a threat to human health.
   A. Canada geese do not spread diseases.
   B. Canada geese are beautiful birds.
V. The solution to problem geese is to use dog patrols.
   A. GeesePeace has had success using dogs to frighten away geese.
   B. The objection of the cost of training dogs is insignificant in comparison to the cost of bad publicity created by killing geese and the bad example set for children.

In contrast, a working outline is more like an initial sketch of how you will arrange the major sections. Jotting down main points and a few sub-points before you begin can be a great help while you are writing. If you have made an idea map (see Figure 3.1), you can easily work from the map to produce a working outline. You can read the complete essay that developed from these outlines in Section 9d.

Problem Geese

<u>Section 1:</u> Begin with my experience with my nephew in the park when I first learned about problem geese.

<u>Section 2:</u> Tell how Canada geese were almost hunted to extinction in the 1950s and then came back.

<u>Section 3:</u> Start with the obvious solution of hunting and explain why it won't work in suburbs.

<u>Section 4:</u> Go through other solutions that have been tried and haven't worked.

<u>Section 5:</u> Describe the bad solution-killing geese.

<u>Section 6:</u> Describe the solution that has worked-trained border collies.

<u>Section 7:</u> Mention the possible objection of cost and explain why the cost is negligible in comparison to the benefits.

EXERCISE 3.7 Look again at the brainstorming list for Exercise 3.1, the freewrite you did for Exercise 3.3, and the summaries and thesis you extracted from the passage in Exercise 3.5. Choose one of these to pursue and write a short outline for a paper that includes three to five main topics.

3e | COMPOSE A DRAFT

A common misconception about successful writers is that they write a finished piece in one sitting without having to go back and change anything. Nothing is further from the truth. The best writers know that nobody gets everything right the first time. They know that the most efficient way of writing is not to get obsessed with getting everything in final form as you are writing. They aim at producing a good draft—not a perfect draft. They know that they can go back and revise later.

Essays typically contain an introduction, body, and conclusion. You do not have to write these parts in that order, though. You may want to begin with your best example, which might be in the third paragraph according to your informal outline. The most important thing about drafting is that you feel comfortable and treat yourself kindly. If the inner critic shows up— that little voice in your mind that has nothing encouraging to say—banish it, refute it, write through it. Remember, the inner critic cannot frustrate you if you are putting words on paper or on the computer screen.

Often students have learned the introduction-body-conclusion formula too well. If you have practiced for state-mandated writing tests, you probably have the three-part essay tattooed on the inside of your skull. Consider this: If a reader cannot remember your line of reasoning in a three-page paper without having your thesis stated, proven, and then re-stated, likely something is wrong with your line of reasoning. You don't have to drop the introduction and conclusion and write an essay that is all body, but you can think of the introduction and conclusion as something other than a statement and reiteration of your main point.

Readers want to be motivated to read what you write. You can offer a short example that illustrates the problem being discussed, as in the essay "Problem Geese" (see Section 9d). You can state a surprising fact. You can begin with a fascinating quotation. Your aim is to interest the reader and to let the reader know the topic of the paper, if not necessarily the thesis. Unless the thesis is striking, often it can wait until you have laid the groundwork that will ready the reader for your thesis.

The body of the essay consists of the primary discussion. Remember to guide readers through the discussion by letting them know where you are going. If your discussion is a road, your readers need road signs to tell them where the road is taking them. Road signs are transition words and phrases such as "consequently," "the third reason is . . . ," and "on the other hand."

The last section, the conclusion, often repeats what has already been said. If the essay has been long and complex, sometimes this repetition is necessary, but usually the repetition is just that—annoying redundancy.

The final paragraph does not have to repeat the main point. It can give a compelling last example or propose a course of action. It can ponder the larger significance of the subject under discussion. It can pose an important question for the reader to think about.

Strategies for writing a draft

1. **If you have an outline, put it on the computer screen or place it beside you.** The outline will give you prompts to help get you started.

2. **Begin writing what you know best.** If you don't know exactly where you are headed, the introduction can be the hardest section to write. The introduction can wait until last.

3. **Resist the urge to revise too soon.** It's more important to keep moving forward. If you stop to polish a section, you will lose momentum, and in the end you may discard that section anyway.

4. **If you get stuck, try working on another section.** Look again at your notes or outline.

5. **If you are still stuck, talk to someone about what you are trying to write.** If your campus has a writing center, talk to a consultant. Reading more about your subject can also help you to get moving again.

3f | WRITE AS A MEMBER OF A TEAM

Until recently, a major difference between writing on the job and writing in college courses was that writing in the workplace—especially important writing tasks like reports, analyses, and proposals—is often done by teams of people. Almost without exception people in occupations that require a college education write frequently on the job, and much of that writing is done in collaboration rather than alone. Even people who don't have experience writing collaboratively find that when they move into managerial positions, they often are responsible for employees who must work and write in teams. Furthermore, they are responsible for all that comes out of their units, so if a particular document is poorly written, they suffer the consequences.

Collaborative writing isn't confined to the workplace. Word processing programs make it easy to compose newsletters and other documents for organizations, and the Internet makes it even easier for several people to work on a project from different locations. The better you understand how to write effectively with other people, the more enjoyable and more productive the process will be for you. If you've played on competitive sports teams, you know that it takes time for a team to come together. Successful athletic teams recognize that their members each have different strengths; they find ways to blend these strengths so that each team member can contribute to the team's goals.

Athletic teams, however, have the advantages of playing together over several months under the direction of a coach who assigns roles, conveys expectations, and assesses progress. In many cases, writing teams collaborate on only one project. Often no one is in a supervisory role, and the team members are expected to determine what needs to be done, decide the necessary roles, and monitor the progress of the project themselves. You may have to be player and coach at the same time, and often you will be under deadline pressure. Successful writing team members have skills that enable them to determine overall goals, the work required, and the people responsible for the various tasks. Team members monitor progress in order to improve constantly and ensure quality in the finished product.

You can become a member of a successful writing team by understanding how a team works effectively.

Determine the goals and identify tasks and roles.

- Write down the goals as specifically as you can and discuss them as a team.
- Determine what tasks are required to meet those goals. Be as specific as you can. Write down the tasks and arrange them in the order they need to be completed.
- Decide whether the team has the skills and resources to perform those tasks. If you do not possess the necessary skills and resources, adjust the goals to what you can realistically expect to accomplish.

Make a work plan.

- Make a time line that lists the dates when specific tasks need to be completed and distribute it to all team members. Charts are useful tools for keeping track of progress.
- Assign tasks to team members. Find out if anyone possesses additional skills that could be helpful to the team.
- Revisit the team's goals often. To succeed, each team member must keep in mind what the team aims to accomplish.
- Decide on a process for monitoring progress. Set up specific dates for review and assign team members to be responsible for reviewing work that has been done.

Understand the dynamics of a successful team.

- Teamwork requires some flexibility. Different people have different styles and contribute in different ways. Keep talking to each other along the way.
- It may be desirable to rotate roles during the project.

Deal with problems when they come up.

- If a team member is not participating, find out why.
- If team members have different ideas about what needs to be done, find time to meet so that the team can reach an agreement.
- Get the team together if you are not meeting the deadlines you established in the work plan and devise a new plan, if necessary.

Have realistic expectations about the pluses and minuses of working as a group.

- The major benefit of working in a group is that you can potentially accomplish a great deal more than you could by working alone. Participating as a team member can be personally rewarding.
- Working in groups can have disadvantages. Groups can require more time because people bring different perspectives that need to be discussed. Two perennial problems with groups are maintaining focus on clearly articulated goals and handling team members who aren't doing their share.

3g | STAY ORGANIZED

If you work on paper, use file folders for your notes, freewrites, drafts, and research. If you work on a computer, label your files and put them in a folder. Develop a system for naming your files of drafts, so you will know which is the most recent (one way is to put a date in the file name). If you decide to cut a section out of a draft, make a new file and save it with a file name such as "assignment1-extra." Or make a folder and label it "assignment1-old" and put the earlier versions in it. You may change your mind later and decide you want to use what you have set aside.

Computer Strategies

Save, save, save

Nothing is more frustrating than putting in a lot of time and effort writing and then losing your work because of a computer glitch. Disks get misplaced or lost, hard drives crash, and files sometimes get overwritten by mistake or mysteriously disappear. Avoid disaster by saving frequently as you write. And create backup files of everything that you do. Save work on your computer to a floppy or zip disk. If you are using a computer at your school, save to two disks.

Chapter 4

Composing Paragraphs

The word *paragraph* derives from a symbol (¶) that was used in medieval manuscripts and later in print to indicate a small shift in topic. It took centuries for the notion of a paragraph to evolve into its modern form, that of a short block of text set off by indentation or space, with all sentences connected in some way to a single topic.

You may have heard a paragraph defined as a unit of thought, but that definition is incomplete. A paragraph is also a device to help readers. If you have ever picked up a book by a classic writer of the nineteenth century (for example, Charles Darwin), you likely found paragraphs that ran on for pages. Most readers today cringe at the sight of paragraphs that fill entire pages, and, as a result, paragraphs have become shorter over the past hundred years. Most important, readers expect that the sequence of paragraphs will set out a line of thought that they can follow.

4a FOCUS YOUR PARAGRAPHS

Readers expect sentences in a paragraph to be closely related to one another. Often writers will begin a paragraph with one idea, but other ideas will occur to them while they are writing. Paragraphs confuse readers when they go in different directions. When you revise your paragraphs, check for focus.

In the following example, notice how much stronger the paragraph becomes when we remove the sentences in green. They distract us from the subject, Royal Chitwan National Park in Nepal and how it is different from Western national parks.

Like everything else in Nepal, Royal Chitwan National Park is different from Western notions of a park. It is a jungle between two rivers, with grass twenty to twenty-five feet tall growing in the swampy land along the rivers. Several rare or endangered species live in the park, including leopards, crocodiles, royal Bengal tigers, and the greater one-horned Asian rhinoceros. In fact, we saw several rhinos during our weeklong visit to the park. To my relief we saw all but one from the safety of an elephant's back. But the boundaries of the park restrict neither the Nepalis nor the animals. The Nepalis cross the river into the park to gather firewood and the tall grass, which they use to make their houses. Some even live within the park. The rhinos and deer raid the Nepalis' fields at night, and the leopards prey on their dogs and livestock. To keep the truce between these competitors, the army patrols the park, mostly to prevent poachers from killing the tigers and rhino. But confrontations do occur; the animals lose habitat and the Nepalis lose their crops and lives.

Use explicit topic sentences

You were probably taught to begin a paragraph with a topic sentence. Topic sentences alert readers to the focus of a paragraph and help writers stay on topic. Topic sentences should explain the focus of the paragraph and situate it in the larger argument. Topic sentences, however, do not have to begin paragraphs, and they need not be just one sentence. You will decide what placement and length will best suit your subject.

Topic sentences at the beginning of a paragraph will quickly orient readers, preparing them for the sentences to come. Each sentence that follows elucidates the topic sentence.

TOPIC SENTENCE AT THE BEGINNING

We live in a world of risks so much beyond our control that it is difficult to think of anything that is risk free. Even the most basic human acts involve risk—having sex in an era of AIDS, eating in an era of genetically altered food, walking outside in an ozone-depleted atmosphere, drinking water and breathing air laden with chemicals whose effects we do not understand. Should we eat more fish in our daily diet? Nutritionists tell us that eating fish reduces the risk of heart disease. Other scientists, however, tell us that fish are contaminated with a new generation of synthetic chemicals.

When a paragraph builds to make a particular point, the topic sentence is more effective at the end of the paragraph.

TOPIC SENTENCE AT THE END

We are continually being summoned to change ourselves for the better—through fitness programs, through various kinds of instruction, through advice columns, through self-help books and videos—and somehow we never quite measure up. The blame always comes back on us. If we had eaten better, or exercised more, or paid more attention to our investments, or learned a new skill, or changed our oil every 3,000 miles, then things would have turned out better. Very rarely do we ask how a different social organization might have made things better. **Our society incorporates critical thinking without being much affected by the consequences of that thinking.**

Use implicit topic sentences in narrative paragraphs

In some cases, particularly in narrative prose, writers omit explicit topic sentences because they would clash with the tone or style of the paragraph. Instead, these paragraphs use tightly connected, focused sentences to make the topic implicitly clear.

IMPLICIT TOPIC SENTENCE

By the mid-1970s in the United States, the temporary advantage of being the only major power with its industries undamaged following World War II had evaporated, and rust-belt industries failed one after the other against competition from a revived Europe and an emergent Asia. The United States seemed to be going the way of other historical world powers, where efficient trading nations beat out bloated military regimes. Japan appeared to be the model for a fast and light capitalism that the rest of the world would imitate. Just a few years later, however, the American decline reversed. The United States again became the economic leader of the world in the 1990s.

The implicit topic sentence is something like "The United States' economy appeared to be in rapid decline in the 1970s, only to bounce back to world leadership in the 1990s."

EXERCISE 4.1 Find the topic sentence in each of the following paragraphs. If it is implied, write what you think it is.

1. I first got interested in the Civil War as a boy. Any Deep South boy, and probably all Southern boys, have been familiar with the Civil War as a sort of thing in their conscience going back. I honestly believe that it's in all our subconsciouses. This country was into its adolescence at the time of the Civil War. It really was; it hadn't formulated itself really as an adult nation, and the Civil War did that. Like all traumatic experiences that you might have had in your adolescence, it stays with you the rest of your life, constantly in your subconscious, most likely in your conscience, too.

—Shelby Foote, *Booknotes*, 1997

2. "NORM!" You want to go where everyone knows your name, right? Especially if it is a hip yuppie bar filled with good-looking and witty people. For years, television viewers tuned in to witness the antics of the crowd at "Cheers": Sam, Diane/Rebecca, Coach/Woody, Carla, Cliff and Norm, the corpulent resident of the corner stool. Frats even developed a drinking game in which each participant had to down a shot every time Norm was greeted by the other regulars. Here comes the regular, and, as the Replacements song goes, "am I the only one to feel ashamed" that both the viewing public and the media celebrate an alcoholic television character?

3. When was the last time you were in the mood for a nice, hearty, basic meal and the only thing that would do was a heaping plate of spaghetti and meatballs? It would have to be about every other day for me. Sometimes, though, a nice light chicken dish with some bread and herb butter would hit the spot. Enter Al Capone's Ristorante Italiano. This little joint on Barton Springs Road is a haven for those who enjoy good home-cooked Italian food and a peaceful atmosphere. When Tex-Mex, Chinese, or steak won't do, Al Capone's proves that it is by far the best place to go for Italian food.

4. But I have said enough. I hope you will treasure up the instructions which I have given you, and make them a guide to your feet and a light to your understanding. Build your character thoughtfully and painstakingly upon these precepts; and by and by, when you have got it built, you will be surprised and gratified to see how nicely and sharply it resembles everybody else's.

—Mark Twain, "Advice to Youth," 1882

4b ORGANIZE YOUR PARAGRAPHS

Logically arrange paragraphs within a paper

An essay usually has a clear beginning, middle, and end. It begins with a paragraph (or section) that introduces the subject and captures the reader's interest. Then a series of body paragraphs develops that subject. If the purpose of the paper is primarily informative, the body of the paper will identify aspects of the subject and discuss those aspects. If the purpose is to make an argument, then the body will offer reasons in support of the writer's position, with an analysis of evidence. And finally, a paragraph (or section) at the end provides the conclusion, by summarizing what has been said, drawing implications, adding examples, or calling for action.

Logically arrange sentences within a paragraph

Well-organized paragraphs in essays usually follow a pattern similar to that of a well-organized paper, but in miniature. Well-organized paragraphs often begin by getting the reader's attention. They introduce the subject with a topic sentence and indicate how the subject fits with what comes before and after. Sometimes well-organized paragraphs draw conclusions that lead to the subject of the next paragraph.

Seven strategies for effectively organizing sentences within a paragraph follow. Remember, the form of the paragraph should follow its function in the paper. Chances are you'll use a combination of these strategies within paragraphs in order to get your point across. These combinations are illustrated in the examples on pages 66 to 72.

The example paragraphs about Nepal are adapted from Lester Faigley, "Nepal Diary: Where the Global Village Ends." *North Dakota Quarterly* 57.3 (1989): 106-29.

Description

Description is a common strategy for informative and narrative writing. Providing concrete details—sights, sounds, smells, textures, and tastes— gives the reader a sensory memory of your subject.

Topic sentence

Details convey a dominant impression.

The airport at Kathmandu resembles one-gate airports in the United States, with a small waiting room and baggage area, except that it is deluged with international tourists. Busloads of young people lug bright nylon rucksacks and duffle bags emblazoned with names like "Australian Wilderness Adventures" and "South Korean Dhaulagiri Winter Expedition." Mingled with them are traders from India and Nepal—some dressed in suits, some in peasant clothes—carrying bulky goods like folding chairs, drums of cooking oil, and boxes of medicine.

This descriptive paragraph relies on a comparison to a place U.S. readers will probably recognize.

As in descriptive writing, in photographs close attention to detail is essential.

Narrative paragraphs tell a story for a reason. Organized by time, narratives explain a series of events in the order they occur. This approach is useful when the temporal order of ideas or events is essential to their logic, such as how-to writing.

The ascent goes easier than they expected. In two hours they reach the yak pastures where they will make the high camp. The view from the high camp is spectacular, with Dhaulagiri in clouds above them and the three sunlit summits of Nilgiri across the valley, with snow plumes blowing from their tops. Jim and Lester drop their packs at the campsite and continue walking to scout the route above the camp that they will follow in the darkness of early morning the next day. They find a steep path that parallels a fern-lined gorge, now rich in fall color. It is the lushest forest they have seen in Nepal. They congratulate each other on their decision to attempt the climb to the Dhaulagiri icefall, unaware that they will soon experience the mountain's furious weather, even on its lower slopes.

Verbs establish the sequence of events to orient the reader in time.

Narrative paragraphs often include description to orient the reader in space.

Paragraphs of comparison assess one subject in terms of its relation to others, usually highlighting what they have in common. Contrasting paragraphs analyze differences between things.

You can organize a comparison or a contrast in two ways: by describing one thing and then describing another, or by moving back and forth between the two items point by point. Often the latter strategy highlights contrasts, as the following paragraph illustrates.

Establishes the terms of the comparison

Each phrase shows the medieval "heart" and the "thin overlay" of Western culture.

Nepal was closed to Europeans from 1843 to 1949 and missed the colonial influences of the British. Consequently, Kathmandu remains a medieval city at heart, with a thin overlay of the last two decades of trendy Western culture: Tibetan women dressed in traditional clothes weave rugs on antique looms while humming Sting tunes; a traffic jam on Kathmandu's only wide street is caused by bulls fighting in an intersection; restaurants play U2 and serve tough buffalo steak under the name *chateau briande*; coffee houses serve cappuccino across the street from women drying rice by lifting it into the air with hoes; nearly naked children wearing burlap sacks grab cake slices out of the hands of gawking tourists emerging from a Viennese pastry shop.

This comparison/ contrast also uses a cause/effect pattern to help organize it. The word *consequently* in the third line is the transition from the cause to the effect.

Much writing in college depends on establishing the definitions of key terms. Consequently, writers often use entire paragraphs for definitions. Paragraphs organized by definition usually begin with the term and then go on to list its distinguishing features, sometimes using examples. Writers may begin with a standard definition and then qualify or add to that definition in unexpected ways.

Definitions are critical to persuasive writing. If your audience accepts your definitions of key terms, usually you will be convincing.

Tranquility in Western countries is usually equated with getting away from it all. Its synonyms are *calmness, serenity,* and *peace of mind,* and no wonder: We live in a world where it is increasingly difficult to get completely away from human-produced noise. In the Hindu and Buddhist traditions, however, tranquility is thought of as an internal quality that is gained when a person no longer is controlled by worldly desires. While this definition of tranquility may seem foreign to us, the internal state of tranquility is evident when you are in the presence of someone who possesses it.

Usual definition

Extended definition adds a new dimension.

If you want to prove a point or bring an issue to life, an organization based on examples and illustrations may work well. This structure usually begins with the main idea or point, then moves to a vivid explanation of one or two examples that illustrate the main idea. Examples and illustrations also can work well in opening and concluding paragraphs.

Point

Illustration

When religious principles clash with practical realities, ingenuity often comes to the rescue. Upon entering Braga, a Buddhist village built into a cliffside high in the Himalayas, Jim and Lester noticed that the men of the village surrounded two yaks, wrestled them to the ground, and tied their feet together. By a stone wall on the side of the field, an old bearded man read from a holy book while the yaks were stabbed in the heart. They lay panting, bleeding little, taking a long time to die. Three young men poured water down the throats of the yaks, while the other men chanted in their Tibetan dialect. As Buddhists, the people of Braga are forbidden to kill animals, yet the environment demands that they eat meat to survive. They resolve the dilemma by helping the animal to assume a higher form when it is reincarnated.

Cause-and-effect paragraphs are structured in two basic ways. The paragraph can begin with a cause or causes, then state its effects, or it can begin with an effect, then state its causes. Insightful analysis often requires you to look beyond the obvious to the underlying causes.

The loss of the world's forests affects every country through global warming, decreased biodiversity, and soil erosion, but few suffer its impact more than Nepal. Deforestation in Nepal has led to economic stagnation and further depletion of forest resources. **Effects**

The immediate cause of deforestation is the need for more fuel and more farmland by an increasing population. The loss of trees in Nepal, however, has been accelerated by government policies. During the eighteenth and nineteenth centuries, Nepal taxed **Obvious cause**

both land and labor. Farmers could avoid these high taxes for three years if they converted forests to farmland. Others could pay their taxes in firewood or charcoal. While these taxes were reduced in the **Underlying cause 1**

twentieth century, the government required farmers to register their land, which encouraged clearing of trees to establish boundaries. Furthermore, the stag- **Underlying cause 2**

nant economy led to families wanting more children to help in the fields at home and to send abroad to find jobs as another source of income. **Underlying cause 3**

Classification and Division

Classification and division are valuable strategies for analyzing and explaining a topic. Classifying places items into categories according to their similarities. Dividing takes a single item or concept and breaks it down into its component parts.

Classifying

Category

Characteristics of specific category

Nepal is classified as one of the poorest and least developed countries in the world. The average annual income of $220 a year places Nepal alongside the poorest nations in Africa. Only 27% of the population is literate, and over 40% of the population lives below the poverty line. The infant death rate of 76 per 1,000 births is one of the highest in the world.

Dividing

Item

Parts of item

Nepal is divided into three distinct regions. In the south is the Terai, the flat river plain of the Ganges, occupying 17% of the country. The central hill region is the largest, containing 64% of the land, including the Kathmandu Valley, the country's urban center. The rugged Himalaya mountain region in the north is above 4,000 meters (13,120 feet) and features eight of the ten highest mountains in the world, including the tallest, Mt. Everest (29,028 feet).

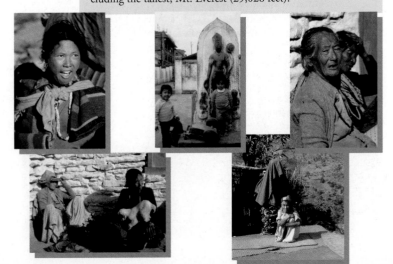

EXERCISE 4.2 A student is writing a paper on Bobby Sands, a member of the IRA who was the first to die during a 1981 hunger strike in a British prison. The strikers wanted political rather than regular criminal status within the prison. The student has the following ideas for paragraphs. Which of the seven common organizational strategies would work best for each?

1. Conditions within a British prison, circa 1980
2. History of the hunger strike as a political tool
3. Treatment of criminal-status prisoners and political-status prisoners
4. What political status is
5. The evolution of the strike
6. The popularity of Bobby Sands and the other strikers
7. Breakdown of the Catholic population in Derry, Northern Ireland, and of the Catholic prison population

EXERCISE 4.3 Find a paper you wrote either for this class or for another class. Choose one paragraph and rewrite it, organizing it according to one of the strategies from this section. Make sure you choose a strategy that is different from the one you used when you first wrote the paragraph!

4c   MAKE YOUR PARAGRAPHS COHERENT

One of your teachers may have told you that your paragraphs should flow. Paragraphs that don't flow make readers struggle to understand how sentences relate to one another, often forcing readers to backtrack. Sentences clash rather than mesh together.

But what exactly does *flow* mean? Writing that flows is coherent. To achieve coherence you must make all the separate parts fit together as a whole. At the level of the paragraph, your task as a writer is first to determine how your sentences fit together. Sometimes you know how your sentences relate to each other as you write them; at other times these relationships become clearer when you are revising. In either case, reiterating key phrases and using transitional terms help writers achieve that elusive quality called flow.

Reiterate key terms and phrases

When you repeat key terms and phrases within paragraphs, your reader will be able to trace major ideas and stay situated in your argument. In the following paragraph, notice that the writer refers back to two central terms, *grass roots activism* and *battleground*. Notice too, that the paragraph isn't repeating itself. Repetition without forward momentum is self-defeating.

> The Web has become the primary medium for **grass roots activism**. Among thousands of the Web sites created by individuals are many pages devoted to media criticism and parodies of advertising. **This activism** has come at a time when the Internet has become the **battleground** for the deregulated corporate giants. On **this battleground**, control of the coaxial cable and fiber-optic conduits represents only a small part of the potential fortunes to be made from an array of services carried through the pipe.

Signal relationships with transitional terms

Transitional terms act like warning signs for readers, preparing them for whatever is around the bend. Notice how transitions in the following paragraph make it easier to read by preparing you for what is coming.

> **In spite of** all the talk about the Internet as cyberspace and a virtual world, the materiality of the Internet as a medium is unavoidable. You sit in front of a machine that has to be turned on and connected to the net. **And if** you want to access the resources of the World Wide Web, you need an Internet service provider, a modem, and a computer with enough memory to support the current versions of Netscape or Internet Explorer. **In the United States** the lines do not go to every neighborhood, and **in the rest of the world** almost the entire continent of Africa outside South Africa is not online. **At present** the Internet continues the one-way flow of information from the First to the Third World. Can the Internet be a factor in promoting a two-way flow between the margins and the center?

Transitional terms

Be sure to use transitional terms accurately in order to signal the relationships between your sentences:

- **To enumerate:** again, also, and, as well, finally, furthermore, first, second, third, in addition, last, moreover, next, too
- **To generalize:** commonly, in general, for the most part, on the whole, usually, typically
- **To offer an example:** for example, for instance, indeed, in fact, of course, specifically, such as, the following
- **To situate in time:** after a month, afterward, as long as, as soon as, at the moment, at present, at that time, before, earlier, followed by, in the meantime, in the past, lately, later, meanwhile, now, preceded by, presently, since then, so far, soon, subsequently, suddenly, then, this year, today, until, when, while
- **To situate in space:** above, below, beyond, close to, elsewhere, far from, following, here, near, next to, there
- **To conclude:** as a result, hence, in conclusion, in short, on the whole, therefore, thus
- **To contrast:** although, but, even though, however, in contrast, conversely, in spite of, instead, nevertheless, nonetheless, on one hand, on the contrary, on the other hand, still, though, yet
- **To compare:** again, also, in the same way, likewise, similarly
- **To signal cause or effect:** as a result, because, consequently, for this reason, hence, if, so, then, therefore, thus
- **To sum up:** as I said, as we have seen, as mentioned earlier, in conclusion, in other words, in short, in sum, therefore, thus
- **To concede a point:** certainly, even though, granted, in fairness, in truth, naturally, of course, to be fair, while it's true

EXERCISE 4.4 Rewrite these paragraphs using the two strategies mentioned in Section 4c to make them cohere. Use each strategy at least once. Note that one of the paragraphs has incorporated one of the strategies, but has done so poorly.

1. Three kids go into the woods to seek out an evil witch who lives in a remote cabin. They lose their way and run out of food. Something mysterious happens when they finally meet the witch. Does this sound familiar? It is the plot of many familiar fairy tales. It is the plot to the blockbuster film *The Blair Witch Project.*

2. In fairy tales from many different cultures, the woods tend to represent a variety of psychological forces. It can represent the dark side of the individual soul, the id. From a social standpoint, the lack of civilization or culture is represented. Most of all, there's a loss of innocence. Children who are in the transition to adulthood are cast out, and must find their way. They must also battle a force out there that robs them of their innocence. If they survive the journey there, they come back to civilization as adults.

3. The woods are also a liminal space. Magical and impossible things happen in the woods. Creatures can adopt roles opposite their nature. Animals can speak. Mortal enemies can be friends. In *Through the Looking Glass*, Alice encounters a baby deer in the woods. She and the deer become friends. They gain comfort from one another. They reach the end of the woods. The deer looks at Alice and recognizes her as its enemy, man. The deer runs away in fright.

4. The college students in *The Blair Witch Project*, one could argue, are in an arrested state of development, as are many college students. Like children, they are titillated by the stories that the locals tell them about the Blair Witch. Like adolescents, they believe that they know it all. In this adolescent state, they mock the locals' superstitions and they mock the Blair Witch. They behave in an adolescent fashion; the girl is bossy and demanding. The boys respond as adolescents, and do things to spite the girl's carefully detailed plans. One boy throws the map away. The other begins to behave erratically and starts to act out physically. In the movie it seems as if the boys' adolescent behavior is being caused by the Blair Witch. It

could be argued that they are just handling the transition from adolescence to adulthood very poorly.

EXERCISE 4.5 Choose a paragraph from a paper you have written for either this class or another class. Underline any transitional words or phrases you used, and mark spaces where you think you need a transitional word or phrase. Write out the relationships expressed by the transitions you underlined. Then, write out the relationship that needs to be expressed in each place that you marked. What transitional word or phrase could you add to make that relationship clear?

4d CONSIDER PARAGRAPH LENGTH

Paragraph breaks can signal various kinds of shifts:

- A new concept
- The next step in an argument
- The end of the introduction
- The beginning of the conclusion
- A new speaker in dialogue
- A shift in time or place
- A logical pause that gives the reader a breather

What is the ideal length for a paragraph? It depends on what sort of paragraphs you are writing. Business letter writers strive for short paragraphs so their readers can see the essential information at a glance. Fiction writers construct paragraphs of various lengths to produce dramatic effects. For instance, Jack Kerouac's description of staying up all night in a skid row movie theater goes on for thirty-two sentences in *On the Road*. But Harper Lee includes a five-word paragraph—*Jem was a born hero.*—in *To Kill a Mockingbird*. Paragraphs in academic essays tend to be about 150 to 200 words long. Academic writers need space to make and support arguments in depth. As a general rule, readers' eyes glaze over when they see paragraphs in an essay that stretch beyond one page. Nevertheless, too many short paragraphs are a sign that the piece lacks either weighty ideas or sufficient development.

Writing in the World

Paragraph length and line length

Newspapers and other documents that use narrow column formats tend to use short paragraphs to increase readability.

Text on Web sites often has short paragraphs for the same reasons. Except for those who have big-screen, high-resolution monitors, text is generally harder to read on the screen than on paper.

To some extent the length of paragraphs is in proportion to the length of lines.

If the column is extremely narrow—five words or fewer—expect nearly every sentence to be a paragraph.

4e | LINK ACROSS PARAGRAPHS

Transitions at the beginnings and ends of paragraphs guide readers. They explain why a paragraph follows from the previous one. They offer writers the opportunity to highlight the turns in their thinking.

Write strong transitions

Thin content is a common source of weak transitions. When writing doesn't progress from paragraph to paragraph, but merely reiterates the same point, transitions have no work to do. Be aware of transitions in your writing. Ask yourself why one main idea leads into the next. What step or shift takes place between paragraphs? How does this step or shift fit into the overall development of the piece? The answer to these questions can become your transition.

The same strategies that make a paragraph coherent will make links between paragraphs coherent. Notice how the repetition of central terms and phrases in the following paragraphs helps the reader track the development of ideas from one paragraph to the next. The first paragraph introduces the metaphor of the "Information Superhighway" and connects the metaphor to the American myth of the frontier. The second paragraph begins with the frontier and examines how roads are also tied to ideas of a free-market economy. The third paragraph repeats the "Information Superhighway" metaphor and shows how it embodies a vision of a new economy on the Internet.

> **The metaphor of the "Information Superhighway,"** popularized by Albert Gore in the 1990s, sprang from a long-standing American myth about the freedom of **the open road.** Throughout the twentieth century the automobile represented freedom of action— not just the pleasures of driving around aimlessly for recreation but the possibility of exploring new territories and reaching **the frontier.** When talking about the Internet, both Republicans and Democrats in the 1990s invoked the idealized highway in the American imagination—**the highway** that leads to **the frontier.**
>
> Exploration of the **frontier** is linked to democracy in this rhetoric. From Thomas Jefferson onward, American leaders have maintained that **good roads** are a prerequisite to democracy. By the end of the last century, **good roads** were the people's answer to the hated railroad monopolies depicted by Frank Norris in *The Octopus.* With **good roads** farmers could transport their crops directly to local markets and competitive railheads. When the Interstate system was proposed, it was advanced as a means of connecting the nation, stimulating the economy, and eliminating poverty in Appalachia and other regions that lacked **good roads.**
>
> **The "Information Superhighway" metaphor** thus associated the economic prosperity of the 1950s and 1960s facilitated by new highways with the potential for vast amounts of commerce to be conducted over the Internet.

EXERCISE 4.6 Find a paper that you've written either for this or another class. Choose a paper that has more than five paragraphs, if possible. Write out the first sentence of each paragraph. Does this list of first sentences tell a coherent story? Mark the places where one sentence links to the next. Did you use a transition or repetition? If you used a transition, underline it and write out the relationship being expressed. If you used repetition, underline the word or idea being repeated.

Now mark the places where the sentences do not connect. Write out the relationship that needs to be expressed and the best method to achieve this, repetition or transition. If repetition, write what word or idea needs to be repeated. If you need a transition, write what relationship needs to be addressed and the word or phrase that would best achieve this.

4f | WRITE EFFECTIVE BEGINNING AND ENDING PARAGRAPHS

Beginning and ending paragraphs of essays should behave like a smart suitor meeting "the parents" for the first time: Dress well; start with a firm handshake; show you are thoughtful and personable; close on a strong note. Because readers are more likely to remember beginning and ending paragraphs than any others, they are your best opportunity to make a good impression.

What beginning paragraphs do

Effective beginning paragraphs convince the reader to read on. They capture the reader's interest and set the tone for the piece. In essays they often state the thesis and briefly map out the way the writing will progress from paragraph to paragraph. Sometimes the work of the beginning paragraph might be carried through three or four paragraphs. A writer might start with a memorable example, then use the example to launch the rest of the essay.

Start beginning paragraphs with a bang

Getting the first few sentences of an essay down on paper can be daunting. Try the following strategies to ease your struggle. Get your reader's attention by beginning with one of the following.

A QUESTION

How valuable are snow leopards? The director of a zoo in Darjeeling, India, was fired when its snow leopard caught a cold and died.

A HARD-HITTING FACT

Poaching is big business—to be exact, a six-billion-dollar business. The only illegal trade that's larger is drugs.

A PITHY QUOTATION

"That the snow leopard is," writes Peter Matthiessen, "that it is here, that its frosty eyes watch us from the mountains—that is enough." And it has to be enough because, while snow leopards are here now, they may not be here much longer.

IMAGES

Tons of animal pelts and bones sit in storage at Royal Chitwan National Park in Nepal. The mounds of poached animal parts confiscated by forest rangers reach almost to the ceiling. The air is stifling, the stench stomach-churning.

AN ANECDOTE

The snow leopard stood so still in the frosty bushes, it wasn't until the goat squealed that we saw it. Its mottled white fur was now spattered with the goat's blood. Steam rose from the animal's wounds. We fumbled for our cameras, hoping to capture this terrible beauty.

A PROBLEM

Ecologists worry that the construction of a natural gas pipeline in Russia's Ukok Plateau will destroy the habitat of endangered snow leopards, argali mountain sheep, and steppe eagles.

A CONCISELY STATED THESIS

If the governments of China and Russia don't soon act decisively, snow leopards will be extinct in a few years.

A CONTRADICTION OR PARADOX

Snow leopards are tremendously versatile animals, strong enough to kill a horse and fast enough to chase down a hare. What they can't do is hide from poachers in Nepal and India. And this may be their downfall.

AN ODD, RIDICULOUS, OR UNBELIEVABLE FACT

Caterpillar fungus is a hot commodity. Traditional healers and their clients are willing to pay handsomely for illegally harvested ingredients for their treatments. As a result, demand for the fungus, along with other poached items like rhinoceros horns and snow leopard bones, drives a lucrative and destructive black market in endangered species.

Essays that begin with obvious, overly general, or exaggerated sentences dampen the readers' interest immediately. Use the first sentence to tell readers something they don't know. Begin with a fresh idea, fact, or image.

What ending paragraphs do

Ending paragraphs remind readers where they've been and invite them to carry your ideas forward. Use the ending paragraph to touch on your key points, but do not merely summarize. Leave your readers with something that will inspire them to continue to think about what you have written.

Conclude with strength

The challenge in ending paragraphs is to leave the reader with something provocative, something beyond pure summary of the previous paragraphs. The following are some strategies for ending an essay:

Issue a Call to Action

Although ecological problems in Russia seem distant, students like you and me can help protect the snow leopard by joining the World Wildlife Fund campaign.

Discuss the Implications of Your Argument

Even though the extinction of snow leopards would be a sad event, their end is not the fundamental problem. Instead, their precarious position is a symptom of a larger dilemma: Environmental damage throughout developing nations in Asia threatens their biodiversity.

Explain the Applications of Your Argument

This study of snow leopard breeding behavior can inform captive breeding programs in zoos.

Make Recommendations

Russia's creditors would be wise to sign on to the World Wildlife Fund's proposal to relieve some of the country's debt in order to protect snow leopard habitat. After all, if Russia is going to be economically viable, it needs to be ecologically healthy.

Speculate about the Future

Unless Nepali and Chinese officials devote more resources to snow leopard preservation, these beautiful animals will be gone in a few years.

Tell an Anecdote that Illustrates a Key Point

Poachers are so uncowed by authorities that they even tried to sell a snow leopard skin to a reporter researching a story on endangered species.

Describe a Key Image

As they watched the pile of confiscated furs and bones burn, Nepali forest rangers flashed proud smiles that seemed to say, "This time we mean business."

OFFER A QUOTATION THAT EXPRESSES THE ESSENCE OF YOUR ARGUMENT

Too often, developed nations impose their high-flown priorities, like protecting snow leopards and tigers, on developing nations. A Russian farmer summed up the disjunction succinctly. Tigers ate two cows in his herd of fifty. When he was compensated for the two he asked, "What's this? Can't the tiger come back and eat the remaining forty-eight?"

ASK A RHETORICAL QUESTION

Generally the larger and more majestic (or better yet, cute) an endangered animal is, the better its chances of being saved. Bumper stickers don't implore us to save blind cave insects; they ask us to save the whales, elephants, and tigers. But snow leopards aren't cave bugs; they are beautiful, impressive animals that should be the easiest of all to protect. If we can't save them, do any endangered species stand a chance?

Resist the urge to end on a bright note if what comes before doesn't warrant it; you don't want your ending to ring hollow.

EXERCISE 4.7 Write an introductory and a concluding paragraph for each of the essays described here. Label what each paragraph does from the lists in Section 4f, such as asking a question or making a recommendation.

1. An essay explaining the process for applying to colleges
2. A description of a moment when you completely changed your mind about a person
3. A proposal to make talking on a cell phone while driving a felony
4. An analysis of a short story, poem, or novel by your favorite author
5. A letter to the editor of a newspaper or magazine, responding to an article, editorial, letter, or advertisement you felt was misinformed or inappropriate, or that presented a viewpoint that opposes your opinion on a subject

Chapter 5

Rewriting, Editing, and Proofreading

Skilled writers know that the secret to writing well is rewriting. Even the best writers often have to revise several times to get the result they want. To be able to revise effectively, you have to plan your time. You cannot revise a paper or a Web site effectively if you wait until the last minute to begin working. Allow at least a day to let what you write cool off. With a little time you will gain enough distance to "re-see" it, which, after all, is what revision means.

You also must have effective strategies for revising if you're going to be successful. The biggest trap you can fall into is starting off with the little stuff first. *Don't sweat the small stuff at the beginning.* When you see a word that's wrong or a misplaced comma, the great temptation is to fix it. But if you start searching for errors, it's hard to get back to the larger concerns.

5a SWITCH FROM WRITER TO READER

First, pretend you are someone who is either uninformed about your subject or holds an opposing view. If possible think of an actual person and pretend to be that person. Read your draft aloud, all the way through. When you read aloud, you will probably hear clunky phrases and outright errors, but do no more in this stage than put checks in the margins so you can find these things later. Once again, you don't want to get bogged down with the little stuff. What you are after in this stage is an overall sense of how well you have accomplished what you set out to do.

Use these questions to evaluate your draft. Note any places where you might make improvements.

Does your paper or project meet the assignment?

- Look again at your assignment and especially at the key words, such as *analyze*, *define*, *evaluate*, and *propose*. Does your paper or project do what the assignment asks?
- Look again at the assignment for specific guidelines, including length, format, and amount of research. Does your work meet these guidelines?

Does your writing have a clear focus?

- Does your project have an explicitly stated thesis? If not, is your thesis clearly implied?
- Is each paragraph related to your thesis?
- Do you get off the track at any point by introducing other topics?

Are your main points adequately developed?

- Do you support your main points with reasons and evidence?
- Can you add more examples and details that would help to explain your main points?
- Would additional research fill in gaps or make your case stronger?

Is your organization effective?

- Is the order of your main points clear to your reader? (You may want to make a quick outline of your draft if you have not done so already.)
- Are there any places where you find abrupt shifts or gaps?
- Are there sections or paragraphs that could be rearranged to make your draft more effective?

Do you consider your potential readers' knowledge and points of view?

- Do you give enough background if your readers are unfamiliar with your subject?
- Do you acknowledge opposing views that readers might have?
- Do you appeal to common values that you share with your readers?

Do you represent yourself effectively?

- To the extent you can, forget for a moment that you wrote what you are reading. What impression do you have of you, the writer?
- Does "the writer" create an appropriate tone?
- Has "the writer" done his or her homework?
- Is the writing project visually effective? Has "the writer" selected an attractive and readable font? Does "the writer" use headings and illustrations where they are helpful?

When you finish, make a list of your goals for the revision. You may have to write another draft before you move to the next stage.

5b   LEARN STRATEGIES FOR REWRITING

Now it's time to go through your draft in detail. You should work on the goals you identified in your review. Also look for other opportunities to improve your work, using this checklist.

1. Sharpen your focus wherever possible. You may have started out with a large topic but find now that most of what you wrote concerns only one aspect. For example, you may have started with the large topic of privacy, but your focus now is on the current practice of some states selling their driver's license databases to companies that build junk mail lists. Revise your thesis and supporting paragraphs as needed.

Check to see that your focus remains consistent throughout the essay. For example, let us say you started out with the large topic of privacy and wrote a whole paragraph about libraries using filters on their computers to prevent minors from accessing pornography. Then you shifted your focus to states selling databases. You should then cut the discussion of libraries' use of filters.

2. Check that key terms are adequately defined. What are your key terms? Are they defined precisely enough to be meaningful? Consider this example:

If people are just in their initial actions (i.e., going to war), they will tend to act justly throughout the situation. If people are unjustified in their initial actions, however, they will have no reason to act justly throughout the rest of the situation. In the Six Day War, the Israelis were justified in going to war and fought a just war throughout. In Vietnam, the Americans had no justification for going to war, and thus they fought unjustly throughout.

What do the words "just" and "unjust" mean in this paragraph? Evidently whatever the writer wants them to mean. This paragraph is a true hall of mirrors. If your argument depends on a critical distinction such as the difference between "just" and "unjust," you are obligated to be as specific as possible in defining these terms.

3. Develop where necessary. Key points and claims may need more explanation and supporting evidence. Look for opportunities to add support without becoming redundant.

Perhaps you are writing about the hardships experienced by an immigrant family: "The Hidalgo family has a hard life," you begin. "They do not have enough money, and they have transportation problems." Each generalization needs a supporting detail to show the reader what you mean.

> The Hidalgo family has a hard life. When Maria walks the seven blocks to the grocery store, she has enough money for rice and beans, but she must choose between meat and cheese. Toothpaste is too expensive. Maria's walk home is difficult carrying two heavy bags of groceries. She hopes that when Carlos gets paid next week, they will have enough to buy a new alternator for their car.

4. Check links between paragraphs. Look for any places where the ideas shift abruptly, and make the transitions smoother or more logical. Check to make sure you signal the relationship between one paragraph and the next (see Section 4e).

5. Consider your title. Many writers don't think much about titles, but they are very important. A good title makes the reader want to read what you have written. Be as specific as you can in your title, and if possible, suggest your stance. "Use of Anabolic Steroids" as a title is vague and bland, and it suggests a topic far too large to be handled well in a few pages. A stronger title would be, "Is Andro a Food Supplement or a Steroid?"

6. Consider your introduction. In the introduction you want to get off to a fast start and convince your reader to keep reading. If your subject is the use of steroids among high school students, don't start with an empty sentence like "Drugs are a big problem in today's high schools." Cut to the chase with a sentence such as "The National Institute of Drug Abuse reports that the number of high school students who abuse anabolic steroids rose steadily during the 1990s, while the perception of the risks involved declined." Then you might follow with a sentence that indicates how you will approach your topic: "My experiences as a high school athlete gave me insights into why students would risk future liver failure, cancer, strokes, heart attacks, and other serious health problems in order to gain a competitive advantage." In two sentences you have established your topic and your own credibility to write about it.

7. Consider your conclusion. Restating your claim usually isn't the best way to finish. The worst endings say something like "in my paper I've said this." Think about whether there is a summarizing point you can make, an implication you can draw, or another example you can include that sums up your position. If you are writing a proposal, your ending might be a call for action.

The essay "Problem Geese" (see Section 9d) ends with a proposed solution to the problem (border collie patrols of areas where geese are bothersome), a rebuttal of a likely objection to the solution of dog patrols (the expense), and a final reason for the solution based on ethics (we should not give children living in an increasingly violent society the impression that killing is a good solution to a problem). This conclusion is strong because it follows logically from the discussion that comes before and drives home the proposed solution by appealing to the audience's higher values.

8. Improve the visual aspects of your text. Does the font you selected look attractive? (See Section 10d.) Do you use the same font throughout? Are you consistent if you use more than one font? Do you include headings and subheadings to identify key sections of your argument? If you include statistical data, would presenting it in charts be effective? (See Section 11e.) Would illustrations help to establish key points? For example, a map could be very useful if you are arguing about the location of a proposed new highway.

5c | RESPOND TO OTHER WRITERS' DRAFTS

Your instructor may ask you to review your classmates' drafts. Writing a response to the work of a fellow student may make you feel uncomfortable. You may think you don't know enough to say anything useful. Remember that you are only charged with letting the writer know how you—one of many potential readers—react.

But you do have to put forth your best effort. Responding to other people's writing requires the same careful attention you give to your own draft. To write a helpful response, you should go through the draft more than once. Before you begin, number the paragraphs, if the writer has not already done so.

First reading

Read at your normal rate the first time through without stopping. When you finish you should have a clear sense of what the writer was trying to accomplish.

- **Main idea:** Write a sentence that summarizes what you think is the writer's main idea in the draft.
- **Purpose:** Write a sentence that summarizes what you think the writer was trying to accomplish in the draft.

Second reading

In your second reading, you should be most concerned with the content, organization, and completeness of the draft. Make notes as you read.

- **Introduction:** Does the writer's first paragraph effectively introduce the topic and engage your interest?
- **Thesis:** Where exactly is the writer's thesis? Note in the margin where you think the thesis is located.
- **Focus:** Does the writer maintain a focus on the thesis? Note any places where the writer seems to wander off to another topic.
- **Organization:** Are the sections and paragraphs ordered effectively? Do any paragraphs seem to be out of place? Do you note any abrupt shifts? Can you suggest a better order for the paragraphs?
- **Completeness:** Do any sections and paragraphs lack key information or adequate development? Where do you want to know more?
- **Sources:** If the draft uses outside sources, are they cited accurately? If there are quotations, are they used correctly and worked into the fabric of the draft?

Third reading

In your third reading, turn your attention to matters of audience, style, and tone.

- **Audience:** Who is the writer's intended audience? What does the writer assume the audience knows and believes?
- **Style:** Is the writer's style engaging? How would you describe the writer's voice?
- **Tone:** Is the tone appropriate for the writer's purpose and audience? Is the tone consistent throughout the draft? Are there places where another word or phrase might work better?

When you have finished the third reading, write a short paragraph on each bulleted item, referring to specific paragraphs in the draft by number. Then end by answering these two questions:

1. What does the writer do especially well in the draft?
2. What one or two things would most improve the draft in a revision?

Responding to comments

Mark Stewart's first draft received these comments from a peer reviewer. The comments helped him to see how he might present his essay in a more effective order.

Problem Geese—draft 1

The problem with geese is one created by people, so we can't expect to get rid of it easily. They were hunted nearly to extinction by the 1950s. Before that Canada geese nested in Canada and wintered in the United States. A flock was found in Minnesota and people started raising geese to bring them back. These farm-raised geese had lost their instinct to migrate, so they started living here all the time (Schnell). They found grass around people, and not many predators, so they stayed. Hunting geese was illegal. Therefore, there was a population explosion of geese.

Killing the geese is cruel, though. Dog patrols are a better solution. Border collies are expensive, but so is killing. In northern Virginia they formed an organization called GeesePeace that tried to find good ways of dealing with the geese. They trained border collies to irritate the geese until the geese would decide to move on. They do not hurt the geese, but the geese don't like them. GeesePeace has tried other things, too, like painting the eggs with corn oil.

I took my nephew Andy to Point Defiance Park last summer. I was locking the car and I heard Andy scream. A large Canada goose was hissing at him. I ran to rescue him. He was crying. His shoes were also covered in goose droppings, and so were mine.

What is the problem with geese? The problem needs to be introduced.

Wait! Killing? Dog patrols? I want to know what methods have been tried and how those methods worked. I also wonder if you should wait until the end to propose your 'solution.' Perhaps talk about the different solutions that have been tried, then introduce your proposal.

This paragraph gives useful background on the goose population explosion, but shouldn't it come later, after we understand the nature of the problem?

Aha! This story is a great illustration of why the geese are a problem. You could lead with this story, then back up and explain how the situation got to this point.

EXERCISE 5.1 Read the following first draft and respond, following the process outlined in Section 5c. Resist the urge to edit sentences and correct mechanical errors.

We've Come Along Way, Baby

Humans has existed on the Earth for approximately 3.4 million years. That's from when the oldest human ancestor, "Lucy," an Australopithecus, discovered by Donald Johnson and M. Taieb. s had been found. Lucy was not only the oldest Australopithecus find, they also found over 40% of her skeleton intact, making her one of the most complete, too. Australopithecus africanus, means "southern ape from Africa" (Lewin).

Australopithecine's looked more like primates than modern-day Homo Sapiens. Although they walked upright, they had low, sloping foreheads, protruding jaws, and thick body hair. They were also only about three feet tall. For some reason, they also didn't seem to show any facial expressions (McKie 50).

Humans have evolved a lot over the past three and a half million years. We are almost 6 feet, have lost most of our body hair, have adapted to walking upright all the time, and we've grown brains that are over three times as large as the first Australopithecine's (Larson 123). Besides, humans (Homo Sapiens) have also developed an advanced material culture. We live in cities now and we don't have to live in trees. We also don't have to dig in the ground for our food; we can just buy it at the store. We also can grasp abstract concepts like time and we have art and literature.

But we haven't changed all that much, really. We still are related to primates in many ways. This can be seen in the way our hands, feet, and over all body is structured. Our faces are even very similar (IHO).

There have been four distinct species of human throughout time: Homo Habilis, Homo Erectus, Homo sapiens Neanderthalesis, and Homo sapiens Sapiens. The first major step in evolution was becoming bipedal, or walking upright (Larson 20). As I said before, Australopithecine's were the first to do this. They were

really clumsy, though; because their skeleton weren't really able to support the weight, they probably spent most of their time on all fours. They were, however, probably really good at climbing trees. This is not the only way they were more similar to primates than homo sapiens, though (McKie 35). They were tiny, with a tiny (orange size) brain, prominent cheekbones, and thick molars. Like chimps, they had small, underdeveloped thumbs. But their toes were shorter than other primates (IHO).

Australiopithicene also probably lived socailly like chimps. Judging from the way fossils were at their sites, they probably lived in one place in small groups. We think they lived in groups because usually about 5 individuals are found in the same place. One site even had had 13 in the same place! (Lewin) Scientists think that these groups usually had one male in charge and this was because of their sexual dimorphism. Sexual dimorphism, or the difference in size between the genders, usually means that males are larger (Lewin). So probably the one guy that was big was in charge.

They also weren't very smart. The only tools they had were sticks and rocks. They were also vegetarians. They may not have known animals could be eaten. If they did know, though, they probably couldn't figure out how to kill one anyway. Homo Habilis, though, figured this out (Larson 145). Homo Habilis is the earliest known member of the Homo genus, and has been found only in Africa. Homo Habilis's brain was about 50% larger than Australopithecine's, he was taller, had flatter nostrils, and their faces were nearly hairless (IHO).

Most importantly, though, Homo Habilis figured out, through scavenging, scientists think, that meat was edible. Their teeth show that they started to add meat to their vegetarian diets. Homo Habilis lived in Africa until about 1.6 million years ago, when Homo Erectus emerged, causing their eventual extinction. Homo Erectus was the next step. He had a much larger brain (1060 cc) than Homo Habilis (Mc Kie 80). "Homo Erectus" means "Man who Walks Upright" (Lewin).

The larger brain is the main physical change from H. Hablis to Homo Erectus. But they did have smaller jaws and teeth. They also had a larger brow. The brow-ridge was also slightly larger than Homo Habilis. "The term *Homo habilis* means *handy man,* a name selected for the deposits of primitive tools found near *H. habilis* fossils (Lewin).

Homo Erectus lived until about 100,000 years ago, when Homo sapiens Neanderthalesis took over. Homo sapiens Neanderthalesis, or the Neanderthals, lived during the most recent Ice Age (Larson 160).

Evolution happens so slowly that it almost can't be seen. The changes occur in tiny mutations; if you possess a mutation that makes you survive better than others, you are more likely to reproduce and spread that mutation into the next generation. If you have a bad mutation, you die and you don't pass that mutation on. There are lots of examples that prove this, from the problems in royal families to skin color differences that are related to climate (Larson 30).

We have to remember, though, that all of these things are just physical. Deep down, all humans are really the same so we should love and respect one another.

Works Cited

Institute of Human Origins (IHO). *Becoming Human.* 2001. 23 February 2002 <http://www.becominghuman.org/>.

Larsen, Clark Spencer, and Robert M. Matter. *Human Origins : The Fossil Record.* Waveland Press, 1998.

Lewin, Roger. "Australopithecines," *Microsoft® Encarta® Encyclopedia 99.* 1998.

---. "Homo habilis," *Microsoft® Encarta® Encyclopedia 99.*

McKie, Robin. *The Dawn of Man: The Story of Human Evolution.* London: DK, 2002.

EXERCISE 5.2 Exchange drafts of a paper you wrote for this class or for another class with another student. Respond to this student's paper following the procedure underlined in Section 5c. Resist the urge to edit sentences and correct mechanical errors.

5d | EDIT FOR PARTICULAR GOALS

In your final pass through your text, you should concentrate on the style of your argument and eliminate as many errors as you can.

1. Check the connections between sentences. Notice how your sentences are connected. If you need to signal the relationship from one sentence to the next, use a transitional word or phrase. For example, when you find two sentences that are closely connected, you should ask what the relationship is. If you need to signal the relationship, use a transitional word or phrase:

Silent Spring was widely translated and inspired legislation on the environment in nearly all industrialized nations. *Silent Spring* changed the way we think about the environment. →

Silent Spring was widely translated and inspired legislation on the environment in nearly all industrialized nations. **Moreover**, the book changed the way we think about the environment.

2. Check your sentences. If you noticed that a sentence was hard to read or didn't sound right when you read your paper aloud, think about how you might rephrase it. Often you can pick up problems with verbs (see Chapters 34 and 35), pronouns (see Chapter 36), and modifiers (see Chapter 37) by reading aloud. If a sentence seems too long, you might break it into two or more sentences. If you notice a string of short sentences that sound choppy, you might combine them. If you notice run-on sentences or sentence fragments, fix them (see Chapter 33).

3. Eliminate wordiness. Writers tend to introduce wordiness in drafts. Look for long expressions that can easily be shortened ("at this point in time" → "now") and unnecessary repetition. Remove unnecessary qualifiers (*rather, very, somewhat, little*). See how many words you can take out without losing the meaning (see Chapter 27).

4. Use active verbs. Any time you can use a verb besides a form of *be* (*is, are, was, were*) or a verb ending in *-ing,* take advantage of the opportunity to make your style more lively. Sentences that begin with "There is (are)" and "It is" often have better alternatives:

> It is true that exercising a high degree of quality control in the manufacture of our products will be an incentive for increasing our market share. $\rightarrow$

> If we pay attention to quality when we make our products, more people will buy them.

Notice too that use of active verbs often cuts down on wordiness (see Chapter 26).

5. Use specific and inclusive language. As you read, stay alert for any vague words or phrases (see Chapter 29). Check to make sure that you have used inclusive language throughout (see Chapter 30).

EXAMPLE OF SENTENCE-LEVEL EDITING

~~It is a widely believed opinion that computers have greatly influenced the lives of the latest generation. I agree with this opinion. I remember back w~~ **W**hen I was in the fourth grade, we had a computer **literacy** class every Friday. ~~The classroom held about~~ **in a room equipped with** 20 Apple IIe computers. Besides learning how to type correctly, we were also given simple graphic programming assignments. ~~Thus, I along with m~~ **M**y fellow classmates~~,~~ **and I** were assigned to input VLIN (Vertical Line) and HLIN (Horizontal Line) commands followed by a color and coordinates~~.~~ ~~When we finished we would have~~ **that created** a picture on the monitor. ~~This was not a photographic quality image by any means.~~ Because the pixels were only slightly smaller than sugar cubes~~,~~ and ~~we were~~ limited to 16 colors, these images made ~~the~~ **our** Nintendo Entertainment System's graphics ~~al output~~ look like the ~~graphic output~~ **quality** of a Hollywood studio production **by comparison.**

5e | PROOFREAD CAREFULLY

In your final pass through your text, eliminate as many errors as you can. To proofread effectively, you have to learn to slow down. Some writers find that moving from word to word with a pencil slows them down enough to allow them to find errors. Others read backward to force themselves to concentrate on each word.

1. Know what your spelling checker can and can't do. Spelling checkers are the greatest invention since peanut butter. They turn up many typos and misspellings that are hard to catch. But spelling checkers do not catch wrong words (e.g., "to much" should be "too much"), missing endings ("three dog"), and other, similar errors. You still have to proofread carefully to eliminate misspellings (see Chapter 31).

2. Check for grammar and mechanics. Nothing hurts your credibility with readers more than a text with numerous errors. Many job application letters get tossed in the reject pile because an applicant made a single, glaring error. Issues of grammar are treated in Chapters 32 through 37. The conventions for using punctuation, capitalization, italics, abbreviations, acronyms, and numbers can be found in Chapters 38 through 46. Get into the habit of referring to these chapters.

5f | LEARN TO EDIT THE WRITING OF OTHERS

Editing someone else's writing is easier than editing your own. In your own writing you know most of the time what you meant to say and often you don't notice where a reader might be stopped or jarred. But editing someone else's writing is also harder because you want to give the writer useful feedback without taking over the writer's task.

1. Make comments in the margins. If you find a sentence hard to read, let the writer know. If you think a sentence is repetitive, let the writer

know. If you think a word was left out, say so in the margin. Also let the writer know when a sentence is especially successful.

> *Word missing here?*
>
> *Same point as sentence 1?*
>
> *Can you join this sentence with the previous sentence?*
>
> *Vivid description!*

2. Use symbols to indicate possible problems. Draw a wavy line under any phrase or sentence where you think there may be a problem. Even if you are not sure what the problem is, you can ask the writer to look carefully at a particular sentence. If you think a word is misspelled, draw a circle around it. If you think words can be deleted, put parentheses around them.

A Web cam is a Web page which hosts images or even live video streams served by a digitel camera attached to a computer. Web cams serve as surveillance, entertainment, control, and many other services. Web cam technology has become quite popular (with people) since the first Web cams hit the world wide web.

Writing in the World

Standard proofreading symbols

More advanced editing requires learning standard proofreading symbols. Authors, editors, and printers use proofreader's marks to indicate changes. Standard proofreading marks are used in pairs. One mark goes in the text where the change is to be made and the other goes in the margin, close to the change. See how this works in the two-column list on page 100.

(continued next page)

Mark in the margin	Mark in the text
ℯ	Delete: take it out
⌒	Close up: foot ball
∧	Caret: insert here
#	Insert a space: a word
ⓣⓡ	Transpose: the in beginning
∧	Add a comma: moreover we
∨	Add an apostrophe: Ellens books
∜ / ∜	Add double quotation marks: James Joyce's Clay
:	Add a colon: 3 45 p.m.
;	Add a semicolon: concluded however, we
⊙	Add a period: last call Next we
¶	Begin a new paragraph
No ¶	No new paragraph
sp	Spell out: 7 dwarfs => seven dwarfs
stet	Ignore correction: in the beginning

EXERCISE 5.3 Choose two consecutive paragraphs from the paper in Exercise 5.1. Make sure that the combined length of the two paragraphs is at least ten sentences. Copy the paragraph out, exactly as it appears, and edit it. Use the proofreading symbols above. Resist the urge to rewrite the paragraphs.

EXERCISE 5.4 Edit a classmate's paper written for this class or another using the standard proofreading symbols. Resist the urge to rewrite the paragraphs.

Writing in College and Beyond 2

Chapter 6

Critical Reading and Viewing

When you write about any major topic, you will be entering ongoing written conversations to which many others have contributed. Consequently, most writing you will do in college requires you to reflect in depth on what you read, a process called **critical reading.** This critical awareness does not stop with reading. College courses often ask you to engage in critical viewing, to think in depth about what you see—whether it be in the form of photographs, drawings, paintings, graphics, advertising, television, film, or the World Wide Web.

6a TWO KINDS OF READING AND VIEWING

Many familiar words are used in slightly different ways in college, and *reading* is one of them. Reading can mean what you normally think of as sitting down with a book, newspaper, or magazine. But reading can also mean thinking about and interpreting almost anything—tattoos, a clever commercial on television, a fashion trend, or a controversial museum exhibit. Reading does not have to mean simply reading words.

Let's take an event as an example. Imagine you are with several friends watching a college football game on television, perhaps one in which your school is participating. For most of the first half, you and your friends watch the game, cheering when your team scores and groaning when the other team scores. You behave as college students do when they watch a game together. For the sake of convenience, let's describe this kind of viewing as **ordinary reading** or viewing. If you observe people carefully, you know that there is no such thing as "ordinary" viewing. Some people pay close attention to the game; others are more interested in talking to each other; and still others wander off. Even though viewing behavior varies, ordinary viewing in this situation means that people don't attempt to do much interpreting beyond praising or more often criticizing the players, coaches, and referees.

In the second half, the game turns one sided and your friends start to get bored. One of your friends starts talking about how unfair it is that the school makes a lot of money off the game but the athletes don't get paid. Another counters by saying that the players get a full scholarship, which allows many who might not otherwise be able to go to college to get a degree. A third friend says that football pays for other sports that don't make money. A fourth complains that student fees are used to support the athletics programs. All of a sudden your friends aren't talking about the game itself but are thinking about it in terms of economics. They are still watching the game, but they are viewing it quite differently—in a way that might be termed critical reading or viewing.

The discussion of the game suggests the different strategies you use for different kinds of reading. When you engage in ordinary reading, one time through is enough. While waiting for a haircut you pick up a magazine and thumb through it. An article catches your eye and you start reading. You get a sense of content and form an initial impression: whether what you are reading is interesting, whether the author has something important to say, whether you agree or disagree. But when you finish, you put the magazine back on the stack and it's unlikely that you will read the article again.

When you read for a specific purpose, you use different strategies. You no longer read to form a sense of the overall content. Often you look for something in particular. You might reread a historian's account of a presidential decision for signs of political bias. You might reread your health insurance contract to find out when emergency room visits are covered. This second kind of reading—often literally a second reading—is critical reading.

Critical reading doesn't mean just criticizing what you read, although certainly that can be one result of critical reading. Critical reading begins with questions and specific goals.

6b   CRITICAL READING

Nearly all the reading required in college courses is critical reading. You cannot get far into an academic discipline with ordinary reading. When you read the work of several people in the same discipline, you quickly realize that they do not have the same point of view—they may not even agree on basic facts. And you also quickly realize that their work builds on the work of others; thus you have to have a sense of how they are interpreting the work of others before you can evaluate their claims.

Previewing

You can become a more effective critical reader if you have a set of strategies and use them while you read. These strategies are illustrated in a sample reading, "A Defense of the Open Road" by Lance Armstrong on page 107.

Critical reading requires thinking about the context first. Begin by asking the following questions:

- Who wrote this material?
- Where did it first appear? In a book, newspaper, magazine, or online?
- What is the topic or issue?
- Where does the writer stand on the topic or issue?
- What else has been written about the topic or issue?
- What social, political, and economic forces and influences can be identified in this piece of writing?
- Why was it written?

When you come to an understanding of the context, certain details take on additional meaning.

Previewing

"A Defense of the Open Road" was first published in the editorial pages of the *Austin American-Statesman* on February 11, 2001. After surviving a life-threatening bout with cancer, the author, Lance Armstrong, won the most demanding and prestigious bicycle race in the world, the Tour de France, in 1999, 2000, 2001, and 2002. Armstrong was training for the racing season with his U.S. Postal team when bills were introduced in the Texas legislature to ban bicycle riding in groups and on certain roads, which if passed would effectively prevent Armstrong from training in his home state. Not surprisingly, Armstrong was strongly opposed to these bills. Armstrong voiced his views in an editorial column in his hometown newspaper.

Summarizing

Make sure you understand exactly what is at issue, usually a claim or question. If the claim or question is not overtly stated, note where you think it is being made or asked. Circle any words or references that you don't know and look them up. You may get a sense of the main points the first time through, or you may have to read the piece slowly a second time. Then summarize by asking yourself these questions:

- What is the writer's main claim or question? (You should be able to paraphrase it.)
- If you do not find a specific claim, what is the main focus?
- What are the key ideas or concepts that the writer considers?
- What are the key terms? How does the writer define those terms?

Summarizing

Lance Armstrong, in "A Defense of the Open Road," makes a strong counterargument against laws banning bicycling in a group and bicycling on certain roads, which were proposed in the 2001 Texas

(continued next page)

legislature. Armstrong maintains that the proposed laws make riding unsafe not only for racers but for a variety of recreational cyclists. He argues that cycling is safer and more efficient when riders are in a group or *peloton* (in bicycle jargon). Furthermore, he points out that the language of proposed laws banning riding from certain roads is vague and does not acknowledge local conditions such as time of day. At the beginning and end, he emphasizes his Texas roots and appeals to the pride of fellow Texans in their state.

Analyzing

On your second reading, start analyzing the structure, using the following questions:

- How is the piece of writing organized?
- What does the writer assume the readers know and believe?
- Where is the evidence? Does this evidence support the thesis and main claims? Can you think of contradictory evidence?
- Does the writer refer to expert opinion or research about this subject? Do other experts see this issue differently?
- Does the writer acknowledge opposing views? Does the writer deal fairly with opposing views?
- What kinds of sources are cited? Are they from books, newspapers, periodicals, or the Web? Are they completely documented?
- How would you characterize the style?
- How does the writer represent herself or himself?

Responding

As you read, write down your thoughts. Something you read may remind you of something else. Jot that down. Ask these questions:

- What points does the writer make to which you should respond?
- What ideas do you find that you might develop or interpret differently?

- What do you need to look up?
- What else should you read before writing?

Read with a pencil in hand so you can make notes in the margin. Pens and highlighters do not erase.

Critical response

A Defense of the Open Road

Lance Armstrong

I learned to love Texas as a teenager cycling on a long, flat road past the plains of Plano to the ranch land and cotton fields, past the wildflowers and mesquite.

Armstrong immediately reminds his Texas audience that he is a native Texan.

Sometimes I'd ride alone and sometimes with friends, racing or pulling each other as a team—working together against the dry, dusty wind. Drafting behind a friend, and then pulling ahead to pull your friends, is part of the camaraderie and teamwork of cycling.

Armstrong explains why teamwork is a valuable part of cycling. He relies on personal experience since he is an expert cyclist.

That's why I'm so disappointed that two Hill Country legislators want to keep cyclists from riding the best roads in Texas. One legislator wants to ban riding with more than one friend on many rural roads, and another wants to ban all riding on certain rural roads.

Going further, Senate Bill 238, in a face-slap of an insult, would make all cyclists—children, adults, amateurs and pros—ride single file on every road, with a Slow Moving Vehicle triangle hanging off our rear ends. This is the anti-sport, nanny-like equivalent of requiring golfers to use a putter off the tee to prevent a hook into the next fairway.

He uses the analogy of forcing golfers to use a putter to prevent errant drives.

Although banning groups might be slightly more convenient for cars, it's vastly more dangerous for cyclists. Riding as a peloton, or group, is safer (not to mention more practical and efficient). Would

Peloton, the bicycling term for riding in a group, is defined and the concept defended.

you prefer your son or daughter to ride with a group or have to ride almost alone?

For example, when the U.S. Postal team holds training camp in Austin, we ride double-pace lines through the Hill Country. The single-file rule and no-peloton rule would outlaw such team training rides. Plus, a single-file rule would make it illegal for riders to even pass each other.

Armstrong appeals to a broad range of people who ride bicycles, not just racers.

The rules also would outlaw families riding together, Saturday-morning rides with friends, organized rides and races, charity rides and fund raisers, and bicycle tours of Texas roads. From the forests of East Texas to the rugged mountains of West Texas, there is nothing like seeing Texas from a bike. These rules would make it an impossibility.

He argues that the current law is based on common sense and is easy to understand.

The current law—stay to the right, ride no more than two abreast and don't impede the reasonable flow of traffic—is based on common sense and thus easy to follow. The examples cited as reasons for the proposed laws seem to be based on a few cyclists disobeying the current law.

His point about law that follows common sense is reiterated.

But a few bad acts shouldn't be the basis for passing a bad bill. Imposing new limits—potholed with exceptions for certain events, situations, speeds or roads—would be a nightmare to follow and to enforce. The more complex a rule, and the more distant it is from common sense, the less likely it can be followed.

The proposed laws are vague because the terms cannot be accurately defined and ignore local circumstances.

Shoulders appear and disappear, and maps don't designate "roads with shoulders" and "roads without." Maps don't designate "high-traffic roads" and "low-traffic roads." Time of day, growth and other factors make this a moving target anyway. Often the road less traveled leads to the road more trafficked, which leads to another road less traveled. Restricting access to some roads is just not practical.

I am proud to be a Texan, and I want Texas to continue to attract riders with the beauty of our long, open roads. The rules of the road should be rules of reason and rules of respect, unencumbered by unworkable, excessive government regulation.

Armstrong concludes by appealing to the pride of Texans in their state and their general resistance to government regulation.

6c | VERBAL FALLACIES

Reasoning depends less on proving a claim than it does on finding evidence for that claim that readers will accept as valid. The kinds of faulty reasoning called *logical fallacies* reflect a failure to provide sufficient evidence for a claim that is being made. Among the most common fallacies are the following:

- **Bandwagon appeals.** *It doesn't matter if I copy a paper off the Web because everyone else does.* This argument suggests that everyone is doing it, so why shouldn't you? But on close examination, it may be that everyone really isn't doing it—and in any case, it may not be the right thing to do.

- **Begging the question.** *People should be able to say anything they want to because free speech is an individual right.* The fallacy of begging the question occurs when the claim is restated and passed off as evidence. In fact, there are many things we cannot and should not say, such as threatening to kill people.

- **Either-or.** *Either we eliminate the regulation of businesses or else profits will suffer.* The either-or fallacy suggests that there are only two choices in a complex situation. Rarely, if ever, is this the case. (In this example, the writer ignores the fact that Enron was unregulated and went bankrupt.)

- **False analogies.** *Japan quit fighting in 1945 when we dropped nuclear bombs on them. We should use nuclear weapons against other countries.* Analogies always depend on the degree of resemblance of one situation to another. In this case, the analogy fails to recognize

that circumstances today are very different from those in 1945, and it is easy to point out how the analogy fails.

- **Hasty generalization.** *We have been in a drought for three years; that's a sure sign of a climate trend.* A hasty generalization is a broad claim made on the basis of a few occurrences. Climate cycles occur regularly over spans of a few years; climate trends must be observed over centuries.

- **Name calling.** *Candidate Smith is a tax-and-spend liberal; candidate Jones is a right-wing reactionary.* Name calling is frequent in politics and among competing groups. Unless these terms are carefully defined, they are meaningless.

- **Non sequitur.** *A university that can raise a billion dollars from alumni should not have to raise tuition.* A non sequitur (which is a Latin term meaning "it does not follow") ties together two unrelated ideas. In this case, the argument fails to recognize that the money for capital campaigns is often donated for special purposes, such as athletic facilities, and is not part of a university's general revenue.

- **Oversimplification.** *No one would run stop signs if we had a mandatory death penalty for doing it.* This claim may be true, but the argument would be unacceptable to most citizens. More complex, if less definitive, solutions are called for.

- **Polarization.** *Feminists are all man haters.* Polarization, like name calling, exaggerates positions and groups by representing them as extreme and divisive.

- **Post hoc fallacy.** *The stock market goes down when the AFC wins the Super Bowl in an even year.* The *post hoc* fallacy (from the Latin *post hoc ergo procter hoc,* which means "after this, therefore because of this") assumes that things that follow in time have a causal relationship.

- **Rationalization.** *I could have finished my paper on time if my printer had been working.* People frequently come up with excuses and weak explanations for their own and others' behavior that avoid actual causes.

- **Slippery slope.** *If we grant citizenship to illegal immigrants, no one will bother to enter the country legally.* The slippery slope maintains that one thing will inevitably lead to another.
- **Straw man.** *Environmentalists won't be satisfied until not a single human being is allowed to enter a national park.* A straw man argument is a diversionary tactic that sets up another's position in a way that can be easily rejected. In fact, only a small percentage of environmentalists would make an argument even close to this one.

EXERCISE 6.1 Build a collection of fallacies. See if you can find examples of all thirteen fallacies mentioned in Section 6c. Make sure you cite the source of your fallacy. Create examples for the ones you can't find. Compare your examples with those of your classmates.

6d CRITICAL VIEWING

Critical viewing is similar to critical reading, although it may be a skill less often practiced. Let's take an example. Usually photographs come in a context—in a book with a caption, in a family photo album, in a magazine advertisement—that tells us a great deal about why the photograph was taken and what purpose it is intended to serve. But even without the external context, there are often clues within a photograph that suggest its origins.

We likely could guess the approximate date of the photograph on page 112 by the content of the billboard. By the end of the 1950s, long-distance travel by passenger train was being replaced by airline travel, so the picture must have been taken before then. The name of the railroad, Southern Pacific, along with the barren landscape indicates that the photograph was taken in the southwestern United States. In fact, this photograph was taken in 1937 by Dorothea Lange (1895-1965), who gave it the title "Toward Los Angeles, California."

One approach to critical viewing is to examine a photograph in terms of its composition. In Lange's photograph the lines of the shoulder of the road, the highway, and the telephone poles slope toward a vanishing point on the horizon, giving the image a sense of great distance. At the same time, the image divides into ground and sky with the horizon line in the center. The two figures in dark clothing walking away contrast to a rectangular billboard with a white background and white frame.

Another approach to critical viewing is to analyze the content. In 1937 the United States was in the midst of the Great Depression and a severe drought, which forced many small farmers in middle America to abandon their homes and go to California in search of work. The luxury portrayed on the billboard contrasts to the two walking figures, who presumably do not have bus fare, much less enough money for a luxury train. By placing the figures and the billboard beside each other (a visual relationship called juxtaposition), Lange is able to make an ironic commentary on the lives of well-off and poor Americans during the depression.

No one set of questions can cover the great variety of images, but a few general questions can assist you in developing a critical response.

Previewing

Critical reading requires thinking about the context first. Begin by asking yourself the following questions:

- Who created this image (film, advertisement, television program, and so on)?
- Why was it created?
- Where did it first appear?
- When did it appear?
- What media are used? (Web sites, for example, often combine images, text, and sound.)
- Who sponsored it?
- What has been written about the creator or the image?

Analyzing

The following analytical questions apply primarily to still images. Animations and motion pictures also provoke questions about their narrative structure.

- What can you say about the composition of the image? See Chapters 2 and 10 for ways to analyze composition.
- Where do your eyes go first? If there is an attention-grabbing element, how does it connect with the rest of the image?
- How is color used?
- How does the image appeal to the values of the audience?
- How does the image relate to its context?
- Was it intended to serve a purpose besides art or entertainment?

Responding

Make notes and write as and after you view the image, with these questions in mind:

- What was your first impression of the image (film, advertisement, television program, and so on)?
- After you have thought more and perhaps read more about it, how has your first impression changed or expanded?

EXERCISE 6.2 Find an interesting photo in your textbook, a magazine, or a newspaper. Write a brief (one- or two-page) analysis of this photo following the process outlined in Section 6d. Pay particular attention to the last question: After you have thought about this picture, how has your first impression changed?

EXERCISE 6.3 Altered photos can have a huge impact, especially when they rewrite history or are used to "prove" the existence of some other-worldly beast. Faced with such grand hoaxes, though, we often overlook the prevalence of altered images in our daily lives. Find an image that has clearly been altered in an advertisement, on TV (you can write a description of the image and cite the source), on the Internet, or in the newspaper (newspapers like the *National Inquirer* and *Weekly World News* routinely alter images). Write a few paragraphs about this image. What has been altered? Is the producer of the image up front about the alteration? What, do you think, was the purpose behind the alteration of this photo? What are the possible implications?

EXERCISE 6.4 Advertising has become so much a part of our lives that we are very nearly blind to its more subtle manifestations. Look around your room; how many corporate logos and brand names do you see? Make a list of all that you find and compare your list with your classmates' lists. Are you surprised by the results?

6e | VISUAL FALLACIES

Misleading images

The era of digital photography has made it possible to create images of almost anything imaginable, including lifelike dinosaurs chasing humans, interactions between people now living and those long dead, and human feats that defy human limits and the laws of physics. What is a "real" stunt in an action

film today matters little to most filmgoers, and readers of newspapers no longer are shocked to find that some news photos are digitally manipulated.

The manipulation of images is not new to the digital era. One of the best-known images from the Civil War is an image of a dead Confederate sharpshooter behind a rock barricade on the Gettysburg battlefield. The photograph reproduced here was made by Alexander Gardner (1821-82) in July 1863. Gardner titled the photograph "The Home of a Rebel Sharpshooter, Gettysburg," and for over a century historians accepted that description. Gardner claimed that he saw the body again in November 1863 in the same place with the rusted rifle still beside him.

A modern historian, William Frassanito, studied other photographs Gardner took at Gettysburg and discovered pictures of the dead soldier in another, much less dramatic location. He also noted that the rifle in the photograph was not the type of weapon used by sharpshooters. Frassanito surmised that Gardner had moved the body and added a rifle as a photographic prop. Furthermore, he doubted that Gardner had seen the body again four months later since all the bodies had been buried by that time and the battlefield had been thoroughly scavenged for souvenirs.

Pictures are not always what they claim to be. Critical viewers ask the same questions about images that they do about texts.

Writing in the World

Accessibility and usability

Two additional criteria important for critical reading and viewing in the workplace are accessibility and usability.

Accessibility refers to the accuracy, completeness, appropriateness, and visual effectiveness of information for a particular audience. If information is not accurate, it is worthless. If the information is not complete, it makes high demands on readers to fill in what has been left out. If the information assumes a level of knowledge that is either too high or too low, readers will either be frustrated because they cannot understand or frustrated because they have to wade through too much they know already to get to what they want. Finally, much information is conveyed visually as well as verbally. If you have ever tried to assemble something and found that the diagrams bore little resemblance to the parts in the package, you know that visual effectiveness involves much more than a handsome look.

Usability refers to the time it takes to find relevant information and whether that information allows readers to accomplish their own tasks. For example, a manual designed to allow you to repair your own car should tell you how to diagnose a particular problem and then how to repair it. If it fails to do either, it is not usable.

Misleading charts

A special category of visual fallacies is misleading charts. For example, the fictitious company, Glitzycorp, might use the chart in Figure 6.1 to attract investors. The chart shows what looks like remarkable growth from 2001 to 2003 and projects additional sales for 2004. But is the picture quite as rosy as it is being painted?

Notice that the bars in this bar chart start at 20 rather than at 0. The effect is to make the $22 million sales in 2002 appear to double the $21 million sales of 2001, even though the increase was less than 5%. Three years is also a short span to use to project a company's future profits. Figure

Figure 6.1

Figure 6.2

6.2 shows the sales of Glitzycorp over seven years, and it tells quite a different story. The big growth years were in the late 1990s, followed by a collapse in 2000 and slow growth ever since.

Glitzycorp's sales charts illustrate how facts can be manipulated in visual presentations.

Chapter 7
Writing to Reflect

When we write to reflect, we consider an idea or experience, and through this consideration come to a greater understanding of its significance. In any venue other than the pages of our personal journal, we intend to share our experience and its significance with others. Reflecting is also a way of understanding ourselves. By connecting memories of the past to our knowledge in the present, we learn about who we were and who we have become.

7a | FIND A REFLECTIVE TOPIC

Reflecting on experience

Reflections, whether they are in print, video, or any other medium, often deal with personal and private experiences. Filmmaker Michelle Citron, for example, makes films that address her childhood abuse and depression—issues that are not usually represented in the snapshots and home movies that families use to chronicle their histories. In her book *Home Movies and Other Necessary Fictions,* Citron reflects on how watching her family's home movies as an adult compelled her to use her art to examine and expose potentially destructive family dynamics:

> I watched my family's home movies over and over, trying to understand why they didn't show what I remembered; why I felt a lie. This family seemed so nice, loving, normal. I was disturbed. I was obsessed. I kept trying to figure out why the images I saw flickering on the wall had no correspondence to the memories flickering in my mind. Sister, friends, strangers came over to my house for dinner. Little did they know there was a price to pay. For after dinner I would sit them down in the darkened living room and make them watch the home movies. What do you see? Does this seem like a happy family to you? Do you think all is as it should be? I badgered them with questions. I'm sure they thought

me meshuggeneh, as my mother would say. But I had to understand the split between what I saw and what I remembered. (14, 16)

Reflections do not have to be based on explicitly personal topics, however. In some cases, being too personal or confessional can limit a writer's ability to connect to his or her audience. The goal of reflection should not be simply to vent pent-up feelings or to expose secrets (although when done well, this can be effective). Instead, its goal should be to allow the audience to share with the writer his or her discovery of the significance of an experience. In "Thru-Hiking," an essay about hiking the entire 2,150-mile length of the Appalachian Trail published in *The Missouri Review*, Eric Lupfer shares his realization that his individual desire to hike the Trail conveys a more generic, yet wholly American, attitude about pilgrimages:

> One of the remarkable things about the Trail is this separateness it keeps as it winds down through the crowded Eastern Mountains. Though it passes through towns and pastures, along roads and sidewalks, the Trail is something set apart from the settled areas from which it is only rarely out of reach. Even weekend hikers feel this, but for thru-hikers, the Trail stands apart from all of the towns, counties and states it passes through in a more profound way. It becomes a separate world, an unfurling narrative of mountains, people and weather. What Dan "Wingfoot" Bruce in *The Thru-Hiker's Handbook* refers to as "modern recreational thru-hiking" seems ultimately an American form of pilgrimage. The idea is not to break new ground, but to follow the official Trail, which has been cleared and flattened by thousands of others. The frontiers you explore are at the edge of your own personal landscape, and the way you go about that is particularly your own. (49)

Discovering a reflective topic

Listing is a good way to identify possibilities for reflective essays based on memories.

- List five people who have been significant in your life.
- List five events that have been important in your life. Think about one-time events, such as getting a scholarship, and recurring events, such as a yearly family get-together.
- List five places that have been important in your life.

- Now look through your lists and check the items that are especially vivid.

Another set of possibilities can be drawn from looking at family photographs (see Melissa Dodd's reflection on a family photograph in Section 7d). In addition to constructing the context for the photograph, you can point to details in the picture that have significance. You can also write about objects that have special significance for your family or just for you, such as a scrapbook that you kept in elementary school.

Once you have selected a topic, try freewriting to stimulate your memories and explore your present perspective (see Section 3b). Take five to ten minutes to write about the event, person, or place as you remember it. Then write for five to ten minutes about how you think about the person, event, or place today. What has changed from your first experience? Why do you feel differently now?

Not all reflective topics are about the past. You can visit a place or go to an event and focus on your interaction with the place or event instead of on the place or event itself. Sylvia Herrera used this strategy in her visit to a museum (see Section 7e).

EXERCISE 7.1 Look at your immediate work space. Are you at home, at the library, at a coffee house, or elsewhere? If you are someplace that is familiar to you, list the first five people that this place makes you think about, the first five things this place makes you think about, and the first five events in your past that you associate with this place. Can you connect any of these into a brief narrative? Write a one-paragraph narrative of a memory this place inspires, using the items from your lists.

If the place isn't familiar to you, choose an object, person, or aspect of the atmosphere that reminds you of something else. Does the smell of the coffee bring back a memory? Does the person napping across the table from you at the library remind you of anyone? Use your moment now to frame a memory you could associate with this particular place.

7b IDENTIFY A FOCUS

While vastly different in subject matter and style, Citron's and Lupfer's reflections have one important thing in common—they both have a **focus**.

In other words, they both aim to communicate a main idea to an audience. The focus, while not necessarily stated as a formal thesis, makes the reflection coherent. Why is this experience important? Why is it memorable? In short, why is it worth writing about?

The purpose of the reflection, then, is the effect the writer wants the main idea to have on the reader. For Citron, the experience of watching her family's home movies was worth writing about because it compelled her first to explore and then to confront the depression and pain that she suffered as a child. Perhaps a reader who has had a similar childhood will be inspired to do the same. For Lupfer, the experience of hiking the Appalachian Trail was worth writing about because it reflected something innately American.

Often the focus comes not in the big idea but in the small details that call for reflection. In one of the most powerful essays ever written about capital punishment, George Orwell, while serving as a minor British colonial official in Burma (now Myanmar), describes the routine execution of a nameless prisoner convicted of a nameless crime. All of those present quietly do their jobs—the prison guards, the hangman, the superintendent, and even the prisoner, who offers no resistance when he is bound and led to the gallows. All is routine until a very small incident changes Orwell's awareness of what is happening: The prisoner, gripped tightly by the guards, steps lightly around a puddle on his way to the gallows. Orwell writes, "It is curious; but till that moment I had never realized what it means to destroy a healthy, conscious man."

Writing in the World

Double-entry journals

Many authors of reflective writing use a double-entry journal, which simply means that they write on only one side of the page when they record their initial impressions. They leave the facing page blank to allow room for later comments. Of course you can do much the same thing with word processing software, using the annotation feature or adding later comments in a different color. The technology is simple; the work is in taking time to write and then going back later to reconsider what you have written.

EXERCISE 7.2 Find a short reflective piece of writing in the newspaper, a magazine, a book, or on the Internet. Many popular magazines, for example, have articles in which celebrities detail their story of a marital break-up, illness, bouts with depression or addiction, or other personal details. Talk shows and interviews are also ripe for this sort of personal narrative. Write a paragraph in which you analyze the format of the message: Does the intended purpose actually line up with the way in which the message is presented and with its intended audience?

7c | DEVELOP A RESPONSE

Choosing details

Writers communicate their experiences to readers by carefully selecting and developing details. For experiences in the past, the challenge is to make them come alive for the reader. Vivid, concrete details are the catalyst for stimulating readers' imaginations.

- Use factual details such as specific dates to provide background information.
- Augment visual details with other sensory details (smells, sounds, tastes, tactile feelings).
- Choose specific words to convey details.
- Identify people by more than how they look. Think about typical mannerisms, gestures, and habits.
- If people interact, use dialogue to convey the interaction.

Organizing your ideas

Some reflections are narratives that tell a story in **chronological order**. Sylvia Herrera's account of a visit to a museum (see Section 7e) follows a chronological order. Melissa Dodd, by contrast, writes about a family photograph (see Section 7d). She briefly tells about the circumstances of the photo, but her focus is on why her mother is not in the photo. Dodd's

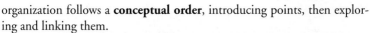

organization follows a **conceptual order**, introducing points, then exploring and linking them.

Chronological order is easier to write because we simply have to put things in the order they occurred. Even if a writer decides to put something out of sequence—for example, starting with a car crash and then telling about the events that led up to it—readers are accustomed to these narrative strategies. Conceptual order, however, does not fall into place easily. You have to think about the main points and how you want to connect them. Melissa Dodd decided to introduce Michelle Citron's point about who gets left out of photographs before describing her own family. Then she links again to Citron near the end. Idea maps can help you to make links (see Section 3b), and outlines can help you organize points in the most effective order (see Section 3d).

Beginning and ending

The beginning of a reflective essay, like those in other kinds of essays, should announce the subject and indicate the writer's stance toward that subject. The introduction in a reflective essay carries the additional burden of signaling the writer's involvement and gaining the reader's interest in the writer's reflection. Sylvia Herrera tells of her curiosity about how a museum can claim to represent *the* story of Texas in a state that has always been diverse. Melissa Dodd begins with a simple description of a family photograph, then raises the stakes in the second paragraph by mentioning who was left out. Both writers succeed in keeping us reading.

Conclusions of reflective essays often invite further reflection. Sylvia Herrera uses the conclusion to offer a summary judgment about the representation of her own history in the museum. Her narrative of the museum led logically to a final evaluation. Melissa Dodd's organization did not lead her to a summarizing conclusion. Her ending is a challenge to herself to learn more about her family and think more deeply about her family's relationships. Herrera's and Dodd's beginnings and endings work because they fit what each writer is trying to accomplish.

Thinking about your voice

Successful reflections convey a sense of a person's voice, and that voice in turn suggests the writer's attitude toward the subject. Melissa Dodd (her essay appears in Section 7d) takes a more distant voice from her subject than does Sylvia Herrera (see Section 7e). Dodd describes the photo in the first paragraph in almost clinical fashion, and she connects Citron's *Home Movies* to her own family with objective language. The details we normally associate with a child's memory of her grandparents' house do not come until the last paragraph ("Grandma's house—its warmth, and that it always smelled like bacon and Dr. Pepper"), and they are qualified as a partial memory of a larger scene that included some unpleasant relationships.

Sylvia Herrera quickly establishes who she is, and her voice is one that asks hard questions. She wonders why Mexicans are not represented in the section on Anglo settlement during the 1820s and 1830s if Texas was a part of Mexico until 1836, and later why Mexican-Americans in the twentieth century are represented almost exclusively as migrant workers. Her voice is not angry, but nevertheless, she is not going to let the museum off the hook easily.

7d | SAMPLE REFLECTIVE ESSAY

After reading excerpts from Citron's book *Home Movies* for her film studies class, Melissa Dodd decided to write her own reflection on a family snapshot. The main idea of Melissa Dodd's reflection is that the objects in a photograph give clues not only to what is missing, but also to the dynamics of the moment the photo claims to capture. Her purpose is to lead others to examine more closely their own family photographs and the memories they depict.

Dodd 1

Melissa Dodd

Professor Mendoza

Introduction to Film

25 April 2002

My Sister and Me on Grandma's Lap

This picture was taken at my paternal grandmother's
house in Enid, Oklahoma. I'm on Grandma's lap, and my sister Rhonda is on the floor. I believe this picture was taken
around 1969 or 1970 because I look about two or three
years old. It is after supper, and Grandma is reading to me.

Dodd begins with
a descriptive
paragraph,
bringing the
reader into the
photo.

Dodd 2

The summary of Citron's *Home Movies* is used to pose a question about why Dodd's mother was missing from the photo.

This photograph is interesting to me because it reflects two points that Michelle Citron makes in her book, *Home Movies*. First, the person taking the picture is asserting control over the interpretation of the memory. Second, there are clues within the frame that signify what has actually been left out of the frame. The item missing from this picture is my mother.

A detail in the photo, the moccasins, leads to a description of conflict between mother and grandmother.

My father took the picture in order to show me wearing the moccasins my maternal grandfather had just bought for me when we visited him in Holdenville, Oklahoma. My mother had remained there, while we went on to Enid. She rarely came with us to visit Grandma because they did not get along. Like her own mother, my mother could be moody, distant, and bad-tempered. Grandma, on the other hand, was somewhat meddlesome, but affectionate, and over-indulgent with us kids. Consequently, they argued over how we should be treated.

Dodd steps back to reflect on the photograph in the context of what was happening in the family.

Grandma is pointing to the moccasins, which signify my mother's absence. In some ways, the photo is a conciliatory gesture; my father is acknowledging his in-laws' contribution to my happiness and well being. In another, less obvious way, it is an act of spite. Since my mother

Dodd 3

refused to be there, my father replaced her with his own mother in this happy family scene he has created.

Her absence is also highlighted by the presence of my sister, Rhonda, who was about nine or ten. When I was a baby, Rhonda and I were always in pictures together. Usually she's playing "mommy" and holding me on her lap. She was very protective of me and would not let me out of her sight. Taking the role of my guardian often got her in trouble, especially when my mother's temper flared. Here, she looks silly and relaxed, more childlike than she does in other family pictures.

Dodd examines how her sister was affected by family conflicts by contrasting her appearance in this photo with her appearance in others.

Citron argues that since they are selective and often taken by men, home movies and family photographs assert a balance of power within the family and strive to promote the "good" memory of family: "parents in control, men in charge, families together" (15). What she does not overtly mention, however, is that these created memories are also punitive. It is the people, things, or events that disrupt the image of the ideal family that are banished from the frame. Importantly, my mother's temper and her refusal to make peace with my grandmother led to her omission from my father's carefully constructed scene of domestic tranquillity.

Dodd moves one step further to explore how good memories are manufactured in family photographs by banishing what is disruptive.

Dodd 4

In the end, what is most significant is the fact that
this manufactured memory works. Until I began to look at
this picture through Citron's eyes, I simply had a memory
of my Grandma's house—its warmth, and that it always
smelled like bacon and Dr. Pepper. Unfortunately, this is
not the whole picture. But this pleasant memory does not
have to go away just because I now see things in more
detail. By recognizing what is missing, I hope I can work
to reconcile the fiction to the reality and come to a more
complete understanding of my family's dynamics.

Dodd 5

Work Cited

Citron, Michelle. <u>Home Movies and Other Necessary</u>
<u>Fictions</u>. Minneapolis: U of Minnesota P, 1999.

 To hear audio commentary on this piece of writing, visit
www.ablongman.com/faigley001.

EXERCISE 7.3 Return to the paragraph you wrote for Exercise 7.1.
Develop this paragraph into a full response using the advice provided in
Section 7c. Find a focus for your response, and add details to make the
reflection come alive for the reader. Remember to give your response an
attention-getting introduction and a thoughtful conclusion.

7e | A REFLECTIVE MAGAZINE ARTICLE

Sylvia Herrera wanted to write an article for a college magazine produced by Mexican American students. She decided to write a review of the Bob Bullock Texas State History Museum in Austin, Texas. To make the review more appealing to her audience, she wrote it as a personal reflection about her first visit to the museum.

Whose Story?
Sylvia Herrera

When the Bob Bullock Texas State History Museum opened in March 2001, it advertised itself as "The Story of Texas." It still calls itself the story of Texas in letters chiseled into the top of the building, on its Web site, on signs directing visitors to the museum, and even on the refrigerator magnets you can buy in the gift shop. When I first saw the slogan, I wondered how there could be "the" story of Texas, since Texas has been culturally diverse throughout its history as a part of Mexico that became a separate nation and later a state. Shortly Texas will have no one group as a majority. I grew up in the Rio Grande Valley, where the great majority of the population, like me, is Mexican American. How was this new museum going to present *my* story? I had to go and find out.

When I first walked into the lobby, I noticed the large mosaic on the floor but I couldn't figure out what it depicted. I just saw a campfire and a bunch of wiggly figures. Someone next to me told their kids that they'd be able to see the entire mosaic from the third floor. I decided to wait and do the same.

The first exhibit I saw was the "It Ain't Braggin' if it's True" (one of my friends told me I had to see the shrine

to Lance Armstrong and the rhinestone car). The name of the exhibit didn't make much sense to me though; aren't all museum exhibits, especially ones about history, supposed to be true? The big banner in the middle of the room didn't help much either. It simply said "Vision" and had a quote about how only those with great vision can see opportunity where others see empty space. Maybe those who have this type of vision get the braggin' rights?

Texas was never a big empty space. The Spaniards and later the French who came here discovered cultures that were centuries old. But history, and the museum itself, begins with European colonization. The history of Texas, one of the signs says, was shaped by the way the different groups of people who came to Texas responded to the land and to each other. So land, and interaction between different groups of people, would be used a lot in the telling of this story of Texas, I assumed. In this first room, though, I noticed something else that would continue throughout the museum. All of the mannequins, no matter what ethnicity they represent, are white—not Caucasian, but a strange plaster white. The only way you know what group they represent is by their costumes.

As I wandered through the "Mission" area of the museum, I noticed that there was little discussion of the violence I had heard about hap-

pening in and around the missions. Everything seemed watered down. Missionaries and soldiers "relied" on the native peoples for supplies. The "Indians" were "indifferent" to attempts to convert them.

The next area was called "Gone to Texas," featuring Stephen F. Austin's attempts to get settlers to move to Texas in order to make it more stable. Texas, it seems, was still an empty space. But what had happened to all of the native peoples? There was a little stump in the middle of the room with a sign that asked the same question. The answers were in a notebook on the back, one page for each group of native peoples, all of which were exterminated or moved out of Texas. I wondered, though, how many visitors actually stopped to page through the book. We were in a section where dioramas lit up and spoke when you pushed buttons.

Where were the Mexicans? Texas was owned by Mexico at this time, but the only people represented here were Europeans, a few African Americans held in slavery, and a few renegade Comanches. Maybe there would be answers to this question upstairs.

A big statue of Sam Houston greeted me as I reached the second floor. Next to him was a sign that said, "Building the Texas Identity 1821-1936." I'd just learned that there were lots of different people in Texas before 1821, and that it was owned by Mexico up to this time, so I was surprised to find that Texas still had no identity. I guess what they meant was an identity separate from Mexico. When I saw the life-size diorama of the first shots fired in the Texas Revolution, I remembered the "It Ain't Braggin'" exhibit I saw downstairs. This diorama showed the shouting Texans with a cannon that they had borrowed and now refused to give back to Mexico. They were shouting and brandishing a flag that said "come and get it." Seizing opportunity, whether it be land, a rhinestone cadillac, or a borrowed cannon, is heroic and the story of Texas.

Throughout the area dealing with the Texas Revolution, the only personal accounts of those who fought and fled during the revolution were by Anglos.

According to a museum display, the population of Texas in 1836 included about 35,000 Anglos, 3,500 Tejanos, 14,200 Indians, and 5,000 African Americans held in slavery. Granted, Anglos were the majority, but didn't any of these groups leave behind a record of their experiences? Maybe not. That would explain why they all seem to disappear for the next 50 or so years that the museum represents.

At the third floor landing, I read this quote, given without a source: "If you work hard, are smart and tough, and get a little bit lucky, Texas can be a bountiful place." The display after this sign tells the story of the ranchos and how the Spanish established the cattle business and the image of the cowboy in Texas. But then there's a sudden shift to farming, and the only Mexican Americans represented anywhere else on the floor (including the sections on the oil business, the military, and the space program) are migrant workers. The gap is never explained unless we take that quote at face value.

I was done, but I still wanted to take in the full view of the mosaic on the lobby floor. I finally realized that it shows a campfire and seated around it, in a bird's-eye view, are the people supposedly represented in the museum (cowboys, Indians, Mexicans, and so on). The legend around the mosaic says: "Born around the campfires of our past, the history of Texas." It presents a nice picture—all these people sitting peacefully around the campfire, as if they had all come together to tell the story they all have in common. I

also looked up to the banners hanging from the ceiling. Each one has a photo of a person of a different ethnicity and the words "It's my story."

It's not my story. The story I know from my family and the land where I grew up is too complicated to fit onto three floors. There is a lot of conflict, a lot of joy, and many, many brown faces. In the year 2000, the population of Texans who claimed Hispanic heritage was 32%, a fact you would never guess from the displays in the Bullock Museum. We are not all migrant workers, dictatorial generals, converted Indians, or romantic figures from stage and screen. We are war heroes, scientists, entrepreneurs, and politicians. We are Texas, and it's time to tell our story too.

To hear audio commentary on this piece of writing, visit **www.ablongman.com/faigley002.**

EXERCISE 7.4 Visit a local museum or event, see an exhibit, watch a documentary, or listen to a radio program that claims to present the true story of something that is central to your identity—your ethnicity, your community, your social group, your sexual orientation, your hometown, your socioeconomic class, or your religion, for example. Write a magazine-style reflection on your experience, using Sylvia's essay as a model. Take photographs, if possible, or use other images to support your text. Remember to stay focused, keep the information organized, and provide vivid details. You must also cite any sources you use (museum information, the documentary you watch, the radio program you listen to, and so on) and get permission from anyone you might interview or photograph.

7f A REFLECTIVE WEB SITE

Many personal Web sites sprang up early on the Web. Most of these personal sites contained little more than a few photos and a list of links. Some personal sites, however, became places for publishing writing, art, photographs, audio, and video. One such site that has gained widespread recognition is **www.maganda.org**, published by Christine Castro. A native of the Philippines, Castro chose the Tagalog word *maganda* (meaning "pretty") as the title of her site (see Figures 7.1 and 7.2).

Castro posts on her site journal entries that reflect on books she has read, television shows she has watched, people she has seen, places she has visited, and other events in her life. She updates the site frequently, keeping the content fresh.

Figure 7.1. Maganda.org combines Christine Castro's writing and art.

Figure 7.2. Christine constructs an online identity by describing herself in words and images.

Chapter 8
Writing to Inform

Much of what you read in college is informative. Even before you enter college, you read about how to apply, and, after you are accepted, how to register for courses. When you begin courses, your textbooks inform you about particular subjects, and you learn more about those subjects by reading in the library and on the Web. You read about what is happening on campus in your college newspaper, and you learn about other campus activities by reading. Likewise, many of the writing tasks assigned in college are informative—from lab reports and essay exams, to analyses of literature, research papers, and case studies.

The emphasis on writing to inform in college is not surprising because nearly every occupation that requires a college degree requires informative writing. The communication product of many professionals, including accountants, engineers, scientists, journalists, and business consultants, to name a few, is a written report. Informative writing has four primary functions: to report new or unfamiliar information; to analyze for meaning, patterns, and connections; to explain how to do something or how something works; and to explore questions and problems.

8a | FIND AN INFORMATIVE TOPIC

At the beginning of any college assignment, especially one that asks for informative writing, it is critical to understand what kind of information your instructor expects. Look at your assignment for key words such as *study, analyze, explain,* and *explore*, which indicate what kind of writing you are expected to produce (see Section 3a).

Reporting information

Reporting information takes many forms, ranging from reports of experimental research (see Section 23g) and reports of library research (see Section 21k) to simple lists of information. In one sense, writing to reflect (discussed in Chapter 7) and writing to persuade (Chapter 9) also report information. The main difference is that the focus of a report and other informative kinds of writing is on the subject, not on the writer's reflections or on changing readers' minds or on getting them to take action. Writers of reports usually stay in the background and keep their language as neutral as possible, giving the impression of an objective, impartial observer.

Analyzing meaning, patterns, and connections

Writers not only report what they read and observe. They often construct meaning through selecting what and what not to include and in organizing that information. Sometimes this construction of meaning is made explicit as **analysis**. You may have experience in analyzing literary texts (see Chapter 22). Writing in and after college requires you to analyze more than literature. The complexity of the world we live in requires making connections. For example, scientists now agree that the earth has become warmer over the last few decades, but to what extent this warming has been caused by the burning of fossil fuels remains controversial. Advertisers know that certain kinds of ads (for example, ones that associate drinking beer with social life) sell the product, but often they do not know exactly how these ads work or why some ads are more effective than others. Historians debate the importance of certain historical events (for example, the Treaty of Versailles following World War I) and how those events led to subsequent events (World War II).

Explaining how

Often what you know well is difficult to explain to others. You may know how to solve certain kinds of difficult problems, such as how to fix a problem in your car's electrical system, but if you have to tell someone else how to do it over the phone, you may quickly become very frustrated.

Often you have to break down a process into steps that you can describe in order to explain it. Explaining a process sometimes requires you to think about something familiar in a new way.

Exploring questions and problems

Not all informative writing is about topics with which you are familiar or ones that you can bring to closure. Often college writing involves issues or problems that perplex us and for which we cannot come to a definitive conclusion. The goal in such writing is not the ending but the journey. Tracing the turns of thought in a difficult intellectual problem can result in writing far beyond the ordinary. Difficult issues often leave us conflicted; readers appreciate it when we deal honestly with those conflicts.

Finding a topic

When your general subject is specified in your assignment, you can make your work more pleasant by choosing a specific topic that is either more familiar to you or that you find particularly interesting. Here are some guidelines you can use when choosing a topic:

- Choose a topic you will enjoy writing about.
- Choose a topic that readers will enjoy reading about.
- Choose a topic that you know something about or can readily find information about.
- Choose a topic for which you can make a contribution of your own, perhaps by viewing something familiar in a new way.
- If you choose an unfamiliar topic, you must be strongly committed to learning more about it.

EXERCISE 8.1 Informative writing in college often involves explaining a concept. Pick a particular academic discipline that interests you (psychology, government, biology, art) or another broad subject area (the environment, college athletics, eating disorders). List at least five central concepts for that discipline or area of interest. When you finish, review your list and select one concept as a possible topic.

Take five minutes to write what you know about that concept. Why does it interest you? What more would you like to know about it?

Next, make a quick survey of information about the concept. If your library has online resources such as specialized encyclopedias, look up the concept. Otherwise, go to the library. Do a Web search using a search engine. After an hour or two, you should know whether you can find enough information to write about this concept.

8b | NARROW YOUR TOPIC AND WRITE A THESIS

A central difficulty with writing to inform is determining where to stop. For any large subject, a lifetime may be insufficient. The key to success is to limit the topic. Find a topic you can cover thoroughly in the space you have. Broad, general topics are nearly impossible to cover in an essay of five pages. Look for ways of dividing large topics such as "the use of steroids among college students" into smaller categories and select one that is promising. "Why college athletes ignore the risks of steroids" is a topic that you are more likely to be able to cover in a short paper.

Often your readers will lack initial interest in your topic. If you ignore their lack of interest, they in turn likely will ignore you. Instead, you can take your readers' knowledge and interest into account when you draft your thesis. For example, someone who knows a lot about birds in the parks of your city might write this informative thesis:

Watching birds in urban areas is interesting because unusual birds often show up in city parks.

It doesn't sound like a topic that most college students would find as interesting as the writer does. But if the writer puts the audience's attitude in the foreground, challenging them to consider a subject they likely have not thought much about, a college audience might read beyond the title:

Although most college students think of bird watching as an activity for retired people, watching birds gives you a daily experience with nature, even in urban areas.

This thesis also gives the writing a stance from which to approach the topic.

EXERCISE 8.2 An informative thesis statement should contain the topic and indicate your particular focus. To sharpen that focus, answer the following questions.

1. Who are your readers? What are they likely to know about your topic?
2. What makes you interested in this topic?
3. What are the major subdivisions of your topic? Which one or ones are you writing about?
4. What key words are important to your topic?

Look at your thesis statement and your answers to the questions. Revise your thesis statement to give it a sharper focus.

8c DEVELOP AND ORGANIZE YOUR IDEAS

Successful reporting of information requires a clear understanding of the subject and clear presentation. How much information you need to include depends on your audience's knowledge of and potential interest in your topic.

Introducing your subject to your audience

Consider these questions about your audience:

- What does my audience already know about the subject?
- What questions or concerns might they have about my subject?
- What is their attitude toward the subject? If it is different from mine, how can I address the difference?

If your audience is unfamiliar with your subject, you will need to supply background information. If key terms are unfamiliar, you should define them.

Organizing your information

The organization of informative writing varies according to the subject. If you are writing about a topic that occurs over time, often a **chronological organization** works best. Andrea Chen used chronological organization in writing about the life of explorer John Wesley Powell (see Section 8d).

Most analyses require you to identify the major aspects of a subject and to discuss each. **Conceptual organization** requires you to make decisions before you start about what is most important and how those concepts relate to each other. Idea maps can help you determine what the key concepts are and how they relate to each other (see Section 3b). A useful strategy for deciding how to organize your information is to make a working outline that sets up the key points (see Section 3d).

Writing in the World

Analyzing causes

One of the most difficult tasks in the workplace is analyzing the causes of a problem. For example, an airport shuttle company was losing a great deal of money on the weekends because passengers didn't get to the airport on time, forcing the company to pay for rescheduling flights. Corporate headquarters hired a consultant to write a report on what was going wrong. She thought she had quickly identified the cause when managers told her that drivers often called in sick on the weekends.

When the consultant audited records, however, she found that the absence rate was no higher than during the week. What the managers had claimed was the obvious cause didn't turn out to be a significant factor. The consultant began riding with the drivers to learn why they were often late. She found that the vans were not well maintained and when they broke down on weekends, there was no one to fix them. Equipment was in short supply, not drivers. She noted that weekend dispatchers were not as experienced as weekday dispatchers, and they were not as clever at routing drivers or at assisting drivers who got lost. Furthermore, she found that the airport was located close to a shopping center that created traffic jams on weekends. Saturday afternoon was a terrible time to get to the airport, sometimes worse than weekday rush hour.

Writing the report was straightforward for the consultant once she had isolated the causes.

If you are reporting on two similar or different things, a **compare and contrast organization** is likely appropriate. The simplest procedure is to describe one thing and then describe the other, ending with a conclusion that summarizes the similarities and differences. Often it is more effective to proceed point by point, explaining how each is similar or different in each aspect.

EXERCISE 8.3 Which of the methods of organization discussed in Section 8c would work best for each of the following topics?

1. How to interview for a job
2. The unseen stresses faced by teenaged girls
3. An analysis of the causes of the Spanish-American War
4. A description of Egyptian burial practices
5. How to install software on a computer
6. A comparison of two different proposals to solve the same problem
7. A description of the Battle of Little Bighorn
8. An analysis of the rhetorical styles of Malcolm X and Martin Luther King, Jr.
9. An analysis of a proposal to make a course in English grammar mandatory for all entering freshmen
10. A continent-by-continent survey of the various styles of Stone Age cave painting

8d SAMPLE INFORMATIVE ESSAY

Andrea Chen was given the following essay assignment in her American history class: "Select a person who lived and wrote in the United States in the nineteenth century whom you find especially important or whose achievements you find especially noteworthy. Read one or more works that the person wrote. Explain what makes him or her historically unique."

Chen chose to write about John Wesley Powell, an explorer who made several trips down the Colorado River. After reviewing her notes from class, doing some research in a few online encyclopedias, and reading Powell's account of his journey down the Colorado River, Chen wrote this essay.

Chen 1

Andrea Chen

Professor Ward

History 102

11 November 2002

The First Descent of the Grand Canyon

John Wesley Powell was one of the foremost explorers in American history, and his first descent down the Colorado River through the Grand Canyon is one of America's greatest adventure stories. Although he is not as well known as other explorers, his travels and his contributions to American history are significant because they represent a spirit of discovery motivated not by self-glory or the acquisition of gold or land, but by a curiosity about and appreciation for both the natural world and the native peoples of the West.

> The thesis is placed early in the paper.

John Wesley Powell pursued knowledge and the uncommon experience his entire life. Born in 1834 in Ohio to a Methodist minister, he became interested in science as a boy and was fortunate to have a neighbor who was both an amateur scientist and a willing teacher (Stegner 13–14). In 1846, the Powell family moved to Wisconsin, where John Wesley struggled to continue his scientific education against the will of his father, who wanted him to become a preacher.

> Background information is arranged chronologically and creates a brief narrative of Powell's life.

Chen 2

In 1857, he set off on his first great adventure: a trip down the Ohio and Mississippi rivers in a rowboat (Stegner 16).

In 1861 Powell enlisted in the Union Army and was elected captain of artillery under U. S. Grant. He was wounded at the Battle of Shiloh in 1862 and lost his right arm. Despite his debility, however, Powell returned to active duty and finished the war (Stegner 17).

Illustrates Powell's courage

After the Civil War, Powell became a professor of science at Illinois Weslyan and curator of the Illinois State Natural History museum. In 1867 he went on his first expedition to Colorado and began his life-long love affair with the American West and the native peoples who lived there. The next year he went back to Colorado and spent the winter among the Utes on the White River, learning their language (Stegner 40).

Shows Powell's interest in and respect for the cultures of the native peoples of the West

Shortly after, he went to Washington to attempt to get support for his expedition down the Colorado River, but was unsuccessful in gaining more than a few scientific instruments from the Smithsonian. Undaunted, he raised his own funds to have three sturdy wooden boats built, and he transported them by rail to Green River, Wyoming, where on May 24, 1869, he began his journey down the Green and Colorado Rivers (Powell, Exploration 1–2). With him were nine other men,

Shows how Powell was different from other nineteenth century explorers

Chen 3

Fig. 1. Tau-gu, Chief of the Paiutes, and
Major John Wesley Powell (Hillers)

including his brother. Powell was the only one interested
in science; the others were, like other men roaming the
West in the years after the Civil War, rowdy adventurers in
search of gold.

Powell hadn't traveled far down the Green before
problems began. His boats were sturdy, but they weren't

Chen 4

Creates drama here and in the next paragraph to avoid losing the reader in list after list of facts and information

built for running rapids. Furthermore, none of the men had life jackets, nor could they swim. They managed to tie ropes to the boats and lower them down many of the rapids, but in the Canyon of Ladore on June 9, one of the boats missed an eddy and was swept downstream into a rapid Powell later named Disaster Falls (see Fig. 2). Luckily, no one drowned. Also, Powell and his men were able to salvage two important things they had feared were lost on the boat—barometers and a keg of whiskey (Powell, Exploration 21).

Powell and his men proceeded to the confluence of the Colorado and Green Rivers and through the severe rapids of Cataract Canyon and the now flooded Glen Canyon. By August 2 they were running low on food. Nevertheless, Powell was busy making side trips, climbing up canyon walls for a view of the surroundings, and taking measurements. When they entered the Grand Canyon, their situation was close to desperate and the strain of the journey began to show. Finally on August 28, at Separation Rapid near the end of the Grand Canyon, three of the men deserted (Powell, Exploration 103). Powell and the others continued downstream, and soon encountered Mormon settlers near the mouth of the Virgin River. Powell's account of this journey, The Exploration of the Colorado River and Its Canyons, is

Chen 5

remarkable for the scope and depth of knowledge exhibited, especially because Powell had very little formal training in science or ethnography.

Fig. 2. Wreck at Disaster Falls

Chen 6

In 1871 Powell made a second expedition down the Colorado River, this time bringing along a photographer. He spent most of the next decade exploring the Colorado Plateau, doing important geologic and ethnographic research. In 1878 he published his <u>Report on the Lands of the Arid Region of the United States</u>, in which he argued *against* extensive settlement of the West—an unpopular idea at the time. In 1879 he became director of the Bureau of Ethnology in Washington, and in 1881 he became director of the U.S. Geological Survey.

In spite of his inability to prevent oversettlement of the West, Powell was a major influence in preserving many of the wonderful canyons of the Colorado Plateau. Ironically, the one lake bearing his name is the same one under which Glen Canyon is buried—the one canyon Powell could not save.

The event that perhaps best represents Powell's dedication to developing an understanding of and appreciation for the West and its native peoples happened in 1870. Powell sought to find out what had happened to the three men who left his expedition at Separation Rapid. He visited the Shivwits Indians, smoked with them, and asked them if they knew anything of the missing men. The Shivwits admitted that they had killed Powell's men, mistaking them for the murderers of an Indian woman, and apologized for

Notes a major contribution Powell made

Supports claim that Powell was uncommon in his dedication to the land and its people

Memorable example used to further support thesis

Chen 7

the error. Instead of demanding retribution, as many others would have done, Powell told the Shivwits it was an honest mistake and shook hands with them. He later wrote of this same tribe's nobility and kindness toward him:

> That night I slept in peace, although these murderers of my men, and their friends, the Uinkarets, were sleeping not 500 yards away. While we were gone to the canyon, the pack train and supplies, enough to make an Indian rich beyond his wildest dreams, were all left in their charge, and were all safe; not even a lump of sugar was pilfered by the children. (Exploration 323)

It is unlikely that anyone in a similar situation, either then or now, would have exhibited such forgiveness and trust.

John Wesley Powell was not only able to see much of the American West before it was forever changed by settlement, but he was also able to see beyond its value in terms of gold or settled land to what really mattered—the natural beauty of the land and the native cultures who lived there. Perhaps it was this understanding that made him fearless and victorious against hardship. Because of his unfaltering dedication to knowledge and the preservation of the West, Powell is truly one of the most significant American explorers of the nineteenth century.

Source material included as required by the assignment

Final paragraph sums up Powell's achievement

Chen 8

Works Cited

Hillers, John K. "Tau-gu, Chief of the Paiutes, and Major
    John Wesley Powell." 1873. National Anthropological
    Archives. Washington: Smithsonian Institution.

Powell, John Wesley. The Exploration of the Colorado River.
    Ed. Wallace Stegner. Chicago: U of Chicago P, 1957.

---. Report on the Lands of the Arid Region of the United States.
    2nd ed. Washington: GPO, 1879.

---. "Wreck at Disaster Falls." Exploration of the Colorado
    River of the West and Its Tributaries. Washington:
    GPO, 1875: 26.

Stegner, Wallace. Beyond the Hundredth Meridian: John
    Wesley Powell and the Second Opening of the West.
    Boston: Houghton Mifflin, 1954.

To hear audio commentary on this piece of writing, visit
www.ablongman.com/faigley003.

EXERCISE 8.4 An informative essay can do several things. It can report information; analyze meaning, patterns, and connections; explain how to do something; and explore questions or problems. Write a three- to five-page informative essay using one of the following questions to help you formulate your thesis.

1. What (or who) is X?
2. How does X work?
3. What are the different opinions on X?
4. What caused X?
5. What effects has X had?

    Use the sample essay in the previous section as a model. Ask your instructor what format you should use for your citations.

8e AN INFORMATIVE BROCHURE

Most businesses, organizations, and clubs use informational documents to tell about themselves and to describe their products, services, and activities. The most common printed documents are brochures, form letters, flyers, and newsletters. Recognizing the need for an informational document is often the first step in writing one. Knowing a document is needed, however, is not the same thing as identifying exactly for whom it is to be written and what the document is intended to achieve. Begin with these questions:

Audience

- Is there a specific target audience?
- What do I know about their age, gender, ethnicity, educational level, and knowledge of the document's subject?
- Is there a broader or secondary audience who might also read the document?

Purpose

- What does the audience need to learn?
- What background information do they need?
- If they are to perform a task, what instructions do I need to give?

Context

- How does the document fit into the overall mission of the business or organization?
- How will the document be used? Will people be required to read it?
- Are there possible legal issues to consider?
- How much time do I have to produce the document? Will others help me?

Creating a brochure

Newsletters, brochures, and other informational documents that used to be difficult to produce are now easy to make using word processing tools and inexpensive to print or photocopy. Some programs have templates that give you a choice of formats for brochures, letters, and newsletters, into which you put your content.

Brochures are one of the most useful informational documents because they can be produced using the front and back of an $8\frac{1}{2} \times 11$ sheet of paper. They fit into standard #10 envelopes and are handy for distribution on tables or racks. Even if you don't use a ready-made template, six-panel brochures are straightforward to design.

1. **Develop a layout.** A typical brochure has six panels—three on the front and three on the back. Take two pieces of standard $8\frac{1}{2} \times 11$ paper, place them together, and fold them into three sections. Separate them, lay one page above the other, and label the sections by number, so you will know which panel fits where (Figure 8.1).

2. **Make a sketch of what you want to put on each panel.** Draw boxes where you want to insert art.

3. **In your software program, open a blank page and change the orientation to horizontal.** In Word, select **Page Layout** under **View**, which will allow you to see the graphics. Under the **File** menu, select **Page Setup**, then select **Landscape**, which will change the orientation of your page.

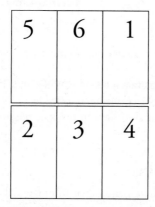

Figure 8.1

4. **Create a text box.** Under the **Insert** menu, select **Text Box**. Your pointer will change to a cross tool, which if you click and drag, creates a box. You can resize the box by clicking on its edges. Make three boxes for the panels on each side.

5. **Format the text box.** Under the **Format** menu, select **Text Box**. You will find options that allow you to change the size, color, and layout of the text box.

6. **Insert images.** You can insert images and other graphics into text boxes by selecting the options under **Picture** in the **Insert** menu.

7. **Check the formatting.** When you finish you will have two pages with three panels each. Place them together and fold them to make sure the panels are in the correct order. Also, check the alignment of the panels and the readability of the text. If you have extra space, consider enlarging the type and inserting blank space to set apart key points.

8. **Edit and proofread.** Errors destroy the effect of an otherwise handsome brochure.

Sample brochure

The Vermont Wilderness Association, a nonprofit umbrella organization dedicated to preserving wild places in Vermont, produced the brochure _Wilderness: A Vermont Tradition_. This typical informational brochure tells the mission of the organization, defines the concept of wilderness, gives a history of efforts to preserve Vermont's wilderness, and provides contact information. Although the pages reproduced in Figure 8.2 on page 152 are foldouts from a larger document, they were designed to be printed as a separate brochure.

Wilderness: A Vermont Tradition differs from the typical brochure in using horizontal rather than vertical panels. This strategy makes the bottom panel the cover when folded. The horizontal layout allows a panoramic landscape image to be placed on the cover.

To hear audio commentary on this piece of writing, visit
www.ablongman.com/faigley004.

The panel at the top of the cover page will be the first one a reader will see after lifting the cover panel. This panel quotes from The Wilderness Act of 1964.

The back cover gives a list of organizations that are part of the Vermont Wilderness Association and leaves enough white space for a mailing address to be added.

The front cover has a prominent script "wilderness" over a panoramic photograph of a wild Vermont forest.

The inside panels display in order from top to bottom when the brochure is unfolded. The top panel asks "What is Wilderness?" and then supplies a definition.

The center panel uses a contrasting color and highlights important dates in the history of protecting Vermont's wilderness areas.

Images work together with text to convey the message of the brochure.

Figure 8.2

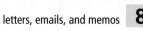

EXERCISE 8.5 Working in a group with two or three other students, create an informative brochure. You can choose as your subject a service, business, or organization located on campus or in the local community. Use the advice given in Section 8e to help you format your brochure. Make sure you clearly identify your audience, your purpose, and your context before you get started.

8f | BUSINESS LETTERS, EMAILS, AND MEMOS

Good business letters, emails, and memoranda get things done. Because they are to the point and action oriented, they communicate effectively with busy professionals. Even if you aren't a businessperson, you'll likely write business correspondence and memoranda somewhere along the way. Following the conventions of business writing increases the chances that your message will be heard. Your reader will appreciate an instantly recognizable, easy-to-read format.

The following general guidelines for business letters apply for the most part to business email and memos.

BUSINESS LETTER GUIDELINES

- Use unlined, white paper.
- Try not to exceed one page.
- Use one-inch margins.
- Single-space lines within addresses and paragraphs.
- Double-space lines between elements.
- Speak in a formal but cordial voice.
- Avoid slang and contractions.
- Construct short paragraphs (under seven lines).

Business letters

ELEMENTS OF A BUSINESS LETTER

- **Your return address:** If you're not using letterhead stationery that includes the name and address of your organization, type your address.

Spell out *street, road,* and so on. Abbreviate the name of the state. (Although it's less common, some writers prefer to write their names on the line above the return address.)

- **Date:** Use month, day, year order (January 30, 2002). Do not abbreviate the month. (Occasionally you will see writers make the date the last line of the return address element instead of skipping a space between the two.)

- **Inside address:** Write the recipient's name, followed by a comma and the recipient's title. Capitalize the initial letters of each word in the title (*Systems Administrator*). In the next lines type the recipient's address. If you are not writing to a specific person, insert a job title (*Sales Manager*), department name (*Division of Customer Service*), or institution name (*Cristado's Bakery*) in place of the recipient's name.

- **Salutation:** Type *Dear,* the recipient's name, and then a colon (*Dear Mr. Marshall:*). Prefix a title—*Mr., Ms., Miss, Mrs.,* or a professional title like *Dr.* or *Rev.*—followed by the last name (*Dear Rev. Miko*). Unless a woman refers to herself otherwise, use *Ms.* If you can't determine the person's gender from the first name, omit the prefix and use the full name instead (*Dear Lee Barger*). Use the recipient's first name exclusively only if you already know one another. *Dear Sir, Dear Madam,* and *To Whom It May Concern* are considered passé; avoid using them. Again, if you aren't writing to a specific person, write a job title, department name, or institution name in place of the recipient's name (*Dear Human Resources*).

- **Body paragraphs:** Double-space between paragraphs. Introduce the reason for the letter right away. Explain what exactly you're asking the recipient to do. If appropriate, give your contact information, and make a plan to get in touch.

- **Closing:** Write a courteous but professional closing like *Sincerely, Sincerely yours, Cordially, Respectfully,* or *Yours truly.* Capitalize only the initial letter of the first word in a closing (*Yours truly*).

- **Name:** Type your name four lines below the closing; that is, enough space to insert your signature in ink. If you are writing in an official capacity, type your title below your name.

- **Enclosures or courtesy copies:** If you have enclosed any other documents with the letter or you have sent a copy of the letter to someone else, indicate so at the end of the letter. For enclosures, type *Encl*, a colon, and the name of the enclosed documents (*Encl: asbestos removal cost estimates*). If you've sent copies to someone else, type *cc*, a colon, the name of the copy's recipient, a comma, and the person's title (*cc: Max Wexler, Professor of Chemistry*).

- **Additional pages:** If a second page is absolutely necessary, place a three-line heading flush left at the top of the page. Type the recipient's name, *page 2*, and the date.

Three business letter formats

Full block. Full block format is considered the most formal business letter format. It calls for aligning all lines flush with the left margin. The sample business letter on page 156 is an example of this format.

Modified block. Modified block format is less formal than full block. It is similar to full block except that it requires writers to align the return address, the closing, the signature, and the name at the right margin.

Block. Block format, the least formal of the three, is the same as modified block form, except that it indents the first line of each paragraph.

Sample business letter

The following letter is an example of full block format.

6814 Beecher Street, 203
Washington, D.C. 20016
March 15, 2002

Robert Turaj, Resources Director
Office of Student Affairs
American University
4400 Massachusetts Avenue
Washington, D.C. 20016

Dear Mr. Turaj:

The India Interest Group would like permission from the Office of Student Affairs to show free outdoor films on the McKinley Quadrangle as part of our India Week festivities. The films would run on the evenings of Friday, April 14 and Saturday, April 15 on a large screen to be erected in front of Bender Library.

For the past three years we have held screenings in Ward Auditorium. They were so well attended that we had to turn people away at the door each year. This year we would like to extend our promotion of India Week events to Georgetown and George Washington Universities in addition to our own campus.

In order to have sufficient time to prepare for the screenings, we would need authorization to use the quadrangle from your office by March 22.

Thank you for considering our request. We appreciate the Office of Student Affairs' support of India Week in the past, and we hope we can count on it again this year. I shall call you Monday, March 15 to discuss any concerns you might have about the film screenings. I look forward to speaking with you.

Sincerely,

Shilpa Kamath

Shilpa Kamath
President, India Week Committee

cc: Vimala Shah, President of India Interest Group

Business email

The informal style of personal email can create problems in business settings. Unlike personal email, business email often serves a documentary function, allowing others in the organization access to decision-making processes long after decisions are made. On many projects hundreds and even thousands of emails are exchanged in the course of development. Because email is so easy to produce and accumulates so rapidly, the ability to sort through a long list of it is critical. Above all, each business email should have a descriptive subject line so it can be identified later. Like other business correspondence, the writing in an email should be to the point.

One function of email is to record what happens at meetings. While what was discussed at a particular meeting may be clear to everyone for a few days, later memories will have faded. And people who did not attend the meeting will have great difficulty reconstructing what happened unless the agenda of the meeting is reported in detail.

Another problem with the ease of sending email is that people sometimes respond too hastily. Misunderstandings can become angry exchanges when people are too quick to send email in response. Email is not a good medium for expressing displeasure with an organization, project, or person. Resist the temptation to send a flaming message to a coworker by email.

Memoranda

Along with email, memos are used for communication within organizations. They are often brief requests, notifications, queries, or instructions. When composing a memo, focus on one topic so the recipient can file it accurately. Use headings and bulleted lists when they make the document easier to read. Strive for brevity.

MEMO GUIDELINES

- Single-space elements in the heading (to, from, date, and subject) and within paragraphs.
- Double-space between the heading and the first paragraph.

- Double-space between paragraphs.
- Align all lines flush left. Do not indent the first lines of paragraphs.

Memo format

The following are the basic conventions of memo format. However, format can vary slightly from organization to organization. If they differ from the format explained here, follow the conventions of your organization.

Heading. The heading consists of four lines:

To: Recipient's Name
From: Your Name
Date: Month Day, Year
Subject: Short description of subject

Capitalize the initial letter of each line. Also capitalize the first letter after the colon in the subject line. Follow the recipient's and sender's names with commas and capitalize their job titles. Spell out the name of the month.

Body paragraphs. Use short paragraphs; one-sentence paragraphs are fine. Begin with the most important information. If you want the recipient to respond or act, say so explicitly.

Copies or enclosures. As with business letters, indicate at the bottom of a memo if you sent a copy to another coworker or you have enclosed other documents with the memo. For copies, type *cc*, a colon, the name of the person receiving the copy, a comma, and the person's job title. For enclosures, type *Encl*, a colon, and the name of the documents.

8g REPORTS

As with all writing in the workplace, ease of reading and clarity are the goals of report writing. Achieving these goals is a bit trickier with reports

Sample Memo

Cleveland Literacy Project
4886 Euclid Ave.
Cleveland, OH

To: Gabriel Rivas, Volunteer Coordinator
From: Shelby Uritz, Director
Date: January 23, 2002
Subject: Web site development meeting

Please plan to attend a Web site development meeting with departmental coordinators on Monday, February 12 at 9:00 in the conference room. The goal of the meeting will be to assess how each department can contribute to a unified Web site.

We have contracted with Claudia Martin, a Web architect with Webtext Designs, to build the site. She will attend the meeting to advise us about our design and technology options. In preparation for the meeting, Claudia asks that you send electronic copies of the following to c.martin@webtext.com:

- Volunteer application form
- 2000–2001 Volunteer Report
- 2002 calendar of volunteer training sessions
- Digital photographs of the Volunteer Picnic last July

Please call me this week to confirm you will attend. I know this is a busy time of year; thank you for making the time to ensure we develop a successful Web site.

because they are usually written for groups of people, rather than one person. Thus, you will likely have to meet several different sets of needs. For instance, imagine you've distributed a report on the advisability of changing your company's health plan. The human resources director will want to know how much effort it will take to administer the new plan, your coworkers will look to see whether the plan includes dental coverage, and the president will want to learn how much the new plan will cost. The way to satisfy all these audiences is to give the necessary background information and construct clear signposts so your readers can find the information they want at a glance.

The lengths and subjects of reports can differ radically. A biology student might write a three-page lab report about a sampling technique, while an economist might write a 200-page report recommending changes in trade policy to the president. Because reports vary widely, their formats vary widely as well. This section explains some basic elements most reports share and lists other elements that may be appropriate to include with only certain kinds of reports.

Basic elements of a report

Heading. The heading gives the most basic information about the report. It can take either of two forms: a memo heading with *To*, *From*, *Subject*, and *Date* lines or a title page, which would dedicate a whole sheet of paper to the report's title, the name(s) of the recipient(s), the author's name, and the completion date.

Introduction. In the space of two or three paragraphs, introduce the substance of the report to the reader. To write an effective introduction, do the following:

- Briefly state the issue at hand.
- Explain how you examined the issue.
- Offer an assessment or recommend a course of action.

Body. The body is the extended version of your introduction. Present the subject, review the previous pertinent work that has been done on the subject, explain how you studied the subject, justify your methodology, present findings, and draw conclusions. If the report exceeds a couple of pages, use descriptive headings to organize your findings. When possible, rely on tables, graphs, and bulleted lists to break your report into easily digestible pieces.

Conclusion. Review the report's central issues, findings, and recommendations.

Other elements of a report

Memo or cover letter. When the heading won't offer enough information to orient your reader, include a memo or cover letter that explains whatever information your readers might need. You may need to explain who you are, why you're sending the report, or to which parts of the report that particular reader should pay attention.

Table of contents. Tables of contents are especially helpful in long reports. They list the titles of the report's sections and subsections along with their page numbers, letting readers see immediately how the report is divided and how it progresses.

Abstract. Abstracts are common in academic writing, particularly in the sciences. They are succinct summaries of reports (less than a page long), similar to the introduction.

Chapter 9
Writing to Persuade

Persuasive writing can take many forms, ranging from simple advertisements to entire books that advance a thesis with many pieces of evidence. Persuasive writing in college is often called **argument**. When you imagine an argument, you might think of two people, or two groups of people, with different views, engaged in a heated exchange—maybe even shouting slogans. In college courses, in public life, and in professional careers, written arguments are aimed at readers who will not immediately accept or reject a **claim** expressed as a slogan. Extended written arguments attempt to change people's minds by convincing them that a new idea or point of view is valid, or that a particular course of action is the best one to take. Written arguments not only offer evidence and reasons, but also often examine the assumptions on which they are based, explore opposing arguments, and anticipate objections.

9a FIND AN ARGUABLE TOPIC

Probably you know at least a few people who will argue about almost anything. If you think long enough, you too can find ways to argue about almost anything. Some topics, however, are much better suited than others for writing an extended argument. One way to get started is to make a list of topics you care about (see Section 3a). Limited, local topics tend to work better for short papers than ones that are vast and have long histories. Try one or more of the invention strategies in Section 3b to identify a topic.

Position arguments and proposal arguments

How you develop a written argument depends on your goals. You may want to convince your readers to change their way of thinking about an issue or perhaps get them to consider the issue from your perspective. Or you may want your readers to take some course of action based on your argument. These two kinds of arguments can be characterized as **position** and **proposal arguments**.

Computer Strategies

Finding arguments on the Web

Because the Web is a grass roots medium with millions of people putting up Web sites, it's no surprise that the Web has turned out to be a vast forum for arguments. Many organizations and individuals have taken advantage of the low cost of the Web to publicize their stands on issues. To get a sense of the range of interest groups that use the Web to publicize their views, go to Yahoo! (**www.yahoo.com**), where you'll find under the "Society and Culture" heading, a sub-heading on "Issues and Causes." As you can see from the list, the issues extend from abortion, affirmative action, and animal rights to weight and nutrition, welfare reform, and xenotransplantation.

Figure 9.1. Yahoo's Issues and Causes index
(**www.yahoo.com/Society_and_Culture/Issues_and_Causes/**)

In a position argument you make a claim about a controversial issue. You

- define the issue,
- take a clear position,
- make a convincing argument, and
- acknowledge opposing views.

In a proposal argument you propose a course of action in response to a recognizable problem. The proposal says what can be done to improve the situation or change it altogether. You

- define the problem,
- propose a solution or solutions, and
- explain why the solution will work and is feasible.

Topics that are not easily argued

Certain topics can be argued only in limited ways.

- **Statements of fact.** Statements of fact are usually not considered arguable since they can usually be verified by doing research. You can easily verify that George W. Bush is the forty-third president of the United States. Claims of fact are arguable only if you can challenge the basis of the fact. For example, since Grover Cleveland served two nonconsecutive terms, he is considered both the twenty-second and twenty-fourth presidents. If you argue for counting Cleveland only once, George W. Bush becomes the forty-second president.
- **Personal taste.** Another category of claims that are not arguable is claims of personal taste. If you hate peas, no argument can convince you that you like them. But just as some statements of fact turn out to be arguable, so too do many claims of personal taste turn out to be value judgments based on arguable criteria.
- **Claims of belief.** Many claims rest on **belief** or **faith**. If a person accepts a claim as a matter of faith or religious belief, that claim is true for that person and cannot be refuted. Of course, people still argue about the existence of God, and which (if any) religion reflects the will of God. But those who hold to irrefutable beliefs will not be convinced by those arguments.

EXERCISE 9.1 Which of the following statements are arguable claims? Which are statements of fact, personal taste, or claims of belief? If a statement seems borderline, how could it be made into an arguable claim?

1. The United States has by far the highest rate of deaths by handguns.
2. Individuals should not be allowed to own handguns.
3. *Lord of the Rings* is the best fantasy movie ever made.
4. Buddhism is superior to other religions because it considers that the root of evil lies in craving—both sensual pleasures and material possessions.
5. Buddhism began in India in the sixth century BCE.
6. Graffiti should be considered art and not vandalism.
7. Any sport performed to music is not really a sport and should not be included in the Olympics.

9b | MAKE AN ARGUABLE CLAIM

Slogans versus arguable claims

The difference between a slogan, such as *Vote for candidate X,* and an arguable claim, such as *Vote for candidate X because she will lower taxes and improve schools,* is the presence of a reason linked to the claim. A reason is typically offered in a ***because* clause**, a statement that begins with the word *because* and provides a supporting reason for the claim. The word *because* signals a **link** between the reason and the claim.

Regardless of their sloganizing, many bumper stickers still can be considered as starting points for written arguments. For example, the bumper sticker in Figure 9.2 offers the beginnings of an arguable claim.

Figure 9.2

We have to do some work to unpack this bumper sticker. First, we may want to know exactly what the writer means by *Buy American,* since the components to many products are made overseas and assembled here. Second, we need to know exactly what the writer means by *It's our future.* Presumably the phrase means that if people in the United States buy products made in the United States, more jobs will be created, which in turn will lead to greater prosperity. When we start fleshing out what the bumper sticker might mean, we find a proposal argument.

Supporting claims with reasons

To move beyond simple assertion—or a shouting match—a claim must have one or more supporting reasons, and the reasons must be linked to the claim in order to be accepted by readers. An argument in college writing, therefore, consists of a claim and a series of appropriately linked supporting reasons:

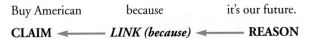

Buy American   because   it's our future.

CLAIM ◄——— *LINK (because)* ◄——— **REASON**

The problem lies in convincing a reader to accept that the reasons provided are linked to the claim. A reader might challenge the bumper sticker's claim by asking *How? So what?* or *Why?*

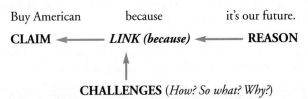

Buy American   because   it's our future.

CLAIM ◄——— *LINK (because)* ◄——— **REASON**

↑

CHALLENGES (*How? So what? Why?*)

The argument should not end simply because it is challenged. Instead, you often must generate a **series of claims**, each of which is supported by evidence that your readers will accept:

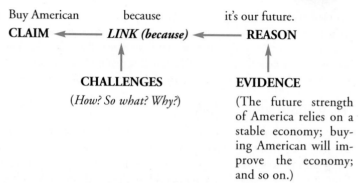

Buy American because it's our future.
CLAIM ◄——— *LINK (because)* ◄——— REASON
⬆ ⬆
CHALLENGES **EVIDENCE**
(*How? So what? Why?*) (The future strength of America relies on a stable economy; buying American will improve the economy; and so on.)

Claims must be specific and contestable

In addition to being supported by reasons that are appropriately linked to it, your claim must also be *specific*. Broad general claims such as *The United States has become too crowded* are nearly impossible to argue effectively. Often general claims contain more restricted claims that can be argued, such as *The United States should increase its efforts to reduce illegal immigration* or *The amount of land in national parks should be doubled to ensure adequate wild spaces for future generations.*

Your claim must also be contestable. Your claim that you like sour cream on a baked potato is specific, but it is not contestable. No matter how many times you are told that a baked potato is less fattening without sour cream, the fact that you like sour cream won't change. You may stop eating the sour cream, but you won't stop wanting to eat it.

EXERCISE 9.2 Collect five slogans from advertisements, posters, the news, T-shirts, even bumper stickers. Expand each slogan into a potential proposal argument by brainstorming evidence that will answer the challenges So what? Why? and How?

9c │ DEVELOP AND ORGANIZE GOOD REASONS

Thinking of reasons to support a claim is not hard. What *is* hard is convincing your audience that your reasons are good ones. When you create an argument, you should imagine critical readers—people who are going to listen carefully to what you have to say but who are not going to agree with you automatically. Whenever you put forward a reason, they will ask *So what?* You will have to have evidence, and you will have to link that evidence to your claim in ways they will accept if they are to agree that your reason is a good reason.

Think about your audience

A good reason works because it includes a link that your readers accept as valid. Your readers are a jury, passing judgment on your good reasons. If your audience accepts your reasons, and if they cannot think of other, more compelling reasons that *oppose* your position, then your argument will convince them. Thus, you need to learn as much as possible about your audience before you begin to construct your argument so that you can decide, first, whether or not it will be possible to persuade them and, second, how you can gather the best information for your subject. Here are a few questions you should ask about your audience:

- What does my audience already know about the topic?
- What is my audience's point of view about the subject?
- Does my audience already agree or disagree with my position?
- What are the chances of changing the opinions and behavior of my audience?
- Are there any sensitive issues I should be aware of?

Most important, if your audience disagrees with your position, make sure you know why they disagree so that you will be able to develop an effective counterargument.

Think about possible lines of argument

In the course of developing your arguments, get in the habit of asking a series of questions. If you ask these questions systematically, you will probably have more good reasons than you need for your arguments.

1. Can you argue by definition—from "the nature of the thing"?

- Can you argue that while many (most) people think X is a Y, X is better thought of as a Z?

Most people think of deer as harmless animals that are benign to the environment, but their overpopulation devastates young trees in forests, leading to loss of habitat for birds and other species that depend on those trees.

- Can you argue that while X is a Y, X differs from other Ys and might be thought of as a Z?

While geology is usually classified as a physical science, John McPhee's books on geology show how dependent geologists are on language and metaphors for their understanding of the earth.

2. Can you argue from value?

- Can you grade a few examples of the kind of thing you are evaluating into good, better, and best (or bad, worse, and worst)?

There were many important leaders in the Civil Rights movement, but none had the brilliance, vision, and eloquence of Martin Luther King, Jr.

- Can you list the features you use to determine whether something is good or bad and then show why one is most important?

Theodore Roosevelt is remembered for his opposition to monopolies, the building of the Panama Canal, and his "big stick" foreign policy, but his most important legacy is the protection of federal lands in the West that later became national parks and wilderness areas.

3. Can you compare or contrast?

- Can you think of items or events or situations that are similar or dissimilar to the one you are writing about?

Television viewing in Great Britain is not plagued by frequent commercials because television programming is financed through a flat-rate fee rather than through advertising

- Can you distinguish why your subject is different from one usually thought of as similar?

While immigrants to the United States are often thought of as a drain on tax dollars, households with at least one naturalized immigrant pay more in taxes ($6,580 a year compared to a national average of $5,080 in 1997) and will pay more in Social Security taxes than they will receive in benefits.

4. Can you argue from consequence?

- Can you argue that good things will happen if a certain course of action is followed, or that bad things will be avoided?

Eliminating league rules against public ownership of professional sports teams would make the teams accountable to the cities in which they are located and end the practice of wealthy sports owners holding cities hostage with threats to move if their demands are not met.

- Can you argue that while there were obvious causes of Y, Y would not have occurred had it not been for X?

College students are called irresponsible when they run up high credit card debts that they cannot pay off, but these debts would not have occurred if credit card companies did not aggressively market cards and offer high lines of credit to students with no income.

- Can you argue for an alternative cause rather than the one many people assume?

The defeat of the Confederate Army at the Battle of Gettysburg in July 1863 is often cited as the turning point in the Civil War, but in fact the South was running out of food, equipment, and soldiers, and lost its only real chance of winning when Great Britain failed to intervene on its side.

5. Can you counter objections to your position?

- Can you think of the most likely objections to your claim and turn them into your own good reasons?

Some people object to light rail and other public transportation systems because of cost, but if fewer people are forced to drive to work, ever more costly highways will not be necessary.

- Can the reverse or opposite of an opposing claim be argued?

New medications that relieve pain are welcomed by runners and other athletes who put their joints and muscles under extreme stress, but these drugs also mask important signals that our bodies send us, increasing the risk of serious injury.

Think about your organization

A typical organization of an argument essay contains these elements. Sometimes they are set out in one-two-three order, but sometimes the writer's position is not given until the background and opposing views have been addressed (see the sample paper in Section 9d for an alternative organization). The three elements are

1. **Introduction:** Captures the reader's attention, defines the issue or problem, and expresses the writer's thesis or indicates the writer's stance.
2. **Body:** Supports the writer's thesis in paragraphs that present reasons, facts, examples, and expert opinions. Opposing views are raised and discussed.
3. **Conclusion:** Presents a summary or strong conclusive evidence—logically drawn from the arguments—that underscores the writer's thesis.

Consider opposing views

You can use several strategies to strengthen your argument and address opposing viewpoints effectively:

- Use facts and examples rather than opinions to support your argument.
- Refer to respected authorities on your topic.

- If the opposition has a good point, admit it. Then show why the point is still not enough to sway your opinion. This is called *conceding a point,* and it will strengthen your credibility.
- Use polite and reasonable language rather than biased or emotionally charged words.

EXERCISE 9.3 Return to your slogans from Exercise 9.2. Choose one that is particularly interesting or that presents a wealth of possible arguments. Try to come up with a thesis based on the slogan for each line of argument (definition, value, comparison/contrast, consequence).

9d | SAMPLE PROPOSAL ARGUMENT

In his government class Mark Stewart was assigned an essay persuading local voters to consider a new solution to an ongoing local problem. The problem of Canada geese in his hometown of Tacoma was still fresh in his mind, so he decided to research the issue and propose a solution to send to members of the city council and possibly publish in the newspaper. Notice that he signals his stance early in the paper, but he does not state his position and his solution until he has defined the problem, given its history nationwide, and examined efforts to solve the problem.

Stewart 1

Mark Stewart
Professor Liu
Government 305
21 November 2002

Introductory paragraphs give a vivid, personal account of the problem. Local voters might have similar memories of Point Defiance Park.

Problem Geese

When I returned to my parents' home in Tacoma, Washington, last summer, I decided to take Andy, my four-year-old nephew, to Point Defiance Park, where I had often

Stewart 2

played as a child. As soon as I had unbelted him from his car seat, Andy ran down the hill toward the small pond below us. Before I could lock the car, I heard him scream and looked up immediately. A large Canada goose was hissing menacingly at him, and three others were just a few feet away. I ran to rescue Andy and picked him up. That's when I noticed that Andy's shoes were covered with goose droppings. I then looked down. Mine were too.

After I cleaned our shoes and took Andy home, I told my mother about the incident with the geese, to which she replied, "You should have seen the park a few months ago. The geese were everywhere. Then the agents started sneaking in during early morning hours, rounding them up, and hauling them away."

"Where did they take them?"

She smiled, "To goose heaven."

I was stunned. I couldn't believe that people in the environmentally conscious Puget Sound area would round up waterfowl and kill them. But at the same time, I found out from experience why the geese are a nuisance. Surely, I thought, there must be a better way to deal with problem geese. I began looking on the Internet and then went to the library to find out what other communities had

In this paragraph, Stewart begins to give anecdotal background information about the problem, which he expands on in the body paragraphs with his research on the issue.

This paragraph does not present Stewart's thesis directly, but explains the direction his essay is going. He doesn't feel that killing the geese is the best solution to the problem, so he will be exploring alternatives.

Stewart 3

done to discourage unwanted geese. I learned just how widespread the goose problem is—from coast to coast—and how many different methods to control the geese had been tried.

The problem with the Canada geese is one that people have created. Before the 1950s, when they were hunted nearly to extinction, the geese nested in Canada and wintered in the United States. Later, conservationists found a surviving flock in Minnesota and began raising the geese to restore the population. Unfortunately, these farm-raised geese had lost their instinct to migrate and began living in the United States the year round (Schnell). Since goose hunting had been made illegal, the Canada geese found friendly habitat in the spreading suburbs, parks, and golf courses, which had plenty of grass and other food and few predators. The result was a population explosion in communities that had not seen a Canada goose in decades.

An obvious solution was to permit Canada geese to be hunted again, which several states have done. This solution works, however, only for geese that migrate. Many Canada geese now live permanently in subdivisions, urban parks, and golf courses where hunting is not allowed.

In this paragraph, Stewart explains the history of the problem. In subsequent paragraphs, he discusses the solutions that have been tried.

Stewart uses parenthetical citations in the text that refer to the works-cited list. See Chapter 21.

In this and subsequent paragraphs, Stewart details each attempt to solve the problem and then explains why it did not work. He shows that he is knowledgeable about the subject and he anticipates possible counter arguments against his solution.

Stewart 4

One approach to getting rid of urban and suburban resident geese has been to scare the birds. Communities have tried fireworks and guns loaded with blanks, which haven't moved the birds for long. Other scare tactics such as flags, scarecrows, fake owls, and plastic swans—the traditional enemy of geese—have been even less successful. Canada geese are too smart to be tricked that easily. Real swans have been tried too, but they are so large and unruly that they too can become a nuisance. Plus, they fly away.

Another approach is to substitute plastic eggs for real goose eggs or to "addle" the eggs by spraying them with corn oil so that the embryos do not get enough air to develop. Plastic eggs, like plastic swans, haven't fooled the geese, and addling eggs has not had much effect on the overall population. Still other ideas have been to spray grass with chemicals that supposedly make it taste bad (about as successful as plastic swans) and to surround ponds with red Mylar ribbon (somewhat successful but ugly and hard to maintain).

Stewart explains a term that might be unfamiliar to his audience.

Out of frustration communities have turned to lethal means to get rid of problem geese. In March 2001 the U.S. Department of Agriculture approved a plan to kill

Stewart 5

Since this is the method he opposes the most, Stewart uses words like "slaughter" and provides graphic details about the method to turn the audience's opinion against it.

4,200 geese in Puget Sound alone, and geese are being slaughtered on a large scale in other states (Lindblom). The geese are captured in the middle of summer when they are molting and cannot fly, loaded into trucks, and then asphyxiated with carbon dioxide gas.

Here, Stewart makes his primary claim: killing the geese is not the solution. He then gives his reasons: the geese are beautiful birds, they are not a threat to public health, and finally, killing is only a short-term solution for a problem that was decades in the making.

The solution to the problem will not be found by killing the geese. They are beautiful birds that become even more breathtaking when they fly in a V formation. They also mate for life. Geese are a nuisance, not a threat. They are not dangerous to public health; no evidence has ever been produced that geese cause giardiassis or any other digestive diseases. In fact, the worst disease that geese have been accused of spreading is swimmer's itch. Finally, killing the geese is only a short-term solution be-cause other geese will move into the vacated habitat, thus forcing another round of slaughter. Since people created the geese problem over decades, it is unrealistic to expect a quick fix.

Here Stewart introduces his solution. He supports his reasons with a description of how the solution would work and provides evidence that it has worked elsewhere.

Other communities have resisted the easy way out. People in northern Virginia formed an organization called GeesePeace that aimed at finding nonlethal ways of deal-ing with problem geese. Not everything they have tried has worked, but they do continue to practice goose birth

Stewart 6

control by addling eggs. Most importantly, however, they have had considerable success training border collies to irritate geese until the geese decide to move on (Hazard). The collies, bred to herd sheep, use their herding instincts on geese. They do not harm geese, but the geese nonetheless see them as a threat. The program has been so successful that the state of Maryland rented border collies from GeesePeace to patrol its state parks (Thomson).

We too can solve our goose problem with dog patrols. Our local government might complain that border collies cost money. A registered border collie does cost about $2,000, and there are the additional costs of training, housing, and feeding the dog. But killing geese also costs money and creates a vicious cycle. Even if the dog solution is slightly more expensive than outright slaughter, the cost of dividing our community is extreme by comparison, not to mention the bad national publicity we receive. Even more important, what message are we sending to children like Andy, who is growing up in a time of violence, when we resort to killing when a problem is not easily resolved?

In his conclusion, Stewart addresses concerns that his audience might have about the feasibility of his proposed solution.

The last sentence is a direct address to the audience.

Stewart 7

Works Cited

Hazard, Holly. "Peace with Geese." 2000. 8 Nov. 2001
      <www.ddal.org/AGSpring00.html>.

Lindblom, Mike. "4,200 Geese Doomed This Year." Seattle
      Times 7 March 2001: B1.

Schnell, Nancy E. "Give Geese a Chance." St. Louis Post-
      Dispatch 5 July 2001: B7.

Thomson, Candus. "State Goes to Dogs to Clean Up Birds'
      Act." Baltimore Sun 23 Aug. 2001: D1.

To hear audio commentary on this piece of writing, visit
www.ablongman.com/faigley005.

EXERCISE 9.4 Using one of the slogan theses you developed in Exercise
9.3, the list of topics you generated for Exercise 3.1, or a topic from Yahoo's
Issues and Causes Web page, write a thesis that follows one of the lines of
argument. Write a complete argument for it. Follow the structure outlined
in Section 9c and use the paper in Section 9d as a model.

To make sure you address possible rebuttals, exchange papers with another student and develop counterarguments for each other's arguments.

9e | A PERSUASIVE LETTER OF APPLICATION AND RÉSUMÉ

When you apply for a job, most often you send a **letter of application** (also called a **cover letter**) with your résumé. Together, the letter and

the résumé are a proposal argument with the goal of a specific action—getting an interview. Letters of application and résumés use different tactics toward the same end. Résumés convey much information about your experience and skills in a small space. Letters of application favor depth and focus over coverage; they allow you to call the employer's attention to your key strengths as an applicant.

Letters of application

In a letter of application don't fall into the trap of emphasizing why the job would be good for you. Successful letters focus on why you are good for the job, placing the reader's needs first. Show the reader that you are a competent, dynamic professional and a pleasant person. Here are some suggestions.

- Limit yourself to one page.
- In the inside address and salutation, use the name and title of the person doing the hiring whenever possible. If you don't know, call the organization to ask for the person's name, its correct spelling, and the person's official title. When responding to a help-wanted advertisement that only lists a post office box, begin the first paragraph after the inside address, omitting the salutation.
- In the first paragraph, explain your purpose for writing and name the position for which you are applying.
- Then explain why your education, experience, and skills make you a good candidate for the position. Try to show some familiarity with the company.
- Next, give the reason you're applying for the position. What role would the job play in meeting your career goals?
- Finally, mention that you've enclosed your résumé or add an enclosure line after the end of the letter. Express interest in speaking to the interviewer. Give your contact information.

Sample letter of application

609 McCaslin Lane
Manitou Springs, CO 80829

November 2, 2002

Ann Darwell
100 Pine Street
Colorado Springs, CO 80831

Dear Ms. Darwell:

Please consider my application for Fox 45's *Kids' Hour* production assistant position.

During my senior year at Boston College, I interned for the Emmy-winning children's program *Zoom*. Through the internship I learned not only the technical skills necessary to produce a weekly, hour-long show, but the finesse required to manage an all-child cast.

My experience as the producer of *All the News* also gave me intensive training in the skills of a successful producer. Under my direction, a staff of fifteen crewmembers and reporters regularly broadcast creative campus news pieces. Because I produced this weekly show for three years, I would need little initial supervision before being able to make significant contributions to *Kids' Hour*.

After one year at *Zoom*, I want to continue production work in a position that offers more responsibility in the field of children's television. My work at *Zoom*, particularly my authoring and producing a series of spots to teach children Spanish, has given me hands-on experience in creating the kind of innovative television for which *Kids' Hour* is known.

Thank you for considering my application. Enclosed is my résumé. I would be happy to send my references if you wish to see them. You can reach me at (719) 555-0405 or c.popolo@hotmail.com. I look forward to speaking with you about the production assistant position.

Sincerely,

Christian Popolo

Christian Popolo

To hear audio commentary on this piece of writing, visit **www.ablongman.com/faigley006.**

Résumés

You should start thinking about what kind of job you want long before you graduate. You may be able to arrange an internship in your chosen field while you are still in school and get paid while gaining valuable experience. When you begin the serious job search, finding the right job depends on writing a successful résumé—one of the most important pieces of writing you will ever compose. The secret of a successful résumé is understanding its purpose. Above all, the purpose of your résumé is to get interviews with potential employers. Great jobs often attract many applicants. A successful résumé will place you among the small group of candidates to be interviewed.

Focus on the employer's needs. Begin by imagining that you are the person who will decide which candidate to hire. It is likely that person will be either the head of or a key member of the team that you hope to join. From that person's perspective, what qualities would the ideal candidate have? What would distinguish that candidate from other well-qualified candidates? Make a list of those qualities and put checks beside the ones you believe are most important. Then assess your own qualifications. What abilities and experiences do you have that match those of the ideal candidate?

Elements of a successful résumé. Many people think of a résumé as a life history beginning with elementary school. Nothing could be duller or less effective in a highly competitive job search. Instead, think of your résumé as an advertisement for yourself. In a very short space, you have to convince the prospective employer that you are competent, energetic, and collegial with coworkers. Successful résumés typically have two critical sections at the beginning: an **objective** section in which you name the position you want and an **overview** of your most important qualifications and experience.

Target the objective section to the position you are applying for. The key is to focus and to be as specific as possible, using the language of the target field. Vague, empty phrases such as *an entry-level position that presents new challenges and will fully utilize my talents* earn your résumé a quick trip to the rejected pile. One method is to name the position, the target location, and the two most important qualities for excelling in that position. For example, look at the following objectives:

> Credit reviewer in Central or South America where familiarity with local banking systems and fluency in Spanish and Portuguese are essential.

> Special education teacher in the greater Atlanta area specializing in brain-injured patients and requiring familiarity with coordinating ARDS and completing IED documentation.

The overview section consists of short statements of the most important qualifications you bring to the position. How you structure this section depends on what you have to offer. List your education in reverse chronological order, beginning with certificates or degrees earned. List work experience in reverse chronological order, focusing on your more recent jobs and including details of your duties and accomplishments, as in the following:

> Two years of experience analyzing computer system requirements and designing computer system specifications based on projected workloads.

> Supervised, trained, and assessed the work of staff (1 to 4) involved in audit assists.

> Reviewed real estate investments and loan portfolios for documentation, structure, credit analysis, risk identification, and credit scoring.

You can conclude with *References available upon request,* but this line is not necessary. You should never include the actual names and addresses of your references, but instead bring them on a separate sheet to the interview.

 To hear audio commentary on the résumé, visit
www.ablongman.com/faigley007.

Sample résumé

Christian Popolo c.popolo@hotmail.com
609 McCaslin Lane
Manitou Springs, CO 80829   (719) 555-0405

OBJECTIVE
Production assistant position for an innovative Colorado television program requiring prior experience in children's television and a strong technical background.

SUMMARY OF SKILLS
On-location production, studio-based production, news production, children's television, management, fundraising, animation, AVID Media Composer, AVID Xpress DV, MSWord, MS Office, fluent Spanish, detail-oriented, articulate, excellent writer

EDUCATION
Bachelor of Arts in Communications, Boston College, May 2001
GPA: 3.65/4.0

WORK EXPERIENCE
Producer, *All the News,* BCTV Campus Television, Chestnut Hill, MA, August 1998-May 2001. Produced a weekly, half-hour campus news program. Supervised seven studio staffers and eight reporters. Spearheaded successful initiative to increase Student Services funding of the program by fifteen percent.

Intern, *Zoom,* Boston, MA, May 2000-May 2001. Interned in the production department of award-winning national children's television program. Assisted in production of on-location shoots. Wrote and produced three 2-minute "Hablamos" segments, designed to teach Spanish phrases.

Technician, Communications Media Lab, Chestnut Hill, MA, August 1997-April 2000. Maintained over $300,000 worth of the latest filming and editing technology. Provided technical support to five to six Communications courses each semester. Led monthly seminars for undergraduates on the Avid nonlinear editing system.

HONORS
Dean's List, Boston College, August 1997-May 2001
Presidential Scholar, August 1997-May 2001
BCTV Excellence Award, May 1999 and May 2000
Georgia Young Memorial Prize, May 2001

REFERENCES
Available upon request from the Career Center, Boston College, Southwell Hall, Chestnut Hill, MA 02467 at (617) 555-3430.

EXERCISE 9.5 Find a job listing in the newspaper or on your school's job database that you would consider applying for. Write a letter of application and a résumé that would make you a strong candidate. Do not, however, pad your résumé with false or misleading information.

Writing in the World

Scannable and traditional résumés

Most career counselors now recommend that you create two printed résumés, a scannable résumé and a traditional résumé. A traditional résumé often includes bullets, italics, boldfacing, and different type sizes. While it may look attractive, it is not well suited for human resource departments at medium and large companies, who typically scan résumés and put them in a database. Bullets, boldfacing, and fancy backgrounds can confuse scanners. The company is interested only in the text on the résumé, which is what goes into the database. The company uses the database to search for qualified applicants when new positions become available.

Your scannable résumé should be clean and simple. Because a machine and not a person screens your résumé, your strategy changes accordingly. Your Web résumé must use words that can be scanned, sorted, and retrieved by the search engine. The employer will do keyword searches on the résumé database, so it's critical to anticipate which keywords the employer might use to find you. For example, an employer might search for *Oracle RDBMS* and *data modeling*. If you have *Oracle RDBMS* and *database administration* but not *data modeling* on your résumé, you will be overlooked. The best strategy is to include as many different nouns as possible that might describe you.

The temptation is to dump a bunch of nouns into a paragraph at the beginning of the résumé; while this tactic might get you recognized by the search engine, it's not going to be effective when the recruiter pulls up your résumé to read. Thus you shouldn't ignore the traditional elements of a résumé, including a work history. You should include your work objective and a summary of your skills at the beginning. Keep these points in mind:

1. Use a 10- or 12-point sans serif font such as Helvetica or Arial.
2. Do not underline, boldface, or use italics because these can confuse scanners.
3. Place your text flush against the left margin.
4. Avoid graphics and lines because scanners do not recognize them.
5. Use white space. The one design element that doesn't confuse scanners is white space.
6. Know the language of the field. Read job descriptions carefully for the words used to describe particular positions.

Visual Rhetoric

Chapter 10

Design Basics

Before typewriters, writers needed to worry about only the legibility of their handwriting. And typewriters required only setting the width of the margins and choosing single or double spacing between lines. Few writers paid attention to design because they had so few tools to work with.

Today the situation is radically different. When type is too small to read or a page is visually confusing, readers blame the writer, not the tools. But if you pay attention to design basics, your main points will be emphasized and readers will appreciate the look and the clarity of your presentation.

10a CREATE VISUAL RELATIONSHIPS

One of the most common design tasks is the flyer. Perhaps you've written one to advertise a school or club activity. The flyer in Figure 10.1 advertises a spring break trip to London sponsored by a drama club. The designer of this flyer uses a typical beginner's strategy—center everything. This design does nothing to support the message.

The flyer in Figure 10.1 has exciting content but it is rendered in a boring way. The destination, London, gets no more attention than the sponsoring club. The list of attractions is not visually sorted. The white space isolates rather than enlivens the information. The typeface is Helvetica, a clean, modern typeface (see Section 10d), but it is one that has been overused and now seems a little dated. Overall, the visual effect is blah. The trip might be a lot of fun, but you do not get this impression from the flyer.

The first questions to ask when creating a design are

1. What are the elements of the design?
2. Which element is most important?

The Drama Club is sponsoring a Spring Break trip to London

March 8-16, 2003

You'll see six outstanding plays including the Royal Shakespeare Company. During the day you'll see the famous sights of London, including Buckingham Palace, the Tower of London, Westminster Abbey, St. Paul's Cathedral, the Houses of Parliament, Big Ben, and 10 Downing Street, the residence of the Prime Minister. We will also visit the National Gallery of Art, the new Tate Modern, the restored Globe Theatre, and the British Museum.

For more information please contact
Karen Clark, President
Drama Club
405 Memorial Union
482-1564

Figure 10.1. Novice designers typically center everything.

On the flyer, there are four elements: the title, the description, the contact information, and the image. Clearly the destination—London—is most important, yet the name is buried in the text. The picture on the flyer is one of the most frequently used images of London, yet it appears to be an afterthought.

Together *London* and the image are a powerful combination. The revised design in Figure 10.2 (page 190) lets the name and image work together: the name appears in the upper left, where readers begin, and the image has been cropped to align with other elements on the page.

In the revised flyer, more than one typeface is used. London is set in Old English Text MS for a traditional look that contrasts with the other typefaces on the page. The attractions of London are divided into three categories with headings. The contact information is set off by ample white space, making it both easy to find and visually appealing.

**Spring Break
March 8-16, 2003**

You'll see

Plays
Six outstanding plays including a
performance by the Royal
Shakespeare Company

Sights of London
Buckingham Palace, the Tower of
London, Westminster Abbey, St.
Paul's Cathedral, the Houses of
Parliament, Big Ben, 10 Downing
Street, the residence of the Prime
Minister

Museums
National Gallery of Art, the new
Tate Modern, the restored Globe
Theatre, the British Museum

Sponsored by the Drama Club

**For information contact
Karen Clark, President
Drama Club
405 Memorial Union
482-1564**

Figure 10.2. Place the most important information where it receives the most emphasis.

10b | MAKE SIMILAR ITEMS LOOK SIMILAR

Headings

Readers increasingly expect writers to divide long stretches of text into chunks and to label those chunks with headings. One method is simply to center all the headings so the result looks like Figure 10.3.

The problem with the example in Figure 10.3 is that no distinction has been made between what is more and less important. You can determine the importance of each heading by making an outline. Look at which

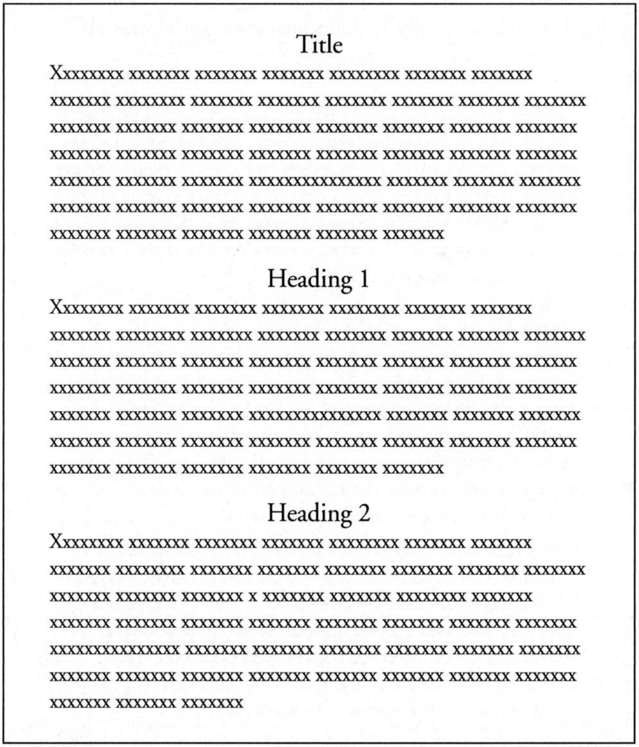

Title

Xxxxxxxx xxxxxxx xxxxxxx xxxxxxx xxxxxxxx xxxxxxx xxxxxxx
xxxxxxx xxxxxxxx xxxxxxx xxxxxxx xxxxxxx xxxxxxx xxxxxxx xxxxxxx
xxxxxxx xxxxxxx xxxxxxx xxxxxxx xxxxxxx xxxxxxx xxxxxxx xxxxxxx
xxxxxxx xxxxxxx xxxxxxx xxxxxxx xxxxxxx xxxxxxx xxxxxxx xxxxxxx
xxxxxxx xxxxxxx xxxxxxx xxxxxxxxxxxxxxxx xxxxxx xxxxxxx xxxxxxx
xxxxxxx xxxxxxx xxxxxxx xxxxxxx xxxxxxx xxxxxxx xxxxxxx xxxxxxx
xxxxxxx xxxxxxx xxxxxxx xxxxxxx xxxxxxx xxxxxxx

Heading 1

Xxxxxxxx xxxxxxx xxxxxxx xxxxxxx xxxxxxxx xxxxxxx xxxxxxx
xxxxxxx xxxxxxxx xxxxxxx xxxxxxx xxxxxxx xxxxxxx xxxxxxx xxxxxxx
xxxxxxx xxxxxxx xxxxxxx xxxxxxx xxxxxxx xxxxxxx xxxxxxx xxxxxxx
xxxxxxx xxxxxxx xxxxxxx xxxxxxx xxxxxxx xxxxxxx xxxxxxx xxxxxxx
xxxxxxx xxxxxxx xxxxxxx xxxxxxxxxxxxxxxx xxxxxxx xxxxxxx xxxxxxx
xxxxxxx xxxxxxx xxxxxxx xxxxxxx xxxxxxx xxxxxxx xxxxxxx xxxxxxx
xxxxxxx xxxxxxx xxxxxxx xxxxxxx xxxxxxx xxxxxxx

Heading 2

Xxxxxxxx xxxxxxx xxxxxxx xxxxxxx xxxxxxxx xxxxxxx xxxxxxx
xxxxxxx xxxxxxxx xxxxxxx xxxxxxx xxxxxxx xxxxxxx xxxxxxx xxxxxxx
xxxxxxx xxxxxxx xxxxxxx xxxxxxx x xxxxxxx xxxxxxx xxxxxxx xxxxxxx
xxxxxxx xxxxxxx xxxxxxx xxxxxxx xxxxxxx xxxxxxx xxxxxxx xxxxxxx
xxxxxxxxxxxxxxxx xxxxxxx xxxxxxx xxxxxxx xxxxxxx xxxxxxx xxxxxxx
xxxxxxx xxxxxxx xxxxxxx xxxxxxx xxxxxxx xxxxxxx xxxxxxx xxxxxxx
xxxxxxx xxxxxxx xxxxxxx

Figure 10.3

headings go with major sections and which with subsections. Then use one style for main headings and another style for subheadings. The style you choose should give the reader visual clues to the importance of the heading. For example, in Figure 10.4 the main heading stands alone on a line and is a larger type size than the subheading.

Consistency in headings

Short papers, business letters, newspaper and magazine articles, reviews, and short reports often do not require headings, but longer documents such as business reports, reports of experiments, instruction manuals, proposals, and in-depth analyses usually include headings. Brochures and other short

Title

xxxxxxx xxxxxxx xxxxxxx xxxxxxx xxxxxxxx xxxxxxx xxxxxxx xxxxxxx xxxxxxxx xxxxxxxx xxxxxxx xxxxxxx xxxxxxx xxxxxxx

Major Heading

xxxxxxx xxxxxxx xxxxxxx xxxxxxx xxxxxxxx xxxxxxx xxxxxxx xxxxxxx xxxxxxxx xxxxxxxxxxxxxxx xxxxxxx xxxxxxx xxxxxxx xxxxxxx xxxxxxx xxxxxxx xxxxxxx xxxxxxx xxxxxxx xxxxxxx xxxxxxx xxxxxxx xxxxxxx xxxxxxx xxxxxxx xxxxxxx xxxxxxx

Level 2 Heading xxxxxxx xxxxxxx xxxxxxx xxxxxxx xxxxxxxx xxxx xxxxxxx xxxxxxx xxxxxxx xxxxxxx xxxxxxx xxxxxxx xxxxxxx xxxx xxxxxxxxxxxxxxx xxxxxxx xxxxxxx xxxxxxx xxxxxxx xxxxxxx xxxxxxx xxxxxxx xxxxxxx xxxxxxx xxxxxxx xxxxxxx xxxxxxx xxxx xxxxxxx xxxxxxx xxxxxxx xxxxxxx

Figure 10.4

documents also provide headings to help readers to locate information. If you decide that you need to use headings, follow a consistent strategy.

Headings should be informative. Headings such as "Introduction" and "Conclusion" tell readers little more than what they could infer by where the headings appear. Often an outline can help you determine what kind of headings you need and where they should be placed. For example, the outline for "Problem Geese" in Section 3d might produce the following headings.

PROBLEM GEESE

Canada geese—an urban nuisance
A problem created by people
Unsuccessful solutions for problem geese
Beautiful birds that cause no health threat
The answer to problem geese—dog patrols

These headings could also be written as questions. The key is to be consistent.

PROBLEM GEESE

Why are Canada geese a nuisance?
How was the problem created?
What solutions have been tried?
Are Canada geese a threat to health?
What is the humane solution to problem geese?

If you are writing instructions or describing a process that you expect someone to follow, you may want to write headings as imperative sentences.

CHANGING A TIRE

Remove the hubcap
Loosen the lug nuts
Remove the spare from the trunk
Jack up the car
Remove the flat tire

Lift the spare onto the lug bolts and tighten the lug nuts
Lower the car to the ground
Tighten the lug nuts
Replace the hubcap

Lists

Other useful tools that word processing programs, Web-page editors, and presentation software offer are several ways of making lists. Bulleted lists are used frequently to present items in a series, as in the example below. Bulleted lists are frequently used as visual aids in verbal presentations (see Chapter 12). Speakers use them to give an overview of a presentation so listeners know where a particular point fits. Bulleted lists, however, can be ineffective if the items in the list are not similar (see Section 28d).

ADVANTAGES OF USING A FLOWCHART

- Allows a team to agree on the steps of a process
- Shows problem areas and unnecessary loops
- Helps to identify steps in a process that could be simplified
- Compares the ideal flow to the way things are done now
- Serves as a training aid for new employees

10c MAKE DIFFERENT ITEMS LOOK DIFFERENT

We tend to follow the principle of consistency because that's what we've been taught and that's what writing technologies—from typewriters to computers—do for us. The flyer in Figure 10.1 is an example of letting the technology (in this case centering everything) determine the design. But the principle of contrast takes some conscious effort on our part to implement. Take the simple résumé in Figure 10.5 as an example (see also Section 9e).

Christian Popolo
609 McCaslin Lane
Manitou Springs, CO 80829
719-555-0405
c.popolo@hotmail.com

OBJECTIVE

Production assistant position for an innovative Colorado television program requiring prior experience in children's television and a strong technical background.

EDUCATION

Bachelor of Arts in Communications, Boston College, May 2001
GPA: 3.65/4.0

WORK EXPERIENCE

Producer, *All the News,* BCTV Campus Television, Chestnut Hill, MA, August 1998–May 2001. Produced a weekly, half-hour campus news program. Supervised seven studio staffers and eight reporters. Spearheaded successful initiative to increase Student Services funding of the program by 15%.

Intern, *Zoom*, Boston, MA, May 2000–May 2001. Interned in the production department of award-winning national children's television program. Assisted in production of on-location shoots. Wrote and produced three 2-minute "Hablamos" segments, designed to teach Spanish phrases.

Technician, Communications Media Lab, Chestnut Hill, MA, August 1997–April 2000. Maintained over $300,000 worth of the latest filming and editing technology. Provided technical support for five to six Communications courses each semester. Led monthly seminars for undergraduates on the Avid nonlinear editing system.

Figure 10.5

The résumé has consistency, but there is no contrast between what is more important and what is less important. The writer seeks a position with an innovative television program, but there is no sign that the writer might be innovative.

The design of a résumé should direct the reader's attention to certain elements and create the right ethos. Use of contrast can emphasize the key features of the résumé and contribute to a much more forceful and dynamic image, as shown in Figure 10.6. Notice that arrangement and con-

---

Christian Popolo

609 McCaslin Lane
Manitou Springs, CO 80829
719-555-0405
c.popolo@hotmail.com

OBJECTIVE

Production assistant position for an innovative Colorado television program requiring prior experience in children's television and a strong technical background.

EDUCATION

May 2001
  Bachelor of Arts in Communications, Boston College
  GPA: 3.65/4.0

EXPERIENCE

August 1998–May 2001
  Producer, *All the News*, BCTV Campus Television, Chestnut Hill, MA
  Produced a weekly, half-hour campus news program. Supervised seven studio staffers and eight reporters. Spearheaded successful initiative to increase Student Services funding of the program by 15%.

May 2000–May 2001
  Intern, *Zoom*, Boston, MA
  Interned in the production department of award-winning national children's television program. Assisted in production of on-location shoots. Wrote and produced three 2-minute "Hablamos" segments, designed to teach Spanish phrases.

Figure 10.6

sistency are also important to the revised résumé. Good design requires that all elements be brought into play to produce the desired results.

Writing in the World

Color

Another element that can provide contrast is color. Until the last few years, color printers were expensive, but ink-jet printers have made color printing affordable. Color costs nothing to add to Web sites; indeed, it's expected.

We're surrounded by so much color that sometimes the strongest effects are created by using color in minimal ways. Limited use of warm colors—yellow, orange, and especially red—can make a strong statement. In the figure below, red is used for the title and headings, which both matches and balances the red uniforms in the image.

London

Spring Break
March 8-16, 2003

You'll see

Plays
Six outstanding plays including a
performance by the Royal
Shakespeare Company

Sights of London
Buckingham Palace, the Tower of
London, Westminster Abbey, St.
Paul's Cathedral, the Houses of
Parliament, Big Ben, 10 Downing
Street, the residence of the Prime
Minister

For information contact
Karen Clark, President
Drama Club
405 Memorial Union
482-1564

Museums
National Gallery of Art, the new
Tate Modern, the restored Globe
Theatre, the British Museum

Sponsored by the Drama Club

10d | UNDERSTAND THE RHETORIC OF TYPE

Until computers and word processing software came along, most writers had little or no control over type style. Most typewriters used Courier, a fact many typists didn't even know. Furthermore, the typewriter gave the user no choice about type size. Nearly all used 10-point or 12-point type. (A point is a printer's measure. One inch equals 72 points.) There was no way to include italics, so the convention was to underline the word or words that the printer would later set in italics. Boldface could be accomplished only by typing the word over again, making it darker.

Use typefaces and fonts effectively

Even if the general public knew little about type styles and other aspects of printing before computers came along, printers had five hundred years' experience learning which type styles are easiest to read and what effects different styles produce. When you open the pull-down font menu of your word processing program, you see a small part of that five-century tradition of developing type styles.

A particular style of type is called a **typeface**, such as Times New Roman or Arial. A specific kind of that typeface, such as Verdana bold, is called a **font**. At first, typefaces may all appear similar, but after you get some practice with using various typefaces, you will begin to notice how they differ.

Serif type

Typefaces are divided into two categories, **serif** and **sans serif**. Serif (rhymes with *sheriff*) faces were developed first. Serifs are the little wedge-shaped ends on letter forms, which scribes produced with wedge-tipped pens. Serif typefaces also have thick and thin transitions on the curved strokes. Five of the most common serif typefaces are

Times
Palatino
Bookman
Garamond
New Century Schoolbook

Serif typefaces were designed to be easy to read. They don't call attention to themselves. Thus they are well-suited for long stretches of text and are used frequently.

Sans serif type

Sans serif (*sans* is French for *without*) typefaces don't have the little wedge-shaped ends on letters, and the thickness of the letters is the same. Popular sans serif typefaces include

Helvetica
Avant Garde
Arial

Sans serif typefaces work well for headings and short stretches of text. They give a crisp, modern look. Some sans serif typefaces are easy to read on a computer screen. Verdana, Helvetica, and Arial are sans serif typefaces that most computers now have installed, which is why they are popular on Web sites.

Script and decorative type

Finally, there are many script and decorative typefaces. These typefaces tend to draw attention to themselves. They are harder to read, but sometimes they can be used for good effects. Script typefaces imitate handwriting or calligraphy, which is why they often appear on diplomas, formal invitations, and similar documents.

Popular script typefaces include Nuptial Script and Wedding Text:

When you want only the very best

Snead, Potter, and Jones, Attorneys at Law

Some decorative typefaces, including Lazyvermont and ComicStrip Classic, are informal, almost irreverent:

That's a no brainer.

Totally awesome!

Use a readable type size

It's easy to change the size of type when you compose on a computer. For long stretches of text, use at least 10- or 12-point type. Use larger type for headings. (Note: In commercial printing, the size effect varies with the font.)

Smaller 8- or 9-point type can also be readable on the printed page, but it is next to impossible to read on the computer screen because the resolution on a screen is not as fine as type on a printed page. Use larger type if you expect people to read text on a screen. For text that is to be projected during a presentation, the minimum size is 18-point, with headings and titles larger (see Section 12c).

type	8 point
type	10 point
type	12 point
type	14 point
type	18 point
type	24 point
type	36 point

type

48 point

type

72 point

Use other effects as needed

Finally, word processing programs allow you to use type fonts such as **boldface**, *italics*, and underlining. All three are used for emphasis.

EXERCISE 10.1 Are the graphics and text in the following flyer for a German Club party effective? Are they attractive? Make a list of suggestions for improving both the flyer's look and its readability.

Chapter 11

Illustrations, Tables, and Charts

Sophisticated software and hard drives with plenty of memory allow you to create attractive illustrations, tables, and charts. The key is understanding when and how to use graphics for effective communication. Visuals should not be used just for decoration but to clarify points, supply additional information, and provide alternate ways of understanding a subject. Visuals that are well integrated into text can make a presentation more powerful.

11a ILLUSTRATIONS

Drawings

You can create drawings the old-fashioned way, with pen or pencil, scan them, and import them into computer files. Professionals use Macromedia FreeHand, Adobe Illustrator, CorelDraw, and other complex drawing programs, all of which take time to learn, but you can make simple drawings using the drawing modules on word processing programs and presentation software. You don't have to be an artist to create simple drawings, such as the one shown in Figure 11.1.

Photographs

You can incorporate photographs in text documents if you get them into a digital format. You can create digital images by taking photographs with a digital camera, by scanning prints, or by using a photo CD service (see Figure 11.2). Once your photographs are in a digital format, you can use an image editor to alter them.

Figure 11.1

Figure 11.2

Clip art

Another source of illustrations is clip art. *Clip art* refers to professionally created drawings and illustrations, such as cartoons, symbols, maps, and backgrounds. Clip art is often bundled with software, including word processing programs. You can find public domain clip art on the Web or purchase clip art on CDs (see Figure 11.3). Clip art can annoy your readers if you toss it into a document without much regard for its effect, but used thoughtfully, it can indicate content and direct readers.

Figure 11.3

Scanners

It's easy to scan drawings and photographs. Computer labs often have scanners, and because scanners have become affordable, many people now own them. Flatbed scanners, which resemble small photocopiers, are the most common type. You place the image facedown on the glass, open the image editor on the computer linked to the scanner, select **Import** or a similar command, and select the scanner you are using. You will then see an interactive menu.

All the controls for the scanner are in the software. Because there are many different types of scanners, the software varies a great deal. If you are new to scanning, pay attention to the settings for type of image and resolution.

- **Type of image.** Some scanning software allows you to indicate what you are scanning—a color photograph, printed matter, or a transparency. Other software will ask you to choose among B/W photo, B/W document, color RGB, and color CMYK. All monitors and most ink-jet printers use RGB rather than CMYK; thus you'll likely select RGB for color images that you scan.

- **Resolution.** Scanning resolution is measured in dots per inch (dpi). Most scanners offer a range from 72 to 1600 dpi. The higher the number, the finer the image, but the file size also becomes larger. Most printers use a resolution from 300 to 600 dpi. Images on the Web or on the screen display at 72 dpi, so resolution higher than 72 is effectively wasted, making the image slower to display without improving the quality.

Writing in the World

Scanning and the law

Images in books and magazines published in the last 75 years are almost always owned by someone. If you copy an image for redistribution of any kind, including putting it on a Web site, you must find out who holds the copyright and obtain permission to use the image. Always give credit for any image that you copy, even if it is in the public domain.

11b | IMAGE EDITORS

Image editors allow you to touch up images, create special effects, and convert image files to the correct format for printing or displaying on a Web site. Image editors range from extensive software used by professionals, including Macromedia Fireworks and Adobe Photoshop, to shareware programs you can download from the Web that allow you to do simple image editing, including Picture Man (for Windows) and GraphicConverter (for Mac). If you own a scanner, you likely have an image editor on your computer. Many computers now come equipped with a photo editor; you can also find free image editors online.

No matter which editor you use, there are a few manipulations that you will need to use frequently. It's always a good idea to copy the image first and work on the copy.

- **Cropping.** Most images can be trimmed to improve visual focus and file size. To crop an image, select the rectangle tool, draw the rectangle over the area you want to keep, and select the **Crop** or **Trim** command (see Figure 11.4). The part of the image outside the

Figure 11.4. Cropping often improves the image. Smaller images use less memory and thus are able to load faster on the screen.

rectangle will be discarded. Every pixel you can squeeze out of an image intended for use on the Web makes the image display faster on a user's screen.

- **Rotating images**. Often you'll find that you held your camera at a slight angle when taking pictures, especially if your subjects were moving. You can make small adjustments by using the **Rotate Image** command. You can also rotate images 90° to give them a vertical orientation.

- **Sizing images.** All photo editors will tell you the height and width of an image. You can resize images to fit in a particular area of a Web page or printed page. You can also change the resolution in the dpi window. Increasing the resolution does not improve the image after it has been scanned but does make the file larger.

- **Optimizing images for the Web.** Macromedia Fireworks and Adobe Photoshop (versions 5.5 and higher) allow you to optimize images for the Web by finding the best mix of color, compression, and quality. These programs allow you to reduce the size of an image file considerably without a great sacrifice in quality. Optimizing images on Web pages makes them load much faster, especially if the user is connecting on a dial-up modem. You will make images for the Web quicker to load by dropping the resolution to 72 dpi.

- **Adjusting colors.** Often the colors in photographs that you scan appear off when you view the image on a computer monitor. The image may appear too dark or lack contrast. Sometimes the color balance appears off and you want to correct it. The basic controls for brightness, contrast, and color saturation are similar to those on your color TV. Be aware that colors look different on different monitors and what you print may not look like the colors on your screen.

- **Special effects.** Advanced editors offer a number of different special effects. You can find a list of these effects under the **Filter** menu. The filters allow you to simulate drawings, watercolors, mosaics, and oil paintings, as shown in Figure 11.5, page 208.

Figure 11.5. The brushstroke filter creates the illusion of a painting.

Computer Strategies

Make a copy of an image before editing it

Always keep a copy of your original scan or digital photo. Once you change an image and save it, you cannot restore what you changed. Use the **Save As** command to make a copy before you start editing an image.

11c | FORMATS AND PRINTERS

Native file formats

Native file formats are the ones used by the software that creates the file. When you create an image file in Photoshop, for example, it will be saved as a Photoshop file unless you specify otherwise. Native file formats often give you more possibilities, such as working in layers in a Photoshop file when using Photoshop. You can print image files in native file formats, but you cannot put them on the Web. You must use the **Save As** or **Export** command to convert the file to a GIF or JPEG image if you plan to put it on a Web page (see Chapter 14).

GIF images

Many images on the Web are in **Graphics Interchange Format (GIF)**, which squeezes down the file size of an image by eliminating redundancies in the data. GIF images have the file ending **.gif**. GIF is the preferred format for images with sharp lines, buttons with text, visual icons, and other small images. GIF uses a "no loss" compression format, which means that all the information in the image is maintained. But the GIF format often makes photographic images splotchy. Thus GIF images are good for icons with sharp lines and solid colors, but not so good for large photographs and complex images. When you save a GIF image in Photoshop, you will first need to open the **Mode** menu, then select **Indexed color** rather than RGB.

JPEG images

JPEG is an acronym for Joint Photographic Experts Group, and, as the name suggests, it is the preferred format for photographs on the Web. JPEG images have the file ending **.jpeg** or **.jpg**. JPEG compresses the data in a photograph and rearranges it so that it tends to blend the colors and loses some of the detail. For this reason it is not suited for print. JPEG compression can be increased to reduce the size of a file as much as 100 times smaller than the original, but as the compression increases, the quality decreases, so at some point you have to decide which is more important—a fast download time or the quality of the image.

Printers

Different kinds of printers are better for different tasks. If you lack the printer necessary for a particular job, you can usually find the right one in a campus computer lab or in a retail copy shop.

- **Ink-jet printers**, which have become affordable for most computer users, can produce outstanding color images, especially on glossy paper. They are also lightweight, making it possible to transport them when necessary. The major disadvantage of ink-jet printers is that they are slow.
- **Laser printers** use a technology similar to photocopying and have the great advantage of speed. Most offices use laser printers because they print documents quickly with crisp text and graphics. Monochrome (black and white) laser printers have become affordable. Color laser printers, however, remain too expensive for most individuals.
- **Dye-sublimation (dye-sub) printers** produce quality color prints but do not print text as well as laser printers. Like ink-jet printers, they are slow; like color laser printers, they are relatively expensive.

11d TABLES

Extensive statistical data can be dull or cumbersome to communicate in sentences and paragraphs. Readers can more quickly and easily grasp data when displayed in a table. For example, a table will allow readers to view an entire set of data at once, or to focus only on relevant aspects.

Tables are easy to create in word processing programs, presentation software, and Web page editors. Usually, the command is **Insert Table** or **Insert** under the **Table** menu. You will then be asked to specify the number of columns and the number of rows. You can use the default width for columns or specify the widths for particular columns. You can also add lines to the table or omit them (see Table 11.1).

11e CHARTS AND GRAPHS

The terms *chart* and *graph* are often used interchangeably, but there is a distinction between them. Graphs are plotted using coordinates on *x*- and *y*-axes; charts are not.

Table 11.1. Earnings by Highest Degree Earned: 1999
(mean earnings in dollars)

	Less than high school	High school graduate	Bachelor's	Master's	Professional	Doctorate
All persons	16,053	23,594	43,782	52,794	95,488	74,712
White men	19,632	29,782	56,620	65,637	112,944	85,837
White women	11,255	18,327	31,406	40,679	67,998	55,793
African-American men	16,013	22,698	42,539	47,951	68,693	46,743
African-American women	11,372	15,892	31,952	39,760	39,109	46,914
Hispanic men	17,756	24,739	40,889	73,362	108,071	90,474
Hispanic women	12,273	15,952	29,317	36,589	45,829	33,407

Source: United States. Census Bureau. *Statistical Abstract of the United States: 2000.* Washington: GPO, 2000. 158.

You can use spreadsheet applications (Microsoft Excel, Lotus 1-2-3, and others) and presentation software (see Section 12c) to create handsome graphs and charts. You can then import these graphs and charts into word processing software or other applications. You need only to type the data into a spreadsheet, then select the kind of chart you want. The program draws the graph or chart for you. You still have to supply the labels for different parts of the chart or graph. You also have to make sure that the chart or graph is legible. If you have too much information to display, you will not have enough space between elements.

Like any graphic, graphs and charts can be used to mislead readers. Small differences can be exaggerated, for example, or relevant data concealed (see Section 6e). You have an ethical responsibility to create accurate graphs and charts.

Bar graphs

Bar graphs are useful for comparing data. Multiple bars can be combined, as shown in Figure 11.6 (page 212), which compares the earnings of men and women according to level of education.

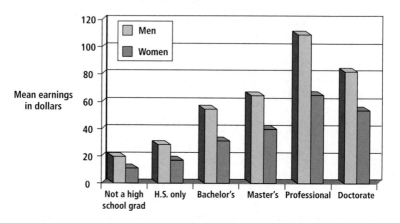

Figure 11.6. Bar graphs are useful for comparing data.

Line graphs

Line graphs are well suited for displaying changes in data across time. Line graphs can have one line, or two or more sets of data can be displayed on different lines, emphasizing the comparative rates of change (see Figure 11.7).

Pie charts

Pie charts are commonly used to represent the relationship of parts to a whole. They provide quick overviews that are easily understood. For example, Figure 11.8 shows that in 1999 half the people in the United States had at least some college education. You must have data in percentages to use a pie chart, and the slices of the pie must add up to 100%. If the slices are too small, a pie chart becomes confusing. Six or seven slices are about the limit for a pie chart that is easy to interpret.

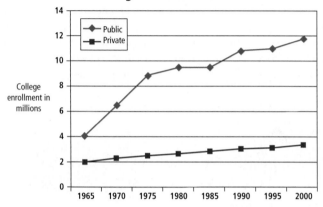

Source: United States. Census Bureau. *Statistical Abstract of the United States: 2000.* Washington: GPO, 2000. 151.

Figure 11.7. Line graphs are useful for displaying data across time.

Educational attainment for persons in the U.S. aged 25 and over: 1999

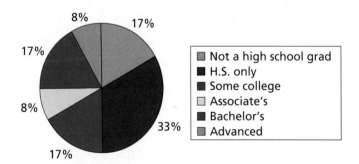

Source: United States. Census Bureau. *Statistical Abstract of the United States: 2000.* Washington: GPO, 2000. 154.

Figure 11.8. Pie charts display the relationship of parts to a whole.

Organizational and flowcharts

Presentation software and the drawing module in word processing programs allow you to create organizational charts and flowcharts (see Figure 28.1 for an example of an organizational chart). You can make organizational and flowcharts by selecting shapes and arrows on the drawing module and inserting them. Select the text tool for typing labels on the shapes (see Figure 11.9).

Stage 1: Planning

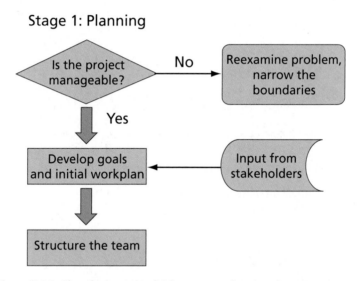

Figure 11.9. Flowcharts are useful for representing steps in a process.

EXERCISE 11.1 Decide what kind of graphic (photo, drawing, table, bar graph, line graph, pie chart, or flowchart) would best represent the following information. In some cases, there might be more than one correct answer.

1. At the time of first European contact, North and South America were inhabited by an estimated 90 million people. There were about 10 million in America north of present-day Mexico; 30 million in Mexico; 11 million in Central America; 445,000 in the Caribbean islands; and 39 million in South America.

2. The estimated date of the earliest migrations into the Americas is about 30,000 years ago. Bone tools have been discovered in the Yukon, however, that have been radiocarbon-dated to 22,000 BCE and campfire remains in central Mexico have been radiocarbon-dated to 21,000 BCE. In a cave in the Peruvian Andes, archaeologists have found stone tools and butchered animal bones that have been dated to 18,000 BCE. A cave in Idaho contains similar items, dated to 12,500 BCE.

3. The social, political, or economic organization of the Cherokee nation

4. The similarities and differences in regard to language, social structure, economy, and culture between the Five Civilized Tribes: the Cherokee, the Choctaw, the Chickasaw, the Creek, and the Seminole

5. The differences in the domestic structures built by Native American groups living in the nine culture areas of North America (the Southwest, the Eastern Woodlands, the Southeast, the Plains, the California-Intermountain region, the Plateau, the Subarctic, the Northwest Pacific Coast, and the Arctic)

6. The number of expeditions to the Americas undertaken per year by European nations

7. The internal structure of a Moche pyramid

8. The size of Native American societies in relation to the amount of food available

9. The qualities of the many varieties of maize grown by Native Americans

10. The percentage of different tribes that make up the population of Native Americans living in the United States today

Chapter 12
Verbal and Visual Presentations

New technologies have blurred the line between oral and written presentations. Often a speech later becomes the basis for a written report, or a written report is summarized in a verbal and visual presentation, perhaps even transmitted by teleconferencing. New technologies make producing high-quality visuals to accompany oral presentations easy, but these technologies also offer many choices that place new demands on speakers. The key to success is remembering that your purpose is to communicate effectively. In any medium, your goals, your subject, and your audience should shape your presentation.

12a PLAN A PRESENTATION

Analyze your task

Successful presentations, like writing assignments, require careful planning. First, consider what kind of presentation you are being asked to give. Look closely at your assignment for words such as *argue for, explain, describe, report, summarize,* and *propose* that indicate what is expected. Some common types of presentations include the following:

- **Informative speeches** explain a concept or analyze a subject (see Chapter 8).
- **How-to presentations** are a subset of informative presentations aimed at providing the audience with the knowledge necessary to perform a task.
- **Persuasive speeches** attempt to change the audience's attitudes and beliefs or to convince them that a particular course of action is best (see Chapter 9).

- **Summaries** give an overview of a report or long document.
- **Group presentations** allow several people to present individual aspects of a subject.

Think about your medium

Audiences now expect that most informative and persuasive presentations will use visuals. Visual elements range from simple transparencies and handouts to elaborate multimedia presentations. Some of the easier visual elements to create are

- Outlines
- Text
- Statistical charts
- Flowcharts
- Photographs
- Models
- Maps

Think about where you will give your presentation

Consider early on where you will be giving the presentation. If you want to use visual elements to support your presentation, make sure the room has the equipment you need. If you know the room is large or has poor acoustics, you may need to arrange for a microphone, amplifier, and speakers. Some rooms have other limitations, such as the inability to darken the room enough for visuals to show up well. Find out in advance what limitations you will face and plan for them.

Select your topic

Choosing and researching a topic for an oral presentation is similar to preparing for a written assignment. If you have a broad choice of topics, make a list of subjects that interest you. Then go through your list and answer these questions:

- Will you enjoy speaking on this topic?
- Will your audience be interested in this topic?
- Does the topic fit the situation for your presentation?
- Do you know enough to speak on this topic?
- If you do not know enough, are you willing to do research to learn more about the topic?

Section 3a describes how to find a topic and Section 3b offers ways of exploring that topic. Remember that enthusiasm for a topic is contagious.

Researching a topic for an oral presentation is similar to researching a written assignment. See Chapter 16 for guidelines for planning your research. You should write a working thesis just as you would for a research paper, then modify the thesis as needed. Consult Chapters 17 and 18 for help on finding and evaluating sources in the library and online. You may also wish to conduct interviews, surveys, and observations (see Section 16f). Remember that you may need to develop a bibliography for a presentation just as you would for a research paper, documenting the sources of your information and providing those sources in your talk or in handouts.

Think about the scope of your topic

Length is a critical consideration. How much time you have determines the depth you can go into. Speakers who ignore this simple principle are often forced to rush toward the end and omit major points, leaving the audience confused about what the speaker had to say.

Consider your audience

Unlike writing for readers you've never seen, when you give a speech, you have your audience directly before you. Your audience will give you concrete feedback during your presentation by smiling or frowning, by paying attention or losing interest, by asking questions or sitting passively.

Think about the general characteristics of your audience—their age, their occupations, their educational level, their ethnic and cultural background, and the mix of men and women. Think specifically about your audience in relation to your topic.

- Will your audience be interested in your topic?
- Are there ways you can get them more interested?
- What is your audience likely to know or believe about your topic?
- What does your audience probably not know about your topic?
- What key terms will you have to define or explain?
- What assumptions do you hold in common with your audience?
- How is your audience most likely to disagree with you?
- What questions is your audience likely to ask?

Organize your presentation

After you have done your research and analyzed your audience, it's time to organize your presentation. Make a list of key points and consider how best to organize them. Your visuals should clearly indicate your major points. These types of organization are common for presentations:

- **Chronological organization** orders major points according to a time sequence.
- **Topical organization** divides a speech into several connected topics and elaborates on those topics.
- **Problem/solution organization** is often used for proposals, where a problem is identified and a solution proposed (see Chapter 9).

Support your presentation

When you have organized your main points, you next need to decide how to support those points. Look at your research notes and think about how best to incorporate the information you found. Consider using one or more of these strategies:

- **Facts.** Speakers who know their facts build credibility.
- **Statistics.** Good use of statistics can give the audience the impression that you have done your homework. Statistics also can indicate that a particular example is representative.
- **Statements by authorities.** Quotations from credible experts can support key points.
- **Narratives.** Narratives are brief stories that illustrate key points. Narratives can hold the attention of the audience—but keep them short or they will become a distraction.
- **Humor.** Humor is one of the primary ways to convince an audence to share your point of view. You have to know the audience well, however, to predict with confidence what they will think is funny.

Plan your introduction

No part of a presentation is more critical than the introduction. You have to get the audience's attention, introduce your topic, convince the audience that it is important to them, present your thesis, and give your audience either an overview of your presentation or a sense of your direction. Accomplishing all this in a short time is a tall order, but if you lose your audience in the first two minutes, you won't recover their attention. You might begin with a compelling example or anecdote that both introduces your topic and indicates your stance.

Plan your conclusion

The second most important part of your presentation is your conclusion. You want to end on a strong note. First, you need to signal that you are entering the conclusion. You can announce that you are concluding, or you can give signals in other ways such as turning off the projector. Touching on your main points again will help your audience remember them. But simply summarizing is a dull way to close. Think of an example or an idea that captures the gist of your speech, something that your audience can take away with them.

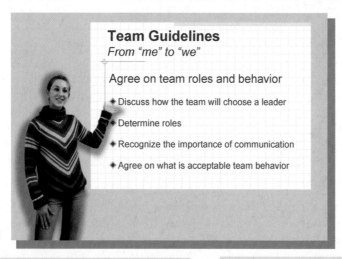

Team Guidelines
From "me" to "we"

Agree on team roles and behavior

◆ Discuss how the team will choose a leader

◆ Determine roles

◆ Recognize the importance of communication

◆ Agree on what is acceptable team behavior

Nervousness

Nervousness is usually invisible. If you make a mistake, remember that your audience will understand. Stage fright is normal, and often you can draw off that energy to make a more forceful presentation. Take a deep breath before you begin, and smile.

Practice

There is no substitute for rehearsing your speech several times.

- You will become more confident.
- You will be able to focus more on your audience and on maintaining eye contact.
- You will be more comfortable using your visuals.
- You will know how long your presentation will take.

Effective techniques

- Practice in advance
- Talk, don't read
- Stand, don't sit
- Make eye contact
- Signal main points with gestures
- Speak loudly
- Use effective visuals
- Focus on main points
- Give an overview in the introduction
- Give a conclusion that ends with a key idea or example
- Finish on time

Writing in the World

Home field advantage

Athletes know that the home field advantage involves much more than having the crowd behind them. Each field and court has its own special characteristics. In many cases small bits of knowledge acquired from playing on the field (such as a position from which the sun is blinding at a certain time of day) can mean the difference between winning and losing. Visiting teams practice on the opponent's field or court before the game to learn as much as possible.

In college many or all presentations will be in your classroom, which can give you your own home field advantage. You'll know whether acoustics are good, whether it is easy to see visuals from everywhere in the room, and so on. In the workplace, you may be required to give presentations in unfamiliar places, such as a client's site. You will have to work a little harder to ensure success.

Practice your presentation in the room where you will deliver it. Bring a friend who can tell you whether you can be heard in the back of the room and whether your visuals can be read at that distance. Make sure any equipment you need is working.

Have a back-up plan for visuals. If your presentation depends on a projector that stops working unexpectedly, think about what you will do if you suddenly cannot use the visuals you brought. For example, you can write a few main points on a white board or flip chart if necessary.

Remember that the audience is with you. Most people are patient when something goes wrong. They have been in similar situations themselves. If, for example, a projector bulb burns out and another one is available, ask the audience to give you a minute or two.

12c | DESIGN EFFECTIVE VISUALS

Advantages and disadvantages of visuals

Visuals focus the attention of the audience. Visuals can keep your audience oriented throughout your presentation while providing you with memory aids. Charts, pictures, and diagrams can help you emphasize major points and provide information that would be tedious to describe verbally. Visuals also give your audience something to look at besides you, which helps you to relax.

At a minimum, consider putting an outline of your talk on an overhead transparency. Most computer printers can make transparencies from blank transparency sheets inserted into the paper feeder. Charts, maps, photographs, and other graphics in digital format can thus be printed directly onto transparencies. Many photocopiers can also make transparencies. Visuals take time to prepare, so start planning them early.

The unplanned use of visuals can be distracting to both you and your audience. If you cannot find the right transparency or lose track of your slides, your presentation may fall apart. Visuals can be frustrating for the audience if they cannot see them. Visuals can also tempt you to look at the screen instead of looking at the audience. Keep practicing with your visuals until you feel comfortable and get your timing right.

Guidelines for creating and using visuals effectively

The following guidelines will help you create better visuals and use them effectively.

- **Keep the text short.** You don't want your audience straining to read long passages on the screen and neglecting what you have to say. Except for quotations, use short words and phrases on transparencies and slides.
- **Always proofread.** Typos and misspelled words make you look careless and can distract the audience from your point.
- **Use dark text on a white or light-colored background.** Light text on a dark background is hard to read. If you use it you may have to

close every window and turn off all the lights in order for your audience to see the text.

- **Use graphics that reproduce well.** Some graphics do not show up well on the screen, often because there isn't enough contrast.
- **Plan your timing when using visuals.** Usually you can leave a slide on the screen for one to two minutes, which allows your audience time to read the slide and connect its points to what you are saying.

Presentation software

If you have taken any large lecture courses, you likely have seen presentations that use presentation software. This software allows you to combine text, images, sounds, animations, and even video clips on computer-generated slides, which can be projected onto a large screen. Presentation software gives you a choice of templates that you can use to format slides, and a variety of backgrounds and color schemes that make your slides attractive. Once you have created the file, you need do no more than click a mouse to move from one slide to another. You can also prepare paper handouts from the slides to accompany the visual presentation. The most popular software is Microsoft PowerPoint, which is bundled with Microsoft Office. Other software includes Adobe Persuasion and Lotus Freelance.

Presentation software is easy to use. It offers quality visuals with no more effort than using a word processing program. It allows you to import charts and other graphics that you have created in other programs. It gives you several options for presentation, including printed handouts and Web pages. Presentation software can be quite portable: You can plug your laptop into a projector to give your presentation. Some speakers when on the road send their presentations on ahead of time on a disk and don't even carry their laptop.

The major drawback of presentation software is perhaps that it is too easy to use. An attractive presentation can be empty in content. The software does not do the planning, researching, and thinking about your audience described in Section 12a. Another is that it is easy to get carried away with the special effects, such as fade-ins, fade-outs, and sound effects. Presentations heavy on special effects often come off as heavy on style and light on substance. They also can be time-consuming to produce.

Common Errors

Too small type

If you put text on transparencies or slides, make sure that the audience can read the text from more than 10 feet away. You may depend on your transparencies and slides to convey important information, but if your audience cannot read the slides, not only will the information be lost but the audience will become frustrated.

Use these type sizes for transparencies and slides.

	Transparencies	Slides
Title	36 pt	24 pt
Subtitles	24 pt	18 pt
Other text	18 pt	14 pt

Remember:

Preview your transparencies and slides from a distance equal to the rear of the room where you will be speaking. If you cannot read them, increase the type size.

EXERCISE 12.1 Think about oral presentations you have recently seen—class lectures, presentations at work, public talks—and choose one that you felt was the most effective and one that you felt was the least effective. Using examples from these presentations, create a list of effective tactics and a list of ineffective or poor tactics.

EXERCISE 12.2 Choose an informative or persuasive paper you have written either for this class or for another class and rework it as an oral presentation. Rewrite your paper to be heard rather than read. Add visuals where necessary or organize your talk with presentation software. Insert anecdotes or some humor where appropriate.

Practice your talk with a group of classmates and get feedback on your material, your visuals, your speaking manner, and your body language. If possible, videotape the practice so that you can do a self-critique.

Writing for the Web 4

13
Web Basics

14
Steps in Creating a Web Site

15
Building a Multipage Site

Chapter 13

Web Basics

On your campus or in the city or town where you live, there are some buildings that you always enjoy walking into and others that make you feel lost or that seem sterile and ugly. These responses are a direct result of the design of a building. Much like the experience of a building, a visitor's response to a Web site is the direct result of the site design—the successful integration of technology, art, and writing on a Web site is made possible by good design.

13a THE ARCHITECTURE OF A WEB SITE

Web sites are described with metaphors of place. You *visit* a *home* page, *navigate* on a Web *site*, participate in a *community*, *travel* on the *information highway*, and *explore worlds*. These metaphors are not accidental. The visual interface that we take for granted today marked a breakthrough in computing because it allowed knowledge to be categorized and accessed in visual as well as verbal forms.

As writers we have been taught to think of beginnings, middles, and endings. However, like places, Web sites often do not have clear beginnings, middles, and especially endings. Instead, we enter a Web site as we enter a building, and when we're inside, we need to see how to move through the site or else we turn around and leave. Because people experience the Web as spatial, Web site designers have a great deal to learn from those who design spaces for people. Buildings that have been in use for many decades and even centuries survive not only because they are structurally sound. Successful buildings endure because they are functional: They provide spaces well suited for the activities that take place there. The best buildings are also aesthetically pleasing; thus, we might define architecture as functional art. Builders of Web sites also combine art and technology to create functional art. They are, like architects, creators of spaces that people interact with and move through. Spaces can be both practical and beautiful.

Successful architects begin by envisioning how people will use a building and how they will encounter and move through it. Architects have long understood the importance of entrances and use them to convey much more than movement from outside to inside. The triumphal arches of ancient Rome were designed to impress upon all those who passed under them the greatness of the Roman Empire. Often the effects of entrances, however, are created with subtlety. The anonymous architect who designed the Mission Espiritu Santo in East Texas in the mid-1700s did not want parishioners to approach the entrance directly (see the series of photographs in Figure 13.1). Instead they would have to contemplate the

Figure 13.1. Approach and doorway of Mission Espiritu Santo (1749) near Goliad, Texas

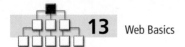

grandeur of the building from beyond an outer wall, then enter a courtyard before turning gradually toward the doorway. A few more steps are required before the intimate carvings surrounding the doorway come into focus. Today the entrance to the mission still evokes a sense of entering a sacred, mystical space.

No part of a Web site is more important than the entrance. This first page is a portal that users pass through to get inside the site. The initial page shapes what users expect to find on a site and how they expect to interact with the site. Designers of Web sites sometimes draw directly on the work of architects in constructing entryways for Web sites. The entry page for the Metropolitan Museum of Art in New York City (Figure 13.2) represents the entrance to the building in the background image.

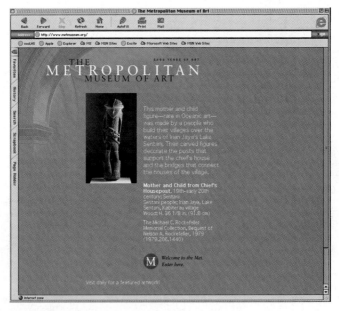

Figure 13.2. Metropolitan Museum of Art, New York
(http://www.metmuseum.org/)

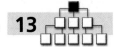

After a visitor enters a building, an architect must next lead that visitor through the building. Because of its complicated floor plan (Figure 13.3), those unfamiliar with the Metropolitan Museum of Art require a map to locate a specific piece of art. The museum is one of the largest in the world, so it's not surprising that navigating through it would be relatively complex. A visitor might have to walk through several rooms and make several turns before finding a particular piece of art. Similarly, some Web sites require you to click through several pages before reaching a specific page. Such a structure can be described as narrow and deep (Figure 13.4, page 232).

In contrast to the museum architecture, a shopping mall typically arranges stores along corridors so that each is easy to access directly. A corresponding Web site with a broad and shallow structure (Figure 13.5, page 232) would present many choices on the entry page so that users can access any page with a click or two.

The kind of structure determines how visitors will experience a Web site. Imagine that you are at a party with a group of people you know. You talk to many different people, but the order is not predictable. Perhaps you might see an old friend on the other side of the room, and you know you will

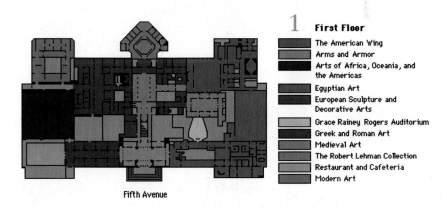

Figure 13.3. Plan of the first floor, Metropolitan Museum of Art, New York

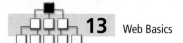

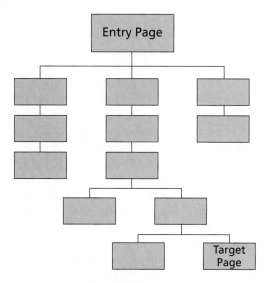

Figure 13.4. A narrow and deep site structure

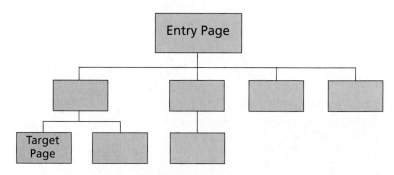

Figure 13.5. A broad and shallow site structure

find her eventually, but before you get to her, you meet some new people on the way. Hypertext structures (Figure 13.6) often work in similar ways. A hypertext structure is still ordered, but it can allow many different paths to reach the same place.

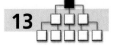

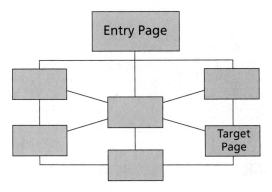

Figure 13.6. A hypertext structure

Computer Strategies

Changing your browser's home page

On your browser, the home page is the page that appears when you start your browser. You can set your home page to whatever site you like; you don't have to use the page selected for you by your browser or Internet service provider. Your school's main page is a good choice because it links to libraries, colleges and departments, catalogs and course schedules, upcoming events, and other important sources of campus information. You can always return to this page quickly by clicking on "home"—the house icon on Netscape and Internet Explorer.

Complete the following steps to change your home page.

Netscape

1. Select **Preferences** from the **Edit** menu.
2. Select **Navigator** from the **Preferences** box.
3. Type the URL (the Web address) of the home page you choose on the Location bar.
4. Click on **OK.**

(continued next page)

Internet Explorer
1. Select **Preferences** from the **Edit** menu.
2. Select **Browser Display** from the **Preferences** box.
3. Type the URL (the Web address) of the home page you choose on the Address bar.
4. Click on **OK.**

13b │ VISUAL DESIGN ON THE WEB

The importance of a visual theme

A consistent look and feel makes a Web site appear unified and supports the content. A Web site does not need a loud background or flashy animations to achieve a visual theme. Instead, the little things such as selecting a simple set of colors for the text, headings, links, and background do more to create a consistent visual theme than an attention-grabbing image. Consistency in navigation tools is one of the most important aspects of the visual theme. Navigation tools should be placed at the top or on the side of the page, not at the bottom of a long page where a user must scroll down to find them. Similar graphics and images should be the same size, and often their placement can be repeated from page to page.

Focal points

Successful Web sites pay close attention to visual focal points on a page and what surrounds those focal points. Any motion on a page will get the user's attention first, so if you put animations on your page, they should not be just ornaments. Lacking motion on a page, images will draw attention next. If a page contains mostly text and does not have a visual center, then readers of English and other European languages begin at the top left of the page. Many users skim texts on the Web, so what gets read depends a great deal on how the site directs the user's eyes.

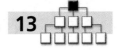

Clutter

The limited screen real estate on the Web is a major headache for novice and professional designers alike. The temptation is to get everything on one page, but this strategy quickly leads to disaster.

Clutter creeps into less extensive Web sites through decorative images that do not contribute to the content, distracting backgrounds, sprawling text that runs across the screen, and annoying animations. Elements on overloaded pages compete with one another so intensely that the overall effect is chaotic. Blank space, called "white space" by designers, is an important design element. It breaks up blocks of text and provides "breathing space" for the eye.

Text on the Web

Long stretches of text on the Web tend not to get read. For users who do not have a large-screen monitor, reading text on the Web is like trying to read a newspaper through a 3-inch-square hole—possible to do but not much fun. Perhaps in the next few years, large-screen monitors will give us an expanse of screen real estate comparable to a newspaper page, but in the meantime, most Web users will still have small-screen monitors, often made even smaller when people do not resize their browsers to fit the entire screen or leave visible all the toolbars. Smart Web designers create pages for the small screen.

An advantage of displaying text on the Web is the ability to create additional layers of information connected by links to the main text. A site can be designed both for those who know a great deal about the subject and want to skip the background information, and for those who know little and need the background. The big disadvantage is the difficulty of placing a long text on the Web in a form that people will read. Some Web designers don't even try. They assume that those who are really interested will download that long text, print it, and read it on paper. That assumption, however, risks losing people who don't want to take the time to print a long text. Whenever possible, good Web designers try to divide text into chunks that fit on a screen or require minimal scrolling.

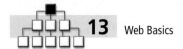
Above all, text on the Web page should be readable. Dark backgrounds make for tough reading.

> ## TEXT IN ALL CAPS IS HARD TO READ ON A BLACK BACKGROUND, *ESPECIALLY IF THE TEXT IS IN ITALICS.*

Electrifying combinations like blue on magenta can have an impact, but they are not pleasant to read for long. Likewise, busy background graphics can be distracting (Figure 13.7) and can make the text hard to read. Background graphics should stay in the background.

Figure 13.7. Text written over a noisy background is unpleasant to read.

13c ESTABLISH GOALS FOR A WEB SITE

The process of creating a Web site is similar in many ways to other kinds of writing. Thinking about your goals at the beginning and keeping them in mind will guide you in making decisions as you compose and revise.

What should your Web site accomplish?

The original purpose of the Web was **informative**—it allowed physicists to share scientific papers quickly and easily. After improved browsers made the Web easy to use, companies rushed to advertise and later to sell goods and services online. Many organizations advocating particular causes also put up Web sites. Even though these sites display a wide range of goals, their general purpose is **persuasive**; they want you to buy something, believe something, or take some action. Individuals have also put up many thousands of Web pages, some informative, some persuasive, some just for the fun of it—to display art work, to post a family album, to list personal interests in hope of meeting like-minded people, to tell a little about themselves. We might classify these sites as **expressive**. Before you begin designing a site, you need to answer these questions.

- What's your main goal?
- What personality do you want your site to project?
- What "look and feel" do you want your site to possess?

Who is your intended audience?

Many times when you write on paper, you have a good sense of who will read your writing. But when you put up a Web site, even one that fulfills a course requirement, you cannot be sure who will visit it. Many students have received email from people in other countries only hours after putting up a site in a trial version. Search engines turn up sites according to key words, so if you have on your site a name or phrase that someone is looking for, the search engine will find it. If your Web site is not password-protected, your potential audience is global. Think about your larger audience as well as your intended audience.

- Are you aiming your site at a target group of viewers? If so, what are they likely to know about your subject? What attitudes will they likely have about your subject?
- How will you identify your target audience on your site? For example, if you are creating a site intended for children, how will you indicate that?
- If you are creating a site for a general audience, what assumptions can you make about that audience? What kinds of general knowledge can you assume they are likely to have?
- Do you want people with relatively slow telephone modem connections to be able to access your site? If so, you will have to make sure that the site loads quickly.
- Will you make your site accessible to people with disabilities?

What do you want visitors to do at your site?

You should make it obvious to visitors how they might use your site.

- Do you want them simply to read the text you have put up?
- Do you want them to navigate around your site?
- Do you want them to follow the links to other Web sites that you have made? If they click on the links to other Web sites, do you want them to come back to your site?
- Do you want them to write anything, such as an entry in a guest book? Do you want them to send you email?

Defining specific goals

To begin to translate a vision of a Web site into specific goals, think about your own experiences on the Web. You might start out by making two lists, such as what you hate about the Web and what you like about the Web. Your "hate" list might look something like this:

What I hate about the Web

1. Sites that take too long to appear
2. Can't find what I'm looking for on a site
3. Pages that are too crowded, hard to read
4. Too many bells and whistles like Java applets and animations that take forever to download and don't add anything
5. Sites that are hard to navigate
6. Poorly written content with many errors

Some of these might sound like technical issues, but in fact they are all design issues. If you put huge image files on your Web pages, the time it takes for a telephone modem user to download your site will be excruciating. In many cases unnecessary graphics and complicated backgrounds contribute to the crowding. Even when a site is visually appealing, if the organization of the site is jumbled and the text poorly written, the site seems sloppy and poorly executed.

Your list of what you like about the Web might look like this:

What I like about the Web

1. Sites that load fast, even on a slow modem connection
2. When information I want is easy to find
3. Content that is up to date and interesting
4. Sites that are visually attractive
5. When navigation is easy—there's always a way back to the start and to other major parts of the site
6. Text that is well written

On a well-designed site, the images contribute to the overall effect without calling unnecessary attention to themselves. Information on the site can be located without difficulty so if you return to the site later, you don't have the frustrating experience of being unable to find something you have seen before. The best Web sites show care with small details. You should include

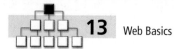
in your goals the characteristics of Web sites that you find most appealing. You want your Web site to be handsome, well organized, easy to navigate, informative, and well written.

Writing in the World

Evaluating a Web site

You can learn a great deal about effective Web design by keeping these criteria in mind when you visit Web sites. Some will be more critical than others, depending on the site. For example, good navigational tools become more important on extensive sites.

1. **Audience and purpose:** How does the site identify its intended audience? How would you characterize its purpose: informative, persuasive, or expressive?
2. **Content:** How informative is the content? Has the site been updated recently? What do you want to know more about? Are there any mechanical, grammatical, or style problems?
3. **Readability:** Is there sufficient contrast between the text and the background to make it legible? Are the margins wide enough? Are there any paragraphs that go on too long and need to be divided? Are headings inserted in the right places, and if headings are used for more than one level, are these levels indicated consistently? Is high-contrast text, including text in boldface and all caps, kept short?
4. **Visual design:** Does the site have a consistent visual theme? Where is the focal point on each page? Do the images contribute to the visual appeal or do they detract from it?
5. **Navigation:** Does the first page indicate what else is on the site? How easy or difficult is it to move from one page to another on the site? Is a consistent navigation scheme used throughout the site? Are there any broken links?

EXERCISE 13.1 Make two lists. On one list, write out the Web sites you always enjoy visiting and why you like them. Are they updated frequently? easy to navigate? quick to load? Do they act as indexes to other useful sites? What else do you like about them?

On the other list, write out the Web sites that you often have to visit but almost always find annoying or frustrating, and explain why you don't like them. Are they slow to load? Do the applications cause your computer to crash? Are they frequently out of date? Are they hard to navigate? What else do you find frustrating about these sites?

EXERCISE 13.2 Choose a Web site that you are very familiar with and write a brief evaluation of it. Focus on the five points mentioned in the Writing in the World box on page 240. Keep your notes; you may return to them in a later exercise.

Chapter 14

Steps in Creating a Web Site

Publishing on the Web requires doing a little legwork at the beginning, but once you get started, you'll find creating a Web page about as easy as word processing. To compose a Web page, you need to learn how to generate HTML files. Although HTML looks complicated when you first view a source page, it's a relatively simple computer language. You can compose Web pages in three ways:

1. With an **editor**—Netscape Composer, Microsoft Front Page, Claris Home Page, Macromedia Dreamweaver, and Adobe PageMill
2. With a **translator**—Microsoft Word, Excel, and PowerPoint, which all have a "save as HTML" command
3. By **hand-coding** HTML with NotePad on Windows, SimpleText on Mac, or any word processing program

Editors and translators offer the great advantage that you don't have to learn any HTML commands, but it's still handy to know a little about HTML. Sometimes the editor doesn't produce exactly the results you want, and you can open the source file, identify the problem, and fix it.

This chapter shows you how to create a Web site using Netscape Composer. You can get Netscape Composer for free as part of the Netscape Communicator package. (Download the most recent version from **http://www.netscape.com**.) Other editors have additional features, but all include the basic elements of Netscape Composer. Composer is a good program for a beginning Web designer. When you become proficient in

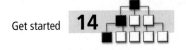

Composer, you may want to move up to an advanced editor such as Macromedia Dreamweaver.

14a | GET STARTED

Getting space on a Web server

When you have a computer and a connection to the Internet, you have most of what you need to become a Web publisher. The missing ingredient is the capability to share the pages you create with people around the world connected to the Web. You gain that capability by putting your pages on a Web server. Most colleges and universities allow students to publish Web pages on servers designated for student use. Before you can publish your Web page, you will need to set up an account and find out how to make your own subdirectory.

Probably your easiest option is to use a server at your college. Your computer center will have step-by-step directions on how to set up your subdirectory, and often these directions are posted on your school's main Web site under "computers" or "computing." Other options for publishing on the Web include

1. Internet service providers such as AOL, Microsoft Network, and Road Runner
2. Free space offered on sites such as GeoCities (**http://www.geocities.com**). The catch about the free space is that you have to put up with a lot of advertising.
3. Your own computer as a Web server (which is considerably more advanced)

Get your space on a server first because you'll want to see your pages on the Web once you make them. Write down the name of the server, your login name, and your password. You'll need them when you put your pages on the Web.

Before you begin making your own Web pages, think about how you will name and organize your files. You will save much time and energy later if you think about these issues now.

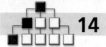
Computer Strategies

Organizing your files

- **Figure out your system for naming files.** Use only lowercase letters because you will eventually get confused if you use capitals. Don't put any spaces or characters like semicolons in filenames because they cause problems for servers. All Web page filenames must end in **.htm** or **.html**. Label image files by their type, either **.gif** (for GIF files) or **.jpg** (for JPEG files). See Section 11c.
- **Put your files in a folder.** Web sites are made up of folders and files just like the folders and files on your desktop. The simplest way to keep track of everything is to keep the folders and files on your computer (the local site) the same as those on the Web server (the remote site). Whenever you make changes, move the entire folder from your computer to the server as soon as you are finished.
- **Back up your work.** It always is a good idea to make backup copies. Save your files on a disk or CD.

Creating a blank Web page with Composer

To create a blank page in Composer, start Netscape and select **New** from the **File** menu, then choose **Blank Page to Edit**. Before you begin working on your page, save your page to a new folder by selecting the **Save** command from the **File** menu. Name your file *index.html*, navigate to the new folder you created, and click on **OK**. You will see the name of the file above the toolbar.

Working in Composer

To see what your page will look like when you put it on the Web, select **Browse Page** from the **File** menu. The Composer window remains open behind the Navigator window, and you can go back and forth as you

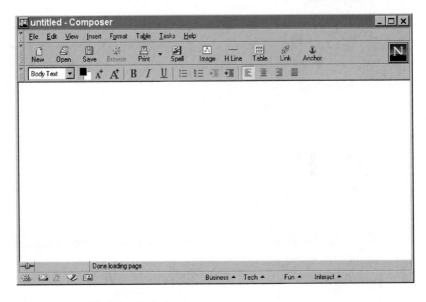

Figure 14.1. Blank page in Composer

make your page to see how your page will look once it's on the Web. The toolbars on Composer have icons for various functions that are quite similar to those on a word processing program (see Figure 14.1). You can find out what each does by moving the mouse pointer over the tool icon without clicking.

Now take a look at Rachel Jones's home page as an example (Figure 14.2, page 246). She introduces herself, then she describes a sea kayaking trip in Alaska.

Jones takes advantage of the possibilities to create links to other pages. She starts off by making links to her university and to her department by highlighting the words and clicking the **Link** button ![Link]. The Link button pulls up the **Link dialog box** (see Figure 14.3, page 247), where Jones types in the URL of the Biochemistry Department.

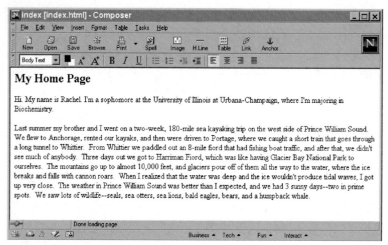

Figure 14.2. Rachel Jones's home page

Adding pictures

Rachel Jones decides she wants to include a picture of a humpback whale. She remembers that the search engine Lycos has a gallery of images that can be copied legally. She switches to the Navigator window and searches for "humpback whale" on the Lycos site at **http://www.lycos.com**. Up pop two thumbnail images of humpback whales from the Alaska Division of Tourism. She views a full-size image that she likes by clicking on it, then copies it.

To insert this saved image into her page, Jones goes to the **Insert** menu and then selects **Image**. She clicks on **Choose File,** finds the image file on her computer, then clicks **OK**. She also remembers to include the caption giving credit for the picture. She wants to distinguish the caption from her text, so she selects **Font** under the **Format** menu and picks **Helvetica**. She reduces the type size from 12 to 9 points.

Customizing a page

With the basic elements of her page now assembled, Jones can concentrate on improving the look of her page. She changes the gray background to white by following these steps:

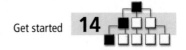

Figure 14.3. Link dialog box in Composer

1. Select **Page Properties** from the **Format** menu, which shows another dialog box.
2. Select **Use Custom Colors**.
3. Select a color (Jones chooses **Black on Off-White** from the list).

Next she makes the links into a bulleted list. She highlights the list, then clicks on the **bullet list** icon on the **Formatting** toolbar (see Figure 14.4, page 248). Jones wants to put her email address at the bottom of her page. She first clicks on the **horizontal line** icon, which puts a line at the bottom of her page. Then she includes her email address.

Giving your page a title

Finally Jones has one last, important step—giving her page a title. The **Page Title** is different from both the filename and the heading on the page.

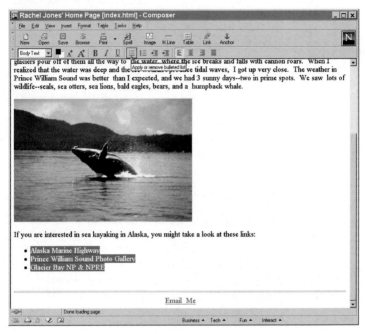

Figure 14.4. Formatting a bulleted list in Composer

The page title shows up on the frame on the top of the page. Giving your page an accurate title helps people remember what's on the page when they have bookmarked it. To give your page a title, follow these steps:

1. Select **Page Properties** from the **Format** menu.
2. Type the name of your page in the **Title** box.
3. Click **OK**.

14b | HOW HTML TAGS WORK

In the 1920s the people who drove Model T Fords had to know how to fix them to keep them going. Today cars can go 100,000 miles without a tune-up, so we don't spend much time under the hood. Nonetheless, it's

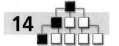

good to know a little about how your car works, even if it's just so you can tell your mechanic what you think needs to be done. Similarly, fewer and fewer people now start by writing HTML when they compose a Web page, but knowing how HTML works enables you to make better use of the tools available on an editor and to troubleshoot if the editor doesn't produce exactly what you want.

In the early days of the Web, most people learned HTML by studying the HTML code on existing Web sites. Anyone can do this by using the **Page Source** command on the **View** menu (see Figure 14.5).

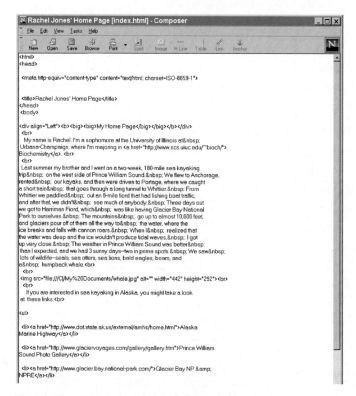

Figure 14.5. HTML source of Rachel Jones's home page

If you haven't looked at HTML before, it probably strikes you as complicated, messy, and ugly. However, there is logic to it. HTML works with a system of tags. Tags generally come in pairs that surround the text they affect. For example, if you want a word boldfaced, you insert a **<B>** tag that turns on the boldfacing before the word and a **</B>** tag that turns off the boldfacing after the word. Most tags use this starting and closing formula to define areas of text.

For a list of HTML tags, go to
www.ablongman.com/faigley008.

Viewing your page with a browser

To view your page, you must first save it. The name of the file must end in **.htm** or **.html.** (If you are using a word processing program for HTML coding, you must choose **Save As** and select **text only.**) Rachel Jones saves her file as *index.html* and opens it in Navigator using the **Open Page** command. She doesn't like what she sees (Figure 14.6).

All of her text has flowed into one big paragraph because browsers don't recognize spacing and formatting. To tell the browser you're starting a

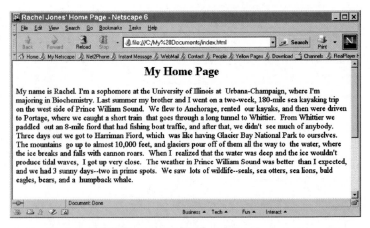

Figure 14.6. Rachel Jones's page without paragraph tags

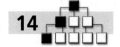

paragraph, you have to use the **<P>** tag. The close paragraph **</P>** tag is optional. The **<P>** tag places an extra line between paragraphs, which makes prose quite readable on a computer screen. If you do not want a blank line inserted, use the line break **
** tag.

"It's not a place**
**
To go to twice," he says**
**
And goes three times.**
**

Fonts in HTML

Web page editors, including Netscape Composer, allow you to control the typeface, size, font, and color of the text your visitors will see. These changes are controlled by **<FONT>** commands. For example, if Jones wanted her first name to jump off the page, she might make it bigger, change the color to red, and change to a contrasting typeface. For the contrasting type-face, she wants Arial. So the command would look like this: **<FONT SIZE="+1" COLOR="#CC0000" FACE="ARIAL">Rachel</FONT>**.

14c | ADD LINKS AND IMAGES

Adding links

Adding links to your site often results in problems, so proceed with care. It's useful to know how the HTML code works for links. Let's start with the link to Rachel Jones's major department, Biochemistry. Jones begins by sur-rounding the area she wants to specify as the clickable link with the **<A>** tag: **<A>Biochemistry</A>**. Next she adds the URL—the address of the page she wants to link to—using the HREF attribute within the opening **<A>** tag: **<A HREF="http://www.scs.uiuc.edu/~bioch/">Biochemistry</A>**. Long URLs are prone to typos. You have to be 100% accurate when you type in a URL or the browser won't find it. URLs are case sensitive on many servers, which means that if you name your file Whale.html and make the link to whale.html, the browser will not find it. When you name files, use only lower-case letters to avoid this problem.

Computer Strategies

The Reload button

When you make changes and want to view them with your browser, you have to save your file first and then click on the **Reload** button. Sometimes you have to hold down the Shift or Option key when you click **Reload** to get the new version. Otherwise, the browser will bring up the previous version saved in its cache, giving you the false impression that the change has not been made.

Absolute versus relative links

There are two kinds of links: links to other pages on your Web site and links to other sites on the Web. When you link to other locations, such as Jones's Biochemistry Department site, you must give the full URL. These links are called **absolute links**. But when you link to other pages on your site, you can and should use a partial URL. If the link is in the same folder as your HTML file, you need only to use the filename. These links are called **relative links**. For example, if Jones posted another page about the whale she saw, the link would look like this: **<A HREF="whale.html">**humpback whale**</A>**. When you're building a small site, using fewer than thirty files, keep all your files in the same folder and use relative links. Relative links allow your site to load faster and make it easier for you when you put your site on the server.

Adding images

Web browsers can read images in two formats: GIF and JPEG (see Chapter 11 for more on preparing images). You can tell that your image is in one of these formats by looking at the end of the filename; files ending with **.gif** or **.jpg** should display on a browser. You tell the browser to include images on your page with an **<IMG>** tag. Rachel saves the image of

the humpback whale to her hard drive in the same folder as her HTML file. She adds it to her page with this tag: **<IMG SRC="whale.jpg">**.

When to hand-code HTML

You may be asking at this point why you should go to so much trouble writing HTML when the editor will do it for you. Resizing images is one example of why it is handy to know a little about how HTML works. You can do some resizing with an editor that gives you handles on the edges of images, but specifying the size commands in pixels puts you in complete control.

Netscape and Internet Explorer allow you to size images in pixels and to build space around your images. Sometimes an image is slightly too big for the space, and being able to squeeze it by a few pixels lets you get it exactly right. Sometimes images appear jammed up against text. The **HSPACE** and **VSPACE** attributes leave some blank space around the image. For example, if you want five pixels of blank space around the top, bottom, and sides of an image, you can insert these attributes: **<IMG SRC="whale.jpg" HSPACE=5 VSPACE=5>**. Knowing HTML allows you to tweak your page.

Another reason it's handy to know some HTML is that editors don't always do everything you want them to do. For example, you might want to include a link that sends mail to your email address. Most Web page editors can do this for you, but Composer does not have this feature. So Rachel Jones might include a tag to make it easy to send her mail: Send mail to **<AHREF="mailto:rachel.jones@uiuc.edu">Rachel</A>**. Composer allows you to insert HTML tags with the command **HTML Tag** on the **Insert** menu.

Still another reason you should know HTML is that editors try to do things for you that you don't necessarily want done. Sometimes you'll find that the spacing seems way off, and often the problem is that the editor has forced in extra space with the command ** **. When you think extra space that you don't want has been added, you can open the file and delete it. Of course you can add space, too. There are many more HTML commands; once you know how some work, you can figure out ones you haven't seen before.

14d | ORGANIZE YOUR WEB SITE

Putting your Web page on the server

When you've set up an account on a server and you have a Web page ready to go, the next step is getting it on the Web. Make sure you've given your page a title and a name with an **.htm** or **.html** extension so that a browser can recognize it as a Web page.

The usual way to get files on a server is with a **file transfer protocol** or **ftp** program. Before Web page editors came along, ftp programs were the only way you could put files on a server from a remote location. The most popular ftp program on Windows is WS_FTP; on Macintosh it is Fetch. Both are easy to use after you practice, but it helps to have someone walk you through them the first time.

Writing in the World

Browser-safe colors

You can choose among millions of colors, but you cannot be confident that they will look the same when someone views your Web page using a different computer or a different browser. If you have access to a lab that has both Windows and Mac computers, try viewing the same image on each; you'll likely be surprised by the difference. Only 216 colors display the same on both Windows and Macs, and on both Netscape and Explorer. For this reason they are called **browser-safe colors**. It follows that if you want others to see the same colors you do, you should stick with these colors. The colors on the Color Picker are all browser safe.

Macs have several tools for selecting colors in addition to the Color Picker, including a Crayon Picker that looks like an open box of crayons. All the colors in the crayon box are browser safe.

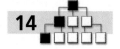

Structuring your site

Web sites often take on a life of their own. For many people, building an extensive Web site becomes a personal hobby. Others become involved in building a large Web site to support an organization they belong to or even a small business. When you start building a site with several pages, the files multiply in a hurry. Be careful to keep them organized. Remember to save each image as a separate file. In addition to pictures, you might want to create icons for making links instead of words. Each icon is a separate file.

Think what your home computer would be like if you didn't have folders to manage all the documents and applications that you've accumulated. It would be tough to sort through all your files each time you wanted to find something. The same is true of your files on a server. Once you start putting many files on a server, sorting them out becomes a problem. The good news is you can organize files in folders on the server just as you can on your home computer. Furthermore, you can upload an entire site, so what's on the server is organized the same way it is on your home machine.

Typically people start by putting everything in the same folder. Rachel Jones's index.html has one associated image file; if both were on the desktop of her home computer and she sent them both to the server, they would look like Figure 14.7.

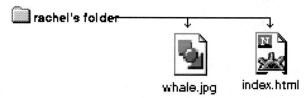

whale.jpg   index.html

Figure 14.7

If Jones were hand-coding her file, the link to the image file on index.html would be **<IMG SRC="whale.jpg">**.

But if Jones plans to expand her site in the future, she might want to create a separate folder named "images" and put whale.jpg in it (see Figure 14.8, page 256).

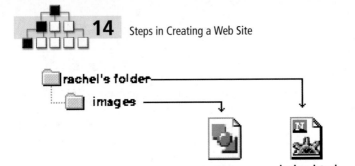

Figure 14.8

Using an images folder, however, requires telling the browser that whale.jpg is in a different folder. The command **<IMG SRC="images/whale.jpg">** means that whale.jpg is in a folder named "images."

Let's say that Jones plans to put other Web sites on her account and wants to keep the files that create her home page in a folder called "home." She wants to keep her images in a separate folder, so her directory would look like Figure 14.9. In order for a browser to find whale.jpg, it would have to go to another folder at the same level as the home folder, which contains index.html. The command **<IMG SRC=". . / images/whale. jpg">** means "go up one level, find the folder images, then find the whale.jpg file." If an image doesn't show up when you put the site on the server, it's probably because you haven't given the browser the correct instructions to find it. These problems are usually easy to fix if you have a basic knowledge of how HTML works.

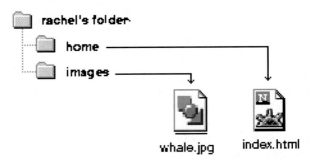

Figure 14.9

EXERCISE 14.1 As you build a Web site for either this class or another, keep a detailed log. What process did you follow? How did you find images? How did you design your site? What problems did you run into? How did you solve these problems?

Chapter 15

Building a Multipage Site

When we look for something in a book, we rely on an elaborate set of navigation tools. At the most basic level, we know that books are continuous. If a sentence doesn't end on a particular page, we can expect to find the remainder at the beginning of the next page. Books we use to find information are divided into chapters, which in turn are often divided into sections with headings, as this one is. They have elaborate tables of contents and detailed indexes that give us specific page references, which we can use to access specific information. When books are collected in a library, we rely on tools that allow us to locate a particular book. These tools seem so natural to use that it is hard to imagine books and libraries without them. The navigation tools of print, however, including page numbers, titles and headings, chapters, tables of contents, indexes, and library classification systems, took centuries to develop.

Few people had heard of the Web before 1994; thus it's no wonder that Web navigation tools often seem so rudimentary. You do see some borrowing of print tools for Web navigation, but their adaptability is limited. The key difference is that navigation tools for print are based on book technology with continuously bound, numbered pages. A Web site does not have to be sequential. Indeed, many sites are like a huge drawer stuffed full of odds and ends, and your task is to arrange what's in the drawer.

15a PRINCIPLES OF NAVIGATIONAL DESIGN

How then do you begin? Many multipage Web sites use a tree structure that spreads outward, as the branches of a tree do. That solution works reasonably well for many subjects, but what happens when you want to get from one side of the tree to the other? Do you have to retrace your path back to the trunk of the tree and then start down another branch? Many users don't want to do that much clicking. Designing a multipage Web site presents many conceptual and design problems, but, as in visual design, there are a few basic principles that can provide solutions for many of these problems.

Making the navigational structure intuitive

The best navigational structures allow users to do what comes naturally. For example, on a Web site with pages in a linear sequence, users expect to be able to move forward and backward easily. Users also expect to find what they are looking for, so you should anticipate their needs. Suppose you are designing a Web site for your club or organization. Think first about who will be likely to visit the site. Some people will be curious to know what the club does, so you will need an "about" page. Some may want to join, so it should be easy to find out how. Members of your club will want to know about activities; you should provide an obvious path to that information.

Making the navigational structure visible

How to move through a Web site should be evident from the beginning. An overview of your site should be presented in the navigation tools on the first page. The tools should reflect the primary subjects of your site.

Making the navigational structure consistent

The format of the navigation tools should be consistent from one page to another. For example, if your main navigation tool is a row of buttons down the left side of the page, subsequent pages should also have a row of buttons down the left side. Colors used for navigation should also remain consistent.

Keeping the user oriented

Visitors to your site should always be able to tell where they are on your site. The navigation tools should indicate where exactly the user is located on a site and should provide a clear path back to the beginning. Users should not have to resort to the back button on the browser.

15b TOOLS FOR NAVIGATION

Just as the basic unit of computing is a binary number or bit, the link is the basic navigation tool on the Web. A multipage Web site without links is like a pizza without cheese—the key ingredient is missing. You have several ways of placing links on your site.

Embedded links

The simplest method of putting links on your site is to make a link using words in your text. You can click on the link icon or select **Link** on your Web page editor, highlight or type in the word or words you want to use for the link, type in the URL, click **OK**, and you've got a link. You can create links quickly using this method, but you won't have created a navigational structure for your site and you won't keep users oriented to their location on your site. Embedded links are useful, but you need additional navigation tools for a multipage site.

Text navigation bars

One of the easiest navigation tools to create is a text bar with links, such as this:

Home | My Courses | My Hobbies | Photos | Links

You can copy the HTML code for the text bar, open the other pages, and paste in the navigation bar. When you make it once, you don't have to make it again. On long pages, even if you have navigation tools at the top, a simple text bar at the bottom saves your visitor from having to scroll back up.

Buttons and icons

Creating a set of navigation buttons is almost as easy as making a text navigation bar. Buttons with or without text can be created quickly in Photoshop and other image editors. Image editors have a text tool that allows you to type on a button image, which you can then save as a GIF file. Once you have inserted the image into your text, you can make the image serve as a link, just as you did for text. If your Web page editor does not have a window to make an image a link in the **Link** dialog box, you can insert the HTML code that links from a button (button.gif) to a new page (newpage.html):
<A HREF="newpage.html"><IMG SRC="button.gif"></A>.

Many clip art sites on the Web and clip art files included with software provide you with ready-to-use buttons. Buttons, icons, and images can add interest and even humor to your site (see Figure 15.1).

When you are designing a site that lends itself well to visual icons, you can use images organic to that site. For example, many art museums use representative images to provide visual guides. The home page of the Art Institute of Chicago uses thumbnail images to represent its major collections (see Figure 15.2, page 262).

Figure 15.1

Figure 15.2. The Art Institute of Chicago, Permanent Collections
(http://www.artic.edu/aic/collections/)

Links within the same page

If you have long pages of text that require scrolling down more than two windows, you should create links that allow the user to move around on that page. These links within pages are called **targets** or **anchors**. Composer and other editors allow you to create targets. On Composer, follow these steps.

1. Put the cursor at the beginning of a line or select some text.
2. Select **Target** on the **Insert** menu.
3. Type in a name for the target in the **Edit** box.
4. Click **OK**. You will see a target icon in the Composer window where you marked the text.
5. Select the text or image that you want to link to the target.
6. Select **Link** on the **Insert** menu.
7. Select **Browse Page** on the **File** menu and click the link you just made.

15c | NAVIGATION ON COMPLEX SITES

Most class projects lend themselves to straightforward navigational schemes because they have fewer than twenty pages. But you may become involved in designing a more complex site for an organization you belong to or for an employer or even for yourself. Often when Web sites grow, they end up serving several different functions. When the mission of a site becomes complex, the navigation tools should reflect that complexity rather than lumping everything together in one chaotic list of links.

Limited options at any given point

On a Web site of ten to fifteen pages, a user is not likely to feel overwhelmed. But when sites grow larger and many choices are offered at a single point, a user can feel overwhelmed if the choices are not grouped. That's when you have to make some hard decisions about your main menu items.

Take a look at your school's Web site. Some colleges and universities follow the organizational structure of the school for defining the major categories. On such sites you'll find that the major links are for administration, libraries, colleges and departments, graduate studies programs, campus life, and so on. Others begin from the perspective of potential users with major categories for students, faculty, staff, alumni, parents, visitors, and businesses. These categories were not selected on the spur of the moment. They reflect long discussions about the mission of the school.

The welcome page for the Allyn & Bacon/Longman Web site (the publisher's Web site) has six main items on the image menu bar at the top, with a text navigation bar below (see Figure 15.3, page 264). On the left side is a link for instructors who wish to examine books, contact their sales representatives, examine Web sites for particular books, and search the catalog. The text body offers information about the content in each of these links. The welcome page makes it easy for both first-time and returning visitors to find what they are looking for.

Figure 15.3. Welcome page for Longman (http://longman.awl.com/)

The "bread crumb trail" approach

If you are putting up page after page on a deep site, you should make it easy for the user to get back to the previous page. Users should always be able to retrace their steps without having to click on the back button. If you have long pages with the navigation tools on the top, then you should put in an anchor that returns the user to the top of the page.

15d | MAKE YOUR SITE ACCESSIBLE

Keep in mind that many users cannot experience everything on the Web because their access is by telephone modem. When users are sitting in front of a blank screen, 15 seconds can seem like an eternity. They may well give up, click on the stop button, and move on to another site.

Writing in the World

Accessible design

In addition to users with small screens and slow connections, many others may not be able to see, hear, move, or process some information easily. To reach the entire community, it is important to have text equivalents for any pictures, audio, or video you might put on your site. Any graphs or charts should have summaries attached. Visually impaired users have access to text through screen reader technology, which reads the text aloud.

Including text equivalents has other advantages. Search engines that might otherwise miss your site have more words to identify when you describe an image with a text equivalent. All users benefit from good navigation tools. The Center for Applied Special Technology (CAST) is committed to making the Web accessible to people with disabilities. They offer a Web-based tool called Bobby that analyzes Web pages for their accessibility to people with disabilities. You can submit your site to Bobby (**http://www.cast.org/bobby/**), which will tell you what potential problems your site might contain for people with disabilities, along with any browser compatibility errors.

The ALT attribute

Perhaps you don't care about users with telephone modem connections. Most Web designers, however, cannot be so casual about tossing out such a big chunk of their potential viewers. Figure 15.4 on page 266 is the home page of a major bank with the images turned off on a browser. What is this bank saying to customers who want to check their bank balances online using a slow connection or to customers who are blind or have low vision and rely on speech synthesis of text?

It doesn't have to be this bad. At the very least, the designer should have provided alternate text attributes for the images on this page, which will supply text for users who have images turned off. When you insert an image

Figure 15.4. Web site of a major bank with images turned off

using an editor, pay attention to the ALT box on your editor. Supply text in the ALT box that describes the image that the user may not be able to see.

Designing for screen size

You can design Web pages with images that nearly all users can access, including those with slow dial-up modem connections, if you take into account the sizes of your users' screens and the sizes of the pictures and graphics you put on your pages. The screens users have now vary widely, from the 640×480 screen many laptops and older computers have, up to the 1600×1200 screens on newer monitors. You can expect most users to be clustered at the bottom end, with 640×480, 800×600, and 832×624 screens. Professional Web designers attempt to stay within these dimensions. They are constantly aware that most users will not spend much time scrolling down a page.

15e │ TEST AND IMPROVE YOUR SITE

Good Web sites take time to complete. Few things are more aggravating on the Web than a Web site with broken links, numerous errors, and entire sections "under construction." Before you upload your site to the server, you should make sure all your links are working and everything appears the way you want it to appear. If possible, you should load your folder on a different platform (e.g., on Windows if you composed it on a Mac), you should look at your site on different screen sizes (e.g., 640 × 480, 832 × 624), and you should try it with both Netscape and Internet Explorer. Remember, different people will visit your site on different computers using different browsers with different connections to the Internet, and all these variables will affect how your site will be viewed.

Next you are ready to make a thorough review of your content.

1. **What kind of experience do you want to create and for whom?**
   - Will your site convey that experience to the people you want to visit your site?
   - If your site is largely informative, how much do you need to explain the subject of your Web site?
   - If you cite other work, is it clear where that work came from? Will a user be able to find it?
2. **What visual message does your site convey?**
   - Is the text easy to read?
   - If you use a background, does it enhance the site?
   - How can you improve the appearance of your site?
3. **How easy is it to navigate on your site?**
   - Do you always know where you are in the site?
   - Can you always get back to the start?
   - Is it easy to move from one page to another?

When you have done a thorough in-house review and made the necessary changes, it's time to put the site on your server. By putting the site on your server, you've declared that it's ready for the world to see. You should have on your site your email address or a way for users to reach you. A few people at least will give you unsolicited feedback. But you should also ask specific people for feedback. If possible, ask people who are not in your class but who might have some interest in the subject of your site. Often they will give you valuable advice. Note that this process takes time, and you have to plan for that time. The biggest mistake professional designers make is not allowing time for the process of testing and improving.

EXERCISE 15.1 Suppose you are an Internet design consultant. Return to the Web site you evaluated in Exercise 13.2 or look at your school's Web site. If you are examining the Web site you evaluated earlier, add a discussion of the site's accessibility to your original evaluation. If you are using your school's Web site, take notes on the five points outlined in Section 13c, and include a discussion of the site's accessibility. Then, using your evaluation, write a brief (one- to two-page) report suggesting ways in which your client can improve the site.

Researching 5

16
Planning Your Research

17
Finding Sources

18
Evaluating Sources

" cite sources "
(Faigley 101)

19
Avoiding Plagiarism When Using Sources

20
Writing the Research Project

Chapter 16

Planning Your Research

You do research every day. If you read movie reviews in your newspaper to decide which movie you want to see, or if you visit travel Web sites to find out where you can get the best deal on airline fares, you are doing research. If you want to settle an argument about which teams made the Final Four in last year's basketball championship, you need to do research. In college, research means both **investigating existing knowledge** that is stored on computers and in libraries, and **creating new knowledge** through original analysis, surveys, experiments, and theorizing. When you start a research task in a college course, you need to understand the different kinds of possible research and to plan your strategy in advance.

16a | ANALYZE THE RESEARCH TASK

If you have an assignment that requires research, look closely at what you are being asked to do. The assignment may ask you to review, compare, survey, analyze, evaluate, or prove that something is true or untrue. The purpose of your research and your potential audience will help guide your strategies for research.

Determine your purpose

Often the assignment itself will tell you what is expected. Look for key words:

- An *analysis* or *examination* requires you to look at an issue in detail, explaining how it has evolved, who or what it affects, and what is at stake.
- A *review of scholarship* requires you to summarize what key scholars and researchers have written about the issue.
- A *survey* requires you to gather opinion about a particular issue, either by a questionnaire or by interviews.
- An *evaluation* requires you to make critical judgments.
- An *argument* requires you to assemble evidence in support of a claim you make.

Ask your instructor for guidance if you remain unsure of what is expected.

Identify your potential readers

Think about whom you are writing for.

- How familiar are your readers likely to be with your subject?
- What are they likely to know and not know about your subject?
- What aspects of your subject might interest them the most?
- What background information will you need to supply?
- If your subject is controversial, what opinions or beliefs are your readers likely to have about it?
- Do you want to inform your readers, change their attitudes, or persuade them to take some action?

Assess the project's length and scope

Think about exactly what you are expected to produce.

- What kind of research are you being asked to do? library research? survey research? field observations?
- How long is the paper you are writing or how extensive is the Web site you are creating?

- How many sources are you expected to include?
- What steps are required by your instructor in advance of the final draft? a topic proposal? a first draft? a working bibliography?

EXERCISE 16.1 Determine the research strategy required for each of the assignment topics below: analysis/examination, review of scholarship, survey, evaluation, or argument.

1. How does the student body feel about a proposed raise in tuition?
2. What do scientists know about the effectiveness of acupuncture in treating various forms of addiction?
3. How historically accurate is the film *Gladiator*?
4. What caused the crash of the technology market in 2000?
5. How far should the government go to prevent terrorism?

16b SET A SCHEDULE

The secret to a successful research project is allowing enough time to do the job well. To use the following schedule, fill in the date your final draft is due and work backward to the present.

Schedule for research project

Task to complete	Date
Find a topic that interests you (16c)	_____
Ask a question and draft a working thesis (16d)	_____
Decide what kind of research you need to do (16e, 16f)	_____
Begin library or Web research (17a–e)	_____
Start a working bibliography (17f)	_____
Read and evaluate your sources (18)	_____
Summarize and paraphrase your sources (19)	_____
Review your goals and thesis (20a)	_____
Plan your organization (20b)	_____
Decide what material from your sources to include (20c)	_____
Write the first draft (20d)	_____

Review your draft (20e)   _____
Revise your draft (20f)   _____
Edit and check formatting of your
     revised draft (20f)   _____
Submit final draft   _____

You can use your schedule to make a research log in which you keep track of your progress.

Writing in the World

Use folders

Writers who make their living doing research rely on both paper and computer folders. Before you begin, get a few paper folders for your handwritten notes, photocopies, and early drafts. Create a folder on your desktop, if you are using a computer, and create subfolders for drafts and sources. Make sure you have a folder labeled something like "old project" and put in it all your early drafts and other material that you decide not to use. You never know when you may want to refer to work you had done earlier but didn't think you would need.

16c   FIND A TOPIC THAT INTERESTS YOU

Ask meaningful questions and research will be enjoyable. Your courses may give you some ideas about questions to ask, or you may simply want to pursue an interest of your own. One good way to begin is by browsing, either in your library or on the Web. Browsing may lead you to topics you hadn't yet considered; it may also show you the breadth of possibilities included in a topic you have already selected. For example, perhaps you're interested in key policy issues that are likely to affect the Internet over the next few years. One issue that is certain to be controversial is privacy, but when you start browsing, you realize privacy is a wide-ranging concept involving many concerns, including Web security, encryption, spam, and employer surveillance of employees. You will need to narrow your topic—perhaps to the issue of "cookies." (A cookie is a small file placed on your computer by a Web server so that it recognizes you the next time you access the site from your browser.)

Browse a Web subject directory

A Web search engine is a set of programs that sort through millions of items with incredible speed. Several Web search sites (Britannica, LookSmart, and Yahoo! are some of the best known) include **subject directories**. Web directories are useful when you want to narrow a topic or learn what subcategories a topic might contain. The most popular subject directory, Yahoo! (**www.yahoo.com**), will retrieve both Web sites indexed by Yahoo! staff members and sites from the entire Web using **search engine** technology. (See Figure 16.1.) In addition to the Web subject directories, the Library of Congress Virtual Reference Shelf (**lcweb. loc.gov/rr/askalib/virtualref.html**) may help you identify sites relevant to your topic.

Consult a general encyclopedia

General encyclopedias, which provide basic information about a wide range of topics, are also a good starting point for browsing. Some encyclopedias are now available online without charge; your library reference room will undoubtedly have others. Two of the best known are the *Columbia Encyclopedia* (**www.bartleby.com**), and *Encyclopaedia Britannica* (**www.eb.com**).

Consult a specialized encyclopedia

Specialized encyclopedias focus on a single area of knowledge, go into more depth about a subject, and often include bibliographies. Specialized encyclopedias are available for virtually any area that may interest you, from the *Encyclopedia of Accounting Systems* to the *Encyclopedia of Zoroastrianism*. Your library may have handouts for specialized encyclopedias and other specialized reference sources, or you can consult Robert Balay's *Guide to Reference Books*, which should be available at the reference desk.

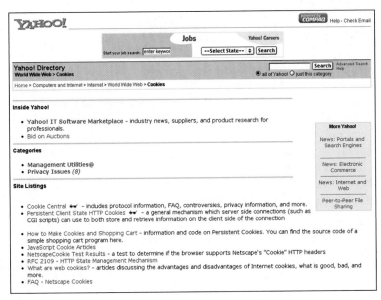

Figure 16.1. Yahoo! subject directory for Web cookies

EXERCISE 16.2 Think of a general topic you might write about for one of your courses (the human genome, the European Union, pragmatism, the National Parks, the Negro Leagues of baseball, or any other). Then, gather lists of subtopics using a Web directory, a general encyclopedia, and a specialized encyclopedia (if applicable). Answer the questions that follow.

1. What subtopics do all of the resources provide for this general topic?
2. Do any of the subtopics lead to other subtopics? Which ones?
3. Which resource produced the most useful list of subtopics for this general topic?
4. Which of the subtopics generated seems the most fruitful to pursue? Why?

16d ASK A QUESTION AND DRAFT A WORKING THESIS

Often you'll be surprised by the amount of information your initial browsing uncovers. Your next task will be to identify in that mass of information a question for your research project. This **researchable question**, to which you may want to formulate an initial answer, or **working thesis**, will be the focus of the remainder of your research and ultimately of your research project or paper.

Research profile: Mary Kingsley

Let's say you are interested in learning more about female explorers. During your research you quickly discover that there were many women who traveled in the 1800s to areas unknown to Europeans. One who interests you is Mary Kingsley (1862-1900), a British woman who journeyed alone in remote areas of West Africa between 1893 and 1895. The information you find suggests that Kingsley was incredibly independent and undeterred by danger and hardship. You'd like to write about her, but you do not have a researchable question. You read more and discover that she defended the beliefs and practices of native Africans and had little good to say about missionaries. A question begins to emerge, and so does your working thesis.

Write your topic, research question, and working thesis on a note card or sheet of paper. Keep your working thesis handy. You may need to revise it several times until the wording is precise.

> TOPIC: Mary Kingsley's travels in West Africa
>
> RESEARCH QUESTION: What was Mary Kingsley's attitude toward the people she encountered in West Africa, both native and European?

WORKING THESIS: Mary Kingsley presented a view of West Africa contrary to the one prevailing in her time, because she valued the great diversity of native peoples, customs, and beliefs, and attacked European missionaries for doing more harm than good.

Research profile: Casino gambling

Take another example. You want to write about the trend toward legalizing casino gambling, but that topic turns out to be massive. You find that the debate over allowing casino gambling on Indian reservations goes back to the early 1980s. In order to narrow your topic, you look at arguments for and against expanding casino gambling. An argument proponents of casino gambling often use is that casinos bring tourist dollars that benefit the entire community. Opponents of casino gambling argue the opposite: People who go to casinos spend money on gambling that they might spend elsewhere. In your initial research, you discover that studies on this issue show that some businesses are helped but others are hurt. This initial research gives you a working thesis.

TOPIC: Economic impacts of casino gambling

RESEARCH QUESTION: How does the presence of a casino affect the economy of the community where it is located?

WORKING THESIS: The economic impact of casino gambling on the communities in which it is located is mixed, with some businesses benefiting and others suffering.

EXERCISE 16.3 Choose one of the subtopics you found for Exercise 16.2. Do some preliminary research on this subject and develop a topic, research question, and working thesis, using the advice given in Section 16d.

16e | DECIDE WHAT KIND OF RESEARCH YOU NEED TO DO

Once you have formulated a research question, you should begin thinking about what kind of research you will need to do to address the question.

Secondary research

Most people who do research rely partly or exclusively on the work of others as sources of information. Research based on the work of others is called **secondary research**. In the past this information was contained almost exclusively in collections of print materials housed in libraries, but today enormous amounts of information are available on the Internet and in various recorded media.

Conducting secondary research means reading the books, articles, or online publications written about your chosen topic. The purpose of secondary research is to familiarize yourself with factual information and arguments established by others. It can be hard to figure out how to find and sort through these sources. (Chapters 17 and 18 offer specific strategies for finding and evaluating sources.) In the initial research stage, try to determine which type or combination of secondary sources seems most promising for your topic.

Imagine you are beginning secondary research on explorer Mary Kingsley (see Section 16d). A quick search of your library's online book catalog lists eleven books on Kingsley. At first you might think that you have found more than enough material and that your source search is complete. But perhaps only two or three of the books focus on your specific research interest: Kingsley's attitudes about the European colonial presence in West Africa. Therefore, you should also consult a periodical index, such as the *Historical Abstracts* online database, for scholarly articles on Kingsley, the effects of colonialism in West Africa, or both. Writers of scholarly journal articles tend to target specific issues and assume aggressive argumentative stances, so there is a good chance that you will find relevant arguments that you can use to reinforce or contrast with your own.

To write on most topics in the humanities, you will need to read both books and articles. If your topic addresses a current event or recent public policy, all of your secondary sources may come from mainstream periodicals or Internet sources. Topics in the natural or social sciences may focus on primary research, but they almost always require a review of secondary literature.

Primary research

Much of the research done at a university creates new information through **primary research**: experiments, data-gathering surveys and interviews, detailed observations, and the examination of historical documents. Although most undergraduates do not do primary research, sometimes you have to gather the needed information yourself. If you are researching a campus issue such as the problem of inadequate parking for students, you may need to conduct interviews, make observations, and take a survey.

EXERCISE 16.4 What kind of research (primary, secondary, or both) would each of the following topics require?

1. The programs a local public radio station should add to or remove from its schedule
2. The history of the color line in American sports
3. How people applying for unemployment could be better served
4. The emotional, physical, and social health of children raised by same-sex parents
5. Japanese *manga* (comic strip narratives) as a working-class art form

16f PLAN YOUR FIELD RESEARCH

Even though much of the research you do for college courses will be secondary research conducted at a computer or in the library, some topics do call for primary research, requiring you to gather information on your own by conducting interviews, making observations, or administering surveys. Field research of this kind can be especially important for exploring local issues.

Interviews

College campuses are a rich source of experts in many areas, both on the faculty and in the surrounding community. Interviewing experts on your research topic can help build your knowledge base. You can use interviews to discover what the people most affected by a particular issue are thinking and feeling. Before you contact anyone, think carefully about your goals; the goals of your interview will help you determine whom you need to interview and what questions you need to ask.

- Decide what you want or need to know, and who best can provide that for you.
- Schedule each interview in advance, and let the person know why you are conducting the interview.
- Plan your questions in advance. Write down a few questions and have a few more in mind. Listen carefully so you can follow up on key points.
- Come prepared with a notebook and pencil. A tape recorder sometimes can intimidate the person you are interviewing. If you want to use a tape recorder, ask for permission in advance.

Effective interviews

Consider the questions you plan to ask from the point of view of the person you are going to interview.

Research scenario: Several fellow students in your introductory composition class have challenged the curriculum set for this course, complaining that the paper assignments are too formulaic. You schedule an interview with the director of the composition program.

Less effective question: Why are the papers so formulaic in this course? (Problem: Question may be perceived as insulting and accusatory, putting the interviewee on the defensive.)

More effective question: What is the rationale behind the writing assignments in this course?

Observations

Local observation can also be a valuable source of data. For example, if you are researching why a particular office on your campus does not operate efficiently, observe what happens when students enter and how they are handled by the staff.

- Choose a place where you can observe with the least intrusion. The less people wonder about what you are doing, the better.
- Carry a notebook and write extensive field notes. Get down as much information as you can, and worry about analyzing it later.
- Record the date, exactly where you were, exactly when you arrived and left, and important details like the number of people present.
- Write on one side of your notebook so you can use the facing page to note key observations and analyze your data later.

Effective observation

Be sure you collect enough of the right kind of information before you start to interpret what you have observed.

Research scenario: You are doing observational research on why a campus office does not function as well as you think it should.

Ineffective method: You visit the office on two separate occasions at the same time of the day, 4 to 5 p.m. You observe that the desk staff seem testy and impatient with the students, and you even witness a hostile confrontation between a staff member and a student. You conclude that this campus office is not operating efficiently because of poor staff-student relations. (Problem: You have not collected an adequate and representative sample.)

More effective method: You visit the office several times at different times of the day. You keep track of the number of staff-student interactions you witness. You devise a coding system to organize your observations systematically with categories such as "student asks question in polite, respectful manner," "student asks question in demanding manner," "student's attitude not easily discerned."

Surveys

Extensive surveys that can be projected to large populations, like the ones used in political polls, require the effort of many people. Small surveys, however, often can provide insight on local issues. You need to decide what exactly you want to know, then design a survey that will provide that information.

- Write a few specific questions. Make sure that they are unambiguous—people will fill out your survey quickly, and if the questions are confusing, the results will be meaningless. To make sure your questions are clear, test them on a few people before you conduct the survey.
- Include one or two open-ended questions, such as "What do you like about X?" "What don't you like about X?" Open-ended questions can be difficult to interpret, but sometimes they turn up information you had not anticipated.
- Decide whom and how many people you will need to survey. For example, if you want to claim that the results of your survey represent the views of residents of your dormitory, your method of selecting respondents should give all residents an equal chance to be selected. Don't select only your friends.
- Decide how you will contact participants in your survey. If you are going to mail or email your survey, include a statement about what the survey is for.
- Think about how you will interpret your survey. Multiple-choice formats make data easy to tabulate, but often they miss key information. Open-ended questions will require you to figure out a way to group responses.

Effective surveys

As you plan your questions, consider how background and assumptions—your own and those of your respondents—may affect your survey.

Research scenario: Some colleges have adopted coed bathrooms on coed dormitory halls. You want to survey the residents of your dormitory about how they feel about coed bathrooms.

Ineffective method: You don't collect demographic information about respondents such as their age, gender, or race/ethnicity. (Problem: You deprive yourself of information about your respondents that may affect their answers.)

More effective method: You preserve the anonymity of respondents but provide separate boxes for age, gender, and race/ethnicity.

Ineffective survey question: Isn't the prospect of coed bathrooms disturbing and embarrassing? (Problem: Bias is built into the question.)

More effective survey question: Are you in favor of or against adopting a policy of coed bathrooms on your dormitory hall? Why?

EXERCISE 16.5 Choose either a research project from Exercise 16.4 that requires primary research, or, if applicable, the research project you began to develop in Exercise 16.3. Decide what form(s) of field research you might have to do (interview, observation, survey, or a combination) and create a plan for gathering the information you need. If you need to conduct interviews, make a list of people you might interview and a list of questions you would ask them. If you need to conduct a survey, decide how you will implement your survey (who, where, when) and design a draft of the survey you will distribute. If you will gather your data through observation, write up a plan (who, what, when, and where) and make a list of the things you expect to find out.

Chapter 17

Finding Sources

Information—and knowing how to find it—is power in the digital era. After you graduate you will often need to find information in your career and in your life in the community. When you begin research projects as an undergraduate, however, the volume of information available in your library and on the Web may seem overwhelming. The distinction between doing research online and in the library is blurring as more and more library resources go online. Many colleges and universities have made most of the major resources in their reference rooms available online. Paper card catalogs are not being updated, so if you look for a book published in the last decade, you must use the online catalog. Newspapers, scholarly journals, and government documents are increasingly being archived in digital form. And all these resources are now being indexed online, so searching online catalogs is the fastest way to find sources, even if the information itself is in print.

17a | RESEARCH IN LIBRARIES AND ON THE WEB

Library resources

You may have heard people say that you can find any information you want on the Web. In reality, relatively few published books are available in their entirety on the Web. A great deal of what you can find in a large library is not on the Web. Most books, films, recordings, scholarly journals, and older copies of newspapers are not available. Many online resources are available to you through your library's Web site only because your library pays for them.

Advantages of library resources	*Disadvantages of library resources*
Comprehensive. Libraries include many books, films, recordings, scholarly journals, and older issues of newspapers not available on the Web.	**Physical limitations.** Most library resources are not online, so you have to go to the library. Sometimes items are checked out or missing.
High quality. Librarians review and select the resources.	**Sometimes out of date.** The most current information may not be available in the library.
Logically organized. Materials are cataloged and can be located easily.	**Sometimes difficult to use.** If the information you need is part of a specialized collection, such as government documents, you may need to use a specialized index to find it.
Permanent. Library materials remain available for many years.	
Free of charge. You do not pay for information in your library.	**Limited hours.** Few libraries are open 24/7.
Supported by staff. You can ask a librarian for help if you have difficulty finding an item.	
Increasing online resources. Online library resources offer the best of both worlds: the quality of library resources and the convenience of Web resources.	

Web resources

Because anyone can publish on the Web, there is no overall quality control and there is no system of organization, as there is in a library. Nevertheless, the Web offers you some resources for current topics that would be difficult or impossible to find in a library. The keys to success are knowing where you are most likely to find current and accurate information about the particular question you are researching, and knowing how to access that information.

Advantages of Web resources	*Disadvantages of Web resources*
Accessible. Web resources are available 24/7 from anywhere in the world connected to the Internet.	**No quality control.** Anyone with access to a server can put up a Web site.
Current. The Web offers up-to-the-minute news, stock quotes, and other information.	**No overall organization.** Individual libraries have catalogs, but there is no catalog for the Web.
Diverse. Nearly every major organization, company, government agency, college, and university has a Web site. You can find public opinion from many countries on the Web.	**Lack permanence.** What you find on the Web one day may be gone tomorrow.
Speedy. Fast connections make it possible to access some information quickly.	**Sometimes not available.** Much information available on the Web is password protected or available only for a fee.
	No one way of searching. Search engines access only a small fraction of the millions of Web pages. Furthermore, particular databases have their own search tools.
	Often difficult to use. Many college writing topics are difficult to research on the Web.

EXERCISE 17.1 Decide where (library, Internet, or both) you might find each of the following. If you could find it in both the library and on the Internet, what are the advantages of one over the other?

1. *Jay's Journal of Anomalies*, by Ricky Jay
2. Reviews of *Jay's Journal of Anomalies*
3. An interview with the writer Ricky Jay
4. A newspaper article from the nineteenth century that describes a magician's performance
5. The 2001 membership roster for the International Brotherhood of Magicians

6. A comprehensive history of the American sideshow
7. The current auction value of several pieces of magic memorabilia
8. The date of Penn and Teller's next television appearance
9. The number of books published about Harry Houdini one year after his death
10. The etymology of the word *mesmerize*

17b | FIND BOOKS

Libraries have well-developed systems for locating books. Nearly all libraries now shelve books according to the Library of Congress Classification System, which uses a combination of letters and numbers to give you the book's unique location in the library. The Library of Congress call number begins with a letter or letters that represent the broad subject area into which the book is classified.

Subject searches

You can search the extensive Library of Congress online catalog (**catalog.loc.gov/**) to find out how your subject might be indexed, or you can go straight to your own library's catalog and conduct a subject search. Here are the letters and titles of the main classes in the Library of Congress classification system:

A—General Works
B—Philosophy, Psychology, Religion
C—Auxiliary Sciences of History
D—History: General and Old World
E, F—History: America
G—Geography, Anthropology, Recreation
H—Social Sciences
J—Political Science
K—Law
L—Education

M—Music and Books on Music
N—Fine Arts
P—Language and Literature
Q—Science
R—Medicine
S—Agriculture
T—Technology
U—Military Science
V—Naval Science
Z—Bibliography, Library Science, Information Resources

Research profile: Browsing the Library of Congress online catalog

Suppose you want to do research on attention deficit disorder, which afflicts 3% to 5% of American children.

1. Start with a subject browse search on the Library of Congress's on-line catalog.
2. Select **Subject Browse** and type "attention deficit disorder" in the box (see Figure 17.1).
3. Click **Search** and the results will be listed (see Figure 17.2).

The search will give you an extensive list of topics. You can click on the in-dividual topics to narrow the search.

Research profile: Conducting a subject search in your library

Say you are interested in doing research on the causes of the U.S.-Mexican War (1846-48). You read that Ulysses S. Grant, commander of the Union armies during the Civil War and later president of the United States, did not support going to war with Mexico. You want to find out why. You do a subject search using Grant's name and find the record for a copy of his *Personal Memoirs* (see page 290).

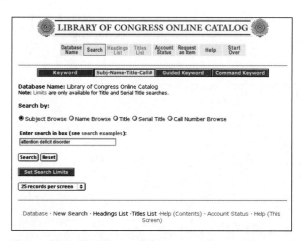

Figure 17.1. The Library of Congress online catalog

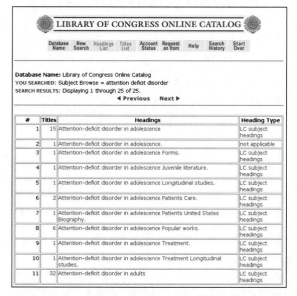

Figure 17.2. Subject Browse results for attention deficit disorder

AUTHOR:
   Grant, Ulysses S. (Ulysses Simpson), 1822–1885

TITLE:
   Personal memoirs of Ulysses S. Grant

PUBLISHED:
   New York, C.L. Webster & Co., 1885–1886

DESCRIPTION:
   2 v. front. (ports.) plates, maps, facsims. 24 cm.

NOTES:
   Includes index.

SUBJECTS:
   Grant, Ulysses S. (Ulysses Simpson), 1822–1885
   United States—History—Civil War, 1861–1865—Campaigns
   United States—History—War with Mexico, 1845–1848—
      Personal narratives

OCLC NUMBER:
   289150
Locations
E 672 G76 1885 V.1 Main Library Stacks
E 672 G76 1885 V.2 Main Library Stacks

Call numbers that begin with letters use the Library of Congress system. Your library may also contain older books that use Dewey Decimal system call numbers, which begin with numbers, but nearly all newer books and many older ones have Library of Congress call numbers. The Library of Congress system groups books by subject, and you can often find other items relevant to your search shelved close to the particular one you are looking for.

The call number will enable you to find the item in the stacks. You will need to consult the locations guide for your library. The locations guide will give the level and section.

Library of Congress Call Numbers

Call number range	*Level and section*
DS 462–DS 885	3Q
DS 886–E 755	3R
E 756–GV	3S
H–HA 1999	4L
HA 2000–HC 106.9	4M

Looking at the table tells you that your book E 672 is within the range DS 886–E 755 and will be shelved on level 3, section R of your library.

The art of keyword searches

If you start a subject search with a precise question in mind, such as why Ulysses S. Grant was opposed to going to war with Mexico, often you can find material quickly. On many other occasions, however, you will not start out with such a limited question. If, for example, you type the word *ethics* into the subject search window on your library's online catalog, you likely will get more than a thousand items, perhaps several thousand.

Subject search tools are similar for libraries and for the Web. They use one or more search terms or **keywords**. If you start with only one keyword, chances are the search will give you too many items to be useful. To narrow your search, you can combine search terms with the word AND. For example, you may have read or heard that attention deficit hyperactivity disorder (ADHD) tends to run in families, so there may be genetic factors involved. You can do additional searches for "attention deficit hyperactivity disorder AND genetics" to narrow the topic.

Most search tools also allow you to use OR to retrieve items that include either term. Note that replacing AND with OR in the previous search would yield very different results, since using OR would make the search retrieve all items about ADHD and all items about genetics, not just items related to genetic influences on ADHD.

Another strategy to limit your search is to specify what you don't want, by using NOT. If, for example, you are interested in ADHD only in adults, you could eliminate items that mention children by typing "attention deficit hyperactivity disorder NOT children."

Computer Strategies

Choosing keywords

Before you begin a keyword search, write a paragraph about your topic in as much detail as possible; the more nouns you use the better. When you finish, read your paragraph and underline or highlight every possible keyword for your subject. Copy these words to a list. Then think of any other words that might apply to your topic, even if they seem harebrained. Think about any synonyms—words that have the same or similar meaning. If you get stuck, consult a specialized dictionary for your subject, a thesaurus, or the Library of Congress online catalog (**catalog.loc.gov/**).

Finding book reviews

You may want to consult book reviews in your research to learn how others understand particular books and if they find them important. You need to know the author's name, the title of the book, and the date of original publication to search for book reviews. Book reviews are included in periodical indexes (see Section 17c). The most comprehensive index dedicated to book reviews is *Book Review Digest* (1905–), which includes excerpts and some full-text reviews. You can find the printed version in your library's reference collection, and your library may subscribe to the online version, which contains reviews written since 1983.

17c FIND ARTICLES IN JOURNALS

Searching for articles in scholarly journals and magazines works much the same way as searching for books. Indexes for scholarly journals and magazines are located in the reference area of your library, and many may also be available on your library's Web site. Online indexes are databases, fully searchable by author, title, subject, or keywords, and they are often

referred to as *databases* instead of *indexes*. Some online indexes even contain the full text of articles, allowing you to copy the contents onto your computer. Others give you a citation, which you then have to find in your library's resources.

Follow these steps to find articles:

1. Select an index appropriate to your subject.
2. Search the index using relevant subject heading(s).
3. Print or copy the complete citation to the article(s).
4. Print or copy the full text if it is available.
5. If the full text is not available, check the periodicals holdings to see if your library has the journal.

Computer Strategies

Subject headings

Often the key to a successful search is finding the right subject headings. Here are some strategies:

1. **Use subject guides.** Many indexes have subject guides or thesauruses that you can browse.
2. **Find a good article and use its subject headings for your search.** If you have one article that targets your subject precisely, look to see how it is indexed. Then use its subject terms for your search.
3. **Make intelligent guesses.** Sometimes a smart guess produces the term that finds the gold.
4. **Use keywords.** Use the same keyword strategies to find articles that you use to find books. Different periodical indexes offer slightly different options for searching their databases, but almost all will offer a keyword search option. As explained in Section 17b, you can combine keywords with the operators AND, OR, and NOT to focus your online search. Another keyword strategy is to use quotation marks around words, which will make the search engine select only sources with that exact phrase or sequence of words. Using quotation marks is an effective way to narrow the number of search results. For example, a search for *"seasonal migration"* with quotation marks will probably yield a more focused set of sources than *seasonal migration* without quotation marks. However, you may narrow your search too much if you put too many words inside the quotation marks. *"The seasonal migration of whooping cranes"* may eliminate relevant sources that address whooping cranes and seasonal migration but that do not have that exact phrasing in the text.

You can find the location of scholarly journals and magazines by using the title search in your library's online catalog. General indexes include the following.

- **Academic Search Premier.** Provides full text for over 3,000 scholarly publications, including social sciences, humanities, education, computer sciences, engineering, language and linguistics, literature, medical sciences, and ethnic studies journals.
- **ArticleFirst.** Indexes over 13,500 journals in business, the humanities, medicine, science, and social sciences.
- **Biography Index.** Indexes biographies, autobiographies, and interviews in 2,700 journals and 1,800 books.
- **CARL Uncover.** Gives citations to over 17,000 multidisciplinary journals.
- **Expanded Academic ASAP.** Indexes 2,300 periodicals from the arts, humanities, sciences, social sciences, and general news, some with full text articles available.
- **LexisNexis Academic.** Provides full text of a wide range of newspapers, magazines, government and legal documents, and company profiles from around the world.

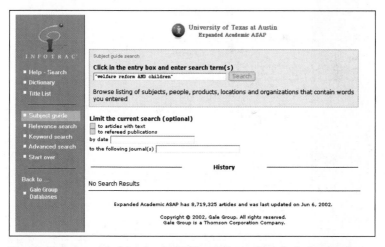

Figure 17.3. Expanded Academic ASAP on Infotrac is typical of online indexes, where you select the kind of search (in this case a subject search), then type the search terms in the entry box.

- **Periodical Abstracts.** Indexes current events and business news from 600 periodicals. Available in print and online.
- **ProQuest.** Indexes thousands of periodicals and newspapers, with the full text of many articles published after 1986.
- **Readers' Guide Abstracts.** Indexes popular periodicals. Available in print and online.

In addition, many specialized indexes list citations to journal articles in various fields. For example, *Medline* indexes articles in medical journals; *ERIC* is a database that indexes articles on education. The *MLA Bibliography* indexes literary criticism articles that can be found in journals or books. Your library will probably have handouts that tell you which specialized index to use for a particular subject. Ask a librarian who works at the reference or information desk to help you. Take advantage of your librarian's experience in searching for information.

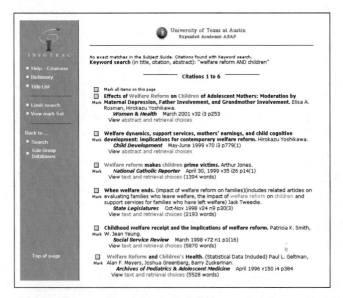

Figure 17.4. A subject search for "welfare reform AND children" produced this result on Expanded Academic ASAP.

Knowing what kinds of articles you want to look for—scholarly, trade, or popular—will help you select the right index. Many indexes include more than one type of journal. Although the difference among journals is not always obvious, you should be able to judge whether a journal is scholarly, trade, or popular by its characteristics. Some instructors frown on using popular journals, but these journals can be valuable for researching current opinion on a particular topic.

Scholarly journals

Scholarly journals are shelved in the periodicals section of your library. They

- Contain long articles typically written by scholars in the field, usually affiliated with a university or research center
- Usually include articles that report original research and have footnotes or a list of works cited at the end
- Assume that readers are other experts in the field
- Display few advertisements or illustrations
- Usually are published quarterly or biannually

Examples of scholarly journals include *American Journal of Mathematics; College English; JAMA: Journal of the American Medical Association; PMLA: Publication of the Modern Language Association;* and *Psychological Reports.*

Trade journals

Trade journals can be found in libraries and on large newsstands. They

- Publish articles related to particular fields, occupations, and interests
- Often give practical information

- Usually include articles that do not report original research and have few or no footnotes, nor a list of works cited at the end
- Contain advertisements aimed at people in specific fields
- Are published weekly, monthly, or quarterly

Examples of trade journals include *Advertising Age, Byte, PC Computing,* and *Teacher Magazine.*

Popular journals

Popular journals are found primarily on newsstands. They

- Publish short articles aimed at the general public
- Contain many advertisements and photos
- Seldom include footnotes or the source of information in detail
- Are published weekly or monthly

Examples of popular journals include *Cosmopolitan, GQ, Rolling Stone, Sports Illustrated,* and *Time.*

EXERCISE 17.2 Decide what kind of periodical (trade, popular, scholarly) you would turn to for information on each of the following topics.

1. Results of a recent study on the long-term physiological effects of Prozac
2. A first-person account of one woman's experiences with depression
3. A review of a self-help book titled *Be Your Own Therapist*
4. An essay arguing that Mary Shelley's *Frankenstein* was heavily influenced by the author's struggles with depression
5. A description of a new reading skills program for students with mild learning disabilities

17d | FIND NEWSPAPER ARTICLES

Newspaper articles are a valuable resource, especially on local topics. They can be found in indexes similar to those for magazines. For issues more than a year old, you likely will have to read the newspaper on microfilm. Nearly all libraries have *The New York Times Index*, which indexes by subject articles in the *New York Times* from 1913 to the present. Also, your library probably has *The Wall Street Journal* index, which is the best source for detailed business news.

For current topics you can now find many newspaper articles online. The best way to begin is to look at the newspaper section on your library's Web site. You will find links to many individual online newspapers and other online collections, such as *NewsBank*, which indexes over 200 newspapers from cover to cover and offers full-text articles. In some libraries you will have to read the articles on microfiche in the library. Other libraries allow you to read the articles in *NewsBank* online.

Nearly every major newspaper now allows you to read current articles online. Be aware, however, that what you find one day may not be available without charge when you return to the newspaper's Web site. You can find links to hundreds of newspapers on these sites:

- **News and Newspapers Online (library.uncg.edu/news/).** This University of North Carolina at Greensboro site offers links to U.S. and foreign newspapers.

- **NewspaperLinks.com (www.newspaperlinks.com)**. This Newspaper Association of America site offers links to U.S. and Canadian newspaper sites, as well as selected links to international newspapers.

- **NewsLink (www.newslink.org)**. Offers links to newspapers, magazines, and radio and TV stations in the United States and other countries.

- **CollegeNews.com (www.collegenews.com)**. Search tool for finding student-run and campus newspapers.

Many newspapers now make some past issues available online for a fee. The most comprehensive directory of online newspaper archives is *U.S. News Archives on the Web* (**www.ibiblio.org/slanews/internet/archives.html**).

Writing in the World

LexisNexis Academic

In addition to college and university libraries, LexisNexis Academic Universe provides online information to businesses, government agencies, law firms, and medical institutions. The Lexis service provides legal information, and the Nexis service is the largest online news and information service. Check your library's Web page to find out if your school has a subscription to LexisNexis Academic Universe. If you have access, you will be able to read full-text articles from over 5,000 publications. LexisNexis Academic is easy to search. It requires you only to type keywords into a window and specify a date range.

EXERCISE 17.3 Find a relevant book, a periodical article, and a newspaper article on the subject you began to develop in the exercises in Chapter 16. Write two paragraphs detailing your research. In the first paragraph, retrace the steps of your research process. Where did you start? What keywords did you use? What problems did you have? Where might you go from here? In the second paragraph, compare your sources. What information do you expect to find in each? What are their relative strengths and weaknesses? Keep these paragraphs. You will be adding to them in future exercises.

17e | FIND INFORMATION ON THE WEB

Search engines versus indexes and catalogs

Search engines designed for the Web work in ways similar to book and periodical indexes and your library's online catalog, with two important differences.

- Catalogs and most indexes, whether online or print, do not give you the full text of an item, only a citation that you can use to find it. Web search engines take you directly to the item, which may or may not exist anywhere except on the Web.
- Catalogs and online indexes typically do some screening of the items they list. Search engines potentially take you to everything on the Web—millions of pages in all. Consequently, you have to work harder to limit searches on the Web or you can be deluged with tens of thousands of items.

Kinds of search engines

A search engine is a set of programs that sort through millions of items at incredible speed. There are four basic kinds of search engines.

1. **Keyword search engines** (e.g., AltaVista, Go.com, Google, Hotbot, Lycos). Keyword search engines use both a **robot**, which moves through the Web capturing information about Web sites, and an **indexer**, which organizes the information found by the robot. They give different results because they assign different weights to the information they find.

2. **Web directories** (e.g., Britannica.com, LookSmart, Open Directory, WebCrawler, Yahoo!). Web directories classify Web sites into categories and are the closest equivalent to the cataloging system used by libraries. On most directories professional editors decide how to index a particular Web site. Web directories also allow keyword searches.

3. **Metasearch agents** (e.g., Dogpile, Metacrawler, ProFusion). Metasearch agents allow you to use several search engines simultaneously. While the concept is sound, metasearch agents are limited by the number of hits they can return and their inability to handle advanced searches.

4. **Natural-language search engines** (e.g., Ask Jeeves). Natural- or real-language search engines allow you to search by asking questions such as "Where can I find a recipe for pound cake?" Natural-language search engines are still in their infancy; no doubt they will become much more powerful in the future.

Computer Strategies

Compare search engines

A good way to compare search engines is to type in your name. You can get some idea of how broadly they search and what they look for by what turns up. (You may discover your name on Web sites you didn't know about!)

Advanced searches

Search engines often produce too many hits to be of use. If you look only at the first few items, you may miss what is most valuable. The alternative is to refine your search. Most search engines give you the option of an advanced search, which gives you the opportunity to limit numbers.

The advanced search on Google gives you the options of using a string of words to search for sites that contain (1) all the words, (2) the exact phrase, (3) any of the words, (4) without certain words. It also allows you to specify the language of the site, the date range, where the words occur (e.g., the title), and the file format. Advanced searches on other search engines such as AltaVista and Yahoo! allow you to use the operators AND, OR, and NOT (see page 291).

Archives

An archive is traditionally a physical place where historical documents, such as manuscripts and letters, are stored. Recently the term has come to mean any collection of documents, typically preserved for educational purposes. All archives focus on preserving materials for posterity. Given the rapidly changing nature of the Web, electronic archives strive to preserve access to their materials. Here are four good electronic archive sites.

- **American Memory: Historical Collections for the National Digital Library** (lcweb2.loc.gov/amhome.html) Library of Congress site offering over 7 million digital items from more than a hundred historical collections.

- **A Chronology of U.S. Historical Documents** (www.law.ou.edu/hist) Sponsored by the University of Oklahoma College of Law, this site contains chronologically ordered primary sources ranging from the Federalist Papers to George W. Bush's 2001 inaugural address.

- **JSTOR: The Scholarly Journal Archive** (www.jstor.org) Electronic archive of the back issues of over a hundred scholarly journals, mainly in the humanities and social sciences fields.

- **University of Michigan Documents Center** (www.lib.umich.edu/govdocs) Huge repository of local, state, federal, foreign, and international government information. Includes extensive subject directory.

Listservs, bulletin boards, and discussion forums

The Internet allows you to access other people's opinions on thousands of topics. A listserv is an electronic discussion forum in which members exchange messages via email. Everyone who is subscribed to the list receives email sent to the list. Bulletin boards and newsgroups post messages on a Web site, often organized in discussion threads. Sometimes you must register to post messages, but you usually can read the messages without registering. Much of the conversation on these sites is undocumented and highly opinionated, but you can still gather important information about people's attitudes and get tips about other sources, which you can verify later.

Several Web sites catalog online discussion forums:

- Cyberfiber Newsgroups (**www.cyberfiber.com**)
- Tile.net (**tile.net/lists/**)
- Topica (**www.liszt.com**)

In addition, the Groups section of Google (**groups.google.com**) has an archive of 700 million messages that can be searched.

Many commercial and nonprofit Web sites also maintain their own discussion or "chat" forums. Depending on your topic, it might be useful to check out these forums. For example, if you wanted to research the psychological support services available for women who have had miscarriages, you might scan the discussion forum on **www.babycenter.com**, a commercial site that offers information and advice on all aspects of pregnancy and childrearing. Or, if you wanted to examine how the negative reports of SUV safety have affected SUV owners, you might look at the Town Hall discussion forum on **www.edmunds.com**, a popular car-buying advice site. Be aware, though, that people who are drawn to participate in the forums on these sites do not represent the general population.

Research profile: Keyword search for Title IX and college wrestling

All too often the obvious keywords turn up too much material in a search. Let's take an example. You may have heard that some people blame Title IX (the law that mandates gender equality for college and high school sports) for the rapid decline in the number of college wrestling programs. If you use AltaVista to search for "Title IX," you will get millions of matches. Clearly, this is too general to be an effective search term. Combining "Title IX" with "wrestling" gets the number down to the thousands, still too

many hits. Adding "Office of Civil Rights" (the agency that enforces Title IX) reduces the number of hits to 220, much better, but still a lot. If you are interested in a particular state, such as Iowa, you can bring the number down to 37, a manageable number (see Figure 17.3).

Research profile: A subject search for ADHD

Subject indexes offered by Web directories like Yahoo! often divide large topics into subcategories. These subcategories can be quite useful in helping you narrow your topic to one that is manageable. To use the subject search, ignore the keyword search box and select one of the subject fields listed below it. You will get a list of narrower topics within the field, from which you can select still narrower subject areas. A subject search, however, is limited by what is already indexed in a Web directory. Expect different Web directories to produce different results and the searches to be less comprehensive than keyword searches.

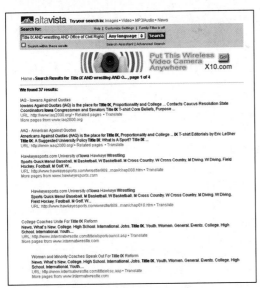

Figure 17.3. AltaVista advanced search

Computer Strategies

Tips for Web searches

HELP! MY SEARCH TURNED UP TOO MANY RESULTS.

- Try more specific search terms.
- Combine the words with AND.
- Use a phrase within quotation marks or specify "the exact phrase."
- Specify NOT for terms you are not interested in finding.
- Limit the search by a date range.

HELP! MY SEARCH TURNED UP TOO FEW RESULTS.

- Check your spelling.
- Try broader search terms.
- Use OR instead of AND, or specify "find any of the words."
- Try another index or search engine.

To start a subject search on ADHD using Yahoo!, begin by selecting the appropriate major category (see Figure 17.4, page 307). For ADHD, Health is the obvious choice. Under Diseases and Conditions is a long list, on which you can find Attention Deficit Disorder. Even before you examine individual Web sites, you can surmise that there is a wide range of opinion on treating ADHD (see Figure 17.5, page 308).

Keep track of Web research

Before the days of the Web and personal computers, most research projects involved taking notes on index cards. Every time you opened a book or journal article, you noted all the information you needed on 3 × 5 cards. While cumbersome, this method did have (and still does have) the advantage of allowing you to spread out the cards to get an overview of how the pieces of information you gathered might be connected. Today

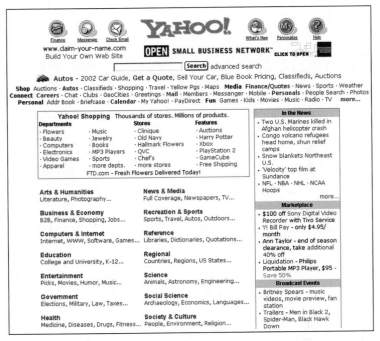

Figure 17.4. Yahoo! (www.yahoo.com)

many researchers copy information to computer files and make notes in those files. One advantage of this method is that you don't have to retype anything. If you choose to track your sources, you will benefit greatly in the long run if you create a system before you start and stick to it.

The Internet makes it easy to find many sources in a hurry—often too many. If you click away on the Web one day and a day later want to go back to a site you visited, locating it may be almost impossible. When you find a Web site you think will be worth consulting again, always click on **Add Bookmark** (on Netscape) or **Add Page** to Favorites (on Internet Explorer). That will allow you simply to open up your Bookmarks or Favorites list on your next visit and return to the site immediately.

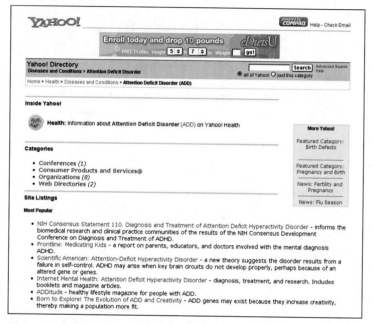

Figure 17.5. Yahoo! Health: Biology: Diseases and Conditions: Attention Deficit Disorder (http://dir.yahoo.com/Health/Diseases_and_Conditions/ Attention_Deficit_Disorder/)

EXERCISE 17.4 Return to the subject you researched for Exercise 17.3 and use two of the search engines listed in Section 17e to find Web sites related to your topic. After choosing the two or three that seem the most relevant and reliable, add two more paragraphs to the narrative you began in Exercise 17.3. In the first paragraph, retrace the steps of your Web research. How did you get started? What keywords did you use? What problems did you run into? How did you evaluate the sites you found? In the second paragraph, compare the information you found on the Web with the print information you've gathered. Does it add any new information or perspectives? How does the information you gathered from the Web compare in reliability and relevance to the print sources?

EXERCISE 17.5 A recent search on Google using the phrase *hate crimes* resulted in a list of the following URLs. Answer the questions that follow with the letter of the correct URL. Use only the clues provided by the URLs to answer the questions.

7 A. http://www.fbi.gov/publish/hatecrime.htm
5 B. http://www.ncjrs.org/hate_crimes/hate_crimes.html
2 C. http://unquietmind.com/hate_crime.html
3 D. http://caag.state.ca.us/civilrights/content/hatecrimes.htm
1 E. http://www.mtv.com/onair/ffyr/anatomy/index.jhtml
6 4 F. http://www.af.mil/news/Oct1999/
8 G. http://www.ou.edu/oupd/hate.htm

1. On which of the sites are you most likely to find advertisements?
2. Which site is most likely to feature the opinions of an individual?
3. Which site is most likely to provide you with information on hate crime legislation in California?
4. Which site probably contains out-of-date information?
5. Which site is probably funded by grants from the government or public donations?
6. Which site is maintained by the U.S. Air Force?
7. Which site provides information from the federal government?
8. Which site might give you information about the frequency of hate crimes on a college campus?

17f | START A WORKING BIBLIOGRAPHY

As you begin to collect your sources, make sure you get full bibliographic information for everything you might want to use in your project: articles, books, Web sites, and other materials. Decide which documentation style you will use. If your instructor does not tell you which style is appropriate, ask. (The major documentation styles—MLA, APA, Chicago, and CSE—are dealt with in detail in Chapters 21 through 25.)

Necessary bibliographic information

For books you will need, at minimum, the following information. This information can typically be found on the front and back of the title page:

- Author's name
- Title of the book
- Place of publication
- Name of publisher
- Date of publication

Computer Strategies

Organize your bookmarks and save them on a disk

Bookmarks on Netscape and Favorites on Explorer allow you to return quickly to Web sites you have visited. But when you do research and frequently add new bookmarks, you'll soon have a long list that makes it hard to find the particular Web site you want to return to. At this point you need to organize your bookmarks into folders:

1. Open the **Bookmarks** menu and select **Edit Bookmarks**. You'll see a list of your bookmarks.
2. Open the **File** menu and select **New Folder**.
3. Name the folder and drag the bookmarks into it.

You can also save your bookmark file on a disk by using the **Save As** command on the **File** menu. Then you can take your bookmarks with you and use them on more than one computer. This is very handy if you do some of your work in a campus computer lab and some at home. You also can have more than one list of bookmarks, but you can see only one list at a time.

You will also need the page numbers if you are quoting directly or referring to a specific passage, and the title and author of the individual chapter if your source is an edited book with contributions by several people.

For journals you will need

- Author's name
- Title of the article
- Title of the journal
- Volume and issue of the journal
- Date of the issue
- Page numbers of the article

For Web sites you will need

- Name of the page
- Author if listed
- Sponsoring organization if listed
- Date the site was posted
- Date you visited
- Complete URL

Compiling bibliographic information from Web pages can be challenging. The interconnected nature of the Web can make it hard to determine where a site begins and ends. Web pages often contain multiple headings and more idiosyncratic style markers (bold, italics, quotation marks) than books or articles, so they require more evaluation from you to determine how the parts fit together.

In general, as you research and develop a working bibliography, the rule of thumb is to write down more information, rather than less. You can always cull unnecessary information when it comes time to format your citations according to your chosen documentation style (APA, MLA, CMS, or CSE), but it is time-consuming to go back to sources to find missing bibliographic information.

Sample notecard

A notecard for Volume 1 of Grant's *Memoirs* would look like this:

> E
> 672
> G76
> 1885
> V.1
>
> Grant, Ulysses S. Personal Memoirs of U.S. Grant. Vol. 1. New York: Webster, 1885.

The same information should appear in any computer file you are generating to build your bibliography.

If you make notes on the source, be sure to distinguish your summary from material you quote directly. You will also need to identify by page number any quoted material. For example, you might want to quote directly the passage where Grant discusses how the war with Mexico was initiated.

> Grant explains how the war with Mexico started.
>
> p. 68 "We were sent to provoke a fight, but it was essential that Mexico should commence it.
>
> "Mexico showing no willingness to come to the Nueces to drive the invaders from her soil, it became necessary for the 'invaders' to approach to within a convenient distance to be struck. Accordingly, preparations were begun for moving the army to the Rio Grande, to a point near Matamoras. It was desirable to occupy a position near the largest
>
> / p. 69
> center of population possible to reach, without absolutely invading territory to which we set up no claim whatsoever."

Alternatives to copying from a source are cutting and pasting into a file (for online sources) or making photocopies (for a print source). Both methods ensure accuracy in copying sources, but in either case make sure you attach full bibliographic information to the file or photocopy. It's easy to get confused about where the material came from.

EXERCISE 17.6 Create a working bibliography using the sources you gathered and the narrative you wrote for Exercises 17.4 and 17.5. Make sure you have the complete bibliographical information for each source. Then write a brief description of the source, the information it contains, and how you intend to use it. Here is a sample entry in MLA format:

> Lee, J.J. *Ireland 1912-1985: Politics and Society*. New York: Cambridge UP, 1989.
>
> This is a comprehensive political history of Ireland. Lee is ambivalent about Irish politics and openly critical of overly romantic or overly emotional interpretations of Irish history. His work will be useful in balancing out the other sources I'm using.

Refer to Chapters 21 to 25 for MLA, APA, Chicago, and CSE formats. Ask your instructor which format you should use for this exercise. Hold onto this bibliography. You will be adding to it in a future exercise.

EXERCISE 17.7 Here are three note cards for a research paper on the battle of the Alamo. One is for a book, one is for a periodical, and one is for an Internet source. What information is missing from the cards or unclear?

1.

> Loewen, <u>Lies My Teacher Told Me</u>. The New Press, 1995.
>
> He says that slavery was a big cause in the Texas War (1835-36).
> "The freedom for which Davy Crockett, James Bowie and the rest fought at the Alamo was the freedom to own slaves!"

2.

Graham, Don. "Mission: Impossible; Dear Ron and John." *Texas Monthly*. February, 2002.

p. 84. This is a letter to the guys who want to make another movie about the Alamo. Graham gives them advice about how difficult it will be because the guys at the Alamo weren't really heroic, but no one in Texas wants to hear that. More recently, other groups have protested naming public schools after Travis (because he championed slavery and abandoned his wife and child) or Bowie (because he was a slave smuggler). In a politically correct age, the heroes of the Alamo are apt to come off as a bit unsavory.

3.

The Alamo. 31 January 2002. 9 February 2002.
<http://www.thealamo.org/>

While the facts surrounding the siege of the Alamo continue to be debated, there is no doubt about what the battle has come to symbolize. People worldwide continue to remember the Alamo as a heroic struggle against overwhelming odds—a place where men made the ultimate sacrifice for freedom. For this reason the Alamo remains hallowed ground and the Shrine of Texas Liberty.

Chapter 18
Evaluating Sources

You may have heard someone say that everything on the Web is either advertising or garbage. Certainly a great deal of what's on the Web is advertising, and since no one is in charge of what appears on the Web, there is also a great deal of misinformation and highly biased information. But the fact that a work is in print doesn't necessarily mean it is accurate or unbiased either. There are many examples of people witnessing the same event and then writing about it in ways so different that it's hard to believe they were in the same place at the same time. Similarly, there are many examples of respected scientists examining the same data and reaching different conclusions. Not everything you find in a library will be true, just as not everything you find on the Web is false. Becoming a successful researcher requires that you take a critical view of all sources you find. In short, you need to evaluate potential sources.

18a | DETERMINE THE RELEVANCE OF SOURCES

Whether you use print or online sources, a successful search will turn up many more items than you can expect to use in your final product. You have to make a series of decisions about what is important and relevant. Return to your research question and working thesis (Section 16d). You should be able to use your research question and working thesis to create guidelines for yourself about importance and relevance.

For example, if your research question asks why the Roman Empire declined rapidly at the end of the fourth and beginning of the fifth centuries AD, you may find older sources as valuable as new ones. Edward Gibbon's three-volume history, *Decline and Fall of the Roman Empire*, remains an important source, even though it was published in 1776 and 1781. But if you ask a research question about contemporary events—for example, to what extent online college courses have replaced courses held in traditional classrooms—you will need the most current information you can find. You also will want to find information on how many students were enrolled in distance education before the advent of the Internet. It is easy to get sidetracked. Likely you will find both glowing and grim predictions about the future of online education, but if your focus is on what has happened, not on what might happen, then these sources are not relevant.

Use these guidelines to determine the importance and relevance of your sources to your research question.

- Does your research question require you to consult primary or secondary sources?
- Does a source you have found address your question?
- Does a source support or disagree with your working thesis? (You should not throw out work that challenges your views.)
- Does a source add to your content in an important way?
- Is the material you have found persuasive?
- What indications of possible bias do you note in the source?

18b DETERMINE THE RELIABILITY OF PRINT SOURCES

Determining the reliability of sources is not a problem new to the Web. Print sources contain their share of biased, inaccurate, and misleading information. But because books are expensive to print and distribute, book publishers generally protect their investment by providing some level of editorial oversight. Print sources in libraries have an additional layer of oversight because someone has decided that a book or journal is worth purchasing and cataloging. Web sites, in contrast, can be put up and changed quickly, so information can be—and often is—posted thoughtlessly. No one filters information that is posted to the Web, and virtually anyone who has access to the Internet can generate it.

Traditional criteria for evaluating print sources

Over the years librarians have developed a set of criteria for evaluating print sources.

1. **Source.** Who published the book or article? Scholarly books and articles in scholarly journals are reviewed by experts in the field before they are published. They are generally more reliable than popular magazines and books, which tend to emphasize what is sensational or entertaining at the expense of accuracy and comprehensiveness. However, the appropriateness of your source depends very much on your topic. Even if a source is a well-researched piece in a reputable scholarly journal, it may not be an effective source for you if it is not relevant. Also, if your topic addresses an issue in contemporary popular culture, such as the outrageous television talk shows (*Jerry Springer* or *Jenny Jones*, for example) you will probably find the most relevant commentary in popular magazines and newspapers such as *Time* or *The New York Times Magazine.*

2. **Author.** Who wrote the book or article? What are the author's qualifications? How extensively has the author written about your chosen topic? As part of your evaluation of an author's claim to expertise, look at the "about the author" section which most books and some articles provide. Keep in mind, though, that these descriptions are usually slanted to present the author favorably because the publisher is interested in selling copies or validating the journal or magazine's credibility. It is probably worth your time to run a search on the author's name through your library's online catalog and through a Web search engine so you can see what other texts the author has written and how others regard the author's work.

3. **Timeliness.** How current is the source? If you are researching a fast-developing subject such as treating ADHD, then currency is very important. Currency might not be so important for an older subject, but even historical topics are subject to controversy or revision. For example, historians and the general public long viewed

Thomas Jefferson as a great man beyond reproach, but more recently, attention has focused on his slaveholding and extramarital relations, resulting in more qualified appraisals of the early president. Because new research or contemporary perspectives can bring an old subject under scrutiny, be aware of the publication date of your source.

4. **Evidence.** Where does the evidence come from—facts, interviews, observations, surveys, or experiments? Is the evidence adequate to support the author's claims? Statistics can be manipulated to serve the author's purpose, but a credible author will demonstrate where the numbers come from, as well as a range of evidence to support a central claim.

5. **Biases.** Can you detect particular biases of the author? How do the author's biases affect the interpretation offered? For topics that address politics or public policy, it is especially important to know the author's political leaning, if any. You can cite writers with strong political views, but you should be aware of the values and assumptions they bring to their writing. The question of bias applies not only to authors but also to publications. All publications reflect a philosophical, political, or religious point of view, some more obviously than others. Most people know that *The Nation* has a liberal bias and that *National Review* has a conservative bias. Do you know the political bias of your local or college newspaper? It may change over the years, depending on the editors. If you don't feel confident assessing publication bias, ask for help from your instructors and reference librarians.

6. **Advertising.** Is advertising a prominent part of the journal or newspaper? How might the ads affect what gets printed? Magazines that run feature articles but that also contain a large fashion component (*Glamour, GQ, Marie Claire*) devote more than half their pages to advertising. Regional magazines such as *Texas Monthly* and *Chicago*, which cover news and entertainment of a particular area, may habitually offer positive commentary on regional subject matter if the magazine's purpose is in part to promote the region.

In an unfortunate trend, some cover stories of some magazines may actually be paid for by a business or organization that wants press coverage.

Writing in the World

Checking sources as a test of reliability

Scholars and researchers often consult the sources used in a particular work as an additional test of reliability. They check quotations for accuracy and context to find out if the writer has used sources responsibly or has misquoted or quoted out of context to support his or her point. Examining how a writer has used and represented the sources gives you a perspective on how careful the writer is in making judgments.

18c DETERMINE THE RELIABILITY OF INTERNET SOURCES

All electronic search tools share a common problem: They often give you too many sources. Web search engines not only pull up thousands of hits, but these hits may vary dramatically in quality. No one regulates or checks information put on the Web, and it's no surprise that much of what is on the Web is highly opinionated or false.

Some Web sites are put up as jokes. Other Web sites are deliberately misleading. Many prominent Web sites draw imitators who want to cash in on the commercial visibility. The Web site for the Campaign for Tobacco-Free Kids (**www.tobaccofreekids.org**), for example, has an imitator (**www. smokefreekids.com**) that sells software for antismoking education. The .com URL is often a tip-off that a site has a profit motive, but other sites are more misleading. The government of Tunisia posted a site on human rights in that country, boasting of great progress. The URL suggests the site belongs to

Amnesty International (**www.amnesty-tunisia.org**). Nothing on the site specifically identifies it as the voice of the government (see Figure 18.1). In response to the Tunisian government site, Amnesty International put up a site (**www.amnesty.org/ailib/intcam/tunisia/**) that includes a point-by-point refutation of what it describes as "official Tunisian propaganda" (see Figure 18.2).

Always approach Web sites with an eye toward evaluating content. The Web site of the National Institute of Mental Health, turned up during an ADHD search, can be verified in several ways, beginning with the URL. Government agencies, for example, will always have **.gov** URLs (see Figure 18.3, page 322).

Other sites may have equally reliable information, but you should be prepared to look at them closely. For example, the Web site "The Fraud of Child Psychiatry" (see Figure 18.4, page 323) includes a list of MDs as au-

Figure 18.1. Government site on human rights in Tunisia
(**www.amnesty-tunisia.org**)

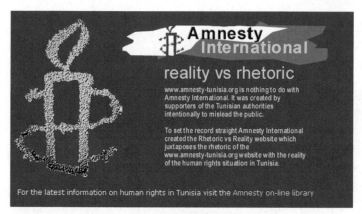

Figure 18.2. Amnesty International site on human rights in Tunisia
(**www.amnesty.org/ailib/intcam/tunisia/**)

thorities. But an examination of the site reveals that it is designed to sell books that take strong positions against psychotherapeutic drugs such as Prozac, Xanax, and Ritalin. The URL (**www.outlookcities.com/children/**), which has a **.com** suffix rather than **.edu**, **.gov**, or **.org**, tells you that this site is on a free or commercial server, not an institutional site. It could have been put up by anyone.

Extending print criteria for evaluating Web sources

The criteria for evaluating print sources can be applied to Web sources if the special circumstances of the Web are acknowledged. For example, when you find a Web page by using a search engine, often you go deep into a complex site without having any sense of the context for that page. To evaluate the credibility of the site, you would need to examine the home page, not just the specific page you get to first.

1. **Source.** Web sites sponsored by organizations often are as reliable as print sources. For example, major newspapers now make some or all of their reportage available on the Web. Look for the site's

NIMH
National Institute
of Mental Health

Attention Deficit Hyperactivity Disorder

Print version **pdf format**
(46 pages, 253KB)

Introduction
Understanding the Problem
What are the symptoms of ADHD?
Can any other conditions produce these
symptoms?
Can other disorders accompany ADHD?
What causes ADHD?
Getting Help
How is ADHD identified and diagnosed?
What are the educational options?
What treatments are available?
Sustaining Hope
Can ADHD be outgrown or cured?
What hope does research offer?
What are sources of information and support?

NIH Publication No. 96-3572
Printed 1994, Reprinted 1996

| Home | Mental Disorder Info |

Attention Deficit Hyperactivity Disorder

Imagine living in a fast-moving kaleidoscope, where sounds, images, and thoughts are constantly shifting. Feeling easily bored, yet helpless to keep your mind on tasks you need to complete. Distracted by unimportant sights and sounds, your mind drives you from one thought or activity to the next. Perhaps you are so wrapped up in a collage of thoughts and images that you don't notice when someone speaks to you.

For many people, this is what it's like to have Attention Deficit Hyperactivity Disorder, or ADHD. They may be unable to sit still, plan ahead, finish tasks, or be fully aware of what's going on around them. To their family, classmates or coworkers, they seem to exist in a whirlwind of disorganized or frenzied activity. Unexpectedly--on some days and in some situations--they seem fine, often leading others to think the person with ADHD can actually control these behaviors. As a result, the disorder can mar the person's relationships with others in addition to disrupting their daily life, consuming energy, and diminishing self-esteem.

ADHD, once called hyperkinesis or minimal brain dysfunction, is one of the most common mental disorders among children. It affects 3 to 5 percent of all children, perhaps as many as 2 million American children. Two to three times more boys than girls are affected. On the average, at least one child in every classroom in the United States needs help for the disorder. ADHD often continues into adolescence and adulthood, and can cause a lifetime of frustrated dreams and emotional pain.

Figure 18.3. Attention Deficit Hyperactivity Disorder site, National Institute of Mental Health (**www.nimh.nih.gov/publicat/adhd.htm**)

ownership in the Web address. If a Web site doesn't indicate ownership, then you have to make judgments about who put it up and why. The suffix can offer clues: **.org** is used by organizations, including nonprofits, **.gov** by government bodies, and **.edu** by educational institutions, generally colleges and universities.

The Fraud of Child Psychiatry, ADD/ADHD, Attention Deficit Disorder, and Ritalin.

"...This elementary fact makes the child psychiatrist one of the most dangerous enemies not only of children, but also of adults who care for the two precious and most vulnerable things in life - children and liberty. Child psychology and child psychiatry cannot be reformed. They must be abolished." - Thomas Szasz M.D., *Cruel Compassion*.

"The pediatrician's wanton prescription of powerful drugs indoctrinates children from birth with the philosophy of 'a pill for every ill'."... "Doctors are directly responsible for hooking millions of people on prescription drugs. They are also indirectly responsible for the plight of millions more who turn to illegal drugs because they were taught at an early age that drugs can cure anything - including psychological and emotional conditions - that ails them. " - Robert S. Mendelsohn, M.D., *How to Raise a Healthy Child...In Spite of Your Doctor*.

Fred A. Baughman, M.D. - Immunize Your Child Against ADD

Ann B. Tracy, PhD – Psychiatric Drugs

Fred A. Baughman, M.D. - What You Should Know About ADD

If You Need Help

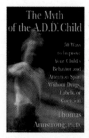 The Myth of the A.D.D. Child, by Thomas Armstrong, Ph.D.

The Myth of the A.D.D. Child exposes the mislabeling of millions of children as A.D.D./ A.D.H.D., and the use of powerful mind-altering drugs such as Ritalin in treating children's hyperactivity. Not long ago, children who behaved in certain ways were called "bundles of energy", "daydreamers," or "fireballs." Now they're considered "hyperactive," "distractible," or "impulsive"-victims of the ubiquitous Attention Deficit Disorder. Tragically, such labeling can follow a child through life. Worse, the mind-altering drugs prescribed for A.D.D./A.D.H.D. are unnecessary-and they are harmful.

Figure 18.4. Fraud of Child Psychiatry site (www.outlookcities.com/children/)

2. **Author.** Often Web sites give no information about their authors other than an email address, if that. In such cases it is difficult or impossible to determine the author's qualifications.

3. **Timeliness.** Many Web pages do not list when they were last updated; thus you cannot determine their currency. Furthermore,

there are thousands of deserted ghost sites on the Web—sites that the owners have abandoned but search engines still turn up.

4. **Evidence.** The accuracy of any evidence found on the Web is often hard to verify. The most reliable information on the Web stands up to the tests of print evaluation, with clear indication of the sponsoring organization. Any factual information should be supported by indicating where the information came from. Reliable Web sites that offer information will list their sources.

5. **Biases.** Many Web sites announce their viewpoint on controversial issues, but others conceal their attitude with a reasonable tone and seemingly factual evidence such as statistics. Citations and bibliographies do not ensure that a site is reliable. Look carefully at the links and sources cited.

6. **Advertising.** Many Web sites are infomercials aimed at getting you to buy a product or service. While they might contain useful information, they are no more trustworthy than other forms of advertising.

Other Internet sources

Other Internet sources, such as online newsgroups, can give you useful ideas but are generally not considered authoritative. Email communication from an expert in the field might be considered an authoritative source, but personal emails are generally not considered worthy of inclusion in a research paper. Remember that a key reason to cite sources is so other researchers can read and evaluate the sources you used.

Computer Strategies

A checklist for evaluating Web sources

- **What organization sponsors or pays for the Web site?** If the name of the organization is not given, determine what you can from the URL. Try cutting off the URL from right to left a step at a time.

- **Is the author of the Web site identified?** Can you get in touch with the author? Be cautious of information on an anonymous site.
- **Are the author's credentials listed on the Web site?** If the credentials are listed, are they relevant to the subject?
- **Is the information on the Web site current?** Can you discover when the Web site was last updated?
- **Are references provided for information given on the site?** References give you one way to check the validity of the information on the site.
- **Are there links to additional information?** Do the links work? Is the linked information reliable?
- **Does the Web site present balanced information or does it chiefly present one point of view?** Many Web sites appear to be balanced but neglect other points of view.
- **Is the Web site an advertisement for a product or service?** Many so-called informative Web sites are trying to sell you something.

EXERCISE 18.1 Return to the working bibliography you wrote for Exercise 17.6. Using the advice given in Chapter 18, evaluate your sources for relevance and reliability. Do any of your sources pose potential problems? Are there still ways you can use them in your argument? For example, a mention of an author's bias might be relevant to a point you wish to make, or a discussion of why a source is questionable might help you either to clarify a particular issue or to illuminate a problem within current discussions of the topic. Add this information to your working bibliography.

EXERCISE 18.2 Here is a working bibliography on hate crimes. Evaluate these sources as if you would be using them for a research paper dealing with hate crime legislation in Texas. Answer these two questions for each:

- How relevant is this source (very, somewhat, slightly, not at all)? Why?
- How reliable is this source (very, somewhat, slightly, not at all)? Look at the evidence used, the author or organization responsible for the source,

the timeliness of the information presented, the potential for bias, and whether or not the author or organization has a commercial motive.

1. United States. Federal Bureau of Investigation. Hate Crime Statistics, 2000. 2002. 17 Sept. 2002. <http://www.fbi.gov/ucr/cius_00/hate00.pdf>. Government site distributing hate crime statistics. The most recent statistics available are for 2000.

2. "Governor of Texas Signs New Hate Crime Bill." Jet 28 May 2001: 16.
   Short article (262 words) about Governor Perry signing the James Byrd Jr. Hate Crime Act.

3. Spong, John. "The Hate Debate." Texas Monthly April 2001: 64. Article dealing specifically with the controversy over hate crime legislation in Texas.

4. Levin, Jack, and Jack McDevitt. Hate Crimes: The Rising Tide of Bigotry and Bloodshed. Boulder, CO: Westview, 2001.
   Scholarly study of the causes of the recent increase in hate crimes in the U.S.

5. National Criminal Justice Referral Service. In the Spotlight: Hate Crimes. 2001. 17 Sept. 2002. <http://www.ncjrs.org/hate_crimes/hate_crimes.html>.
   Site for a nonprofit organization affiliated with the Department of Justice. The site is a clearinghouse for various forms of information about hate crimes (statistics, legal information, reports, links to other sites).

6. Ratcliffe, R. G. "Number of Hate Crimes up 7% in Texas Last Year." The Houston Chronicle 20 July 2001: A35.
   Article about the rise in racially motivated attacks in Texas in 2001.

Chapter 19
Avoiding Plagiarism When Using Sources

From a student's point of view, documenting sources can seem like learning Latin—something obscure and complicated that has little use in daily life. You don't see footnotes or lists of works cited in magazines and newspapers, so you may wonder why they are so important in college writing. Careful documentation of sources, however, is essential to developing knowledge and allows scholars and researchers to build on the work of other scholars and researchers. Large bodies of knowledge have accumulated over many years that allow a scholar to reinterpret the fall of the Roman Empire or a researcher to advance a new hypothesis about how moving plates shape the surface of the earth.

19a   THE PURPOSE OF DOCUMENTING SOURCES

Knowledge building

Knowledge is built through ongoing conversations that take place in writing as well as talking. The practice of citing sources provides a disciplinary map, indicating the conversation in which the writer is participating and how that writer responds to what has been said before. Often knowledge building does not move in a straight line but reflects wrong turns and backtracking. Tracing these movements would be extremely difficult if writers did not acknowledge their sources. Accurate referencing of sources allows you or any reader the opportunity to consult those sources. For example, historians who write about the distant past must rely on different kinds of evidence, including letters, records, public documents, newspaper articles, legal records, and other material from that time; they also take into account the work of contemporary scholars. Other historians working in the same area must be able to find and read these primary sources to assess the accuracy of the interpretation. The system of citing sources requires that summaries and paraphrases be accurate, any strings of words taken from the original be set off in quotation marks, and full information be provided to locate the source.

Fairness

Another basic issue is fairness. If historians draw on the interpretations of other historians, they should give those historians credit. In this respect citing sources builds community with writers of both the present and the past. When you begin to read the published research in an academic discipline, your awareness of that community takes shape. But the issue of fairness also is part of the much larger issues of intellectual property and scholastic honesty—issues that need to be considered carefully when you use sources.

19b | INTELLECTUAL PROPERTY AND SCHOLASTIC HONESTY

Intellectual property and copyright

The concepts of intellectual property and copyright date back to the royal patent grants that accompanied the development of printing in the late 1400s, when monarchs sought to control the production of printed books. The modern concept of copyright took shape in the 1700s. In 1710, the Statute of Anne was passed in England, giving authors the rights to what they produced for a limited duration; by the end of the century other countries, including the United States, had passed laws to protect written intellectual property. With the development of new technologies in the twentieth century, these rights have been extended to music, recordings, photographs, films, radio and television broadcasts, computer software, and many other kinds of likenesses.

Plagiarism

Plagiarism is usually associated with writing, but different kinds of work can be lifted and passed off as one's own. Plagiarism means claiming credit for someone else's intellectual work no matter whether it's to make money or get a better grade. And it's not strictly a question of intent. Reputable authors have gotten into trouble through carelessness by taking notes from published sources without acknowledging those sources. A number of famous people have had their reputations tarnished by accusations of plagiarism, and several prominent journalists have lost their jobs and careers for copying the work of other writers and passing it off as their own.

The Internet likely has increased instances of plagiarism in college. Some students view the Internet as a big free buffet where they can grab anything, paste it in a file, and submit it as their own work. Cut-and-paste plagiarism is easy to do, but instructors quickly recognize when a student's writing style changes in mid-essay. It's also easy to use the Internet to trace sources stolen off the Internet.

Writing in the World

The consequences of plagiarism

Most colleges and universities consider plagiarism a serious form of cheating that deserves severe penalties, including failure of a course for first-time offenders and expulsion for those who are caught cheating more than once. Colleges have to take a strong stance against plagiarism. They attempt to make the playing field level for all students; if some get by without doing the required work, it affects every other student. Professional schools and employers look down on graduates of schools that have a reputation for tolerating scholastic dishonesty. Students who blatantly plagiarize often do not realize how much harm they might do to themselves down the road. Employers do not want to hire students who have been caught cheating.

Businesses also have to take a hard line on plagiarism. In many professions, the product is a written document. If that document turns out to be plagiarized, the reputation of the entire company is tarnished.

Copyright, plagiarism, and the Web

The issues of intellectual property and copyright concerning the Web are far from settled. Copyright law is designed to protect the financial interests of the copyright holder; thus if you use a single image from a site and your motive is not for profit, the copyright owner has to establish that your use of that image caused him or her financial harm (see the Fair Use Test at **www.utsystem.edu/ogc/intellectualproperty/copypol2.htm**). It's unlikely that you will be sued for grabbing an image from another site. Nonetheless, whether or not you get caught, taking someone else's work without acknowledgment is plagiarism. It's only fair to give other people credit for the work they have done. Unless a site is clearly labeled for public use, ask permission when you take something from another site, and always give credit to the source.

EXERCISE 19.1 Decide which of the following are instances of plagiarism or scholastic dishonesty and which are not.

1. You cut and paste information from a Web site into your notes for an economics paper that is due tomorrow. Unfortunately, you lose track of what information you quoted directly, what you paraphrased, and what you summarized. You do your best to sort out which ideas are yours and which came from the Web site, but you don't have time to check everything before your paper is due.

2. A paper for a required government course is due on the same day that a really important paper for a core class in your major is due. You borrow a paper from your roommate, but you rewrite it in your own words and you hand it in.

3. A passage in your English paper is a paraphrase of a lecture your history instructor gave. Your English instructor did not require you to use any outside sources, so you do not create a works-cited sheet for the paper.

4. You are in a real crunch for time, so your friend, an English major, edits your paper. She rewrites a few awkward sentences and corrects a few of your facts. You type in her changes before turning in the paper.

5. You scan a picture from the cover of a CD to put on your personal Web site. Everyone knows where the picture came from, so you don't cite the source.

19c | AVOID PLAGIARISM

You know that copying someone else's paper word for word or taking an article off the Internet and turning it in as yours is plagiarism. That's plain stealing, and people who take that risk should know that the punishment can be severe. But if plagiarism also means using the ideas, melodies, or images of someone else without acknowledging them, then the concept is much broader and more difficult to define. If you think about it, you might wonder whether it is possible to avoid plagiarizing in the strictest sense when you write. How many phrases and ideas are truly original? And how can you know where every idea comes from?

What you don't have to document

Fortunately, common sense governs issues of academic plagiarism. The standards of documentation are not so strict that the source of every fact you cite must be acknowledged. Suppose you are writing about the causes of maritime disasters and you want to know how many people drowned when the *Titanic* sank on the early morning of April 15, 1912. You check the *Britannica Online* Web site and find that the death toll was around 1,500. Since this fact is available in many reference works, you would not need to cite *Britannica Online* as the source.

But let's say you want to challenge the version of the sinking offered in the 1998 movie *Titanic,* which repeats the usual explanation that the *Titanic* sideswiped an iceberg, ripping a long gash along the hull that caused the ship to go down. Suppose that, in your reading, you discover that a September 1985 exploration of the wreck by an unmanned submersible did not find the long gash previously thought to have sunk the ship. The evidence instead suggested that the force of the collision with the iceberg broke the seams in the hull, allowing water to flood the ship's watertight compartments. You would need to cite the source of your information for this alternative version of the *Titanic*'s demise.

What you do have to document

For facts that are not easily found in general reference works, statements of opinion, and arguable claims, you should cite the source. You should also cite the sources of statistics, research findings, examples, graphs, charts, and

Common Errors

Plagiarism in college writing

If you find any of the following problems in your academic writing, it is likely you are plagiarizing someone else's work. Because plagiarism is usually inadvertent, it is especially important that you understand what constitutes using sources responsibly.

1. **Missing attribution.** The author of a quotation has not been identified. A lead-in or signal phrase that provides attribution to the source is not used, and no author is identified in the citation.
2. **Missing quotation marks.** Quotation marks do not appear around material quoted directly from a source.
3. **Inadequate citation.** No page number is given to show where in the source the quotation, paraphrase, or summary is drawn from.
4. **Paraphrase relies too heavily on the source.** Either the wording or sentence structure of a paraphrase follows the source too closely.
5. **Distortion of meaning.** A paraphrase or summary distorts the meaning of the source, or a quotation is taken out of context, resulting in a change of meaning.
6. **Missing Works Cited entry.** The Works Cited page does not include all the works cited in the paper.
7. **Inadequate citation of images.** A figure or photo appears with no label, number, caption, or citation to indicate the source of the image. If material includes a summary of data from a visual source, no attribution or citation is given for the graph being summarized.

 For step-by-step discussion, examples, and practice, go to **www.ablongman.com/faigley009.**

illustrations. As a reader you should be skeptical about statistics and research findings when the source is not mentioned. When a writer does not cite the sources of statistics and research findings, there is no way of knowing how reliable the sources are or whether the writer is making them up. From the writer's perspective careful citing of sources lends credibility. If you take your statistics from a generally trusted source, your readers are more likely to trust your conclusions. When in doubt, always document the source.

Be careful when taking notes and copying material online

The best way to avoid unintentional plagiarism is to take care to distinguish source words from your own words. Don't mix words from the source with your own words. If you copy anything from a source when taking notes, you need to place those words in quotation marks and note the page number(s) where those words appear (see Section 17f). You should also write down all the information you need for a list of works cited or a list of references (see Chapters 21, 23, 24, and 25).

If you copy words from an online source, you need to take special care to note the source. You could easily copy online material and later not be able to find where it came from. Instead of cutting and pasting words straight from an online document, print out the entire source so you can refer to it later. Having photocopies of printed sources also allows you to double-check later that you haven't used words from the source by mistake and that any words you quote are accurate.

EXERCISE 19.2 Which of the following pieces of information require a citation and which do not?

1. Elvis Presley was born in Tupelo, Mississippi, on January 8, 1935.
2. Peter Guralnick wrote *Last Train to Memphis*, which chronicles Elvis's youth in Tupelo, Mississippi, and Memphis, Tennessee.
3. In this book, Guralnick tries to present as complete a picture as possible of Elvis as a teenager, and not as the superstar he was to become.
4. Frank Sinatra thought that Elvis's music inspired destructive behavior in young people.

5. Critics denounce Elvis for stealing the style, rhythms, and, in some cases, the actual lyrics of black music, but many black artists, like Jackie Wilson, felt that this was not the case.

6. Graceland, Elvis Presley's former home, is in Memphis.

7. On December 31, 1956, the *Wall Street Journal* reported that sales of Elvis Presley memorabilia had grossed over $22 million in the past few months.

8. Elvis's mother, Gladys, died on August 14, 1958.

9. Friends and family say Elvis and his mother shared a special bond that made others, including Elvis's father Vernon, feel like outsiders.

10. Elvis Presley died at Graceland on August 16, 1977.

19d | QUOTE SOURCES WITHOUT PLAGIARIZING

Most people who get into plagiarism trouble lift words from a source and use them without quotation marks. Where the line is drawn is easiest to illustrate with an example. In the following passage, Steven Johnson takes sharp issue with the metaphor of surfing applied to the Web:

> The concept of "surfing" does a terrible injustice to what it means to navigate around the Web. . . . What makes the idea of cybersurf so infuriating is the implicit connection drawn to television. Web surfing, after all, is a derivation of channel surfing—the term thrust upon the world by the rise of remote controls and cable panoply in the mid-eighties. . . . Applied to the boob tube, of course, the term was not altogether inappropriate. Surfing at least implied that channel-hopping was more dynamic, more involved, than the old routine of passive consumption. Just as a real-world surfer's enjoyment depended on the waves delivered up by the ocean, the channel surfer was at the mercy of the programmers and network executives. The analogy took off because it worked well in the one-to-many system of cable TV, where your navigational options were limited to the available channels.
>
> But when the term crossed over to the bustling new world of the Web, it lost a great deal of precision. . . . Web surfing and channel surfing are genuinely different pursuits; to imagine them as

equivalents is to ignore the defining characteristics of each medium. Or at least that's what happens in theory. In practice, the Web takes on the greater burden. The television imagery casts the online surfer in the random, anesthetic shadow of TV programming, roaming from site to site like a CD player set on shuffle play. But what makes the online world so revolutionary is the fact that there *are* connections between each stop on a Web itinerant's journey. The links that join those various destinations are links of association, not randomness. A channel surfer hops back and forth between different channels because she's bored. A Web surfer clicks on a link because she's interested.

> —Johnson, Steven. *Interface Culture: How New Technology Transforms the Way We Create and Communicate.* New York: Harper, 1997. 107-09.

If you were writing a paper or putting up a Web site that concerned Web surfing, you might want to mention the distinction that Johnson makes between channel surfing and surfing on the Web. Your options are to paraphrase the source or to quote it directly.

If you quote directly, you must place quotation marks around all words you take from the original:

> One observer marks this contrast: "A channel surfer hops back and forth between different channels because she's bored. A Web surfer clicks on a link because she's interested" (Johnson 109).

Notice that the quotation is introduced and not just dropped in. This example follows Modern Language Association (MLA) style, where the citation goes outside the quotation marks but before the final period. In MLA style, source references are made according to the author's last name, which refers you to the full citation in the works-cited list at the end. Following the author's name is the page number where the quotation can be located. (Notice also that there is no comma after the name.) If you want to cite a newspaper article without a byline or another anonymous source, you use the first important word or two of the title to make the reference. This system allows you to find the reference easily in the list of works cited, since the list is arranged alphabetically by author and title.

If the author's name appears in the sentence, cite only the page number, in parentheses:

> According to Steven Johnson, "A channel surfer hops back and forth between different channels because she's bored. A Web surfer clicks on a link because she's interested" (109).

If you want to quote material that is already quoted in your source, use single quotes for that material:

> Steven Johnson uses the metaphor of a Gothic cathedral to describe a computer interface: " 'The principle of the Gothic architecture,' Coleridge once said, 'is infinity made imaginable.' The same could be said for the modern interface" (42).

EXERCISE 19.3 Using the following excerpts from two sources and an essay that incorporates quotations from both, rewrite the essay to correct punctuation and citation errors.

Source 1: Brice, Chris. "Literary Illusion?" <u>The Advertiser.</u> 9 Feb. 2002: M20.

American author Armistead Maupin's latest novel [*The Night Listener*] is tangled up in the divide between truth and fiction, and not even he can be sure which is which. It centers around the bizarre story of Anthony Godby Johnson, the boy author of a best-selling book who was once described as "the bravest teen in America." [. . .]

[. . .] Maupin is just one of many thousands of people who have been moved by Tony Johnson's 1993 memoir, *A Rock and a Hard Place,* published when Johnson was just 15 years old, and telling of a life of horrific physical and sexual abuse. [. . .]

[. . .] Maupin now says *The Night Listener* was not entirely "a fanciful concoction on the part of a novelist with far too vivid imagination," but was drawn from his own experiences of the "real-life Hitchcockian mystery of Tony Johnson."

Source 2: Friend, Tad. "Virtual Love." The New Yorker. 26 Nov. 2001.

[. . .] Tony has become a symbol of modern victimhood, his body torn apart by the most appalling end-of-the millennium traumas—child abuse and AIDS. (88) [. . .]

[. . .]When I visited Maupin again recently, I noticed that he had removed Tony's picture from his living room. But he told me, "Tony's still more real to me than many people who demonstrably do exist. I wrote the ending of the book the way I'd like it to be in life, because I'd have great trouble killing that child in my head." (99)

Essay

Tony Johnson, child survivor of abuse and AIDS as well as the author of the best-selling book *A Rock and a Hard Place*, has a problem. Many of his celebrity friends don't believe he exists. One of the most outspoken of these friends is Armistead Maupin, who is one of many thousands of people who have been moved by Tony Johnson's 1993 memoir. But why have so many people been taken in by this boy author? According to Friend, "Tony has become a symbol of modern victimhood, his body torn apart by the most appalling end-of-the millennium traumas—child abuse and AIDS." No one, however, has ever met Tony Johnson.

After a series of events that caused him to doubt Tony's existence, Maupin wrote the novel, *The Night Listener*, in which the lives of characters Donna and Pete bear a striking resemblance to that of Tony and his adopted mother, Vicki Johnson. The novel was published in 2000 and was met with instant controversy. Maupin, however, afraid that Tony still might actually exist, insisted that the story was "a fanciful concoction on the part of a novelist with far too vivid imagination." ("Literary" 20) Later, he admitted that the book was inspired by his own experiences as a character in the real-life Hitchcockian mystery of Tony Johnson (Friend 20). However, the novel and its controversial story line do not signify that Maupin bears Tony, whoever or whatever he may be, any ill will. Quite the contrary:

> When I visited Maupin again recently, I noticed that he had removed Tony's picture from his living room. But he told me, "Tony's still more real to me than many people who demonstrably do exist. I wrote the ending of the book the way I'd like it to be in life, because I'd have great trouble killing that child in my head.

To this day, no one really knows if Tony Johnson ever existed.

19e SUMMARIZE AND PARAPHRASE SOURCES WITHOUT PLAGIARIZING

Summarize

When you summarize, you state the major ideas of an entire source or part of a source in a paragraph or perhaps even a sentence. The key is to put the summary in your own words. If you use words from the source (see pages 334–335), you have to put those words in quotation marks.

PLAGIARIZED

Steven Johnson argues in *Interface Culture* that the concept of "surfing" is misapplied to the Internet because channel surfers hop back and forth between different channels because they're bored, but Web surfers click on links because they're interested. [Most of the words are lifted directly from the original.]

ACCEPTABLE SUMMARY

Steven Johnson argues in *Interface Culture* that the concept of "surfing" is misapplied to the Internet because users of the Web consciously choose to link to other sites while television viewers mindlessly flip through the channels until something catches their attention.

Paraphrase

When you paraphrase, you represent the idea of the source in your own words at about the same length as the original. You still need to include the reference to the source of the idea. The following example illustrates what is not an acceptable paraphrase.

PLAGIARIZED

Steven Johnson argues that the concept of "surfing" does a terrible injustice to what it means to navigate around the Web. What makes the idea of Web surfing infuriating is the association with television. Surfing is not a bad metaphor for channel hopping, but it doesn't fit what people do on the Web. Web surfing and channel surfing are truly different activities; to imagine them as the same is to ignore their defining characteristics. A channel surfer skips around because she's bored while a Web surfer clicks on a link because she's interested (107-09).

Even though the source is listed, this paraphrase is unacceptable. Too many of the words in the original are used directly here, including much or all of entire sentences. When a string of words is lifted from a source and inserted without quotation marks, the passage is plagiarized. Changing a few words in a sentence is not a paraphrase. Compare these two sentences:

SOURCE

Web surfing and channel surfing are genuinely different pursuits; to imagine them as equivalents is to ignore the defining characteristics of each medium.

UNACCEPTABLE PARAPHRASE

Web surfing and channel surfing are truly different activities; to imagine them as the same is to ignore their defining characteristics.

The paraphrase takes the structure of the original sentence and substitutes a few words. It is much too similar to the original.

A true paraphrase represents an entire rewriting of the idea from the source.

ACCEPTABLE PARAPHRASE

Steven Johnson argues that "surfing" is a misleading term for describing how people navigate on the Web. He allows that "surfing" is appropriate for clicking across television channels because the viewer has to interact with what the networks and cable companies provide, just as the surfer has to interact with what the ocean provides. Web surfing, according to Johnson, operates at much greater depth and with much more consciousness of purpose. Web surfers actively follow links to make connections (107-09).

Even though there are a few words from the original in this paraphrase, such as *navigate* and *connections*, these sentences are original in structure and wording while accurately conveying the meaning of the source.

EXERCISE 19.4 Two sources dealing with Abraham Lincoln and his association in American pop culture with the log cabin are excerpted here. Decide whether the numbered paraphrases and summaries of the two sources are correct. If not, rewrite to eliminate problems.

Source 1: "Lincoln, Abraham," Microsoft Encarta Encyclopedia 99. 1993-1998. Microsoft Corporation.

In December 1808 the Lincolns moved to a 141-hectare (348-acre) farm on the south fork of Nolin Creek near what is now Hodgenville, Kentucky. On February 12, 1809, in a log cabin that Thomas Lincoln had built, a son, Abraham, was born. Later the Lincolns had a second son who died in infancy. [. . .]

In the winter of 1816 the Lincolns took their meager possessions, ferried across the Ohio River, and settled near Pigeon Creek, close to what is now Gentryville, Indiana. Because it was winter, Thomas Lincoln immediately built a crude, three-sided shelter that served as home until he could build a log cabin. A fire at the open end of the shelter kept the family warm. At this time southern Indiana was a heavily forested wilderness. Lincoln described it as a "wild region, with many bears and other wild animals in the woods." [. . .]

Source 2: Loewen, James W. <u>Lies My Teacher Told Me:</u> <u>Everything Your American History Textbook Got Wrong.</u> New York: The New Press, 1995. 178.

The strange career of the log cabin in which Abraham Lincoln was born symbolizes in a way what textbooks have done to Lincoln. The actual cabin fell into disrepair probably before Lincoln became president. According to research by D. T. Pitcaithley, the new cabin, a hoax built in 1894, was leased to two amusement park owners, went to Coney Island, where it got commingled with the birthplace cabin of Jefferson Davis (another hoax), and was finally shrunk to fit inside a marble pantheon in Kentucky, where, re-assembled, it still stands. The cabin also became a children's toy: Lincoln Logs, invented by Frank Lloyd Wright's son John in 1920, came with instructions on how to build both Lincoln's log cabin and Uncle Tom's cabin! The cabin still makes its archetypal appearance in our textbooks, signifying the rags-to-riches legend of Abraham Lincoln's upward mobility. No wonder one college student could only say of him, in a much-repeated blooper, "He was born in a log cabin which he built with his own hands."

1. The description the encyclopedia gives of Lincoln's childhood—the hard work, the honest poverty, and the succession of hand-hewn log cabins—is the story we are taught as schoolchildren.

2. James Loewen, in his book *Lies My Teacher Told Me*, focuses instead on the career of the log cabin Lincoln grew up in. He argues that the cabin's story symbolizes in some way what the textbooks students read have done to Lincoln (178).

3. It is interesting how the depiction of Lincoln's life in the *Encarta* encyclopedia is so focused on the domestic details. We can almost see the Lincoln family, huddled in the corner of their three-sided shelter, a small fire burning, as they wait for Father to build yet another log cabin.

4. According to Loewen, however, Lincoln's cabin has led a comparatively unhealthy life. In his research he found that a new "Lincoln" cabin, a hoax built in 1894, was leased to two amusement park owners, went to

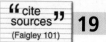
Coney Island, where it got commingled with the birthplace cabin of Jefferson Davis. The cabin, shrunk down to fit inside a marble pantheon, now stands in Kentucky (178). Has the legend of Lincoln suffered the same fate?

EXERCISE 19.5 Using the two sources from Exercise 19.4, write one or two paragraphs in which you correctly paraphrase, quote, and summarize both of the sources. You can either continue the discussion started in Exercise 19.4 or choose another way to bring the information together. Do not spend too much time thinking about what to write, however; focus instead on using the sources correctly.

Chapter 20

Writing the Research Project

Once you've completed the research portion of a research paper, it is time to report on your findings. Research writing may seem formidable at first, but if you've kept your materials organized during the research phase, you can complete the writing phase on schedule with excellent results.

20a | REVIEW YOUR GOALS AND THESIS

Before you begin writing your paper, you should review the assignment and your goals (see Chapter 16). Your review of the assignment will remind you of your purpose (analysis, review, survey, evaluation, argument), your potential readers, your stance on your subject, and the length and scope you should aim for.

By now you should have formulated a working thesis, which will be the focus of your paper. You should also have located, read, evaluated, and taken notes on enough source material to write your paper (see Chapters 17, 18, and 19). At this stage in the writing process, your working thesis will probably be somewhat rough and may change as you write your draft, but having a general idea of what you hope to argue will help keep your paper focused.

EXERCISE 20.1 Go back to the working thesis you developed in Exercise 16.3. After doing research on this topic for the exercises in Chapter 17, you probably changed your thesis, and perhaps even your topic and research questions. Revise your topic, research questions, and thesis to reflect these changes.

20b | PLAN YOUR ORGANIZATION

After you have drafted a thesis, you should look back over your notes and determine how to group the ideas you researched. Decide what your major points will be, and how those points support your thesis. Group your research findings so that they match up with your major points.

Now it is time to create a working outline. Always include your thesis at the top of your outline as a guiding light. Some writers create formal outlines with roman numerals and the like; others compose the headings for the paragraphs of their paper and use them to guide their draft; still others may start writing and then determine how they will organize their draft when they have a few paragraphs written. Experiment and decide which method works best for you.

EXERCISE 20.2 Using the advice given in Section 3d and in Chapter 20, develop an outline for your research paper (Exercise 20.1). Remember that your outline does not have to be formal; use a system that works best for you.

20c | INCORPORATE QUOTATIONS, SUMMARIES, AND PARAPHRASES EFFECTIVELY

The purpose of using sources is to *support* what you have to say, not to say it for you. Next to plagiarism, the worst mistake you can make with sources is to string together a series of long quotations. This strategy leaves your readers wondering whether you have anything to say. Relying too much on quotations from others also makes for a bumpy read.

When to quote and when to paraphrase

The general rule in deciding when to include direct quotations and when to paraphrase lies in the importance of the original wording. If you want to refer to an idea or fact and the original wording is not critical, make the point in your own words. Save direct quotations for language that is memorable or gives the character of the source.

Suppose you are writing about the effects of the Internet on literacy, and you want to acknowledge those who maintain that the effects are largely negative. You find books by Sven Birkerts (*The Gutenberg Elegies: The Fate of Reading in an Electronic Age*), Mark Slouka (*War of the Worlds: Cyberspace and the High-Tech Assault on Reality*), and Clifford Stoll (*Silicon Snake Oil*) that argue the Internet is a disorganized wasteland that discourages people from thinking for themselves. You also find a book by Jay David Bolter (*The Writing Space: The Computer, Hypertext and the History of Writing*), someone more sympathetic to digital technologies who also sees them as a threat to the power of prose. You could paraphrase each argument, but you realize that there are common themes that run through these books, so you decide to summarize these sources by making a list of the themes expressed. You want to use a direct quote from Bolter that articulates the themes. You might write:

> The rapid spread of the Internet has produced many critics, such as Sven Birkerts, Mark Slouka, and Clifford Stoll, who all complain about how the Internet is destroying the foundations of literacy—that critical thinking and reflection, a sense of order, logical relations in texts, depth of analysis, trails of sources, and the reform mission of public discourse are going to be lost. Even those who take a more balanced view fear the multimedia capability of the Web will undermine the power of prose. Jay David Bolter writes,
>
> > The new media [. . .] threaten to drain contemporary prose of its rhetorical possibilities. Popular prose responds with a desire to emulate computer graphics. Academic and other specialized forms respond by a retreat into jargon or willful anachronism. (270)
>
> The coming of the Web, however, does not have to be viewed as a loss to literacy. Images and words have long

coexisted on the printed page and in manuscripts, but relatively
few people possessed the resources to exploit the rhetorical potential of images combined with words.

You would include all four books in your works-cited list.

Block quotations

If a direct quotation is long, it is indented from the margin instead of
being placed in quotation marks. In MLA style, a quotation longer than
four lines should be indented ten spaces. A quotation of forty words or
longer is indented five spaces in APA style. In both MLA and APA styles,
long quotations are double-spaced. When you indent a long quotation this
way, it is called a **block quotation**. (There is an HTML **<BLOCKQUOTE>**
tag that allows you to make block quotations on a Web page.) You still need
to integrate a block quotation into the text of your paper. Block quotations
should be introduced by mentioning where they came from. Note three
points about form in the block quotation.

1. There are no quotation marks around the block quotation.
2. Words quoted in the original retain the double quotation marks.
3. The page number appears after the period at the end of the block
   quotation.

It is a good idea to include at least one or two sentences following the quotation to describe its significance to your thesis.

Whether they are long or short, you should double check all quotations you use to be sure they are accurate and that all words belonging to
the original are set off with quotation marks or placed in a block quotation.
If you wish to leave out words from a quotation, indicate the omitted
words with ellipses placed inside brackets [. . .], but make sure you do not
alter the meaning of the original quote. If you need to add words of your
own to a quotation to make the meaning clear, place your words in square
brackets (see Chapter 43).

Sample block quotation

For her tenth birthday, Dervla Murphy was given an atlas and a bicycle, and in 1963, twenty-one years later, she fulfilled a lifelong dream of riding a bicycle alone from Ireland to India, passing through Iran, Iraq, Afghanistan, and Pakistan on her way, a journey she later described in *Full Tilt*. When she arrived in Kabul and met a young Dutch couple who had just flown in and were suffering culture shock, Murphy reflected that after leaving Istanbul,

> the roads became daily less road-like, the mountains higher, the atmosphere rarer, the clothes stranger, the chairs scarcer, the Moslems more Islamic, the sanitary arrangements more alarming, the weather hotter, the stenches stronger, and the food dirtier. By the time I arrived at the Afghan frontier it seemed quite natural, before a meal, to scrape the dried mud off the bread, pick the hairs out of the cheese, and remove the bugs from the sugar. I had also stopped registering the presence of fleas, the absence of cutlery and the fact that I hadn't taken off my clothes or slept in a bed for ten days. (96)

In spite of the hardships of travel, Murphy preferred traditional Afghan life, claiming that there was more happiness and peace in an Afghan village than in industrial Europe.

Works Cited

Murphy, Dervla. *Full Tilt: Ireland to India with a Bicycle*. London: Murray, 1965.

Integrate quotations, summaries, and paraphrases

You should also check to see whether all sources are well integrated into the fabric of your paper. Introduce quotations by attributing them in the text:

Even those who fought for the United States in the U.S.-Mexican War of 1846 were skeptical of American motives: "We were sent to

provoke a fight, but it was essential that Mexico should commence it"
(Grant 68).

This quotation is used correctly, but it loses the impact of the source.
Compare it with the following:

> Many soldiers who fought for the United States in the U.S.-Mexican
> War of 1846 were skeptical of American motives, including Civil War
> hero and future president Ulysses S. Grant, who wrote: "We were sent
> to provoke a fight, but it was essential that Mexico should commence
> it" (68).

Summaries and paraphrases likewise need introductions. The following paragraph is the summary of a book. The source is noted at the end,
but the reader cannot tell exactly which ideas come from the source.

> In 2001 it became as fashionable to say the Internet changes nothing
> as it had been to claim the Internet changes everything just two years
> before. While the profit-making potential of the Internet was over-
> rated, the social effects were not. The Internet is demolishing old cas-
> tles of expertise along with many traditional relationships based on
> that expertise (Lewis).

In contrast, in the following summary signal phrases make it clear
which ideas come from the source. The summary also indicates the
stance of Lewis and includes a short quotation that gives the flavor of the
source.

> In 2001 it became as fashionable to say the Internet changes nothing
> as it had been to claim the Internet changes everything just two years
> before. In the midst of the Internet gloom, one prominent contrarian
> has emerged to defend the Internet. Michael Lewis observes in *Next:
> The Future Just Happened* that it's as if "some crusty old baron who
> had been blasted out of his castle and was finally having a look at his
> first cannon had said, 'All it does is speed up balls'" (14). Lewis claims
> that while the profit-making potential of the Internet was overrated,
> the social effects were not. He sees the Internet demolishing old cas-
> tles of expertise along with many traditional relationships based on
> that expertise.

Verbs that introduce quotations and paraphrases

acknowledge	claim	emphasize	offer
add	comment	explain	point out
admit	compare	express	refute
advise	complain	find	reject
agree	concede	grant	remark
allow	conclude	illustrate	reply
analyze	contend	imply	report
answer	criticize	insist	respond
argue	declare	interpret	show
ask	describe	maintain	state
assert	disagree	note	suggest
believe	discuss	object	think
charge	dispute	observe	write

EXERCISE 20.3 For each of the following rhetorical situations, decide whether you would quote, paraphrase, or summarize the sources mentioned. In some cases, you may want to do more than one.

1. You are writing an article arguing that a local judge is a racist. You have collected several inappropriate remarks made by this judge as she conducted the business of the court.

2. You are writing an email to your mother comparing two recipes for chicken and dumplings you got from shows on the Food Network.

3. You are trying to get the school computer lab you work at to buy some new multimedia software. Your supervisor hands you a stack of technical manuals and asks you to submit a proposal for the ones you think the school should purchase.

4. You are writing a paper on how Poe uses coded language in the poem "Annabel Lee" to criticize his deceased wife's family.

5. You are writing a response to a letter in the newspaper. You want to emphasize the other author's lack of information about the subject.

EXERCISE 20.4 Write a response (either positive or negative) to the following letter to the editor of a newspaper about a recent layoff at the largest technology firm in the city. Correctly incorporate a quote, a paraphrase, a summary, and a block quote.

October 13, 2002

To the editor,

I was laid off yesterday from my position as technical writer at TWMA.net. I had worked for TWMA.net for five years, had received stellar performance reviews, and had banked my future in the company's 401k plan. Imagine my surprise when I came in yesterday to a nearly empty building. It was nearly 10 A.M. and my supervisor, his supervisor, and even her supervisor could not be found. The few employees that were on my floor that day were milling about, wondering what was going on. At 10:15, over the loudspeaker, came the announcement. "TWMA.net regrets this decision, but due to the recent state of the market, TWMA.net has to make sacrifices. In order to keep the company viable, we have had to cut all of your jobs. We are sorry. Please leave your entry badge with the guard as you leave the building." Our computers were shut off at exactly 10:45. At 11:00, there were guards guiding us all to the doors. "It's not you . . . it's me," I could almost hear my ex-boyfriend saying. But we all know what he, and TWMA.net really meant with their hollow apologies: "So long, sucker!"

Over the past twenty-four hours, I've had nothing to do but worry and think. Here's what I've come up with so far—my proposed changes to the layoff process. (1) supervisors and executives have to be there to see the anguish on their employees' faces as they get the axe. The guilt might be good for their souls. (2) No layoffs should be allowed until the company has made cuts in other areas, especially the company cars driven by the salespeople, executive travel, business lunches, extravagant gifts for clients, and upper management salaries. Only after the last sales-person has had to relinquish the keys to his or her Lexis SUV and the last CFO (Chief Financial Officer) has had to bring a sack lunch for the third week in a row can a regular employee be laid off. (3) Employees must be protected from their company's mismanagement of retirement funds. If an employee cannot re-trieve the funds they have worked so hard to save, someone in an Armani suit should go to jail.

As I left the building with my belongings (and whatever office supplies I could grab), I made a mental list of all the people who got to keep their jobs: the supervisors, the salespeople, the ac-countants, and those guys who work in Customer Service and spend all day gaming on-line. My job was sacrificed for theirs. TWMA.net has decided that they are worth more than I am.

I will openly admit that I am bitter. But I'm not the only one. And until the corporate world makes some changes, my brothers and sisters and I will be siphoning off unemployment like there's no tomorrow. 'Cause the way things are going, there just might not be.

Pounding the pavement,

Mary N. O'Connor

20d | WRITE YOUR DRAFT

Before you begin writing your first paragraph, organize your notes in the order in which you plan to use them. Some writers prefer to write their introductory paragraphs first; others wait until they have written the body of the paper to decide how they want to introduce their topic. No matter what order you write your paper in, you should announce your thesis in your introductory section.

20e REVIEW YOUR DRAFT

After you've finished your first draft, you'll want to get comments from other writers. A good source of help is fellow students. Your instructor may include a peer review session as part of the assignment. Before going to your peer review session, run one last spell-check, then print a double-spaced version of your paper for each member of your group.

Reading another student's paper

It is usually best to read through a paper twice, looking at different levels (see Chapter 5). The first time you read through a paper, concentrate on comprehension and overall impressions. See if you can summarize the paper after reading it once. Ask yourself whether the writing is convincing or informative.

On your second reading show the writer where you got confused or highlight parts that were especially good by adding comments in the margins. Consider the following questions when reading a research paper:

- Does the title describe the subject of the paper? Does it create interest in the subject?
- Are the introductory paragraphs effective and relevant to the paper that follows?
- Is the thesis clearly stated in the beginning paragraphs of the paper?
- Does the writer offer support for the thesis from a variety of valid and reliable sources?
- Does the paper go into enough detail to support the thesis, and are the details relevant to the thesis?
- Do the arguments presented in the paper flow logically? Is the paper well organized?
- Is the tone of the paper consistent throughout? Is the word choice varied and appropriate throughout?
- Did you have to read some parts more than once to fully understand them?
- Are quotations properly introduced and integrated into the text?
- Are all facts and quotations that are not common knowledge documented?

- Is the documentation in the correct form?
- Is the paper free of errors of grammar and punctuation?

Once you've read through the paper a second time, write concluding suggestions and comments about how the writer could improve the paper, using the questions as your guide. Be specific. Saying "I liked your paper" or "It's a good first draft" does not help the writer. Comments like "You need to cite more sources," "You might consider switching paragraphs 2 and 4," or "Try to use a more formal tone in your introductory and concluding paragraphs" give the writer specific areas to concentrate on in the revision. It is important to be supportive in the peer editing process, so try to offer comments that are positive and encouraging.

Reading your own paper

If others read and comment on your paper, you cannot expect them to tell you everything you need to do in a revision. You need to be able to read your own draft with the same distance that you have when you read the drafts of others. Sometimes you will not have another person available who can comment on your paper.

Reading your paper aloud to yourself will help you find rough places. Parts that are difficult for you to speak aloud are going to be hard for your readers to get through. Try to imagine yourself as a reader who does not know much about your subject or who holds a viewpoint different from yours. What could you add that would benefit those readers?

Writing in the World

Scholarly review

Articles published in academic journals and scholarly books undergo an extensive review process. Articles submitted to scholarly journals are sent to reviewers who recommend that the article be accepted, rewritten, or rejected. Of those articles accepted, nearly all are rewritten, often several times. Ask your professors about how many times they have revised the work they have published. You may be surprised by their answers.

20f | REVISE, EDIT, AND CHECK FORMATTING

After you've gone through the peer editing process or assessed your own draft, sit down with your paper and consider the changes you need to make. Start from the highest level, reorganizing paragraphs and possibly even cutting large parts of your paper and adding new sections (see Sections 5b and 5c). If you make significant revisions, likely you will want to repeat the overall evaluation of your revised draft when you finish.

When you feel your draft is complete, you should begin the editing phase. Use the guidelines in Section 5d to revise style and grammatical errors. Finally, you should proofread your paper, word by word, checking for mistakes (see Section 5e). After you print out the final paper, check each page for printer or formatting errors. Make sure all the pages were printed and that all are readable.

You can read a student's completed paper in Section 21k.

Computer Strategies

Documenting sources on a Web site

Web sites provide you the opportunity to link directly to other Web sites. Thus when you make a reference to another Web site, you can make a link from the author's name or the title of the Web site that takes you directly to it. By clicking these links, a visitor to your site can immediately consult the source.

Nonetheless, it's still a good idea to include a works-cited list. One reason is that you don't necessarily want your visitors leaving your site in the middle of what you have to say. If you link off the works-cited list to other Web sites, the visitor will have at least had a chance to read your text first. It's also a good idea to have all of your references in one place. Third, because Web sites change so quickly and often disappear, the date you accessed the source you cite is important. That date is included in the works-cited entry.

Documenting 6

Chapter 21
MLA Documentation

The two styles of documentation used most frequently are the American Psychological Association (APA) style and the Modern Language Association (MLA) style. The APA style is followed in the social sciences and education (see Chapter 23), while the MLA style is the norm for the humanities and fine arts disciplines. If you have questions that the examples in this chapter do not address, consult the *MLA Handbook for Writers of Research Papers*, sixth edition (2003) and the *MLA Style Manual and Guide to Scholarly Publishing*, second edition (1998).

In-text citations

Each use of a source in MLA style is indicated by a citation in parentheses. When readers find a parenthetical reference to a source in the body of a paper, they can turn to the works-cited list and find the full publication information.

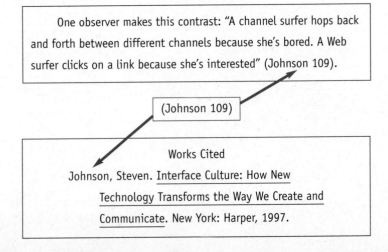

One observer makes this contrast: "A channel surfer hops back and forth between different channels because she's bored. A Web surfer clicks on a link because she's interested" (Johnson 109).

(Johnson 109)

Works Cited

Johnson, Steven. Interface Culture: How New Technology Transforms the Way We Create and Communicate. New York: Harper, 1997.

The writer quotes a passage from page 109 of Johnson's book. The reader can use the information in the works-cited list to locate the book and check whether the writer accurately represents Johnson and how the point quoted fits into Johnson's larger argument. See Section 21a (pages 362–365) for further information on in-text citations.

Entries in the works-cited list

The works-cited list is organized alphabetically by authors' last names. MLA style uses three basic forms for entries in the works-cited list: books, periodicals (scholarly journals, newspapers, magazines), and online sources.

Books

Entries for books have three main elements:

Author's name. Title of book. Publication information.

For examples of book entries see Sections 21b and 21c.

> List the author's name in reverse order for alphabetizing. Use a period after the name. List any additional authors by first and last name.

> Find the exact title on the title page, not the cover. Underline the title and put a period at the end.

McCullough, Malcolm. Abstracting Craft: The Practiced Digital Hand. Cambridge, MA: MIT P, 1998.

> Find the place of publication on the title page. List only the first city if more than one is given. Add an abbreviation for state or country if the name of the city may be ambiguous or unfamiliar. Put a colon after it.

> Find the publisher on the title page. Shorten the name. Abbreviate Press (P) and University Press (UP). Put a comma after it.

> Find the date of publication in the copyright notice on the back of the title page. End the entry with a period.

Periodicals

Entries for periodicals have three main elements:

Author's name. "Title of article." Publication information.

For examples of periodical entries see Sections 21d and 21e.

List the author's name in reverse order, followed by a period.	Place the title of the article inside quotation marks. Put the period before the closing quotation mark.

Welsh, Susan. "Resistance Theory and Illegitimate Reproduction."

College Composition and Communication 52 (2001): 553-73.

Underline the title of the journal.	Volume number	Date of publication and colon	Page numbers

Online sources

Entries for online sources may have five main elements:

Author's name. "Title of document" and/or title of Web site. Print publication information. Electronic publication information. Date of access <URL>.

There are many formats for the different kinds of electronic publications, which are described in Sections 21g and 21h. Here is the format of an entry for a professional Web site.

List the author's name in reverse order.	Place the document title inside quotation marks.	Underline the title of the Web site.	List the date of publication if available.

Zarozinski, Michael. "Suing Video Game Companies."

Louder than a Bomb! 20 Jan. 2000.

Louder than a Bomb! Software. 24 Nov. 2002.

<http://www.LouderThanABomb.com/vg_law_suits.htm>.

Give the name of the organization that sponsors the site.	List the date of access.	Place the URL inside angle brackets, followed by a period.

Formatting the works-cited list

Type the list of works cited on a separate page at the end of the paper.

Suarez 9

Works Cited ◄———— Center "Works Cited"

Agre, Phil. "The Internet and Public Discourse." First
   Monday 3.3 (March 1998). 14 July 2001 <http://
   www.firstmonday.dk/issues/issue3_3/agre/>.

Kleiner, Kurt. "Calling All Geeks." New Scientist 15 May
   1999: 10.

Mallia, Joseph. "Authorities React to Abuse of Tax-funded
   Internet." Boston Herald 13 May 1999: 6.

Murphy, Dervla. Cameroon with Egbert. Woodstock, NY:
   Overlook, 1990.

———. Full Tilt: Ireland to India with a Bicycle. London:
   Murray, 1965.

———. One Foot in Laos. London: Murray, 1999.

National Center for Education Statistics. Internet Access
   in Public Education. Feb. 1998. NCES. 4 Jan. 2002
   <http://nces.ed.gov/pubs98/98021.html>.

"The Net Is Where the Kids Are." Business Week
   10 May 1999: 44.

Side annotations:

Alphabetize each entry by the last name of the author or by title if no author is listed.

Double-space all entries. Indent all but the first line five spaces.

Where there are two or more entries by the same author, list the name for the first entry only and three hyphens for the next entries. Alphabetize entries by title.

For works with no author listed, alphabetize by the first content word in the title (ignore *a*, *an*, and *the*).

Informational notes

The MLA style is designed to avoid the need for either footnotes or endnotes. Documentation should be handled using in-text citations and a list of works cited. Two kinds of notes sometimes appear in MLA style.

Content notes supply additional information that would interrupt the flow of the text, yet may be important to provide the context of a source.

Much speculation has blamed electronic media, especially television, for an alleged decline in literacy, following Newton N. Minow's famous 1961 description of television as a "vast wasteland."[1]

The note explains who Minow was and why the remark was newsworthy.

[1] Minow, the newly appointed chairman of the Federal Communications Commission, told the assembled executives of the National Association of Broadcasters in May 1961 that "[w]hen television is bad, nothing is worse" (Adams). Minow's efforts to upgrade programming were met with cries of censorship from the television industry, and Minow resigned two years later.

Works Cited

Adams, Val. "F.C.C. Head Bids TV Men, Reform 'Vast Wasteland.'"
New York Times 10 May 1961, late ed.: 1+.

Bibliographic notes give either evaluative comments about sources or additional references.

"Fordism" is a summary term for the system of mass production consolidated by Henry Ford in the early decades of this century.[1]

The note gives the origin of the term "Fordism."

[1] The term Fordism was first used by Italian political theorist Antonio Gramsci in his prison notebooks, written while he was jailed under Mussolini's fascist dictatorship.

Works Cited

Gramsci, Antonio. <u>Selections from the Prison Notebooks of</u>
<u>Antonio Gramsci.</u> Ed. and trans. Quintin Hoare and
Geoffrey Nowell Smith. New York: International, 1971.

21a In-text citations in MLA style

Paraphrase, Summary, or Short Quotation

A short quotation takes less than four lines in your paper.

In 1997, the Gallup poll reported that 55% of adults in the United States think secondhand smoke is "very harmful," compared to only 36% in 1994 (Saad 4).

HOW MANY AUTHORS ARE THERE?

1 The author's last name comes first, followed by the page number. There is no comma.

(Bell 3)

2 or 3 The authors' last names follow the order of the title page. If there are two authors, join the names with *and*. If there are three, use commas between the first two names and a comma with *and* before the last name.

(Francisco, Vaughn, and Lynn 7)

4 or more You may use the phrase *et al.* (meaning "and others") for all names but the first, or you may write out all the names. Make sure you use the same method for both the in-text citations and the works-cited list.

(Abrams et al. 1653)

Group Treat the group or organization as the author, but try to identify the group author in the text and place only the page number in the parentheses. Shorten terms that are commonly abbreviated.

According to the Irish Free State Handbook, published by the Ministry for Industry and Finance, the population of Ireland in 1929 was approximately 4,192,000 (23).

No author named Use a shortened version of the title that includes at least the first important word. Your reader will use the shortened title to find the full title in the works-cited list.

A review in The New Yorker of Ryan Adams's new album focuses on the artist's age ("Pure" 25).

Notice that "Pure" is in quotation marks because it refers to the title of an article. If it were a book, the short title would be underlined.

WHERE DO YOU PUT THE AUTHOR'S NAME?

You have two choices:

1. As in the example above, place the author's name inside the parentheses.
2. Put the author's name in a signal phrase in your sentence. You may want to add the author's title or organizational affiliation to show how authoritative the source is:

Sociologist Daniel Bell called this emerging U.S. economy the "postindustrial society" (3).

Quotations Four Lines or Longer

In her article "Art for Everybody," Susan Orlean attempts to explain the popularity of painter Thomas Kinkade:

> People like to own things they think are valuable . . . .
> The high price of limited editions is part of their appeal:
> it implies that they are choice and exclusive, and that
> only a certain class of people will be able to afford
> them. (128)

This same statement could possibly also explain the popularity of phenomena like PBS's Antiques Road Show.

WHEN DO YOU PROVIDE A PAGE NUMBER?

- If the source is longer than one page, provide the page number for each quotation, paraphrase, and summary.
- If an online source includes paragraph numbers rather than page numbers, use *par.* with the number.

  (Cello, par. 4)

- If the source does not include page numbers, consider citing the work and the author in the text rather than in the parentheses.

  In a hypertext version of James Joyce's Ulysses, . . .

WHERE DOES THE PERIOD GO?

Short quotations (in the text):

After the parentheses.

Long quotations (indented):

Before the parentheses.

HOW DO YOU CITE A WORK IN AN ANTHOLOGY?

Cite the name of the author of the work within an anthology, not the name of the editor of the collection. Alphabetize the entry in the list of works cited by the author, not the editor. For example, Melissa Jane Hardie published the chapter "Beard" in *Rhetorical Bodies*, a book edited by Jack Selzer and Sharon Crowley.

In "Beard," Melissa Jane Hardie explores the role assumed by Elizabeth Taylor as the celebrity companion of gay actors including Rock Hudson and Montgomery Cliff (278-79).

If the citation had been completely parenthetical, Hardie, not Selzer and Crowley, would still be cited.

(Hardie 278-79)

21a In-text citations in MLA style, continued

How Do You Cite . . . ?

- Two or more works written by the same author
- Two or more authors with the same last name
- Two or more authors in a single sentence
- A source quoted in another source
- Two or more volumes of a multivolume work
- Poems, plays, and classic works

TWO OR MORE WORKS WRITTEN BY THE SAME AUTHOR

Use the author's last name and then a shortened version of the title of each source.

The majority of books written about coauthorship focus on partners of the same sex (Laird, Women 351).

Note that *Women* is underlined because it is the name of a book; if an article were named, quotation marks would be used.

TWO OR MORE AUTHORS WITH THE SAME LAST NAME

If your list of works cited contains items by two or more different authors with the same last name, include the initial of the first name in the parenthetical reference.

Web surfing requires more mental involvement than channel surfing (S. Johnson 107).

Note that a period follows the initial.

TWO OR MORE AUTHORS IN A SINGLE SENTENCE

Place each citation directly after the statement it supports.

Many sweeping pronouncements were made in the 1990s that the Internet is the best opportunity to improve education since the printing press (Ellsworth xxii) or even in the history of the world (Dyrli and Kinnaman 79).

If two sources support a single point, separate them with a semicolon.

(McKibbin 39; Gore 92)

A SOURCE QUOTED IN ANOTHER SOURCE

When you do not have access to the original source of the material you wish to use and only an indirect source is available, put the abbreviation *qtd. in* (quoted in) before the information about the indirect source.

National governments have become increasingly what Ulrich Beck, in a 1999 interview, calls "zombie institutions"—institutions which are "dead and still alive" (qtd. in Bauman 6).

TWO OR MORE VOLUMES OF A MULTIVOLUME WORK

If you refer to more than one volume of a multivolume work, give the volume number in the parenthetical reference before the page number, with a colon separating the two.

Contrary to the legend that Vincent van Gogh succumbed to personal demons before his suicide in 1890, his letters from the last two months describe feelings of calmness and an end to his recurrent nightmares (Walther and Metzger 2: 647).

POEMS, PLAYS, AND CLASSIC WORKS

Poems

If you quote all or part of two or three lines of poetry that do not require special emphasis, put the lines in quotation marks and separate the lines using a slash (/) with a space on each side.

John Donne's "The Legacy" associates the separation of lovers with death: "When I died last, and, Dear, I die / As often as from thee I go" (lines 1-2).

If they are available, use line numbers, not page numbers, in the parentheses. Use the word *line* or *lines* when you cite a line number. In subsequent references give only the numbers. If the poem is separated into parts, give the part number first, then the line numbers.

(2: 34-35).

Plays

Give the act, scene, and line numbers when the work has them, the page numbers when it does not.

(<u>Ham</u>. 3.2.120-21).

Classic Works

To supply a reference to classic works, you sometimes need more than a page number from a specific edition. Readers should be able to locate a quotation in any edition of the book. Give the page number from the edition that you are using, then a semicolon and other identifying information.

"Marriage is a house" is one of the most memorable lines in <u>Don Quixote</u> (546; pt. 2, bk. 3, ch. 19).

21b Books in MLA-style works cited

Lewis, Michael. Next: The Future Just Happened. New York: Norton, 2001.

BOOK TITLE

- Use the exact title, which appears on the book's title page.
- Underline the title (or italicize it if your instructor agrees or you will publish on the Web). If the title contains the title of another book or a word normally italicized, do not underline that title or word: Critical Essays on Toni Morrison's Beloved.
- All nouns, verbs, and pronouns, and the first word of the title are capitalized. Do not capitalize any article, preposition, coordinating conjunction, or *to* in an infinitive, unless it is the first word of the title or the first word after a colon.
- If the title is in a foreign language, copy it exactly as it appears on the title page.

AUTHOR'S OR EDITOR'S NAME

How many authors are there?

1 The author's last name comes first, followed by a comma, the first name, and a period. If an editor, follow the name with a comma and the abbreviation *ed*.

Kavanagh, Peter, ed. Lapped Furrows. New York, Hand, 1969.

Two or more books by the same author: in the entry for the first book, include the author's name. In the second entry, substitute three hyphens and a period for the author's name. List the titles of books by the same author in alphabetical order.

Behan, Brendan. Borstal Boy. 1958. London: Corgi-Transworld, 1970.

---. Confessions of an Irish Rebel. London: Hutchinson, 1965.

2 or 3 The second and subsequent authors' names appear first name first. A comma separates the authors' names. If all are editors, use *eds.* after the names.

McClelland, Deke, and Katrin Eismann.

4 or more You may use the phrase *et al.* (meaning "and others") for all authors but the first, or you may write out all the names. You need to use the same method in the in-text citation as you do in the works-cited list.

Unknown Begin the entry with the title.

Revised by second author Place the editor's name after the book title:

Strunk, William. Elements of Style. Ed. E. B. White. 4th ed. Boston: Allyn, 2000.

Group or Organization Treat the group as the author of the work.

PLACE OF PUBLICATION

- Only the city name is used when the city is well known and unambiguous.
- Add the state's postal abbreviation when the city is not well known: *Foster City, CA.*
- If more than one city is given, use only the first.

PUBLISHER'S NAME

Use a short form of the name.

- Omit words such as *Press, Publisher,* and *Inc.*
- For university presses, use *UP: U of Chicago P.*
- Shorten the name. For example, shorten *Alfred A. Knopf* to *Knopf; Houghton Mifflin* to *Houghton;* and *W. W. Norton & Co.* to *Norton.*

You may omit the publisher for books published prior to 1900.

Use a hyphen to attach the special imprint to the publisher's name.

O'Brien, Flann. The Poor Mouth. London: Flamingo-Harper, 1993.

YEAR OF PUBLICATION

- Give the year as it appears on the copyright page (often the back side of the title page).
- If no year of publication is given, but can be approximated, put a *c.* ("circa") and the approximate date in brackets: [c. 1999]. Otherwise, put *n.d.* ("no date").

  Cambridge: Harvard UP, n.d.

- For works of fiction that have been printed in many different editions or reprints, give the original publication date after the title.

  Shelley, Mary. Frankenstein. 1818. New York: Bantam, 1991.

21c Parts of a book, volumes, editions, translations in MLA-style works cited

How Do You Cite . . . ?

- Parts of a book
- Religious texts
- Volumes of a multivolume work
- Editions of a book
- Books: A focus on author, editor, or translator

PARTS OF A BOOK

Introduction, Foreword, Preface, or Afterword

Give the author and then the name of the specific part being cited. Next, name the book. Then, if the author for the whole work is different, put that author's name after the word *By*. Place inclusive page numbers at the end.

Walker, Franklin. Introduction. Heart of Darkness. By Joseph Conrad. New York: Bantam, 1981. vii-xiv.

Single chapter written by same author as the book

Greenblatt, Stephen J. "Filthy Rites." Learning to Curse: Essays in Early Modern Culture. New York: Routledge, 1992. 59-79.

Selection in an anthology or a chapter in an edited collection

Auden, W. H. "1929." W. H. Auden: Collected Poems. Ed. Edward Mendelson. New York: Vintage-Random, 1991. 45-49.

Article in a reference work

You can omit the names of editors and most publishing information for an article from a familiar reference work. Identify the edition by date. There is no need to give the page numbers when a work is arranged alphabetically. Give the author's name, if known.

"Utilitarianism." The Columbia Encyclopedia 6th ed. 2001.

A full entry is required for less familiar works.

RELIGIOUS TEXTS

In MLA format, use a period to separate the chapter and verse in the in-text note.

In-text

(John 3.16)

Works Cited

Holy Bible. King James Text: Modern Phrased Version. New York: Oxford UP, 1980.

VOLUMES OF A MULTIVOLUME WORK

One volume

Identify both the volume you have used and the total number of volumes in the set.

Theweleit, Klaus. Male Fantasies. Vol. 1. Minneapolis: U of Minnesota P, 1993. 2 vols.

More than one volume

Identify the specific volume in your in-text citations, and list the total number of volumes in Works Cited.

Theweleit, Klaus. Male Fantasies. 2 vols. Minneapolis: U of Minnesota P, 1993.

A book that is part of a series

Give the series name just before the publishing information. Do not underline or italicize the series name.

Kavanagh, Peter, ed. Patrick Kavanagh: Man and Poet. Man and Poet Series. Orono, ME: National Poetry Foundation, 1986.

EDITIONS OF A BOOK

Include the number of the edition after the title.

Hawthorn, Jeremy, ed. A Concise Glossary of Contemporary Literary Theory. 2nd ed. London: Arnold, 1994.

BOOKS: A FOCUS ON AUTHOR, EDITOR, OR TRANSLATOR

Book, edited—focus on the original author with an editor

In-text

(Hardy 55)

Works Cited

Hardy, Thomas. Jude the Obscure. Ed. Norman Page. New York: Norton, 1999.

Book, edited—focus on the editor

In-text

(Page vii)

Works Cited

Page, Norman, ed. Jude the Obscure. By Thomas Hardy. New York: Norton, 1999.

Book, with more than one editor

In-text

(Kaplan and Monod x-xi)

Works Cited

Kaplan, Fred, and Sylvère Monod, eds. Hard Times. By Charles Dickens. New York: Norton, 2001.

Book with a translator

In-text

(Nicholson-Smith 6)

Works Cited

Nicholson-Smith, Donald, trans. The Society of the Spectacle. By Guy Debord. New York: Zone, 1994.

21d Journals and magazines in MLA-style works cited

Margolis, Stacy. "Huckleberry Finn; or, Consequences." PMLA 116
(2001): 329-43.

AUTHOR'S NAME

How many authors are there?

1 The author's last name comes first, followed by a comma and the first name. For two or more works by the same author, see page 359.

2 or 3 The second and subsequent authors' names are printed in regular order, first name first:

McClelland, Deke, and Katrin Eismann.

Notice that a comma separates the authors' names.

4 or more You may use the phrase *et al.* (meaning "and others") for all authors but the first, or you may write out all the names. You need to use the same method in the in-text citation as you do in the works-cited list.

Unknown Begin the entry with the title.

TITLE OF ARTICLE

- Use the exact title, which appears at the top of the article.
- Put the title in quotation marks. If there is a title of a book within the title, underline it. If there is a title in the title that requires quotation marks, use single marks.

  Berthold, Dennis. "Class Acts: The Astor Place Riots and Melville's 'The Two Temples.'" American Literature 71 (1999): 429-61.

- All nouns, verbs, and pronouns, and the first word of the title are capitalized. Do not capitalize any article, preposition, coordinating conjunction, or *to* in an infinitive, unless it is the first word of the title.
- If the title is in a foreign language, copy it exactly as it appears on the title page, paying special attention to accent marks and capitalization.

DATE OF PUBLICATION

- For magazines and journals identified by the month or season of publication, use the month (or season) and year in place of the volume. Abbreviate the names of all months except May, June, and July.

  Barlow, John Perry. "Africa Rising: Everything You Know about Africa Is Wrong." Wired Jan. 1998: 142-58.

- For weekly or biweekly magazines, give both the day and month of publication, as listed on the issue. Note that the day precedes the month and no comma is used.

  Toobin, Jeffrey. "Crackdown." New Yorker 5 Nov. 2001: 56-61.

NAME OF JOURNAL

- Underline the title (or italicize it if your instructor agrees or you will publish on the Web).
- Abbreviate the title of the journal, if it commonly appears that way.

VOLUME, ISSUE, AND PAGE NUMBERS

Scholarly journals may be paginated (1) separately, each issue starting with page 1, or (2) continuously from issue to issue. In a continuously paginated journal, if issue 1 of volume 12 ends on page 240, issue 2 within that same volume will start on page 241.

1. For journals paginated separately in each issue, list the volume number, a period, and then the issue number (here, *2/3*) before the year and page numbers.

   Davis, Jim. "Rethinking Globalisation." <u>Race and Class</u> 40.2/3 (1999): 37-48.

2. For continuously paginated journals, such as *PMLA* in the first example on page 370, include the volume number before the year, but do not include the issue number.

   <u>PMLA</u> 116 (2001): 329-43.

HOW DO YOU CITE . . . ?

A review

Provide the title, if given, and name the work reviewed. If there is no title, just name the work reviewed.

   Berger, Sidney E. Rev. of <u>The Evolution of the Book</u>, by Frederick G. Kilgour. <u>Library Quarterly</u> 69 (1999): 402.

A letter to the editor

Add the word *Letter* after the name of the author.

   Patai, Daphne. Letter. <u>Harper's Magazine</u> Dec. 2001: 4.

If it is a reply to a previous letter, add *Reply to the letter of [name]* followed by a period.

An editorial

If the editorial is unsigned, put the title first.

   "Stop Stonewalling on Reform." Editorial. <u>Business Week</u> 17 June 2002: 108.

A published interview

   Olson, Gary A., and Lester Faigley. "Language, Politics, and Composition: A Conversation with Noam Chomsky." <u>JAC</u> 11 (1991): 1-35.

An article on microfilm

Cite an article on microfilm or microfiche as you would the original.

Boyd, Robert S. "Solar System Has a Double." Montreal Gazette 14
June 2002, final ed.: A1.

AUTHOR'S NAME

How many authors are there?

1 The author's last name comes first, followed by a comma and the first name. For two or more works by the same author, see page 359.

2 or 3 The second and subsequent authors' names are printed in regular order, first name first:

McClelland, Deke, and Katrin Eismann.

Notice that a comma separates the authors' names.

4 or more You may use the phrase *et al.* (meaning "and others") for all authors but the first, or you may write out all the names. You need to use the same method in the in-text citation as you do in the works-cited list.

Unknown Begin the entry with the title.

TITLE OF ARTICLE

- Use the exact title, which appears at the top of the article.
- Put the title in quotes. If there is a title of a book within the title, underline it. If there is a title in the title that requires quotation marks, use single marks.

  McFarling, Usha Lee. "Solar System Like Ours Is Called 'Missing Link.'" Los Angeles Times 14 June 2002, home ed.: 1.

- All nouns, verbs, and pronouns, and the first word of the title are capitalized. Do not capitalize any article, preposition, coordinating conjunction, or *to* in an infinitive, unless it is the first word of the title.
- If the title is in a foreign language, copy it exactly as it appears on the title page, paying special attention to accent marks and capitalization.

DATE OF PUBLICATION AND EDITION

- Give the complete date for a newspaper—day, month, and year.
  7 Feb. 2003
- Abbreviate the names of all the months except May, June, and July.
- Do not give the volume and issue numbers for newspapers.
- Specify the edition if one is given on the masthead: *natl. ed., late ed., home ed.*
- Place a colon after the edition if an edition name or number is given. If no edition is listed, place the colon after the date.
  18 Mar. 2003, late ed.:
  26 Dec. 2002:

NAME OF NEWSPAPER

- Underline the name (or italicize it if your instructor agrees or you will publish on the Web).

  Chicago Tribune

  Columbus Dispatch

- Omit introductory articles.

  New York Times, not The New York Times

  Denver Post, not The Denver Post

- If the city is not mentioned in the name of the newspaper, add it in square brackets after the name.

  Commercial Appeal [Memphis]; Daily Telegraph [Sydney]

SECTIONS AND PAGE NUMBERS

- Provide the section label (usually A, B, C, etc.)
- Include the page number. If the article continues to a nonconsecutive page, add a plus sign after the number of the first page.

  Kaplow, Larry, and Tasgola Karla Bruner. "U.S.: Don't Let Taliban Forces Flee." Austin American-Statesman 20 Nov. 2001, final ed.: A1+.

HOW DO YOU CITE . . . ?

A review

Fox, Nichols. "What's for Dinner?" Rev. of Eating in the Dark: America's Experiment with Genetically Engineered Food by Kathleen Hart. Washington Post 16 June 2002: T9.

A letter to the editor

Canavan, Jim. Letter. Boston Globe Dec. 2001: 4.

An editorial

Add the word *Editorial* after the name of the author. If the editorial is unsigned, put the title first.

"High Court Ruling Doesn't Mean Vouchers Will Work." Editorial. Atlanta Journal and Constitution 28 June 2002, home ed.: A19.

An article on microfilm

Cite an article on microfilm or microfiche as you would the original.

21f Government documents, pamphlets, dissertations, letters in MLA-style works cited

How Do You Cite . . . ?

- Government document
- Conference proceeding
- Bulletin or pamphlet

- Dissertation or thesis
- Letters

GOVERNMENT DOCUMENTS

Government document

If you are citing a congressional document other than the *Congressional Record*, be sure to identify the congress, and, when necessary, the session after the title of the document.

In-text

(Malveaux 10)

If there is no author, try to mention the document in the text and place only the page number in parentheses.

Works Cited

Malveaux, Julianne. "Changes in the Labor Market Status of Black Women." A Report on the Study Group on Affirmative Action to the Committee on Education and Labor. U.S. 100th Cong., 1st sess. H. Rept. 100-L. Washington: GPO, 1987. 231-55.

United States. Office of the Surgeon General. The Health Consequences of Involuntary Smoking: A Report of the Surgeon General. Rockville, MD: U.S. Public Health Service, 1986.

Congressional Record

Works Cited

Cong. Rec. 8 Feb. 2000: 1222-46.

PUBLISHED PROCEEDINGS OF A CONFERENCE

Works Cited

Zelazny, John, and J. Scott Feierabend, eds. Proceedings of a Conference: Increasing Our Wetland Resources, Washington, October 4-7, 1987. Washington: National Wildlife Federation, 1988.

BULLETIN OR PAMPHLET

If there is no author, try to mention the document in the text.

Works Cited

The Common Cold. Austin, TX: U of Texas Health Center, 2001.

DISSERTATION OR THESIS

Published

When the dissertation you are citing has been published by University Microfilms International (UMI), provide the order number as the last item in the works-cited entry.

In-text

(Price 34)

Works Cited

Price, Jennifer Jaye. Flight Maps: Encounters with Nature in Modern American Culture. Diss. Yale, 1998. Ann Arbor: UMI, 1998. 9835237.

Unpublished

In-text

(Schorn 10)

Works Cited

Schorn, Susan. "The Merciful Construction of Good Women: Actresses in the Marriage-Plot Novel." Diss. U of Texas, 2000.

LETTERS

Published

In-text

(Gramsci 121)

Works Cited

Gramsci, Antonio. "To Teresina." 20 Feb. 1928. In Letters from Prison: Antonio Gramsci. Ed. Lynn Lawner. New York: Noonday-Farrar, 1989. 120-21.

Unpublished

Mentioning the letter and the information from the letter in the text itself is preferable to a parenthetical citation.

Works Cited

O'Nolan, Brian. Letter to Longman's. 1 May 1939. Morris Library, Boston.

21g Online publication sources in MLA-style works cited

Kaplan, Nancy. "E-literacies: Politexts, Hypertexts, and Other Cultural

　　Formations in the Late Age of Print." Working paper, 24 Jan.

　　1995. 2 July 1999 <http://raven.ubalt.edu/staff/kaplan/lit/>.

AUTHOR'S NAME OR ASSOCIATED INSTITUTION OR ORGANIZATION

Known author or creator

Authorship is sometimes hard to discern for online sources. If you know the author or creator, follow the rules for periodicals and books (see page 366).

Group or organization only

If the only authority you find is a group or organization, list its name after the date of publication or date of revision.

Author and group affiliation

If both an author and an organization or institution are affiliated with the site, list the name of the organization or institution after the publication date or revision date.

Edwards, Rebecca. "Socialism." 1896. 2000. Vassar College. 20 Nov. 2001
　　<http://iberia.vassar.edu/1896/socialism.html#debs>.

Pseudonyms and unconventional names

If the author's or creator's name is a pseudonym or is unconventional, list it exactly as it appears on the Web site.

Mordeci. Home page. 20 Nov. 2001. 4 Feb. 2003 <http://homepages.msn.com/
　　IvyHall/mordecix/>.

NAME OF SITE AND TITLE OF PAGE OR ARTICLE

- Web sites are often made up of many separate pages or articles. Each page or article on a Web site may or may not have a title. If you are citing a page that has a title, treat the title like that of an article in a periodical. Otherwise, treat the name of the Web site itself as you would a book, as in the following example.

  The Valley of the Shadow: Two Communities in the American Civil War. Ed. Edward L. Ayres, 2001. Virginia Center for Digital History, U of Virginia. 1 July 2002 <http://www.iath.virginia. edu/vshadow2/>.

- The name of a Web site will usually be found on its index or home page. If you cannot find a link back to the home page on the page you are on, look at the URL for clues. You can work your way back through the URL, deleting sections (separated by slashes) until you come to a home or index page.
- If there is no title for the Web site, list it by author or creator. If it is a personal home page, place the words *Home page* after the name of the owner of the page.

DATES

List two dates for each Web site.

1. List the date the site was produced or last revised (usually at the bottom of the page; might also be copyright date) after the name of the site. This date might be just a year.
2. List the date you accessed the site. Place this second date just before the URL. Notice that there is no period before the angle bracket.

URLS

- Copy the address exactly as it appears in your browser window. You can even copy and paste the address into your text for greater accuracy.
- Test your URLs as a part of your proofreading process.
- If the URL is excessively long and complicated, give the URL of the site's search page. If the document is from a subscription service, give the URL of the service's home page and the keyword assigned, preceded by the word *Keyword*. You can also give the sequence of links you followed, preceded by the word *Path*. Place a colon after *Keyword* or *Path*.

21g Online publication sources in MLA-style works cited, continued

How Do You Cite . . . ?

- Article in an online scholarly journal
- Article in an online newspaper
- Article in a popular magazine online
- Online book
- Document within a scholarly project or information database
- Work from a library subscription service
- Work from a personal subscription service
- Online government publication

ONLINE PERIODICALS

Because most online periodicals do not have page numbers, you should identify the site in the text. That way, you can avoid awkward parenthetical citations.

Article in a scholarly journal

The volume and issue number follow the name of the journal. The date in parentheses is the date of publication.

Agre, Phil. "The Internet and Public Discourse." First Monday 3.3 (Mar. 1998). 14 July
    1999 <http://www.firstmonday.dk/issues/issue3_3/agre/>.

Article in a newspaper

The first date is the date of publication, the second is the date of access.

Erard, Michael. "A Colossal Wreck." Austin Chronicle 16 Nov. 2001. 21 Nov. 2001
    <http://www.austinchronicle.com/issues/dispatch/2001-11-16/pols_feature.html>.

Article in a popular magazine

The first date is the date of publication, the second is the date of access.

Cohen, Jesse. "When Harry Met Maggie." Slate 16 Nov. 2001. 21 Nov. 2001 <http://
    slate.msn.com/?id=2058733&>.

ONLINE BOOKS

Glantz, Stanton A., and Edith D. Balbach. Tobacco War: Inside the
    California Battles. Berkeley: U of California P, 2000. 22 May
    2002 <http://escholarship.cdlib.org/ucpress/ tobacco-war.xml>.

WHAT IF YOU NEED TO CITE . . . ?

A document within a scholarly project or information database

Give, in MLA format, the author and title of the work first, as well as its date and place of publication if it is a book. Then give the name of the project or database, its editor, version or revision date, affiliation, and date of access. The address is the address of the document itself.

> Calhoun, John C. "The Southern Address." Nineteenth Century Documents Project. Ed. Lloyd Bensen. 2000. Furman U. 21 Nov. 2001 <http://www.furman.edu/~benson/docs/calhoun.htm>.

A work from a library subscription service

Begin with the print publication information, then state the name of the database (underlined), the name of the service, the name of the library or library system, date of access, and the URL of the service's home page.

> Snider, Michael. "Wired to Another World." Maclean's 3 March 2003: 23-24. Academic Search Premier. EBSCO. Founders Memorial Lib., Northern Illinois U. 14 March 2003 <http://www.epnet.com/>.

A work from a personal subscription service

For a personal subscription service that allows you to retrieve material by entering a keyword, write *Keyword* followed by a colon and the word you entered at the end of the entry.

> "Anasazi." Compton's Encyclopedia Online. Vers. 2.0. 1997. America Online. 12 Dec. 2001. Keyword: Compton's.

Online government publication

Begin with the same information you would give for printed government works and conclude with information for the electronic source.

> United States. Dept. of the Treasury. Your Rights as a Taxpayer. August 2000. 24 Nov. 2001 <http://www.irs.gov/forms_pubs/pubs.html>.

21h CD-ROM, software, and unedited online sources in MLA-style works cited

How Do You Cite . . . ?

- A publication on CD-ROM
- Computer software
- Unedited online sources (synchronous communication, email, or newsgroup or listserv posting)
- Course home page
- A publication in more than one medium

PUBLICATION ON CD-ROM

When page numbers aren't available, use the author's name in the text to avoid an awkward parenthetical citation.

Boyer, Paul, et al. The Enduring Vision, Interactive Edition. 1993 ed. CD-ROM. Lexington, MA: Heath, 1993.

Periodically revised database on CD-ROM

For a CD-ROM database that is often updated (e.g., *ProQuest* or *InfoTrac*), provide the publication dates for the article you are citing as well as for the data disc itself.

(Roper 425)

Roper, Jill. "Why Don't We Teach Reading in High School?" Journal of Secondary Education 22 (1999): 423-40. ProQuest General Periodicals. CD-ROM. UMI-ProQuest. June 2000.

Multidisc CD-ROM

Follow the publication medium with either the total number of discs or the number of the specific disc you are using. Mentioning the CD-ROM in the text itself is preferable to a parenthetical citation.

The Norton Anthology of English Literature Audio Companion. CD-ROM. 2 discs. New York: Norton, 2001.

SOFTWARE

Provide the author's name (if known), the version number (if any), the manufacturer, and the date. You can also list the operating system, if relevant. Also, if you have downloaded the software from the Internet, list the URL for the download site. For in-text notes, mentioning the software in the text itself is preferable to a parenthetical citation.

AOL. Vers. 6.0. America Online, 2001.

UNEDITED ONLINE SOURCES

For all of these sources, mentioning the source in your text is preferable to an awkward parenthetical citation.

Synchronous communication (MOOs, MUDs)

Provide the speaker and/or site, the title and date of the session, the forum for communication (if specified), the date of access, and the electronic address.

Sirius, B. Discussion of popularity of <u>Harry Potter</u>. 12 December 2000. LinguaMOO. 24 Nov. 2001 <telnet:lingua.utdallas.edu 8090>.

An email message

Give the name of the writer, the subject line, a description of the message, and the date.

Wilson, Samuel. Email to the author. 18 Sept. 2002.

A newsgroup or listserv posting

Give the author's name (or alias), the subject line, the descriptor *Online posting*, the date of posting, the name of the newsgroup or listserv, the date of access, and the URL of the posting.

IrishMom. "Re: Spain Will Send Troops to Aid US." Online posting. 2 Nov. 2001. Ireland List. 21 Nov. 2001 <ireland_list-og@email.rutgers.edu>.

HOME PAGE FOR A COURSE

Begin with the instructor's name, the name of the course, the words *Course home page*, the dates of the course, the name of the department, school, date of access, and URL.

Kirkpatrick, Judith. American Literature Online. Course home page. Jan.-May 2003. Dept. of English. Kapi'olani CC. 21 Feb. 2003. <http://www2.hawaii.edu/~kirkpatr/s03/s03250syllabus.html>.

PUBLICATION IN MORE THAN ONE MEDIUM

Specify all of the media that constitute the publication (book, CD-ROM, diskette, etc.) or list only the media you used. Mentioning the work in the text itself is preferable to an awkward parenthetical citation.

Suffredini, Ana, ed. <u>German Complete Course</u>. Book, audio cassettes. New York: Random, 1998.

21i Visual sources in MLA-style works cited

How Do You Cite . . . ?

- Visual sources in print (cartoon, advertisement, graph, map, table)
- A painting, sculpture, or photograph
- Visual sources online (map, art, cartoon)

VISUAL SOURCES IN PRINT

For all of these sources, a mention in the text is preferable to an awkward parenthetical citation.

Cartoon

Chast, Roz. "First-Period Algebra." Cartoon. New Yorker 19 Nov. 2001: 69.

Advertisement

Discover Card. Advertisement. Newsweek 29 October 2001: 40-41.

Map, graph, or chart

Treat a map, graph, or chart as an anonymous book, but add the appropriate descriptive label.

Baltimore Street Map and Visitor's Guide. Map. Baltimore: MAP, 1999.

Table reproduced in text

This is how a table might appear in your text:

In The Republic, Plato explains how the three parts of the individual soul should be repeated in the structure of the ideal city-state (see Fig. 1).

Soul	Reason	Courage	Appetites
State	Elite guardians	Soldiers	Masses

Fig. 1. Plato's politics, chart from Richard Osborne, Philosophy for Beginners (New York: Writers and Readers, 1992) 15.

Plato's Politics. Chart. New York: Writers and Readers, 1992. 15.

PAINTING, SCULPTURE, OR PHOTOGRAPH

Provide the artist's name, the title of the work, the name of the institution or individual who owns the work, and the city. If you are citing a photograph of a work, give the information for the work, followed by the publication information for the source that you got the photograph from. Include the slide, plate, figure, or page number, as relevant. In the text, mentioning the work and the artist in the text itself is preferable to a parenthetical citation.

Cloar, Carroll. Odie Maude. 1990. David Lusk Gallery, Memphis, TN.

VISUAL SOURCES ONLINE

For all of these sources, a mention in text is preferable to an awkward parenthetical citation.

Online map

"The Political World." Map. National Geographic.com. National Geographic
    Society. 24 Nov. 2001.

Online work of art

Lawrence, Jacob. Street Shadows. 1959. Museum of Modern Art, New York. 24
    Nov. 2001 <http://www.moma.org/docs/exhibitions/current/index.htm>.

Online cartoon

Cullum, Leo. "Roaming Charges." Cartoon. Cartoonbank.com. 19 October 1998.
    24 Nov. 2001 <http://www.cartoonbank.com/>.

21j Multimedia sources in MLA-style works cited

How Do You Cite . . . ?

- A musical composition
- A sound recording
- An online video or sound file
- A film
- A video or DVD
- A television or radio program
- An interview
- A musical, dramatic, dance, or artistic performance
- A speech, debate, mediated discussion, or public talk

MUSIC AND SOUND

Mentioning the work and the artist in your text is preferable to an awkward parenthetical citation.

Musical composition

If you have the sheet music or a score, list the publication information. If not, just provide the composer, the title of the composition, and the year.

Gershwin, George. "Cuban Overture." 1932.

Sound recording

Tedeschi, Susan. Just Won't Burn. Tone-Cool Records, 1998.

Online video or sound file

"Isabella." Perf. James Gandolfini and Edie Falco. The Sopranos. 1998. HBO. 24 Nov. 2001 <http://www.hbo.com/sopranos/show/episode/season1/episode_12.shtml#>.

FILM, TV, AND RADIO

Film

The Blair Witch Project. Dir. Daniel Myrick and Eduardo Sánchez. Perf. Heather Donahue, Michael C. Williams, and Joshua Leonard. Haxan Films, 1999.

Video or DVD

Note the format of the work in the citation.

Long Shots: The Life and Times of the American Basketball Association. Prod. George Roy and Steven Stern. Videocassette. HBO, 1997.

Television or radio program

Provide the title of the episode or segment, followed by the title of the program and series (if any). After the titles, list any performers, narrators, directors, or others who might be pertinent. Then give the name of the network, call numbers and city for any local station, and the broadcast date.

"Commendatori." The Sopranos. Perf. James Gandolfini and Edie Falco. HBO. 16 Dec. 2001.

PERFORMANCE

For all of these sources, mentioning the source in your text is preferable to an awkward parenthetical citation.

Interview

McConaughey, Matthew. Telephone interview. 27 May 1999.

For interviews conducted for broadcast on radio or TV, add the broadcast information.

Cage, Nicholas. Interview. Fresh Air. WHYY-FM. Philadelphia. 13 June 2002.

Musical, dramatic, dance, or artistic performance

Lipstick Traces. By Griel Marcus. Adapted by Kirk Lynn. Dir. Shawn Sides. Perf. Lana Lesley and Jason Liebrecht. Off Center. Austin, TX. 31 Aug. 2000.

Speech, debate, mediated discussion, or public talk

Jobs, Steve. Remarks at Macworld. New York. 21 July 1999.

21k | SAMPLE RESEARCH PAPER WITH MLA DOCUMENTATION

Chapters 16 through 20 discuss how to plan and write a research paper. The sample informative research paper that follows was written by Grace Bernhardt; it is documented and formatted according to MLA guidelines. The paper is annotated to show specific features of MLA style and to show how the works-cited page is organized.

Include your last name and page number as page header, beginning with the first page, 1/2" from the top.

MLA style does not require a title page. Check with your instructor to find out whether you need one.

Center the title. Do not underline the title, put it inside quotation marks, or type it in all capital letters.

Specify 1" margins all around. Double-space everything.

Bernhardt 1

Grace Bernhardt

Professor Faigley

Technology, Literacy, and Culture 321

8 March 2001

Secondhand Smoke: The Risk and the Controversy

We all know that smoking poses a significant risk to our health. We can make an educated decision about whether or not to smoke, and if we do decide to smoke, we should be willing to accept any negative effects such as lung cancer and heart disease later in our lives. But what about exposure to secondhand smoke? At this point, we don't always have a choice in exposure to the smoke of others. The Office of the Surgeon General (OGS) has documented a high level of exposure to secondhand smoke among nonsmoking adults and children in the United States. Blood tests of nonsmokers for the

Bernhardt 2

presence of cotinine, a chemical produced by nicotine, indicate that 88% of nonsmoking Americans are exposed to secondhand smoke (US, OGS, Clean).

In 1972, the Surgeon General released a landmark report, The Health Consequences of Smoking, warning of the dangers of smoking. The report also warned of the risks of breathing secondhand smoke, also called "passive smoking" or "environmental tobacco smoke." Throughout the 1970s, numerous studies were conducted that pointed to the risks of breathing secondhand smoke and the risks to unborn children of smoking mothers (summarized by Shephard). In 1986, both the National Research Council and the United States Surgeon General (Health Consequences of Involuntary Smoking) published independent reports that secondhand smoke causes respiratory infections in children and reduces their lung capacity. Nonetheless, at the International Symposium on Environmental Tobacco Smoke held at McGill University in 1989, critics of the research argued that studies of the effects of secondhand smoke could not rule out the influences of other pollutants. In the summary of the proceedings volume from the conference, Joseph Wu concluded that research had yet to prove that secondhand smoke is a health hazard (375).

Indent each paragraph five spaces (1/2" on the ruler in your word processing program).

Cite publications within the text by the name of the author (here, an organization). If more than one publication is by the same author, cite by title.

Give page numbers for paraphrases as well as direct quotations.

Bernhardt 3

Only in 1992 did the United States Environmental Protection Agency (EPA) issue a report, <u>Respiratory Health Effects of Passive Smoking: Lung Cancer and Other Disorders</u>, asserting that secondhand smoke definitely causes cancer in nonsmoking adults and harms the respiratory health of children. The EPA determined that secondhand smoke is a Group A carcinogen, a classification of pollutants that have been proven to cause cancer. The tobacco industry responded to the report with a well-funded advertising, public relations, and legal counterattack. Since then, controversy over the topic has spread, both politically and socially. But what exactly are the risks associated with secondhand smoke, and how has the American public responded to those risks?

Secondhand smoke is most harmful to young children, especially those with asthma or other respiratory diseases. The EPA notes that 43% of children in the United States under the age of 11 live in a home with at least one smoker. Children exposed to secondhand smoke tend to have more bronchitis, pneumonia, respiratory infections, fluid in the middle ear, and asthma. And if both parents smoke, or if the child is frequently exposed to smoke, the child's chances of showing symptoms of these diseases increase (US, EPA, <u>Indoor</u>).

These two questions serve as Grace's thesis.

Do not include a page number for items without pagination, such as Web sites.

Bernhardt 4

Infants and toddlers up to 18 months of age suffer between 150,000 and 300,000 cases of lung infections because of secondhand smoke, according to EPA estimates. Secondhand smoke produces symptoms of asthma in an additional 200,000 to 1,000,000 children, and it increases fluid in the middle ear, which often requires hospitalization for surgery in children (US, EPA, Indoor).

To determine the risk of secondhand smoke for adult nonsmokers, the EPA considered the results of thirty epidemiologic studies, that examined the effects of secondhand smoke on nonsmoking partners of smokers (US, EPA, Respiratory). Every study found that the level of risk increased according to exposure to secondhand smoke. When the results of the studies were considered together, the probability of the increased rates of lung cancer among nonsmokers occurring by chance was less than one in a billion. The EPA concluded that approximately 3,000 nonsmokers die of lung cancer caused by secondhand smoke each year in the United States; 800 of these cases stem from exposure to secondhand smoke at home and 2,200 from exposure in work or social situations (US, EPA, Respiratory 4).

The EPA's 1992 report was a legal bombshell because it raised the possibility that nonsmokers could sue tobacco

Bernhardt 5

companies. The report and other subsequent studies also
greatly increased public concern over secondhand smoke.
In 1997, the Gallup poll reported that 55% of adults in the
United States think secondhand smoke is "very harmful,"
compared to only 36% in 1994 (Saad 4). As a result of increased public pressure, many local governments now ban
or restrict smoking in public places and workplaces.

"Smoking or non?" This question used to be part of the
standard greeting of waitresses across America. However, following the reports on the harm of secondhand smoke, many
cities have banned or restricted smoking altogether in restaurants. Maine, Vermont, and Utah have placed statewide bans
on smoking in restaurants, and California prohibits smoking
in bars as well as restaurants ("Smoking"). According to the
American Nonsmokers' Rights Foundation, in early 2001, 221
communities have 100% smoke-free workplaces, 787 have
some restriction on smoking in workplaces, and 300 have
100% smoke-free restaurants.

These bans remain causes of intense controversy. In
New York City, a City Council push to ban smoking at all
restaurants in winter 2001 was met with strong opposition
including Mayor Giuliani's (Lombardi). Typical of citizen resistance to smoking bans in the United States and Canada

If a source
appears on a
single page, do
not give the page
number in the
citation.

Bernhardt 6

is Christa Wagner's letter to the editor over the Canadian ban of smoking in prisons: "To ban smoking in restaurants and bars is bad enough. To ban it in prisons is inhuman. What a sad, oppressed society we have become." Others disagree with methods for the enforcement of smoking bans in public places, saying that the government should not and cannot put smoking bans into place. Citing the difficulty in enforcement and the fact that "most people don't want it," the writer of an editorial in the Wisconsin State Journal thinks "there are more important issues facing the city for its council members to get sidetracked on than an unenforceable piece of feel-good legislation like this" ("Place Smoking Ban").

Nonsmokers are perhaps even more adamant that they should not have to breathe secondhand smoke. Dozens of editorials, letters to the editor, and articles about anti-smoking activism that insist on the total elimination of secondhand smoke have been published in recent years. This example from the Pittsburgh Post-Gazette is typical of the anti-smoking arguments. Myles Lampenfeld writes:

> The current policy of segregating smokers and nonsmokers is ineffective. Yet to be developed is the ventilation system that prevents smoke from finding its way into the nonsmoking section.

Quotations of four lines or more should be indented 1" or ten spaces. Do not use quotation marks. Introduce block quotations rather than just dropping them into the text.

Bernhardt 7

Because the source of this quotation appeared on a single page, no page number is given. For block quotations from longer works, the page number is given in parentheses after the period.

In some restaurants, the arbitrary boundary between sections results in patrons trying to enjoy a smoke-free meal while sitting next to smokers . . . . Smoke-free restaurants have been the standard in many states for several years. Backlash and protest have been short-lived, with no economic impact on the restaurant industry.

Regardless of whether government should be the one enforcing smoking bans, many workplaces and restaurants have already put restrictions in place. The Office of the Surgeon General reports that employers are implementing policies for smoke-free workplaces in order to save money. These savings include costs associated with fire risk, damage to furnishings, cleaning, workers' compensation, and life insurance. The estimated cost savings are $1,000 per smoking employee based on 1988 dollars (US, OSG, Clean). The legislative initiative against secondhand smoke is also reducing the amount of smoke in the air. In 2000, Congress passed and President Clinton approved legislation that bans smoking in nearly all public places where the federal government gives aid for services to children (US, EPA, Setting).

Bernhardt 8

In addition to bans, other research is being conducted
on how the harmful effects of secondhand smoke can be
limited. Among the workers who endure the highest concen-
trations of secondhand smoke in the workplace are those
employed by casinos in Nevada. A study is being done with
nonsmoking casino workers to see if the use of vitamins can
reduce the amount of damage from long-term exposure to
secondhand smoke ("Do Vitamins"). In the decade following
the release of the 1992 EPA report, significant steps have
been taken to reduce the hazards of secondhand smoke.
Nevertheless, there still is a long way to go. Only one
state—California—now meets the nation's Healthy People
2010 objective to eliminate exposure to secondhand smoke
by banning indoor smoking or restricting smoking to separately ventilated areas (US, OSG, Clean).

> Use the first
> several words of
> a title when
> citing a work
> with an unnamed
> author.

Bernhardt 9

Works Cited

American Nonsmokers' Rights Foundation. U.S.

> Communities with Local Tobacco Control Ordinances.
>
> 9 Jan. 2001. 21 Feb. 2001 <http://www.no-smoke.org/
>
> ordcount.html>.

> Center "Works
> Cited" on a
> new page.

Bernhardt 10

Double-space all entries. Indent all but the first line in each entry five spaces.

"Do Vitamins Stem Hazards of Secondhand Smoke?
University of Nevada to Conduct Clinical Trial on
Casino Workers." <u>AScribe Newswire</u> 8 Nov. 2000.
<u>Academic: News</u>. LexisNexis. U of Texas Lib., Austin.
20 Feb. 2001 <http://www.lexisnexis.com/>.

Alphabetize entries by the last names of the authors or by the first important word in the title if no author is listed.

Lampenfeld, Myles. "A Ban on Smoking in Restaurants
Would Protect Everyone." <u>Pittsburgh Post-Gazette</u>
12 July 2000, late ed.: A14.

Lombardi, Frank. "Butts Ban on Menu: Flap Looms over
New Restaurant Cig Limits." <u>New York Daily News</u>
25 Jan. 2001, final ed.: 27.

National Research Council. <u>Environmental Tobacco
Smoke: Measuring Exposures and Assessing Health
Effects</u>. Washington: National Academy Press, 1986.

"Place Smoking Ban in Political Ashtray: Madison's Proposal to
Stamp Out Smoking Is an Unenforceable Intrusion into

Underline the titles of books and periodicals.

Citizens' Private Lives." <u>Wisconsin State Journal</u> 19 Feb.
2001. <u>Academic: News</u>. LexisNexis. U of Texas Lib.,
Austin. 20 Feb. 2001 <http://www.lexisnexis.com/>.

Saad, Lydia. "A Half-Century of Polling on Tobacco: Most
Don't Like Smoking but Tolerate It." <u>Public
Perspective</u> 9 (1998): 1-4.

Shephard, Roy J. <u>The Risks of Passive Smoking</u>. New York:
Oxford UP, 1982.

Bernhardt 11

"Smoking to Be Banned in Restaurants in Maine." New York
Times 18 Sept. 1999, late ed.: A18.

United States. Environmental Protection Agency. Indoor
Air Pollutants: Environmental Tobacco Smoke.
Updated 1 Jan. 2000. 23 Feb. 2001
<http://www.epa.gov/children/air.htm#tobacco>.

---. ---. Respiratory Health Effects of Passive Smoking: Lung
Cancer and Other Disorders. EPA/600/6-90/006 F.
Washington: US Environmental Protection Agency,
1992.

---. ---. Setting the Record Straight: Secondhand Smoke Is
a Preventable Health Risk. June 1994. Updated 26
June 2000. 23 Feb. 2001 <http://www.epa.gov/
iedweb00/pubs/strsfs.html>.

---. Office of the Surgeon General. Clean Indoor Air
Regulations Fact Sheet. 11 Jan. 2001. 23 Feb. 2001
<http://www.cdc.gov/tobacco/sgr/sgr_2000/
factsheets/factsheet_clean.htm>.

---. ---. The Health Consequences of Involuntary Smoking:
A Report of the Surgeon General. Rockville, MD: US
Public Health Service, 1986.

---. ---. The Health Consequences of Smoking: A Report of
the Surgeon General. Washington: US Public Health
Service, 1971.

If an author has more than one entry, list the entries in alphabetical order by title. Use three hyphens in place of the author's name for the second and subsequent entries. See also page 360.

Bernhardt 12

Wagner, Christa B. "Inhuman Ban." Ottawa Citizen 24 July
    2000: A11.

Wu, Joseph M. "Summary and Concluding Remarks."
    Environmental Tobacco Smoke: Proceedings of the
    International Symposium at McGill University, 1989.
    Ed. Donald J. Ecobichon and Joseph M. Wu.
    Lexington, MA: Lexington, 1990. 367-75.

Go through your text and make sure all the sources you have used are in the list of works cited.

To hear audio commentary on this student paper, visit
www.ablongman.com/faigley010.

Writing in the World

Putting an MLA works-cited list on a Web site

The convention of putting the URL inside angle brackets creates no difficulties for a works-cited list on paper. Anything in angle brackets on a Web site, however, will be interpreted by your browser as an HTML tag, and it will not show up on your Web page. To get the angle brackets on a Web page requires using a special name for the opening and closing brackets.

<   for <
>   for >

You may have to go into the HTML file and type in these special names for the angle brackets if your Web-page editor does not do it for you. You will know that the conversion to the special names has not been made if the angle brackets and what is inside them do not show up on your Web page.

Chapter 22
Writing about Literature

Less experienced readers sometimes believe that literature is a game played between writers and readers. The writer of literature hides the "real meaning" of a text beneath layers of symbols, images, metaphors, and other fancy literary tricks, daring the reader to find it. Literature is not three-card monte. Literary texts strive to open ground where your imagination and intellect can roam. Instead of hunting for the author's secret meaning, concentrate on developing a reading of your own. Experienced readers read texts several times before they become comfortable with them. They read methodically, recording their ideas in marginal notes.

22a BECOME A CRITICAL READER OF LITERATURE

Reading literature requires a set of practices different from those you might use while reading the Sunday paper or a memo from your boss. Think of yourself as an active critical observer. Your goal is not merely to soak up the text as you might a magazine article. Instead, carry on a dialogue with the text using marginal notes. Resist the urge to use a highlighter; highlighted text will help you identify passages that seemed significant during a previous reading, but it won't help you remember *why* they seemed so. Although writing in the margins as you read may seem like extra work at first, you will soon discover that it saves time and, before long, sharpens your reading skills. Keeping a record of your reading will force you to engage with a text; being an active reader is practice toward being a thoughtful reader. And marginal comments will be your best source from which to generate a paper topic.

The following is a partial list of aspects of a literary text you may want to note as you read:

your gut response
questions or points of confusion
shifts in tone, plot, or character
patterns
things that go against expectations
important passages
contradictions
odd passages
word choice
repeated words, sounds (alliteration), images, or motifs
the effect of hard sounds (like *d*, *k*, *p*, and *t*) or soft sounds (like *f*, *h*, *o*, and *s*)
the effect of the narrative technique
what doesn't get said
interesting imagery
interesting metaphors
allusions to other works

When reading poetry you may also want to note:

rhyme scheme
meter
line breaks
punctuation
stanza breaks

22b DEVELOP AN ORIGINAL ARGUMENT

Assignments for English classes tend to be more open-ended than writing assignments in other disciplines. Use the freedom that an open-ended assignment offers to focus on an aspect of the text that interests you. Take a stand. Develop an original idea. Your job is to enlighten readers

Common Errors

Confusing narrator with author

It's easy but incorrect to assume that the narrator of a work of fiction or the speaker of a poem is the author. *Narrator* and *author* are not interchangeable. Think of the narrator as you think of other characters: the author's creative construction. True, narrators, like authors, sometimes have the power to see more than other characters. But even this special knowledge is colored by the way the author constructs it. A narrator is a kind of filter for a work of literature, shading the work in specific ways, emphasizing some aspects and downplaying or omitting others. Thus, refer to the speaker of a work of literature as the narrator rather than as the author.

Remember: Do not refer to the narrator as the author.

 For step-by-step discussion, examples, and practice of this common error, go to **www.ablongman.com/faigley011**.

with your analysis of a literary text. Challenge conventional readings. Show readers something they may not have noticed or offer a new analysis of an old observation. Ideally your audience will see the text differently after reading your argument.

Questions to consider as you form your ideas about literature

The work's construction
Title: What insight does the title lend to the work as a whole? What is its tone? Is it ironic? Does it allude to something else?

(continued next page)

Plot: How does the story progress? How does the writer keep the reader's attention? Where does the tension reach its peak? How is the tension resolved?

Setting: Where and when does the work take place? How does this setting or settings affect the way we read the work? How does the writer manipulate the passage of time? What effect do shifts in setting have?

Character: How does the work construct its characters? How do the characters interact? Do the characters reflect larger social and political concerns of the day? What would you expect someone in the character's situation to be like? How does the writer meet or diverge from those expectations?

Genre: What form of literature does the work take: novel, short story, poem, play? How does the writer meet or subvert the conventions of the genre? Does the work take advantage of the genre's strengths? Does it exceed its limitations?

Style: How does the writer construct the prose or verse? How would you describe the writer's voice? How does the writer handle the interplay between the characters' thoughts and their dialogue? Do the characters speak in dialect?

Point of view: From whose perspective(s) are we told the story? Is the narrator reliable?

The work's content

Social and political context: What was going on in the world in the writer's day and how does it color the work? Does the work make a political statement or social commentary?

Gender: How is gender constructed in the work? Does it argue for certain advantages or limitations in these constructions? Is there a conflict between or among men and women? Do the characters see a difference between their gender identity and the social formulation of gender? What are the consequences?

Race: How does the work depict race? Is there conflict between or within races? Do the characters notice a difference between their own experiences of racial identity and the social construction of it? How does this difference manifest itself?

Class: How does the work depict social class? What are the relationships between characters of different social classes? How does social class affect characters?

National identity: How does the work depict the expression of national identities? Does this depiction offer an argument about actual historical events? Are there clashing identities? How do characters establish or seek to free themselves from national identity? What resistance do they face?

The work's history

Influence: What and who influenced the work's author? How do these influences inform our reading of the work?

Reception: How have different audiences received the work? At what times was it at its most popular, ignored, or controversial? Have the settings in which the work was read changed? For instance, did it go from being a serial in the popular media to a piece anthologized in college literary anthologies?

Publication: Works of literature are material objects, subject to the influence of printing and publishing processes, designers, and financial concerns. Did the work's manner of distribution affect how it was received? Have variations among different printings affected how it has been read?

Opinion versus argument

Papers about literature are often called *critical analyses*. Don't let the term trip you up. *Critical* in this sense doesn't mean judgmental. The fact is, your understanding of the text is much more interesting to a reader than whether you like it or not. Avoid making an argument about your opinion of a text unless the assignment specifically asks for one. Instead, develop a complex argument that illuminates some aspect of the text.

Simple versus complex arguments

If developing an original argument sounds like a tall order, you'll have an easier time once you learn to distinguish between simple and complex arguments.

Simple arguments are usually obvious and basic. Because they lack the meatiness of a complex argument, they tend to read like a list; each paragraph simply piles up more evidence to prove the same point. Simple arguments tend to fall into generalizations about broad topics or offer observations about a text without developing it into an analysis. They may be well supported, but they won't compel the reader to view the text in a new way.

Complex arguments don't rest with easy or obvious answers. By concentrating on a sufficiently narrow topic, they can go into depth. While simple arguments generate black-and-white answers, complex arguments delve into gray areas. Each paragraph plays a role in unfolding an original analysis. Notice in the following example that the simple argument doesn't go beyond initial observation. The writer will be stuck illustrating the same idea again and again. The complex argument, on the other hand, refuses to accept tidy generalizations. Instead, it delves into the novel's subtleties.

SIMPLE ARGUMENT

In *The Country of the Pointed Firs*, Sarah Orne Jewett's characters are connected to the land.

COMPLEX ARGUMENT

Despite what appears at first glance to be her characters' harmonious connection to the land, Jewett refuses to allow the reader to lapse into pastoral fantasies. The narrator shows us a particularly unsettling view of the Bowden family reunion, which, in her eyes, reveals the fallen empire of an invading army, a gingerbread house crumbling to bits. The militaristic language of the chapter forces us to question not only whether the Bowdens' dominion over the land is natural, but whether it is ethical.

Develop a complex argument

One way to develop a complex argument is to ask yourself *what*, *how*, and *why* questions. These questions lead you from observation, to exploration, to an argument.

Observation: What's going on in the text?

Single out your most interesting marginal notes. What did you observe in the text that was unexpected, odd, powerful, or central? What questions did you ask? Wonderful arguments frequently evolve from a question or confusion about the text.

> Why does the concluding scene of *Pride and Prejudice* feature the Gardiners, two secondary characters?
>
> Why do parts of *Moby-Dick* read a bit like a play?

Although you won't have an argument yet, answering *why* questions will help you narrow your focus to a potentially fruitful topic for argument.

Exploration: How does the text do what it's doing?

The answer to this question may consider technical, stylistic, or thematic aspects of the text. At this point you'll begin to develop the first stages of your argument.

> How does Austen feature the Gardiners in the last scene of *Pride and Prejudice*? Throughout the novel Austen shows us strained or broken marriages, but the Gardiners are an exception. She presents them as a well-matched, well-adjusted couple.
>
> How does *Moby-Dick* read a bit like a play? Some of the chapter titles read like stage directions. Also, the chapters themselves sometimes draw on theatrical conventions like soliloquies and asides. In the larger context of the novel, plays are just one genre with which Melville experiments. He also includes songs, journalism, histories, poetry, and others.

Analysis and argument: Why does the text do what it's doing?

At this stage, you should begin to develop a complex argument. Consider to what end or for what purpose the text functions as it does. What are the ultimate implications of this feature of the text? Frequently answers will fall into one of the following lines of inquiry:

1. It advances or complicates a major theme of the text.
2. It engages in commentary about larger political, social, philosophical, or literary issues of the author's day.

3. It reflects the influence of another writer or text.
4. It advances the plot or adds depth to a character.
5. It's attempting to be technically innovative. It highlights a capability or limitation in the author's choice of theme, genre, structure, stylistic elements, or narrative technique.

Why does the end of *Pride and Prejudice* feature secondary characters, the Gardiners? The Gardiners exemplify successful marriage. By ending the novel with them, Austen lends a note of hope for Elizabeth and Darcy's union. The novel, then, is not a condemnation of marriage as an institution but of the social forces that promote bad matches. We can analyze Austen's characterization of the Gardiners to better understand the kind of marriage making she wants to advocate.

Why do parts of *Moby-Dick* read a bit like a play? Plays are one of many genres from which Melville draws. By using so many different forms of art he furthers the sense that the novel is a working-out of the limits of a symbol. He muses on the whale through drama, poetry, song, and so on to attempt to penetrate the surface of the symbol. The question implicit in these explorations is, Are our symbols based on an objective reality or are they merely frail attempts to rationalize an unknowable world?

THESIS STATEMENT

Pride and Prejudice delights in painting a dark portrait of marriage—so much so, in fact, that Elizabeth may seem doomed no matter whom she weds. Jane Austen employs difficult marriages to both offer social critique and create dramatic tension. However, her handling of the Gardiners suggests that not all marriages are bad, merely ones entered into for the wrong reasons. Ultimately, the Gardiners' minor presence in the novel is a major influence on the way we interpret the central union in the story, the marriage of Elizabeth and Darcy.

THESIS STATEMENT

Herman Melville explores the symbol Moby Dick from every possible perspective to show again and again that human knowledge fails to grasp how the whale generates its mystical power. The author's incorporation of many literary genres resonates in a way that makes us reassess the role of the book itself—or words in general—in making meaning. Melville asks readers to look at words the same way we look at Moby Dick: Although we can see them from every possible perspective, we still cannot know what reality lurks behind language.

Writing in the World

The literary present tense

The disciplinary convention in English is to employ the literary present tense. The literary present tense requires the use of present tense when analyzing any literary text such as a poem, a play, a work of fiction, an essay, or a sermon. Also use the present tense when discussing literary criticism.

INCORRECT　In *Song of Myself* Walt Whitman **tempered** [PAST TENSE] his exuberant language with undercurrents of doubt about whether language **could** [PAST TENSE] do all he **asked** [PAST TENSE] of it.

CORRECT　In *Song of Myself* Walt Whitman **tempers** [PRESENT TENSE] his exuberant language with undercurrents of doubt about whether language **can** [PRESENT TENSE] do all he **asks** [PRESENT TENSE] of it.

However, you should employ the past tense when discussing literary history. The author's life, the creation of the text, the text's publication, and the critical reception of the text all exist outside the work

(continued next page)

itself and require the past tense. The following passage uses the past tense to discuss the publication history and critical reception of *Leaves of Grass*.

Beyond doubting whether his audience would under-
stand the spirit of his verse, Whitman **worried** [PAST TENSE] that
Leaves of Grass would never reach an audience at all. He
[PAST TENSE] **was** so concerned, in fact, that he **published** [PAST TENSE] reviews of
the book under false names to drum up publicity.

22c | ORGANIZE YOUR ARGUMENT

Once you have a thesis statement, you can organize your paper. Decide what the major sections of your argument should be. Ask yourself what steps you should take to prove the thesis. Writing an outline, formal or informal, will help you order the paper.

Informal outlines

Informal outlines are best when you're most concerned about determining and ordering the main sections of your paper and less concerned about evidence and how you might weight each part of the argument.

THESIS STATEMENT

Pride and Prejudice delights in painting a dark portrait of marriage—so much so, in fact, that Elizabeth may seem doomed no matter whom she weds. Jane Austen employs difficult marriages to both offer social critique and create dramatic tension. However, her handling of the Gardiners suggests that not all marriages are bad, merely ones entered into for the wrong reasons. Ultimately, the Gardiners' minor

presence in the novel is a major influence on the way we interpret
the central union in the story, the marriage of Elizabeth and Darcy.

INFORMAL OUTLINE

- Austen represents the main marriages in the novel as negative.
- The first function of negative marriages—to create dramatic tension in the novel
- The second function—social critique
- But the social critique doesn't condemn marriage as a whole, despite the attention the marriages get. The Gardiners' happy marriage shows Austen is only condemning bad marriages.
- The Gardiners have a minor role but play a major part in readers' understanding of Austen's take on marriage.
- Analysis of the Gardiners' scenes show they enter the novel at the most pivotal moments, giving perspective about marriage in general and Elizabeth and Darcy's marriage in particular.

Formal outlines

Formal outlines are most useful when you have a clear sense of the main sections of your paper. Since it is more detailed, a formal outline will give you the opportunity to organize supporting evidence, and the hierarchical structure will help you see clearly which ideas are primary and which are secondary.

THESIS STATEMENT

Herman Melville explores the symbol Moby Dick from every possible perspective to show again and again that human knowledge fails to grasp how the whale generates its mystical power. The author's incorporation of many literary genres resonates in a way that makes us reassess the role of the book itself—or words in general—in making meaning. Melville asks readers to look at words the same way we look at Moby Dick: Although we can see them from every possible perspective, we still cannot know what reality lurks behind language.

I. Melville explores the whale from as many perspectives as he can to prove that, as a symbol, the source of its power is unknowable.

    A. Melville shows us the whale in every way he can.

        1. In "Etymology" he breaks down the word *whale* into different languages.

        2. In "Extracts" he collects quotes about whales from literature, science, and history.

        3. In "Cetology" he gives a methodical biological classification of whales.

    B. Ahab argues to Starbuck that he's chasing Moby Dick to find the reality behind it as a symbol.

II. Melville covers the different genres of literature just as comprehensively as he covers the exploration of whales. The novel argues that, like the whale, words are a set of symbols behind which we cannot see.

    A. The novel incorporates other genres.

        1. The "Midnight, Forecastle" chapter reads like a play.

        2. "The Town-Ho's Story" is a short story within the novel.

        3. Melville also includes scattered selections of verse.

    B. Ahab's argument about the relationship of Moby Dick to words as symbols can be applied.

C. The implication of calling into question the power of words as symbols is that we must reconsider the power of the novel to represent or create reality.

22d | SUPPORT YOUR ARGUMENT

Using the text as evidence

Have you ever worked to use the text as evidence in your paper only to have your instructor write in the margins "Don't summarize"? The trick is to employ the text in a way that creates analysis rather than summary. First, keep your audience in mind. Those who have already read the work will be bored by plot recaps. Quote or paraphrase passages that advance your argument. Second, never use the text as evidence without analyzing it. Your analysis should be a close reading of the text that explains how the text you've chosen illustrates your argument. A close reading looks at the details of the text; refer to the list in Section 22a for elements of the text you may want to discuss in a close reading.

Look at how the following paragraphs use the text as evidence. The first uses the text as evidence by focusing on specific passages and explaining how those passages illustrate the argument. The writer not only quotes and paraphrases, but explains those passages in light of the thesis. The second paragraph merely summarizes the plot without explaining how the plot advances the argument.

ANALYZES TEXT

As she grows to realize a vision of her selfhood, Janie tries to find the life that will allow her to be herself. Gradually becoming a stronger person and growing toward who she truly is, she continually reframes her understanding and finds new relationships that grow with her. Several times during major changes in her life, Janie says things like, "So new thoughts had to be thought and new words said" (77). Through language, through articulating her growing understanding, she becomes more herself. She is like most women who "forget all those things they don't want to remember, and remember everything they don't want to forget" (1). Through new thoughts and new language she shapes her reality to her dream. In the beginning of the novel, Hurston writes that, for women, "The dream is the truth" (1). Janie only grows to understand this after she shares men's dreams for most of her life. She is sometimes a victim of others' dreams, but it teaches her to be flexible, to grow stronger, and to move on. The men in her life end up alone or dead, while Janie moves toward understanding that "The dream is the truth" (1).

MERELY SUMMARIZES

Janie fails to find love with Logan Killicks; he becomes abusive and she becomes discontent. She elopes with Joe Starks, who offers the promise of a new town and freedom from farming. Joe and Janie get rich from their store, but Joe also becomes abusive to his wife. When he dies, Tea Cake comes along and charms Janie. They play checkers and go fishing. They fall in love, marry, and live together in Florida. In her new life with Tea Cake, Janie swaps tall tales with her neighbors and learns to hunt. When Tea Cake dies, she returns to Joe's town very different than when she left.

Incorporating literary criticism

When you tackle an assignment that asks you to address literary criticism, you take on an additional responsibility in your argument. If you're writing about *Hamlet*, for instance, you have to enter a conversation among critics that has been going on for several hundred years. Don't panic. The challenge becomes manageable once you break down the task into smaller steps.

If your instructor doesn't select critical sources for you, your first task is to narrow your scope to the point where the body of criticism you must address is not intimidating. Ask your instructor to list the major critical books and articles that deal with your topic. As you read them, identify common concerns, points of contention, and issues of interpretation. Once you understand the critical works, figure out how to use them in an argument. Your goal should be to contribute to the ongoing critical conversation, not merely to affirm or oppose it. Consider ways you can advance or revise the conversation about your topic. Does your interpretation of the text advance or complicate an existing critical perspective? Is there a scene or aspect of the text that the critics don't consider but should? Are the critics taking the historical, political, or social context of the work into account sufficiently? By developing original responses to these questions, you can enter the critical conversation.

Computer Strategies

Electronic resources for writing about literature

While libraries are still the best places for literary research, you can find a number of handy resources online.

- **Bartleby.com** (**www.bartleby.com**) features free e-texts of well-known poetry, prose, and reference works, including the *Cambridge History of English and American Literature*.
- **Great Books: Texts and Fully Searchable Concordances** (**www. concordance.com/**) contains concordances to well-known works of literature, allowing visitors to search for where and how often a word appears in a text.

(continued next page)

- **Literature Resource Center** (www.galenet.com/servlet/LitRC/ ?finalAuth=true) is a database of biographical, bibliographic, and critical information about authors.
- **MLA Bibliography** is an expansive searchable bibliography (available through the online reference site of most research libraries) of literary criticism.
- **Oxford English Dictionary** (dictionary.oed.com/entrance.dtl) is an electronic version of the OED, as it's commonly called, which records the history of a word's meaning, tracking where it first appeared and how its definition has changed through the years.
- **Project Gutenberg** (www.gutenberg.net/) offers free e-texts of hundreds of works of literature.

22e | SAMPLE LITERARY ANALYSIS

The following student paper responds to the assignment topic, "What does Zora Neale Hurston tell us about her concepts of men and women in the first two paragraphs of *Their Eyes Were Watching God*?"

West 1

Naomi West

Professor Louder

Literature and Culture

3 May 2002

Men and Women in Their Eyes Were Watching God

The difference between men and women characters in

Their Eyes Were Watching God lies essentially in the fact

West 2

that Janie is a changing person, while the male characters are more static. The male characters see their "ship" with their "wishes on board" (1). In other words, they spend their lives with their eyes trained on a goal. The image of the ship is passive; they wait for the tide to bring their wishes in to shore or carry them out beyond their reach. Women, on the other hand, take an active role in shaping their reality to fit their dreams. Women, Janie especially (who is the only female character Zora Neale Hurston develops in the novel), "forget all those things they don't want to remember, and remember everything they don't want to forget" (1). Janie has goals, hopes, and dreams, but they are more flexible than those of the men around her. They are more flexible because they have to be. As a woman, Janie is expected to take on the dreams of her husband.

In some ways, Janie is a victim of her circumstances early in her life. Her grandmother, a former slave, never has the luxury of realizing a dream because she is tied down with raising children, earning money, and surviving. She tries to give her granddaughter a better life by marrying her off to Logan Killicks, but the result is that Janie is forced to follow Logan's static vision of the future. He makes her nothing more than another mule on his farm.

Later in her life Janie realizes that she hates her grandmother because she sold her into a different kind of
slavery—a woman's subservience to a man.

Janie spends a large part of her life trying to latch onto
men who have the dreams she wants to share. She becomes a
victim of Logan's and then Joe's stagnant dreams; they both
have their eyes fixed on a ship on the horizon. On Joe's
deathbed Janie tells him, "You changes everything but nothin'
don't change you—not even death" (82). Both Joe and Logan
have a static vision of their worlds and of Janie. They understand her in terms of how much work she can do, like a mule,
and how well she fulfills their visions of what a wife should be.

Janie and Tea Cake have such a strong relationship
because he gives Janie the most freedom to find her dream
and to be herself. With Tea Cake, she shares a man's dream
willingly for the first time because there's enough room in
his dream for her to find her own dream.

As she grows to realize a vision of her selfhood, Janie
tries to find the life that will allow her to be herself. Gradually
becoming a stronger person and growing toward who she truly
is, she continually reframes her understanding and finds new
relationships that grow with her. Several times during major
changes in her life, Janie says things like, "So new thoughts

had to be thought and new words said" (77). Through language, through articulating her growing understanding, she becomes more herself. She is like most women who "forget all those things they don't want to remember, and remember everything they don't want to forget" (1). Through new thoughts and new language she shapes her reality to her dream. In the beginning of the novel, Hurston writes that, for women, "The dream is the truth" (1). Janie only grows to understand this after she shares men's dreams for most of her life. She is sometimes a victim of others' dreams, but it teaches her to be flexible, to grow stronger, and to move on. The men in her life end up alone or dead, while Janie moves toward understanding that "The dream is the truth" (1).

Early in her life, her flexibility makes her a weak character; she sacrifices her dreams and becomes, essentially, Logan Killicks' servant. "She knew now that marriage did not make love. Janie's first dream was dead, so she became a woman" (24). The death of dream is inherent in womanhood.

Work Cited

Hurston, Zora Neale. <u>Their Eyes Were Watching God</u>. Philadelphia: Lippincott, 1937.

Chapter 23
APA Documentation

Social sciences disciplines, including government, linguistics, psychology, sociology, and education, frequently use the American Psychological Association (APA) documentation style. The APA style is similar to the MLA style in many ways. Both styles use parenthetical citations in the body of the text, with complete bibliographical citations in the list of references at the end. Both styles avoid using footnotes for references. For a detailed treatment of APA style, consult the *Publication Manual of the American Psychological Association*, fifth edition (2001).

APA style emphasizes the date of publication. When you cite an author's name in the body of your paper, always include the date of publication. Notice too that the APA style includes the abbreviation for page (p.) in front of the page number. A comma separates each element of the citation.

> Johnson (1997) makes this contrast: "A channel surfer hops back and forth between different channels because she's bored. A Web surfer clicks on a link because she's interested" (p. 109).

If the author's name is not mentioned in the sentence, the reference looks like this:

> One observer makes this contrast: "A channel surfer hops back and forth between different channels because she's bored. A Web surfer clicks on a link because she's interested" (Johnson, 1997, p. 109).

The corresponding entry in the references list would be

> Johnson, S. (1997). *Interface culture: How new technology transforms the way we create and communicate.* New York: HarperCollins.

Writing in the World

APA reports of research

Reports of experimental research follow a specific organization in APA style, with an abstract that gives a brief summary of the contents and four distinct sections—introduction, method, results, and discussion—followed by the list of references. This organization allows other researchers to identify information quickly.

- **The introduction** identifies the problem, reviews previous research, and states the hypothesis that was tested.
- **The methods section** describes how the experiment was conducted and how the participants were selected.
- **The results section** reports the findings of the study. This section often includes tables and figures that provide statistical results and tests of statistical significance. Tests of statistical significance are critical for experimental research because they give the probability that the results could have occurred by chance.
- **The discussion section** interprets the findings and often refers to previous research.

APA documentation

23a In-text citations in APA style

Paraphrase, Summary, or Short Quotation

In APA style a short quotation has fewer than 40 words.

In 1997, the Gallup poll reported that 55% of adults in the United States think secondhand smoke is "very harmful," compared to only 36% in 1994 (Saad, 1997, p. 4).

WHERE DO YOU PUT THE AUTHOR'S NAME?

You have two choices:

1. As in the example above, place the author's name inside the parentheses.
2. Put the author's name in a signal phrase right in your sentence, particularly when you can add the person's title or affiliation to indicate the authority of the source.

Influential sociologist Daniel Bell (1973) noted a shift in the United States to the "post-industrial society" (p. 3).

HOW DO YOU DISTINGUISH TWO WORKS BY ONE AUTHOR WITH THE SAME COPYRIGHT DATE?

Assign the dates letters (a, b, etc.) according to their alphabetical arrangement in the references list.

The majority of books written about coauthorship focus on partners of the same sex (Laird, 2001a, p. 351).

HOW MANY AUTHORS ARE THERE?

1 The author's last name is followed by the date and page number. There are commas between each element: (Bell, 1973, p. 3)

2 List both authors' last names, joined with an ampersand. (Suzuki & Irabu, 2002, p. 404). If you cite the authors' names in a sentence, use *and* in place of the ampersand: Suzuki and Irabu (2002) report . . .

3 to 5 The authors' last names follow the order of the title page: (Francisco, Vaughn, & Romano, 2001, p. 7). Subsequent references can use the first name and *et al*.: (Francisco et al., 2001, p. 17)

6 or more Use the first author's last name and *et al.* for all in-text references.

Group Treat the group or organization as the author, but try to identify the group author in the text and place only the page number in the parentheses. If you do use the name of the group in an in-text citation, put its acronym (if there is one) in brackets. Use the acronym in subsequent in-text citations.

(National Institute of Mental Health [NIMH], 1999)

Subsequent references: (NIMH, 1999)

Unknown Use a shortened version of the title (or the full title if it is short) in place of the author's name. Capitalize all key words in the title. If it is an article title, place it in quotation marks. ("The Net," 1999, p. 44)

Quotations 40 Words or Longer

Orlean (2001) has attempted to explain the popularity of the painter Thomas Kinkade:

> People like to own things they think are valuable. . . . The high price of limited editions is part of their appeal; it implies that they are choice and exclusive, and that only a certain class of people will be able to afford them. (p. 128)

IN-TEXT CITATIONS OF WEB SITES

If you mention a Web site in your text you can give the address directly in your paper. You do not need to cite the Web site on the references list.

More information is available at the Museum of Jurassic Technology's Web site (http://www.mjt.org/).

WHERE DO YOU PUT THE DATE?

You have two choices. You can put the date (1) in your text in parentheses:

Zhang, Liu, and Cao (2001) specify . . .

or (2) between the author's name and the page number in the citation note.

. . . visual languages (Zhang, Liu, & Cao, 2001, p. 192).

For translations, reprints, and later editions, either put *trans.* or *revised* before the date of the source you have, or give the original date, if known.

(O'Brien, trans. 1973) or (O'Brien 1941/1973).

WHEN DO YOU NEED TO GIVE A PAGE NUMBER?

- Give the page number for all quotations and paraphrases.
- For electronic sources that do not provide page numbers, give the paragraph number when available. Use the abbreviation *para.* or the symbol ¶.
- If the source does not include page numbers, it is preferable to reference the work and the author in the text.

In Wes Anderson's 1998 film *Rushmore,* . . .

WHAT IF YOU NEED MORE THAN ONE CITATION IN A SENTENCE?

- Place each citation directly after the statement it supports.
- If you need to cite two or more works within the same parentheses, list them in the order they appear in the references list and separate them with a semicolon.

(Alford, 2001; Laird, 2001)

HOW DO YOU CITE A WORK DISCUSSED IN A SECONDARY SOURCE?

Name the work and give a citation for the secondary source.

Saunders and Kellman's study (as cited in McAtee, Luhan, Stiles, & Buell, 1994)

23b Books in the APA-style references list

Hardt, M., & Negri, A. (2000). *Empire*. Cambridge, MA: Harvard University Press.

AUTHOR'S OR EDITOR'S NAME

How many authors are there?

1 The author's last name comes first, followed by a comma and the author's initials. If an editor, put the abbreviation *Ed.* in parentheses after the name.

Kavanagh, P. (Ed.). (1969). *Lapped furrows*. New York: Hand Press.

2 Join two authors' names with a comma and ampersand. If editors, use *(Eds.)* after the names.

McClelland, D., & Eismann, K.

3 or more Write out all of the authors' names up to six. The seventh and subsequent authors can be abbreviated to *et al.*

With authors If authors are listed with the word *with*, include them in the reference in parentheses.

Bettinger, M. (with Winthorp, E.).

Unknown Begin the entry with the title. Italicize book titles.

Group or organization Treat the group as the author of the work.

YEAR OF PUBLICATION

- Give the year the work was copyrighted in parentheses.
- If no year of publication is given, write *n.d.* ("no date") in parentheses: Smith, S. (n.d.).
- If it is a multivolume edited work, published over a period of more than one year, put the span in parentheses: Smith, S. (1999–2001).
- For works of fiction that have been printed in many different editions or reprints, give the original publication date.

Shelley, M. (1991). *Frankenstein*. New York: Bantam. (Original work published 1818)

BOOK TITLE

- Italicize the title (or underline, if you are working on a typewriter).
- Capitalize only the first word, proper nouns, and the first word after a colon.
- If the title is in a foreign language, copy it exactly as it appears on the title page.
- Enclose information necessary for identification of the source (e.g., edition, report no., volume no.) in parentheses after the title. Do not italicize the information in parentheses.

Theweleit, K. (1993). *Male fantasies*. (Vol. 1.) Minneapolis: University of Minnesota Press.

PUBLISHER'S NAME

Do not shorten or abbreviate words like *University* or *Press*.

PLACE OF PUBLICATION

- List the city without a state abbreviation or country for major cities known for publishing (New York, Boston).
- Add the state abbreviation or country for other cities (Foster City, CA).
- If more than one city is given, use the first.

HOW DO YOU CITE . . . ?

Two or more books by the same author

Arrange according to the date, or alphabetically according to the names of additional authors. If all of these are the same, arrange them according to the title (excluding beginning articles *A* or *The*). To clarify the in-text citation, assign a letter (a, b, c) to the repeated dates.

Bell, B. (1965a). *Confessions of a rebel.* London: Hutchinson.

Bell, B. (1965b). *Derelict boy.* London: Corgi-Transworld.

A translated book

Voltaire. (1959). *Candide* (R. Aldington, Trans.). Garden City, NY: Hanover. (Original work published 1759)

A selection reprinted from another source

Thompson, H. S. (1997). The scum also rises. In K. Kerrane & B. Yagoda (Eds.), *The art of fact* (pp. 302–315). New York: Touchstone. (Reprinted from *The great shark hunt*, by H. S. Thompson, 1971, New York: Simon & Schuster)

A revised or later edition of a book

Hawthorn, J. (Ed.). (1994). *A concise glossary of contemporary literary theory* (2nd ed.). London: Arnold.

Technical and research reports

Austin, A., & Baldwin, R. (1991). *Faculty collaboration: Enhancing the quality of scholarship and teaching* (ASCHE-ERIC Higher Education Report 7). Washington, DC: George Washington University.

HOW DO YOU CITE ONLY PART OF A BOOK?

A single chapter written by the same author as the book

Add the word *In* after the chapter title and before the book title.

Savage, G. (1996). The ministry of labour: Accentuating the negative. In *The social construction of expertise* (pp. 130–157). New York: Routledge.

A selection in an anthology or a chapter in an edited collection

Add the word *In* after the selection title and before the names of the editor(s).

McCracken, J. L. (1995). Northern Ireland, 1921–66. In T. W. Moody & F. X. Martin (Eds.), *The course of Irish history* (pp. 313–323). Niwot, CO: Roberts Rinehart.

A chapter in a volume in a series

List the series editor first and the volume editor second.

Jackson, E. (1998). Politics and gender. In F. Garrity (Series Ed.) & M. Halls (Vol. Ed.), *Political library: Vol. 4. Race, gender, and class* (2nd ed., pp. 101–151). New York: Muse.

An article in a reference work

If the entry has no author listed, place the title in the author position.

Viscosity. (2001). *The Columbia encyclopedia* (6th ed.). New York: Columbia University Press.

How Do You Cite . . . ?

- Poster sessions and conference papers
- Dissertations and theses
- Religious or classical texts
- Government and legal documents
- Bulletins or pamphlets
- Interviews and letters

POSTER SESSIONS AND CONFERENCE PAPERS

Published conference proceedings

Hoffman, D. (1999). Science, technology and political change. *Proceedings of the 20th International Congress of History of Science.* Turnhout, Belgium: Brepols Publishers.

Unpublished paper presented at a symposium or meeting

Give the month of the symposium, if possible.

Davis, V. (2000, March). *I probably won't vote anyway.* Paper presented at the CWRL Colloquium, University of Texas, Austin.

Poster session

Give the month of the meeting, if possible.

Rawles, J., & Potter, L. (2001, July). *Real magic: Get kids to read and keep them reading!* Poster session presented at the annual meeting of Reading Teachers of America, Boise, ID.

DISSERTATIONS AND THESES

Unpublished dissertation or thesis

Schorn, S. (2000). *The merciful construction of good women: Actresses in the marriage-plot novel.* Unpublished doctoral dissertation, University of Texas, Austin.

Published dissertation or thesis

If the dissertation you are citing is published by University Microfilms International (UMI), provide the order number as the last item in the entry.

Price, J. J. (1998). Flight maps: Encounters with nature in modern American culture. *Dissertation Abstracts International, 59* (5), 1635. (UMI No. 9835237)

RELIGIOUS OR CLASSICAL TEXTS

Reference entries are not required for major classical works or the Bible, but in the first citation, identify the edition used.

In-text

John 3.16 (Modern Phrased Version)

GOVERNMENT AND LEGAL DOCUMENTS

For a more detailed description of government and legal documents, see Appendix D of the *Publication Manual of the American Psychological Association* (5th ed.).

Government document

When the author and publisher are identical, use the word *Author* as the name of the publisher.

In-text

(U.S. Environmental Protection Agency [EPA], 1992)

References

U.S. Environmental Protection Agency. (1992). *Respiratory health effects of passive smoking: Lung cancer and other disorders*. (EPA Publication No. 600/6-90/006 F). Washington, DC: Author.

Congressional record (Senate resolution)

In-text

(S. Res. 103, 2001)

References

S. Res. 103, 147th Cong., Cong. Rec. 5844 (2001) (enacted).

Online government publication

In-text

(U.S. Public Health Service [USPHS], 2001)

References

U.S. Public Health Service. Office of the Surgeon General. (2001, January 11). *Clean indoor air regulations fact sheet*. 11 Jan. 2001. Retrieved February 12, 2001, from http://www.cdc.gov/tobacco/sgr/sgr_2000/factsheets/factsheet_clean.htm

INTERVIEWS AND LETTERS

A published interview

In-text

(Bush, 2001, p. 124)

References

Bush, L. (2001, April). [Interview with P. Burka]. *Texas Monthly*, pp. 80–85, 122–124.

Unpublished letter

Personal communications are not listed on the references list; they are cited in text only.

In-text

(B. O'Nolan, personal communication, May 1, 1999).

BULLETINS OR PAMPHLETS

University Health Center. (2001). *The common cold* [Brochure]. Austin, TX: Author.

23d Periodical sources in the APA-style references list

Kellogg, R. T. (2001). Competition for working memory among writing processes. *American Journal of Psychology, 114,* 175–192.

AUTHOR'S NAME

How many authors are there?

1 The author's last name comes first, followed by the author's initials.

Dobbs, S. E. (2002).

2 Join two authors' names with a comma and an ampersand.

McClelland, D., & Eismann, K. (1998).

3 or more Write out all of the authors' names, up to six authors. The seventh and subsequent authors can be abbreviated to *et al.*

With authors If authors are listed with the word *with*, include them in the reference in parentheses.

Bettinger, M. (with Winthorp, E.).

Unknown Begin the entry with the title of the article.

The net is where the kids are. (1999, May 10). *Business Week,* 44.

Group or organization Treat the group as the author of the work.

DATE OF PUBLICATION

Most popular magazines are paginated per issue. These periodicals might have a volume number, but are more often referenced by the season or date of publication.

- For weekly or biweekly magazines, give the year, then the day and month of publication as listed on the issue. Provide the volume number in italics, if available.

  Toobin, J. (2001, November 5). Crackdown. *The New Yorker,* 56–61.

- For monthly publications, provide the year and the month.

  Barlow, J. P. (1998, January). Africa rising: Everything you know about Africa is wrong. *Wired,* 142–158.

- If an article is awaiting publication, put *(in press)* instead of the date.

NEWSPAPERS

- Include introductory articles (e.g., *The New York Times,* not *New York Times*).
- Give the section and page numbers for articles (use *p.* or *pp.* before page numbers). If pages are discontinuous, list each page number, separated by commas.

  Kaplow, L., & Bruner, T. K. (2001, November 20). U.S.: Don't let Taliban forces flee. *Austin American-Statesman,* pp. A1, A5.

- If an article has no author, list and alphabetize by the first significant word in the title of the article.

TITLE OF ARTICLE

- Do not use quotation marks. If there is a book title in the article title, italicize it.

  Nadel, A. (1993, Winter). Replacing *The Wasteland*: James Merrill's quest for transcendental authority. *Texas Studies in Literature and Language, 43*(4), 154–176.

- The first word of the title, the first word of the subtitle, and any proper nouns in the title are capitalized.

NAME OF JOURNAL

- Italicize the journal name (or underline if you are working on a typewriter).
- All nouns, verbs, and pronouns, and the first word of the title are capitalized. Do not capitalize any article, preposition, or coordinating conjunction unless it is the first word of the title or subtitle.

VOLUME, ISSUE, AND PAGE NUMBERS

Continuous pagination

Most scholarly journals use continuous pagination for an entire volume. Thus, if issue 1 stops on page 322, issue 2 will start on page 323. For continuously paginated journals, include only the volume number and the year, not the issue number.

Pagination issue by issue

For scholarly journals paginated separately in each issue, list the issue number in parentheses (not italicized) after the volume number.

  Davis, J. (1999). Rethinking globalisation. *Race and Class, 40*(2/3), 37–48.

HOW DO YOU CITE . . . ?

Abstract from original source

de Watteville, C. (1904). On flame spectra. [Abstract]. *Proceedings of the Royal Society of London, 74,* 84.

Abstract from printed secondary source

Van Schaik, P. (1999). Involving users in the specification of functionality using scenarios and model-based evaluation. *Behaviour and Information Technology, 18,* 455–466. Abstract obtained from *Communication Abstracts, 2000, 23,* 416.

Article on microfilm or microfiche

Cite as you would the original.

Electronic copy of an abstract retrieved from a database

Putsis, W. P., & Bayus, B. L. (2001). An empirical analysis of firms' product line decisions. *Journal of Marketing Research, 37*(8), 110–118. Abstract obtained from PsychINFO database.

A review

Provide the title, if given, and name the work reviewed in brackets. If the review is not titled, provide the title of the work reviewed in brackets.

Berger, S. E. (1999). [Review of the book *The evolution of the book*]. *Library Quarterly, 69,* 402.

A letter to the editor or editorial

Add in brackets *Letter to the editor* or *Editorial* after the title of the letter (if available) and before the title of the periodical.

Wilkenson, S. E. (2001, December 21). When teaching doesn't count [Letter to the editor]. *The Chronicle of Higher Education,* p. B21.

Kelty, C. (2000). *Scale, or the fact of.* Retrieved January 2, 2002, from
http://kelty.org/or/papers/scaleUS.pdf

AUTHOR'S NAME, ASSOCIATED INSTITUTION, OR ORGANIZATION

- Authorship is sometimes hard to discern for online sources. If you do have an author or creator to cite, follow the rules for periodicals and books.
- If the only authority you find is a group or organization, list its name as the author.
- If there is both an author and a sponsor or host organization or institution, identify the host before giving the URL for the document itself. Precede the URL with a colon.

Edwards, R. (2000). Socialism. *1896.* Retrieved November 20, 2001, from Vassar College Web
site: http://iberia.vassar.edu/1896/socialism

- If the author or organization is not identified, begin the reference with the title of the document.

Halloween costumes from my warped mind. (n.d.). Retrieved November 26, 2001, from http://home.att.net/~jgola/hallow01.htm

ONLINE PERIODICALS

Article online based on a print journal

Many print articles are now duplicated on the Web. If you access an article online that is identical to the printed version, note in brackets after the title *Electronic version.*

Gomez, T. (2001, July). Bungee! Combing DVD with Tivo and Replay TV [Electronic version]. *Camcorder and Computer Video, 18,* 40–43.

Article in an online scholarly journal

Lowe, C. (2001, Fall). Open source. *Kairos, 6*(2). Retrieved February 24, 2002, from http://english.ttu.edu/kairos/6.2/binder.html?news/opensource.htm

Article in an online newspaper

Erard, M. (2001, November 16). A colossal wreck. *Austin Chronicle.* Retrieved November 21, 2001, from http://www.austinchronicle.com/issues/dispatch/2001-11-16/pols_feature.html

Article in an online magazine

Cohen, J. (2001, November 16). When Harry met Maggie. *Slate.* Retrieved November 21, 2001, from http://slate.msn.com/?id=2058733&

DATES

You need to list two dates for a Web site. First, list the date the site was produced or last revised (sometimes the copyright date) after the author. This date might be just a year. If no copyright or revision date is given, use *(n.d.).* Second, list the date you accessed the site. Place this second date just before the URL.

NAME OF SITE AND TITLE OF PAGE OR ARTICLE

- Web sites are often made up of many separate pages or articles. Each page or article on a Web site may or may not have a title. If you are citing a page or article that has a title, treat the title like an article in a periodical. Otherwise, treat the name of the Web site itself as you would a book.
- The name of a Web site will usually be found on its index or home page. If you cannot find a link back to the home page on the page you are on, look at the address for clues. You can work your way backward through the URL, deleting sections (separated by slashes) until you come to a home or index page.
- If there is no title for the Web site, list it by author or creator. If it is a personal home page, place the words *Home page* after the name of the owner of the page.

URL

- Copy the address exactly as it appears in your browser window. You can even copy and paste the address into your text for greater accuracy.
- Note that there are no angle brackets around the URL and no period after it.
- Test your URLs as a part of your proofreading process. If readers cannot access your source, you should consider taking it out of your paper.
- The *Publication Manual of the American Psychological Association*, 5th edition, specifies that the exact source page, not a menu or home page, should be cited for an electronic source. The APA has a Web site with a few examples at <www.apastyle.org.elecref.html>.
- If you access an article via file transfer protocol (ftp), make sure your URL begins with *ftp://*.

HOW DO YOU CITE . . . ?

Message posted to a newsgroup or electronic mailing list

Name the author, the date of posting, the subject line, and any identifier for the message (in brackets). End the reference with *Message posted to* and the address of the newsgroup. Only use messages that are archived and accessible.

Fisher, R. (2001, November 11). CFP: The idea of education [I.D. 129100]. Message posted to http://www2. h-net.msu.edu/announce/

Material from an index or database

Increasingly, articles are read online through indexes and databases. APA recommends giving the original publication information and the date of retrieval from the database.

Clark, J. P. (1989). Marx's inorganic body. *Environmental Ethics*, *11*, 243–258. Retrieved November 27, 2001, from Expanded Academic ASAP database.

Online encyclopedia

Semiconductor. (1999). *Encyclopaedia Britannica Online*. Retrieved November 30, 2002, from http://search.eb.com/bol/ topic?eu=68433&sctn=1#s_top

Email

Email sent from one individual to another should be cited as a personal communication. Since personal communication is often not recoverable, it is usually cited only in the text.

(S. Wilson, personal communication, August 18, 1999)

How Do You Cite . . . ?

- A television program
- A film, video, or DVD
- A musical recording
- Audio recording
- Computer software
- Graphic, audio, or video files

MULTIMEDIA

Television program

List writers first, followed by the director (identify the function after the name). Specify, in brackets after the title, whether you are citing an episode from a series, an entire series, or a single broadcast. List the name of the producer before the series title.

> Manos, J., & Chase, D. (Writers). (1999). College. [Television series episode]. In D. Chase (Producer), *The sopranos*. New York: HBO.

Film, Video, or DVD

List the director or producer or both. Give the motion picture's country of origin. (Note that some movie studios produce films in different countries.)

> Columbus, C. (Director). (2001). *Harry Potter and the sorcerer's stone* [Motion picture]. United States: Warner Brothers.

Musical recording

List both the title of the song and the title of the album or CD. In the in-text citation, include side or track numbers.

> Waits, T. (1980). Ruby's arms. On *Heartattack and vine* [CD]. New York: Elektra Entertainment.

Audio recording

> King, M. L. Jr. (Speaker). (1968). *In search of freedom* [Record No. SR61170]. Los Angeles: Mercury Records.

COMPUTER SOFTWARE

You do not need to cite standard, off-the-shelf software and programming languages. For other software, provide the author's name (if known), the date, the name of the software, and the version number (if any). Also give the place of manufacture (if known) and the manufacturer. You can also list the operating system, if relevant. If you have downloaded the software from the Internet, list the URL for the download site.

In-text Give the proper name of the software and version in the text rather than in a parenthetical citation.

> References
>
> Benjamin, B., Seising, G., & Osborn, A. (1998). Critical Tools [Computer software]. Austin, TX: College of Liberal Arts, University of Texas.

GRAPHIC, AUDIO, OR VIDEO FILES

> East Timor awaits referendum. (1999, August 31). *NPR Online*. Retrieved August 31, 1999, from http://www.npr.org/ramfiles/atc /1990830.atc.10.ram

23g SAMPLE PAPER WITH APA DOCUMENTATION

This paper is a shortened version of a research report by Michael Moshenrose and his faculty advisor, Keli A. Braitman. The original report was published in the online journal *Psych-E* (**truth.boisestate.edu/psyche/ archives/vol3/moshen.html**).

Body Objectification 1

Running head: BODY OBJECTIFICATION

Body Objectification: Relationship with
Fashion Magazines and Weight Satisfaction

Michael Moshenrose and Keli A. Braitman
Southern Illinois University-Carbondale

APA style uses a title page.

Include page header and page number, beginning with the title page.

Type the running head (the shortened title) for publication in all caps, flush left.

Center the title, name of author(s), and name of school.

Continue to use the running head with the page number in the top right.

Body Objectification 2

Abstract

This study examined the relationship between objectified body consciousness and the utilization of fashion magazines for information about fashion and beauty, comparison to models, and weight satisfaction. Participants were 180 female undergraduate students. We hypothesized that highly body-conscious individuals would read more fashion magazines than low body-conscious women and also rate magazine advertisements and articles as important for influencing fashion and beauty ideals. We also hypothesized that highly body-conscious women would compare themselves to models and be less satisfied with their weight as compared to low body-conscious women. A multivariate analysis of variance indicated that significant differences between the groups existed, but that group differences were opposite to hypotheses. Possible explanations for findings are discussed.

The abstract appears on a separate page with the title *Abstract*.

Double-space the abstract.

Do not indent the first line of the abstract.

The abstract must be brief. The limit is 120 words.

Body Objectification 3

Give the full title at the beginning of the body of the report.

Body Objectification: Relationship with Fashion Magazines and Weight Satisfaction

Introduction

Center the heading *Introduction*.

The cultural preoccupation with physical beauty has generated much research regarding how a woman's

Body Objectification 4

perception of her body contributes to negative body esteem. Feminist theorists argue that the female body is often treated as an object to be looked at. This objectification causes women to perceive their bodies as detached
observers, which means they are attempting to see themselves as others see them. An internalization of the cultural body standards results in women believing that they
created these standards and can achieve them. Therefore,
objectified body consciousness (OBC) refers to perceiving
the body as an object and the beliefs that sustain this
perception (McKinley, 1995). McKinley and Hyde (1996)
developed the 24-item instrument to assess OBC, and the
three scale facets are body surveillance, control beliefs,
and body shame. In order to conform to cultural body
standards, women engage in self-surveillance to avoid
negative evaluations (McKinley & Hyde, 1996). Thus,
women are constantly seeing themselves as others see
them, and this act of mental disassociation can have
negative consequences for women.

The next aspect of OBC is that internalizing cultural
body standards can cause women to experience intense
shame (McKinley & Hyde, 1996). Because the cultural ideal
of a "perfect" body is excessively thin, most women are

Specify 1-inch margins.

Include the date in parentheses when you mention authors in the text.

Include authors and date in parentheses when you do not mention authors in the text.

Indent each paragraph five to seven spaces (1/2" on the ruler in the word processing program).

unable to achieve that standard. Consequently, many women experience a discrepancy between their actual bodies and their ideal bodies (Noll & Fredrickson, 1998). Any comparisons that women make between the ultra-thin standard and their bodies will produce body shame. The final component of OBC are control beliefs, which assert that women are responsible for their physical characteristics and can alter their appearance to conform to cultural standards (McKinley & Hyde, 1996). However, women must first be convinced that they are responsible for how they look in order to accept attractiveness as a reasonable standard by which to judge themselves. When women perceive the attainment of the cultural body standards as a choice, they are more likely to believe that appearance can be controlled (McKinley & Hyde, 1996).

Related to the concept of self-objectification is exposure to appearance-related information via fashion and beauty magazines. Levine, Smolak, and Hayden (1994), for example, found that fashion magazines were instrumental in providing motivation and guidance for women striving to mirror the thin-ideal. Further, nearly half of the respondents in a sample of middle school girls indicated that

Body Objectification 6

they read fashion magazines frequently, and that the magazines were moderately important sources of information about beauty (Levine et al., 1994).

Given that fashion magazines are seen as sources of information about beauty ideals, it seems likely that women scoring high on objectified body consciousness would be more likely to utilize fashion magazines for these purposes. The objective of this study was to examine the relationship between objectified body consciousness and attitudes and behaviors regarding fashion magazines. Specifically, we hypothesized that women scoring high on the OBC scale were more likely to read fashion magazines and to rate both magazine articles and advertisements as important in influencing their fashion and beauty ideas. Further, we hypothesized that highly body-conscious individuals would compare themselves to fashion models and be less satisfied with their bodies in comparison to women who were low on body consciousness.

Methods

Participants

Participants were 180 Caucasian females from undergraduate psychology classes. However, only the data from participants scoring above the median on all three OBC scales or below the median on all OBC scales were analyzed. Thus, data from only 56 participants were analyzed. The mean age of the participants was 19.0 (SD = 1.33). Participants were recruited through general psychology classes and received partial course credit for participation.

Instruments

Instruments were administered to measure (1) the extent to which an individual reads or is exposed to fashion magazines, (2) the importance of magazine *advertisements* in influencing fashion and beauty ideals, (3) the importance of magazine *articles* in influencing fashion and beauty ideals, (4) the extent to which an individual compares herself to fashion magazines on a variety of domains such as happiness and physical appearance, and (5) weight satisfaction.

To measure the magazine-related factors, a media questionnaire was created through a synthesis and modification of Levine et al.'s (1994) Media Questionnaire and Strowman's (1996) Media Exposure and Comparison to Models survey. The first 15 items of the instrument comprised the Exposure subscale. Participants were

Body Objectification 8

asked to rate how often they view a variety of listed magazines. Although the focus of the study explored exposure to fashion magazines, nonfashion magazines were also included in the list to make the focus of the study less apparent. A subscale score indicating exposure to fashion magazines was obtained by summing responses to each fashion magazine item, with a high score indicating higher exposure to fashion magazines.

The next 16 items of the instrument comprised the magazine information subscales. The first six of these items assessed the importance of magazine advertisements for providing information about beauty and fashion, and the remaining 10 items assessed the importance of magazine articles for the same purpose. Eight additional items comprised the Comparison to Models subscale, which assessed the extent to which participants compare themselves to models. To assess weight satisfaction, we employed the Weight Satisfaction subscale of the Body Esteem Scale (Franzoi & Shields, 1984). The entire instrument was administered, but only scores for weight satisfaction were included in the analysis. Subscale scores were obtained by summing items for the weight satisfaction scale.

Body Objectification 9

A demographics survey was included at the end of the questionnaire. This survey contained items assessing such characteristics as age, race, height, weight, and exercise habits. Based on self-reported height and weight, the body mass of each participant was calculated using the following formula: Weight (kg)/Height2 (m2).

Procedure

Participants were solicited from general psychology courses and were tested in small groups ranging in size from one to ten. The participants were provided with a packet marked only with an identification number. They were instructed to remove the informed consent form from the packet and read along with the experimenter as she read the informed consent aloud. The participants were told that the project was examining the effects of marketing on college students. Participants agreeing to participate then removed the scantrons and seven-page questionnaire from the packets and began working. Without a time limit being imposed, participants completed the questionnaire and were then presented with a debriefing form describing the true nature of the experiment. Participants were encouraged to contact the researcher if they had any additional questions about the research project.

To identify participants who were either high or low scorers on objectified body consciousness, a median split was conducted for all OBC scales. Participants scoring above the median on all three scales were identified as high on objectified body consciousness, and those scoring below the median on all three OBC scales were identified as low on objectified body consciousness. We then conducted both multivariate and univariate analyses of variance.

Results

Table 1 presents the mean exposure score for each fashion magazine, and Table 2 presents the means, standard deviations, and F-values of the dependent variables for the high and low objectified body consciousness groups.

Body Objectification 11

Number tables and figures.
Give each table and figure a descriptive title. Begin the title flush left and in italics.

Table 1

Means and Standard Deviations for Magazines Included in the Media Exposure Scale

Magazine	Mean	SD
Seventeen	2.93	1.35
Cosmopolitan	2.93	1.17
Glamour	2.79	1.17
YM	2.57	1.26
Vogue	2.55	1.06
Mademoiselle	2.45	1.22
Newsweek	2.32	1.25
National Geographic	2.27	1.05
Reader's Digest	2.13	1.13
Marie Claire	1.93	1.25
Self	1.84	1.04
Better Homes and Gardens	1.80	0.88
In Style	1.80	1.00
Elle	1.67	0.97
Redbook	1.64	0.97
Shape	1.63	0.97
Fitness Magazine	1.54	0.97
US News & World Report	1.52	0.83
Model	1.39	0.78
Vanity Fair	1.23	0.66
Playboy	1.18	0.51

Double-space notes to tables.

Note. 5-point scale: 1 = never look at it; 2 = look through it rarely; 3 = glance through it sometimes; 4 = look through it often; 5 = look through every new issue

Table 2

Means and Standard Deviations for the Objectified Body Consciousness Groups

Dependent Variable	Objectified Body Consciousness				
	Low (n = 25)		High (n = 31)		
	M	SD	M	SD	F(1,53)
Fashion Magazines	30.12	15.40	20.65	13.67	5.26
Magazine Advertisements	18.16	4.67	12.84	4.06	19.59***
Magazine Articles	3.24	7.37	21.90	6.14	37.55***
Comparison to Models	21.72	4.84	14.13	5.85	25.82**
Weight Satisfaction	19.36	5.82	26.16	7.65	12.08**

Asterisks are normally used for notes of statistical probability.

Note. ** $p < .01$, *** $p < .001$.

Multivariate analyses of variance indicated that the two groups differed significantly on their mean profiles based on the five fashion magazine and weight satisfaction measures (Wilks' Lambda = .45, F (5, 49) = 12.01, $p < .001$; effect size = .55). Follow-up univariate tests indicated that these groups differed significantly with respect to the importance placed on both magazine advertisements and articles for obtaining information about beauty and fashion, with low objectifiers placing more importance on these items. Low objectifiers were also more likely to compare themselves to fashion models and were less satisfied with their weight than were high objectifiers. Furthermore, low objectifiers also looked at fashion magazines more frequently than did high objectifiers, but this difference was not statistically significant despite the relatively large mean difference between the groups.

Discussion

In contrast to our hypotheses, low objectifiers (1) were more influenced by magazine advertisements and articles than were high objectifiers, (2) were more likely to compare themselves to models, and (3) were less satisfied with their weight. Because our findings counter certain aspects of what the objectification theory predicts, there may be several reasons why this theory was not supported. First, it is assumed that women compare themselves to a cultural beauty ideal when they engage in self-objectification. The question then becomes: how are women exposed to the cultural ideal? In our study, we assumed that women obtain information about the cultural ideal from fashion magazines. The difficulty with this proposition is that the women in our study were not frequently exposed to fashion magazines. Table 1 shows that the highest mean

Body Objectification 14

frequency of exposure to any magazine was 2.93, for both *Seventeen* and *Cosmopolitan*. This frequency approached the level of women "glancing through it sometimes." Because of a lack of exposure to fashion magazines, women may not be influenced by the cultural ideals of beauty presented within their pages. Consequently, women may be procuring information regarding cultural standards from alternative media sources, such as television, films, and the Internet. Future research may address the influence of these media sources in regard to their impact on women's self-perception.

Another possibility is that women may be making lateral comparisons to members of their peer group as opposed to making upward comparisons to models. According to the social comparison theory, individuals can make upward, lateral, or downward comparisons. It may be that women may accept the fact that they can never achieve the standard of beauty portrayed by the media. Hence, they may decide that the only salient standard for them to achieve is to look as good as their peers. In addition, women may experience intense stress by believing they must conform to a certain standard of appearance; thus, they may make downward social comparisons to regain self-esteem. These women may compare themselves to others whom they consider to be unattractive in order to feel better about themselves.

Although some women may make downward social comparisons, other women who rate highly on body consciousness may decide to invest more resources in their appearance. Because they are concerned with and aware of their appearance, these women may actively engage in activities that help to improve their appearance. According to the preceding logic, high objectifiers would then be more satisfied with their weight than low objectifiers. In support of this idea, Smith, Thompson, Raczynski, and Hilner (1999) found that physical appearance is more important to African-American women and men than to Caucasian women and men, but also that African Americans are more satisfied with their appearance compared to their Caucasian counterparts. Thus, these results support the idea that the more individuals value and invest in their physical characteristics, the more satisfied they will be with their appearance.

The generality of our study is limited by the use of a Caucasian, female, college-age sample. However, this sample is appropriate to study because research examining the

Body Objectification 16

influence of ethnicity on body satisfaction has found that
Caucasian women tend to be less satisfied with their appearance compared to African-American and Asian-
American women (Akan & Grilo, 1995; Altabe, 1998; Cash &
Henry, 1995). In addition to ethnicity, men and women
also tend to differ in body image, with women being less
satisfied with their appearance than men (Mintz & Betz,
1986; Serdula, Collins, Williamson, Anda, Pamuk, & Byers,
1993). Thus, both sex and race differences exist in regard
to body image, and these factors should therefore be considered when conducting body-image studies. For this reason, the findings of the present study should be general-
ized only to Caucasian females. Future studies may explore
whether the findings from this study are replicated in samples of individuals of different ethnicity and sex. However,
the questions in the instruments may need to be slightly
modified to be appropriate with a male sample. For example, the fashion magazines included in the exposure subscale may not be the same magazines that would be appropriate for males. In particular, magazines such as *Seventeen*
and *Glamour* may need to be replaced by magazines mar-
keted to men and focusing on the male physique, such as
weight-lifting or fitness magazines.

444 ψ **23** APA Documentation

Center
References.

Alphabetize
entries by last
name of the
author.

References

Akan, G. E., & Grilo, C. M. (1995). Sociocultural influences on
eating attitudes and behaviors, body image, and psychological functioning: A comparison of African-American,
Asian-American, and Caucasian college women.
International Journal of Eating Disorders, 18, 181–187.

Altabe, M. N. (1998). Ethnicity and body image:
Quantitative and qualitative analysis. *International
Journal of Eating Disorders, 23,* 153–159.

Cash, T. F., & Henry, P. E. (1995). Women's body images:
The results of a national survey in the U.S.A. *Sex
Roles, 33,* 19–28.

Franzoi, S. L., & Shields, S. A. (1984). The Body Esteem
Scale: Multidimensional structure and sex differences
in a college population. *Journal of Personality
Assessment, 48,* 173–178.

Levine, M. P., Smolak, L., & Hayden, H. (1994). The relation of sociocultural factors to eating attitudes and
behaviors among middle school girls. *Journal of
Early Adolescence, 14,* 471–490.

McKinley, N. M. (1995). Women and objectified body
consciousness: A feminist psychological analysis.
Dissertation Abstracts International, 56, 05B.
(UMI No. 9527111)

Double-space all
entries.

Indent all but the
first line of each
entry five spaces.

Body Objectification 18

McKinley, N. M., & Hyde, J. S. (1996). The Objectified Body Consciousness Scale: Development and validation. *Psychology of Women Quarterly, 20,* 181–216.

Mintz, L. B., & Betz, N. E. (1986). Sex differences in the nature, realism, and correlates of body image. *Sex Roles, 15* (3/4), 185–195.

Noll, S. M., & Fredrickson, B. L. (1998). A mediational model linking self-objectification, body shame, and disordered eating. *Psychology of Women Quarterly, 22,* 623–636.

Serdula, M. K., Collins, M. E., Williamson, D. F., Anda, R. F., Pamuk, E., & Byers, T. E. (1993). Weight control practices of U.S. adolescents and adults. *Annals of Internal Medicine, 119,* 667–671.

Smith, D. E., Thompson, J. K., Raczynski, J. M., & Hilner, J. (1999). Body image among men and women in a biracial cohort: The CARDIA Study. *International Journal of Eating Disorders, 25,* 71–82.

Strowman, S. R. (1996). *Media exposure survey.* Unpublished manuscript, University of New Hampshire, Durham.

Go through your text and make sure that everything you have cited, except for personal communication, is in the list of references.

To hear audio commentary on this student paper, visit **www.ablongman.com/faigley012.**

Chapter 24
CMS Documentation

Writers who publish in business, social sciences, fine arts, and humanities outside the discipline of English often use the *Chicago Manual of Style* (CMS) method of documentation. CMS guidelines allow writers a clear way of using footnotes and endnotes (rather than MLA and APA in-text citations) for quotations, summaries, and paraphrases. This chapter explains how to use CMS documentation in your writing. If you have further questions, you can consult the full CMS style manual, *The Chicago Manual of Style*, fourteenth edition (Chicago: The University of Chicago Press, 1993), or visit the University of Chicago Press Web site (**http://www.press. uchicago.edu/Misc/Chicago/cmosfaq.html**).

In-text citations

Unlike MLA and APA, which both use parenthetical documentation to cite sources within a text, CMS uses a superscript number directly after any quotation, paraphrase, or summary. Notes are numbered consecutively throughout the text. This superscript number corresponds to either a footnote, which appears at the bottom of the page, or an endnote, which appears at the end of the text.

> In *Southern Honor: Ethics and Behavior in the Old South*, Wyatt-Brown argues that "paradox, irony, and guilt have been three current words used by historians to describe white Southern life before the Civil War."[1]

NOTE	BIBLIOGRAPHY
1. Bertram Wyatt-Brown, *Southern Honor: Ethics and Behavior in the Old South* (Oxford: Oxford Univ. Press, 1983) 3.	Wyatt-Brown, Bertram. *Southern Honor: Ethics and Behavior in the Old South*. Oxford: Oxford Univ. Press, 1983.

Footnotes and endnotes

Footnotes appear at the bottom of the page on which each citation appears. Begin your footnote four lines from the last line of text on the page. Footnotes are single-spaced, but you should double-space between multiple notes on a single page.

Endnotes are compiled at the end of the text on a separate page entitled *Notes*. Center the title at the top of the page and list your endnotes in the order they appear within the text. The entire endnote section should be double-spaced—both within and between each entry.

CMS Bibliography

Because footnotes and endnotes in CMS format contain complete citation information, a separate list of references is often optional. This list of references can be called the *Bibliography*, or if it only has works referenced directly in your text, *Works Cited, Literature Cited*, or *References*. Generally, CMS bibliographies follow the MLA works-cited format.

CMS documentation

24a Books in CMS style citations

Note

1. Elizabeth Bowen, *The Mulberry Tree: Selected Writings* (London: Vintage, 1999), 33–41.

Bibliography

Bowen, Elizabeth. *The Mulberry Tree: Selected Writings*. London: Vintage, 1999.

AUTHOR'S OR EDITOR'S NAME

How many authors are there?

1 *Note:* the author's name is given in normal order. In subsequent references, cite the author's last name only: 2. Bowen, 231. If the reference is to the same work as the reference before it, you can use the abbreviation *Ibid.*: 3. Ibid., 231.

Bibliography: give the author's name in reverse order. If an editor, put *ed.* after the name.

Kavanagh, Patrick, ed. *Lapped Furrows*. New York: Hand Press, 1969.

2 or 3 *Note:* put all authors' names in normal order. For subsequent references, give only the authors' last names: 4. McClelland and Eismann, 32.

Bibliography: give second and third authors' names in normal order.

McClelland, Deke, and Karin Eismann. *Web Design Studio Secrets*. Foster City, CA: IDG Books, 1998.

4 or more *Note:* give the name of the first author listed, followed by *et al.* or *with others.*

5. William J. Andrews et al., *The Literature of the American South* (New York: Norton, 1998), 69.

Bibliography: either list all of the authors (inverting only the first author's name), or give the first author and use *et al.* for the others. Use whichever style you choose consistently.

Unknown Begin both the note and the bibliography entries with the title.

Group or organization Treat the group or organization as the author of the work.

BOOK TITLE

- Use the exact title, which appears on the title page (not on the cover).
- Italicize the title (or underline, if you are working on a typewriter).
- Capitalize all nouns, verbs, and pronouns, and the first word of the title and subtitle.
- The title of a longer work within the title may be in Roman type: Keane, John B. The Field *and Other Irish Plays*
- Titles of works published prior to 1900 may retain their original spellings and capitalization.

FACTS OF PUBLICATION

In a note, the place of publication, publisher, and year of publication are in parentheses. While the use of the full facts is preferred, there are two alternatives: listing the place and date only, or listing the date only. Whichever style you choose, use it consistently.

Publisher's name

- You may use acceptable abbreviations.
- For works published prior to 1900, the place and date are sufficient.

Place of publication

- Add the state's postal abbreviation or country when the city is not well known (*Foster City, CA*) or ambiguous (Cambridge, MA, or Cambridge, UK).
- If more than one city is given, use the first.

Year of publication

- If no year of publication is given, write *n.d.* ("no date") in place of the date.
- If it is a multivolume edited work published over a period of more than one year, put the span of time as the year.

HOW DO YOU CITE ONLY PART OF A BOOK?

A single chapter written by same author as the book

Note

1. Gail Savage, "The Ministry of Labour: Accentuating the Negative," chap. 5 in *The Social Construction of Expertise* (New York: Routledge, 1996), 130–57.

Bibliography

Savage, Gail. "The Ministry of Labour: Accentuating the Negative." Chap. 5 in *The Social Construction of Expertise*. New York: Routledge, 1996.

A selection in an anthology or a chapter in an edited collection

Note

2. J. L. McCracken, "Northern Ireland, 1921–66," in *The Course of Irish History*, eds. T. W. Moody and F. X. Martin (Niwot, CO: Roberts Rinehart, 1995), 313–23.

Bibliography

McCracken, J. L. "Northern Ireland, 1921–66." In *The Course of Irish History*, edited by T. W. Moody and F. X. Martin. Niwot, CO: Roberts Rinehart, 1995.

Article in a reference work

Publication information is usually omitted from citations of well-known reference volumes. The edition is listed instead. The abbreviation *s.v.* (*sub verbo* or "under the word") replaces an entry's page number.

4. *Benet's Reader's Encyclopedia*, 1987 ed., s.v. "Lampoon."

24b Other book and nonperiodical sources in CMS style

How Do You Cite . . . ?

- A book, with the focus on author, editor, or translator
- A book in a revised edition; work in volumes or a series
- Government documents
- Religious texts
- Dissertations
- Letters

BOOKS: A FOCUS ON . . .

Book with an editor, but with the focus on the original author

Note

    1. Thomas Hardy, *Jude the Obscure*, ed. Norman Page (New York: Norton, 1999), 35.

Bibliography

Hardy, Thomas. *Jude the Obscure*. Edited by Norman Page. New York: Norton, 1999.

Book with the focus on the editor

Note

    2. Norman Page, ed., *Jude the Obscure*, by Thomas Hardy (New York: Norton, 1999).

Bibliography

Page, Norman, ed. *Jude the Obscure*, by Thomas Hardy. New York: Norton, 1999.

Book with a translator, but with the focus on the original author

Follow the style of the first entry above, but substitute "trans." for "ed." in the note and "Translated" for "Edited" in the bibliographic entry.

Book with a focus on the translator

Follow the style of the second entry above, but substitute: "trans." for "ed." in note and bibliography.

BOOKS: REVISED, VOLUME, SERIES

A revised or later edition of a book

Note

    1. Jeremy Hawthorn, ed., *A Concise Glossary of Contemporary Literary Theory*, 2nd ed. (London: Arnold, 1994), 30.

Bibliography

Hawthorn, Jeremy, ed. *A Concise Glossary of Contemporary Literary Theory*. 2nd ed. London: Arnold, 1994.

Work in more than one volume

Note

    1. Oscar Wilde, *The Complete Works of Oscar Wilde*, vol. 3 (New York: Dragon Press, 1998), 1024.

Bibliography

Wilde, Oscar. *The Complete Works of Oscar Wilde*. Vol. 3. New York: Dragon Press, 1998.

Work in a series

Note

    3. Peter Kavanagh, ed., *Patrick Kavanagh: Man and Poet*, Man and Poet Series (Orono, ME: National Poetry Foundation, 1986), 35.

Bibliography

Kavanagh, Peter, ed. *Patrick Kavanagh: Man and Poet*. Man and Poet Series. Orono, ME: National Poetry Foundation, 1986.

GOVERNMENT DOCUMENTS

Government document

Note

> 5. United States Department of Health and Public Safety, *Grade School Hygiene and Epidemics* (Washington, D.C.: GPO, 1998), 21.

Bibliography

United States Department of Health and Public Safety. *Grade School Hygiene and Epidemics*. Washington, D.C.: GPO, 1998.

Congressional Record

Identify the Congress, the session, the year, the volume, the part, and the page numbers.

Note

> 6. *Congressional Record,* 100th Cong., 2d sess., 1987, 70, pt. 2:750–51.

Bibliography

Congressional Record. 100th Cong., 2d sess., 1987. Vol. 70, pt. 2.

RELIGIOUS TEXTS

Citations from religious texts appear in the notes, but not in the bibliography. Traditionally a colon is used between chapter and verse. A period is also acceptable.

Note

> 4. John 3:16 King James Version.

DISSERTATIONS

Unpublished dissertation

Note

> 7. James Elsworth Kidd, "The Vision of Uncertainty: Elizabethan Windows and the Problem of Sight" (Ph.D. diss., Southern Illinois University, 1998), 236.

Bibliography

Kidd, James Elsworth. "The Vision of Uncertainty: Elizabethan Windows and the Problem of Sight." Ph.D. diss., Southern Illinois University, 1998.

LETTERS

Published letter

Give full publication information.

Note

> 5. Antonio Gramsci to Teresina, 20 February 1928. *Letters from Prison: Antonio Gramsci*, ed. Lynn Lawner (New York: Noonday-Farrar, Straus and Giroux, 1989), 120–21.

Bibliography

Gramsci, Antonio. Letter to Teresina. 20 February 1928. In *Letters from Prison: Antonio Gramsci*, edited by Lynn Lawner, 120–21. New York: Noonday-Farrar, Straus and Giroux, 1989.

Personal letter to author

Personal communications are not usually listed in the bibliography because they are not accessible to the public.

Note

> 7. Ann Williams, letter to author, 8 May 2000.

24c Periodical sources in CMS style

Note

1. Stacy Margolis, "*Huckleberry Finn*; or, Consequences," *PMLA* 116 (2001): 329–43.

Bibliography

Margolis, Stacy. "*Huckleberry Finn*; or, Consequences." *PMLA* 116 (2001): 329–43.

AUTHOR'S OR EDITOR'S NAME

How many authors are there?

1 *Note:* the author's name is given in normal order. In subsequent references, cite the author's last name only: 2. Margolis, 331.

If the reference is to the same work as the reference before it, you can use the abbreviation *Ibid.*: 3. Ibid., 331.

Bibliography: the author's name is given in reverse order.

2 or 3 *Note:* all authors' names are printed in normal order. For subsequent references, give both authors' last names.

4. Matthews and O'Farrell, 4.

Bibliography: the second and third authors' names are given in normal order.

Matthews, Pamela R., and Mary Ann O'Farrell. "Introduction: Whose Body?" *South Central Review* 18, no. 3-4 (Fall-Winter 2001): 1–5.

More than 3 *Note:* give the name of the first listed author, followed by *et al.* or *with others.*

Bibliography: either list all of the authors (inverting only the first author's name), or give the first author and use *et al.* for the others. Whichever style you choose, use it consistently throughout your references.

Unknown Begin both the note and the bibliography entries with the title.

Group or organization Treat the group or organization as the author of the work.

TITLE OF ARTICLE

- Put the title in quotation marks. If there is a title of a book within the title, italicize it. If there is a title within the title that requires quotation marks, use single marks.

  2. Dennis Berthold, "Class Acts: The Astor Place Riots and Melville's 'The Two Temples,'" *American Literature* 71 (1999): 429–61.

- Capitalize nouns, verbs, and pronouns, and the first word of the title and subtitle.
- If the title is in a foreign language, copy it exactly as it appears on the title page, paying special attention to accent marks and capitalization.
- Do not put titles of regular features or departments of a magazine in quotation marks.

  3. This Week Online, *Newsweek,* 19 November 2001, 4.

NAME OF JOURNAL

- Italicize the name of the journal.
- Journal titles are normally not abbreviated in the arts and humanities unless the title of the journal is an abbreviation (*PMLA, ELH*). See *Periodical Title Abbreviations*, published by the Gale Group, for the abbreviations of titles of journals from many scientific fields.

VOLUME, ISSUE, PAGE NUMBERS, AND DATE

Volume

- Place the volume number after the journal title without intervening punctuation.
- When citing an entire article, with no page numbers, place the abbreviation *vol.* before the volume number.

Issue

- For journals that are paginated from issue to issue within a volume, do not list the issue number.

> 4. Susan Welsh. "Resistance Theory and Illegitimate Reproduction." *College Composition and Communication* 52 (2001): 553–73.

- For journals that are paginated separately in each issue, list the issue number after the volume number.
- The issue number can be placed either after the volume number, a comma, and the abbreviation *no.*, or in parentheses after the volume number (without a comma and *no.*). If you use parentheses, the date goes after the page numbers.

> 5. Pamela R. Matthews and Mary Ann O'Farrell, "Introduction: Whose Body?" *South Central Review* 18 (3-4): 1–5 (Fall-Winter 2001).

Whichever style you choose, be consistent throughout your references.

Date

- The date or year of publication is given in parentheses after the volume number, or issue number, if provided. When the issue number is put in parentheses, the date goes after the page numbers.
- For a weekly or biweekly popular magazine, give both the day and month of publication as listed on the issue. Note that the date is not in parentheses.

> 5. Roddy Doyle, "The Dinner," *The New Yorker*, 5 February 2001, 73.

WHAT IF YOU NEED TO CITE . . . ?

A review

Provide the title, if given, and name the work reviewed. If there is no title, just name the work reviewed.

> 1. Barbara Erlich, "Far and Away from Irish History," review of *Far and Away* (Universal movie), *The Irish Observer*, 12 April 1994, 32–33.

A letter to the editor or an editorial

Add *letter* or *editorial* after the name of the author (if there is one). If there is no author, start with the descriptor.

> 2. Daphne Patai, letter, *Harper's Magazine*, December 2001, 4.

WHAT IS DIFFERENT ABOUT NEWSPAPERS?

This is a typical citation from a newspaper:

> 1. Larry Kaplow and Tasgola Karla Bruner, "U.S.: Don't Let Taliban Forces Flee," *Austin American-Statesman*, 20 November 2001, final edition.

- The day, month, and year are essential in citations of materials from daily newspapers.
- For an item in a large city newspaper that has several editions a day, give the edition after the date.
- If the newspaper is published in sections, include the name, number, or letter of the section after the date: **sec. C.**
- Page numbers are usually omitted. If you put them in, use *p.* and *col.* (column) to avoid ambiguity.

24d Online and computer sources in CMS style

How Do You Cite . . . ?

- A Web site
- An online book
- An online article
- An online government publication
- Computer software
- Email

THREE FEATURES OF ELECTRONIC SOURCES

The Chicago Manual of Style, 14th edition, focuses on three features in citations of electronic sources:

1. a description of the electronic source in brackets, such as [Web site];
2. the date the material was accessed, updated, or cited; and
3. an electronic address, following the phrase *available from*.

The examples in this section are based on general CMS guidelines. Because CMS does not provide detailed instruction on citing electronic sources, writers using CMS style may also consult the guidelines for electronic citation presented in the MLA citation chapter of this handbook (Section 21h).

WEB SITE

Note

10. *The Museum of Jurassic Technology* [Web site] (2001); available from http://www.mjt.com/; Internet; accessed 2 December 2001.

Bibliography

The Museum of Jurassic Technology. Web site. 2001. Available from http://www.mjt.org/. Internet. Accessed 2 December 2001.

ONLINE BOOK

Note

12. Angelina Grimké, *Appeal to the Christian Women of the South* [book online] (New York: New York Anti-Slavery Society, 1836); available from http://history.furman.edu/~benson/docs/grimke2.htm; Internet; accessed 2 June 2001.

Bibliography

Grimké, Angelina. *Appeal to the Christian Women of the South*. Book online. New York: New York Anti-Slavery Society, 1836. Available from http://history.furman.edu/~benson/docs/grimke2.htm. Internet. Accessed 2 June 2001.

ONLINE ARTICLE

Note

13. Phil Agre, "The Internet and Public Discourse," *First Monday* 3:3, March 1998 [journal online]; available from http://www.firstmonday.dk/issues/issue3_3/agre/; Internet; accessed 14 July 1999.

Bibliography

Agre, Phil. "The Internet and Public Discourse." *First Monday* 3:3, March 1998. Journal online. Available from http://www.firstmonday.dk/issues/issue3_3/agre/. Internet. Accessed 14 July 1999.

ONLINE GOVERNMENT PUBLICATION

Note

1. United States Department of the Treasury, *Your Rights as a Taxpayer* (August 2000) [govt. document online]; available from http://www.irs.gov/forms_pubs/pubs.html; accessed 24 November 2001.

Bibliography

United States Department of the Treasury. *Your Rights as a Taxpayer* (August 2000). Govt. document online. Available from http://www.irs.gov/forms_pubs/pubs.html. Internet. Accessed 24 November 2001.

COMPUTER SOFTWARE

Note

14. AOL Ver. 6.0, America Online, 2001.

Bibliography

AOL Ver. 6.0. America Online, 2001.

EMAIL

Since personal emails are not usually available to the public, they are not usually listed in the bibliography.

Note

11. Samuel Wilson, "Advantages of Flash 3," email to author, 18 August 1999.

24e Multimedia sources in CMS style

How Do You Cite . . . ?

- A musical recording
- A film or video
- An interview
- Speech, debate, mediated discussion, or public talk

AUDIO AND VIDEO

Musical recording

Note

8. Judy Garland, "Come Rain or Come Shine," on *Judy at Carnegie Hall: Fortieth Anniversary Edition*, Capitol compact disc B000059QY9.

Bibliography

Garland, Judy. "Come Rain or Come Shine." On *Judy at Carnegie Hall: Fortieth Anniversary Edition*. Capitol compact disc B000059QY9.

Film or Video

Note

9. *Harold and Maude*, dir. Hal Ashby, Paramount Pictures, 1971. videocassette.

Bibliography

Ashby, Hal, dir. *Harold and Maude*. Paramount Pictures, 1971. Videocassette.

INTERVIEW

It is not necessary to list interviews in the bibliography, but if you include an interview, follow this format.

Note

15. Ira Glass, interview by Terry Gross, *Fresh Air*, National Public Radio, 17 November 2000.

Bibliography

Glass, Ira. Interview by Terry Gross. *Fresh Air*. National Public Radio, 17 November 2000.

SPEECH, DEBATE, MEDIATED DISCUSSION, OR PUBLIC TALK

Note

16. Ellen Arthur, "The Octoroon, or Irish Life in Louisiana" (paper presented at the 2001 Annual Convention of the American Conference for Irish Studies, New York, June 2001).

Bibliography

Arthur, Ellen. "The Octoroon, or Irish Life in Louisiana." Paper presented at the 2001 Annual Convention of the American Conference for Irish Studies, New York, June 2001.

Writing in the World

Footnotes versus endnotes

Word processing programs give you a choice of using footnotes or endnotes. Footnotes allow a reader to find the source without turning the page. Some writers use notes to provide additional explanation for material in the text. These explanatory notes may be a paragraph in length and work best as endnotes.

24f **SAMPLE PAGES WITH CMS DOCUMENTATION**

1

Jason Laker

American History 102

January 9, 2002

THE ELECTORAL COLLEGE: DOES IT HAVE A FUTURE?

Until the presidential election of 2000, few Americans thought much about the Electoral College. It was something they had learned about in civics class and had then forgotten about as other, more pressing bits of information required their attention. In November 2000, however, the Electoral College took center stage and sparked an argument that continues today: Should the Electoral College be abolished?

The founding fathers established the Electoral College as a compromise between elections by Congress and those by popular vote.[1] The College consists of a group of electors

2

who meet to vote for the president and vice president of the United States. The electors are nominated by political parties within each state and the number each state gets relates to the state's congressional delegation.[2] The process and the ideas behind it sound simple, but the actual workings of the Electoral College remain a mystery to many Americans.

The complicated nature of the Electoral College is one of the reasons why some people want to see it abolished. One voter writes in a letter to the editor of the *New York Times* that the elimination of the Electoral College is necessary "to demystify our voting system in the eyes of foreigners and our own citizenry."[3] Other detractors claim that it just does not work and cite the presidential elections of 1824, 1876, 1888, and, of course, 2000 as representative of the failures of the College. Those who defend the Electoral College, however, claim that the failures of these elections had little to do with the Electoral College itself.[4]

According to Gary Gregg, director of the McConnell Center for Political Leadership, a new study shows that much of what Americans think we know about the Electoral College is wrong. Consequently, we should actively question the wisdom of those who want to see it abolished.[5]

3

NOTES

1. Lawrence D. Longley and Neal R. Peirce, *The Electoral College Primer 2000* (New Haven: Yale University Press, 1999).

2. Office of the Federal Register, "A Procedural Guide to the Electoral College," Electoral College Homepage; available from http://www.nara.gov/fedreg/elctcoll/proced.html; Internet; accessed 2 January 2002.

3. William C. McIntyre, "Revisiting the Electoral College," *New York Times*, 17 November 2001, final edition, sec. A.

4. Avagara, *EC: The Electoral College Webzine* (1999) [journal online]; available from http://www.avagara.com/e_c/; Internet; accessed 2 January 2002.

5. Gary Gregg, "Keep the College," *National Review Online* (7 November 2001) [journal online]; available from LexisNexis [database online] at http://www.lexisnexis.com/universe/; accessed 3 January 2002.

4

WORKS CITED

Avagara. *EC: The Electoral College Webzine* (1999) [journal online]. Available from http://www.avagara.com/e_c/. Internet. Accessed 2 January 2002.

Gregg, Gary. "Keep the College." *National Review Online* (7 November 2001) [journal online]. Available from LexisNexis [database online] at http://www.lexisnexis.com/universe/. Accessed 3 January 2002.

Longley, Lawrence D., and Neal R. Peirce. *The Electoral College Primer 2000*. New Haven: Yale University Press, 1999.

McIntyre, William C. "Revisiting the Electoral College." *New York Times*. 17 November 2001. Final edition, sec. A.

Office of the Federal Register. "A Procedural Guide to the Electoral College." Electoral College Homepage. Available from http://www.nara.gov/fedreg/elctcoll/proced.html. Internet. Accessed 2 January 2002.

Chapter 25
CSE Documentation

Within the disciplines of natural and applied sciences, citation styles are highly specialized. Many disciplines follow the guidelines of particular journals or style manuals within their individual fields. One of these guides, published by the Council of Science Editors (formerly the Council of Biology Editors), is *Scientific Style and Format: The CBE Manual for Authors, Editors, and Publishers,* sixth edition (1994). The *CBE Manual* is influential and widely followed by writers in the sciences.

Name-year and citation-sequence systems

CSE style allows writers two alternative methods for documenting sources: the **name-year system** and the **citation-sequence system**. In the CSE name-year system, both the author's last name and the year of publication appear together in parentheses directly following cited material in the text.

> The Red-cockaded Woodpecker (*Picoides borealis*) typically uses a single cavity for nesting (Ligon 1970, Walters et al. 1988).

In the CSE citation-sequence system, citations in the body of the text are marked by a superscript number placed inside punctuation. For example,

> Cold fingers and toes are common circulatory problems found in most heavy cigarette smokers[1].

This number corresponds to a numbered entry on the CSE source list, entitled *References*.

The CSE References page lists all sources cited in the paper. To create a CSE Reference page, follow these guidelines:

1. Title your page "References," and center this title at the top of the page.
2. Double-space the entire References page, both within and between citations.
3. For papers using the **citation-sequence system**, list citations in the order they appear in the body of the paper. Begin each citation with its citation number, followed by a period, flush left.
4. For papers using the **name-year system**, list references, unnumbered, in alphabetical order. Begin each citation flush left. Indent any subsequent lines of the citation five spaces.
5. Authors are listed by last name, followed by initials. Capitalize only first words and proper nouns in cited titles. Titles are not underlined, and articles are not placed in quotations. Names of journals should be abbreviated where possible.
6. Cite publication year, and volume or page numbers if applicable.

Writing in the World

The National Library of Medicine

The CSE recommendations for citations and references are based on the *National Library of Medicine Recommended Formats for Bibliographic Citation* (1991). Additionally, the National Library of Medicine (NLM) has an extensive supplement on Internet formats available at **www.nlm.nih.gov/pubs/formats/internet.pdf**.

25a In-text citations in CSE style

Name-year system (N-Y)

In 1997, the Gallup poll reported that 55% of adults in the United States think secondhand smoke is "very harmful," compared to only 36% in 1994 (Saad 2000).

Citation-sequence system (C-S)

In 1997, the Gallup poll reported that 55% of adults in the United States think secondhand smoke is "very harmful," compared to only 36% in 1994[1].

PLACEMENT OF AUTHOR'S NAME AND DATE (NAME-YEAR SYSTEM)

You have two choices:

1. As in the example above, place the author's name and the year of publication inside parentheses following the material cited.
2. Put the author's name in a signal phrase right in your sentence. Then, put the year in parentheses right after.

Sociologist Daniel Bell (1973) called this emerging U.S. economy the "postindustrial society."

NUMBER OF AUTHORS (NAME-YEAR SYSTEM)

1 The author's last name comes first, followed by the year of publication: (Barron 2001)

2 The authors' last names follow the order of the title page and are joined by *and*: (Monastersky and Allen 1998)

If the authors have the same surname, add their initials: (Allen SR and Allen TJ 1997)

3 or more Use the last name of the first author, followed by *and others*, and the year of publication: (Barker and others 1972)

Group Treat the group or organization as the author, but abbreviate if possible. If there are relatively few citations in the text, the full name may be acceptable: (WHO 2001)

WHAT IF YOU NEED MORE THAN ONE CITATION IN A PASSAGE?

N-Y When you cite two or more sources at once, your citation should be arranged chronologically, from the earliest publication to the latest. Each citation is separated by a semicolon.

(Radhost 1969; Barker and others 1972; WHO 2001)

If your sources are published in the same year, arrange these citations alphabetically:

(Earhart and others 1997; Smythe 1997; Matina 1999)

C-S If the numbers are consecutive, separate with a dash. If nonconsecutive, use a comma.

The previous work [1,3,5-8,11] . . . .

25b Books in CSE-style references

Name-Year (N-Y)

Nance JJ. 1991. What goes up: the global assault on our atmosphere.
New York: W Morrow. 324 p.

Citation-Sequence (C-S)

1. Nance JJ. What goes up: the global assault on our atmosphere. New York:
W Morrow; 1991. 324 p.

BOOK TITLE

- Do not italicize or underline titles.
- Capitalize only the first word and proper nouns.
- Place information needed to identify the source (i.e., edition, report no., volume no.) after the title.

N-Y Clarke JJ. 1903-1916. Protozoa and disease. Part III, The cause of cancer. New York: W Wood.

C-S 5. Clarke JJ. Protozoa and disease. Part III, The cause of cancer. New York: W Wood; 1903-1916.

AUTHOR'S OR EDITOR'S NAME

The NLM recommends using the full first name for an author. Whichever you choose, be consistent throughout your references. How many authors are there?

1 author/editor The author's last name comes first, followed by the initials of the author's first name and middle name (if provided). If an editor, put the word *editor* after the name:

N-Y Minger TJ, editor. 1990. Greenhouse glasnost: the crisis of global warming. New York: Ecco Press. 292 p.

C-S 2. Minger T, editor. Greenhouse glasnost: the crisis of global warming. New York: Ecco Press; 1990. 292 p.

2 or more authors/editors

N-Y O'Day DH, Horgen PA, editors. 1981. Sexual interactions in eukaryotic microbes. New York: Academic Press. 407 p.

C-S 3. O'Day DH, Horgen PA, editors. Sexual interactions in eukaryotic microbes. New York: Academic Press; 1981. 407 p.

Group or organization In **N-Y**, the full name is given, preceded by the abbreviation, in brackets.

N-Y [IAEA] International Atomic Energy Association. 1971. Manual on radiation haematology. Vienna: IAEA. 430 p.

C-S 4. IAEA. Manual on radiation haematology. Vienna: IAEA; 1971. 430 p.

YEAR OF PUBLICATION

- In **N-Y**, the year comes after the author(s). In **C-S**, the year comes after the other publication information. It follows a semicolon.
- If it is a multivolume edited work, published over a period of more than 1 year, give the span of years.

PAGE NUMBERS

- When citing an entire book, give the total number of pages: *324 p.*
- When citing part of a book, give the page range for the selection: *p. 60-90.*

HOW DO YOU CITE PART OF A BOOK?

A single chapter written by the same author as the book

Put the title of the chapter, part, or section after the year of publication. Provide the page numbers of the selection at the end, after a semicolon.

N-Y   Ogle M. 2000. All the modern conveniences: American household plumbing, 1840-1890. Baltimore: Johns Hopkins Univ Pr; Convenience embodied; p. 60-92.

C-S   6. Ogle M. All the modern conveniences: American household plumbing, 1840-1890. Baltimore: Johns Hopkins Univ Pr; 2000. Convenience embodied; p. 60-92.

A selection in an anthology or a chapter in an edited collection

The author of the selection is listed first. The year given is for the collection. Put the word *In* and a colon before the editor of the collection.

N-Y   Kraft K, Baines DM. 1997. Computer classrooms and third grade development. In: Green MD, editor. Computers and early development. New York: Academic. p. 168-79.

C-S   7. Kraft K, Baines DM. Computer classrooms and third grade development. In: Green MD, editor. Computers and early development. New York: Academic; 1997. p. 168-79.

WHAT IF YOU NEED TO CITE . . . ?

Two or more books by the same author

In **C-S**, number the references according to the order in which they appear in the text. In **N-Y**, arrange them by date, or alphabetically according to names of additional authors. If the date and the additional authors are the same, arrange according to title. To clarify in-text citation, assign a letter (a, b, c) to the repeated dates.

Clarke JJ. 1903a. Protozoa and disease. New York: W Wood.

Clarke JJ. 1903b. Rhizopod protozoa. New York: W Wood.

Technical and research reports

N-Y   Austin A, Baldwin R, editors. 1991. Faculty collaboration: enhancing the quality of scholarship and teaching. ASCHE-ERIC Higher Education Report 7. Washington, DC: George Washington University.

C-S   9. Austin A, Baldwin R, editors. Faculty collaboration: enhancing the quality of scholarship and teaching. ASCHE-ERIC Higher Education Report 7. Washington, DC: George Washington University; 1991.

Published conference proceedings

N-Y   Hoffman D, editor. 1999. Science, technology and political change. Proceedings of the 20th International Congress of History of Science; 1997 July 20-26; Liege, Belgium: Brepols.

C-S   10. Hoffman D, editor. Science, technology and political change. Proceedings of the 20th International Congress of History of Science; 1997 July 20-26; Liege, Belgium: Brepols; 1999.

25d Periodical sources in CSE-style references

Name-Year (N-Y)

Board J. 2001. Reduced lodging for soybeans in low plant population is related to light quality. Crop Science 41:379-87.

Citation-Sequence (C-S)

1. Board J. Reduced lodging for soybeans in low plant population is related to light quality. Crop Science 2001;41:379-87.

AUTHOR'S NAME

Use either the first name or initials, but be consistent.

1 author The author's last name comes first, followed by the initials of the author's first name and middle names (if provided).

2 or more authors/editors

N-Y Simms K, Denison D. 1997. Observed interactions between wild and domesticated mixed-breed canines. J. Mamm 70:341-2.

C-S 2. Simms K, Denison D. Observed interactions between wild and domesticated mixed-breed canines. J. Mamm 1997; 70:341-2.

Group or organization In C-S list the abbreviation only. In N-Y, give the abbreviation in brackets, followed by the full name.

N-Y [CSPI] Center for Science in the Public Interest. 2001 Apr 1. Meat labeling: help! Nutrition Action Health Letter: 2.

No identifiable author
In both **N-Y** and **C-S**, use [*Anonymous*].

TITLE OF ARTICLE
• Do not put the title in quotation marks.
• Capitalize only the first word and proper nouns in the title.

NAME OF JOURNAL
• Do not abbreviate single-word titles. Abbreviate multiple-word titles according to the National Information Standards Organization (NISO) list of serials.
• Capitalize the journal title, even if abbreviated.

DATE OF PUBLICATION, VOLUME, AND ISSUE NUMBERS
• For continuously paginated journals, include only the year and volume number, not the issue number.
• Use the month or season of publication (and day, if given) for journals paginated by issue. Include the issue number in parentheses after the volume number.

N-Y Barlow JP. 1998 Jan. Africa rising: everything you know about Africa is wrong. Wired:142-58.

C-S 8. Barlow JP. Africa rising: everything you know about Africa is wrong. Wired 1998 Jan:142-58.

• If the article has not yet been published, place the word *Forthcoming* at the end of the citation.

Scientific Style and Format: The CBE Manual for Authors, Editors, and Publishers (6th edition, 1994) briefly covers electronic citation. For expanded guidelines, see the *National Library of Medicine Recommended Formats for Bibliographic Citations* supplement on Internet formats, available at <www.nlm.nih.gov/pubs/formats/internet.pdf>.

Name-year (N-Y)

Lowe C. 2001. Speech recognition: sci-fi or composition? Currents in Electronic
Literacy [serial online]. 4. Available from: http://www.cwrl.utexas.edu/
currents/archives/spr01/lowe.html. Accessed 2001 June 10.

Citation-sequence (C-S)

1. Lowe C. Speech recognition: sci-fi or composition? Currents in Electronic
Literacy [serial online] 2001;4. Available from: http://www.cwrl.utexas.edu/
currents/archives/spr01/lowe. Accessed 2001 June 10.

AUTHOR'S NAME, ASSOCIATED INSTITUTION, OR ORGANIZATION

- Authorship of online sources is sometimes hard to discern. If you do have an author to cite, follow the rules for periodicals and books.
- An organization or institution can also be an author.

N-Y [WHO] World Health Organization. c2001. [Internet]. Washington: WHO/OMS; Available from: http://www.who.int/home-page/index.en.shtml. Accessed 2001 Dec 21.

C-S 2. WHO. [Internet]. Washington: WHO/OMS; c2001. Available from: http://www.who.int/home-page/index.en.shtml. Accessed 2001 Dec 21.

- If the author is not the publisher, sponsoring organization, or institution, list the name of the organization or institution after the place of publication.
- If there is more than one author, list all, up to three. If there are more than three, list the first three followed by *et al.*
- If no author can be discerned, list by title.

DATES

Include three dates in a Web site reference: (1) the publication date; if not given, the copyright date: *c 2002*; (2) the most recent revision date, placed after the publication date: *[revised 1991 Dec]*; (3) the date you accessed the site, placed at citation's end.

NAME OF SITE AND TITLE OF PAGE OR ARTICLE

If the page on a Web site has a title, treat the title like a periodical article. Otherwise, treat the name of the Web site itself as you would a book and put the format (e.g., serial/journal online, monograph online, Internet) in parentheses.

Effective Style and Language 7

26
Write with Power

30
Write to Be Inclusive

27
Write Concisely

31
Write with Accurate Spelling

28
Write with Emphasis

29
Find the Right Words

Chapter 26
Write with Power

Make your writing a pleasure to read rather than a confusing slog for your readers. Keeping a few principles in mind can turn a correct but boring style into one that is emphatic and memorable, a style that gives your words power.

26a RECOGNIZE ACTIVE AND PASSIVE VOICE

When you were a very young child, you learned an important lesson about language. Perhaps you can remember the day you figured out how to push a chair over to the counter in order to reach the cookie jar. But the inevitable happened: The jar fell off the counter and smashed on the floor. You knew Mom would be rushing to the kitchen. What would you say? Would you 'fess up and say, "I knocked over the jar"? Probably not. Instead, you might have said, "The jar got broken." This short sentence accomplishes an amazing sleight of hand. Who broke the jar and how the jar was broken remain mysterious. Apparently, it just broke.

"Got" is often used for "was" in informal speech. In written language, the sentence would read, "The jar was broken," which is an example of the passive voice. Passives can be as useful for adults as for children to conceal who is responsible for an action:

The hard disks containing the top secret files **were misplaced**.

Who misplaced the hard disks? Who knows?

Sentences with transitive verbs (verbs that need an object; see Section 32c) can be written in the active or passive voice. In the active voice the subject of the sentence is the actor. In the passive voice the subject is being acted upon.

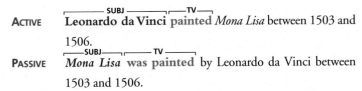

ACTIVE   ┌──── SUBJ ────┐ ┌─TV─┐
           Leonardo da Vinci painted *Mona Lisa* between 1503 and
           1506.
           ┌──SUBJ──┐ ┌─── TV ───┐
PASSIVE   *Mona Lisa* was painted by Leonardo da Vinci between
           1503 and 1506.

The passive is created with a form of *be* and the past participle of the main
verb. In a passive voice sentence, you can either name the actor in a *by*
phrase following the verb or omit the actor altogether.

PASSIVE   *Mona Lisa* was painted between 1503 and 1506.

Most of the time you are not out to conceal but rather to communicate. To write with power, consider different ways of saying the same thing.
The extra effort will bring noticeable results. Listen to the difference:

PASSIVE   The pear tree in the front yard ┌──── TV ────┐
           was demolished by the
           unexpected storm.

ACTIVE   The unexpected storm ┌── TV ──┐
           demolished the pear tree in the
           front yard.

PASSIVE   A request on your part for special consideration based on your
           experience working in the profession ┌── TV ──┐
           will be reviewed by
           the admissions committee.

ACTIVE   If you ask for special consideration because you have
           worked in the profession, the graduate admissions commit-
           tee ┌── TV ──┐
           will review your request.

Writing in the World

When you need to use passives

Whether you are writing for the world of work or the academic
world, you will find there are times when passives are required.
Passive sentences are used when (continued next page)

- you want to keep the focus on the person or thing being acted on,
- you don't know the actor, or
- you and your readers know the actor's identity.

1   Our January sales **were increased** substantially by our deep
     discounts.

2   Analog, digital, and sampled data **are simulated** together
     before the company commits to the expense of manufacture.

3   The suspect **was apprehended** within ten minutes of the
     convenience store robbery.

In sentence 1, the focus is on *increased January sales*, not *deep dis-counts*. In sentence 2, the process of simulation is the focus, not the unknown people who actually perform the simulations. In sentence 3, the actors who do the apprehending are assumed to be the police. The focus is on the suspect.

Use passives when you want to keep the focus on the person or thing being acted on.

EXERCISE 26.1 Underline the active or passive verbs in the following paragraph. If a sentence contains a passive, rewrite the sentence to make it active.

EXAMPLE   Many kinds of human behavior <u>are now being under-
           stood</u> as the products of brain structures by researchers
           in neuroscience.

REWRITE   Researchers in neuroscience now understand many
           kinds of human behavior as the products of brain
           structures.

It has been reported by researchers in neuroscience that food advertising often succeeds because of the structure of our brains. Some people are surprised by this finding. That people buy things they don't need because of advertising has long been rejected by economists. Studies using brain imaging have proven otherwise. When people see and smell their favorite food, a brain structure called the dorsal striatum is stimulated. This brain structure was found to be different from the neural circuits that are stimulated when we are truly hungry. When the dorsal striatum is activated, food is desired to be consumed, even if we are not hungry. Probably the dorsal striatum was important for human survival in past times when food wasn't plentiful. Food needed to be eaten and stored in our bodies for times when food wouldn't be available. But today with food everywhere, an epidemic of obesity is caused by the drive to eat when we aren't hungry.

26b | USE ACTION VERBS

Where are the "action words"?

A teacher may once have told you that verbs are "action words." Where are the action words in the following paragraph?

> The 1980 Olympic games were in Moscow. Two months before the start of the Olympics was the Soviet invasion of Afghanistan. President Jimmy Carter was unhappy about the Soviet invasion and other allies were in sympathy. Consequently, the U.S. Olympic team and teams from 61 other countries were not at the 1980 games. There is still bitterness among hundreds of athletes about the boycott of the 1980 Olympics.

No action words here! The paragraph describes a series of actions, yet the only verbs are forms of *be (is, was, were)*. These sentences are not in the passive voice, but they typify writing that uses *be* verbs when better alternatives are available. Think about what the actions are and choose powerful verbs that express those actions.

> Just two months before the 1980 Olympic games were to be held in Moscow, the Soviet Union **invaded** Afghanistan. President Jimmy Carter **denounced** the invasion and **declared** an American boycott

of the Olympics. Sixty-one other nations also **withdrew** from the Olympics in protest. Today, athletes from those nations who were **denied** the opportunity to participate in the Olympics **remain** bitter about the boycott.

Express actions as verbs

Many sentences contain words that express action, but those words are nouns instead of verbs. Often the nouns can be changed into verbs. For example:

The arson unit ~~conducted an investigation of~~ **investigated** the mysterious fire.

The committee ~~had a debate over~~ **debated** how best to spend the surplus funds.

Notice that changing nouns into verbs also eliminates unnecessary words.

EXERCISE 26.2 The following paragraph includes nouns used to express action. Underline all nouns that show action and the *to be* verbs they follow. Then rewrite the entire paragraph, changing the underlined nouns to verbs and deleting *be* verbs. More than one set of correct answers is possible.

> EXAMPLE   An amputee <u>is likely to have the experience of</u> "phantom limb sensations," as the brain can misinterpret activity from the nervous system.

> REWRITE   An amputee may feel "phantom limb sensations," as the brain can misinterpret activity from the nervous system.

Though few people celebrate the experience of pain, the human body is dependent on unpleasant impulses for survival. Without pain, an individual is at a disadvantage in terms of self-preservation. When a diseased brain is a failure at communication, the entire body is in jeopardy. Pain is a signal to the body of injured or strained joints, bones, or muscles and is integral in forcing an individual to alter his or her behavior to aid the healing process. Those who are without the ability to sense pain often die by early adulthood, as unchecked infections and injuries overwhelm the body.

26c | NAME YOUR AGENTS

The agent is the person or thing that does the action. The most powerful writing usually puts the agents in sentences.

Include people

Read the following sentence aloud:

Mayoral approval of the recommended zoning change for a strip mall on Walnut Street will negatively impact the traffic and noise levels of the Walnut Street residential environment.

It sounds dead, doesn't it? Think about the meaning of the sentence for a minute. It involves people—the mayor and the people who live on Walnut Street. Putting those people in the sentence makes it come alive:

WITH PEOPLE
If the mayor approves the recommended zoning change to allow a strip mall on Walnut Street, people who live on the street will have to endure much more noise and traffic.

Here is another example.

WITHOUT PEOPLE
The use of a MIDI keyboard for playing the song will facilitate capturing it in digital form on our laptop for the subsequent purpose of uploading it to our Web site.

WITH PEOPLE
By playing the song on a MIDI keyboard, we can record the digitized sound on our laptop and then upload it to our Web site.

Including people makes your writing more emphatic. Most readers relate better to people than to abstractions. Putting people in also introduces active verbs because people do things.

Common Errors

Sentences that begin with infinitive phrases followed by a passive

An infinitive is the verb form that begins with *to: to give, to receive, to play, to drive*. When you begin a sentence with an infinitive phrase, you should not follow it with the passive voice. Instead, name the agent.

INCORRECT   To drive to Beaver Stadium from the west, **the Mount Nittany Expressway** should be used.

CORRECT   To drive to Beaver Stadium from the west, **you** should take the Mount Nittany Expressway.

Remember: Sentences that begin with infinitives followed by a main clause must name the agent after the first comma.

 For step-by-step discussion, examples, and practice of this common error, go to **www.ablongman.com/faigley013**.

If you are not writing about people, keep the focus on the agents. Read this short section from a report written by an engineer who was asked to recommend which of two types of valves an oil company should purchase for one of its refineries.

The refinery now uses two systems for grease lubrication: one made by Farval, the other by Alemite. Although the two systems function similarly, Farval valves have two distinct advantages. First, Farval grease valves include a pin indicator that shows whether the valve is

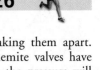

working. Alemite valves must be checked by taking them apart. Second, Farval valves have metal seals, while Alemite valves have rubber grommet seals. If an Alemite valve fails, the pressure will force grease past the rubber grommet seals, creating a grease puddle on the floor. By contrast, Farval's metal seals contain the grease if the valve fails.

It's hard to imagine a duller subject. Nonetheless, this engineer not only makes a definite recommendation supported by reasons, she also makes her report easy to read by keeping the focus on the two types of valves she is comparing. The clarity and confidence of her style speak to her competence as an engineer.

EXERCISE 26.3 In the following paragraph, underline the subject of each sentence. Then rewrite the entire paragraph so that living agents are performing the actions expressed by the verbs.

EXAMPLE   <u>Halloween customs and traditions</u> have been traced back in time to the ancient Druids.

REWRITE   Historians have traced Halloween customs back to the times of the ancient Druids.

The observation of these old customs in parts of Europe where the inhabitants are Celtic proves their Druid origin. To mark the beginning of winter, the burning of fires on November 1 was customary. These Halloween fires are lit even today in Scotland and Wales. Also, it was the belief of Druid custom that on the night of November 1, the earth was roamed by such groups as witches, demons, and evil spirits. To greet the beginning of "their season," Halloween was the night when these demons celebrated the long nights and early sunsets of the coming winter. It was important to have fun at the expense of mortals on this night, and to offer treats as appeasement was the only way mortals could stop the evil, demonic tricks. To give these treats became a tradition, which has continued into modern Halloween celebrations.

26d | VARY YOUR SENTENCES

Read the following passage.

On the first day Garth, Jim, and I paddled fourteen miles down
Johnstone Strait. The strait is off the northeast coast of Vancouver
Island. The morning was moist and deceptively calm. We stopped to
watch a few commercial fishing boats net salmon on the way. Then
we set up camp on a rocky beach. We headed down the strait about
five more miles to Robson Bight. It is a famous scratching place for
orcas. The Bight is a small bay. We paddled out into the strait so we
could see the entire Bight. There were no orcas inside. By this time
we were getting tired. We were hungry. The clouds assumed a wintry
dark thickness. The wind was kicking up against us. Our heads were
down going into the cold spray.

The subject matter is interesting, but the writing isn't. The passage is a series of short sentences, one after the other, that have a thumpety-thump,
thumpety-thump rhythm. When you have too many short sentences one
after the other, try combining a few of them.

For example, the second sentence ("The strait is off the northeast coast
of Vancouver Island") and third ("The morning was moist and deceptively
calm") can be merged into the first sentence as modifiers:

On the first day Garth, Jim, and I paddled fourteen miles down
Johnstone Strait off the northeast coast of Vancouver Island on a
moist and deceptively calm morning.

The choppiness of the last five sentences destroys the effect of impending
danger ("By this time we were getting tired. We were hungry. The clouds
assumed a wintry dark thickness. The wind was kicking up against us. Our
heads were down going into the cold spray.") These sentences can easily be
combined:

By this time we were tired and hungry, the clouds had assumed a wintry dark thickness, and the wind was kicking up against us—our heads dropped going into the cold spray.

The next passage suffers from a different problem. The sentences are not short, but too many are linked by *and*.

Ahead of us we heard what sounded like a series of distant shotgun blasts, and when it happened again, we could see the fins of a pod of orcas, and we stopped paddling. The orcas were feeding on the salmon, and they were surfacing at six- to eight-second intervals, and they were coming straight at us. They swam in twos and threes, and there were at least twelve of them. There was a mix of the long fins of the bulls and the shorter, more rounded fins of the cows, and the noise of their exhaling was becoming louder and louder. Their course did not vary, and when they surfaced fifty yards in front of us, we realized the next time they came up, they would be almost exactly where we were, and we waited a six-second eternity until a pair came up right beside us. The cow was near enough to touch had I extended my paddle, and following were three more orcas with a big bull in the middle, and they too came up beside us, and the bull performed a 360-degree barrel roll out of the water.

The passage builds to a climax, but as in the previous passage, the effect is lost. The use of too many *and*s becomes monotonous. The passage becomes more intense when the paddlers first see the orcas swimming toward them. The sentence should reflect this intensity, speeding up the pace as the paddlers' hearts start racing. Several of the *and*s can be eliminated and short sentences joined.

The orcas were feeding on the salmon, surfacing at six- to eight-second intervals, coming straight at us, swimming in twos and threes, at least twelve of them, a mix of the long fins of the bulls and the shorter, more rounded fins of the cows, the noise of their exhaling becoming louder and louder.

The result of combining some (but not all) short sentences and revising other statements joined by *and* is the paragraph whose sentences match the interest of the subject and control the pace.

On the first day Garth, Jim, and I paddled fourteen miles down Johnstone Strait off the northeast coast of Vancouver Island on a moist and deceptively calm morning. We stopped to watch a few commercial fishing boats net salmon on the way before we set up camp on a rocky beach and headed down the strait about five more miles to Robson Bight, a small bay known as a famous scratching place for orcas. We paddled out into the strait so we could see the entire Bight, but there were no orcas inside. By this time we were tired and hungry, the clouds had assumed a wintry dark thickness, and the wind was kicking up against us—our heads dropped going into the cold spray.

Ahead of us we heard what sounded like a series of distant shotgun blasts, and when it happened again, we could see the fins of a pod of orcas. We stopped paddling. The orcas were feeding on the salmon, surfacing at six- to eight-second intervals, coming straight at us, swimming in twos and threes, at least twelve of them, a mix of the long fins of the bulls and the shorter, more rounded fins of the cows, the noise of their exhaling becoming louder and louder. Their course did not vary, and when they surfaced fifty yards in front of us, we realized the next time they came up, they would be almost exactly where we were. We waited a six-second eternity until a pair came up right beside us. The cow was near enough to touch had I extended my paddle. Following were three more orcas with a big bull in the middle, and they too came up beside us, the bull performing a 360-degree barrel roll out of the water.

Another kind of sentence monotony sets in when sentences are consistently long and complex. The solution to this problem is to simplify some of them and eliminate excess words (see Chapter 27).

26e | PROJECT PERSONALITY

Nobody likes listening to the voice of a robot. Good writing—no matter what the genre—has two unfailing qualities: a human personality that bursts through the page or screen and a warmth that suggests the writer genuinely wishes to engage the readers.

You can project personality in your writing by putting fifteen exclamation points in an email message, but that tactic quickly becomes tiresome when you write at length. In fact, personality often is reflected in the lack of gimmicks. Stephen Covey begins his international best-seller, *The Seven Habits of Highly Effective People*, with this sentence:

> In more than twenty-five years of working with people in business, university, and marriage and family settings, I have come in contact with many individuals who have achieved an incredible degree of outward success, but have found themselves struggling with an inner hunger, a deep need for personal congruency and effectiveness and for healthy, growing relationships with other people.

In one sentence Covey establishes his own credentials and sets out the central issues that the book addresses. He also accomplishes the two things you have to do before you can get anyone to take you seriously. First, convince your readers that what you want to talk about is worth their time. Second, convince them that you are genuinely interested in reaching out to them.

Chapter 27

Write Concisely

Much writing is plagued by unnecessary words, inflated constructions, and excessive jargon. Cut them out. With the pace of daily life growing faster and the demands on our attention multiplying, we have little patience for untangling complicated prose. Now that much writing is read on the computer screen instead of on the printed page, concise writing is more important than ever. Many people are unwilling to scroll down a long page of unbroken text. If you don't make your points quickly and concisely, your writing won't get read.

27a ELIMINATE UNNECESSARY WORDS

Empty words resemble the foods that add calories without nutrition. Put your writing on a diet.

Redundancy

Some words act as modifiers, but when you look closely at them, they repeat the meaning of the word they pretend to modify. These unnecessary words are *redundant*. Have you heard someone refer to a *personal friend*? Aren't all friends personal? Likewise, you may have heard expressions such as *red in color*, *small in size*, *round in shape*, *several in number*, *past history*, *attractive in appearance*, *visible to the eye*, or *honest truth*. Imagine *red* not referring to color or *round* not referring to shape. Similarly, if you watch sports, you no doubt have heard an announcer say something like "The 350-pound tackle is big size-wise," or "The sprinter is fast speed-wise." Nearly all modifiers that end in *-wise*, one of the ugliest constructions in English, say the same thing twice.

Common Errors

Empty intensifiers

Intensifiers modify verbs, adjectives, and other adverbs, and they often are overused. One of the most overused intensifiers is *very*. Take the following sentence as an example:

The new copper roof was **very bright** on a sunny day.

A new copper roof reflects almost all light. *Very bright* isn't an accurate description. Thus another adjective would be more accurate:

The new copper roof was **blinding** on a sunny day.

Very and *totally* are but two of a list of empty intensifiers that usually can be eliminated with no loss of meaning. Other empty intensifiers include *absolutely*, *awfully*, *definitely*, *incredibly*, *particularly*, and *really*.

Remember: When you use *very*, *totally*, or another intensifier before an adjective or adverb, always ask yourself whether there is a more accurate adjective or adverb you could use to express the same thought.

For step-by-step discussion, examples, and practice of this common error, go to **www.ablongman.com/faigley014**.

Legalese

Perhaps the best-known parody of legal language appears in the Marx brothers 1935 classic comedy, *A Night at the Opera*. Groucho Marx's character unrolls a singer's contract many feet long and begins reading it to the singer's manager: "The party of the first part shall be called in this contract the party of the first part." After they haggle and tear off the top of the contract, Groucho begins reading again, "The party of the second part shall be called in this contract the party of the second part."

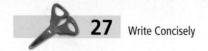

Legal language often attempts to remove ambiguity through repetition and redundancy. As in the example from *A Night at the Opera*, writers and speakers sometimes mimic legal language. Think about what a flight attendant says when your plane arrives:

> Please remain seated, with your seatbelt fastened, until the airplane has come to a full and complete stop; when you deplane from the airplane, be sure to take with you all your personal belongings.

Is there a difference between a *full* stop and a *complete* stop? Can you *deplane* from anything but an airplane? Would you have any *nonpersonal* belongings?

Some speech situations may require redundancy to ensure that listeners understand, but in writing, say it once.

EXERCISE 27.1 The following paragraph is littered with redundant words and phrases. Rewrite wordy sentences to make them concise.

EXAMPLE ~~Threatening in concept,~~ ᴮblack holes are often incorrectly
thought of as ~~an~~ *threatening* astronomical force that possesses a pull
so strong ~~in force~~ it can engulf anything in its path.

Because we cannot visibly see a black hole up close distance-wise, we must use our own imaginations to consider its characteristic properties. For example, imagine taking a jumping leap feet first into a black hole. As you fell, you would descend downward at a slow speed; however, from your personal perception you would seem to be falling faster in speed as time elapsed. In fact, a personal friend observing your downward descent would see that you were in fact moving more and more slowly. In addition, that self-same friend would see that your body was being elongated lengthwise as the center of the black hole pulled more strongly in force on the part of your body which was closest in distance to its center. Simultaneously, your body would begin to start collapsing toward its center, as the forceful force pulled both sides of your body toward the middle of the black hole's center. Unlike in science fiction make-believe, black holes do not serve as either a menacing threat to human life or as a possible means of space or time travel.

EXERCISE 27.2 In the following paragraph, underline empty intensifiers and the modifiers they intensify. Replace them with more specific and effective modifiers.

EXAMPLE   The American CIA conducted a <u>very long</u> search for a drug that could serve as a truth serum.

REWRITE   The American CIA conducted an **extensive** search for a drug that could serve as a truth serum.

In 1942, the American Office of Strategic Services (OSS) Chief William Donovan gathered six incredibly respected scientists to develop a truth serum. The American Psychiatric Association and the Federal Bureau of Narcotics, both very respectable organizations, also participated in this rather secretive search for the truth drug. After definitely varying results and very interesting visions occurred with drugs such as peyote and scopolamine, the group turned to marijuana as a really serious possibility. Creating very different forms of the drug, both strong and diluted, the group tested knowing and unknowing subjects. They tried incredibly unique methods of administering the drug, such as placing a laced gel in foods or injecting a serum into cigars or cigarettes, but they found it very hard to settle on an exact dosage or suitable method. Also, they discovered that individuals did not react very regularly, and the drug could cause a subject to become either absolutely too talkative or particularly quiet. Despite the initial setbacks with marijuana, the American government would really pursue its quest to find a really good substance to serve as a truth serum.

27b | REDUCE WORDY PHRASES

We acquire bad habits because we read and hear so much wordy language. Why does the meteorologist on television say "At the present time we are experiencing significant precipitation," instead of simply "It's raining hard"? Perhaps the meteorologist thinks that "it's raining hard" is too simple. But if the meteorologist said "it's raining hard," we might look outside instead of dismissing the report as background noise.

Many inexperienced writers use phrases like "It is my opinion that" or "I think that" to begin sentences. These phrases are deadly to read. If you find them in your prose, cut them. Unless a writer is citing a source, we assume that the ideas are the writer's. (See "When to Use *I*" in Section 29b.)

Coaches are among the worst at using many words for what could be said in a few:

> After much deliberation about Brown's future in football with regard to possible permanent injuries, I came to the conclusion that it would be in his best interest not to continue his pursuit of playing football again.

The coach might have said simply:

> Because Brown risks permanent injury if he plays football again, I decided to release him from the team.

Perhaps the coach wanted to sound impressive, authoritative, or thoughtful. But the result is the opposite. Speakers and writers who impress us are those who use words efficiently.

Writing in the World

Wordy phrases

Certain stock phrases plague writing in the workplace, in the media, and in academia. Many wordy phrases can be replaced by one or two words with no loss in meaning.

Wordy	Concise
at this point in time	now
at that point in time	then
due to the fact that	because
for the purpose of	for
have the ability to	can
in order to	to
in spite of the fact that	although
in the event that	if
in the modern world of today	today
in the neighborhood of	about
it is possible that there might be	possibly
make an attempt	try
met with her approval	she approved

EXERCISE 27.3 The following paragraph includes many wordy phrases. Rewrite each sentence to eliminate wordiness. Make sure you retain the original meaning of each sentence.

EXAMPLE ~~Due to the fact that at this point in time~~ historians dispute the origin of the necktie, I will not ~~make an at-tempt~~ to provide one conclusive answer.
(handwritten: Because / now / try)

    In the modern world today, it seems the necktie is considered one of the oldest fashion creations and one of the earliest items created for the sole purpose of decorating the human form. One of the main theories locates the predecessor of the modern necktie in the neighborhood of the mid-sixteen hundreds when Croatian soldiers arrived in France adorned with tasseled scarves of linen and muslin. It was at this point in time when the French dubbed these types of garments "croates," which soon became "cravats." In a very real sense, this garment with regard to social practice developed a significance for the purpose of determining levels of proper masculinity; as a matter of fact, at one point in time, the ability to properly tie a necktie served as an initiation ritual for marriage or military service. In spite of the fact that the emphasis placed on tie tying has waned, some historians use this association of proper masculinity with the practice of tie tying in order to explain the short life of the clip-on tie.

27c | SIMPLIFY TANGLED SENTENCES

Long sentences can be graceful and forceful. Such sentences, however, often require several revisions before they achieve elegance. Too often long sentences reflect wandering thoughts that the writer did not bother to go back and sort out. Two of the most important strategies for untangling long sentences are described in Chapter 26: using active verbs (Section 26b) and naming your agents (Section 26c). Here are some other strategies.

Revise expletives

Expletives are empty words that can occupy the subject position in a sentence. The most frequently used expletives are *there is*, *there are*, and *it is*.

WORDY   **There is** another banking option that gives you free checking.

To simplify the sentence, find the agent and make it the subject.

REVISED   Another **banking option** gives you free checking.

WORDY   **There were** several important differences between their respective positions raised by the candidates in the debate.

REVISED   The **candidates** raised several important differences between their respective positions in the debate.

WORDY   **It is** always important to read and follow directions when applying pesticides.

REVISED   Always read and follow directions when applying pesticides.

Here the agent is implied, not stated: *you*.

A few kinds of sentences—for example, *It is raining*—do require you to use an expletive. In most cases, however, expletives add unnecessary words, and sentences usually read better without them.

Use expletives with purpose

You can begin a sentence with *there is* or *it is* if you want to focus readers' attention on a topic you intend to discuss extensively. For example, you might write *There is one overriding reason for my decision* if you plan to go into detail about that reason.

Use positive constructions

Sentences become wordy and hard to read if they include two or more negatives such as the words *no*, *not*, and *nor*, and the prefixes *un-* and *mis-*. For example:

DIFFICULT   A not uncommon complaint among employers of new college graduates is that they cannot communicate effectively in writing.

REVISED   Employers frequently complain that new college graduates cannot write effectively.

EVEN SIMPLER   Employers value the rare college graduate who can write well.

Phrasing sentences positively usually makes them more economical. Moreover, it makes your style more forceful and direct.

Simplify sentence structure

Long sentences can be hard to read, not because they are long but because they are convoluted and hide the relationships among ideas. Take the following sentence as an example.

When the cessation of eight years of hostility in the Iran-Iraq war occurred in 1988, it was not the result of one side defeating the other but the exhaustion of both after losing thousands of people and much of their military capability.

This sentence is hard to read. To rewrite sentences like this one, find the main ideas, then determine the relationships among them.

After examining the sentence, you decide there are two key ideas:

1. Iran and Iraq stopped fighting in 1988 after eight years.
2. Both sides were exhausted from losing people and equipment.

Next ask what the relationship is between the two ideas. When you identify the key ideas, the relationship is often obvious; in this case (2) is the cause of (1). Thus the word you want to connect the two ideas is *because.*

Iran and Iraq stopped fighting after eight years of an indecisive war because both sides had lost thousands of people and most of their equipment.

The revised sentence is both clearer and more concise, reducing the number of words from forty-three to twenty-five. Notice too that nominalizations have been removed (*cessation, hostility, exhaustion*). See Section 26b.

EXERCISE 27.4 The following paragraph includes negative constructions and expletives (*there is, it is,* etc.). Rewrite the sentences for clarity and concision. Some expletives may remain.

EXAMPLE   ~~Not unlike~~ Similar to anthropology and sociology, the discipline of paleontology ~~is an attempt~~ attempts to uncover information ~~that is yet unknown~~ about both living things and civilizations.

There are a number of ways fossils can help paleontologists gain additional information about ancient eras. Though not without problems and informational gaps, fossils aid in locating data that are missing regarding location, time, and traits of both past and future organisms. For example, data have been determined by the not uncontested notion of "uniformitarianism," a theory that assumes certain interactions of matter have not been inconsistent throughout time. Because there is this assumption regarding the constancy of certain processes, it is not illogical to believe there is a way by which fossil age and other characteristics may be determined by considering the effects of constant processes on the aged relic. There is controversy in the scientific community, however, regarding the constancy of such scientific processes and interactions.

Chapter 28
Write with Emphasis

Your writing will be easy to read if you use the structure of each sentence to help readers distinguish more important ideas from less important ones. When you emphasize key ideas, your writing also gains energy.

28a MANAGE EMPHASIS WITHIN SENTENCES

Put your main ideas in main clauses

Chapter 32 discusses a grammatical hierarchy that runs from word to sentence. Within a sentence the clauses that can stand by themselves—the main or independent clauses—are more important than those that must be attached to another clause—the subordinate clauses and phrases.

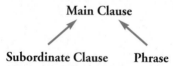

Main Clause

Subordinate Clause   **Phrase**

Placing more important information in main clauses and less important information in subordinate clauses emphasizes what is important.

In the following paragraph all the sentences are main clauses:

> Lotteries were common in the United States before and after the American Revolution. They eventually ran into trouble. They were run by private companies. Sometimes the companies took off with the money. They didn't pay the winners.

This paragraph is grammatically correct, but it does not help the reader understand which pieces of information the author wants to emphasize. Combining the simple sentences into main and subordinate clauses and phrases can significantly improve the paragraph.

First, identify the main ideas:

Lotteries were common in the United States before and after the American Revolution. They eventually ran into trouble.

These ideas can be combined into one sentence:

Lotteries were common in the United States before and after the American Revolution, but they eventually ran into trouble.

Now think about the relationship of the three remaining sentences to the main ideas. Those sentences explain why lotteries ran into trouble; thus the relationship is *because*.

Lotteries were common in the United States before and after the American Revolution, but they eventually ran into trouble **because** they were run by private companies that sometimes took off with the money instead of paying the winners.

Use positions of emphasis within clauses

Read these sentences aloud:

1   The star of the classic teen film *Rebel without a Cause*, made in 1955, was James Dean.

2   The classic teen film *Rebel without a Cause*, starring James Dean, was made in 1955.

3   James Dean starred in the 1955 classic teen film *Rebel without a Cause*.

Probably your voice became a little louder when you read the elements at the end: *James Dean* in sentence 1, *made in 1955* in sentence 2, and *Rebel without a Cause* in sentence 3. Two elements of a clause receive the most emphasis: the beginning and the end. Typically a little more weight is given to the end because that's where we expect to find the point of the clause.

Most often what is at the front of a clause is what is known: the topic. What is at the end is new information about the topic. What is in the middle is subordinate information. If a paragraph is about James Dean, we would not expect the writer to choose sentence 2 over 1 or 3. In sentence 2 Dean is buried in the middle of the clause.

Writing in the World

Use punctuation to show emphasis

Punctuation is not just a matter of correctness, even though students who have learned about punctuation solely in English classes may believe so. If you have read widely and learned about punctuation from novels, news reports, and nonfiction articles, you understand that punctuation is also a matter of style and impact. Compare the following three sentences. All are punctuated correctly, but each has a different rhetorical effect.

1 What our team needs to become a winner is unselfishness, confidence, enthusiasm, trust, and that secret ingredient, hard work.

2 What our team needs to become a winner is unselfishness, confidence, enthusiasm, trust, and that secret ingredient: hard work.

3 What our team needs to become a winner is unselfishness, confidence, enthusiasm, trust, and that secret ingredient— hard work.

If you want to give *hard work* the maximum emphasis, you will select either sentence 2 or sentence 3. The lightest punctuation mark is the comma. Heavier marks are the colon and dash.

Similarly, dashes can be used to make an element in the middle of a sentence stand out. Compare these sentences:

1 My best friend, my mother, inspired me to go on to college.

2 My best friend—my mother—inspired me to go on to college.

For more on using dashes for rhetorical effects, see Chapter 41.

EXERCISE 28.1 The following paragraph includes many short sentences. Locate the main and subordinate ideas, and combine groups of sentences into longer, more concise, and clearer sentences. In the revised sentences, underline the main information twice and the subordinate information once.

EXAMPLE

~~Muscular Christianity was~~ ^ppopular in the late nineteenth and early twentieth centuries. *Muscular Christianity sought to regain* ~~It focused on regaining~~ the church for men. ^{by changing} ~~It sought to change~~ the image of Jesus Christ.

REWRITE

Popular in the late nineteenth and early twentieth centuries, Muscular Christianity sought to regain the church for men by changing the image of Jesus Christ.

American religion was thought of as very feminine in the nineteenth century. It catered to moralism. Some thought it deterred market capitalism. There were more women than men in congregations. Pictures of Jesus Christ portrayed a sickly, effeminate man. Men wanted to reclaim religion. They did not want to aspire to an effeminate God. They wanted to change the image of Jesus. They refocused on Jesus' carpentry. Carpentry was associated with America's self-made man. Billy Sunday was a major spokesman for Muscular Christianity. He was an ex-professional baseball player. He had left baseball. He disapproved of the fact that one did not need morality for success in baseball. He demanded men be manly like Jesus. He was popular. *American Magazine* voted him the eighth greatest man in the United States. This vote was in 1914. This helped to rejuvenate religion. Men were allowed to be religious. They were also allowed to be strong.

28b FORGE LINKS ACROSS SENTENCES

When your writing maintains a focus of attention across sentences, the reader can distinguish the important ideas and how they relate to each other. To achieve this coherence, you need to control which ideas occupy the positions of greatest emphasis. The words you repeat from sentence to sentence act as links.

Link sentences from front to front

In front-to-front linkage, the subject of the sentence remains the focus from one sentence to the next. In the following sequence, sentences 1 through 5 are all about James Dean. The subject of each sentence refers to the first sentence with the pronouns *he* and *his*.

1   **James Dean** was raised on a farm near Fairmount, Indiana, by his uncle and aunt.

2   **He** went to New York as a stage actor and received rave reviews, which earned him a ticket to Hollywood.

3   After a few bit roles, **his** breakthrough came in the 1955 classic *Rebel without a Cause*.

4   **He** also starred in *East of Eden* and *Giant*.

5   **His** career was cut short by a car accident on September 30, 1955, while he was finishing the filming of *Giant*.

Each sentence adds more information about the repeated topic, James Dean.

Link sentences from back to front

In back-to-front linkage, the new information at the end of the sentence is used as the topic of the next sentence. Back-to-front linkage allows new material to be introduced and commented on.

1   James Dean's breakthrough film was the 1955 classic ***Rebel without a Cause***.

2   ***Rebel without a Cause*** featured two other young actors soon to become famous: **Sal Mineo and Natalie Wood**.

3   **Mineo and Wood**, like James Dean, also died tragically.

Back-to-front linkage is useful when ideas need to be advanced quickly, as when you are telling stories. Rarely, however, will you use either front-to-front linkage or back-to-front linkage for long. You will mix them, using front-to-front linkage to add more information and back-to-front linkage to move the topic along.

Check the links between your sentences to find any gaps that will cause your readers to stumble. Where in the following paragraph is your attention disrupted?

> In February 1888, Vincent van Gogh left cloudy Paris for Arles in the sunny south of France. Later that year he persuaded fellow painter Paul Gauguin to join him. Gauguin, who had traveled in the tropics, did not find Arles colorful and exotic. Critics hail this period as the most productive in van Gogh's brilliant but short career.

The last sentence connects distantly with what has come before by mentioning art and van Gogh, but it jars you when you read it because new information, "critics," comes where we expect to find old information. Adding a clause provides a bridge between the old and new information:

> In February 1888, Vincent van Gogh left cloudy Paris for Arles in the sunny south of France. Later that year he persuaded fellow painter Paul Gauguin to join him. Gauguin, who had traveled in the tropics, did not find Arles colorful and exotic. **Although van Gogh and Gauguin argued and soon parted company,** critics hail this period as the most productive in van Gogh's brilliant but short career.

28c USE PARALLEL STRUCTURE WITH PARALLEL IDEAS

Use parallelism in coordinate relationships

In this chapter we have looked at how more important information can be emphasized and less important information downplayed. But what happens when you have two or more items of equal importance? A visual representation of hierarchy is an organizational chart, such as the one shown in Figure 28.1 (page 498).

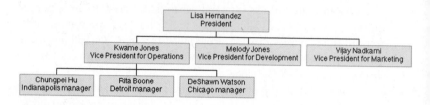

Figure 28.1. Organizational chart

Organizational charts reflect two basic kinds of relationships—those between people on different levels (subordinate) and those between people on the same level (coordinate). Our language works much the same way. We've talked about how to signal subordinate relationships; now we'll turn to coordinate relationships—those at the same level. Again, following a simple principle can make a huge difference in your writing: If the ideas are coordinate, then the structure should be similar.

Writers who use parallel structure often create memorable sentences:

"Give me liberty or give me death."

—Patrick Henry

"No one means all he says, and yet very few say all they mean, for words are slippery and thought is viscous."

—Henry Adams

"Uncommon valor was a common virtue."

—Chester Nimitz describing the Marines at Iwo Jima

"Bread that must be sliced with an ax is bread that is too nourishing."

—Fran Lebowitz

"If a free society cannot help the many who are poor, it cannot save the few who are rich."

—John F. Kennedy

Use parallelism with coordinating conjunctions

When you join elements at the same level with coordinating conjunctions, including *and, or, nor, yet, so, but,* and *for,* normally you should use parallel grammatical structure for these elements.

AWKWARD
In today's global economy, the method of production and where factories are located has become relatively unimportant in comparison to the creation of new concepts and marketing those concepts.

PARALLEL
In today's global economy, how goods are made and where they are produced has become relatively unimportant in comparison to creating new concepts and marketing those concepts.

Use parallelism with correlative conjunctions

Make identical in structure the parts of sentences linked by correlative conjunctions: *either . . . or, neither . . . nor, not only . . . but also, whether . . . or.*

AWKWARD
Purchasing the undeveloped land **not only** gives us a new park **but also** is something that our children will benefit from in the future.

PARALLEL
Purchasing the undeveloped land **not only** will give our city a new park **but also** will leave our children a lasting inheritance.

The more structural elements you match, the stronger the effect the parallelism will achieve.

CORRECT
Either we find a way to recruit new members or we settle for the current number of sailboats.

IMPROVED
Either we find a way to recruit new members or we drop the plan to increase our fleet.

The first sentence is correct but still a bit clunky. The parallelism is limited to *we find/we settle*. The second sentence delivers more punch by extending the parallelism: *we find a way to recruit new members/we drop the plan to increase our fleet*. Matching structural elements exactly—verb for verb, article for article, adjective for adjective, object for object—provides the strongest parallelism.

Common Errors

Faulty parallel structure

When writers neglect to use parallel structure, the result can be jarring. Reading your writing aloud will help you catch problems in parallelism. Read this sentence aloud:

> At our club meeting we identified problems in **finding** new members, **publicizing** our activities, and **maintenance** of our Web site.

The end of the sentence does not sound right because the parallel structure is broken. We expect to find another verb + *ing* following *finding* and *publicizing*. Instead, we run into *maintenance*, a noun. The problem is easy to fix: Change the noun to the *-ing* verb forms.

> At our club meeting we identified problems in finding new members, publicizing our activities, and **maintaining** our Web site.

Remember: Use parallel structure for parallel elements.

For step-by-step discussion, examples, and practice of this common error, go to **www.ablongman.com/faigley015**.

EXERCISE 28.2 The following paragraph contains many examples of nonparallel sentence structure. Find the faulty constructions and either delete them or replace them with parallel constructions, as necessary.

EXAMPLE   *Sesame Street* introduced America to educational chil-

dren's television and ~~providing~~ *provided* children with informa-

tional furry friends.

Sesame Street entered the American consciousness in 1969, playing, singing, and to teach. Joan Ganz Cooney, a major mastermind of *Sesame Street*, proposed to join child-friendly techniques with commercial television standards, and accelerating the speed of teaching. These standards and techniques would aid teachers' goals of teaching symbolic representation, cognitive processes, and teaching social and physical environments. These goals were accomplished with the help of live actors, using puppeteers, and animation. In its more than thirty-year run, *Sesame Street* has managed to educate three generations of school children, finding a home in over 140 countries, and garner more Emmys than any other show in history.

28d | USE PARALLEL STRUCTURE WITH LISTS

Lists are an effective way of presenting a series of items at the same level of importance. Lists are frequently used in visual aids for oral presentations and in announcements, brochures, instructions, and other kinds of short texts. Word processing programs, PowerPoint, and Web-page editors make it simple to format bulleted lists. The effectiveness of a bulleted list is lost, however, if the items are not in parallel form. For example, in a list of action items, such as a list of goals, beginning each item with a verb emphasizes the action.

Sailing Club goals

- Increase the membership by 50% this year.
- Compete in all local regattas.
- Offer beginning and advanced classes.
- Purchase eight new Flying Juniors.
- Organize spring banquet.
- Publicize all major events.

Another common type of list contains instructions. Again, using parallel structure consistently makes the instructions easy to understand.

Creating an animation with GIF Construction Set

1. Select New from the File menu.
2. Click on Insert and select Loop.
3. Click on Insert again and select Control block. Set the delay to 1/100th of a second.
4. Click on Insert again and add the first animation frame.
5. Repeat steps 3 and 4 until all frames are added.

EXERCISE 28.3 You're invited to Howard's party on Saturday. The following directions to Howard's house contain several examples of faulty parallelism. Revise the directions, making the structure of each parallel to the first entry.

Directions to Howard's

1. Turn left onto Route 22 N at the end of Maple Street.
2. You'll come to the Dewdrop Inn after following Route 22 N 3 miles.
3. There's a sharp right turn onto Geoffrey Drive at the fourth traffic signal after the Dewdrop.
4. The red mailbox you're looking for is halfway down the block.
5. Directly across from the mailbox there's a driveway—turn in there.
6. You can reverse the directions and follow them to come home.

28e | USE PARALLEL STRUCTURE IN PARAGRAPHS

Use parallelism to create rhythm

Parallel structure does not have to be used in rigid, mechanical ways. Repeating elements of structure can build a rhythm that gives your prose a distinctive voice.

> If you don't like my book, write your own. If you don't think you can write a novel, that ought to tell you something. If you think you can, do.
> —Rita Mae Brown, from *A Note*

Use parallel structure to pair ideas

Parallel structure is also useful to pair ideas. The closer the similarity in structure, the more emphasis you will achieve.

> Being a grown-up means assuming responsibility for yourself, for your children, and—here's the big curve—for your parents. In other words, you do get to stay up later, but you want to go to sleep sooner.
> —Wendy Wasserstein, from *Bachelor Girls*

Chapter 29
Find the Right Words

Suppose you want to email a friend about a new song you heard on the radio. You might be impressed by the words, which you praise to your friend. Now imagine in your English class you are asked to find an example of common poetry, such as song lyrics or an advertising jingle, and to describe that poetry. You realize the song you like will fulfill the assignment and you write about the lyrics. The language you use in each case will likely be very different.

In the email to your friend, you might use contractions and slang to describe the music. In the college assignment, and in most workplace writing, you will probably use what writers call edited American English.

29a | RECOGNIZE VARIETIES OF ENGLISH

In its negative definition, **edited American English** is what remains after you rid the language of its slang, jargon, regional expressions, and colloquialisms—some of the language's most colorful and striking features. While that definition is certainly true, it doesn't tell the whole story. As a general concept, edited American English is a dialect that is used in most academic, business, and public contexts. We use this dialect when we wish to be understood by the widest possible audience. That goal requires that we eliminate, or at least explain, words that have particular meanings for particular groups, and especially words that are used only by certain groups. You will write most of your college essays in edited American English, the variety of English that is best suited for a broad university audience in the United States.

English is the primary language for written communication in many countries, but what is considered standard written English varies a great deal across English-speaking countries. Within countries, what is considered standard written English also varies according to occupation. Consequently, there is no one standard English, either written or spoken. Even within a particular discipline, there is still much variation. For example, a team of scientists writing an environmental impact statement will likely adjust the language of their report depending on who they believe will eventually read it. If only other scientists will read the report, the writers may use more technical language than if some readers will be members of the general public.

Slang

The most conspicuous kind of language that is usually avoided in edited American English is slang. The next time a friend talks to you, listen closely to the words he or she uses. Chances are you will notice several words that you probably would not use in a college writing assignment. Slang words are created by and for a particular group—even if that group is just you and your friend.

Aside from being a fun way to play with language, slang asserts a sense of belonging. The issue is not whether slang is good or bad, but under what circumstances a primarily oral form of language used within a group becomes effective for writing to people outside that group. If the main purpose is to express the identity of the group, slang is often effective. Sometimes slang can be incorporated into more formal writing if the goal is to convey a sense of a particular group. But if the goal is to write about a matter of broad interest for a broad audience, slang often gets in the way.

Jargon

Jargon is the specialized language of a discipline or occupation, such as "knowledge base of knowledge," which in some workplaces means simply what is already known about a subject. (Some people use the word *jargon* to refer to wordy, unnecessarily complex language, which you should always avoid.) Using jargon in appropriate situations can be an effective way to communicate. When you start a new job or a new class, you often must learn a new jargon, words specific to a particular activity or field of study. For instance, mail carriers need to know that *marriage mail* has nothing to do with weddings, and freestyle skiers know that a *dinner roll* is a trick, not food.

Your decision about when to use discipline-specific language in place of words a general audience would understand will depend on your audience. A doctor can say to another doctor, "The x-rays show a fracture in the fifth metatarsal." But a patient might prefer that the doctor say, "Your foot is broken." Jargon is often the most efficient and precise way for experts in a field to communicate. However, to a nonexpert audience, jargon may sound self-important if common language would do just as well. Avoid using jargon when writing to nonexpert readers. Instead of impressing nonexperts with your knowledge, you will frustrate them with your inability to communicate clearly. An exception is when your audience needs to learn important key terms. In these cases, be sure to define the specialized terms that your readers may not know. One common way to define a specialized term is to treat the definition as an appositive, setting it off with commas.

> Discerning diners claim tripe, the lining of a cow's stomach, is tastiest when cooked for at least 12 hours.

Euphemisms

Euphemisms are rephrasings of harsh terms; they attempt to avoid offending or to skirt an unpleasant issue. For instance, the Federal Reserve Board is fond of calling a bad market "a market imbalance." A well-chosen euphemism can be tactful in a sensitive situation. A bereaved person might rather hear, "I was sorry to hear of your grandmother's passing" than "I was sorry to hear your grandmother died." However, poorly chosen euphemisms can hurt a writer's ethos if they are used to make excuses or downplay the sufferings of others. In the wake of the Clinton-Lewinsky scandal, Representative Henry Hyde admitted to having had a four-year affair with a married woman when he was in his late thirties. Yet Hyde rationalized the affair by saying, "The statute of limitations has long since passed on my *youthful indiscretions*."

Regional varieties of English

Before radio, television, interstate highways, and airplanes, people often revealed where they were from by the regional variety of English they spoke. Today, just as we find the same fast food restaurants across America, so too do we hear younger people speaking much the same English we hear daily on television.

If we listen carefully, however, regional differences are still evident. A native of the upper Midwest may say *Do you want to come with?* instead of *Do you want to come with me?* Many Southerners still say *you all* when addressing more than one person, and many Bostonians still pronounce words using the broad *a* of *father* and shortening their *r*s so those from other regions hear *pahk the cah near Hahvahd Yahd* (park the car near Harvard Yard). Most of these differences in pronunciation do not show up in writing unless the writer is trying consciously to imitate speech. Even then, it's more of a trick for the eye to read *I'm goin'* rather than *I'm going*. Final letters are often not pronounced no matter what region the speaker is from.

Ethnic varieties of English

The United States is composed of people of many national origins and ethnicities, and each of their languages has influenced American English. Think about the names of food we eat every day: *bananas, yams* (West African languages); *hominy, squash* (American Indian languages); *barbeque, potatoes* (Cuba and West Indies); *brandy, crullers* (Dutch); *crepes, omelettes* (French); *hamburgers, pretzels* (German); *pizza, spaghetti* (Italian); *burritos, salsa* (Spanish); *bagel, lox* (Yiddish); and many others. Indeed, the language used for entire subject matters testifies to these influences. For example, the origins of cowboy culture are clearly indicated by the many terms adapted from the Spanish of the Mexican *vaqueros—bronco, chaps* (short for *chaperejos*), *cinch, corral, lariat* (from *la reata*, "the rope"), *lasso, mustang, pinto, poncho, ranch, rodeo, stampede* (from *estampedia*), and many others.

Unlike regional varieties of English, which have been gradually fading away for the past hundred years, ethnic varieties of English remain very much a part of American life. African-American vernacular English has been used for hundreds of years in various forms and, like edited American English, is more a collection of dialects than a single dialect. African-American vernacular English has had major impacts on the language spoken in the United States, and it continues to be a powerful force in revitalizing

the language. Similarly, the long-standing influence of Spanish has intensified with recent increased immigration, producing many bilingual speakers and writers. In the near future American English no doubt will be influenced by Mandarin, Korean, Japanese, and other Asian languages.

EXERCISE 29.1 The following paragraph, taken from a research paper, contains slang that may not be appropriate for its audience, a women's studies professor. Revise the paragraph to make all the sentences edited American English.

EXAMPLE

Sally Ride is ~~super famous~~ *most famous* as the first American woman in space and as the youngest astronaut to orbit in the *Challenger* Shuttle.

In her youth, Ride was a radical tennis player. However, instead of becoming a professional athlete, she went to Stanford and received her doctorate in x-ray physics. While at Stanford, Ride was selected out of a group of 8,000 other folks to be part of NASA's astronaut class. On June 18, 1983, Ride took her totally extreme first trip to space. In 1989, Ride split NASA and became a professor of physics at USSD, where she directs the California Space Institute. Ride was so awesome in space that she totally had an impact on women in scientific and technical careers.

29b | BE AWARE OF LEVELS OF FORMALITY

Formality

While you may get plenty of practice in informal writing—emails and notes to friends and family members—mastering formal writing is essential in academic and professional settings. How formal or informal should your writing be? That depends on your audience and the writing task at hand.

Look at the following emails. They address the same subject, but the first is written to a coworker who is a friend. The second is written to a supervisor. Notice changes in language and format.

EMAIL TO FRIEND AND COWORKER

Hey, Brenda. When you get a chance, could you let me know what you think about the attached offer from Jansen Corp.? Should we take them up on it? Thanks!

—Simone

EMAIL TO A SUPERVISOR

To: Helen Winters

From: Simone Brooks

Subject: Jansen Corporation offer

I have attached the Jansen Corporation's offer to provide human resources services for the next fiscal year. Could you please give us your recommendation on whether we should accept it or pursue other offers? Thank you for giving this your attention.

Sincerely,

Simone Brooks

Benefits Coordinator

Differences between formal and informal writing

Formal	Informal
edited American English	slang, regional expressions, colloquialisms
no contractions	contractions
strict business or academic formats	less strict formats
formal titles, few abbreviations	abbreviations, first names

Regardless of whether a writing task is formal or informal, a clear, concise style remains paramount.

- Who is your audience?
- What is the occasion?
- What level of formality is your audience accustomed to in similar situations?
- What impression of yourself do you want to give?
- How formal have the communications you received from your audience been?

Colloquialisms

Colloquialisms are words or expressions that are used informally, often in conversation but less often in writing. Think of the many terms used to indicate lack of intelligence:

He's about **three bricks shy of a load**.

She's a **dim bulb**.

He's a **bonehead** and his wife **doesn't have a clue**.

Aside from carrying meanings that aren't always obvious to your reader, colloquialisms usually indicate a lack of seriousness that runs counter to what you'll be trying to accomplish in most academic and professional writing. Colloquialisms can suggest a flippant attitude, carelessness, or even thoughtlessness. Sometimes colloquialisms can be used for ironic or humorous effect in formal writing, but as a general rule, if you want to be taken seriously, avoid using them.

Using edited American English does not mean, however, that you should try to use big words when small ones will do as well, or that you should use ten words instead of two. Formality does not mean being pretentious or wordy.

WORDY   In this writer's opinion, one could argue that the beaches on the west coast of Florida are far superior in every particular to their counterparts on the east coast.

BETTER   I think Florida's west coast beaches are better in every way than those on the east coast.

Writing in the World

When to use *I*

You may have been taught to avoid the first person (*I, we*) in academic and professional writing. Though some instructors and workplace conventions still require that all first-person references be eliminated or rewritten (*I believe* would become *this author believes*), this rule is less commonly enforced than it used to be.

Some instructors feel that first-person references reflect self-indulgence that is inappropriate outside of autobiography. Sentences beginning with *I* refer to the author and make him or her the subject, or at least a fellow subject. In a sentence such as *I think Florida's west coast beaches are better in every way than those on the east coast*, the reader's attention is divided between the beaches and the person evaluating the beaches.

Another reason some instructors prohibit use of the first person is the tendency of writers to overuse it. Some writers feel that nothing can be invalidated as long as each potentially arguable assertion starts with *I think* or *I feel. I* becomes a shield, which the writer uses to escape the work of building an argument.

Occasionally, the use of *I* is redundant. In the following sentence, the nature of the assertion clearly indicates that it's the writer's opinion:

REDUNDANT *I*   I think "Rock the Casbah" is a great song!

Here you can safely drop *I think* without changing the sentence's meaning. Sometimes, however, you will want to indicate plainly that an assertion is tentative. *I* is critical to the meaning of this sentence:

TENTATIVE *I*   I thought that the dim, distant light was a planet.

If you're unsure whether or not first-person references are permissible, ask your instructor.

EXERCISE 29.2 Sue Mills wrote the following note to thank her friend Hannah Le Chat for dinner. How would the language of the note change if Sue Mills were writing a letter to a potential employer, thanking her for a luncheon interview? Rewrite the note, making the potential employer the audience. Note how eliminating colloquialisms changes a letter's level of formality.

> Dear Hannah,
>
> Thanks again for that dinner Friday night. I swear, your cooking could stop a clock. The gumbo tasted like heaven, and that lemonade was tastier than ice water in the desert. I'm a few cards short of a full deck when it comes to culinary intelligence, or as you so tactfully put it, in the kitchen I'm dumb as a post. When you make gumbo it looks easy as pie, but I bet you have some secret skills. Drop me a line with the recipe sometime. It was great to catch up with you and hear how things are going. Let's get together again soon.
>
> Remember, you're the superchef,
>
> Sue

EXERCISE 29.3 The following paragraph was taken from a rough draft of a research paper for an environmental ecology class. The instructor asked the writer to eliminate any use of first person, colloquial language, unnecessarily big words, and wordiness. Use the advice from this section to revise the paragraph according to the instructor's comments.

> EXAMPLE Many geologists and conservationists in the United States have views that are diametrically opposed on whether to support or fight mining and commercialization in sacrosanct public acreage.

> REWRITE Many U.S. geologists and conservationists disagree on whether to mine or commercialize public lands.

> David Brower, who died in 2000, was a person who was the president of the American wilderness preservation club called the Sierra Club. As this organization's preeminent leader he was

the human personification of preservation. Brower took a no-holds-barred approach to fighting the infidels of mining and tourism in America's wilderness areas. I think his most perspicacious campaign against these factors that threaten the wilderness must have been when he published an ad to fight the commercialization of the Grand Canyon. His placement of newspaper advertisements telling people about plans to open businesses at the base of the canyon deterred this development. I think that most who believe in conservation would agree that these achievements make David Brower a hero for the American environment.

29c BE AWARE OF DENOTATION AND CONNOTATION

When you see a Jeep covered with mud, you know the driver has probably been off the pavement. Of course car manufacturers take advantage of these associations. While some advertisements show shiny new cars, ads for Jeeps and similar vehicles show them caked with mud, emphasizing their ruggedness.

Words likewise carry associations from the places they have been. Words have both literal meanings, called **denotations**, and associated meanings, called **connotations**. The contrast is evident in words that mean roughly the same thing but have different connotations. For example, some people are set in their opinions, a quality that can be described positively as *persistent*, *firm*, and *steadfast* or negatively as *stubborn*, *bull-headed*, and *close-minded*. The language of advertisements is carefully selected for connotative meanings. A brand of toothpaste might claim to have a *bold, new taste*. What exactly does *bold* taste mean? As a denotative adjective, *bold* is meaningless as the modifier of a brand of toothpaste. Nevertheless, *bold* carries positive connotations that the advertiser wishes to link to the brand.

Politicians also are well aware of the connotations that words carry. They typically describe themselves and their ideas using words such as *change*, *opportunity*, *courage*, *reform*, *prosperity*, *children*, *family*, *candid*,

principle, duty, tough, listen, help, lead, vision, success, empower(ment), dream, freedom, peace, rights, flag, confident, initiative, incentive, common sense, and *passionate.* When they talk about their opponents, they use words such as *decay, failure, crisis, bureaucracy, waste, pessimistic, excuses, intolerant, extremist, insensitive, status quo, disgrace, radical,* and *hypocrisy.* In the language of politicians, most of these words are used without reference to any specific meaning. They make us feel good about the candidate and bad about the opponent without telling us anything about either.

In college and professional writing, writers are expected not to rely on the connotations of words to make important points. For example, the statement *It's only common sense to have good schools* carries high positive connotations. Most people believe in common sense, and most people want good schools. What is common sense for one person, however, is not common sense for another; how a good school is defined varies greatly. Except for common function words such as *and, to,* and *the,* all words carry connotative meanings. Consequently, you cannot write in an entirely neutral language, but you can be forthright about any value judgments you make. You have the obligation in college writing to support any judgment with evidence.

Take a look at three versions of a letter of recommendation to Clown College that drama professor Ryan Claycomb wrote for his student Cynthia Miller. All denote essentially the same thing, but only the third would improve Cynthia's chances of getting in. The first contains words with poor connotations. The second contains better connotations but lacks evidence. The third combines strong positive connotations with evidence.

POOR CONNOTATIONS

I am pleased to recommend Cynthia Miller for admission to Clown College. Cynthia first appeared to be a rather run-of-the-mill student. However, she demanded my attention immediately. She has fallen into the position of being one of our best bets as a comedic actress. The clearest sign of her outrageous maturity is her ability to pressure the rest of the cast to improve their performances. Her obsession with her craft pushed the level of our production up to a professional caliber.

STRONG CONNOTATIONS WITHOUT EVIDENCE

I am pleased to recommend Cynthia Miller for admission to Clown College. Cynthia first appeared to be a rather unassuming student. However, she commanded my attention immediately. She has distinguished herself as one of our most promising comedic actresses. The clearest sign of her exceptional maturity is her ability to improve the performances of the rest of the cast. Her commitment to her craft lifted the level of our performance to a professional caliber.

STRONG CONNOTATIONS WITH EVIDENCE

I am pleased to recommend Cynthia Miller for admission to Clown College. When she first began my Acting 101 class in her freshman year, Cynthia appeared to be a rather unassuming student. However, she commanded my attention immediately by becoming the first freshman to win a lead role in a university production; she played a masterful Antigone in the fall of 2001. In the four productions in which I directed Cynthia, she has distinguished herself as one of our most promising comedic actresses—no small feat in a 200-student department. The clearest sign of her exceptional maturity is her ability to raise the performances of the rest of the cast. In our 2001 production of *The Producers*, Cynthia treated every rehearsal like opening night and challenged the other actors to do the same. Her commitment to her craft lifted the level of the performance to a professional caliber. In fact, she received the Drama Circle award for best supporting actress, and the show received a four-star rating in the *Cleveland Press*.

EXERCISE 29.4 The following sets of words have similar denotative meanings but differ in connotation. Put a plus sign (+) over words that have positive connotations and a minus sign (–) over words that have negative connotations. Put an equal sign (=) over words that are neutral in connotation. If you are unsure of the meaning of a word, use a dictionary.

1. thin, skinny, gaunt, slender, sleek, lean, emaciated, bony, skeletal, slight, lanky
2. music, cacophony, noise, tune, song, discord, racket, harmony, clamor
3. hard worker, drudge, diligent, nose to the grindstone, workaholic, industrious, plodder, assiduous, painstaking, drone, thorough

EXERCISE 29.5 Jon Antonioni's political science professor asks his students to write a brief self-evaluation about each paper they write. The following passage is Antonioni's self-evaluation of his paper arguing that the United States should not renew most-favored-nation status for China. Jon knows he did not do his best work on the paper, and he wants to be honest about that but avoid hurting his ethos as a student who cares about the class. As practice in using words with the right connotations, revise his evaluation to (1) strengthen his ethos without bending the truth and (2) offer evidence to back up his assertions.

Jon Antonioni
Politics in the United States
Self-assessment

This is my worst paper of the semester. After beginning my research at 11 the night before it was due, I realized I was in deep trouble. I was stupid to assume the issue of MFN status could be mastered in a few hours. However, I did my best, cramming in as much research as I could before I started writing. Because it was so late, I decided to skip writing a boring outline. But when I started cranking out the draft, the thesis started to seem ridiculous a few paragraphs in. I got confused about where the thesis was headed. Instead of going back to the beginning, though, I kept churning out pages. The result was that I had a different argument at the beginning than I did at the end. With the little time I had left, I squeezed in as much revising as I could to try to make the thesis consistent throughout. I think the argument I ended up with would have worked all right, had I not chosen to play video games all week instead of starting my paper.

29d | USE SPECIFIC LANGUAGE

Be precise

Effective writing conveys information clearly and precisely. Words such as *situation*, *sort*, *thing*, *aspect*, and *kind* often signal undeveloped or even lazy thinking.

VAGUE	The movie was sort of a documentary-like thing.
BETTER	The movie resembled a documentary.

VAGUE	The violence aspect determines how video games are rated.
BETTER	The level of violence determines how video games are rated.

VAGUE	Joe DiMaggio's hitting streak lasted many games.
BETTER	Joe DiMaggio's hitting streak lasted 56 games.

When citing numbers or quantities, be as exact as possible. A precise number, if known, is always better than slippery words like *several* or *many*, which some writers use to cloak the fact that they don't know the quantity in question. If you know an approximate quantity, indicate the quantity but qualify it: *about 25* tells readers much more than *many*.

Use a dictionary

There is no greater tool for writers than the dictionary. Always have a dictionary handy when you write—either a book or an online version—and get into the habit of using it. In addition to checking spelling, you can find additional meanings of a word that perhaps you had not considered, and you can find the etymology—the origins of a word. In many cases knowing the etymology of a word can help you use it to better effect. For example, if you want to argue that universities as institutions have succeeded because they bring people together in contexts that prepare them for their lives after college, you might point out the etymology of *university*. *University* can be traced back to the late Latin word *universitas*, which means "society or guild," thus emphasizing the idea of a community of learning.

Common Errors

Words often confused

Words with different meanings that are pronounced in the same way are called **homonyms**. Be particularly careful that you select the correct one. In addition to the common homonym errors listed in Section 31b, these pairs can cause confusion.

bare—unadorned
bear—(1) an animal; (2) to carry

capital—(1) government seat; (2) material wealth; (3) uppercase letter
capitol—a building housing a government seat

cite—(1) to make mention of; (2) to quote as an example
sight—something seen
site—place, location

coarse—rough
course—plotted-out site or matter

counsel—(1) advice; (2) lawyer; (3) to advise
council—a deliberative body

complement—to go with, as in *That tie complements that suit.*
compliment—to flatter

fair—(1) just; (2) carnival
fare—(1) ticket price; (2) to get along

hear—to listen to
here—location

passed—went by
past—time before the present

patience—the state of calmly waiting
patients—people receiving medical care

peace—serenity
piece—a part of

plain—(1) simple; (2) level land

plane—(1) short for airplane; (2) level surface; (3) carpenter's tool

principal—(1) head of an organization; (2) a sum of money

principle—a basic law or guideline

wear—(1) to don clothes; (2) to erode

where—location

weather—climatic condition

whether—if

Other words do not sound exactly alike, only similar. The words in thez following pairs are frequently confused:

accept—to receive

except (as preposition)—excluding

adverse—difficult

averse—against

advice—a suggestion

advise—to suggest

affect—to act upon or to have an effect on something or somebody

effect—a change caused by an action

allude—to make reference to

elude—to evade

allusion—an indirect reference

illusion—a false impression

censor—to suppress controversial material

censure—to reprimand

conscience—moral compass

conscious—aware

continually—(1) consistently; (2) regularly

continuously—without stopping

(continued next page)

desert—(1) geographical feature; (2) to abandon
dessert—sweet snack

elicit—to bring out
illicit—unlawful

loose—not tight
lose—(1) to misplace; (2) to fail to win a game

personal—(1) individual; (2) private
personnel—staff

presence—opposite of absence
presents—(1) gifts; (2) introduces

respectfully—demonstrating respect
respectively—in the given order

Remember: Use a dictionary to check that you are using the right word.

 For step-by-step discussion, examples, and practice of this common error, go to **www.ablongman.com/faigley016**.

EXERCISE 29.6 This paragraph, from a research paper about space exploration, contains vague and incorrect language. Revise it to eliminate vague language, misused homonyms, and misused sound-alike words. Information you may need to eliminate vague language is included in parentheses.

EXAMPLE   Astronauts have been **exploiting** space for **quite a few years now**.

REWRITE   Astronauts have been **exploring** space **since at least the 1960s**.

Space missions can adversely affect an astronaut's health. A more than minor culprit is the lack of gravity in space; one of the affects that weightlessness has on astronauts is that it causes bone loss, which might be really bad. A sort-of older (45) astronaut may have such serious bone deterioration that after a mission, her bones resemble those of an old lady (like an 80-year-old). Other continuous effects are the interruption of sleeping patterns and the deterioration of the immune system and mussels. But perhaps the scariest affect sited by experts is radiation exposure, especially during visits to Mars. None knows what the cancer risks from this exposure might be.

EXERCISE 29.7 Circle the correct word in parentheses in the following paragraph. Look up the words in a dictionary if you are not sure of their meaning.

Butchering a hog requires (patience, patients) and hard work. First, find a (cite, sight, site) outside (wear, where) you will have plenty of space. After killing the pig, dunk it in hot water to loosen the (coarse, course) hair. Scrape the hair with a knife (continually, continuously) until the skin is completely (bare, bear). Thread a gambling stick (threw, through) the hamstrings, and hang the pig head-down from a post. Remove the head, cut down the length of the underbelly, and remove the organs. Then cut down the length of the spine and remove the tenderloin, fatback, ribs, middlin' meat, shoulders, and hams (respectfully, respectively). While some people are squeamish about eating hogs' heads and organs, in (principal, principle) nearly every part of the animal is edible.

29e | USE EFFECTIVE FIGURATIVE LANGUAGE

Figurative language—figures of speech that help readers get a more vivid sense of an object or idea—is what you use when literal descriptions seem insufficient.

LITERAL   The prosecutor presented a much stronger legal case than did the attorney.

FIGURATIVE   The prosecutor took the attorney apart like a dollar watch.

The two most common figures of speech are the simile and the metaphor. A **simile** usually begins with *as* or *like*, and makes an explicit comparison between two unlike objects.

A tie in soccer is *like* kissing your dog.

Metaphor is from a Greek term that means "carry over," which describes what happens when you encounter a metaphor: You carry over the meaning from one word to another. Metaphor makes a comparison without using *like* or *as*.

She reached the **pinnacle** of her profession.

[highest point ⟶ best]

Two other forms of figurative language are the **synechdoche**, in which the part is used to represent the whole (a hood ornament that represents a car) and **metonymy**, in which something related stands in for the thing itself (*White House* for the executive branch; *brass* for military officers). The purpose of all figurative language is to suggest, or sometimes to create, a resemblance or link between two otherwise distinct objects and to convey a larger, more complex idea than a simple presentation of the unadorned facts could impart.

If not used imaginatively, figurative language merely dresses up a literal description in fancy clothes without adding to the reader's understanding of the object or idea. The purpose of figurative language is to convey information vividly to help the reader grasp your meaning.

You'll also want to avoid **clichés**, which are relics of figurative language, phrases used so often that they have become tired and stripped of meaning. Among countless others, the following expressions have hardened into clichés.

better late than never	out like a light
blind as a bat	playing with fire
easier said than done	pride and joy
hard as a rock	thin as a rail
ladder of success	water under the bridge
nutty as a fruitcake	wise as an owl

You might find yourself resorting to clichés when you're low on inspiration or energy. Read your drafts aloud to yourself to identify clichés, listening for the phrases that you've used or heard before. Make a note of them and either change the clichés to literal description or, better still, create fresh new phrases to convey what you were trying to say with the cliché.

EXERCISE 29.8 Using the types of figurative language stated in parentheses, invent sentences that convey the ideas represented in the following paragraph.

EXAMPLE The 1956 explosion of Bezymianny, a Russian volcano, was **shocking** to area residents since the volcano was assumed to be dormant. (simile)

REWRITE The 1956 explosion of Bezymianny, a Russian volcano, **came like the return of Lazarus** to area residents; the volcano was assumed to be dormant.

After the 1956 explosion, Bezymianny's ash covered everything around it; days later, the ash had even reached Alaska and Britain. (metaphor) Trees fifteen miles away were knocked down by the explosion. (metaphor) The same as Mount St. Helens, the Bezymianny eruption began with a large avalanche and then exploded sideways. (metonymy) Since its 1956 eruption, Bezymianny has erupted every so often, causing its neighbors to fear the volcano in their midst. (synecdoche)

EXERCISE 29.9 The following paragraph is filled with clichés. Underline each cliché and replace it with fresh language.

EXAMPLE Cephalopods are a group of marine mollusks that many Americans **would not touch with a ten-foot pole.**

REWRITE Cephalopods are a group of marine mollusks that many Americans **find distasteful.**

However, in Japan and in the Mediterranean, squid, octopus, and cuttlefish are an important food source and sell like hot cakes. Unfortunately, myths about giant squid sinking boats and octopus drowning swimmers persist in the United States, and information that giant squid are weak as kittens and that an octopus has never drowned anyone falls on deaf ears. The Japanese attitude is a step in the right direction; they see the octopus as a cheerful, friendly creature and often use its image as a toy or mascot. Our culinary pleasures could grow by leaps and bounds if more of us opened our minds to the joys of fried calamari dipped in marinara sauce and squid sushi with plenty of wasabi. We need to wake up and smell the coffee in the United States that cephalopods are an underexploited marine resource.

Chapter 30
Write to Be Inclusive

Except for comedians and angry people, few writers want to insult their readers. When readers are offended by a writer's language, most of the time the writer did not intend this result. Instead, the writer likely expressed assumptions that readers rejected as biased. If you want to reach all your potential readers, you should avoid biased language.

Writers who use inclusive language will also be more accurate. Writing *man* to refer to *men and women* only conveys half of what you mean. And perhaps the best reason to strive for inclusiveness is that your writing shapes public discourse, even in the classroom. Exclusionary language perpetuates biases. Writing does not only reflect reality; it shapes reality.

This chapter explains current conventions for avoiding bias in your writing toward specific groups of people. While the conventions of inclusiveness change continually, three guidelines for inclusive language toward all groups remain constant:

1. Do not point out people's differences unless those differences are relevant to your argument.
2. Call people whatever they prefer to be called.
3. When given a choice of terms, choose the more accurate one.

30a | BE AWARE OF STEREOTYPES

Reject stereotypes

A **stereotype** makes an assumption about a group of people by applying a characteristic to all of them based on the knowledge of only a few of them. The idea that Asian women are submissive, for instance, is a stereotype; it tries to apply one personality trait to many individuals whose only shared characteristics are their gender and ethnicity. Such a stereotype is just as ridiculous as a belief that all Idahoans are potato farmers. Since individuals in any group are different, stereotypes present a reductive picture of the group being described.

Of course you want to avoid obviously harmful, not to mention inaccurate, stereotypes, such as *People on welfare are lazy*, *gays are effeminate*, or *NASCAR fans are rednecks*. More subtle stereotypes, however, may be harder to identify and eliminate from your writing. If you want to offer an engineer as an example, will you make the engineer a man? If you want your reader to envision a child living in subsidized housing, will you describe the child as an African American? Instead of using these examples that perpetuate stereotypes, try to choose cases that go against them.

Avoid using stereotypes even if they seem flattering, such as *Asians are smart*, *African Americans dance well*, and *women are nurturing*. Flattering stereotypes are just as inaccurate as unflattering ones, and they can be just as harmful. For instance, the stereotype that women are nurturing has been used to argue that women's only natural role is to raise children, that women aren't suited to work outside the home. By extension, the argument goes, fathers don't have the same responsibility to care for their children because fathers aren't as naturally nurturing. The stereotype that women are nurturing could ultimately offend both women and men.

Be careful when establishing a normal group

Establishing a normal, regular, or general group of people can create bias if you are not careful. Establishing a normal group is dangerous, first, because the writer's notion of normal is usually just a euphemism for the people with whom the writer is most comfortable. Second, establishing a norm implies other people are abnormal, which inevitably implies a value judgment. How can you revise the following statements to be more inclusive?

PROBLEMATIC NORM

While normal people learn about the Civil War in school, hard-core re-enactors don musty uniforms, grab slabs of old bacon, and live the war during weekend battles.

BETTER

Not satisfied with learning about the Civil War through books, hard-core re-enactors don musty uniforms, grab slabs of old bacon, and live the war during weekend battles.

PROBLEMATIC NORM

Gloria Nuñez isn't like regular sprinters at the Greater Detroit Meet; while other runners gingerly settle their feet into the blocks, Nuñez plants her prosthetic foot in the block and waits for the starting gun.

BETTER

Gloria Nuñez is one sprinter at the Greater Detroit Meet who might surprise you; while other runners gingerly settle their feet into the blocks, Nuñez plants her prosthetic foot in the block and waits for the starting gun.

Writing in the World

Stereotypical images

Sign over a service station in New Mexico

Most Americans now realize that overtly racist images are offensive. The notable exception is representations of American Indians. Currently over eighty college sports team (along with a few professional teams) have American Indian mascots. These mascots have long been controversial. Most were adopted in the early decades of the twentieth century when European Americans enjoyed putting on paint and feathers and "playing Indian." Supporters of the mascots claim that they honor American Indians. Critics argue that

(continued next page)

the mascots perpetuate stereotypes of American Indians as primitive, wild, and bellicose. Furthermore, fans of schools that compete with those that have Indian mascots often shout derogatory slogans and create derogatory images of American Indians.

Subtle stereotyping comes through the media. Based on images in the news media, many Americans think that women in Islamic countries cover their faces in public, but this practice is typical only in Saudi Arabia and the most conservative sectors of Islamic society. The majority of men in Islamic countries do not have long beards. Again, the issue is accuracy. Some people in Holland still wear wooden shoes, but wooden shoes do not represent everyday Dutch footwear.

EXERCISE 30.1 The following paragraph includes numerous assertions based on stereotypes, both positive and negative. Rewrite the sentences to eliminate the stereotypes. More than one correct answer may be possible.

EXAMPLE   **Surly, artistic, and foreign,** New Yorkers exemplify **the American melting pot.**

REWRITE   With their **diverse cultural heritage,** New Yorkers represent the **American mosaic.**

Throughout the New York City boroughs, widely diverse groups live and work together. Manhattan's single women brazenly forgo family lives for careers, high-powered suits, and Park Avenue apartments, while gays and literary types make an artistic home in Greenwich Village. Modern-day geisha and samurai abound in North America's largest Chinatown, where visitors can find an Asian feast most any time of day. A jazzy dance north brings one to Harlem, famous for the Apollo Theater, where one can see African Americans display their musical abilities, and Sylvia's Soul Food, a restaurant rivaled only by its greasy-spoon counterparts in the Deep South. New York City is the perfect place for a wide-eyed Texan or Midwesterner to escape the cultural sameness of their home regions and experience a true American city.

30b | BE INCLUSIVE ABOUT GENDER

Gender is a term that refers to the social designations of men, women, and their sexual orientations.

Avoid exclusive nouns and pronouns

Don't use masculine nouns and pronouns to refer to both men and women. *He, his, him, man,* and *mankind* are outmoded and inaccurate terms for both genders. Eliminate gender bias by using the following tips:

- Don't say *boy* when you mean *child.*
- Use *men and women* or *people* instead of *man.*
- Use *humanity* or *humankind* in place of *mankind.*

Eliminating *he, his,* and *him* when referring to both men and women is more complicated. Many readers consider *he/she* to be an awkward alternative. Try one of the following instead:

- Make the noun and its corresponding pronoun plural. The pronoun will change from *he, him,* or *his* to *they, them,* or *theirs.*

  BIASED MASCULINE PRONOUNS
  An undercover agent won't reveal **his** identity, even to other agents, if **he** thinks it will jeopardize the case.

  BETTER
  Undercover agents won't reveal **their** identities, even to other agents, if **they** think it will jeopardize the case.

- Replace the pronoun with an article (*the, a,* or *an*)

  BIASED MASCULINE PRONOUN
  Each prospective driving instructor must pass a state test before receiving **his** license.

  BETTER
  Each prospective driving instructor must pass a state test before receiving **a** license.

Use parallel construction when writing about men and women

When discussing men and women together, use parallel construction to apply the same standards to each. For instance, avoid describing the way a woman looks if you don't also describe a man's appearance. If you write *the lovely Dina Lopez and her brother Eric Lopez,* the physical description of Dina is inappropriate. Likewise, writing *Anthony Kinney and Mrs. Kinney* defines the wife in terms of her husband. Change *Mrs. Kinney* to *Evelyn Kinney* to eliminate the bias.

BIASED, UNPARALLEL	BETTER, PARALLEL
Joshua Baines and his wife	Joshua Baines and Anne Claycomb-Baines
men and girls	men and women (or) boys and girls
Rita Rando and Mr. Rando	Rita and Julius Rando
man and wife	man and woman (or) husband and wife

Use gender-neutral names for professions

Professional titles that indicate gender—*chairman, waitress*—falsely imply that the gender of the person doing the job changes the essence of the job being done. Use gender-neutral terms for professions. Likewise, avoid adding a gender designation to a gender-neutral professional title. Terms like *woman doctor* and *male nurse* imply that a woman, working as a doctor and a man working as a nurse are abnormal. Instead, write simply *doctor* and *nurse*. The following list suggests alternatives to gender-specific professional terms.

BIASED, GENDER-SPECIFIC	BETTER, GENDER-NEUTRAL
businessman	businessperson
chairman	chair, chairperson
clergyman	member of the clergy
congressman	representative or senator

BIASED, GENDER-SPECIFIC	BETTER, GENDER-NEUTRAL
fireman	firefighter
foreman	supervisor
hostess	host
laundress	launderer, dry cleaner
mailman	mail carrier
manpower	personnel, staff
poetess	poet
policeman	police officer
salesman	salesperson
stewardess	flight attendant
waitress	server
weatherman	meteorologist
workmen	workers

Eliminate bias when writing about sexual orientation

Sexual orientation refers to a person's identification as bisexual, heterosexual, homosexual, or transsexual. *Heterosexual* and *homosexual* carry a somewhat clinical connotation. Referring to people who are homosexual as *gays* can lead to confusion: It sometimes connotes men and women, sometimes just men. Instead, use *gay men* and *lesbians*. Likewise, writing *bisexual man* or *bisexual woman* is more accurate than simply *bisexual*. Again, the principle is to use terms that individuals in specific groups prefer.

EXERCISE 30.2 The writing in the following paragraph is not inclusive with regard to gender and sexual orientation. Rewrite the sentences to make them more inclusive.

EXAMPLE Controversy followed the 1993 "Don't Ask, Don't Tell" policy, which altered the ban on **homosexuals** in the military.

REWRITE Controversy followed the 1993 "Don't Ask, Don't Tell" policy, which altered the ban on **gay men, lesbians, and bisexual men and women** in the military.

Fulfilling his campaign promise, President Clinton pursued the elimination of the military policy that limited the enlistment of servicemen based on sexual preference. In 1993 a compromise called "Don't Ask, Don't Tell" went into effect, thereby permitting the enlistment of any soldier as long as he avoided any public disclosure of his sexual orientation. Because of the semantics of the policy, effeminate men and masculine girls are still under threat of witch-hunts and discharges. Under the current policy, if a soldier has revealed his homosexuality to anyone (including a parent, clergyman, or psychologist), he can be discharged. Though "Don't Ask, Don't Tell" arose out of an attempt to alleviate bias toward gays in the military, the boys and girls in Congress merely reconfigured the presence of bias in the armed forces.

30c | BE INCLUSIVE ABOUT RACE AND ETHNICITY

Use the terms for racial and ethnic groups that the groups use for themselves. Use *black* to write about members of the Black Coaches' Association and *African American* to write about members of the Society for African American Brotherhood.

If you are still in doubt, err on the side of specificity. For instance, while *Latino(a)*, *Hispanic*, and *Chicano(a)* are all frequently accepted terms for many people, choosing a term that identifies a specific country (*Mexican* or *Puerto Rican*) would be more accurate. Broad regional terms (*European*, *African*, *Caribbean*) are flimsier because they do not acknowledge the uniqueness of each nation within the region. *Asian* is currently preferred over *Oriental*; however, terms like *Vietnamese* and *Japanese* are even more specific. Also, *English* and *British* are different. The people who live in England are English, but people from elsewhere in Great Britain—Scotland, Wales, Northern Ireland—will be quick to tell you that they are not English. Again, be specific. Call people from Wales *Welsh* and those from Scotland *Scots*.

When discussing an American's heritage, often the best term to use is the country of origin plus the word *American*, as in *Swedish American* or *Mexican American*. Capitalize the initial letters of both words and do not use a hyphen unless you are using the term as an adjective. Currently *black* and *African American* are acceptable. Some people prefer *Native American* over *American Indian*, but both terms are used in edited American English. Use the name of the specific American Indian group (*Ute, Dakota, Inupiat*) if you are writing about specific people. *Inuit* is currently the term preferred over *Eskimo*.

30d | BE INCLUSIVE ABOUT OTHER DIFFERENCES

Writing about people with disabilities

The *Publication Manual of the American Psychological Association* (5th ed.) offers some good advice: "Put people first, not their disability" (75). Write *people who are deaf* instead of *the deaf* and *a student who is quadri-plegic* instead of *a quadriplegic student*. Discuss *a man who has depression,* not *a depressive* and *a woman who uses a wheelchair,* not *a wheelchair-bound woman.* Avoid naming someone as a victim; *a person with cancer* is better than *a cancer victim. Disability* is the term preferred over *handicap.* The word *handicap* derives from *hand-in-cap,* a term referring to begging that carries negative connotations.

Writing about people of different ages

Avoid bias by choosing accurate terms to describe age. If possible, use the person's age rather than an adjective, like *elderly* or *older,* which might offend. *Eighty-two-year-old Adele Schumacher* is better than *elderly Adele Schumacher* or *Adele Schumacher, an older resident.*

Writing about people of different financial statuses

When writing about financial status, be careful not to make assumptions (*People who live in trailer parks are uneducated*) or value judgments (*Dishwashing is a less respectable job than managing a restaurant*). While *upper class* and *middle class* are acceptable terms, *lower class* implies a bias. Instead use *working class.* Also, use the word *homeless* as an adjective, not a noun. Instead of writing *the homeless,* write *a homeless person* or, better yet, *a person who is homeless.* Be aware that words like *upper crust* and *white trash* imply value judgments based on a person's financial means.

Writing about people of different religions

Avoid making assumptions about someone's beliefs or practices based on religious affiliation. Even though the Vatican opposes capital punishment, many Roman Catholics support it. Likewise, not all Jewish men wear yarmulkes. The tremendous variation within religions and among individual practitioners makes generalizations questionable.

EXERCISE 30.3 Some of the writing in the following paragraph is not inclusive. Underline these words or phrases and replace them with better alternatives.

EXAMPLE   American census data examine both <u>poor, uneducated blacks</u> and <u>rich Orientals</u>.

REWRITE   American census data examine **the diverse ethnic and socioeconomic groups living in the United States**.

Various organizations gather census data in order to observe patterns of growth or decline in many areas of American life. For example, questions regarding politics, special interests, and marketing can be answered by identifying where old people live. Florida has one of the highest and Utah one of the lowest percentages of people over the age of sixty-five. Once they identify this pattern, marketers can target the elderly. Statistics regarding employment of the old are also found to intersect with those regarding handicapped people, since old people are usually also handicapped. A recent poll showed that the dumb and lame had less than a 25% employment rate. Based on the data provided, it would be wise to guess that these unfortunates also live in Florida.

Chapter 31

Write with Accurate Spelling

A few misspelled words can ruin the impression of an otherwise well-written paper. Reserve time near the end of your writing process to check for spelling mistakes. Computer spelling checkers are a good tool for identifying certain kinds of spelling errors, but they do not eliminate the need for careful proofreading. Some writers find it helpful to read both forward and backward. First, read your text from beginning to end, looking for mistakes with homonyms. Then read the text backward, from the last word to the first. Errors often jump out when you aren't caught up in reading sentences for content.

This chapter explains spelling rules that will help you catch mistakes—even the ones that spelling checkers overlook. Once you identify misspelled words, use a dictionary to determine the correct spellings. General dictionaries are indispensable. If you are using the vocabulary of a specific discipline, you will also need a specialized dictionary that contains words and definitions specific to that discipline.

31a | KNOW THE LIMITATIONS OF SPELLING CHECKERS

Spelling checkers actually help you to become a better speller. But spelling checkers are also quite limited and miss many errors. If you type *ferry tail* for *fairy tale*, your spelling checker will not catch the errors.

What spelling checkers can do for you:

- Identify typos
- Identify spelling errors (unless the misspelling is another word)

Computer Strategies

Electronic dictionaries

A number of reputable dictionaries now maintain searchable electronic versions on CD or on the Internet. If you don't own a dictionary, these Web sites offer a convenient, inexpensive alternative.

General Dictionaries

American Heritage Dictionary	**bartleby.com/61/**
Merriam-Webster Dictionary	**www.m-w.com/**
Oxford English Dictionary	Most research libraries offer access to an online version free to people with borrowing privileges.

Specialized Dictionaries

The Web site *yourDictionary.com* at **www.yourdictionary.com/diction4.html** lists specialized electronic dictionaries from a variety of disciplines.

What spelling checkers cannot do for you:

- Indicate when you have used the wrong words
- Determine that you have used apostrophes correctly
- Identify the correct spelling of most proper names
- Determine the correct spelling of some jargon (discipline-specific language) and other words not included in its database

Don't always take the advice of your spelling checker. In addition to missing certain kinds of misspelled words, it can flag correctly spelled words as incorrect. The following sentence illustrates the limitations of spelling checkers. It contains four errors a spelling checker wouldn't catch and two correctly spelled words that the checker would mark as misspellings.

Greenen Electronix, a Miami **megastore**, offers **to** of the most cutting-edge digital **videos** players on the market today, one of which is manufactured on **sight** by **Green** engineers.

Greenen Electronix (flagged incorrectly, a proper name)
megastore (flagged incorrectly, a word not in the checker's database)
to (two, unflagged homonym error)
videos (video, unflagged error with plurals)
sight (site, unflagged homonym error)
Green (Greenen, unflagged misspelling that spells another word)

Writing in the World

American versus British spelling

Among the many things that interested Benjamin Franklin was spelling reform. Franklin made sweeping proposals that never gained much support, but he convinced Noah Webster to take up the cause. While the changes included in Webster's first small dictionary in 1806 were not radical, they did become influential and led to the characteristic differences between American and British spelling.

Following the lead of Noah Webster, Americans write *color, favor, honor,* and other words without the *u* of British *colour, favour,* and *honour.* Americans put an *s* in words like *defense* and *offense* instead of the *c* the British use: *defence, offence.* Americans write *er* instead of *re* in words like *center, fiber,* and *theater* (instead of *centre, fibre,* and *theatre*). Perhaps the most confusing spelling is *judgment. Judgment* is the preferred spelling in American English and in British legal texts; British nonlegal texts use *judgement.*

EXERCISE 31.1 The author of the following paragraph ran it through a spelling checker and took all of the checker's advice. The checker missed some errors and created a few new errors. Correct all the spelling mistakes in the paragraph.

EXAMPLE ~~Its~~ *It's* indicative of ~~Despond~~ *Desmond* Tutu's feelings of solidarity

with his parishioners that he opted to live in ~~Sowed~~ *Soweto*, a

poor black neighborhood, rather than in Houghton, a

rich suburb.

Archbishop Despond Tutu's message to the peoples of South Africa is that all are "of infinite worth created in the image of god," and "to be treated . . . with reverence" (Wepman 13). Tutu maintains that this is true fore whites as well as blacks, a position that isn't popular wit some South African. It can be scene from the many awards tutu has received, not least among them the Nobel Peace Prize in 1984, that his commitment to morality and human freedom have had an effect the world over. Archbishop Despond Tutu is a ban who does not waist the potential of hiss powerful role as religious leader. On the contrary, the Archbishop seas many political problems as moral ones and speaks out frequently on human rights issues.

31b DISTINGUISH HOMONYMS

Homonyms are pairs (*your*, *you're*) and trios (*their*, *there*, *they're*) of words that sound alike but have different spellings and meanings. They are tricky words to spell because we don't learn to distinguish them in spoken language, and spelling checkers don't flag them as errors because they correctly spell other words in their databases. It's easy to type *there* for *their* or *Web sight* for *Web site* and not catch the error when you proofread.

The best way to avoid homonym errors is to be aware of the pairs and trios that cause the most errors.

all ready—completely prepared
already—as of now
all together—totally united
altogether—in sum
sense—(1) to perceive; (2) a perception
since—because

than—used with comparison
then—moment in time

their—possessive pronoun
there—location
they're—contraction for *they are*

threw—tossed
through—(1) completed; (2) via

to—preposition
too—(1) also; (2) excessive
two—a number

who's—contraction for *who is*
whose—possessive for *who*

your—belongs to you
you're—contraction for *you are*

There are also many other homonyms and near homonyms that are easy to confuse and misspell. You can find a list of these pairs in Section 29d.

EXERCISE 31.2 Circle the correct homophones in the paragraph that follows.

EXAMPLE   (Except/Accept) for the ethnic cleansings in Rwanda in 1995, one of the worst incidents of genocide in history occurred in the Southeast Asian country of Cambodia.

Modern Cambodia, or Kampuchea, gained its independence from France in 1953, but (by/buy) the early 1970s the country was embroiled in bloody civil war. In 1975, Khmer Rouge guerrillas secured the Cambodian (capital/capitol), Phnom Penh, (where/wear) they ruled the country until 1979. Once in power, the Khmer Rouge killed over 25% of their fellow Cambodians; (all together/altogether) they murdered over 2 million people. Most of those killed met their deaths at a (sight/site) (write/right) outside of Phnom Penh, known today as the "Killing Fields." The (affects/effects) of the Khmer Rouge's brief, yet defining rule remain all (to/too) apparent in contemporary Cambodia.

31c | LEARN SPELLING RULES

This section addresses four major categories of spelling rules: *i* before *e*; prefixes; suffixes; and plurals. While you'll see that each rule carries a number of exceptions, learning the rules is an important first step toward becoming a better speller.

I before *e*, except after *c* or when pronounced as *ay*

I before *e* is the classic spelling rule you probably learned in grade school. An *i* goes before an *e* except in two cases. The *i* follows the *e* when these letters follow *c* or when they are pronounced *ay*.

> *i* before *e*: *brief, hierarchy, obedient*
> except after *c*: *receipt, perceive, ceiling*
> or when pronounced as *ay*: *eight, neighbor, heir*

Exceptions to the *i* before *e* rules

ancient	feisty	science
being	foreign	seismic
caffeine	forfeit	seize
conscience	height	species
counterfeit	heist	weird
efficient	leisure	
either	neither	

Prefixes

When adding a prefix to a word, retain the spelling of the root word. (See Section 40a for help determining when a prefix–root word combination should be hyphenated.)

> mis + spelling = misspelling
> hemi + sphere = hemisphere
> un + believable = unbelievable
> un + nerve = unnerve

Suffixes

Double the root word's final consonant if

1. The root word ends in a consonant, and
2. A single vowel comes before the consonant, and
3. The root word is one syllable or the last syllable of the root is stressed.

   rappel + ed = rappelled
   control + ing = controlling
   recur + ence = recurrence
   hit + able = hittable

Do not double the root word's final consonant if

1. The root wood ends in two consonants.
   lift + ing = lifting
   remind + ed = reminded

2. Two vowels come before the consonant.
   head + ing = heading
   repeat + ed = repeated

3. The last syllable of the root is not stressed.
   fó-cus + ed = focused
   tra-vél + ed = traveled
   lá-bel + ing = labeling

Drop the final *e* from a root word if the suffix begins with a vowel.

When adding a suffix that begins with a vowel to a root word that ends with an unpronounced *e*, drop the *e*.

fate + al = fatal
opportune + ity = opportunity
Greece + ian = Grecian

Exceptions. Keep the *e* if it is preceded by a *c* (*enforceable*, *noticeable*) or a soft *g* (*advantageous*, *courageous*).

Keep the final _e_ in a root word if the suffix begins with a consonant.

Keep the root word's final unpronounced _e_ when the suffix begins with a consonant.

> subtle + ty = subtlety
> fortunate + ly = fortunately
> appease + ment = appeasement

✳ **Exceptions** ✳

> acknowledge + ment = acknowledgment
> argue + ment = argument
> awe + ful = awful
> judge + ment = judgment
> true + ly = truly
> whole + ly = wholly

When adding a suffix to a root word ending with a consonant and _y_, change the _y_ to an _i_.

> beauty + ful = beautiful
> crazy + ness = craziness
> glory + fy = glorify
> hungry + est = hungriest

Exceptions. When the suffix begins with an _i_, keep the _y_ (as in _study_, _studying_ and _dandy_, _dandyism_) in order to avoid a double _i_. Also keep the _y_ when adding _'s_ (_July's_ heat, the _spy's_ house). Other individual exceptions: _dryness_, _wryly_, _spryly_.

When adding a suffix to a root word ending with a vowel and _y_, retain the _y_.

> pay + ment = payment
> stay + ing = staying
> boy + hood = boyhood
> annoy + ance = annoyance

Exceptions

day + ly = daily	lay + ity = laity
gay + ty = gaiety	pay + ed = paid
lay + ed = laid	say + ed = said

EXERCISE 31.3 Each of the following root words ends in a consonant-vowel-consonant combination. Write the correct spelling of each word.

occur + ed = occurred
stop + ing = stopping

1. slap + ed
2. refer + ing
3. drop + ed
4. ship + ment
5. dim + er

6. run + ing
7. refer + ence
8. benefit + ed
9. commit + ment
10. forget + able

EXERCISE 31.4 Each of the following root words ends in a silent e. Write the correct spelling of each word. Pay attention to whether the first letter of the suffix is a consonant or a vowel.

continue + ous = continuous
state + ly = stately

1. definite + ly
2. pure + ist   *purist*
3. spine + less   *spineless*
4. exercise + ing *exercising*
5. imagine + ation *imagination*

6. hate + ful   *hateful*
7. judge + ment   *judgment*
8. debate + able *debatable*
9. like + able   *likable*
10. nine + th   *nineth*

Plurals

You can make most words plural simply by adding *s*. Exceptions abound, however. The following rules will help you determine which words do not just take an *s* in the plural.

Compound nouns: Make the most important word plural.

To indicate more than one of a compound noun (several words combining to make a noun) make the most important word plural. Note that the last word isn't always the most important.

sisters-in-law

attorneys general

courts-martial

brigadier generals

passersby

power plays

Add *es* to words ending with *ch, s, sh, x, z,* or a consonant and an *o*.

Add *es* to words that end in *ch, s, sh, x,* or *z,* as well as to words that end with a consonant followed by an *o*.

ending with *ch*:   church, churches   catch, catches

ending with *s*:   dress, dresses   trellis, trellises

ending with *sh*:   wash, washes   radish, radishes

ending with *x*:   ax, axes   box, boxes

ending with *z*:   buzz, buzzes   quiz, quizzes

ending with consonant

 and an *o*:   hero, heroes   tomato, tomatoes

Exceptions

memo, memos   photo, photos

piano, pianos   solo, solos

With words ending in a consonant and *y*, change the *y* to an *i* and add *es*.

Words ending in a consonant followed by a *y* become plural by replacing the *y* with an *i* and adding *es*.

spy, spies

derby, derbies

philosophy, philosophies

With words ending in a vowel and *y*, add *s*.

If a vowel precedes the *y*, simply add an *s* to make the word plural.

day, days

buoy, buoys

lackey, lackeys

Irregular plurals

Some words are irregular in the plural; they don't follow any set rules in English. Some are Latin words that retain their Latin plural endings. The following is a partial list of irregular plurals.

Singular	Plural	Singular	Plural
alumnus	alumni	man	men
analysis	analyses	medium	media
axis	axes	memorandum	memoranda
bacterium	bacteria	mouse	mice
basis	bases	octopus	octopi
cactus	cacti	ox	oxen
child	children	parenthesis	parentheses
crisis	crises	phenomenon	phenomena
criterion	criteria	radius	radii
curriculum	curricula	self	selves
datum	data	species	species
deer	deer	stimulus	stimuli
dice	die	stratum	strata
fish	fish	syllabus	syllabi
focus	foci	thesis	theses
half	halves	thief	thieves
hypothesis	hypotheses	vertebra	vertebrae
life	lives	woman	women
locus	loci		

EXERCISE 31.5 In the following paragraph, singular words that should be plural are underlined. Make all the underlined words plural. Where necessary, change verbs so that they agree with the plural words.

> EXAMPLE   Why Oscar Wilde, in 1885, brought Lord Queens-
>
> bury to trial on charges of libel remains one of the
>
> great mystery of literary history.
> *(mysteries written above "mystery")*

Wilde, a successful author with two <u>child</u> and multiple <u>follower</u> in literary London, made a mistake when he pressed <u>charge</u> against the famous lord. By all account, Wilde was in jovial spirit when he arrived at the Old Bailey courthouse on April 3, 1895. Passerby may have seen the famous writer make one of his characteristically fantastic entrance: Wilde's carriage was outfitted with two horse, several servant, and all the pomp and circumstance his public character demanded. But the series of event that followed led up to one of the great crash of the Victorian era. Wilde lost the libel suit and was then himself tried, twice, based on the body of evidence amassed against him in the first trial. The medium were not sympathetic to Wilde, who had come to embody the multiple threat of moral indecency for conservative Victorian. In the day following his two trial and ultimate conviction for the newly illegal crime of gross indecency, both print article and caricature presenting story from the trial served as knife in the artist's back. Wilde was sentenced to two year "hard labor," and upon his release from prison fled to France in exile. He died two year later. Wilde lived two life in his brief 47 years; he lived the first under the spotlight of fame, and the second under the glare of infamy. But his philosophy of art and beauty survive, as Wilde predicted they would.

Common Errors

Commonly misspelled words

Is *accommodate* spelled with one *m* or two? Is *harass* spelled with one *r* or two? You'll find a list of words commonly misspelled at the URL below.

Remember: Always check a dictionary when you are unsure of how a word is spelled.

www.ablongman.com/faigley017

EXERCISE 31.6 The words in the following paragraphs illustrate all the rules explained in Section 31c, Learn Spelling Rules. Some are spelled correctly and some are spelled incorrectly. Rewrite any words that are spelled incorrectly.

Their are several kinds of sleep disorders, the most common being insomnia. Sleepyness during daytime hours can often be a sign of needing more rest during the night. Insomnia is defined as a disatisfaction with the amount or quality of sleep aquired. It is interesting to note that many people who identifeid themselves as insomniacs for a study were found to be awake less than 30 min. per night. It is possable that these test subjects were sleeping lightly and suffered from a lack of "good" sleep.

There are a number of sugestions for increasing your chances of getting proper sleep. First, stick to a scedule. Even on weekends it is a good idea to rise at the same time as during the week. Second, avoid alcohol and stimulants such as caffeine. Alchohol can disturb sleep cycles and even a small amount of caffeine can remain in the blood stream for a long period of time. Regular exercise can actually help sleeping, but a workout right before bed sresses your chances of good sleep. Perhaps the most important criteerion for proper sleep is relaxation. Meditative exercieses or relaxing music can reduce stress and help get you ready for restfull sleep. Also, reserch actually supports the old tale that a warm glass of milk before bed can help you get a good nights sleep.

32
Grammar Basics

33
**Fragments, Run-Ons, and
Comma Splices**

34
Subject-Verb Agreement

35
Verbs

36
Pronouns

37
Modifiers

Chapter 32

Grammar Basics

Many people feel uncomfortable when they hear the word *grammar*. They think of grammar as a set of mysterious rules that they are constantly in danger of violating. In fact, people know intuitively the grammar of their native language or else they couldn't speak it. What they often don't know is how grammar works. Just as you can drive a car without knowing much about an engine, you can also write without knowing much about the concepts of grammar. But if you know a little about how your car works, you can keep it running better and longer. Similarly, if you understand a few concepts of grammar, you can be more confident about many aspects of writing.

32a SENTENCE BASICS

Sentences are the basic units in writing. Many people think of a sentence as a group of words that begins with a capital letter and ends with a period, but that definition includes grammatically incomplete sentences called **fragments** (see Section 33a).

Subjects and predicates

Regular sentences must have a subject and a predicate that includes a main verb. Typically the subject announces what the sentence is about and the predicate says something about that subject or conveys the action of the subject.

SUBJECT	PREDICATE
I	**want** a new monitor.
Your Web site	**loads** quickly.
By 1910, 26 million Americans	**were going** to the movies at nickelodeon theaters every week.

The exception to this rule is a class of sentences called **imperatives**, in which the subject is usually implied. In these sentences, we know that the subject is *you* without stating it.

> Quit bothering me.
> Help me carry in the groceries.

English is unlike several other languages in requiring a subject for sentences. In Spanish, Chinese, and Japanese, for example, speakers can say the equivalent of *is raining* without inserting a subject. But speakers of English must insert a dummy subject in such cases (*it is raining*) even though *it* refers to nothing.

Sentence patterns

Sentences can be classified into four major patterns according to function.

- **Declaratives.** Declarative sentences make statements.

  The house on the corner was built in 2001.

- **Interrogatives.** Interrogatives are usually referred to as questions.

  Who will be the first to volunteer?

- **Imperatives.** Imperatives request or demand some action.

  Stop complaining.

- **Exclamations.** Exclamations are used to express strong emotion.

  What an incredible performance you gave!

Sentences can be classified as either **positive** or **negative**. A sentence can be made negative by inserting a negative word, usually *not* or a contracted form of *not* (*can't, isn't*).

POSITIVE   Juanita has worked here for a year.

NEGATIVE   Juanita has **not** worked here for a year.

Sentences with transitive verbs (see Section 32c) can be considered as **active** or **passive**. Sentences can be made passive by changing the word order.

> **ACTIVE** The House of Representatives selected Thomas Jefferson as president in 1800 when the electoral vote ended in a tie.
>
> **PASSIVE** Thomas Jefferson **was selected** president by the House of Representatives in 1800 when the electoral vote ended in a tie.

The subject in an active sentence can be dropped in a passive sentence or another noun or noun phrase can take its place.

> Thomas Jefferson was selected president in 1800 when the electoral vote ended in a tie.

For more on active versus passive sentences, see Section 26a.

EXERCISE 32.1 Classify each of the following sentences as declarative, interrogative, imperative, or exclamatory. Then classify it as positive or negative. Finally, decide whether it is passive or active.

> **EXAMPLE** America boasts some of the world's strangest museums, from the American Sanitary Plumbing Museum to the Museum of Questionable Medical Devices. (Declarative, positive, active)

1. Don't miss the Spam memorabilia display in Austin, Minnesota's First Century Museum.
2. The Combat Cockroach Hall of Fame in Plano, Texas, displays a roach dressed like Marilyn Monroe!
3. Does the Elvis Is Alive Museum in Wright City, Missouri, really have a Tomb Room?
4. Stand in the mouth of a four-and-a-half-story-high fiberglass muskie at the National Fresh Water Fishing Hall of Fame in Hayward, Wisconsin.
5. The Desert of Maine Museum was not built in a desert at all, but in snowy Freeport, Maine.

32b WORD CLASSES

Like players in a team sport who are assigned to different positions, words are classified into parts of speech. The different positions on a team have different functions. The forwards in soccer and hockey do most of the scoring; goalies are responsible for preventing scoring. The parts of speech also serve different functions in sentences. And just as individuals can play more than one position on a team, so too can individual words belong to more than one part of speech. *Try* is a noun in *The third try was successful,* but a verb in *I would not try it.*

Nouns

A noun is the name of a person, place, thing, concept, or action. Names of particular persons, places, organizations, companies, titles, religions, languages, nationalities, ethnicities, months, and days are called **proper nouns** and are almost always capitalized. More general nouns are called **common nouns** and are seldom capitalized unless they begin a sentence (see Section 45a). Most common nouns can be made plural, and most are preceded by articles (*a, an, the*). Nouns have several functions:

- **Subject:** The **cat** climbed the tree.
- **Object:** Please feed the **cat.**
- **Subject complement:** This is the **cat.**
- **Object of a preposition:** This is for the **cat.**
- **Modifier of other nouns:** She moved on **cat** feet.
- **Appositive of other nouns:** My best friend, my **cat,** eats mice.
- **Possessive noun:** The **cat's** ball is under the sofa.

Nonnative speakers should see Chapter 47 for more on count and noncount nouns.

EXERCISE 32.2 The underlined words in the following paragraph are nouns. Identify the function of each. Does it serve as the subject, object, subject complement, object of a preposition, or modifier of another noun?

EXAMPLE

SUBJ   OBJ OF PREP   SUBJECT COMPLEMENT

The original title for *Casablanca* was *Everybody Comes to Rick's.*

The boyish Ronald Reagan was the studio's first choice for the male lead. Instead, the studio chose Humphrey Bogart, the shrapnel-scarred tough guy, to portray the owner of Rick's nightclub. The Swedish actress Ingrid Bergman was eventually cast as the female lead. The unexpected chemistry between Bergman and Bogart made *Casablanca* one of the greatest films of all time.

Pronouns

Pronouns are a subclass of nouns and are generally used as substitutes for nouns. Pronouns themselves are divided into several subclasses.

- **Personal pronouns:** *I, you, he, she, it, we, they, me, him, her, us, them*

  I gave my old racquet to **her**. **She** gave **me** a CD in return.

- **Possessive pronouns:** *my, mine, his, hers, its, our, ours, your, yours, their, theirs*

  My old racquet is now **hers**.

- **Demonstrative pronouns:** *this, that, these, those*

  Those are the mittens I want.

- **Indefinite pronouns:** *all, any, anyone, anybody, anything, both, each, either, everyone, everything, many, neither, no one, none, nothing, one, some, someone, somebody, something*

  Everyone was relieved that the driver's injuries were minor.

- **Relative pronouns:** *that, which, what, who, whom, whose, whatever, whoever, whomever, whichever*

  The house, **which** hung off a steep ridge, had a stunning view of the bay.

- **Interrogative pronouns:** *who, which, what, where*

  What would you like with your sandwich?

- **Reflexive pronouns:** *myself, ourselves, yourself, yourselves, himself, herself, itself, themselves*

  The twins behaved **themselves** around their grandfather.

- **Reciprocal pronouns:** *each other, one another*

  The brothers didn't like **each other**.

See Chapter 36 for more on pronouns.

EXERCISE 32.3 The underlined words in the following paragraph are pronouns. Identify the function of each. Does it serve as a personal, possessive, demonstrative, indefinite, relative, interrogative, reflexive, or reciprocal pronoun?

> EXAMPLE   On November 20, 1820, a sperm whale rammed and sank the whaleship *Essex*, but all the sailors escaped
> **POSS**
> with their lives.

The ramming was no accident; after the whale hit the *Essex* once, it turned around to hit the ship a second time. The sailors found themselves adrift in three whaleboats, 1,200 miles from the nearest islands. However, the crew feared that those were populated by cannibals. After a month starving at sea, the sailors found a small island, which offered little to eat. Crushed by hunger, the crew convinced each other to eat a fellow sailor who had died of starvation. Who could say that anybody would act differently if placed in similar circumstances? Their chances of survival weakened with each passing day. Yet, first mate Owen Chase navigated his whaleship for eighty-eight days until the crew was rescued by a merchant ship.

Verbs

Verbs indicate actions, states of mind, occurrences, and states of being. Verbs are divided into two primary categories: **main verbs** and **auxiliaries**. A main verb must be present in the predicate. The main verb may be the only word in the predicate.

> She **slept**.
>
> When he heard the starting gun, Vijay **sprinted**.

Auxiliaries (often called *helping verbs*) include forms of *be*, *have*, and *do*. A subset of auxiliaries are **modals**: *can, could, may, might, must, shall, should, will, would*.

> You **will be** satisfied when you see how well they painted your car.
>
> She **might have been** selected for the lead role in the ballet if her strained muscle **had** healed.

See Chapters 34 and 35 for more on verbs.

> **EXERCISE 32.4** Underline the verbs in the following paragraph. Decide whether each verb is a main verb or an auxiliary verb. If it is an auxiliary verb, note whether or not it is a modal verb.
>
> AUX NOT
> MODAL MAIN
>
> **EXAMPLE**   Fred Rogers has hosted his children's television program *Mister Rogers' Neighborhood* since 1965.
>
> Mr. Rogers has written all the songs and scripts for the nearly 900 episodes of *Mister Rogers' Neighborhood*. Children know the show best for Rogers' puppets, his soothing manner, and his cardigan sweaters. Rogers could have made a fortune from the show, but he has decided not to keep any of the profits. While some television personalities might preach one lifestyle and live another, Rogers abstains from smoking and drinking. And, in keeping with his unpretentious style, all of his sweaters are hand knit by his mother.

Verbals

Verbals are forms of verbs that function as nouns, adjectives, and adverbs. The three kinds of verbals are infinitives, participles, and gerunds.

- **Infinitives:** An infinitive is the base or *to* form of the verb. Infinitives can be used in place of nouns, adjectives, or adverbs.

  ┌NOUN┐
  To fly has been a centuries-old dream of people around the world.

  ┌ADJECTIVE┐
  Keeping your goals in mind is a good way **to succeed**.

- **Participles:** Participles are either present (*flying*) or past (*defeated*). They always function as adjectives.

  The **flying** insects are annoying.
  Napoleon's **defeated** army faced a long march back to France.

- **Gerunds:** Gerunds have the same form as present participles, but they always function as nouns.

  Flying was all that she wanted to do in life.

EXERCISE 32.5 Underline the verbals in the following paragraph and identify whether they are infinitives, participles, or gerunds. In addition, specify whether the participle is past or present.

	┌GERUND┐	PAST ┌PARTICIPLE┐

EXAMPLE <u>Casting</u> the "evil eye" is a superstition <u>recognized</u> in cultures around the world.

The evil eye is a focused gaze, supposedly causing death and destruction. Writings of the Assyrians, Babylonians, Greeks, and Romans all document an abiding belief in this supernatural concept. Old women and those thought to be witches are often accused of having the evil eye. To ward off the effects of the evil eye, people have resorted to praying, hand gestures, and purifying rituals.

Adjectives

Adjectives modify nouns and pronouns. Some adjectives are used frequently: *good, bad, small, tall, handsome, green, short.* Many others are recognizable by their suffixes: *-able (dependable), -al (cultural), -ful (hopeful), -ic (frenetic), -ive (decisive), -ish (foolish), -less (hopeless), -ous (erroneous).*

The **forgetful** manager was always backed up by her **dependable** assistant.

Adjectives often follow linking verbs.

That drumbeat is **relentless**.

Numbers are considered adjectives.

Only **ten** team members showed up for practice.

See Chapter 37 for more about adjectives and adverbs.

Adverbs

Adverbs modify verbs, other adverbs, adjectives, and entire clauses. The usual suffix for adverbs is *-ly.* Many adverbs do not have suffixes (*then, here*) and others have the same form as adjectives (*fast, hard, long, well*).

That drummer plays **well**. [modifies the verb *plays*]
That drummer plays **very** well. [modifies the adverb *well*]
That answer is **partly** correct. [modifies the adjective *correct*]
Frankly, I could care less. [modifies the clause *I could care less*]

Conjunctive adverbs often modify entire clauses and sentences. Like coordinating conjunctions, they indicate the relationship between two clauses or two sentences. Commonly used conjunctive adverbs include *also, consequently, furthermore, hence, however, indeed, instead, likewise, moreover, nevertheless, otherwise, similarly, therefore, thus.*

The Olympics brings together the best athletes in the world; **however**, the judging often represents the worst in sports.

EXERCISE 32.6 The underlined words in the following paragraph are modifiers. Label each modifier as adjective or adverb, and state which word it modifies.

> **ADV**
> **MOD. LIVING**
> **ADJ**
> **MOD.**
> **WOMAN**
> **ADJ**
> **MOD.**
> **WOMAN**
>
> EXAMPLE   After <u>initially</u> living the life of an <u>average</u> <u>middle-class</u>
>
> **ADV MOD. BECAME**
> woman, Dorothy Parker <u>ultimately</u> became one of the
>
> **ADV MOD.**
> **INFAMOUS**
> **ADJ MOD.**
> **WITS**
> **ADJ MOD. CENTURY**
> <u>most</u> <u>infamous</u> wits of the <u>twentieth</u> century.

Parker's father encouraged her to pursue "<u>feminine</u> arts" such as piano and poetry, but <u>just</u> following his <u>death</u> in 1913, she rushed into what turned out to be a <u>profitable</u> foray into the world of literature. <u>Almost</u> <u>immediately</u>, *Vanity Fair* purchased one of her poems, leading <u>her</u> into a <u>full-time</u> <u>writing</u> position with *Vogue*. It was <u>life-changing</u>, as Parker's flair for <u>clever</u> prose <u>swiftly</u> led her into the <u>inner</u> sanctum of New York <u>literary</u> society. Parker was fired from *Vanity Fair*'s editorial board in 1919 after <u>harshly</u> panning an advertiser's film. Despite her <u>early</u> departure from magazines, Parker gained <u>lasting</u> fame as a <u>prolific</u> writer and critic.

Prepositions

Prepositions indicate the relationship of nouns or pronouns to other parts of a sentence. Prepositions come before nouns and pronouns, and in this sense prepositions are "prepositioned." The noun(s) or pronoun(s) that follow are called the objects of prepositions.

> **PREP**   **OBJ**   **PREP** ┌──────OBJ──────┐
> She took the job **of speechwriter for the president.**

Here are some common prepositions.

about	behind	from	than
above	below	in	through
across	beside	inside	to
after	between	into	toward
against	but	off	under
among	by	on	until
around	despite	out	up
as	down	over	upon
at	during	past	with
before	for	since	without

Some prepositions are compounds.

according to	due to	in front of	next to
as well as	except for	in spite of	out of
because of	in addition to	instead of	with regard to

EXERCISE 32.7 Underline the prepositional phrases in the following paragraph and circle the prepositions.

EXAMPLE (During) the 1964 presidential campaign, Lyndon B. Johnson waged a dynamic campaign (against) Barry Goldwater (with) great success.

Johnson's campaign, inspired by the New Deal of Franklin Roosevelt's administration, was attractive to members of both political parties. According to Johnson's idea of the "Great Society," America would eliminate prejudice, poverty, and other social ills. In addition to the support of Democrats and social liberals, Johnson received approval from a large portion of the American media, which had traditionally lauded Republican candidates.

Conjunctions

Conjunctions indicate the relationship between words or groups of words. The two classes of conjunctions are **coordinate**, indicating units of equal status, and **subordinate**, indicating that one unit is more important than the other.

- **Coordinating conjunctions:** The seven coordinating conjunctions are *and, but, or, yet, for, so,* and *nor.*

  Do you want cake **or** ice cream?

  I graduated a semester early, **but** I had to go to work immediately to pay off loans.

- **Subordinating conjunctions:** Subordinating conjunctions introduce subordinate clauses. Common subordinating conjunctions are *after, although, as, because, before, if, since, that, unless, until, when, where, while.*

  After the value of the NASDAQ dropped by over two thirds between March 2000 and April 2001, some of the new dotcom millionaires found out the party was over.

EXERCISE 32.8 Fill in the blanks in the following paragraph with an appropriate coordinating or subordinating conjunction. More than one conjunction may fit.

> EXAMPLE   Scientists used to believe that sharks attacked people intentionally, _but_ they now assert that sharks attack humans only when mistaking them for natural prey.

Only four of the 400 species of shark attack humans: bull sharks, whitetips, tiger sharks, _____ great whites. _____ sharks committed 74 fatal attacks in the past 100 years, 75% of all shark attack victims have survived. Peter Benchley, the author of *Jaws*, describes sharks as "fragile" _____ their numbers seem to be declining. _____ the populations of some shark species have declined by 80%, some nations have enacted laws to protect them. People are coming to see sharks as an important part of ocean environments, _____ they are acting accordingly.

Articles

There are two classes of articles:

- **Definite article:** *the*
- **Indefinite article:** *a, an*

Nonnative speakers should see Section 47d for more on articles.

Interjections

Interjections are words like *oops, ouch, ugh,* and *ah.* They are usually punctuated separately and they do not relate grammatically to other words.

EXERCISE 32.9 Each underlined word in this paragraph represents one of the word classes explained in this section. Identify nouns, pronouns, verbs, verbals, adjectives, adverbs, prepositions, conjunctions, articles, and interjections.

NOUN
EXAMPLE   The <u>explosion</u> at the Chernobyl nuclear power plant in

1986 released one hundred times as much radiation as

PREP
the atomic bombs dropped <u>on</u> Hiroshima and Nagasaki.

Although the Chernobyl explosion was the worst nuclear disaster ever, the implicit Russian response seemed to be, "<u>Oops!</u>" They downplayed the significance of the disaster. The <u>massive</u> amounts of radiation <u>affected</u> Belarus, Poland, Scandinavia, <u>and</u> the Ukraine. Most of the <u>radiation</u> released <u>into</u> the air <u>settled</u> on Northern Ukraine and Southern Belarus. Some of the <u>radiation</u> released <u>by</u> the disaster has <u>a</u> half-life of over thirty years. Thus, scientists surmise that the <u>full</u> <u>medical</u> and environmental effects have yet to be felt. <u>Birth defects</u> in regions surrounding Chernobyl have increased <u>dramatically</u> since 1986. <u>Hiking</u> is under the question in forests surrounding the plant; <u>those</u> near the epicenter <u>of</u> the disaster continue to be affected by <u>large</u>, lingering doses of radioactivity.

32c | CLAUSES

Clauses are the grammatical structures that underlie sentences. Each clause has a subject and a predicate, but not all clauses are sentences. The variety of clauses is nearly infinite because phrases and other clauses can be embedded within them in a multitude of ways. Nevertheless, a few basic patterns are central to English clause structure.

Subject-verb-object

On the predicate side of a clause, you always find a main verb and often a direct object that is affected by the action of the verb.

┌─ S ─┐ ┌─ V ─┐ ┌── DO ──┐
Ahmad **kicked** the ball.

This basic pattern, called **subject-verb-object** or **S-V-O**, is one of the most common in English. Verbs that take objects (*kick, revise*) are called **transitive verbs**. Some transitive verbs can take two objects: a **direct object** that completes the sentence and an **indirect object**, usually a person, indirectly affected by the action.

┌─ S ─┐ ┌─ V ─┐ ┌── DO ──┐ ┌─ IO ─┐
Ahmad **kicked** the ball to Sally.

Clauses without objects

Not all clauses have objects.

┌─ S ─┐ ┌─ V ─┐
Maria **slept**.

┌─── S ───┐ ┌─ V ─┐
The engine **runs** rough. (*Rough* is an adverb, not an object.)

┌─── S ───┐ ┌─── V ───┐
The staff **cannot work** on weekends. (*On weekends* is a prepositional phrase.)

This clause pattern is **subject-verb** or **S-V**. Verbs that do not require objects are called **intransitive verbs**. Many verbs can be both transitive and intransitive.

INTRANSITIVE	Ginny **runs** fast.
TRANSITIVE	Ginny **runs** the company.

For more on the verbs *lay/lie, set/sit,* and *raise/rise,* see Section 35c.

Linking-verb clauses

A third major pattern links the subject to a noun or adjective following the verb that restates or describes the subject. The most commonly used verbs for this pattern are forms of *be*.

McKinley was president in 1900.
Rosalia Fernandez is the assistant manager.
The results of the MRI **were negative**.

What follows the verb is the subject complement, either a noun or noun phrase (*president, assistant manager*) or a predicate adjective describing the subject (*negative*).

Other linking verbs besides *be* are *appear, become, feel, look, remain,* and *seem*. These linking verbs often refer to people's perceptions or senses.

Jennifer **felt** nervous when she accepted the award.

Main versus subordinate clauses

All the examples of clauses we have looked at up to now can stand by themselves as sentences. These clauses are called **main** or **independent clauses**. Other clauses have the necessary ingredients to count as clauses—a subject and a main verb—yet they are incomplete as sentences.

Where you choose to go to college
Which was the first to be considered
As fast as my legs could pedal

These clauses are examples of **subordinate** or **dependent** clauses. They do not stand by themselves, but must be attached to another clause:

I rode my bike *as fast as my legs could pedal*.

Subordinate clauses serve three main functions.

- **Noun clauses:** Noun clauses serve all the functions that nouns perform, including subjects, objects, complements, and appositives. They usually are formed with either a relative pronoun (*that, which, what, who, whom, whose, whatever, whoever, whichever*) or with *when, where, why,* or *how*.

AS SUBJECT	**That the entry fee included all the food** made the price reasonable.
AS DIRECT OBJECT	I could not **find where it was located**.
AS SUBJECT COMPLEMENT	**The newest version** is what she wants.
AS APPOSITIVE	**The reason** that I am here today is obvious.
AS OBJECT OF PREPOSITION	He listened **to what she had to say**.

- **Adjective clauses:** Adjective clauses modify nouns and pronouns. They are also called **relative clauses** and usually begin with a relative pronoun.

  Steroids that are used to increase muscle density have many harmful side effects.

  The site where the fort once stood was washed away by a hurricane.

- **Adverb clauses:** Adverb clauses function as adverbs, modifying verbs, other adverbs, adjectives, and entire clauses. They begin with a subordinating conjunction such as *after, although, as, because, before, if, since, that, unless, until, when, where, while*.

MODIFIES VERB	She **arrived** after we had carried all of our furniture into our new apartment.

MODIFIES ADVERB   Jeff laughed **nervously** whenever the
                   boss came around.

MODIFIES ADJECTIVE The forward was not as **tall** as the media
                   guide listed.

MODIFIES CLAUSE   When you see a person faint, **you
                   should call 911**.

EXERCISE 32.10 Identify which of the three main clause patterns each of the following sentences exemplifies: subject-verb-object, subject-verb, or subject-linking verb.

> EXAMPLE   In 1954, the United States Supreme Court ordered
>   school desegregation. (Subject–verb–object)

1. Arkansas Governor Orval Faubus refused to obey the order.
2. The Arkansas militia seemed impenetrable.
3. Nine African-American students retreated from the school.
4. President Dwight Eisenhower ordered National Guard troops to escort the African-American students.
5. The guardsmen were successful.

EXERCISE 32.11 The subordinate clauses in the following sentences are in italics. Identify whether they are noun, adjective, or adverb clauses.

> **ADVERB CLAUSE**
> EXAMPLE   *Although many cultures abhor the practice of cannibalism,*
>
> **NOUN CLAUSE**
>   *that it has taken place in many areas* is indisputable.

1. Tribes in the West Indies *who sought dominance over neighboring peoples* often ate human flesh.
2. Some practitioners in New Guinea and West Africa believed *that consuming the body of an enemy would transfer the special attributes of the conquered to themselves.*
3. It is important to note that not all tribes *who practiced human sacrifice* necessarily condoned consumption of the dead.

4. *Unless there were dire circumstances of famine* most tribes perceived cannibalism solely as a byproduct of military conquest.

5. *That cannibalism is a purely non-Western phenomenon* is a common misconception; *because Mediterranean histories cite instances of cannibalism*, we must concede that it has had a long and diverse cultural existence.

32d PHRASES

Along with clauses, phrases add to sentences groups of words that modify or develop parts of the sentence. Some phrases can be confused with clauses, but phrases lack either a subject or a main verb.

Prepositional phrases

Prepositional phrases consist of a preposition and its object, including modifiers of the object. They can modify nouns, verbs, or adjectives.

The **carton** of orange juice froze solid.

They will **bring** the pizza on time.

She was **rich** in spirit.

Verbal phrases

Each of the three kinds of verbals—infinitives, participles, and gerunds— can be used to create phrases.

- **Infinitive phrases:** Infinitive phrases can function as nouns, adverbs, and adjectives. As nouns they can be subjects, objects, or complements.

To succeed where others had failed was her goal.

- **Participial phrases:** Participial phrases are formed by either present participles (*flying*) or past participles (*defeated*); they function as adjectives.

  The freighter, **listing noticeably to the port side,** left the port without balancing the load.

- **Gerund phrases:** Gerund phrases formed from the present participle (*-ing*) function as nouns.

  ┌─────── SUBJECT ───────┐
  Feeding stray cats became my next-door neighbor's obsession.

Appositives

Appositive phrases modify nouns and are often set off by a pair of commas. They usually follow the noun they modify. They are quite useful as identifying tags for nouns.

Andy, **my old linguistics teacher,** became one of my best friends.

Absolutes

Absolute phrases are nearly clauses because they include a noun or pronoun and a verb; however, the verb is a participle ending in *-ing* or *-ed* and not a main verb. Absolute phrases can appear anywhere in a sentence and are set off by commas.

He struggled at the beginning of his speech, **his voice trembling.**

EXERCISE 32.12 Identify the italicized phrases in the following sentences. Are they prepositional, verbal, appositive, or absolute phrases? If they are verbal phrases, specify whether they are infinitive phrases, participial phrases, or gerund phrases.

PARTICIPIAL PHRASE
EXAMPLE   *Reaching peak capacity between 1892 and 1924,* Ellis
PREPOSITIONAL PHRASE
Island was the initial point of contact *for countless new*

American immigrants.

1. *Arriving on Ellis Island,* immigrants *seeking American citizenship* were herded *into long lines for medical inspection.*
2. *Surviving this process* enhanced one's chances *of remaining here.*
3. *To check immigrants' eyelids* for diseases was a procedure examiners commonly performed *with nonmedical objects, including hairpins and buttonhooks.*
4. Trachoma, an eye disease, was often diagnosed *in immigrants* and resulted *in their deportation.*
5. Judgments *of the immigrants' mental stability* also affected entry status, *decisions often seeming highly subjective.*

32e SENTENCE TYPES

Simple sentences

A simple sentence consists of one main clause and no subordinate clauses. Simple sentences can be quite short.

⌐SUBJ⌐ ⌐VERB⌐
The two toy **figures spun** together.

Simple sentences can become quite long if phrases are added.

⌐———————— MAIN CLAUSE ————————⌐
The two toy figures spun together, standing on top of their round metal pedestal, teetering back and forth in a jerky, clockwise motion, slowing gradually.

Compound sentences

Compound sentences have two or more main clauses and no subordinate clauses. The main clauses are connected in one of three ways: (1) by a semicolon, (2) by a comma and coordinating conjunction (*and, but, or, for, so, nor, yet*), or (3) by punctuation and a conjunctive adverb (*furthermore, however, indeed, nevertheless, therefore*).

⌐——— MAIN CLAUSE ———⌐ ⌐——— MAIN CLAUSE ———⌐
Mike walked to his car, **and** he opened the trunk.

┌──────── MAIN CLAUSE ────────┐   ┌──── MAIN CLAUSE ────┐
The theater enjoyed record attendance; **however,** rising costs took all
└──┘
the profits.

Complex sentences

Complex sentences have one main clause and one or more subordinate clauses.

┌──── MAIN CLAUSE ────┐┌─── SUBORDINATE CLAUSE ───┐
Mike walked to his car **when** he got out of class.

Compound-complex sentences

Compound-complex sentences have at least two main clauses and at least one subordinate clause.

┌──── MAIN CLAUSE ────┐┌─── SUBORDINATE CLAUSE ───┐   ┌──── MAIN CLAUSE ────┐
Mike walked to his car when he got out of class, **but** he had to go back
└──┘
for his briefcase.

Writing in the World

Descriptive grammar versus prescriptive grammar

Read this pair of sentences:

I wore my green new coat yesterday.

I wore my new green coat yesterday.

If you grew up speaking English, you know that *I wore my green new coat yesterday* is not a correct English sentence. English has a rule for adjectives that requires more inherent qualities (such as color) to be placed closer to the noun than less inherent qualities (such as age). Even though you may never have heard this rule stated, you internalized it before you started the first grade. This rule is *descriptive* because it states what speakers of English recognize as English.

Consider another pair:

Don't blame the mess on me.

Don't blame me for the mess.

Both sentences may sound correct to you. Some people, however, avoid using *blame on* and prefer the second sentence. Rules that express preferences of one alternative over another are called *prescriptive*. Prescriptive rules deal with questions of usage.

You can think of prescriptive rules as a kind of etiquette of language. The more formal the occasion for writing, the more you want to pay attention to the fine distinctions of prescriptive rules.

EXERCISE 32.13 In each of the following sentences, underline the main clause. If there are subordinate clauses, underline them twice. Then identify what type each sentence is: simple, compound, complex, or compound-complex.

> EXAMPLE Although many cultures consider death an ending or something to fear, various Meso-American civilizations see it as something to embrace, and it is this belief that gives rise to the celebration known as The Day of the Dead. (Compound-complex)

1. The dead reappear during the month-long celebration.
2. The goddess Mictecaclhuati presides over all the festivities, but each culture celebrates the festival in its own unique way.
3. Some revelers celebrate by eating candy skulls with the names of their deceased relatives written on the foreheads.
4. In some parts of Mexico, family members picnic at the spots where the deceased have been buried.
5. Because Spaniards found the ritual blasphemous, they attempted to replace it with the Christian holiday All Saints' Day, but their efforts failed and the celebration still thrives today.

EXERCISE 32.14 The following are simple sentences. Rewrite each as compound, complex, and compound-complex sentences.

SIMPLE   Baseball, America's national pastime, has endured decades of poor attendance, scandals, and players' strikes.

COMPOUND   Baseball has endured decades of poor attendance, scandals, and players' strikes, yet it is still America's national pastime.

COMPLEX   Baseball, which many consider America's national pastime, has endured decades of poor attendance, scandals, and players' strikes.

COMPOUND-   While it has been called America's national pastime
COMPLEX   for over a century, baseball has endured many trials, yet the game has survived decades of poor attendance, scandals, and players' strikes.

1. Philip K. Wrigley, chewing gum entrepreneur, founded the All-American Girls Professional Baseball League in 1943, bolstering waning interest in baseball during World War II, when many major league players were away fighting.
2. The league attracted women from all over the United States and Canada, providing them with a previously absent national venue to showcase their athletic talents.
3. The league peaked in 1948 with ten teams and over 900,000 paying fans.
4. Promoting an image of femininity among female athletes, the league insisted on strict regulations regarding dress and public behavior.
5. Lacking audience interest, the league folded in 1954.

Chapter 33
Fragments, Run-ons, and Comma Splices

The most common sources of sentence errors are fragments, run-ons, and comma splices.

33a | FRAGMENTS

Fragments in speech and writing

Fragments are incomplete sentences. They are punctuated to look like sentences, but they lack a key element—often a subject or a verb—or else are a subordinate clause or phrase. In spoken language we usually pay little attention to fragments.

MISSING SUBJECT; MISSING VERB	Nothing like a hot shower when you're cold and wet.
MISSING SUBJECT	I was completely hooked on the game. And played it constantly.
MISSING VERB	You too?
SUBORDINATE CLAUSE	If you think so.

In writing, however, fragments usually interrupt the reader. Consider another example of a full sentence followed by a fragment:

The university's enrollment rose unexpectedly during the fall semester. **Because the percentage of students who accepted offers of admission was much higher than previous years and fewer students than usual dropped out or transferred.**

Such fragments compel a reader to stop and reread. When a sentence starts with *because*, we expect to find a main clause later. Instead, the *because* clause refers back to the previous sentence. The writer no doubt knew that the fragment gave reasons why enrollment rose, but a reader must stop to determine the connection.

Common Errors

Recognizing fragments

If you can spot fragments, you can fix them. Grammar checkers can find some of them, but they miss many fragments and identify other sentences wrongly as fragments. Ask these questions when you are checking for sentence fragments.

- **Does the sentence have a subject?** Except for commands, sentences need subjects:

  Jane spent every cent of credit she had available. And then applied for more cards.

- **Does the sentence have a complete verb?** Sentences require complete verbs. Verbs that end in *-ing* must have an auxiliary verb to be complete.

  Ralph keeps changing majors. He trying to figure out what he really wants to do after college.

- **If the sentence begins with a subordinate clause, is there a main clause in the same sentence?**

  Even though Seattle is cloudy much of the year, no American city is more beautiful when the sun shines. Which is one reason people continue to move there.

Remember:

1. **A sentence must have a subject and complete verb.**
2. **A subordinate clause cannot stand alone as a sentence.**

For step-by-step discussion, examples, and practice of this common error, go to **www.ablongman.com/faigley018**.

In formal writing you should avoid fragments. Readers expect words punctuated as a sentence to be a complete sentence. They expect writers to complete their thoughts rather than force readers to guess the missing element.

Basic strategies for turning fragments into sentences

If you can identify fragments, you can fix them easily.

Incorporate the fragment into an adjoining sentence. In many cases you can incorporate the fragment into an adjoining sentence.

She saw him coming. And looked away. *(a)*

I was hooked on the game. Playing day and night. *(game, playing)*

Add the missing element. If you cannot incorporate a fragment into another sentence, add the missing element.

He studying more this semester. *(is)*

When aiming for the highest returns, and also thinking about the possible losses. *(investors should think)*

Watch for these fragments

1. Pay close attention to sentences that begin with transitional words, coordinating conjunctions, and subordinating conjunctions. Among the most common are fragments that begin with a transitional word (*also, therefore, however, consequently*), a coordinating conjunction (*and, but, or*), or a word indicating a subordinate clause (*although, because, if, since*). Prepositional or verbal phrase fragments are also common.

Transitional words and phrases such as *also, however,* and *therefore* mark movement from one idea to another, such as introducing another example, a change in direction, or a conclusion. Writers often produce fragments when trying to separate these shifts with a period.

Susan found ways to avoid working during her shift. ~~T~~, ~~t~~herefore making more work for the rest of the employees.

Compound predicates are linked by a coordinating conjunction such as *and, but,* or *or.* Because compound predicates share the same subject, the solution for a coordinating conjunction fragment is to incorporate it into the sentence with the subject.

Heroin use among urban professionals is on the rise in the United States. ~~A~~ *a*nd also in Europe, after several decades during which cocaine was the preferred drug among this group.

Subordinate clauses resemble sentences because they contain subjects and verbs. But subordinate clauses cannot stand alone as sentences because their meaning is dependent on another clause. Subordinate clauses begin with words such as *although, after, before, despite, if, though, unless, whether, while, when, who,* and *that.* Subordinate clause fragments often follow the sentence to which they actually belong. You can fix the subordinate clause fragment by incorporating it into the preceding sentence.

The movie *Gladiator* is fiction, but it is based on extensive research with much of the plot inspired by actual people and historical events. ~~W~~ , *w*hich explains why it seems more realistic than earlier movies about Rome such as *Spartacus.*

Or you can fix the subordinate clause fragment by turning it into a sentence.

The movie *Gladiator* is fiction, but it is based on extensive research with much of the plot inspired by actual people and historical events. This attention to historical detail, if not historical accuracy, explains why *Gladiator* seems more realistic than earlier movies about Rome such as *Spartacus*.

2. Look for phrase fragments. Phrases also cannot stand alone as sentences because they lack either a subject, a verb, or both. There are many different kinds of phrase fragments. Prepositional phrase fragments are easy to spot and fix.

As Helen looked over the notes for her autobiography, she mused about how much her life had changed. ~~I,~~ in ways she could not have predicted.

Andrew accepted the university's award for outstanding dissertation. ~~W~~ with great dignity and humility.

Appositive phrases, which rename or describe a noun, are often fragments.

For his advanced English Tudor history course, Professor Levack assigned J. J. Scarisbrick's *Henry VIII.* ~~A,~~ an older text historians still regard as essential when studying sixteenth-century English history and politics.

Verbal phrase fragments are sometimes difficult to spot because verbals look like verbs. But remember: They function as adjectives, nouns, or adverbs.

On their last trip to Chicago, Greta went to the Art Institute, but Roger didn't go. ~~Roger,~~ having visited that museum twice already.

3. Watch for list fragments. Do not isolate a list from the sentence that introduces it. Words or phrases such as *for example, for instance, namely,* and *such as* often introduce lists or examples. Make sure these lists are attached to a sentence with a subject and verb.

Several Ben and Jerry's ice cream flavors are puns. ~~S,~~ such as Cherry Garcia, Phish Food, and The Full VerMonty.

Writing in the World

Intentional fragments

Most academic and professional writers avoid fragments. Consequently, fragments are not acceptable in formal college writing. If you read carefully, however, you will find fragments in certain kinds of writing.

Fragments used for emphasis

In informal writing that imitates spoken language, you will find fragments used occasionally for emphasis.

> The door-to-door salesman tried to convince us that frozen vegetables taste better than ones picked off the vine. **Nonsense.**

Fragments in advertising

Advertising copy often uses fragments.

> **New and improved! 100% more cleaning power!**

Fragments in literary prose

Fragments are common in fiction and literary nonfiction. For example, they can be effective for adding descriptive details if you want those details to stand out.

> An immature bald eagle stood on the bank only thirty feet away, its speckled white and black breast feathers ruffling in the breeze, its massive talons clutching a dead king salmon. **Wings spread in the indecision of retreat. Powerful beak locked. Eyes and head moving, missing nothing.**

This series of details might have been punctuated with commas. Setting off the final three clauses with periods adds additional pauses, as if the writer is moving in to take close-up shots. This strategy, however, should be reserved for special effects. If the ordinary details are punctuated with periods, the result is choppy writing that appears incorrect, even in fiction.

EXERCISE 33.1 Revise each of the following to eliminate the sentence fragment.

> EXAMPLE   Certain mammals, like flying squirrels and sugar gliders,
>
> are varieties that actually ~~glide. Which~~ *glide, which* enables them to
>
> survive when they are being hunted by nimble predators.

1. Flying squirrels, like typical squirrels except they have flaps of skin that allow them to glide.
2. Flying squirrels glide gracefully. From tree to tree with surprising ease.
3. To gain speed and momentum, flying squirrels often free-fall for several feet. Then to turn in midair, lower one arm.
4. The Japanese giant flying squirrel is one of the largest known varieties. Spanning two feet long from its head to its furry tail.
5. By gliding, escape predators and gather food quickly.

EXERCISE 33.2 Find the fragments in the following paragraph and revise the paragraph to eliminate them.

> Barton Springs still seems like a place not in Texas for those who come from elsewhere. Surrounding hills covered by live oaks and mountain juniper. And ground around the pool shaded by pecan trees whose trunks are a dozen feet in circumference. Banana trees and other tropical plants grow in the roofless dressing areas of the pool. With grackles whistling jungle-like sounds outside. The pool is in a natural limestone creek bed. Which is an eighth of a mile long. Fed by 27,000,000 gallons of 68° water bubbling out of the Edwards Aquifer each day.

33b | RUN-ON SENTENCES

Run-on sentences are the opposite of sentence fragments. While fragments are incomplete sentences, run-ons jam together two or more sentences, failing to separate them with appropriate punctuation. And while fragments are sometimes acceptable, especially in informal writing, run-on sentences are never acceptable.

Common Errors

Recognizing run-on sentences

When you read this sentence, you realize something is wrong.

> I do not recall what kind of printer it was all I remember is that it could sort, staple, and print a packet at the same time.

The problem is that the two main clauses are not separated by punctuation. The reader must look carefully to determine where one main clause stops and the next one begins.

> I do not recall what kind of printer it was | all I remember is that it could sort, staple, and print a packet at the same time.

A period should be placed after *was*, and the next sentence should begin with a capital letter:

> I do not recall what kind of printer it was. All I remember is that it could sort, staple, and print a packet at the same time.

Run-on sentences are major errors.

Remember: Two main clauses must be separated by correct punctuation.

 For step-by-step discussion, examples, and practice of this common error, go to **www.ablongman.com/faigley019.**

Fixing run-on sentences

Take three steps to fix run-on sentences: (1) identify the problem, (2) determine where the run-on sentence needs to be divided, and (3) choose the punctuation that indicates the relationship between the main clauses.

1. Identify the problem. When you read your writing aloud, run-on sentences will often trip you up, just as they confuse readers. You can also search for subject and verb pairs to check for run-ons. If you find two main clauses with no punctuation separating them, you have a run-on sentence.

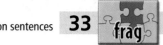
┌──────SUBJ──────┐┌──VERB──┐
Internet businesses are not **bound** to specific locations or old ways of
┌─S─┐┌─V─┐
running a business **they are** more flexible in allowing employees to
telecommute and to determine the hours they work.

2. Determine where the run-on sentence needs to be divided.

Internet businesses are not bound to specific locations or old ways of
running a business | they are more flexible in allowing employees to
telecommute and to determine the hours they work.

3. Determine the relationship between the main clauses. You will
revise a run-on more effectively if you first determine the relationship between the main clauses and understand the effect or point you are trying to
make. There are several punctuation strategies for fixing run-ons.

- **Insert a period.** This is the simplest way to fix a run-on sentence.

  Internet businesses are not bound to specific locations or old ways of
  running a business. They are more flexible in allowing employees to
  telecommute and to determine the hours they work.

  However, if you want to indicate the relationship between the two
  main clauses more clearly, you may want to choose one of the following strategies.

- **Insert a semicolon (and possibly a transitional word indicating
  the relationship between the two main clauses).**

  Internet businesses are not bound to specific locations or old ways of
  running a business; therefore, they are more flexible in allowing employees to telecommute and to determine the hours they work.

- **Insert a comma and a coordinating conjunction (*and, but, or,
  nor, for, so, yet*).**

  Internet businesses are not bound to specific locations or old ways of
  running a business, so they are more flexible in allowing employees to
  telecommute and to determine the hours they work.

- **Make one of the clauses subordinate.**

  Since Internet businesses are not bound to specific locations or old ways of running a business, they are more flexible in allowing employees to telecommute and to determine the hours they work.

EXERCISE 33.3 Correct the following run-on sentences.

                                                                         1600s. Its

    EXAMPLE   Japanese Kabuki theater surfaced in the early ~~1600s its~~ origins are often linked to the public, improvised performances of Izumo Grand.

1. The original Kabuki troupes were mostly comprised of female dancers however male performers replaced them after the art became associated with prostitution.
2. Performances included several thematically linked elements such as dance, history, and domestic drama they lasted up to twelve hours.
3. In the 1700s, choreographers and special schools became commonplace Kabuki dance became more complex.
4. Kabuki costumes are often quite elaborate actors sometimes need assistance preparing for performances.
5. Since World War II, Western influences have altered the social position of Kabuki ticket prices have risen, making performances more accessible to tourists, but not the average Japanese citizen.

33c   COMMA SPLICES

Comma splices are a kind of run-on sentence. They do include a punctuation mark—a comma—but it is not a strong enough punctuation mark to separate two main clauses. Comma splices often do not cause the same problems for readers as run-ons. The following sentence can be read aloud with no problem.

Most of us were taking the same classes, if someone had a question, we would all help out.

On the page such sentences may cause confusion because commas are used to distinguish between elements within sentences, not to mark the boundary between sentences. Most readers see comma splices as errors, which is why you should avoid them.

Common Errors

Recognizing comma splices

When you edit your writing, look carefully at sentences that contain commas. Does the sentence contain two main clauses? If so, are the main clauses joined by a comma and coordinating conjunction (*and, but, for, or, not, so, yet*)?

INCORRECT   The **concept** of "nature" **depends** on the concept of human "culture," the **problem is** that "culture" is itself shaped by "nature." *(Two main clauses joined by only a comma)*

CORRECT   Even though the concept of "nature" depends on the concept of human "culture," "culture" is itself shaped by "nature." *(Subordinate clause plus a main clause)*

CORRECT   The concept of "nature" depends on the concept of human "culture," but "culture" is itself shaped by "nature." *(Two main clauses joined by a comma and coordinating conjunction)*

Treating the word *however* as a coordinating conjunction produces some of the most common comma splice errors. *However* is a conjunctive adverb that does not function grammatically like the coordinating conjunctions *and, but, or, nor, yet, so,* and *for* (see Section 32b).

INCORRECT   The White House press secretary repeatedly vowed the Administration was not choosing a side between the two countries embroiled in conflict, however the developing foreign policy suggested otherwise.

CORRECT   The White House press secretary repeatedly vowed the Administration was not choosing a side between the two countries embroiled in conflict; however, the developing foreign policy suggested otherwise. *(Two main clauses joined by a semicolon)*

Remember: Do not use a comma as a period.

For step-by-step discussion, examples, and practice of this common error, go to **www.ablongman.com/faigley020**.

Fixing comma splices

You have several options for fixing comma splices. Select the one that best fits where the sentence is located and the effect you are trying to achieve.

1. Change the comma to a period. Most comma splices can be fixed by changing the comma to a period.

It didn't matter that I worked in a windowless room for 40 hours a ~~week, on~~ *week. On* the Web I was exploring and learning more about distant people and places than I ever had before.

2. Change the comma to a semicolon. A semicolon indicates the close connection between the two main clauses.

It didn't matter that I worked in a windowless room for 40 hours a ~~week,~~ *week;* on the Web I was exploring and learning more about distant people and places than I ever had before.

3. Insert a coordinating conjunction. Other comma splices can be repaired by inserting a coordinating conjunction (*and, but, or, nor, so, yet*) to indicate the relationship of the two main clauses. The coordinating conjunction must be preceded by a comma.

Digital technologies have intensified a global culture that affects us daily in large and small ways**, yet** their impact remains poorly understood.

4. Make one of the main clauses a subordinate clause. If a comma splice includes one main clause that is subordinate to the other, rewrite the sentence using a subordinating conjunction.

Because community
~~Community~~ is the vision of a great society trimmed down to the size of a small town, it is a powerful metaphor for real estate developers who sell a mini-utopia along with a house or condo.

5. Make one of the main clauses a phrase. You can also rewrite one of the main clauses as a phrase.

Community—the vision of a great society trimmed down to the size of a small town—is a powerful metaphor for real estate developers who sell a mini-utopia along with a house or condo.

EXERCISE 33.4 The following sentences all contain comma splices. Eliminate the splices using the methods indicated in the parentheses.

EXAMPLE Accused Nazi propagandist Leni Riefenstahl was born

in Germany in ~~1902, her~~ *1902. Her* films *Triumph of the Will* and

Olympia are said to have captured the essence of the

Nazi era. (Split into two sentences.)

1. Riefenstahl spent her early days performing in Germany as a dancer. *A* 1924 knee injury derailed her dance career, detouring her into a successful *yet* scandal-ridden life in film. (Split into two sentences; add a conjunctive adverb.)
2. Early editing work prepared her to direct her first film, *The Blue Light;* however, national recognition was slow to come. (Add a semicolon.)
3. The year 1935 saw the release of Riefenstahl's film *Triumph of the Will,* which stunningly captured a Nazi Party rally. ~~to be sure,~~ *T*his film forever cast a shadow over the director's career. (Split into two sentences.)
4. Her documentary of the 1936 Berlin Olympics, *Olympia,* captured the spirit of athletics. ~~her~~ pioneering techniques such as the underwater camera solidified her place in film history. (Convert one clause to a participial phrase.)
5. ~~Her~~ *Because* films were deemed Nazi propaganda, the French imprisoned Riefenstahl. *H*er film career was forever damaged by insinuations, despite the eventual ruling that she was not an active member of the Nazi Party. (Make into a compound-complex sentence.)

Chapter 34

Subject-Verb Agreement

A verb must match its subject. If the subject is singular (*I, you, he, she,* or *it*), the verb must take a singular form. If the subject is plural (*we, they*), the verb must take a plural form. Therefore, verbs are said to *agree in number* with their subjects. This single rule determines subject-verb agreement.

34a   AGREEMENT IN THE PRESENT TENSE

When your verb is in the present tense, agreement in number is straightforward: The subject takes the base form of the verb in all but the third person singular. For example, the verb *walk,* in the present tense, agrees in number with most subjects in its base form:

First person singular: I walk
Second person singular: You walk
First person plural: We walk
Second person plural: You walk
Third person plural: They walk

Third person singular subjects are the exception to this rule. When your subject is in the third person singular (*he, it, Fido, Lucy, Mr. Jones*) you need to add an *s* or *es* to the base form of the verb.

THIRD PERSON SINGULAR (ADD *S*)	He walks. It walks. Fido walks.
THIRD PERSON SINGULAR (ADD *ES*)	Lucy goes. Mr. Jones goes.

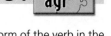

EXERCISE 34.1 Choose the correct present tense form of the verb in the following sentences.

1. Aaron (play) the piano.
2. The sisters (resemble) their mother.
3. I (want) a new DVD player.
4. He (go) for days without taking a bath.
5. You (make) me laugh.

34b │ SINGULAR AND PLURAL SUBJECTS

Sometimes it will be difficult to determine whether your subject is singular or plural, especially when subjects joined by *and* refer to the same thing or idea (*toast and jam, peace and quiet*) or when subjects are linked by *either . . . or* or *neither . . . nor*. Follow these rules when you have trouble determining whether to use a singular or plural verb form.

Subjects joined by *and*

When two subjects are joined by *and*, treat them as a compound (plural) subject.

Mary and Jane are leaving for New York in the morning.

The teacher and the lawyer are headed west to start a commune.

Some compound subjects are treated as singular. These kinds of compounds generally work together as a single noun. Although they appear to be compound and therefore plural, these subjects take the singular form of the verb:

Gin and tonic is a ritual before dinner in Bermuda.

Rock and roll remains the devil's music, even in the twenty-first century.

Also, when two nouns linked by *and* are modified by *every* or *each*, these two nouns are likewise treated as one singular subject:

Every hill and valley **is** aglow with light.

Each night and day **brings** no new news of you.

An exception to this rule arises when the word *each* follows a compound subject. In these cases, usage varies depending on the number of the direct object.

The army and the navy each **have** their own air forces.

The owl and the pussycat each **has** a personal claim to fame.

Subjects joined by *or, either . . . or,* or *neither . . . nor*

If a subject is joined by *or, either . . . or,* or *neither . . . nor,* make sure the verb agrees with the subject closest to the verb.

┌─ SING ─┐   ┌──── PLURAL ────┐ ┌PL┐
Is it **the sky or the mountains** that **are** blue?

┌──── PLURAL ────┐   ┌─ SING ─┐   ┌── SING ──┐
Is it **the mountains or the sky** that **surrounds** us?

┌──── PLURAL ────┐   ┌── SING ──┐┌ SING ┐
Neither the animals nor the zookeeper knows how to relock the gate.

┌── SING ──┐   ┌──── PLURAL ────┐┌PL┐
Either a coyote or several dogs were howling last night.

Subjects *along with* another noun

Verbs agree with the subject of a sentence, even when a subject is linked to another noun with a phrase like *as well as, along with,* or *alongside.* These modifying phrases are usually set off from the main subject with commas.

┌──────────── IGNORE THIS PHRASE ────────────┐
Chicken, alongside various steamed vegetables, **is** my favorite meal.

┌─ IGNORE THIS PHRASE ─┐
Besides B. B. King, **John Lee Hooker and Muddy Waters are** my favorite blues artists of all time.

Phrases to ignore when determining subject-verb agreement

as well as
in addition to
accompanied by
together with

along with
alongside
besides

We use these phrases in appositives, which are set off by commas and offer additional but not essential information. Thus, do not take these phrases and the nouns they modify into account when making decisions about subject-verb agreement.

Common Errors

Subjects separated from verbs

The most common agreement errors occur when words come between the subject and verb. These intervening words do not affect subject-verb agreement. To ensure that you use the correct verb form, identify the subject and the verb. Ignore any phrases that come between them.

┌─────── IGNORE THIS PHRASE ───────┐

INCORRECT Students at inner-city Washington High **reads** more than suburban students.

CORRECT Students at inner-city Washington High **read** more than suburban students.

Students is plural and *read* is plural; subject and verb agree.

INCORRECT The whale shark, the largest of all sharks, **feed** on plankton.

CORRECT The whale shark, the largest of all sharks, **feeds** on plankton.

(continued next page)

The plural noun *sharks* that appears between the subject *the whale shark* and the verb *feeds* does not change the number of the subject. The subject is singular and the verb is singular. Subject and verb agree.

Remember: When you check for subject-verb agreement, identify the subject and the verb. Ignore any words that come between them.

 For step-by-step discussion, examples, and practice of this common error, go to **www.ablongman.com/faigley021**.

Ignore the subject complement when determining agreement

In sentences that follow the subject-linking verb-subject complement pattern, ignore the subject complement when deciding to make the verb (**v**) singular or plural (see Section 32c). A subject complement further identifies the subject but should not be confused with the subject itself.

┌──────────── SUBJECT ────────────┐ ┌ **VERB** ┐ ┌──── SUBJECT COMPLEMENT ────┐
Tantrums and runny noses are the reality of living with toddlers.

INCORRECT ┌──────── PLURAL SUBJECT ────────┐ **SING V**
Tantrums and runny noses is the reality of living with toddlers.

CORRECT ┌──────── PLURAL SUBJECT ────────┐ **PL V**
Tantrums and runny noses are the reality of living with toddlers.

┌──────────── SUBJECT ────────────┐ **V** ┌──── SUBJECT COMPLEMENT ────┐
The beauty of my plan is its simplicity and economy.

INCORRECT ┌──────── SINGULAR SUBJECT ────────┐ **PL V**
The beauty of my plan are its simplicity and economy.

CORRECT ┌──────── SINGULAR SUBJECT ────────┐ **SING V**
The beauty of my plan is its simplicity and economy.

Make the verbs agree with the antecedents of relative pronouns: *who, whom, whose, which,* and *that*

The relative pronouns *who, whom, whose, which,* and *that* begin clauses that modify nouns. For instance, in the following sentence a clause beginning with *who* modifies *engineer*.

CLAUSE MODIFYING ENGINEER

The engineer **who works in this lab** has twenty-two patents.

To determine whether a verb should be singular or plural, use the antecedent to the relative pronoun. In other words, find the noun that the relative pronoun refers to.

SING ANTECEDENT   RELATIVE PRON   SING VERB

The **engineer** who works in this lab **has** twenty-two patents.

PL ANTECEDENT   RELATIVE PRON   PL VERB

The **greyhounds** that play in North Park **are** all **retired** from dog racing.

SING ANTECEDENT   RELATIVE PRON   SING VERB

The **mechanic** whose tools are all over the garage always **loses** his wrench.

PL ANTECEDENT   RELATIVE PRON

My **daughters**, to whom I give a fifteen-dollar allowance weekly,

PL VERB

claim they are always broke.

SINGULAR ANTECEDENT   RELATIVE PRON   SING VERB

Baklava, which most Greek restaurants serve, **is** difficult to make.

Titles, institutional and business names, words used as words, and gerunds take singular verbs

Titles of works, institutional and business names, words used as words, and gerunds are all singular subjects, even if they end in *-s*. Thus, they all take singular verbs.

TITLE OF A WORK	SINGULAR SUBJECT SING VERB *The Decline and Fall of the Roman Empire* **is** Edward Gibbon's most popular book.
TITLE OF A WORK	SING SUBJECT SING VERB *Kids* **shocks** moviegoers with its sex and drug-laden portrayal of teenagers.
INSTITUTIONAL NAME	SINGULAR SUBJECT SING VERB Big Brothers and Big Sisters **hosts** a bowling tournament fundraiser each May.
BUSINESS NAME	SING SINGULAR SUBJECT VERB Armstrong Bikes **does** the best repairs in town.
WORDS USED AS WORDS	SING SINGULAR SUBJECT VERB *Old and Leaky* **is** a better name for our boat than *Hale and Hearty*.
WORDS USED AS WORDS	SING SUBJECT SING VERB *Hamburgers* **is** no longer visible on the Sandwich Paradise sign.

Gerunds are *-ing* verbs that act as nouns. They are always singular. Thus, when a gerund or gerund phrase is the subject of a sentence, the verb should be singular as well, in order to agree.

INCORRECT	SING SUBJECT PL VERB Loitering outside of schools **are** illegal.
CORRECT	SING SUBJECT SING VERB Loitering outside of schools **is** illegal.
INCORRECT	SING SUBJECT PL VERB Riding buses **reduce** pollution.
CORRECT	SING SUBJECT SING VERB Riding buses **reduces** pollution.

EXERCISE 34.2 Underline the subject in the following sentences and decide whether it should be treated as singular or plural. Next, circle the verb. If the verb doesn't agree in number with the subject, revise so that it agrees.

EXAMPLE   Various <u>regions</u> in Italy—including Tuscany, Lazio,
and Umbria—possesses rich cultures that revolve *(possess)*
around food preparation and meals. ("Regions" is
plural, so the verb needs to be changed to "possess.")

1. Some cite Rome's Marcus Gavius Apicius as the author of the first
   cookbook, written in the first century.
2. Each Italian city and town in Italy possess a historical rationale for the
   gastronomical traditions of today.
3. People in central Italy enjoy eating many types of meat, but neither
   beef nor liver outshine the popularity of the region's top meat, pork.
4. Cheese, as well as foods such as balsamic vinegar and olive oil, is
   sometimes named for the region where it is produced.
5. Almost every man and woman in America knows spaghetti balls from
   Italy, but many fail to learn about the rich and varied Italian tradition
   of food.

Writing in the World

Agreement with *one of those who*

Many writers find using the construction *one of those . . . who* especially difficult when it comes to subject-verb agreement. The verb
that follows *who* is always plural, even though it can seem counterin-
tuitive. Consider this sentence:

Ellen is one of those women who never **seem** to get enough rest.

The verb is *seem*, and not *seems*, because the subject of the clause,
who, refers to *those women*; hence it is plural. If we change the order
of the sentence, the reason the verb is plural becomes clear:

Of women who never **seem** to get enough rest, Ellen is one.

However, if you add the word *only* to the phrase *one of those*, the subject becomes singular, so the verb is singular:

(continued next page)

> Ellen is the **only** one of those women who never **seems** to rest.
> The use of *only* singles out an individual from the group *of those women*. Consequently, the verb is singular.

EXERCISE 34.3 Each of the following sentences uses a "one of those . . . who" construction. Underline the subject and circle the verb. Correct the verb if it does not agree in number with the subject.

EXAMPLE   Babe Didrikson Zaharias is only one of those great
           female <u>athletes</u> who ⟨is⟩ ^are^ lost to younger generations,
           often overshadowed by the splashy television images of
           athletes of the second half of the twentieth century.

           ("Athletes" is plural, so the verb needs to be changed to "are.")

1. Born in south Texas in 1911 and overcome with a passion for sports, Didrikson Zaharias was not one of those <u>girls</u> who ⟨was⟩ wiling away the hours dreaming of wearing dresses, catching boys, and settling down.

2. Because she qualified for five events for the 1932 Olympics, Didrikson Zaharias was the only one of those <u>women</u> who ⟨was af-⟩ fected by the regulation prohibiting female athletes from competing in more than three Olympic contests.

3. The United States Golf Association president was only one of those <u>officials</u> who ⟨banned⟩ Didrikson Zaharias from tournaments in order to prevent her from overwhelming the competition.

4. In addition to excelling in basketball, tennis, bowling, baseball, and track and field and winning three Olympic gold medals, Didrikson Zaharias was one of those <u>athletes</u> who ⟨was⟩ responsible for creating the Ladies Professional Golf Association.

5. Didrikson Zaharias stands as one of those <u>women</u> who ⟨defy⟩ the notion that girls cannot swing, throw, or run; yet her early death from cancer stands as a stark reminder of the frailty of even the most impressive human form.

34c | INDEFINITE PRONOUNS AS SUBJECTS

The choice of a singular or plural pronoun is determined by the **antecedent**—the noun that pronoun refers to. For instance, the sentence *My friend likes soup* might be followed by another sentence, *She makes a new kind daily*. The pronoun must be singular because *she* refers to the singular noun *friend*.

Indefinite pronouns, such as *some, few, all, someone, everyone*, and *each*, often do not refer to identifiable subjects; hence they have no antecedents. Most indefinite pronouns are singular and agree with the singular forms of verbs. Some, like *both* and *many*, are always plural and agree with the plural forms of verbs. Other indefinite pronouns are variable and can agree with either singular or plural verb forms, depending on the context of the sentence.

Agreement with indefinite pronouns

Indefinite pronouns that are always singular

anybody	everyone	one
anyone	everything	somebody
anything	neither*	someone
each	nobody	something
either*	no one	
everybody	nothing	

*Note: Although *either* and *neither* are treated as singular when written, they may be treated as singular or plural in spoken English.

Indefinite pronouns that are always plural

both	few
many	several

Indefinite pronouns that are sometimes singular and sometimes plural

all	more	some
any	most	
half	none	

Common Errors

Agreement errors using *each*

The indefinite pronoun *each* is a frequent source of subject-verb agreement errors. If a pronoun is singular, its verb must be singular. This rule holds true even when the subject is modified by a phrase that includes a plural noun.

A common stumbling block to this rule is the pronoun *each*. *Each* is always treated as a singular pronoun in college writing. When *each* stands alone, the choice is easy to make:

INCORRECT   Each **are** an outstanding student.

CORRECT   Each **is** an outstanding student.

But when *each* is modified by a phrase that includes a plural noun, the choice of a singular verb form becomes less obvious:

INCORRECT   Each of the girls **are** fit.

CORRECT   Each of the girls **is** fit.

INCORRECT   Each of our dogs **get** a present.

CORRECT   Each of our dogs **gets** a present.

Remember: *Each* is always singular.

For step-by-step discussion, examples, and practice of this common error, go to **www.ablongman.com/faigley022**.

EXERCISE 34.4 The indefinite pronouns in each of the following sentences have been underlined. Identify each indefinite pronoun as singular or plural. Then circle the verb and correct it if it does not agree in number with the subject.

> **EXAMPLE**   Because stand-up comedy has traditionally been a
> male-dominated industry, <u>each</u> of the successful *singular*
> female comics ⟨have⟩ struggled against the grain. ("Each" *has*
> is singular, so the verb needs to be changed to "has.")

1. Of those who overcame the gender barrier, <u>few</u> are more beloved than Lily Tomlin, the creator of Ernestine the telephone operator and Edith Ann, the precocious child in the jumbo rocking chair.

2. <u>Each</u> of her characters were introduced to the American public when she burst onto the scene in the 1960s and 1970s on shows such as *Laugh-In, Sesame Street,* and *Saturday Night Live.*

3. <u>Most</u> of Tomlin's films in the 1980s—including *9 to 5, All of Me,* and *The Incredible Shrinking Woman*—were greeted with mixed reviews.

4. <u>Neither</u> Tomlin's cultural critiques nor her sketch comedy were whole-heartedly embraced by the networks. *was*

5. <u>Each</u> of the many female comics of today owe homage to women like Lily Tomlin, Phyllis Diller, and Joan Rivers for paving the way.

34d COLLECTIVE NOUNS AS SUBJECTS

Collective nouns refer to groups (*administration, audience, class, committee, crew, crowd, faculty, family, fleet, gang, government, group, herd, jury, mob, public, team*). When members of a group are considered as a unit, use singular verbs and singular pronouns.

The **audience was** patient with the novice performer.

The **crowd is** unusually quiet at the moment, but **it** will get noisy soon.

The **fleet leaves** port on June 29, and **it** will not return until next year.

When members of a group are considered as individuals, use plural verbs and plural pronouns.

The **brigade are** in **their** positions on both flanks.

The **faculty have their** differing opinions on how to address the problems caused by reduced state support.

Sometimes collective nouns can be singular in one context and plural in another. Writers must decide which verb form to use based on sentence context.

The **number** of people who live downtown **is** increasing.

A **number** of people **are** moving downtown from the suburbs.

Sports is one of the four main buttons on the newspaper's Web site.

Sports are dangerous for children under five.

EXERCISE 34.5 The following paragraph contains collective nouns that can be considered either singular or plural depending on the context. Select the form of the verb that agrees with the subject in the context given.

> **EXAMPLE** The jury (is/are) ready to deliberate. (*Jury* is considered singular.)
>
> The jury (believe/believes) that they will resolve their differences in judgment. (*Jury* is considered plural.)

   The administration usually (try/tries) to avoid responsibility for issues concerning students living off campus, but also (listen/listens) when the city government (complain/complains) about student behavior. The public (is/are) upset about large parties that last into the morning. The university formed a committee of students, faculty, and neighborhood residents to investigate the problem. Unfortunately, the committee (disagree/disagrees) about the causes of excessive noise.

34e INVERTED WORD ORDER

   In English a sentence's subject usually comes before the verb: *The nights are tender.* Sometimes, however, you will come across a sentence with inverted word order: *Tender are the nights.* Here, the subject of the sentence, *nights*, comes after the verb, *are.* Writers use inverted word order most often in forming questions. The statement *Cats are friendly* becomes a question when you invert the subject and the verb: *Are cats friendly?* Writers also use inverted word order for added emphasis or for style considerations.

Do not be confused by inverted word order. Locate the subject of your sentence, then make sure your verb agrees with that subject.

PLURAL VERB   PLURAL SUBJECT

Wise **are** the **people** who listen first and speak later.

SING VERB   SING SUBJECT

Uneasy **rests** the **head** that wears the crown.

PL VERB   PLURAL SUBJECT

There **are statues** of Robert E. Lee dotting the South.

SING VERB   SING SUBJECT

There **is** a massive **vault** in the National Archives building that protects the Constitution.

34f   AMOUNTS, NUMBERS, AND PAIRS

Subjects that describe amounts of money, time, distance, or measurement are singular and require singular verbs.

Three days is never long enough to unwind.

Two hundred dollars stands as the asking price.

Some subjects, such as courses of study, academic specializations, illnesses, and even some nations, are treated as singular subjects even though their names end in *-s* or *-es*. For example, *economics, news, ethics, measles,* and *the United States* all end in *-s* but are all singular subjects.

Economics is a rich field of study.

News keeps getting more and more commercial.

The United States is a global power.

Other subjects require a plural verb form even though they refer to single items such as *jeans, slacks, glasses, scissors,* and *tweezers.* These items are all pairs.

Your **jeans** look terrific.

My **glasses** are scratched.

EXERCISE 34.6 Each of these sentences contains a tricky subject. Identify whether the underlined subject is singular or plural. Circle the verb and correct the verb if it does not agree in number with the subject.

EXAMPLE Despite the racist overtones of nineteenth-century
minstrel shows, the United States <u>have</u> a rich tradition
singular *has*
of African-American theater dating back to the 1820s.

(The subject is singular so the verb needs to be changed to "has.")

1. African-American <u>theatrics</u> dates back to 1821, the year John Brown organized the first troupe of African-American actors.

2. Despite the controversy connected to Brown's involvement in the Harper's Ferry riots, <u>thanks</u> is due to him for creating a space where African Americans could publicly perform works such as *Richard III* and *Othello*.

3. Because American <u>politics</u> was incongruous with supporting serious African-American art, the troupe's lead actor, Ira Aldridge, moved to London.

4. <u>Politics</u>, not talent or ambition, was a driving force in determining the success of non-Anglo performers for decades.

5. Despite the success of twentieth-century actors such as Sidney Poitier, James Earl Jones, and Alfre Woodard, nearly <u>one hundred and thirty years</u> are a long time for African-American actors to wait for popular acceptance.

Chapter 35

Verbs

As a reader you've had the experience of stumbling over a sentence, reading it three or four times before it makes sense. Often the cause of the confusion is a verb problem. Problems with verbs, fortunately, are easy to spot and fix if you know what to look for.

35a | BASIC VERB FORMS

Almost all verbs in English have five possible forms. The exception is the verb *be*. Regular verbs follow this basic pattern:

Base form	Third person singular	Past tense	Past participle	Present participle
jump	jumps	jumped	jumped	jumping
like	likes	liked	liked	liking
talk	talks	talked	talked	talking
wish	wishes	wished	wished	wishing

Irregular verbs do not follow this basic pattern. See Section 35b for the forms of irregular verbs.

Base form

The base form of the verb is the one you find listed in the dictionary. This form indicates an action or condition in the present.

I **like** New York in June.

They **wish** they could attend the party.

We **talk** often on weekends.

Third person singular

The base form of the verb expresses actions or conditions in the present. The only exception to this rule occurs with third person singular subjects. Third person singular subjects include *he, she, it,* and the nouns they replace, as well as other pronouns, including *someone, anybody,* and *everything.* (See Section 34c.) Present tense verbs in the third person singular end with an *s* or an *es*.

Ms. Nessan **speaks** in riddles.

Everything **fades** with time.

The president **falters** when he speaks in public.

He **watches** too much television.

Common Errors

Missing verb endings

Verb endings are not always pronounced in speech, especially in some dialects of English. It's also easy to omit these endings when you are writing quickly. Spelling checkers will not mark these errors, so you have to find them while proofreading.

INCORRECT	Jeremy **feel** as if he's catching a cold.
CORRECT	Jeremy **feels** as if he's catching a cold.
INCORRECT	Sheila **hope** she would get the day off.
CORRECT	Sheila **hoped** she would get the day off.

Remember: Check verbs carefully for missing *s* or *es* endings in the present tense and missing *d* or *ed* endings in the past tense.

 For step-by-step discussion, examples, and practice of this common error, go to **www.ablongman.com/faigley023**.

Past tense

The past tense describes an action or condition that occurred in the past. For most verbs, the past tense is formed by adding *d* or *ed* to the base form of the verb.

I **called** at nine, but there was no answer.

She **inhaled** the night air.

Many verbs, however, have irregular past tense forms. (See Section 35b.)

Past participle

The past participle is used with *have* to form verbs in the perfect tense, with *be* to form verbs in the passive voice (see Section 26a), and to form adjectives derived from verbs.

PAST PERFECT	They **had gone** to the grocery store prematurely.
PASSIVE	The book **was written** thirty years before it was published.
ADJECTIVE	In the eighties, **teased** hair was all the rage.

Present participle

The present participle functions in one of three ways. Used with an auxiliary verb, it can describe a continuing action. The present participle can also function as a noun, known as a **gerund**, or as an adjective. The present participle is formed by adding *ing* to the base form of a verb.

PRESENT PARTICIPLE	Wild elks **are competing** for limited food resources.
GERUND	**Sailing** around the Cape of Good Hope is rumored to bring good luck.
ADJECTIVE	We looked for shells in the **ebbing** tide.

Make sure every sentence has a verb

What is the one grammatical component you need to make a sentence? You only need a verb. A sentence is not a sentence without one. While writers usually include a verb in each sentence, verbs can occasionally be dropped accidentally, especially when linking or helping verbs are used. Learn to identify the situations where you need linking and helping verbs to ensure you include them.

Linking verbs join subjects with subject complements:

$$\underbrace{\text{SUBJ}}_{} \quad \underbrace{\substack{\text{LINKING} \\ \text{VERB}}}_{} \quad \underbrace{\text{SUBJ COMPLEMENT}}_{}$$

Jeremiah **was** a bullfrog.

A subject complement further identifies or renames a subject, just as *a bull-frog* further identifies *Jeremiah*. The linking verb is often a form of *to be*, although verbs like *appear, become, grow, feel, look, make, prove, remain, seem, smell, stay, sound,* and *taste* can act as linking verbs when they stand between subjects and subject complements. Be careful not to omit a linking verb between a subject and a subject complement.

INCORRECT	Dogs a great home security system.

$$\underbrace{\text{SUBJ}}_{} \quad \underbrace{\substack{\text{LINKING} \\ \text{VERB}}}_{} \quad \underbrace{\text{SUBJ COMPLEMENT}}_{}$$

CORRECT	Dogs **are** a great home security system.

INCORRECT	The kindergartners sick.

$$\underbrace{\text{SUBJ}}_{} \quad \underbrace{\substack{\text{LINKING} \\ \text{VERB}}}_{} \quad \underbrace{\substack{\text{SUBJ} \\ \text{COMPLEMENT}}}_{}$$

CORRECT	The kindergartners **seem** sick.

You may also use a contraction—such as *I'm, you're, Jim's, she's, it's, we're,* and *they're*—that combines the subject and the linking verb.

$$\underbrace{\substack{\text{SUBJ +} \\ \text{LINKING VERB}}}_{} \quad \underbrace{\text{SUBJ COMPLEMENT}}_{}$$

They**'re** interns on Capitol Hill.

$$\underbrace{\substack{\text{SUBJ +} \\ \text{LINKING VERB}}}_{} \quad \underbrace{\text{SUBJ COMPLEMENT}}_{}$$

Augie**'s** a talented pianist.

Auxiliaries or helping verbs are verbs that combine with main verbs. The following are verbs that can act as auxiliaries:

forms of *to be*	could	shall
forms of *to do*	may	should
forms of *to have*	might	will
can	must	would

Be sure not to omit auxiliaries when they are necessary before a main verb.

| | **MAIN VERB** |
| INCORRECT | Civil unrest **erupt** at any moment. |

| | **AUXILIARY**
MAIN VERB |
| CORRECT | Civil unrest **could erupt** at any moment. |

| | **MAIN VERB** |
| INCORRECT | We **going** to the disco tonight. |

| | **MAIN**
AUXILIARY VERB |
| CORRECT | We **are going** to the disco tonight. |

Like linking verbs, auxiliaries may also be used in contractions. Possible helping verb contractions include *I'd, you'll, he's, we've,* and *they'll.*

SUBJ + MAIN
AUXILIARY VERB
You**'ll hear** from my lawyer.

SUBJ + MAIN
AUXILIARY VERB
Houston, we**'ve got** a problem.

EXERCISE 35.1 Underline the verbs in the following paragraph and write the verb form for each. You may find some forms more than once. Choose from the following:

base form	past participle—adjective
-*s*/-*es* form	present participle—present perfect
past tense	present participle—gerund
past participle—past perfect	present participle—adjective
past participle—passive	

| PRESENT PARTICIPLE—
GERUND | | PRESENT PARTICIPLE—
ADJECTIVE |

EXAMPLE   Animal <u>baiting</u>, a gruesome predecessor to <u>dueling</u>

PAST

cocks, <u>found</u> great success in the medieval era.

Recent lobbying efforts by animal rights groups are illustrating how drastically contemporary beliefs regarding animal safety differ from beliefs in medieval times. History shows that the torturing of taunted animals such as bears and bulls was considered a sport in medieval times. At bullbaitings, organizers tethered a bull to a pivot point in the middle of an arena and unleashed a snarling dog that taunted the bull. Once the bull ceased to amuse the crowd, he found himself on the quick route to the nearest butcher shop.

35b | IRREGULAR VERBS

A verb is **regular** when its past and past participle forms are created by adding *ed* or *d* to the base form. If this rule does not apply, the verb is considered an **irregular** verb. Here are some common irregular verbs and their basic conjugations.

Common irregular verbs

Base form	Past tense	Past participle
arise	arose	arisen
be (is, am, are)	was, were	been
bear	bore	borne or born
beat	beat	beaten
become	became	become
begin	began	begun
bend	bent	bent
break	broke	broken

Base form	Past tense	Past participle
bring	brought	brought
buy	bought	bought
choose	chose	chosen
cling	clung	clung
come	came	come
cost	cost	cost
creep	crept	crept
deal	dealt	dealt
dig	dug	dug
dive	dived or dove	dived
do	did	done
draw	drew	drawn
drink	drank	drunk
drive	drove	driven
eat	ate	eaten
fall	fell	fallen
feed	fed	fed
feel	felt	felt
fight	fought	fought
fling	flung	flung
fly	flew	flown
forbid	forbade or forbad	forbidden
forget	forgot	forgotten or forgot
forgive	forgave	forgiven
freeze	froze	frozen
get	got	got or gotten
give	gave	given
go	went	gone
grow	grew	grown

(continued next page)

Base form	Past tense	Past participle
hang	hung	hung
have	had	had
know	knew	known
lay	laid	laid
lend	lent	lent
lie	lay	lain
make	made	made
read	read	read
run	ran	run
say	said	said
see	saw	seen
send	sent	sent
shine	shone	shone
show	showed	shown or showed
sit	sat	sat
sleep	slept	slept
speak	spoke	spoken
spring	sprang or sprung	sprung
swim	swam	swum
take	took	taken
teach	taught	taught
tell	told	told
think	thought	thought
understand	understood	understood
wear	wore	worn
write	wrote	written

Use *to be* correctly in the past and present

To be is irregular in the present and past tenses.

	Present tense		Past tense	
	singular	plural	singular	plural
First person:	I am	we are	I was	we were
Second person:	you are	you are	you were	you were
Third person:	he/she/it is	they are	he/she/it was	they were

Not all dialects of English use these forms, however. Some use *be* in place of the other present tense forms of the verb, *is* in place of *are*, or *was* in place of *were*. Also, some speakers use *ain't* in place of *am not*, *isn't*, and *aren't*. In cases where edited American English is called for, be sure to choose the forms of *to be* that correspond to the subject of the sentence.

DIALECT

3RD PERSON, SING · INFINITIVE

He **be** repainting his house this weekend.

EDITED AMERICAN ENGLISH

3RD PERSON, SING · 3RD PERSON, SING

He **is** repainting his house this weekend.

DIALECT

1ST PERSON, PL · 3RD PERSON, SING

My friends and I **is** tired of reading nothing but bad news in the paper.

EDITED AMERICAN ENGLISH

1ST PERSON, PL · 1ST PERSON, PL

My friends and I **are** tired of reading nothing but bad news in the paper.

DIALECT

1ST PERSON, PL · 1ST OR 3RD PERSON, SING

We **was** in the right.

EDITED AMERICAN ENGLISH

1ST PERSON, PL · 1ST PERSON, PL

We **were** in the right.

DIALECT

3RD PERSON, SING | NONSTANDARD 3RD PERSON, SING

Petula **ain't** going to take care of any more pets.

EDITED
AMERICAN ENGLISH

3RD PERSON, SING | 3RD PERSON, SING

Petula **isn't** going to take care of any more pets.

Use *to have* correctly in the past and present

To have is regular in the present tense except for *has* in the third person singular. Some English speakers use *have* in place of *has* and vice versa. When edited American English is appropriate, use *has* in the third person singular present form only and *have* in all the other present tenses.

DIALECT

3RD PERSON, PL | 3RD PERSON, SING

My **pet rats has** more personality than most people think they do.

EDITED
AMERICAN ENGLISH

3RD PERSON, PL | 3RD PERSON, PL

My **pet rats have** more personality than most people think they do.

DIALECT

3RD PERSON, SING | 3RD PERSON, PL

John **have** chicken pox.

EDITED
AMERICAN ENGLISH

3RD PERSON, SING | 3RD PERSON, SING

John **has** chicken pox.

Use *to do* correctly in the past and present

To do is regular in the present tense except in the third person singular form, *does*. The negative of the third person singular form is *does not* or *doesn't*. And the negative of all the other present forms is *do not* or *don't*. Speakers of some dialects of English will use *don't* in place of *doesn't*. In cases where you want to use edited American English, however, be sure to use *doesn't* when forming the negative third person singular.

	3RD PERSON, SING	ALL FORMS EXCEPT 3RD PERSON, SING
DIALECT	My instructor	**don't** accept late papers.

	3RD PERSON, SING	3RD PERSON, SING
EDITED AMERICAN ENGLISH	My instructor	**doesn't** accept late papers.

Common Errors

Confusing the past tense and past participle forms of irregular verbs

The past tense and past participle forms of irregular verbs are often confused. The most frequent error is using a past tense form instead of the past participle with *had*.

PAST TENSE

INCORRECT She had never **rode** a horse before.

PAST PARTICIPLE

CORRECT She had never **ridden** a horse before.

PAST TENSE

INCORRECT He had **saw** many alligators in Louisiana.

PAST PARTICIPLE

CORRECT He had **seen** many alligators in Louisiana.

Remember: Change any past tense verbs preceded by *had* to past participles.

For step-by-step discussion, examples, and practice of this common error, go to **www.ablongman.com/faigley024.**

EXERCISE 35.2 Underline the correct form of the irregular verbs in the following paragraph.

> **EXAMPLE** *I Love Lucy*, (thinked/<u>thought</u>) of by many as that funny show with the zany redhead, (<u>drove</u>/drived) many television innovations.

After marrying in 1940, Lucille Ball and Desi Arnaz (strived/ strove) to create their own television situation comedy. However, the networks feared audiences would not accept a Cuban leading man married to an Anglo woman and (sought/seeked) to block their project. Thus, Ball and Arnaz decided to fund the show independently, and within a short time the couple (got/gotten) together the money, created Desilu Studios, and (began/begun) shooting their pilot. Soon Americans (eated/ate), (drunk/drank), and (slept/sleeped) *I Love Lucy*. With innovations like the three-camera technique, Desilu Studios (laid/lain/layed) the groundwork for future sitcoms and (rode/ride/rided) into television history.

35c | TRANSITIVE AND INTRANSITIVE VERBS

Lay/lie, set/sit, and raise/rise

Do you know whether you raise or rise from bed in the morning? Do your house keys lay or lie on the kitchen table? Does a book set or sit on the shelf? *Raise/rise*, *lay/lie*, and *set/sit* are transitive and intransitive verbs that writers frequently confuse. Transitive verbs take direct objects, nouns that receive the action of the verb. Intransitive verbs act in sentences that lack direct objects.

The following charts list the trickiest pairs of transitive and intransitive verbs and the correct forms for each verb tense. Pay special attention to *lay* and *lie*, which are irregular.

	lay (put something down)	**lie (recline)**
Present	lay, lays	lie, lies
Present participle	laying	lying
Past	laid	lay
Past participle	laid	lain

TRANSITIVE   Once you complete your test, please **lay** your pencil (direct object, the thing being laid down) on the desk.

INTRANSITIVE   After working a double shift, I **lie** on the couch for hours, too exhausted to move.

	raise (elevate something)	**rise (get up)**
Present	raise, raises	rise, rises
Present participle	raising	rising
Past	raised	rose
Past participle	raised	risen

TRANSITIVE   We **raise** our glasses (direct object, the things being raised) to toast Uncle Han.

INTRANSITIVE   The sun **rises** over the bay.

	set (place something)	**sit (take a seat)**
Present	set, sets	sit, sits
Present participle	setting	sitting
Past	set	sat
Past participle	set	sat

TRANSITIVE   Every morning Stanley **sets** two dollars (direct object, the things being set) on the table to tip the waiter.

INTRANSITIVE   I **sit** in the front seat if it's available.

EXERCISE 35.3 Decide whether each of the sentences in the following paragraph calls for a transitive or intransitive verb and underline the correct choice.

EXAMPLE   The eastern diamondback rattlesnake (will set/<u>will sit</u>) immobile for hours, sometimes coiled and sometimes stretched to its full length of seven feet.

A rattlesnake will often (lay/lie) in wait for its favorite meal: a rat. When you encounter one of these poisonous snakes, (set/sit) aside your assumptions about aggressive snakes; many are timid. You can tell a rattlesnake feels threatened if its tail (rises/raises) and you hear a sharp rattling sound. If you are hiking in the desert in the southwestern United States, do not (sit/set) down without carefully surveying the ground. To (rise/raise) your chances of avoiding a rattlesnake bite, make noise when you are hiking in wilderness areas.

35d | SHIFTS IN TENSE

Appropriate shifts in verb tense

Changes in verb tense are sometimes necessary to indicate a shift in time.

PRESENT
TO PAST

               PRESENT TENSE   PAST TENSE
I never shop online anymore because I heard that
               PAST TENSE
hackers have stolen thousands of credit card numbers used in Internet transactions.

PAST
TO FUTURE

               PAST TENSE   FUTURE TENSE
Because Oda won the lottery, she will quit her job at
                                PRESENT TENSE
the hospital as soon as her supervisor finds a qualified replacement.

Writing in the World

Verb tenses in academic writing and in reviews

Texts and ideas

Use the present tense to discuss another author's work or ideas. Texts and ideas are enduring; they never become part of the past.

Garcia and Brink's review of the control groups in fifty-two
PRESENT TENSE **PRESENT TENSE**
medical studies **concludes** that doctors grossly **overestimate** the placebo effect.

Be careful to shift tenses when necessary. The sentence that follows cites one pundit's analysis (analysis calls for present tense) about a past event (past events call for past tense).

ANOTHER'S ENDURING IDEA;   A COMPLETED EVENT;
USE PRESENT TENSE   USE PAST TENSE
Gerreau **argues** that the Monica Lewinsky scandal **was** the defining event of the Clinton presidency.

However, if you are writing in the sciences and using APA style, use past tense when referring to completed studies and events in the past. Stick to the present tense when dealing with your current research, ongoing issues or problems, and accepted ideas.

COMPLETED STUDY	**PAST TENSE** Bahl (1999) **showed** that children in day care are no more likely to have depression than children cared for at home.
EVENT IN THE PAST	**PAST TENSE** The 1986 meteor shower **was** the biggest ever recorded.
CURRENT RESEARCH	**PRESENT TENSE** My study suggests bunions **play** a role in shin injuries.

(continued next page)

ONGOING PROBLEM

PRESENT TENSE

Melting rates of the polar icecaps **indicate** the intensification of global climate change.

ACCEPTED IDEA

PRESENT TENSE

The earth **revolves** around the sun.

Works of art

Use the present tense when discussing works of art, which, like ideas, endure. (See Section 22b for a discussion of the literary present tense.)

PRESENT TENSE

Rilke's "Archaic Torso of Apollo" **captures** the potential

PRESENT TENSE

energy of a frozen block of stone. The poem's imagery **refuses** to portray the headless, limbless sculpture of a Greek god as anything less than a powerful, twisting, glowing whole.

Remember to shift verb tenses when your argument shifts from an analysis of an art object, requiring present tense, to a discussion of historical events, requiring past tense.

PAST TENSE,
HISTORICAL EVENT

PAST TENSE

Rilke **met** the sculptor Auguste Rodin in 1902, **worked**

PAST TENSE

as his secretary for a time, and later **wrote** a book about him. His

PRES TENSE, ANALYSIS OF ARTWORK

experience with Rodin **accounts** for Rilke's keen eye for the plastic arts in his poetry. The "Archaic Torso of Apollo" in particular

PRESENT TENSE

PRESENT TENSE

illustrates how the fluidity of words **instills** an ancient, cold block of stone with new vitality.

Inappropriate shifts in verb tense

Be careful to avoid confusing your reader with unnecessary shifts in verb tense. Once you reach the proofreading stage of your writing, dedicate one careful reading of your text to finding inappropriate tense changes.

Common Errors

Unnecessary tense shift

Notice the tense shift in the following example.

INCORRECT Several years ago the Melissa virus **ravaged** [PAST TENSE] computers around the world before Microsoft programmers **were** [PAST TENSE] **able** to write a program to neutralize it. For days, unsuspecting email users **click** [PRESENT TENSE] open their accounts and unwittingly **send** [PRESENT TENSE] the voracious, memory-eating virus to everyone in their address books.

The second sentence shifts unnecessarily to the present tense, confusing the reader. Did the Melissa virus have its heyday several years ago, or is it still wreaking havoc now? Changing the verbs in the second sentence to the past tense eliminates the confusion.

CORRECT Several years ago the Melissa virus **ravaged** [PAST TENSE] computers around the world before Microsoft programmers **were** [PAST TENSE] **able** to write a program to neutralize it. For days, unsuspecting email users **clicked** [PAST TENSE] open their accounts and unwittingly **sent** [PAST TENSE] the voracious, memory-eating virus to everyone in their address books.

Remember: Shift verb tense only when you are referring to different time periods.

For step-by-step discussion, examples, and practice of this common error, go to **www.ablongman.com/faigley025**.

INCORRECT While Brazil **looks** [PRESENT TENSE] to ecotourism to fund rainforest preservation, other South American nations **relied** [PAST TENSE] on foreign aid and conservation efforts.

The shift from present tense (*looks*) to past tense (*relied*) is confusing. The sentence attempts to compare Brazil with other South American countries, but the shift in tenses muddles the comparison. Correct the mistake by putting both verbs in the present tense.

PRES TENSE

CORRECT   While Brazil **looks** to ecotourism to fund rainforest
PRES TENSE
preservation, other South American nations **rely** on
foreign aid and conservation efforts.

EXERCISE 35.4 Read the entire paragraph and underline the correct verb tenses.

EXAMPLE   The American Indian Movement (AIM) (originated/ originates) in Minneapolis in 1968.

Native American activists, including Dennis Banks and Russell Means, (created/create) AIM, a militant organization that fights for civil rights for American Indians. AIM members (participate/participated) in a number of famous protests, including the occupation of Alcatraz Island (1969–1971) and the takeover of Wounded Knee (1973). The group (has helped/helps) Indians displaced by government programs, (will work/has worked) for economic independence for Native Americans, and (agitates/has agitated) for the return of lands (seize/seized) by the U.S. government. In his book *Agents of Repression: The FBI's Secret War Against the Black Panther Party and the American Indian Movement*, Ward Churchill (documented/documents) how the FBI (infiltrated/infiltrates) AIM in an attempt to destroy it. While most local chapters of AIM (have disbanded/disband), Native American activists today still (fight/fought) for their autonomy and for compensation for centuries of oppression and economic injustice.

35e | SHIFTS IN MOOD

Indicative, imperative, and subjunctive verbs

Verbs can be categorized into three moods—indicative, imperative, and subjunctive—defined by the functions they serve.

Indicative verbs state facts, opinions, and questions.

FACT | The human genome project **seeks** to map out human DNA.

OPINION | The scientific advances spurred by the human genome project, including cloning and designer genes, **will allow** normal people to play God.

QUESTION | How long **does** it **take** to map out the entire human genome?

Imperative verbs make commands, give advice, and make requests.

COMMAND | **Research** the technology being used to carry out the human genome project.

ADVICE | **Try** to join a high-profile research project like the human genome project if you want to make a name for yourself in the scientific community.

REQUEST | **Could** you please **explain** the role you played in the human genome project?

Subjunctive verbs express wishes, unlikely or untrue situations, hypothetical situations, requests with *that* clauses, and suggestions.

WISH | We **wish** that unlocking the secrets of our DNA **were** a surefire way to cure genetic diseases.

UNLIKELY OR UNTRUE SITUATION | If the genome project **were** as simple as the news media made it out to be, scientists could complete it over a long weekend.

HYPOTHETICAL SITUATION	If the genome project **were** to lose government funding, the scientists working on it would not be able to afford the equipment they need to complete it.

The subjunctive in past and present tenses

Subjunctive verbs are usually the trickiest to handle. In the present tense subjunctive clauses call for the base form of the verb (*be, have, see, jump*).

It is essential that children **be** immunized before they enter kindergarten.

In the past tense they call for the standard past tense of the verb (*had, saw, jumped*), with one exception. In counterfactual sentences the *to be* verb always becomes *were*, even for subjects that take *was* under normal circumstances.

INDICATIVE	I **was** surprised at some of the choices she made.
SUBJUNCTIVE	If I **were** in her position, I'd do things differently.
INDICATIVE	The young athletes found that gaining muscle **was** not easy.
SUBJUNCTIVE	If being muscular **were** easy, everyone would look like Arnold Schwarzenegger.

EXERCISE 35.5 Identify the mood of the underlined verbs in the following paragraph: indicative, imperative, or subjunctive.

EXAMPLE	When elected in 1960, John Fitzgerald Kennedy INDICATIVE <u>became</u> the nation's youngest and its first Roman Catholic president.

Using the slogan "Let's <u>get</u> this country moving again," Kennedy <u>fought</u> against unemployment and a sluggish economy. His insistence that U.S. technology <u>be</u> on a par with that of the

Soviets <u>contributed</u> to his popularity. In his inaugural speech, he <u>expressed</u> his desire that Americans "<u>bear</u> the burden of a long <u>twilight</u> struggle . . . against the common enemies of man: tyranny, poverty, disease, and war itself." His desire that all citizens <u>regard</u> themselves as participants in a growing democracy is evident in his famous words, "<u>Ask</u> not what your country can do for you—ask what you can do <u>for</u> your country."

EXERCISE 35.6 Underline the correct subjunctive form of the verbs in the following paragraph.

EXAMPLE   If you (are/<u>were</u>) to go more than 100 feet below the surface during a deep sea dive, you might experience what is commonly called "rapture of the deep."

Rapture of the deep results when nitrogen levels elevate in the bloodstream because of added pressure, and the diver begins to feel as if she (was/were) invincible. Often the combination of nitrogen and excessive oxygen overwhelms the diver, causing her to wish that she could (gets/get) free of the breathing apparatus. If a diver (was/were) at the surface, she would experience one atmosphere of pressure. At 100 feet below, however, the pressure is tripled. It is crucial that a diver (prepare/prepares) for the possibility of rapture. To get used to this disorienting sensation, some divers inhale nitrous oxide to see how they would handle themselves if they (are/were) in the throes of rapture of the deep.

Chapter 36

Pronouns

Pronouns are little words like *he, she, it, we, our, who,* and *mine* that stand for nouns and other pronouns. They are among the most frequently used words in English, but they also are a frequent source of problems in writing.

36a PRONOUN CASE

Pronoun case refers to the forms pronouns take to indicate their function in a sentence. Pronouns that function as the subjects of sentences are in the **subjective case**. Pronouns that function as direct or indirect objects are in the **objective case**. Pronouns that indicate ownership are in the **possessive case**.

Subjective pronouns	Objective pronouns	Possessive pronouns
I	me	my, mine
we	us	our, ours
you	you	your, yours
he	him	his
she	her	her, hers
it	it	its
they	them	their, theirs
who	whom	whose

People who use English regularly usually make these distinctions among pronouns without thinking about them.

     _s   _o   _p   _s   _o _o   _s   _o

I let him use my laptop, but he lent it to her, and I haven't seen it since.

Nonetheless, choosing the correct pronoun case sometimes can be difficult.

Pronouns in compound phrases

Picking the right pronoun sometimes can be confusing when the pronoun appears in a compound phrase.

If we work together, you and **me** can get the job done quickly.

If we work together, you and **I** can get the job done quickly.

Which is correct—*me* or *I*? Removing the other pronoun usually makes the choice clear.

INCORRECT   **Me** can get the job done quickly.

CORRECT   **I** can get the job done quickly.

Similarly, when compound pronouns appear as objects of prepositions, sometimes the correct choice isn't obvious until you remove the other pronoun.

When you finish your comments, give them to Isidora or **I**.

When you finish your comments, give them to Isidora or **me**.

Again, the choice is easy when the pronoun stands alone:

INCORRECT   Give them to **I**.

CORRECT   Give them to **me**.

We and *us* before nouns

Another pair of pronouns that can cause difficulty is *we* and *us* before nouns.

Us friends must stick together.

We friends must stick together.

Which is correct—*us* or *we*? Removing the noun indicates the correct choice.

INCORRECT   **Us** must stick together.

CORRECT   **We** must stick together.

EXERCISE 36.1 Underline the pronoun in each sentence of the following paragraph and replace the pronoun if it is incorrect.

EXAMPLE   You and ~~me~~ should pay more attention to what we eat.
                    ^I

If you and a friend go on a road trip, the ADA suggests that you and her limit your stops at fast food restaurants. The association suggests us snack in the afternoon, provided we choose foods that are healthy for you and I. If your friend wants a cheeseburger for lunch, you should respond that you and her could split the meal. For your sake and me, it is not a good idea to snack after dark.

Who versus *whom*

Choosing between *who* and *whom* is often difficult, even for experienced writers. When you answer the phone, which do you say?

1. To **whom** do you wish to speak?
2. **Who** do you want to talk to?

Probably you chose 2. *To whom do you wish to speak?* may sound stuffy, but technically it is correct. The reason it sounds stuffy is that the distinction between *who* and *whom* is disappearing from spoken language. *Who* is more often used in spoken language, even when *whom* is correct.

Pronouns in subordinate clauses

With complex sentences that have one or more subordinate clauses, it can be especially tricky figuring out whether to use *who* or *whom*. Substituting subjective and objective pronouns will help, but first you must (1) isolate the subordinate clause, (2) rearrange the clause so that it leads with the subject, (3) substitute the subjective and objective pronouns to see which sounds right, and (4) choose *who* if the subjective prounoun sounds right and *whom* if the objective pronoun sounds right.

EXAMPLE   The technology company gave stock options to all employees [who, whom] the Board of Trustees recommended.

1. Isolate the subordinate clause: [who, whom] the Board of Trustees recommended.
2. Rearrange: The Board of Trustees recommended _____.
3. Substitute: The Board of Trustees recommended they. The Board of Trustees recommended them.
4. Choose subjective or objective case: The Board of Trustees recommended whom.

CORRECT   The technology company gave stock options to all employees whom the Board of Trustees recommended.

Pronouns in phrases and clauses that function as objects of prepositions

When a phrase or clause functions as the object of a preposition, the objective pronoun is not automatically the correct choice. Decide whether the pronoun (*who, whom, whoever,* or *whomever*) functions as the subject or object of the verb in the clause.

CORRECT   Phil was excited to meet the film director about **whom so much had been written.**

CORRECT   Struggling with a bad phone connection, Sylvia tried to speak to **whoever was on the other end of the phone.**

Pronouns that function as subject complements

When the pronoun functions as a subject complement, always use who.

I am **who I am.**

My mother is **the kind of person who likes to cook elaborate meals.**

Pronouns that function as subjects or objects of infinitives

When the pronoun functions as the subject or object of an infinitive, always use *whom.*

As Hyun began her job search, she thought about **whom to ask for advice.**

Common Errors

Who or *whom*

In writing, the distinction between *who* and *whom* is still often observed. *Who* and *whom* follow the same rules as other pronouns: *Who* is the subject pronoun; *whom* is the object pronoun. If you are dealing with an object, *whom* is the correct choice.

INCORRECT	Who did you send the letter to?
	Who did you give the present to?
CORRECT	To **whom** did you send the letter?
	Whom did you give the present to?

Who is always the right choice for the subject pronoun.

CORRECT	Who gave you the present?
	Who brought the cookies?

If you are uncertain of which one to use, try substituting *she* and *her* or *he* and *him*.

INCORRECT	You sent the letter to **she[who]**?
CORRECT	You sent the letter to **her[whom]**?
INCORRECT	**Him[Whom]** gave you the present?
CORRECT	**He[Who]** gave you the present?

Remember: *Who* = subject
             ***Whom* = object**

For step-by-step discussion, examples, and practice of this common error, go to **www.ablongman.com/faigley026**.

Whoever versus *whomever*

With the same rule in mind, you can distinguish between *whoever* and *whomever*. Which is correct?

Her warmth touched **whoever** she met.
Her warmth touched **whomever** she met.

In this sentence the pronoun functions as a direct object: Her warmth touched everyone she met, not someone touched her. Thus *whomever* is the correct choice.

EXERCISE 36.2 In the following sentences, fill in the blank with the correct pronoun: *who, whom, whoever,* or *whomever*.

EXAMPLE   Soon the Japanese people will select new members of Parliament, some of __*whom*__ are prominent celebrities.

1. Seats in the Japanese Parliament have lately gone to candidates _____ have high ambitions, fame, and no political experience.
2. Atsushi Onita is a professional wrestler _____ cries "Fire!" when he enters the ring and _____ believes in strict parental disciplining of children.
3. One of the candidates for _____ many will vote is Emi Watanabe, a former Olympic figure skater _____ deplores the mounting costs of health care.
4. _____ the Japanese vote for, one thing is certain.
5. _____ wins will have done so after an unprecedented wave of sports star campaigning.

Pronouns in comparisons

When you write a sentence using a comparison that includes *than* or *as* followed by a pronoun, usually you will have to think about which pronoun is correct. Which of the following is correct?

Vimala is a faster swimmer than **him**.
Vimala is a faster swimmer than **he**.

The test that will give you the correct answer is to add the verb that finishes the sentence—in this case, *is*.

INCORRECT   Vimala is a faster swimmer than **him is**.

CORRECT   Vimala is a faster swimmer than **he is**.

Adding the verb makes the correct choice evident.

In some cases the choice of pronoun changes the meaning. Consider these examples:

She likes ice cream more than **me**. (A bowl of ice cream is better than hanging out with me.)

She likes ice cream more than **I**. (I would rather have frozen yogurt.)

In such cases it is better to complete the comparison:

She likes ice cream more than **I do**.

Possessive pronouns

Possessive pronouns at times are confusing because possessive nouns are formed with apostrophes but possessive pronouns do not require apostrophes. Pronouns that use apostrophes are always **contractions**.

It's	=	It is
Who's	=	Who is
They're	=	They are

The test for whether to use an apostrophe is to determine whether the pronoun is possessive or a contraction. The most confusing pair is *its* and *it's*.

INCORRECT   **Its** a sure thing she will be elected. (Contraction)

CORRECT   **It's** a sure thing she will be elected. (**It is** a sure thing.)

INCORRECT   The dog lost **it's** collar. (Possessive)

CORRECT   The dog lost **its** collar.

Whose versus *who's* follows the same pattern.

INCORRECT	**Who's** bicycle has the flat tire? (Possessive)
CORRECT	**Whose** bicycle has the flat tire?
INCORRECT	**Whose** on first? (Contraction)
CORRECT	**Who's** on first? (**Who is** on first?)

Possessive pronouns before *ing* verbs

Pronouns that modify an *-ing* verb (called a *gerund*) or an *-ing* verb phrase (*gerund phrase*) should appear in the possessive.

INCORRECT	The odds of **you** making the team are excellent.
CORRECT	The odds of **your** making the team are excellent.

Subject complements

Pronouns that function as subject complements are in the subjective case in formal writing. A subject complement is a word that follows a linking verb such as a form of *to be*. Objective pronouns are common in informal contexts, especially *It's me* instead of the more formal *It is I*.

INFORMAL	Driving home, Thomas thought he saw his wife exit the grocery store and later confirmed it **was her**.
FORMAL	Driving home, Thomas thought he saw his wife exit the grocery store and later confirmed it **was she**.

Appositives

When a pronoun functions as an appositive, put it in the same case as the noun to which it refers.

SUBJECTIVE CASE	The three company **principals**, Gary, Michelle, and **I**, decided to hire a financial analyst.
OBJECTIVE CASE	My English teacher asked two **students**, Jennifer and **me**, to stay after class.

Subjects and objects of infinitives

Many people mistakenly put the pronoun subject of an infinitive in the subjective case. But when a pronoun is either the subject or object of an infinitive, it must be in the objective case.

INCORRECT SUBJECT OF INFINITIVE	Our landlord wanted my roommate and **I to replace** the stained carpet.
CORRECT SUBJECT OF INFINITIVE	Our landlord wanted my roommate and **me to replace** the stained carpet.
INCORRECT OBJECT OF INFINITIVE	My father asked my sister and me **to visit** our mother and **he** next summer.
CORRECT OBJECT OF INFINITIVE	My father asked my sister and me **to visit** our mother and **him** next summer.

EXERCISE 36.3 The following sentences include all the pronoun situations explained in this section. Underline the correct pronoun in each sentence.

EXAMPLE   (We/Us) scholars generally look at subjects from a critical distance, but we must never forget to impose that critical distance on our own lives too.

1. The gurkhas are a division in the British armed forces (who/whom) originate from Nepal.
2. Between 1814 and 1816 several Nepalese hill tribes successfully contained the advancing British army, even though the British were far more technically advanced than (they/them).
3. Thinking that "(us/we) warriors should stick together," the British enlisted the Nepalese tribesmen to fight in the specially formed gurkha division.
4. (Whomever/Whoever) wished to join the gurkhas had to know someone already serving in the British army; it was an extremely prestigious battalion to be a part of.
5. (Its/It's) amazing to think that nearly 200 years later, money earned from gurkha pensions and salaries constitutes the largest single source of foreign exchange for the Nepalese economy.

36b | PRONOUN AGREEMENT

Because pronouns usually replace or refer to other nouns, they must match those nouns in number and gender. The noun that the pronoun replaces is called its **antecedent**. If pronoun and antecedent match, they are in **agreement**. When a pronoun is close to the antecedent, usually there is no problem.

> **Maria** forgot **her** coat.
>
> The band **members** collected **their** uniforms.

When pronouns and the nouns they replace are separated by several words, sometimes the agreement in number is lost.

> When the World Wrestling Federation (WWF) used **wrestlers** [PLURAL] to represent nations, there was no problem identifying the **villains**. **He** [SING] was the enemy if **he** [SING] came from Russia. But after the Cold War, **wrestlers** [PLURAL] can switch from **good guy** to **bad guy**. We don't immediately know how **he** [SING] has been scripted—good or bad.

Careful writers make sure that pronouns match their antecedents.

Common Errors

Indefinite pronouns

Indefinite pronouns (such as *anybody, anything, each, either, everybody, everything, neither, none, somebody, something*) refer to unspecified people or things. Most take singular pronouns.

INCORRECT	**Everybody** can choose **their** roommates.
CORRECT	**Everybody** can choose **his or her** roommate.

(continued next page)

Because it can be laborious to read *his or her*, especially when the phrase is used repeatedly, one effective solution is to make the subject plural, thereby making the correct pronoun the single word *their*.

CORRECT   **All students** can choose **their** roommates.
ALTERNATIVE

A few indefinite pronouns (*all, any, either, more, most, neither, none, some*) can take either singular or plural pronouns.

CORRECT   **Some** of the shipment was damaged when **it** became overheated.

CORRECT   **All** thought **they** should have a good seat at the concert.

The choice depends on the named entity. In the first example, *shipment* is a singular concept, even though a shipment may consist of multiple items, so the singular pronoun *it* is more appropriate. In the second example, *All* obviously refers to the unnamed entity *people*, so the plural pronoun *they* is more appropriate in this case.

A few are always plural (*few, many, several*).

CORRECT   **Several** want refunds.

Remember: Words that begin with *any*, *some*, and *every* are usually singular.

 For step-by-step discussion, examples, and practice of this common error, go to **www.ablongman.com/faigley027**.

Collective nouns

Collective nouns (such as *audience, class, committee, crowd, family, herd, jury, team*) can be singular or plural depending on whether the emphasis is on the group or on the particular individuals.

CORRECT   The **committee** was unanimous in **its** decision.

CORRECT   The **committee** put **their** opinions ahead of the goals of the unit.

In the first example, the singular pronoun *its* is the correct choice because the committee acts in unison and the sentence conveys that the committee should be regarded as a single entity. In the second example, the mention of the committee's opinions draws attention to the fact that the committee is made up of individuals who each have an opinion. The emphasis on plurality here makes the plural pronoun *their* the correct choice. Often a plural antecedent is added if the sense of the collective noun is plural.

> CORRECT   The individual committee **members** put **their** opinions ahead of the goals of the unit.

Generic nouns

Related to collective nouns are categorical nouns that identify a person, place, or thing as a member of a particular class or type. With a categorical noun we tend to think immediately of the plural concept and often slip into plural pronoun usage. But you should always look at how the noun functions grammatically in the sentence.

> INCORRECT   Each French professor at the local college had **their** own office.

> CORRECT   Each French professor at the local college had **his or her** own office.

Common Errors

Pronoun agreement with compound antecedents

Antecedents joined by *and* take plural pronouns.

> CORRECT   **Moncef and Driss** practiced **their** music.

Exception: When compound antecedents are preceded by *each* or *every*, use a singular pronoun.

> CORRECT   **Every male cardinal and warbler** arrives before the female to define **its** territory.

(continued next page)

When compound antecedents are connected by *or* or *nor*, the pronoun agrees with the antecedent closer to it.

INCORRECT **Either the Ross twins or Angela** should bring **their** CDs.

CORRECT **Either the Ross twins or Angela** should bring **her** CDs.

BETTER **Either Angela or the Ross twins** should bring **their** CDs.

When you put the plural *twins* last, the correct choice becomes the plural pronoun *their*.

Remember:
1. **Use plural pronouns for antecedents joined by *and*.**
2. **Use singular pronouns for antecedents preceded by *each* or *every*.**
3. **Use a pronoun that agrees with the nearest antecedent when compound antecedents are joined by *or* or *nor*.**

 For step-by-step discussion, examples, and practice of this common error, go to **www.ablongman.com/faigley028.**

EXERCISE 36.4 In the following sentences, pronouns are separated from the nouns they replace. Underline the antecedent and fill in the pronoun that agrees with it in the blank provided.

EXAMPLE Ironically, greyhounds are rarely gray; _their_ fur can be all shades of red, brown, gray, and brindle.

1. Canine experts disagree on the origin of the name "greyhound," but many believe _____ derives from "Greek hound."
2. For over 5,000 years, greyhounds have been prized for _____ regal bearing and grace.
3. Greyhounds were introduced into England by the Cretans around 500 BC, but _____ are best known as the mascot for America's number-one bus line.

4. King Cob was the first notable greyhound sire recorded after England
   began documenting canine pedigrees in 1858, and _____ fathered
   111 greyhounds in three years.

5. Each greyhound King Cob fathered was of the purest pedigree, even
   though _____ great-grandfather was a bulldog.

EXERCISE 36.5 Underline the indefinite pronouns, collective nouns, and
compound antecedents in the paragraph that follows. Circle the related
pronouns, and, if necessary, revise them to agree with their antecedents.
In some cases, you may have to decide whether the emphasis is on the
group or individuals within the group.

> EXAMPLE   Almost everyone can remember the first time he or she
>
> saw *The Sound of Music*, the story of the nanny and
>
> her Austrian family who use their ingenuity to escape
>
> the Nazi Anschluss.

   Neither the three films nor the stage play used their time to
tell the complete and accurate story of the real Maria von Trapp;
however, the audience often believe(s) what they see(s). Americans
associate Maria with the pixie-ish icon Julie Andrews, but few
would recognize the real Maria if he saw her. As in the American
musical, Maria, Captain von Trapp, and the children fled her
home. The real family did use its singing skills to evade the Nazis
during a concert, but afterward, it settled in a lodge in Stowe,
Vermont. Everyone who visits the lodge finds themselves surrounded by a bit of cultural history.

36c PROBLEMS WITH PRONOUNS AND GENDER

   English does not have a neutral singular pronoun for a group of mixed
genders or a person of unknown gender. Referring to a group of mixed
genders using male pronouns is unacceptable to many people. Unless the
school in the following example is all male, many readers would object to
the use of *his*.

Sexist   **Each student** must select **his** courses using the online registration system.

Several strategies can help you avoid sexist language. One strategy is to use *her or his* or *his or her* instead of *his*.

Correct   Each student must select **his or her** courses using the online registration system.

Some readers, however, find the use of *his or her* awkward. To avoid using this phrase, try substituting a plural pronoun. Remember that you must also make the subject plural so that it agrees with the plural pronoun.

Better   **All students** must select **their** courses using the online registration system.

If you have a string of sentences that use singular pronouns, another strategy is to alternate using *his* and *her*. However, keep the pronoun gender consistent within each individual sentence.

Better   Each student must select **her** courses using the online registration system. First the student must log into the system using **his** password and then select **his** courses.

In some cases, however, using *his or her* is necessary.

Common Errors

Problems created by the pronoun *one* used as a subject

Some writers use *one* as a subject in an attempt to sound more formal. At best this strategy produces writing that sounds stilted, and at worst it produces annoying errors.

Sexist   **One** can use **his** brains instead of a calculator to do simple addition.

Incorrect   **One** can use **their** brains instead of a calculator to do simple addition. (Agreement error: *Their* does not agree with *one*.)

<table>
<tr><td>INCORRECT</td><td>When **one** runs a 10K race for the first time, **you** often start out too fast. (Pronoun shift error: *One* changes to *you*.)</td></tr>
<tr><td>CORRECT</td><td>**One** can use **his or her** brains instead of a calculator to do simple addition.</td></tr>
<tr><td>CORRECT</td><td>**One** can use **one's** brains instead of a calculator to do simple addition.</td></tr>
</table>

You're better off avoiding using *one* as the subject of sentences.

BETTER	Use **your brain** instead of a calculator for simple addition.

Remember: Avoid using the pronoun *one* as a subject.

 For step-by-step discussion, examples, and practice of this common error, go to **www.ablongman.com/faigley029.**

EXERCISE 36.6 The following sentences contain examples of gender bias. Rewrite the sentences using subject and pronoun formations that are unbiased. Try to avoid using "his or her" constructions.

EXAMPLE	When an American turns eighteen, he is bombarded with advertisements that market easy credit.

REWRITE	When **Americans** turn eighteen, **they** are bombarded with advertisements that market easy credit.

1. When someone is financially overextended, he often considers credit cards as a way of making ends meet.
2. One might begin to convince himself that credit is the only way out.
3. But each adult must weigh the advantages and disadvantages of her own credit card use.

4. Eventually, one may find himself deep in debt because of high credit rates and overspending.

5. Then, one option might be for the individual to find a debt consolidator to assist him.

36d VAGUE REFERENCE

Pronouns can sometimes refer to more than one noun, thus confusing readers.

> The **coach** rushed past the injured **player** to yell at the **referee**. **She** was hit in the face by a stray elbow.

You have to guess which person *she* refers to—the coach, the player, or the referee. Sometimes you cannot even guess the antecedent of a pronoun.

> The new subdivision destroyed the last remaining habitat for wildlife within the city limits. **They** have ruined our city with their unchecked greed.

Whom does *they* refer to? the mayor and city council? the developers? the people who live in the subdivision? or all of the above?

Pronouns should never leave the reader guessing about antecedents. If different nouns can be confused as the antecedent, then the ambiguity should be clarified.

> **VAGUE**   Mafalda's pet boa constrictor crawled across Tonya's foot. **She** was mortified.
>
> **BETTER**   When Mafalda's pet boa constrictor crawled across Tonya's foot, **Mafalda** was mortified.

If the antecedent is missing, then it should be supplied.

> **VAGUE**   Mafalda wasn't thinking when she brought her boa constrictor into the crowded writing center. **They** got up and left the room in the middle of consultations.
>
> **BETTER**   Mafalda wasn't thinking when she brought her boa constrictor into the crowded writing center. **A few students** got up and left the room in the middle of consultations.

Remote pronouns

Pronouns are also vague if they are too far removed from their antecedents. It is confusing and annoying for a reader to have to search back through several sentences to find the noun to which the pronoun refers.

> INCORRECT   Last summer, Joel worked as an intern at the *City Star*, his hometown's local newspaper. His immediate supervisor was Cathy Simon, the features editor. Joel had hoped he would be able to write some feature stories on local environmental issues but soon discovered his job mainly entailed making copies and answering phone calls. After the internship was over, Joel wrote a letter to **her**, making suggestions about how the internship program might be improved for future interns.

> BETTER   Last summer, Joel worked as an intern at the *City Star*, his hometown's local newspaper. His immediate supervisor was Cathy Simon, the features editor. Joel had hoped he would be able to write some feature stories on local environmental issues but soon discovered his job mainly entailed making copies and answering phone calls. After the internship was over, Joel wrote a letter to **Simon**, making suggestions about how the internship program might be improved for future interns.

Vague use of *which* and *it*

Writers often use *which* or *it* vaguely or too broadly when they assume the reader will know what the pronoun refers to, or when they are uncertain about a point or idea.

> VAGUE   This semester, three students were caught copying their papers from the Internet and were only reprimanded, **which** shows how much the school has changed over the past twenty years.

Which fact shows how much the school has changed—the fact that students are cheating or the school's response to the cheating? To avoid vague usage, supply a clear antecedent for the pronoun.

BETTER   This semester, three students were caught copying their papers from the Internet and were only reprimanded, **a policy which** shows how much the school has changed over the past twenty years.

Implied antecedents

Pronouns should refer to specifically named antecedents. Pronouns cannot refer to an implied noun.

INCORRECT   Because Susan had enjoyed reading Don Delillo's novel *White Noise*, she went to **his** book signing at the local bookstore.

CORRECT   Because Susan had enjoyed reading Don Delillo's novel *White Noise*, she went to **the author's** book signing at the local bookstore.

People commonly mistake a modifier for an antecedent, especially in the case of possessives, as illustrated in the incorrect example. The pronoun *his* requires the antecedent *Delillo*—not *Delillo's*, a word that functions as an adjective modifying *novel* in this sentence.

Indefinite use of *it*

Avoid using *they* and *it* as indefinite pronouns. Indefinite pronouns refer to unspecified people or things (see Section 36b), but *they* and *it* should refer to clear antecedents.

INCORRECT   In the novel *Middlemarch*, **it** details Dorothea Brooke's struggle to escape the constraints of her oppressive marriage to Edward Causabon.

CORRECT   The novel *Middlemarch* details Dorothea Brooke's struggle to escape the constraints of her oppressive marriage to Edward Causabon.

Common Errors

Vague use of *this*

Always use a noun immediately after *this, that, these, those,* and *some.*

VAGUE   Enrique asked Meg to remove the viruses on his computer. This was a bad idea.

Was it a bad idea for Enrique to ask Meg because she was insulted? Because she didn't know how? Because removing viruses would destroy some of Enrique's files?

BETTER   Enrique asked Meg to remove the viruses on his computer. This imposition on Meg's time made her resentful.

Remember: Ask yourself "*this* what?" and add the noun that *this* refers to.

 For step-by-step discussion, examples, and practice of this common error, go to **www.ablongman.com/faigley030.**

People versus animals and things

Use *who, whom,* or *whose* to refer to persons. Use *which* or *that* to refer to objects. With named animals (pets) it is common to use *who, whom,* or *whose,* but *which* or *that* for unnamed animals.

CORRECT   My springer spaniel, Lily, is the kind of dog **who** loves to sleep all day.

CORRECT   The deer **that** live near suburban homes eat as much garbage as foliage.

Writing in the World

Pronouns in legal writing

Legal writing is often difficult to read, in part because lawyers often don't use many pronouns. The following paragraph is typical.

LEGALESE

Cancellations by participants received within thirty days of departure are subject to loss of the deposit paid in advance by participant plus cancellation costs for services rendered by the travel agency unless a substitute participant is found by the participant or the letter of cancellation from the participant is accompanied by a letter from a physician stating that the participant is not able to travel due to medical reasons, in which case the participant will not pay cancellation costs.

Legal writing does not have to be this difficult to understand. Some attorneys and others who write legal language wrongly believe that they can avoid any possible misunderstanding by not using pronouns. In fact, many states now require consumer contracts to be written in plain English. Using pronouns makes the contract readable.

PLAIN ENGLISH

If you cancel within thirty days of departure, you will lose your deposit and you must pay for any services we have provided unless (1) you find a substitute, or (2) you send a letter from a physician stating that you cannot travel for medical reasons, in which case you lose only the deposit.

EXERCISE 36.7 In the paragraph that follows, underline the vague pronoun references and replace them with logical antecedents as needed. More than one answer will be acceptable.

EXAMPLE   <u>They</u> had no warning before the Great Galveston Hurricane of 1900 destroyed their city.

REWRITE   **The citizens of Galveston** had no warning before the Great Galveston Hurricane of 1900 destroyed their city.

On September 8, 1900, Sister Elizabeth Ryan and Mother Gabriel visited St. Mary's Infirmary in Galveston. She was worried about the oncoming storm and thought she should leave the infirmary if it grew worse. It did grow worse, and Sister Elizabeth began to make her way back to St. Mary's Orphan Asylum, where she worked. It was located on the western edge of the city, which bordered the beach, and it would be hard to reach because of this. Therefore, they began to prepare them for the rising water of the hurricane. They tied them together with lengths of clothesline, and then attached them to their habits. Tied together with rope and secured to their caregivers for dear life, they became a symbol for the resilience of a city facing tragedy.

Chapter 37

Modifiers

Modifiers can limit or elaborate on your words. They make your eggs *scrambled* and your shower *hot*; they allow you to sleep *soundly* and laugh *loudly*. But if you're not careful they can also create unintentionally funny sentences.

> **Mired in the swampy muck**, the alligator swam toward the fisherman.

Who's mired in the muck, the fisherman or the alligator?

> Jason returned the new car his parents purchased **after denting a fender**.

The sentence has the parents purchasing a new car after denting the fender. Modifiers are effective when they are both carefully selected and carefully placed.

Modifiers come in two varieties: adjectives and adverbs. The same words can function as adjectives or adverbs, depending on what they modify.

ADJECTIVES MODIFY
nouns—*iced* tea, *power* forward
pronouns—He is *brash*.

ADVERBS MODIFY
verbs—*barely* reach, drive *carefully*
adjectives—*truly* brave activist, *shockingly* red lipstick
other adverbs—*not* soon forget, *very* well
clauses—*Honestly*, I find ballet boring.

Only adverbs can modify verbs, adjectives, clauses, and other adverbs, but people sometime incorrectly use adjectives to modify verbs and other adjectives.

INCORRECT	The new version of that computer program works **won-derful**, and I will recommend it to all my colleagues.
CORRECT	The new version of that computer program works **won-derfully**, and I will recommend it to all my colleagues.

Adjectives answer the questions *Which one? How many?* and *What kind?* Adverbs answer the questions *How often? To what extent? When? Where? How?* and *Why?*

37a | CHOOSE THE CORRECT MODIFIER

Use the correct forms of comparatives and superlatives

As kids, we used comparative and superlative modifiers to argue that Superman was *stronger* than Batman and recess was the *coolest* part of the day. Comparatives and superlatives are formed differently; all you need to know to determine which to use is the number of items you are comparing.

Comparative modifiers weigh one thing against another. They either end in *er* or are preceded by *more*.

Road bikes are **faster** on pavement than mountain bikes.

The **more courageous** juggler tossed flaming torches.

Superlative modifiers compare three or more items. They either end in *est* or are preceded by *most*.

April is the **hottest** month in New Delhi.

Wounded animals are the **most ferocious**.

When should you add a suffix instead of *more* or *most*? The following guidelines work in most cases:

ADJECTIVES

- For adjectives of one or two syllables, add *er* or *est*.

  redder, heaviest

- For adjectives of three or more syllables, use *more* or *most*.

  more viable, most powerful

ADVERBS

- For adverbs of one syllable, use *er* or *est*.

  nearer, slowest

- For adverbs with two or more syllables, use *more* or *most*.

  more convincingly, most humbly

Some frequently used comparatives and superlatives are irregular. The following list can help you become familiar with them.

Adjective	Comparative	Superlative
good	better	best
bad	worse	worst
little (amount)	less	least
many, much	more	most
Adverb	**Comparative**	**Superlative**
well	better	best
badly	worse	worst

Do not use both a suffix (*er* or *est*) and *more* or *most*.

INCORRECT The service at Jane's Restaurant is **more slower** than the service at Alphonso's.

CORRECT The service at Jane's Restaurant is **slower** than the service at Alphonso's.

Be sure to name the elements being compared if they are not clear from the context.

UNCLEAR COMPARATIVE	Mice are **cuter**.
CLEAR	Mice are **cuter than rats**.
UNCLEAR SUPERLATIVE	Nutria are the **creepiest**.
CLEAR	Nutria are the **creepiest rodents**.

Absolute modifiers cannot be comparative or superlative

Absolute modifiers are words that represent an unvarying condition and thus aren't subject to the degrees that comparative and superlative constructions convey. How many times have you heard something called *very unique* or *totally unique*? *Unique* means "one of a kind." There's nothing else like it. Thus something cannot be *very unique* or *totally unique*. It is either unique or it isn't. The United States Constitution makes a classic absolute modifier blunder when it begins, "We the People of the United States, in Order to form a more perfect Union. . . ." What is a *more perfect Union*? What's more perfect than perfect itself? The construction is nonsensical.

Absolute modifiers should not be modified by comparatives (*more* + modifier or modifier + *er*) or superlatives (*most* + modifier or modifier + *est*). Note the following list of common absolute modifiers.

absolute	impossible	unanimous
adequate	infinite	unavoidable
complete	main	uniform
entire	minor	unique
false	perfect	universal
fatal	principal	whole
final	stationary	
ideal	sufficient	

EXERCISE 37.1 Decide whether each word in parentheses should be comparative or superlative. Rewrite the word, adding either the correct suffix (*-er* or *-est*) or *more* or *most*. If you find an absolute modifier (a word that should not be modified), underline it.

EXAMPLE   With over 23 million models sold since 1966, the
            most popular
            (popular) car in the world is the Toyota Corolla.

1. The (good) selling car in the United States is the Toyota Camry, closely followed by the Honda Accord and the Ford Taurus.
2. At 41,907 the United States has the (high) number of road deaths per year; however, the (bad) motor vehicle accident occurred in Afghanistan in 1982, when 300 people died after an oil tanker exploded in a tunnel.
3. If you are traveling a long distance, a car might not be the (convenient) form of transportation.
4. A train can travel at speeds exceeding 160 miles per hour, but if you want something (fast) the U.S. military's X-15 aircraft travels an (incredible) 4,520 miles per hour!
5. London's Heathrow, the world's (busy) airport, serves over 48 million travelers per year.

Double negatives

In English, as in mathematics, two negatives equal a positive. Avoid using two negative words in one sentence, or you'll end up saying the opposite of what you mean. The following are negative words that you should avoid doubling up:

barely	nobody	nothing
hardly	none	scarcely
neither	no one	

INCORRECT, **DOUBLE NEGATIVE**	**Barely no one** noticed that the pop star lip-synched during the whole performance.
CORRECT, **SINGLE NEGATIVE**	**Barely anyone** noticed that the pop star lip-synched during the whole performance.
INCORRECT, **DOUBLE NEGATIVE**	When the pastor asked if anyone had objections to the marriage, **nobody** said **nothing**.
CORRECT, **SINGLE NEGATIVE**	When the pastor asked if anyone had objections to the marriage, **nobody** said **anything**.

EXERCISE 37.2 Revise the following paragraph to eliminate double negatives. More than one answer may be correct in each case.

EXAMPLE   One ~~can't~~ ^can^ hardly survey the history of the American film

industry without encountering the story of the Holly-

wood Ten, a group of artists targeted as communists.

After the creation of the House Un-American Activities Committee (HUAC), Cold War paranoia could not barely hide itself in post-World War II America. HUAC followed on the coattails of the 1938 Special Committee on Un-American Activities. This earlier committee did not focus not solely on communists; extremists from both the far left and the far right were targeted. By the 1940s, however, HUAC focused not on neither white supremacist nor pro-Nazi groups, but instead on the supposed communist infiltration of Hollywood. Scarcely no one could escape the grasp of HUAC; actors, producers, and directors all came under scrutiny. By the end of the proceedings, not hardly nobody remained unscathed. Hundreds in the entertainment industry were either fired or appeared on the infamous HUAC blacklist.

Common Errors

Irregular adjectives and adverbs

Switch on a baseball interview and you will likely hear numerous modifier mistakes.

> Manager: We didn't play **bad** tonight. Martinez hit the ball **real good**, and I was glad to see Adamski pitch **farther** into the game than he did in his last start. His fastball was on, and he walked **less** hitters.

While this manager has his sports clichés down pat, he makes errors with five of the trickiest modifier pairs. In three cases he uses an adjective where an adverb would be correct.

(continued next page)

Adjectives	Adverbs
bad	badly
good	well
real	really

Bad, an adjective modifying the noun *call*: The umpire made a **bad** call at the plate.

Badly, an adverb modifying the verb *play*: We didn't play **badly**.

Good, an adjective modifying the noun *catch*: Starke made a **good** catch.

Well, an adverb modifying the verb *hit*: Martinez hit the ball **well**.

Exception: *Well* acts as an adjective when it describes someone's health: Injured players must stay on the disabled list until they feel **well** enough to play everyday.

Real, an adjective modifying the noun *wood*: While college players hit with aluminum bats, the professionals still use **real** wood.

Really, an adverb modifying the adverb *well*: Martinez hit the ball **really** well.

The coach also confused the comparative adjectives *less* and *fewer*, and the comparative adverbs *farther* and *further*.

ADJECTIVES

less—a smaller, uncountable amount
fewer—a smaller number of things

LESS   Baseball stadiums with pricey luxury suites cater **less** to families and more to business people with expense accounts.

FEWER   He walked **fewer** hitters.

ADVERBS

farther—a greater distance
further—to a greater extent, a longer time, or a greater number

FARTHER   Some players argue that today's baseballs go **farther** than baseballs made just a few years ago.

FURTHER   The commissioner of baseball curtly denied that today's baseballs are juiced, refusing to discuss the matter **further**.

Remember: *Bad, good, real, less* (for uncountables), and *fewer* (for countables) are adjectives. *Badly, well, really, farther* (for distance), and *further* (for extent, time, or number) are adverbs. *Well* is an adjective when it describes health.

 For step-by-step discussion, examples, and practice of this common error, go to **www.ablongman.com/faigley031**.

EXERCISE 37.3 The following words in parentheses are tricky adjective-adverb pairs. Underline the word(s) being modified in the sentence, and circle the correct adjective or adverb from the pair.

EXAMPLE   To ensure the success of their missions, NASA has tackled the challenge of enabling astronauts to <u>eat</u> (healthy/healthily) in space so that <u>they</u> can stay (good/well).

In the early days of manned space missions, NASA had (fewer/less) problems feeding astronauts. But the (further/farther) astronauts traveled, the (further/farther) NASA had to go to ensure healthy eating in space. For example, the Mercury missions of the

early 1960s took (fewer/less) time than an actual meal, so NASA's (real/really) challenge didn't come until crews were in space for longer periods of time. However, these shorter trips worked (good/well) as tests for experimental astronaut foods. By the mid-1960s, those on the Gemini missions were offered better ways to prepare and enjoy food in space. Engineers eventually discovered that packaging food in an edible liquid or gelatin container would prevent it from crumbling and damaging the equipment (bad/badly). By the Space Shuttle expeditions of the 1980s and 1990s, (real/really) headway had been made in terms of (good/well) dining technology, and crew members could devise their own menus.

37b PLACE ADJECTIVES CAREFULLY

As a general rule, the closer you place a modifier to the word it modifies, the less the chance you will confuse your reader. This section and the next elaborate on this maxim, giving you the details you need to put it into practice. Most native speakers have an ear for many of the guidelines presented here, with the notable exception of limiting modifier placement, which is explained in Section 37c.

Place adjective phrases and clauses carefully

Adjective clauses frequently begin with *when*, *where*, or a relative pronoun like *that*, *which*, *who*, *whom*, or *whose*. An adjective clause usually follows the noun or pronoun it modifies.

> **Adjective clause modifying *salon*:** The **salon where I get my hair styled** is raising its prices.

> **Adjective clause modifying *stylist*:** I need to find a **stylist who charges less**.

Adjective phrases and clauses can also come before the person or thing they modify.

> **Adjective phrase modifying *girl*:** **Proud of her accomplishment**, the little **girl** showed her trophy to her grandmother.

Adjective phrases or clauses can be confusing if they are separated from the word they modify.

CONFUSING   **Watching from the ground below,** the kettle of broadwing hawks circled high above the observers.

Is the kettle of hawks watching from the ground below? You can fix the problem by putting the modified subject immediately after the modifier or placing the modifier next to the modified subject.

BETTER   The kettle of broadwing hawks circled high above the **observers** who were watching from the ground below.

BETTER   **Watching from the ground below,** the **observers** saw a kettle of broadwing hawks circle high above them.

See dangling modifiers in Section 37e.

EXERCISE 37.4 Underline the adjective phrases and clauses in the following sentences. If any phrases or clauses could apply to two subjects, revise the sentence to eliminate ambiguity.

EXAMPLE   Arriving June 19, 1865, the Texas slaves were informed of their freedom by Union soldiers two years after the signing of the Emancipation Proclamation.

REWRITE   Arriving June 19, 1865, two years after the signing of the Emancipation Proclamation, Union soldiers informed Texas slaves of their freedom.

1. Now known as Juneteenth, Texas celebrates the day Texan slaves discovered their freedom.
2. A people's event that has become an official holiday, freed slaves celebrated annually their day of emancipation.
3. Celebrated vigorously in the 1950s and 1960s, the Civil Rights movement sparked a renewed interest in the Juneteenth holiday.
4. Still going strong, entertainment, education, and self-improvement are all activities included in the annual celebration.

Place one-word adjectives before the modified word(s)

One-word adjectives almost always precede the word or words they modify.

Pass the **hot** sauce, please.

When one-word adjectives are not next to the word or words being modified, they can create misunderstandings.

UNCLEAR Before his owner withdrew him from competition, the **fiercest** rodeo's bull injured three riders.

Readers may think *fiercest* modifies *rodeo's* instead of *bull*. Placing the adjective before *bull* will clarify the meaning.

BETTER Before his owner withdrew him from competition, the rodeo's **fiercest** bull injured three riders.

Exception: predicate adjectives follow linking verbs

Predicate adjectives are the most common exception to the norm of single-word adjectives preceding words they modify. Predicate adjectives follow linking verbs such as *is, are, was, were, seem, feel, smell, taste,* and *look.* Don't be fooled into thinking they are adverbs. If the word following a linking verb modifies the subject, use a predicate adjective. If it modifies an action verb, use an adverb. Can you identify the word being modified in the following sentence?

I feel **odd.**

Odd modifies the subject *I,* not the verb *feel.* Thus, *odd* is a predicate adjective that implies the speaker feels ill. If it were an adverb, the sentence would read *I feel oddly.* The adverb *oddly* modifying *feel* would imply the speaker senses things in unconventional ways. Try the next one:

The bruise looked **bad.**

Since *bad* modifies *bruise, bad* is a predicate adjective implying a serious injury. *Looked* is the linking verb that connects the two. If we made the modifier an adverb, the sentence would read *The bruise looked badly*, conjuring the creepy notion that the bruise had eyes but couldn't see well. You can avoid such bizarre constructions if you know when to use predicate adjectives with linking verbs.

Put subjective adjectives before objective adjectives

When you have a series of adjectives expressing both opinion and more objective description, put the subjective adjectives before the objective ones. For example, in

the sultry cabaret singer

sultry is subjective and *cabaret* is objective.

Put determiners before other adjectives

Determiners are a group of adjectives that include possessive nouns (such as *woman's* prerogative and *Pedro's* violin), possessive pronouns (such as *my*, *your*, and *his*), demonstrative pronouns (*this, that, these, those*), and indefinite pronouns (such as *all, both, each, either, few,* and *many*). When you are using a series of adjectives, put the determiners first.

our finest hour
Tara's favorite old blue jeans
those crazy kids

When you are using a numerical determiner with another determiner, put the numerical determiner first.

both those tattoos
all these people

EXERCISE 37.5 Underline the one-word adjectives in the following paragraph. If any are placed ambiguously or incorrectly, revise them.

EXAMPLE   The <u>incomparable</u> Loretta Lynn was the ~~female first~~ *first female*

singer to be inducted into the Songwriters Hall of Fame.

Lynn rose from a Kentucky sheltered childhood to earn the title "First Lady of Country Music," garnering awards various and honors. At fourteen, a pregnant Lynn felt lost as she joined her husband Doolittle in Washington state, but their both lives would change when he bought Lynn her first guitar. Country music lovers were receptive to prolific Lynn's lyrics and tales of female strength. Maintaining a music successful career, Lynn has continued to write and perform these all years.

37c PLACE ADVERBS CAREFULLY

For the most part, the guidelines for adverb placement are not as complex as the guidelines for adjective placement.

Place adverbs before or after the words they modify

Single-word adverbs and adverbial clauses and phrases can usually sit comfortably either before or after the words they modify.

Dimitri **quietly** **walked** down the hall.

Dimitri **walked** **quietly** down the hall.

Conjunctive adverbs—*also, however, instead, likewise, then, therefore, thus,* and others—are adverbs that show how ideas relate to one another. They prepare a reader for contrasts, exceptions, additions, conclusions, and other shifts in an argument. Conjunctive adverbs can usually fit well into more than one place in the sentence. In the following example, *however* could fit in three different places.

BETWEEN TWO MAIN CLAUSES
Professional football players earn exorbitant salaries; **however,** they pay for their wealth with lifetimes of chronic pain and debilitating injuries.

WITHIN SECOND MAIN CLAUSE
Professional football players earn exorbitant salaries; they pay for their wealth, **however,** with lifetimes of chronic pain and debilitating injuries.

AT END OF SECOND MAIN CLAUSE

Professional football players earn exorbitant salaries; they pay for their wealth with lifetimes of chronic pain and debilitating injuries however.

Subordinating conjunctions—words such as *after, although, because, if, since, than, that, though, when,* and *where*—often begin **adverbial clauses**. Notice that we can place adverbial clauses with subordinating conjunctions either before or after the word(s) being modified:

> After some thought, he **stepped** back from the door of the airplane.
>
> He **stepped** back from the door of the airplane after some thought.

While you have some leeway with adverb placement, follow the advice in Section 37d: Avoid distracting interruptions between the subject and verb, the verb and the object, or within the verb phrase. A long adverbial clause is usually best placed at the beginning or end of a sentence.

Avoid squinting modifiers

In some situations placing a modifier next to the word or phrase it modifies is still unclear; the modifier needs to be on one side or the other. Be especially careful to avoid a **squinting modifier**, an adverb between two verb phrases. The reader won't know which verb phrase it modifies.

> CONFUSING   Tim grabbed the plate hungrily carried by the waiter.

Who's hungry, Tim or the waiter? Placing the adverb before the verb it modifies will clarify.

> BETTER   Tim hungrily grabbed the plate carried by the waiter.
>
> CONFUSING   The Chens left the kittens sadly playing in a cage at the pound.

Who's sad, the kittens or the Chens? Again, the sentence will be clearer if we place the adverb before the verb it modifies.

> BETTER   The Chens sadly left the kittens playing in a cage at the pound.

Common Errors

Placement of limiting modifiers

Words such as *almost, even, hardly, just, merely, nearly, not, only,* and *simply* are called limiting modifiers. Although people often play fast and loose with their placement in everyday speech, limiting modifiers should always go immediately before the word or words they modify in your writing. The following example illustrates how many different meanings a limiting modifier can convey according to its placement. This cumbersome sentence uses *just* in four places, and in all four places it carries different connotations.

> **Just** twenty new people **just** volunteered **just** for the sea turtle rescue program **just** for the spring.

Just twenty new people: "merely," implying the number was lower than expected

just volunteered: "in the immediate past"

just for the sea turtle rescue program: "alone," implying it was one of several well-staffed programs

just for the spring: "only," implying volunteer numbers were high in other seasons too

Many writers have difficulty with the placement of *only.* Like other limiting modifiers, *only* should be placed immediately before the word it modifies.

INCORRECT   The Gross Domestic Product **only** gives one indicator of economic growth.

CORRECT   The Gross Domestic Product gives **only** one indicator of economic growth.

Remember: Place limiting modifiers immediately before the word(s) they modify.

For step-by-step discussion, examples, and practice of this common error, go to **www.ablongman.com/faigley032.**

EXERCISE 37.6 Rewrite each of the following sentences, moving the adverb to eliminate squinting modifiers. Place adverbs where they make the most logical sense within the context of the sentence. Underline the adverbs in your revised sentences.

EXAMPLE   In the mid-1800s, Father Gregor Mendel developed experiments ingeniously examining the area of heredity.

REWRITE   In the mid-1800s, Father Gregor Mendel <u>ingeniously</u> developed experiments examining the area of heredity.

1. Mendel's work focused on initially hybridizing the Lathyrus, or sweet pea.
2. The Lathyrus possessed variations conveniently composed of differing sizes and colors.
3. Hybridizing the plants easily allowed Mendel to view the mathematical effects of dominant and recessive trait mixing.
4. By crossing white-flowered pea pods with red-flowered pea pods, Mendel proved successfully existing pairs of hereditary factors determined the color characteristics of offspring.
5. Though published in 1866, Mendel's theory of heredity remained unnoticed mostly by the biological community until the early 1900s.

37d | REVISE DISRUPTIVE MODIFIERS

The fundamental way readers make sense of sentences is to identify the subject, verb, and object. Modifiers can sink a sentence if they interfere with the reader's ability to connect the three. Usually, single-word modifiers do not significantly disrupt a sentence. However, avoid placing modifying clauses and phrases between a subject and a verb, between a verb and an object, and within a verb phrase.

DISRUPTIVE   The forest fire, **no longer held in check by the exhausted firefighters**, jumped the firebreak. (Separates the subject from the verb)

BETTER	No longer held in check by the exhausted fire-fighters, the forest fire jumped the firebreak. (puts the modifier before the subject)
DISRUPTIVE	The fire's heat seemed to melt, at a temperature hot enough to liquefy metal, the saplings in its path. (separates the verb from the object)
BETTER	At a temperature hot enough to liquefy metal, the fire's heat seemed to melt the saplings in its path. (puts the modifier before the subject)
DISRUPTIVE	The firefighters would, when the wind shifted, risk being trapped by the flames. (interrupts the verb phrase)
BETTER	When the wind shifted, the firefighters would risk being trapped by the flames. (puts the modifier before the subject)

Writing in the World

Split infinitives

An infinitive is *to* plus the base form of a verb. A split infinitive occurs when an adverb separates *to* from the base verb form.

INFINITIVE = *TO* + BASE VERB FORM

Examples: **to feel, to speak, to borrow**

SPLIT INFINITIVE = *TO* + MODIFIER + BASE VERB FORM

Examples: **to strongly feel**, **to barely speak**, **to liberally borrow**

If you have ever studied Latin or a language derived from Latin (French, Italian, Portuguese, and others), you know that you cannot split an infinitive because it is one word. Using the example of Latin, grammarians in the eighteenth century ruled that infinitives in English should not be split, even though English has a different system for marking infinitives.

Grammarians of today tend to frown on split infinitives but also understand that in some cases split infinitives are the preferable alternative. The most famous split infinitive in recent history occurs in the opening credits of *Star Trek* episodes: "to boldly go where no one has gone before." The alternative without the split infinitive is "to go boldly where no one has gone before." The writers in *Star Trek* no doubt were aware they were splitting an infinitive, but they chose *to boldly go* because they wanted the emphasis on *boldly*, not *go*.

Nevertheless, many split infinitives are considered awkward for good reason.

AWKWARD	You have to get away from the city lights **to better appreciate** the stars in the night sky.
BETTER	You have to get away from the city **to appreciate** the stars in the night sky **better**.
AWKWARD	**To, as planned, stay** in Venice, we need to reserve a hotel room now.
BETTER	**To stay** in Venice **as planned**, we need to reserve a hotel room now.

When a sentence would sound strange without the adverb splitting the infinitive, you can either retain the split or, better yet, revise the sentence to avoid the problem altogether.

ACCEPTABLE	When found by the search party, the survivors were able **to barely whisper** their names.
ALTERNATIVE	When found by the search party, the survivors **could barely whisper** their names.

EXERCISE 37.7 Underline the disruptive modifiers in the following paragraph. You may find a modifying clause or phrase that separates major components of a sentence, or you may find a split infinitive. Rewrite the paragraph to eliminate the disruptions. More than one way of revising may be correct.

EXAMPLE   The Catholic papacy, <u>because of conflict in the Papal States</u>, resided in France for more than seventy years.

REWRITE   Because of conflict in the Papal States, the Catholic papacy resided in France for more than seventy years.

In the thirteenth and fourteenth centuries, the Italian Papal States, because of militantly rivaling families, were consumed in chaos. In 1305 the cardinals elected, unable to agree on an Italian, a Frenchman as the new pope. He decided to temporarily remain in France. The papacy would, because of various religious and political reasons, remain in France until 1378. Rome, during the papacy's seventy-year absence, would lose both prestige and income.

37e   REVISE DANGLING MODIFIERS

Some modifiers are ambiguous because they could apply to more than one word or clause. Dangling modifiers are ambiguous for the opposite reason; they don't have a word to modify. In such cases the modifier is usually an introductory clause or phrase. What is being modified should immediately follow the phrase, but in the following sentence it is absent.

After bowling a perfect game, Surfside Lanes hung Marco's photo on the wall.

Neither the subject of the sentence, *Surfside Lanes,* nor the direct object, *Marco's photo,* is capable of bowling a perfect game. Since a missing noun or pronoun causes a dangling modifier, simply rearranging the sentence will not resolve the problem. You can eliminate a dangling modifier in two ways:

1. Insert the noun or pronoun being modified immediately after the introductory modifying phrase.

   After bowling a perfect game, **Marco** was honored by having his photo hung on the wall at Surfside Lanes.

2. Rewrite the introductory phrase as an introductory clause to include the noun or pronoun.

   After **Marco** bowled a perfect game, Surfside Lanes hung his photo on the wall.

EXERCISE 37.8 Each of the following sentences contains a dangling modifier. Revise the sentences to eliminate dangling modifiers according to the methods described in Section 37e. More than one way of revising may be correct.

EXAMPLE   Though it preceded Woodstock, popular music history often obscures the Monterey Pop Festival.

REWRITE   Though the Monterey Pop Festival preceded Woodstock, it is often obscured by popular music history.

1. Lasting for three days in June of 1967, over thirty artists performed.
2. The largest American music festival of its time, attendance totaled over 200,000.
3. With artists such as Ravi Shankar, Otis Redding, and The Who, the fans encountered various musical genres.
4. Performing live for the first time in America, fans howled as Jimi Hendrix set his guitar on fire.
5. Establishing a standard for future festivals, Woodstock and Live Aid would eventually follow suit.

Understanding Punctuation and Mechanics 9

38
Commas

39
Semicolons and Colons

40
Hyphens

41
Dashes and Parentheses

42
Apostrophes

43
Quotation Marks

44
Other Punctuation Marks

caps/italic
45
Capitalization and Italics

abbr., number
46
Abbreviations, Acronyms, and Numbers

Chapter 38

Commas

Commas give readers vital clues about how to read a sentence. They tell readers when to pause and indicate how the writer's ideas relate to one another.

38a COMMAS WITH INTRODUCTORY ELEMENTS

Introductory elements like conjunctive adverbs and introductory phrases usually need to be set off by commas. Introductory words or phrases signal a shift in ideas or a particular arrangement of ideas; they help direct the reader's attention to the writer's most important points. Commas force the reader to pause and take notice of these pivotal elements.

Common introductory elements

Conjunctive adverbs	Introductory phrases
however	of course
therefore	above all
nonetheless	for example
also	in other words
otherwise	as a result
finally	on the other hand
instead	in conclusion
thus	in addition

When a conjunctive adverb or introductory phrase begins a sentence, the comma follows.

Therefore, the suspect could not have been at the scene of the crime.

Above all, remember to let water drip from the faucets if the temperature drops below freezing.

Adverb - modifies a verb, adjetive, or other adverb
Conjunctive - joins two ideas
Commas with introductory elements **38** **⌐** **667**

When a conjunctive adverb comes in the middle of a sentence, set it off with commas preceding and following.

> If you really want to prevent your pipes from freezing**,** *however,* you should insulate them before the winter comes.

Conjunctive adverbs and phrases that do not require commas

Occasionally the conjunctive adverb or phrase blends into a sentence so smoothly that a pause would sound awkward.

AWKWARD	Of course**,** we'll come.
BETTER	Of course we'll come.
AWKWARD	Even if you take every precaution, the pipes in your home may freeze**,** *nevertheless.*
BETTER	Even if you take every precaution, the pipes in your home may freeze *nevertheless.*

Sometimes the presence or absence of a comma can affect the meaning. For example:

> Of course, we'll come. [Be reassured that we will come.]
>
> Of course we'll come. [There is no doubt we will come.]

Common Errors

Commas with long introductory modifiers

Long subordinate clauses or phrases that begin sentences should be followed by a comma. The following sentence lacks the needed comma.

| **INCORRECT** | Because cell phones now have organizers and email**,** Palm Pilots may soon become another technology of the past. |

(continued next page)

When you read this sentence, you likely had to go back to sort it out. The group of words *organizers and email Palm Pilots* tend to run together. When the comma is added, the sentence is easier to understand because the reader knows where the subordinate clause ends and where the main clause begins:

CORRECT   Because cell phones now have organizers and email, Palm Pilots may soon become another technology of the past.

How long is a long introductory modifier? Short introductory adverbial phrases and clauses of five words or fewer can get by without the comma if the omission does not mislead the reader. Using the comma is still correct after short introductory adverbial phrases and clauses:

CORRECT   In the long run stocks have always done better than bonds.

CORRECT   In the long run, stocks have always done better than bonds.

Remember: Put commas after long introductory modifiers.

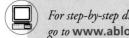

For step-by-step discussion, examples, and practice of this common error, go to www.ablongman.com/faigley033.

EXERCISE 38.1 Underline conjunctive adverbs, introductory phrases, and long introductory modifiers in the following sentences. Then set off those elements with commas when necessary.

EXAMPLE   Although king cobras have small fangs, one bite is

poisonous enough to kill an elephant.

1. King cobras in fact have a poisonous bite from the moment they are born.
2. Even though king cobras carry lethal venom women in Thailand's King Cobra Club dance with the snakes' heads in their mouths.
3. Also many Southeast Asian countries worship the king cobra.
4. Above all avoid provoking king cobras; they are not aggressive animals if left undisturbed.
5. An antidote is available however if you are bitten by a cobra.

38b | COMMAS WITH COMPOUND CLAUSES ✳

Two main clauses joined by a coordinating conjunction (*and, or, so, yet, but, nor, for*) form a compound sentence (see Section 32e). Writers sometimes get confused about when to insert a comma before a coordinating conjunction.

Use a comma to separate main clauses

Main clauses carry enough grammatical weight to be punctuated as sentences. When two main clauses are joined by a coordinating conjunction, place a comma before the coordinating conjunction in order to distinguish them.

Sandy borrowed two boxes full of records on Tuesday, and she returned them on Friday.

Very short main clauses joined by a coordinating conjunction do not need commas.

She called and she called, but no one answered.

Do not use a comma to separate two verbs with the same subject

INCORRECT   Sandy borrowed two boxes full of records on Tuesday, and returned them on Friday.

Sandy is the subject of both *borrowed* and *returned*. This sentence has only one main clause; it should not be punctuated as a compound sentence.

> **CORRECT**   Sandy borrowed two boxes full of records on Tuesday
> **and** returned them on Friday.

Exceptions to this rule occur when there is a lapse of time or after *said*.

> He did not study, and failed.
>
> "That's fine," he said, and went on reading.

Common Errors

Identifying compound sentences that require commas

The easiest way to distinguish between compound sentences and sentences with phrases that follow the main clause is to isolate the part that comes after the conjunction. If the part that follows the conjunction can stand on its own as a complete sentence, insert a comma. If it cannot, omit the comma.

> **MAIN CLAUSE PLUS PHRASES**
> Mario thinks he lost his passport while riding the bus or by absentmindedly leaving it on the counter when he checked into the hostel.

Look at what comes after the coordinating conjunction *or*:

> by absentmindedly leaving it on the counter when he checked into the hostel

This group of words is not a main clause and cannot stand on its own as a complete sentence. Do not set it off with a comma.

> **MAIN CLAUSES JOINED WITH A CONJUNCTION**
> On Saturday Mario went to the American consulate to get a new passport, but the officer told him that replacement passports could not be issued on weekends.

Read the clause after the coordinating conjunction *but*:

> the officer told him that replacement passports could not be issued on weekends

This group of words can stand on its own as a complete sentence. Thus, it is a main clause; place a comma before *but*.

Remember:

1. **Place a comma before the coordinating conjunction (*and, but, for, or, nor, so, yet*) if there are two main clauses.**

2. **Do not use a comma before the coordinating conjunction if there is only one main clause.**

For step-by-step discussion, examples, and practice of this common error, go to **www.ablongman.com/faigley034.**

Do not use a comma to separate a main clause from a restrictive clause or phrase

When clauses and phrases that follow the main clause are essential to the meaning of a sentence, they should not be set off with a comma.

INCORRECT	Sandy plans to borrow Felicia's record collection, while Felicia is on vacation.
CORRECT	Sandy plans to borrow Felicia's record collection while Felicia is on vacation.
INCORRECT	Sandy plans to borrow Felicia's records while Felicia is on vacation, in order to convert them to CDs.
CORRECT	Sandy plans to borrow Felicia's records while Felicia is on vacation in order to convert them to CDs.

Common Errors

Do not use a comma to set off a *because* clause that follows a main clause

Writers frequently place unnecessary commas before *because* and similar subordinate conjunctions that follow a main clause. *Because* is not a coordinating conjunction; thus it should not be set off by a comma unless the comma improves readability.

INCORRECT	I struggled to complete my term papers last year, because I didn't know how to type.
CORRECT	I struggled to complete my term papers last year because I didn't know how to type.

But do use a comma after an introductory *because* clause.

INCORRECT	Because Danny left his red jersey at home Coach Russell benched him.
CORRECT	Because Danny left his red jersey at home, Coach Russell benched him.

Remember: Use a comma after a *because* clause that begins a sentence. Do not use a comma to set off a *because* clause that follows a main clause.

 For step-by-step discussion, examples, and practice of this common error, go to **www.ablongman.com/faigley035**.

EXERCISE 38.2 Decide which of the coordinating conjunctions in the following sentences should be preceded by commas and add them.

> **EXAMPLE** In their heyday, ABBA topped the charts in the United States and Britain ⌃and only Volvo was a bigger export in Sweden.

1. The band ABBA was together only from 1974 to 1982⌃yet their hit "Dancing Queen" is still popular today.

2. ABBA is best know for its music, but the group also made a movie entitled *ABBA— The Movie.*
3. The quartet's two married couples had success as musicians, but not as husbands and wives.
4. After their divorces, group members parted ways and began solo careers.
5. ABBA's songs no longer top the charts, but in 2001 their music was featured in a Broadway musical called *Mamma Mia.*

38c | COMMAS WITH NONRESTRICTIVE MODIFIERS

Imagine that you are sending a friend a group photo that includes your aunt. Which sentence is correct?

In the back row the woman wearing the pink hat is my aunt.

In the back row the woman, wearing the pink hat, is my aunt.

Both sentences can be correct depending on what is in the photo. If there are three women standing in the back row and only one is wearing a pink hat, this piece of information is necessary for identifying your aunt. In this case the sentence without commas is correct because it identifies your aunt as the woman wearing the pink hat. Such necessary modifiers are **restrictive** and do not require commas.

If only one woman is standing in the back row, *wearing the pink hat* is extra information and not necessary to identify your aunt. The modifier in this case is **nonrestrictive** and is set off by commas.

Distinguish restrictive and nonrestrictive modifiers

You can distinguish restrictive and nonrestrictive modifiers by deleting the modifier and then deciding whether the remaining sentence is changed. For example, delete the modifier *still stained by its bloody Tianamen Square crackdown* from the following sentence:

Some members of the Olympic Site Selection Committee wanted to prevent China, **still stained by its bloody Tianamen Square crackdown,** from hosting the 2008 games.

Participle usually ends in "–ing"

The result leaves the meaning of the main clause unchanged.

Some members of the Olympic Site Selection Committee wanted to prevent China from hosting the 2008 games.

The modifier is nonrestrictive and should be set off by commas.

In contrast, deleting *who left work early* does change the meaning of this sentence:

The employees **who left work early** avoided driving home in the blizzard.

Without the modifier the sentence reads:

The employees avoided driving home in the blizzard.

Now it sounds as if all the employees avoided driving home in the blizzard instead of just the ones who left early. The modifier is clearly restrictive and does not require commas.

Recognize types and placement of nonrestrictive modifiers

Nonrestrictive modifiers are used frequently to add details. You can add several kinds of nonrestrictive modifiers to a short, simple sentence (see Sections 32c and 32d).

The student ran across campus,

- which left him panting when he got to class. *[adjective clause]*
- his backpack swaying back and forth. *[absolute phrase]*
- weaving his way down the crowded sidewalks. *[participial phrase]*

Participle →

Nonrestrictive modifiers can be placed at the beginning of sentences.

- When he realized his watch had stopped, *[adverb clause]*
- With his thoughts on the intramural championship later that afternoon, *[prepositional phrase]*
- Rushing to get to class, *[participial phrase]*

the student ran across campus.

They also can be placed in the middle of sentences.

The student,

- who woke up only fifteen minutes before class, *[adjective clause]*
- my old roommate, *[appositive]*
- wearing a ripped black trenchcoat, *[participial phrase]*
- with one arm in a cast and the other clutching a stack of books, *[prepositional phrase]*

ran across campus.

Pay special attention to appositives

Clauses and phrases can be restrictive or nonrestrictive, depending on the context. Often the difference is obvious, but some modifiers require close consideration, especially appositives. An **appositive** is a noun or noun phrase that identifies or adds information to the noun preceding it. Consider the following pair.

1. The best-selling vehicles SUVs usually rate the lowest on fuel efficiency.
2. The best-selling vehicles, SUVs, usually rate the lowest on fuel efficiency.

Which is correct? The appositive *SUVs* is not essential to the meaning of the sentence and offers additional information. Thus, it is a nonrestrictive appositive and should be set off with commas. Sentence 2 is correct.

Here's another pair.

1. Civil rights activist Jesse Jackson runs an organization called the Rainbow Coalition.
2. Civil rights activist, Jesse Jackson, runs an organization called the Rainbow Coalition.

The name *Jesse Jackson* is essential to identify which of the many civil rights activists is under discussion. Thus, it is a restrictive appositive and should not be set off with commas. Sentence 1 is correct.

Use commas around nonrestrictive clauses within a *that* clause

Restrictive clauses beginning with *that* sometimes have a nonrestrictive clause embedded within them.

> INCORRECT   I want you to know that **despite all the arguments we have had over the past few months** I still value your advice.

> CORRECT   I want you to know that **, despite all the arguments we have had over the past few months,** I still value your advice.

Use commas to mark off parenthetical expressions

A **parenthetical expression** provides information or commentary that usually is not essential to the sentence's meaning.

> INCORRECT My mother much to my surprise didn't say anything when she saw my pierced nose.

> CORRECT My mother, much to my surprise, didn't say anything when she saw my pierced nose.

Some parenthetical expressions are essential to the point of the sentence, especially ones that make contrasts, but they too are set off by commas.

> INCORRECT The candidate's conversational skills not her résumé landed her the job.

> CORRECT The candidate's conversational skills, not her résumé, landed her the job.

However, do not use a comma if the parenthetical expression is one word and its function not obviously parenthetical.

> INCORRECT The Freshmen Studies course is, fundamentally, an introduction to writing arguments.

> CORRECT The Freshmen Studies course is fundamentally an introduction to writing arguments.

Use commas to mark off absolute phrases

An **absolute phrase** contains at least one noun or pronoun and at least one participle (see Section 32d). Absolutes can modify a noun or a whole sentence.

INCORRECT	Her project completed Marianne decided to splurge on a beach vacation.
CORRECT	Her project completed, Marianne decided to splurge on a beach vacation.
INCORRECT	Their recess privileges taken away the boys sat slumped in the classroom's uncomfortable chairs.
CORRECT	Their recess privileges taken away, the boys sat slumped in the classroom's uncomfortable chairs.

Common Errors

Commas with *that* and *which* clauses

Writers often confuse when to use commas to set off modifying phrases beginning with *that* and *which*. *That* clauses follow a hard and fast rule: They are used only as restrictive modifiers.

A *THAT* CLAUSE IS A RESTRICTIVE MODIFIER: OMIT COMMAS

Two other women were wearing the same dress that Sherice bought specifically to wear to the awards banquet.

Which clauses are usually used as nonrestrictive modifiers. While *which* clauses can also function as restrictive modifiers, careful writers observe the difference and change *which* to *that* if the clause is restrictive.

A *WHICH* CLAUSE IS A NONRESTRICTIVE MODIFIER: USE COMMAS

A student government committee is recommending the allocation of an additional $10,000 for Black History Month festivities, which take place in February, in order to bring a nationally known speaker to campus.

(continued next page)

WHEN A *WHICH* CLAUSE ACTS AS A RESTRICTIVE MODIFIER CHANGE
WHICH TO *THAT*

INCORRECT   The uncertainty **which** surrounded the selection of the new coach was created by the sudden and unexpected resignation of her predecessor.

CORRECT   The uncertainty **that** surrounded the selection of the new coach was created by the sudden and unexpected resignation of her predecessor.

Remember:
1. *That* clauses are restrictive modifiers and do not take commas.
2. *Which* clauses can be either restrictive or nonrestrictive, but careful writers use them as nonrestrictive modifiers and set them off with commas.

For step-by-step discussion, examples, and practice of this common error, go to **www.ablongman.com/faigley036**.

EXERCISE 38.3 The underlined portions of the following paragraph are modifiers. Identify each modifier as either restrictive or nonrestrictive. Then set off the nonrestrictive modifiers with commas.

EXAMPLE   Marcus Ulpius Traianus ‸ <u>a successful governor and soldier</u> ‸ became emperor of the Roman Empire in the year AD 98. (Nonrestrictive modifier)

Trajan decided to use the Empire's coffers <u>which were brimming with war booty</u> to begin a massive building program. He commissioned the market <u>Mercati Traianei</u> and a lush new forum. In AD 113 he also built a column <u>still on display in Rome today</u> adorned with reliefs depicting his military victories. But the conditions <u>that many Romans faced from day to day</u> stood in stark contrast to the splendor Trajan created. <u>Living in cramped apartment buildings</u> people coped with dark, dirty, and sometimes cold homes.

38d | COMMAS WITH ITEMS IN A SERIES

In a series of three or more items, place a comma after each item but the last one. The comma between the last two items goes before the coordinating conjunction (*and, or, nor, but, so, for, yet*).

> Health officials in Trenton**,** Manhattan**,** and the Bronx have all reported new cases of the West Nile virus.

Writing in the World

Commas between the last two items in a series

Whether you should insert a comma between the last two items in a series depends on what kind of writing you're doing. In newspapers and magazines, the comma is typically omitted; however, academic, business, and professional writing includes a comma before the last series item. Omitting the comma sometimes causes confusion.

JOURNALISTIC CONVENTION

I thank my parents, Robert Pirsig and Harley-Davidson for my outlook on life.

ACADEMIC CONVENTION

I thank my parents, Robert Pirsig **,** and Harley-Davidson for my outlook on life.

EXERCISE 38.4 Insert commas to separate items in a series, following the academic convention. Some sentences may not require commas.

> EXAMPLE   Suburban residents unknowingly spread diseases among deer by feeding them salt⸍ corn ⸍and pellets.

1. White-tailed deer ground squirrels gray squirrels foxes raccoons coyotes opossums and armadillos often wander across my back yard.
2. White-tailed deer and coyotes are among the animals that have adapted best to urban habitats.

3. Deer find cover in urban green belts and thrive on young trees shrubs and flowers that homeowners plant.
4. White-tailed deer reproduce quickly because they have always been prey animals for wolves coyotes mountain lions bobcats and bears.
5. Elimination of predators curtailment of hunting and a high birth rate have led to deer overpopulation in many urban areas.

38e | COMMAS WITH COORDINATE ADJECTIVES

Coordinate adjectives are two or more adjectives that each modify the same noun independent of one another. Coordinate adjectives that are not linked by *and* must be separated by a comma.

After the NASDAQ bubble burst in 2000 and 2001, the Internet technology companies that remain are no longer the **fresh-faced, giddy** kids of Wall Street.

Distinguish coordinate adjectives

You can recognize coordinate adjectives by reversing their order; if their meaning remains the same, the adjectives are coordinate and must be linked by *and* or separated by a comma. In the following example when the order of the adjectives changes, the description of *lifestyles* retains the same meaning:

Because border collies are bred to herd sheep, their energetic temperaments may not suit city dwellers' more **sedentary, staid** lifestyles.

Because border collies are bred to herd sheep, their energetic temperaments may not suit city dwellers' more **staid, sedentary** lifestyles.

Do not use commas to link cumulative adjectives

Commas are not used between cumulative adjectives. Cumulative adjectives are two or more adjectives that work together to modify a noun:

deep blue sea, inexpensive mountain bike. If reversing their order changes the description of the noun (or violates the order of English, such as *mountain inexpensive bike*), the adjectives are cumulative and should not be separated by a comma.

The following example doesn't require a comma in the cumulative adjective series *massive Corinthian.*

Visitors to Rome's Pantheon pass between the **massive Corinthian** columns flanking the front door.

We know they are cumulative because reversing their order to read *Corinthian massive* would alter the way they modify *columns*—in this case, so much so that they no longer make sense.

EXERCISE 38.5 Identify each underlined adjective series as either coordinate or cumulative. Then insert commas to separate coordinate adjectives.

EXAMPLE   Although the eating of pork is prohibited by many religions, the tender⌃succulent meat is the most widely eaten in the world today. (Coordinate)

While an average meat-eating American eats approximately 70 pounds of pork per year, China leads the world in total pork consumption. Prior to 1900 pork was the most popular meat in the United States; however today, the other white meat is less widely eaten than beef. Since no part of the pig goes unused and it can be easily preserved, pork is an economical versatile meat. In addition, the wily resourceful pig can forage for food when its owner cannot provide for it. It seems likely that meat eaters across the globe will continue to enjoy various pork products, like bacon, ham, and sausage, daily.

38f   COMMAS WITH QUOTATIONS

Properly punctuating quotations with commas can be tricky unless you know a few rules about when and where to use commas.

When to use commas with quotations

Commas set off phrases that attribute quotations to a speaker or writer, such as *he argues*, *they said*, and *she writes*.

"When you come to a fork in the road**,**" said Yogi Berra **,** "take it!"

If the attribution follows a quotation that is a complete sentence, replace the period that normally would come at the end of the quotation with a comma.

INCORRECT	"Simplicity of language is not only reputable but perhaps even sacred**.**" writes Kurt Vonnegut.
CORRECT	"Simplicity of language is not only reputable but perhaps even sacred**,**" writes Kurt Vonnegut.

When an attribution is placed in the middle of a quotation, put the comma preceding the attribution within the quotation mark just before the phrase.

INCORRECT	"Nothing is at last sacred**"**, wrote Emerson in his 1841 essay, "but the integrity of your own mind."
CORRECT	"Nothing is at last sacred**,**" wrote Emerson in his 1841 essay, "but the integrity of your own mind."

When not to use commas with quotations

Do not replace a question mark or exclamation point with a comma.

INCORRECT	"Who's on first**,**" Abbott asked Costello.
CORRECT	"Who's on first **?**" Abbott asked Costello.

Not all phrases that mention the author's name are attributions. When quoting a term or using a quotation within a subordinate clause, do not set off the quotation with commas.

"Stonewall ❡" Jackson gained his nickname at the First Battle of Bull Run when General Barnard Bee shouted to his men that ❡ "Jackson is standing like a stone wall."

Even a quotation that is a complete sentence can be used in a subordinate clause. Such quotations should not be set off with commas. Pay special attention to quotations preceded by *that*, *which*, and *because*; these words are the most common indicators of a subordinate clause.

> It was Benjamin Franklin's conviction that "Those who would give up essential liberty to purchase a little temporary safety deserve neither liberty nor safety."

EXERCISE 38.6 Proofread the following paragraph for errors in comma usage with quotations. Some are used correctly. Cross out unnecessary commas, move misplaced commas, and add omitted commas.

EXAMPLE   When inspecting a painting for authenticity, try looking for an angle that catches the glare of lights. "You will not be able to see what the paintings show," asserts author James Elkins, "but you'll get a good look at the *craquelure.*"

Craquelure is "the fine network of cracks that scores the surface of . . . paintings" (Elkins 20). Elkins explains that "few museum visitors realize how many paintings have been seriously damaged" and goes on to list possible hazards, such as damage by "fire, water, vandalism, or just the wear and tear of the centuries" (20). Not all cracks are signs of legitimate age; indeed, "Counterfeiters have faked cracks by putting paintings in ovens, and they have even rubbed ink in the cracks to make them look old" (Elkins 22). Though cracks often happen with mishandling, Elkins explains that, "most cracks in paintings that are not caused by accidents are due to the flexing of the canvas or the slow warping of the wood" (22). If you are serious about art history, you may want to learn how to read the cracks in art work. "*Craquelure* is not a hard-and-fast method of classifying paintings," admits Elkins, "but it comes close" (24).

38g COMMAS WITH DATES, NUMBERS, TITLES, AND ADDRESSES

Some of the easiest comma rules to remember are the ones we use every day in dates, numbers, personal titles, place names, direct address, and brief interjections.

Commas with dates

Use commas to separate the day of the week from the month and to set off a year from the rest of the sentence.

March 25, 1942
Monday, November 18, 2002
On October 1, 2003, Ray Charles plans to release his next album.

Do not use a comma when the month immediately precedes the year.

12 June 1988
April 2003

Commas with numbers

Commas mark off thousands, millions, billions, and so on.

16,500,000

However, do not use commas in street addresses or page numbers.

page 1542
7602 Elm Street

Commas with personal titles

When a title follows a person's name, set the title off with commas.

Roy Jones, Jr.
Marcus Welby, M.D.

Jackie Hart, Vice President for Operations, reported that her company's earnings are far ahead of projections.

Commas with place names

Place a comma between street addresses, city names, state names, and countries.

Poughkeepsie, New York

Lima, Peru

Write to the president at 1600 Pennsylvania Avenue, Washington, DC 20500.

Commas in direct address

When addressing someone directly, set off that person's name in commas.

I was happy to get your letter yesterday, Jamie.

Yes, Virginia, there is a Santa Claus.

Commas with brief interjections

Use commas to set off brief interjections like *yes* and *no*, as well as short questions that fall at the ends of sentences.

The director said that, no, the understudy will not have to stand in for the lead tonight.

Have another piece of pie, won't you?

EXERCISE 38.7 The fictional business letter that follows on page 686 is missing commas with dates, numbers, personal titles, place names, direct addresses, and brief interjections. Insert commas where they are needed.

Mazaces' Headquarters
Cairo Egypt
December 13 332 BC

Parmenio
Commander of Syria
Damascus Syria

Dear Parmenio:

Thank you for your latest correspondence dated December 9 332 BC. I am pleased to hear the streets of Damascus remain quiet since our arrival in October 333 and that mighty Syria has adjusted herself to our presence.

To other matters. I write to request 4,000 of your most rested troops be sent to Egypt to arrive no later than January 1 331 BC. The fighting in Gaza was bitter and our enemy merciless; my soldiers are tired and need to recuperate before marching westward.

I busy myself with the construction of the city of Alexandria. Address future correspondence to 12 Conquest Avenue Alexandria where I will soon move in order to oversee the construction directly. Deinocrates head architect has seen to every detail, but of course detail requires time. I remain here until the spring when I intend for our armies to reunite and travel west to Thapsacus Mesopotamia where we will meet Darius King of Persia and secure his defeat for our mutual triumph and to the glory of Greece.

Sincerely,
Alexander the Great (Alex)

38h | COMMAS TO AVOID CONFUSION

Certain sentences can confuse readers if you do not indicate where they should pause within the sentence. Use a comma to guide a reader through these usually compact constructions.

UNCLEAR	With supplies low prices of gasoline and fuel oil will increase.

This sentence could be read as meaning *With supplies, low prices will increase.*

CLEAR	With supplies low, prices of gasoline and fuel oil will increase.

EXERCISE 38.8 Some of the sentences in the following paragraph are confusing because they lack clarifying commas. Add commas where readers need more clues about how to read the sentences.

EXAMPLE	Using new ways of dating, scientists can now apply multiple techniques to determine an object's age.

Because geologists used both radiometric and fossil dating, we now know that the Colorado River only started carving the Grand Canyon five or six million years ago. Scientists were able to accurately date the Shroud of Turin, believed by many Catholics to be Christ's burial covering, to between AD1260 and 1390. This particular example of carbon dating challenged some believers to weigh faith against science. The mysterious Sphinx, stands before the pyramid of Khafre, dated using the "star method." Scientists determined that the Sphinx and its host pyramid are approximately seventy years younger than was originally believed.

38i UNNECESSARY COMMAS

Do not place a comma between a subject and predicate

INCORRECT	American children of immigrant parents, often do not speak their parents' native language.
CORRECT	American children of immigrant parents often do not speak their parents' native language.

However, you do use commas to set off modifying phrases that separate subjects from verbs.

> **INCORRECT** Steven Pinker author of *The Language Instinct* argues that the ability to speak and understand language is an evolutionary adaptive trait.

> **CORRECT** Steven Pinker**,** author of *The Language Instinct***,** argues that the ability to speak and understand language is an evolutionary adaptive trait.

Do not use a comma with a coordinating conjunction unless it joins two main clauses

> **INCORRECT** Susana thought finishing her first novel was hard**,** but soon learned that getting a publisher to buy it was much harder.

> **CORRECT** Susana thought finishing her first novel was hard but soon learned that getting a publisher to buy it was much harder.

> **CORRECT** Susana thought finishing her first novel was hard**,** but **she** soon learned that getting a publisher to buy it was much harder.

Do not use a comma after a subordinating conjunction such as *although, despite*, or *while*

> **INCORRECT** Although**,** soccer is gaining popularity in the States, it will never be as popular as football or baseball.

> **CORRECT** Although soccer is gaining popularity in the States, it will never be as popular as football or baseball.

Do not use a comma before *than*

Some writers mistakenly use a comma with *than* to try to heighten the contrast in a comparison.

INCORRECT   Any teacher will tell you that acquiring critical think-ing skills is more important**,** than simply memorizing information.

CORRECT   Any teacher will tell you that acquiring critical think-ing skills is more important than simply memorizing information.

Do not use a comma before a list

A common mistake is to place a comma after *such as* or *like* before in-troducing a list.

INCORRECT   Many hourly workers, such as**,** waiters, dishwashers, and cashiers, do not receive health benefits from their employers.

CORRECT   Many hourly workers, such as waiters, dishwashers, and cashiers, do not receive health benefits from their employers.

Chapter 39

Semicolons and Colons

Semicolons and colons are punctuation marks that link closely related ideas. They allow writers to emphasize the relationships between elements of a sentence, often using dramatic pauses to direct readers' attention to the most important ideas. Notice how semicolons and colons direct our attention in the following examples:

> "My life has been incredible**;** I don't believe a word of it," wrote Katherine Anne Porter.

> Will Rogers said, "I do not belong to any organized political party**:** I'm a Democrat."

39a | SEMICOLONS WITH CLOSELY RELATED MAIN CLAUSES

Why use semicolons? Sometimes we want to join two main clauses to form a complete sentence in order to indicate their close relationship. We can connect them with a comma and a coordinating conjunction like *or*, *but*, or *and*. However, using those constructions too often can make your writing cumbersome. Instead you can omit the comma and coordinating conjunction, and insert a semicolon between the two clauses.

Semicolons can join only clauses that are grammatically equal. In other words, they join main clauses only to other main clauses, not to phrases or subordinate clauses. Look at the following examples:

INCORRECT

————————————— MAIN CLAUSE —————————————
Gloria's new weightlifting program will help her recover
————————————— PARTICIPIAL PHRASE —————————————
from knee surgery; doing a series of squats and presses

with a physical therapist.

INCORRECT

————————————— MAIN CLAUSE —————————————
Gloria's new weightlifting program will help her regain
————————————— SUBORDINATE CLAUSE —————————————
strength in her knee; which required surgery after she

injured it skiing.

CORRECT

————————————— MAIN CLAUSE —————————————
Gloria's new weightlifting program will help her recover
————————————— MAIN CLAUSE —————————————
from knee surgery; a physical therapist leads her through

a series of squats and presses.

Common Errors

Main clauses connected with conjunctive adverbs and transitional phrases

Closely related main clauses sometimes use a conjunctive adverb (such as *however, therefore, moreover, furthermore, thus, meanwhile, nonetheless, otherwise, rather*; see the list in Section 38a) or a transition (*in fact, for example, that is, for instance, in addition, in other words, on the other hand, even so*) to indicate the relationship between them. When the second clause begins with a conjunctive adverb or a transition, a semicolon is needed to join the two clauses. This sentence pattern is frequently used; therefore, it pays to learn how to punctuate it correctly.

INCORRECT
(COMMA SPLICE)

The police and city officials want to crack down on drug use at raves, however, their efforts have been unsuccessful so far.

CORRECT

The police and city officials want to crack down on drug use at raves; however, their efforts have been unsuccessful so far.

(continued next page)

The semicolon separates the second main clause from the first. Note that a comma is also needed to separate *however* from the rest of the second clause.

INCORRECT
(COMMA SPLICE)
The poster design left much to be desired**,** for example, the title was printed in garish red, orange, and green.

CORRECT
The poster design left much to be desired**;** for example**,** the title was printed in garish red, orange, and green.

Note that in addition to the semicolon, a comma separates *for example* from the rest of the second clause.

Remember: Main clauses that use a conjunctive adverb or a transitional phrase require a semicolon to join the clauses.

 For step-by-step discussion, examples, and practice of this common error, go to **www.ablongman.com/faigley037.**

Do not use a semicolon to introduce quotations

Use a comma or colon instead.

INCORRECT
Robert Frost's poem "Mending Wall" contains this line **;** "Good fences make good neighbors."

CORRECT
Robert Frost's poem "Mending Wall" contains this line **:** "Good fences make good neighbors."

Do not use a semicolon to introduce lists

INCORRECT
William Shakespeare wrote four romance plays at the end of his career **;** *The Tempest, The Winter's Tale, Cymbeline,* and *Pericles.*

CORRECT   William Shakespeare wrote four romance plays at the end of his career : *The Tempest, The Winter's Tale, Cymbeline,* and *Pericles.*

39b │ SEMICOLONS TOGETHER WITH COMMAS

When an item in a series already includes a comma, adding more commas to separate it from the other items will only confuse the reader. Use semicolons instead of commas between items in a series that have internal punctuation.

CONFUSING   The church's design competition drew entries from as far away as Gothenberg , Sweden , Caracas , Venezuela , and Athens , Greece.

CLEARER   The church's design competition drew entries from as far away as Gothenberg, Sweden ; Caracas, Venezuela ; and Athens, Greece.

EXERCISE 39.1 Decide where semicolons should go in the following paragraph. Add any semicolons that would repair run-on sentences, fix comma splices, or clarify a list. Also eliminate any incorrectly used semicolons and insert the correct punctuation.

EXAMPLE   In the summer of 1947 a flying object crashed in eastern New Mexico ‸the incident feeds speculation that the government hides evidence of UFOs.

The media reported that the wreckage of a flying saucer had been discovered on a ranch near Roswell, military spokespeople came up with another explanation. They asserted that the flying saucer was actually a balloon, people stationed at the base, however, reported seeing unidentifiable bodies removed from the wreckage. Initially even UFO enthusiasts believed the government's reports; which seemed plausible at the time. The Air Force has declared the case closed they stated that the bodies at the crash sites were test dummies. Roswell, New Mexico joins the list of rumored

UFO hot spots that includes Delphos, Kansas, Marshall County, Minnesota, Westchester, New York, and Gulf Breeze, Florida.

39c | COLONS IN SENTENCES

Like semicolons, colons can join two closely related main clauses (complete sentences). Colons indicate that what follows will explain or expand on what comes before the colon. Use a colon in cases where the second main clause interprets or sums up the first.

> Internet retailers have a limited customer base: Only those who have Internet access can become e-shoppers.

You may choose to capitalize the first word of the main clause following the colon or leave it lowercase. Either is correct as long as you are consistent throughout your text.

Colons linking main clauses with appositives

A colon calls attention to an appositive, a noun, or a noun phrase that renames the noun preceding it. If you're not certain whether a colon would be appropriate, put *namely* in its place. If *namely* makes sense when you read the main clause followed by the appositive, you probably need to insert a colon instead of a comma. Remember, the clause that precedes the colon must be a complete sentence.

> I know the perfect person for the job, **namely** me.

The sentence makes sense with *namely* placed before the appositive. Thus, a colon is appropriate.

> I know the perfect person for the job: me.

Never capitalize a word following a colon unless the word starts a complete sentence or is normally capitalized (see Section 45a).

Colons joining main clauses with quotations

Use a colon to link a main clause and a quotation that interprets or sums up the clause. Be careful not to use a colon to link a phrase with a quotation.

INCORRECT: NOUN PHRASE–COLON–QUOTATION

President Roosevelt's strategy to change the nation's panicky attitude during the Great Depression **:** "We have nothing to fear," he said, "but fear itself."

CORRECT: MAIN CLAUSE–COLON–QUOTATION

President Roosevelt's strategy to end the Great Depression was to change the nation's panicky attitude **:** "We have nothing to fear," he said, "but fear itself."

Also, a colon is often used after a main clause to introduce an indented block quotation (see Section 20c).

Writing in the World

Punctuation following quotations

Writing often requires quoting someone else's words. Use the correct sequence of punctuation marks when sharing a quotation with readers.

PLACE SEMICOLONS AND COLONS OUTSIDE QUOTATION MARKS

Commas and periods that come after a quotation sit inside the quotation marks. The rule is different, however, for semicolons and colons: They sit outside the quotation marks. Because commas and periods always appear inside the quotation marks, semicolons and colons may seem incorrectly placed if you don't know that they follow a different rule.

PUT COMMAS AND PERIODS INSIDE THE QUOTATION MARKS

"The length of a film **,"** said Alfred Hitchcock, "should be directly related to the endurance of the human bladder."

PUT SEMICOLONS OUTSIDE QUOTATION MARKS

Chicago mayor Richard Daley said, "The police are not here to create disorder. They're here to preserve disorder **";** his misstatement hit at the truth underlying the violent treatment of protestors at the 1968 Democratic Convention.

(continued next page)

PUT COLONS OUTSIDE QUOTATION MARKS

"I believe, absolutely, that if you do not break out in that sweat of fear when you write, then you have not gone far enough ": Dorothy Allison reassures would-be writers that they can begin on guts alone.

Remember: Little dogs (commas, periods) sleep in the house. Big dogs (semicolons, colons) sleep outside.

For more on using quotation marks correctly, see Chapter 43.

39d | COLONS WITH LISTS

Use a colon to join a main clause to a list. The main clauses in these cases sometimes include the phrases *the following* or *as follows*. Remember that a colon cannot join a phrase or an incomplete clause to a list.

INCORRECT: NOUN PHRASE–COLON–LIST
Three posters decorating Juan's apartment: an old Santana concert poster, a view of Mount Rainier, and a Diego Rivera mural.

CORRECT: MAIN CLAUSE–COLON–LIST
Juan bought three posters to decorate his apartment: an old Santana concert poster, a view of Mount Rainier, and a Diego Rivera mural.

INCORRECT: INCOMPLETE CLAUSE–COLON–LIST
Volunteers aid biologists in: erosion control, trail maintenance, tree planting, and clean-up.

CORRECT: MAIN CLAUSE WITHOUT A COLON
Volunteers aid biologists in erosion control, trail maintenance, tree planting, and clean-up.

Common Errors

Colons misused with lists

Some writers think that anytime they introduce a list, they should insert a colon. Colons are used correctly only when a complete sentence precedes the colon.

INCORRECT	Jessica's entire wardrobe for her trip to Cancun included **:** two swimsuits, one pair of shorts, two T-shirts, a party dress, and a pair of sandals.
CORRECT	Jessica's entire wardrobe for her trip to Cancun included two swimsuits, one pair of shorts, two T-shirts, a party dress, and a pair of sandals.
CORRECT	Jessica jotted down what she would need for her trip **:** two swimsuits, one pair of shorts, two T-shirts, a party dress, and a pair of sandals.

Remember: A colon should be placed only after a clause that can stand by itself as a sentence.

 For step-by-step discussion, examples, and practice of this common error, go to **www.ablongman.com/faigley039.**

EXERCISE 39.2 Decide where colons should go in the following sentences; add any that are necessary. Eliminate any incorrectly used colons and insert correct punctuation.

EXAMPLE Sandra Cisneros has written a number of books, including ꞉ *My Wicked, Wicked Ways; Woman Hollering Creek;* and the acclaimed novel, *The House on Mango Street.*

1. *The House on Mango Street* tells the story of a Mexican-American girl who has a telling name, Esperanza (Hope).
2. Because *The House on Mango Street* consists of forty-four short vignettes, critics disagree on the book's genre, autobiography, short story, novel, or poetry.
3. Whatever its genre, *The House on Mango Street* has attracted the attention of feminist and Chicano literary critics both groups appreciate the complex portrayal of racism and sexism from a young girl's perspective.
4. Cisneros dedicates the novel to women of the barrio whose stories she wants to tell "For the ones I left behind, for the ones who cannot get out."

Chapter 40

Hyphens

Hyphens are handy punctuation marks when you want to link words or parts of words. They often give the reader clues about the meaning of a word or sentence. See how a hyphen would clarify the meaning of the word *coop* in the following example.

> This afternoon I'm going to the **coop** to get some eggs.

Is the speaker going to a *chicken coop* or a *grocery co-op* (short for co-operative)? A hyphen indicates a trip to the grocery store:

> This afternoon I'm going to the **co-op** to get some eggs.

Hyphens (-) are frequently confused with dashes (–), which are similar but longer. Dashes are used to separate phrases. Hyphens are used to join words.

40a   HYPHENS WITH COMPOUND MODIFIERS

When to hyphenate
Hyphenate a compound modifier that precedes a noun.

When a compound modifier precedes a noun, you should usually hyphenate the modifier. A compound modifier consists of words that join together as a unit to modify a noun. Since the first word modifies the second, compound modifiers will not make sense if the word order is reversed.

middle-class values	self-fulfilling prophecy
best-selling novel	tough-minded friend
well-known musician	ill-mannered child

Hyphenate a phrase when it is used as a modifier that precedes a noun.

out-of-body experience   step-by-step instructions
all-you-can-eat buffet   all-or-nothing payoff
devil-may-care attitude   over-the-counter drug

Hyphenate the prefixes *pro-*, *anti-*, *post-*, *pre-*, *neo-*, and *mid-* before proper nouns.

pro-Catholic sentiment   mid-Atlantic states
neo-Nazi racism   anti-NAFTA protests
pre-Columbian art   post-Freudian theory

Hyphenate a compound modifier with a number when it precedes a noun.

eighteenth-century drama   one-way street
tenth-grade class   47-minute swim

When not to hyphenate

Do not hyphenate a compound modifier that follows a noun.

Avoid using hyphens in compound modifiers when they come after the noun.

The instructor's approach is student centered.
Among country music fans Lyle Lovett is well known.

Do not hyphenate compound modifiers when the first word is *very* or ends in *ly*.

newly recorded data   very cold day
freshly painted bench   very jolly baby

Do not hyphenate chemical terms.

calcium chloride base   hydrochloric acid solution

Do not hyphenate foreign terms used as adjectives.

     a priori decision   *post hoc* fallacy

EXERCISE 40.1 In the following sentences, decide where hyphens should be placed. Some sentences may require more than one hyphen and some sentences may need hyphens deleted.

> EXAMPLE   Since there are few clear enemies of the state in the post Soviet era, political parties lack a galvanizing issue.

1. Some people consider the Electoral College to be un democratic.
2. Independent candidates are often viewed as fly by night long shots with little-or-no hope of winning positions of power.
3. The tension surrounding the five week wait for the 2000 presidential election results was palpable.
4. Mudslinging political ads are becoming more common.
5. Local candidates' political debates are rarely considered important enough to interrupt regularly scheduled programming.
6. Candidates with *laissez faire* economic policies are often popular with large corporations, which in turn make substantial donations to the candidates with favorable platforms.

40b   HYPHENS WITH COMPOUND NOUNS

A compound noun is made up of two or more words that work together to form one noun. You cannot change the order of words in a compound noun or remove a word without altering the noun's meaning. No universal rule guides the use of hyphens with compound nouns; the best way to determine whether a compound noun is hyphenated is to check the dictionary.

SOME HYPHENATED COMPOUND NOUNS

T-shirt	one-bagger	time-out
sister-in-law	heart-to-heart	baby-sitter
play-by-play	speed-reading	run-through

SOME COMPOUND NOUNS THAT ARE NOT HYPHENATED

picture window	oneself	time zone
hedgehog	heartland	baby boom
open house	speed of light	playbook

While there's no set rule for all cases of compound nouns, some prefixes and suffixes that commonly require hyphens are *ex-*, *all-*, and *self-* and the suffix *-elect*.

All-American	president-elect
self-conscious	ex-employee

Common Errors

Hyphens with numbers

Whole numbers between twenty-one and ninety-nine are hyphenated when they are written as words.

INCORRECT	twentysix
CORRECT	twenty-six
INCORRECT	sixteen-hundred
CORRECT	sixteen hundred
INCORRECT	fiftytwo
CORRECT	fifty-two

Also, hyphens connect the numerators and denominators in most fractions.

The glass is one-half full.

A few fractions used as nouns, especially fractions of time, distance, and area, do not take hyphens.

A half century passed before the mistake was uncovered.

(continued next page)

Remember: Numbers between twenty-one and ninety-nine and most fractions are hyphenated when written as words.

For step-by-step discussion, examples, and practice of this common error, go to **www.ablongman.com/faigley040.**

40c | HYPHENS THAT DIVIDE WORDS AT THE ENDS OF LINES

A hyphen can show that a word is completed on the next line. Hyphens divide words only between syllables.

The Jackson family waited out the tornado in their storm cellar.

Unless you have a special reason for dividing words at the ends of lines, you should not hyphenate. One special situation might be the need to fit as much text as possible on each line of the narrow columns in a newsletter format. Another might be the need to fit text inside the cells of a table.

Writing in the World

Automatic hyphenation

Word processing programs, including Microsoft Word, allow automatic hyphenation of your document. Hyphenations that break words at the ends of lines are common in newspaper and magazine articles that are printed in narrow columns. However, this use of hyphens is rarely necessary in academic papers. Unless you are creating a brochure or other document with narrow columns, leave the automatic hyphenation turned off.

40d | HYPHENS FOR CLARITY

Certain words, often ones with the prefixes *anti-*, *re-*, and *pre-*, can be confusing without hyphens. Adding hyphens to such words will show the reader where to pause to pronounce them correctly.

The courts are in much need of **repair**.

The doubles final will **re-pair** the sister team of Venus and Serena Williams.

Reform in court procedure is necessary to bring cases quickly to trial.

The thunderclouds **re-formed** after the hard rain, threatening another deluge.

Chapter 41

Dashes and Parentheses

Dashes and parentheses can be excellent tools for setting off and calling attention to information that comments on your ideas. They serve as visual cues to the reader of a sudden break in thought or change in sentence structure. Both should be used sparingly. Too-numerous parentheses and dashes indicate that the writer needs to work harder to integrate ideas.

41a DASHES AND PARENTHESES VERSUS COMMAS

Like commas, parentheses and dashes enclose material that adds, explains, or digresses. However, the three punctuation marks are not interchangeable. The mark you choose depends on how much emphasis you want to place on the material. Dashes indicate the most emphasis. Parentheses offer somewhat less, and commas offer less still.

COMMAS INDICATE A MODERATE LEVEL OF EMPHASIS
Bill covered the new tattoo on his bicep, a pouncing tiger, because he thought it might upset our mother.

PARENTHESES LEND A GREATER LEVEL OF EMPHASIS
I'm afraid to go bungee jumping (though my brother tells me it's less frightening than a roller coaster).

DASHES INDICATE THE HIGHEST LEVEL OF EMPHASIS, AND SOMETIMES, SURPRISE AND DRAMA
Christina felt as though she had been punched in the gut; she could hardly believe the stranger at her door was really who he claimed to be—the brother she hadn't seen in twenty years.

EXERCISE 41.1 Look at the modifying phrases that are underlined in the following paragraph. Use commas, parentheses, or dashes to set them off, based on the level of emphasis you want to create.

EXAMPLE   Coffee, one of the most significant crops of all time, has its origins in Africa (like so many other cornerstones of civilization).

Coffea arabica the official name for the bean was made popular in Yemen. The Shadhili Sufi used coffee to inspire visions and to stimulate ecstatic trances making coffee drinking a spiritual experience. The use of the beverage spread largely through other Muslims the Sufi had contact with, and by 1500 it was well known throughout the Arab world. Cafes originated in the Middle East. These early cafes one of the few secular public spaces Muslims could congregate were seen as subversive.

41b DASHES AND PARENTHESES TO SET OFF INFORMATION

Dashes and parentheses call attention to groups of words. In effect, they tell the reader that a group of words is not part of the main clause and should be given extra attention. Compare the following sentences.

When Shanele's old college roommate, Traci, picked her up at the airport in a new car, a Lexus SC 430 convertible, she knew that Traci's finances had changed for the better.

When Shanele's old college roommate, Traci, picked her up at the airport in a new car (a Lexus SC 430 convertible), she knew that Traci's finances had changed for the better.

When Shanele's old college roommate, Traci, picked her up at the airport in a new car—a Lexus SC 430 convertible—she knew that Traci's finances had changed for the better.

The Lexus SC 430 convertible is weighted differently in these three sentences because of punctuation. In the first, it is the name of the car. But in the third, it's as if an exclamation point were added—a Lexus SC 430 convertible!

The lesson here is simple enough. If you want to make an element stand out, especially in the middle of a sentence, use parentheses or dashes instead of commas.

Dashes with final elements

A dash is often used to set off an element at the end of a sentence that offers significant comments about the main clause. This construction is a favorite of newscasters, who typically pause for a long moment where the dash would be inserted in writing.

> The *Titanic* sank just before midnight on April 14, 1912, at a cost of over 1,500 lives—a tragedy that could have been prevented easily by reducing speed in dangerous waters, providing adequate lifeboat space, and maintaining a full-time radio watch.

Dashes can also anticipate a shift in tone at the end of a sentence.

> A full-sized SUV can take you wherever you want to go in style—if your idea of style is a gas-guzzling tank.

Parentheses with additional information

Parentheses are more often used for identifying information, afterthoughts or asides, examples, and clarifications. You can place full sentences, fragments, or brief terms within parentheses.

> Some argue that SUVs (the best-selling vehicles on the market for three years running) are the primary cause of recent gas shortages.

Common Errors

Do not use dashes as periods

Do not use dashes to separate two main clauses (clauses that can stand as complete sentences). Use dashes to separate main clauses from subordinate clauses and phrases when you want to emphasize the subordinate clause or phrase.

> INCORRECT: MAIN CLAUSE–DASH–MAIN CLAUSE
> I was one of the few women in my computer science classes—most of the students majoring in computer science at that time were men.

> CORRECT: MAIN CLAUSE–DASH–PHRASE
> I was one of the few women in computer science—a field then dominated by men.

Remember: Dashes are not periods and should not be used as periods.

 For step-by-step discussion, examples, and practice of this common error, go to **www.ablongman.com/faigley041.**

EXERCISE 41.2 Insert dashes and parentheses in the following sentences to set off information.

> EXAMPLE Naples⌐founded by the Greeks, enlarged by the Romans, and ruled later by the Normans, Hohenstaufen, French, and Spanish⌐is one of the few European cities where the links to the ancient world remain evident.

1. Naples is a dirty and noisy metropolis in a spectacular setting a city that sprawls around the Bay of Naples with Mount Vesuvius at its back facing out to the islands of Procida, Ischia, and Capri.

2. The most famous eruption of Mt. Vesuvius the eruption that destroyed Pompeii and Herculaneum occurred in AD 79.
3. The eruption came so suddenly that Pompeii was stopped in time carbonized loaves of bread still in the oven.
4. The minor details in Pompeii graffiti scrawled on the walls give the city a living presence.
5. Herculaneum also known as Ercolano to the west of Pompeii was buried by a mudslide in the same eruption.

41c OTHER PUNCTUATION WITH PARENTHESES

Parentheses with numbers or letters that order items in a series

Parentheses around letters or numbers that order a series within a sentence make the list easier to read.

Angela Creider's recipe for becoming a great novelist is to **(1)** set aside an hour during the morning to write, **(2)** read what you've written out loud, **(3)** revise your prose, and **(4)** repeat every morning for the next thirty years.

Parentheses with abbreviations

Abbreviations made from the first letters of words are often used in place of the unwieldy names of institutions, departments, organizations, or terms. In order to show the reader what the abbreviation stands for, the first time it appears in a text the writer must state the complete name, followed by the abbreviation in parentheses.

The University of California, Santa Cruz **(UCSC)** supports its mascot, the banana slug, with pride and a sense of humor. And although it sounds strange to outsiders, UCSC students are even referred to as "the banana slugs."

Parentheses with in-text citations

The various documentation styles require that information quoted, paraphrased, or summarized from an outside source be indicated with a research citation. In several of the styles, including MLA (see Chapter 21) and APA (see Chapter 23), the citation is enclosed in parentheses.

> E. B. White's advice on writing style is to use your natural voice **(**Strunk and White 70**)**.

Common Errors

Using periods, commas, colons, and semicolons with parentheses

When an entire sentence is enclosed in parentheses, place the period before the closing parenthesis.

INCORRECT	Our fear of sharks, heightened by movies like *Jaws*, is vastly out of proportion with the minor threat sharks actually pose. **(**Dying from a dog attack, in fact, is much more likely than dying from a shark attack**)**.
CORRECT	Our fear of sharks, heightened by movies like *Jaws*, is vastly out of proportion with the minor threat sharks actually pose. **(**Dying from a dog attack, in fact, is much more likely than dying from a shark attack.**)**

When the material in parentheses is part of the sentence and the parentheses fall at the end of the sentence, place the period outside the closing parenthesis.

INCORRECT	Reports of sharks attacking people are rare **(**much rarer than dog attacks.**)**
CORRECT	Reports of sharks attacking people are rare **(**much rarer than dog attacks**)**.

(continued next page)

Place commas, colons, and semicolons after the closing parenthesis.

INCORRECT   Although newspaper editors generally prize concise letters to the editor, **(**the shorter the better**)** they will occasionally print longer letters that are unusually eloquent.

CORRECT   Although newspaper editors generally prize concise letters to the editor **(**the shorter the better**)**, they will occasionally print longer letters that are unusually eloquent.

Remember: When an entire sentence is enclosed in parentheses, place the period inside the closing parenthesis; otherwise, put the punctuation outside the closing parenthesis.

For step-by-step discussion, examples, and practice of this common error, go to **www.ablongman.com/faigley042**.

EXERCISE 41.3 Decide where to add parentheses in the following sentences. Be careful to place them correctly in relation to other punctuation marks.

EXAMPLE   Performing at the Grand Ole Opry (broadcast from
Nashville, Tennessee) was the ultimate professional
goal of all country and western hopefuls.

1. To get on the show, an artist had to have 1 style, 2 twang, and 3 the Nashville sound.
2. The Grand Ole Opry GOO began under the name Barn Dance in 1925.
3. Historians place the Grand Ole Opry firmly within the tradition of early twentieth-century vaudeville Stambler and Landon 274.
4. The first performer was bearded fiddler Uncle Jimmy Thompson. Uncle Jimmy died in 1931.
5. In the late 1960s GOO constructed a new amphitheater complete with 4,000 seats, which became the main attraction at Opryland.

41d │ OTHER PUNCTUATION WITH DASHES

Dashes with a series of items

Dashes can set off a series. They are especially appropriate when the series comes in the middle of a sentence or when the series simply elaborates on what comes before it without changing the essential meaning of the sentence. Normally commas enclose nonessential clauses; however, placing commas around items separated by commas would confuse readers about where the list begins and ends.

> Baseball journeyman Glenallen Hill pulled off the highlight of his career when he hit for the cycle—a single, a double, a triple, and a home run—in last night's game against the White Sox.

Dashes with interrupted speech

Dashes also indicate that a speaker has broken off in the middle of a statement.

> "Why did everybody get so quiet all of a—"; Silvia stopped in her tracks when she noticed that the customer had a pistol pointed at the clerk.

Writing in the World

Dashes in formal writing

A common misconception about dashes is that they are not appropriate for formal writing tasks like academic papers or business letters. Dashes can lend a sense of informality to certain sentences, especially when they set off information at the end of a sentence. But they can also be effective when used sparingly in writing that requires a more formal tone.

> "Unfortunately, moral beauty in art—like physical beauty in a person—is extremely perishable."
>
> —Susan Sontag, *Against Interpretation*

Common Errors

The art of typing a dash

Although dashes and hyphens look similar, they are actually different marks. The distinction is small but important because dashes and hyphens serve different purposes. A dash is a line twice as long as a hyphen. If you're using a typewriter, indicate a dash by typing two hyphens side by side. Most word processing programs will create a dash automatically when you type two hyphens together. Or you can type a special character to make a dash. Your manual will tell you which keys to press to make a dash.

Do not put any spaces between a dash or a hyphen and the words that come before and after it. Likewise, if you are using two hyphens to indicate a dash, do not put any spaces between the hyphens.

INCORRECT   A well – timed effort at conserving water may prevent long – term damage to drought – stricken farms – – if it's not already too late.

CORRECT   A well-timed effort at conserving water may prevent long-term damage to drought-stricken farms—if it's not already too late.

Remember: Do not put spaces before or after hyphens and dashes.

For step-by-step discussion, examples, and practice of this common error, go to **www.ablongman.com/faigley043**.

Chapter 42

Apostrophes

Apostrophes have three basic functions: to indicate possession, to mark contractions and omitted letters, and to form certain plurals.

42a POSSESSIVES

Nouns and indefinite pronouns (e.g., *everyone, anyone*) that indicate possession or ownership are in the **possessive case**. The possessive case is marked by attaching an apostrophe and an *-s* or an apostrophe only to the end of the word.

Singular nouns and indefinite pronouns

For singular nouns and indefinite pronouns, add an apostrophe plus *-s: -'s.* Even singular nouns that end in *-s* usually follow this principle.

Iris**'s** coat
everyone**'s** favorite
a woman**'s** choice
today**'s** news
the team**'s** equipment

There are a few exceptions to adding *-'s* for singular nouns:

- **Awkward pronunciations** *Herodotus' travels, Jesus' sermons*

- **Official names of certain places, institutions, companies** *Governors Island, Teachers College of Columbia University, Mothers Café, Saks Fifth Avenue, Walgreens Pharmacy.* Note, however, that many companies do include the apostrophe: *Denny's Restaurant, Macy's, McDonald's, Wendy's Old Fashioned Hamburgers.*

Plural nouns

For plural nouns that do not end in *-s*, add an apostrophe plus *-s*: *-'s*.

women**'s** rights
media**'s** responsibility
children**'s** section

For plural nouns that end in *-s*, add only an apostrophe at the end.

dancers**'** costumes
attorneys**'** briefs
the Kennedys**'** legacy

Compound nouns

For compound nouns, add an apostrophe plus *-s* to the last word: *-'s*.

my mother-in-law**'s** house
mayor of Cleveland**'s** speech

Two or more nouns

For joint possession, add an apostrophe plus *-s* to the final noun: *-'s*.

mother and dad**'s** yard
Ben & Jerry**'s** Ice Cream

When people possess or own things separately, add an apostrophe plus *-s* to each noun: *-'s*.

Roberto**'s** and Edward**'s** views are totally opposed.
Dominique**'s**, Sally**'s**, and Vinatha**'s** cars all need new tires.

Common Errors

Possessive forms of personal pronouns never take the apostrophe

INCORRECT   *her's, it's, our's, your's, their's*

The bird sang in it**'s** cage.

CORRECT   *hers, its, ours, yours, theirs*

The bird sang in it**s** cage.

Remember: It's = It is

For step-by-step discussion, examples, and practice of this common error, go to **www.ablongman.com/faigley044.**

EXERCISE 42.1 The apostrophes have been omitted from the following paragraph. Insert apostrophes in the appropriate places to indicate possession.

EXAMPLE   Pompeii˅s ruins were excavated during the past two centuries.

Its destruction was caused by an eruption of Mount Vesuvius in AD 79. Survivors stories contain accounts of tunneling through up to sixteen feet of debris after the disaster. The Naples Museums collection contains painted stuccos and other art objects from Pompeii that illustrate the delicate nature of the artisans techniques. More than five hundred residents bronze seals were found, and these helped identify the occupants of many destroyed homes. Pompeiis ruins provide the worlds most accurate snapshot of Hellenistic and Roman times.

42b | CONTRACTIONS AND OMITTED LETTERS

In speech we often leave out sounds and syllables of familiar words. These omissions are noted with apostrophes.

Contractions

Contractions combine two words into one, using the apostrophe to mark what is left out.

I am	⟶ I'm		we are	⟶ we're
I would	⟶ I'd		they are	⟶ they're
you are	⟶ you're		cannot	⟶ can't
you will	⟶ you'll		do not	⟶ don't
he is	⟶ he's		does not	⟶ doesn't
she is	⟶ she's		will not	⟶ won't
it is	⟶ it's			

Omissions

Using apostrophes to signal omitted letters is a way of approximating speech in writing. They can make your writing look informal and slangy, but overuse can become annoying in a hurry.

rock and roll ⟶ rock 'n' roll

the 1960s ⟶ the '60s

neighborhood ⟶ 'hood

42c | PLURALS OF LETTERS, SYMBOLS, AND WORDS REFERRED TO AS WORDS

When to use apostrophes to make plurals

The trend is away from using apostrophes to form plurals of letters, symbols, and words referred to as words. In a few cases adding the apostrophe and *s* is still used, as in this old saying:

Mind your p's and q's.

The apostrophe is still used when omitting it would cause confusion.

as   is   us
a's   i's   u's

Words used as words are italicized and their plural formed by adding an *s* not in italics, instead of an apostrophe and *s*.

Take a few of the *and*s out of your writing.

Words in quotation marks, however, typically use apostrophe and *s*.

She had too many "probably's" in her letter for me to be confident that the remodeling will be finished on schedule.

Writing in the World

Apostrophes are not used with the plural of numbers and acronyms

The style manuals of the Modern Language Association (MLA) and the American Psychological Association (APA) do not use apostrophes for indicating plurals of numbers and acronyms. They add only -*s*.

1890s	four CEOs	several VCRs
eights	these URLs	the images are all JPEGs

When not to use apostrophes to make plurals

Do not use an apostrophe to make family names plural.

INCORRECT	You've heard of keeping up with the Jones's.
CORRECT	You've heard of keeping up with the Joneses.

Common Errors

Do not use an apostrophe to make a noun plural

INCORRECT The two government**'s** agreed to meet.

CORRECT The two governments agreed to meet.

INCORRECT The video game console**'s** of the past were one-dimensional.

CORRECT The video game console**s** of the past were one-dimensional.

Remember: Add only *-s* = plural
 Add apostrophe plus *-s* = possessive

For step-by-step discussion, examples, and practice of this common error, go to **www.ablongman.com/faigley045.**

EXERCISE 42.2 In the following sentences some of the apostrophes were placed correctly, some were placed incorrectly, and others were omitted altogether. Cross out incorrectly used apostrophes, and add apostrophes where necessary.

> **EXAMPLE** Americans have often loved their presidents ˅ nick-
> names more than they loved the ~~president's~~ themselves.
> *presidents*

1. Texas VIP's and international diplomats alike affectionately referred to Lyndon B. Johnson as "Big Daddy."
2. There were no *ifs, ands,* or *buts* when the "Rough Rider," Theodore Roosevelt, rode into town.
3. Similarly, when old "Give 'Em Hell," also known as Harry Truman, was on the Hill, congressmen could never catch up on their *Z*'s.
4. Jimmy Carter's staff learned quickly of his attention to small details, down to the dotting of *i*s and crossing of *t*s.
5. The last twenty years have seen two George Bush's in the White House.
6. In the 1990's, George Bush Senior was known as "No New Taxes."

Chapter 43
Quotation Marks

Quotation marks, of course, set off quotations from surrounding text. But they also do other jobs that lend clarity to writing, like indicating certain kinds of titles, noting the novel use of a word, and showing that a word is being used as a word. Quotation marks are among the most commonly used and misused marks of punctuation.

43a | DIRECT QUOTATIONS

Use quotation marks to enclose direct quotations

Enclose direct quotations—someone else's words repeated verbatim—in quotation marks.

> Anne Lamont advises writers to look at everything with compassion, even something as seemingly inconsequential as a chipmunk: "I don't want to sound too Cosmica Rama here, but in those moments, you see that you and the chipmunk are alike, are part of a whole" (98).

Even brief direct quotations, such as the repetition of someone else's original term or turn of phrase, require quotation marks.

> Though she fears appearing overly "Cosmica Rama," Anne Lamont argues that with compassion, writers' observations can be spiritually transcendent (98).

Do not use quotation marks with indirect quotations

Do not enclose an indirect quotation—a paraphrase of someone else's words—in quotation marks. However, do remember that you need to cite your source not only when you quote directly but also when you paraphrase or borrow ideas.

Anne Lamont encourages writers to become compassionate observers who ultimately see themselves as equals to everything else, even something as seemingly inconsequential as a chipmunk (98).

Do not use quotation marks with block quotations

When a quotation is long enough to be set off as a block quotation, do not use quotation marks. MLA style defines long quotations as four or more lines of prose or poetry. APA style defines a long quotation as one of more than forty words. In the following example, notice that the long quotation is indented and quotation marks are omitted. Also notice that the parenthetical citation in long quotations comes after the period.

Complaints about maintenance in the dorms have been on the rise ever since the physical plant reorganized its crews into teams in August. One student's experience is typical:

> When our ceiling started dripping, my roommate and I went to our resident director right away to file an emergency maintenance request. Apparently the physical plant felt that "emergency" meant they could get around to it in a week or two. By the fourth day without any word from a maintenance person, the ceiling tiles began to fall and puddles began to pool on our carpet. (Trillo)

The physical plant could have avoided expensive ceiling tile and carpet repairs if it had responded to the student's request promptly.

For guidance in handling quotations within quotations, see the *Common Errors* box in Section 43e.

Writing in the World

Quotations spanning more than one paragraph

Quotations are frequent in narrative writing and reports of interviews. When a quotation from a single speaker continues for more than one paragraph, do not place a closing quotation mark until the end of the entire quotation. Do place an opening quotation mark at the beginning of each new paragraph in the quotation to remind the reader that you are still quoting.

> According to Emma Alvarez, whose family has been farming their land in Kansas for three generations, corporate farms are driving family farms like hers out of business. "We are hanging on," said Alvarez, "but I don't know how much longer we can keep competing with the big companies. Their costs are lower, so they sell their produce for less.
>
> "When I was a girl I helped my father just like he helped his, and we never wanted for anything. It was natural for me to go into farming. Now I'm not sure if I want my own children to have this life when they're grown."

EXERCISE 43.1 The following sentences contain direct quotations and paraphrases from Tony Horowitz's *Confederates in the Attic: Dispatches from the Unfinished Civil War* (New York: Pantheon, 1998, pages 84–87). Use attribution and punctuation clues to help you decide how to punctuate the quotations and paraphrases.

EXAMPLE   After completing his wild and often contradictory ride through two full years, fifteen states, and the contemporary landscape of what he terms the "South's Unfinished Civil War," award-winning journalist and cultural historian Tony Horowitz concluded: "the pleasure the Civil War gave me was hard to put into words" (387).

1. Horowitz's difficulty was finding words that might make sense as he puts it to anyone other than a fellow addict (387).

2. There are, Horowitz allows, clear and often-cited reasons why one might develop a passion for the Civil War, however. Everywhere, people spoke of family and fortunes lost in the war (384), Horowitz writes.

3. He notes that many Southerners, nostalgic for old-time war heroism, still revere men like Stonewall Jackson, Robert E. Lee, and Nathan Bedford Forrest, officers, Horowitz reminds his readers, who were often not what he calls marble men of Southern myth (385).

4. Civil War heroes were, after all, human. And these men, who for some command the status of gods, were also, in Horowitz's words, petty figures who often hurt their own cause by bickering, even challenging each other to duels (385).

5. The Civil War was also unique because it marked the first war in which the rural landscape of the nineteenth-century United States met a new kind of war technology. Horowitz states:

> It was new technology that made the War's romance and rusticity so palpable. Without photographs, rebs and Yanks would seem as remote to modern Americans as Minutemen and Hessians. Surviving daguerreotypes from the 1840s and 1850s were mostly stiff studio portraits. So the Civil War was as far back as we could delve in our own history and bring back naturalistic images attuned to our modern way of seeing. (386)

43b TITLES OF SHORT WORKS

While the titles of longer works such as books, magazines, and newspapers are italicized or underlined, titles of shorter works should be set off with quotation marks. Use quotation marks with the following kinds of titles:

SHORT STORIES	"Light Is Like Water," by Gabriel García Márquez
MAGAZINE ARTICLES	"Race Against Death," by Erin West
NEWSPAPER ARTICLES	"Cincinnati Mayor Declares Emergency," by Liz Sidoti

SHORT POEMS	"We Real Cool," by Gwendolyn Brooks
ESSAYS	"Self-Reliance," by Ralph Waldo Emerson
SONGS	"Purple Haze," by Jimi Hendrix
SPEECHES, LECTURES, AND SERMONS	"Zero to Web Page in Sixty Minutes," by Jean Lavre
CHAPTERS	"Last, Best Hope of Earth," Chapter 8 of *The Civil War*, by Shelby Foote
SHORT FILMS	"Bed Head," by Robert Rodriguez
EPISODES OF TELEVISION SHOWS	"Treehouse of Horror," an episode of *The Simpsons*
EPISODES OF RADIO SHOWS	"Fiasco," an episode of *This American Life*

The exception. Don't put the title of your own paper in quotation marks. If the title of another short work appears within the title of your paper, retain the quotation marks around the short work. The title of a paper about Jimi Hendrix, for instance, might read as follows:

The History of Hendrix: Riffs on "Purple Haze"

43c | OTHER USES OF QUOTATION MARKS

Quotation marks to indicate the novel use of a word

Quotation marks around a term can indicate that the writer is using the term in a novel way, often with skepticism, irony, or sarcasm. The quotation marks indicate that the writer is questioning the term's conventional definition. Notice the way quotation marks indicate skepticism about the conventional definition of *savages* in the following passage:

In the early days of England's empire building, it wasn't unusual to hear English anthropologists say that conquered native people were savages. Yet if we measure civilization by peacefulness and compassion for fellow humans, those "savages" were really much more civilized than the British.

Quotation marks to indicate that a word is being used as a word

Italics are usually used to indicate that a word is being used as a word, rather than standing for its conventional meaning. However, quotation marks are correct in these cases as well.

Beginning writers sometimes confuse "their," "they're," and "there."

43d | MISUSES OF QUOTATION MARKS

Do not use quotation marks for emphasis

It's becoming more and more common to see quotation marks used to emphasize a word or phrase. Resist the temptation in your own writing; it's an incorrect usage. In fact, because quotation marks indicate that a writer is using a term with skepticism or irony, adding quotation marks for emphasis will highlight unintended connotations of the term.

INCORRECT   "fresh" seafood

By using quotation marks here, the writer seems to call into question whether the seafood is really fresh at all.

CORRECT   fresh seafood

INCORRECT   Enjoy our "live" music every Saturday night.

Again, the quotation marks unintentionally indicate that the writer is skeptical that the music is live.

CORRECT   Enjoy our live music every Saturday night.

You have better ways of creating emphasis using your word processing program: **boldfacing**, <u>underlining</u>, *italicizing*, and **using color**.

Do not use quotation marks around indirect quotations or paraphrases (also see Section 43a)

INCORRECT	The airport security guard announced that "all bags will be searched and then apologized for the inconvenience to the passengers."
CORRECT	The airport security guard announced, "All bags will be searched. I apologize for the inconvenience." (*direct quotation*)
CORRECT	The airport security guard announced that all bags will be searched and then apologized for the inconvenience to the passengers. (*indirect quotation*)

Avoid using quotation marks to acknowledge the use of a cliché

You may have seen other writers enclose clichés in quotation marks. Avoid doing this; in fact, avoid using clichés at all. Clichés are worn out phrases; fresh words engage readers more.

INCORRECT	To avoid "letting the cat out of the bag" about forthcoming products, most large companies employ security experts trained in preventing commercial espionage.
CORRECT BUT STALE	To avoid letting the cat out of the bag about forthcoming products, most large companies employ security experts trained in preventing commercial espionage.
CORRECT AND EFFECTIVE	To prevent their savvy competitors from peeking at forthcoming products, most large companies employ security experts trained in preventing commercial espionage.

EXERCISE 43.2 Decide whether the underlined words in the following sentences require quotation marks. Add quotation marks to indicate the novel use of a word, or a word being used as a word. Delete any quotation marks that are unnecessary. Be careful not to enclose words in quotation marks merely for emphasis.

EXAMPLE   Biologists define ⁶race⁹ as groups within a species that differ significantly from one another.

1. Humans have been divided into several "primary" races according to physical traits.
2. Many assume these divisions to be natural, but these <u>natural</u> categories are not <u>natural</u> at all.
3. The word <u>race</u> represents more than mere biological categories.
4. When <u>politicians</u> talk about race, for example, they often are not referring only to biological "<u>classifications</u>."
5. The catchword <u>race</u> has become a political firearm, but for such a culturally powerful concept, its meaning remains broad and unclear.
6. To talk about "<u>race</u>" in the United States, however, often means to discuss contemporary racial tensions within our <u>color-blind</u> society.

43e OTHER PUNCTUATION WITH QUOTATION MARKS

The rules for placing punctuation with quotation marks fall into three general categories. *The only things outside are Colons and semi colons*

Periods and commas with quotation marks

Place periods and commas inside closing quotation marks.

INCORRECT   "The smartest people", Dr. Geisler pointed out, "tell themselves the most convincing rationalizations".

CORRECT   "The smartest people," Dr. Geisler pointed out, "tell themselves the most convincing rationalizations."

Exceptions occur when a parenthetical citation follows a short quotation. In MLA and APA documentation styles, the period follows the closing parentheses.

INCORRECT   "The smartest people," Dr. Geisler pointed out, "tell themselves the most convincing rationalizations." (52)

CORRECT	"The smartest people," Dr. Geisler pointed out, "tell themselves the most convincing rationalizations" (52).

Colons and semicolons with quotation marks

Place colons and semicolons outside closing quotation marks.

INCORRECT	"From Stettin in the Baltic to Trieste in the Adriatic, an iron curtain has descended across the Continent;" Churchill's statement rang through Cold War politics for the next fifty years.
CORRECT	"From Stettin in the Baltic to Trieste in the Adriatic, an iron curtain has descended across the Continent"; Churchill's statement rang through Cold War politics for the next fifty years.

Exclamation points, question marks, and dashes with quotation marks

When an exclamation point, question mark, or dash belongs to the original quotation, place it inside the closing quotation mark. When it applies to the entire sentence, place it outside the closing quotation mark.

IN THE ORIGINAL QUOTATION
"Are we there yet?" came the whine from the back seat.

APPLIED TO THE ENTIRE SENTENCE
Did the driver in the front seat respond, "Not even close"?

Common Errors

Quotations within quotations

Single quotation marks are used to indicate a quotation within a quotation. In the following example single quotation marks clarify who is speaking. The rules for placing punctuation with single

(continued next page)

quotation marks are the same as the rules for placing punctuation with double quotation marks.

INCORRECT When he showed the report to Paul Probius, Michener reported that Probius "took vigorous exception to the sentence "He wanted to close down the university," insisting that we add the clarifying phrase "as it then existed"" (Michener 145).

CORRECT When he showed the report to Paul Probius, Michener reported that Probius "took vigorous exception to the sentence 'He wanted to close down the university,' insisting that we add the clarifying phrase 'as it then existed'" (Michener 145).

Remember: Single quotation marks are used for quotations within quotations.

For step-by-step discussion, examples, and practice of this common error, go to **www.ablongman.com/faigley046.**

EXERCISE 43.3 The following sentences use a variety of punctuation marks with quotations. Some are used correctly and some are not. Move the punctuation marks that are incorrectly placed in relation to the quotation marks.

EXAMPLE In her essay "Survival Is the Least of My Desires," the novelist Dorothy Allison describes herself as being "born poor, queer, and despised."

1. What does Allison mean when she tells gay and lesbian writers, "We must aim much higher than just staying alive if we are to begin to approach our true potential"?

2. She elaborates, "I want to write in such a way as to literally remake the world, to change people's thinking as they look out of the eyes of the characters I create" (212).

3. "I believe in the truth"; this declaration forms the cornerstone of the philosophy Allison wants to pass on to gay and lesbian writers.

4. According to Allison, "I write what I think are "moral tales." That's what I intend, though I grow more and more to believe that telling the emotional truth of people's lives, not necessarily the historical truth, is the only moral use of fiction." (217).

5. "If I am to survive, I need to be able to trust your stories, to know that you will not lie even to comfort."

    I believe the secret in writing is that fiction never exceeds the reach of the writer's courage," says Allison.

Chapter 44
Other Punctuation Marks

Periods, question marks, and exclamation points indicate the conclusion of a sentence and tell the reader how to read it. Brackets, ellipses, and slashes occur much less often, but they also have important uses.

44a PERIODS

Periods at the ends of sentences

Place a period at the end of a complete sentence if it is not a direct question or an exclamatory statement. As the term suggests, a direct question asks a question outright. Indirect questions, on the other hand, report the asking of a question.

DIRECT QUESTION	Mississippi opponents of the Confederate-themed state flag wonder, "Where does the state's pride in its heritage end and its respect for those offended begin?"
INDIRECT QUESTION	Mississippi opponents of the Confederate-themed state flag wonder where the state's pride in its heritage ends and its respect for those offended begins.

Periods with quotation marks and parentheses

When a quotation falls at the end of a sentence, place the period inside the closing quotation marks.

Although he devoted decades to a wide range of artistic and political projects, Allen Ginsberg is best known as the author of the poem "Howl**.**"

When a parenthetical phrase falls at the end of a sentence, place the period outside the closing parenthesis.

Mrs. Chen, a grandmother in Seneca Falls, is training for her first 10K race (6.2 miles**).**

When parentheses enclose a whole sentence, place the period inside the closing parenthesis.

True to their quirky success, ABBA found a receptive audience in Australia before Americans embraced them. (Australia, in fact, carries the distinction of being the first country to place ABBA at the top of its music charts**.)**

Periods with abbreviations

Many abbreviations require periods; however, there are few set rules. Use the dictionary to check how to punctuate abbreviations on a case-by-case basis.

John F**.** Kennedy	Mr**.**	misc**.**	Wed**.**
a**.**m**.**	p**.**m**.**	a**.**s**.**a**.**p**.**	etc**.**

The rules for punctuating two types of abbreviations do remain consistent: Postal abbreviations for states and most abbreviations for organizations do not require periods.

OH for Ohio	ACLU for the American Civil Liberties Union
CA for California	NRA for the National Rifle Association

When an abbreviation with a period falls at the end of a sentence, do not add a second period to conclude the sentence.

INCORRECT   If the registrar doesn't allow Shilpa to transfer the classes she took at Andrews Community College, she will fall nine credits shy of a B.A**..**

CORRECT If the registrar doesn't allow Shilpa to transfer the classes she took at Andrews Community College, she will fall nine credits shy of a B.A.

Periods in citations of poetry and plays

Use a period to separate the components of the following kinds of literary citations.

A POEM DIVIDED INTO SECTIONS SUCH AS BOOKS OR CANTOS
book.lines   *The Inferno* 27.79-84

A PROSE PLAY
act.scene   *Beyond Therapy* 1.4

A VERSE PLAY
act.scene.lines   *Twelfth Night* 3.4.194-198

Periods as decimal points

Decimal points are periods that separate integers from tenths, hundredths, and so on.

99.98% pure silver	98.6° Fahrenheit
on sale for $399.97	2.6 liter engine

Since large numbers with long strings of zeros can be difficult to read accurately, writers sometimes shorten them using decimal points. Notice how the decimal points make the second sentence easier to read than the first.

With the national debt approaching **6,400,000,000,000** dollars, some senators are salivating at the idea of using a portion of the projected **2,170,000,000,000**-dollar budget surplus to pay it down.

With the national debt approaching **$6.4 trillion**, some senators are salivating at the idea of using a portion of the projected **$2.17 trillion** budget surplus to pay it down.

Periods with computer file names and Internet addresses

A period separates a computer file name from the file extension. The file extension designates the file type.

paper1.doc	index.html
manifesto.txt	jamesdean.jpg

Read as *dot*, a period also separates the components of an Internet address.

n.nguyen@hotmail.com	www.upenn.edu
www.pbs.org	www.onion.com

EXERCISE 44.1 Periods have been omitted from the paragraph that follows. You can see how confusing writing becomes without proper period placement. Add periods to clear up the confusion.

EXAMPLE   The origins of second wave American feminism are often traced to Ms⊙ Betty Friedan of Peoria, Illinois⊙

Ms Friedan was born February 4, 1921 History will record her as one of the major contributors to modern US feminism In 1963, Friedan penned the monumental *Feminine Mystique* The book investigated the contemporary malaise of the postwar US housewife which she dubbed "the problem that has no name" Friedan spoke for the millions of housewives who were wondering why they were discontent as mothers and wives In 1966, she cofounded the National Organization of Women (NOW was co-conceptualized by African-American feminist/minister Pauli Murray at the 1966 National Conference of the Commission on the Status of Women in Washington DC) Friedan went on to serve as president of NOW (wwwnoworg) until 1970, and she has since published works such as *It Changed My Life*, *The Second Stage,* and *Life So Far*

44b | QUESTION MARKS

Question marks with direct questions

Place a question mark at the end of a direct question. A direct question is one which the questioner puts to someone outright. In contrast, an indirect question merely reports the asking of a question. Question marks give readers a cue to read the end of the sentence with rising inflection. Read the following sentences aloud. Hear how your inflection rises in the second sentence to convey the direct question.

INDIRECT QUESTION
Desirée asked whether Dan rides his motorcycle without a helmet.

DIRECT QUESTION
Desirée asked, "Does Dan ride his motorcycle without a helmet?"

Question marks with quotations

When a quotation falls at the end of a direct question, place the question mark outside the closing quotation mark.

Did Abraham Lincoln really call Harriet Beecher Stowe "the little lady who started this big war"?

Place the question mark inside the closing quotation when only the quoted material is a direct question.

Slowly scientists are beginning to answer the question, "Is cancer a genetic disease?"

When quoting a direct question in the middle of a sentence, place a question mark inside the closing quotation mark and place a period at the end of the sentence.

Market researchers estimate that asking Burger World's customers "Do you want fries with that?" is responsible for a 15% boost in their french fries sales.

Question marks to indicate uncertainty about dates or numbers

Place a question mark in parentheses after a date or number whose accuracy is in question.

After his escape from slavery, Frederick Douglass (1817**?**-95) went on to become a great orator and statesman.

EXERCISE 44.2 Periods and question marks have been omitted from the paragraph that follows. Place them where they are needed.

EXAMPLE   What was so Earth-shattering about Friedan's naming of the "problem with no name"**?**

Betty Friedan's *The Feminine Mystique* addressed the question, "Is this all" She examined why millions of women were sensing a gnawing feeling of discontent Friedan asked, "Can the problem that has no name somehow be related to the domestic routine of the housewife" and examined women's shifting place in postwar America What were women missing In asking these questions, Friedan legitimized the panic and uneasiness of many women who found the roles of mother and wife not wholly satisfying However, did this naming solve the "problem with no name"

44c | EXCLAMATION POINTS

Exclamation points to convey strong emotion

Exclamation points conclude sentences and, like question marks, tell the reader how a sentence should sound. They indicate strong emotion. As with any display of strong emotion, occasional doses can be invigorating, but too many exclamation points quickly become grating. Instead of relying on exclamation points to convey heightened emotion, use strong words and careful phrasing. Use exclamation points sparingly in formal writing; they are rarely appropriate in academic and professional prose.

Exclamation points with emphatic interjections

Exclamation points can convey a sense of urgency with brief interjections. Interjections can be incorporated into sentences or stand on their own.

Run! They're about to close the doors to the jetway.

Use commas to set off interjections that are not emphatic.

One study has found that, yes, humans can contract a strain of mad cow disease.

Exclamation points with quotation marks

In quotations, exclamation points follow the same rules as question marks. If a quotation falls at the end of an exclamatory statement, place the exclamation point outside the closing quotation mark.

The singer forgot the words of "America the Beautiful"!

When quoting an exclamatory statement at the end of a sentence that is not itself exclamatory, place the exclamation point inside the closing quotation mark.

Jerry thought his car would be washed away in the flood, but Anna jumped into action, declaring, "Not if I can help it!"

When the quotation of an exclamatory statement does not fall at the end of a sentence, place the exclamation point inside the closing quotation mark and place a period at the end of the sentence.

Someone yelled "Loser!" when the candidate walked on stage.

44d BRACKETS

While brackets (sometimes called *square brackets*) look quite similar to parentheses, the two perform different functions. Brackets have a narrow set of uses.

Brackets to provide clarification within quotation marks

Quoted material sometimes requires clarification because it is removed from its context. Adding clarifying material in brackets can allow you to make the quotation clear while still accurately repeating the exact words of your source. In the following example the writer quotes a sentence with the pronoun *they*, which refers to a noun in a previous, unquoted sentence. The material in brackets clarifies to whom the pronoun refers.

> The Harris study found that "In the last three years, they [Gonzales Junior High students] averaged 15% higher on their mathematics assessment tests than their peers in Northridge County."

Brackets within parentheses

Since parentheses within parentheses might confuse readers, use brackets to enclose parenthetical information within a parenthetical phrase.

> Representative Patel's most controversial legislation (including a version of the hate crimes bill [HR 99-108] the house rejected two years ago) has a slim chance of being enacted this session.

Writing in the World

Using quotations that contain errors

In scholarly writing you should copy quotations exactly as they appear in your source, but you must also produce a paper free of grammatical and mechanical errors. So how should you handle a source that contains an error? One way is to rephrase the quotation in your own words, crediting your source for the idea. However, if the quotation is so eloquent or effective that you decide to include it despite the error, use *[sic]* (an abbreviation of the Latin "sicut," meaning *thus*) to indicate that the original source is responsible for the mistake.

(continued next page)

SPELLING ERROR IN ORIGINAL SOURCE (*TO* INSTEAD OF *TOO*)
"One taste tester reported that the Carb Charge energy bar was to dry; she said it had the consistency of sawdust" (Cisco 22).

REPHRASED
One of the participants in the taste test likened the Carb Charge energy bar to sawdust because it had so little moisture (Cisco 22).

QUOTATION USING [SIC]
"One taste tester reported that the Carb Charge energy bar was to [sic] dry; she said it had the consistency of sawdust" (Cisco 22).

44e | ELLIPSES

Ellipses let a reader know that a portion of a passage is missing. You can use ellipses to keep quotations concise and direct readers' attention to what is important to the point you are making. An ellipsis is a string of three periods with spaces separating the periods. MLA style formerly required square brackets around the three periods. Your instructor may prefer that you use brackets surrounding ellipses when you delete words from quotations.

Ellipses to indicate an omission from a prose quotation

When you quote only a phrase or short clause from a sentence, you usually do not need to use ellipses.

Mao Tse-tung first used "let a hundred flowers blossom" in a Peking speech in 1957.

Except at the beginning of a quotation, indicate omitted words with an ellipsis.

THE ORIGINAL SOURCE

"The female praying mantis, so named for the way it holds its front legs together as if in prayer, tears off her male partner's head during mating. Remarkably, the headless male will continue the act of mating. This brutal dance is a stark example of the innate evolutionary drive to pass genes onto offspring; the male praying mantis seems to live and die only for this moment."

AN ELLIPSIS INDICATES OMITTED WORDS

"The female praying mantis . . . tears off her male partner's head during mating."

When the ellipsis is at the end of a sentence, place the period or question mark after the bracket and follow with the closing quotation mark.

WORDS OMITTED AT THE END OF A SENTENCE

"This brutal dance is a stark example of the innate evolutionary drive to pass genes onto offspring . . . ."

Ellipses to indicate the omission of a whole line or lines of poetry

Using more than three periods is appropriate in just one instance: to signal the omission of a full line or lines of poetry in the middle of a poetry quotation. In such instances, use an entire line of spaced periods.

ORIGINAL

My Shakespeare, rise; I will not lodge thee by
Chaucer or Spenser, or bid Beaumont lie
A little further, to make thee a room;
Thou art a monument, without a tomb,
And art alive still, while thy book doth live,
And we have wits to read, and praise to give.

—Ben Jonson, "To the Memory of My Beloved,
the Author, Mr. William Shakespeare" (1623)

OMITTED LINES OF POETRY IN **MLA** STYLE

My Shakespeare, rise;

. . . .

Thou art a monument, without a tomb,
And art alive still, while thy book doth live,
And we have wits to read, and praise to give.

Ellipses to indicate a pause or an interrupted sentence

Ellipses can provide a visual cue that a speaker is taking a long pause or that a speaker has been interrupted.

"And the winner is . . . David Goldstein."

"That ball is going, going, . . . gone!"

"Be careful that you don't spill . . ."

EXERCISE 44.3 In the following quotations and A. E. Houseman's poem "To an Athlete Dying Young," delete the underlined passages and punctuate the quotations with ellipses where necessary. Be sure to leave in clarifying punctuation.

EXAMPLE   Robert Ward states, "The American culture positions its heroes such that they are destined to end in turmoil, problematizing the desire for eminent success. By elevating them to the position of gods, society gives heroes nowhere to go but down."

REWRITE   Robert Ward states, "The American culture positions its heroes such that they are destined to end in turmoil . . . . By elevating them to the position of gods, society gives heroes nowhere to go but down."

Ward notes, "The phenomenon of the waning star is heavily represented in the last century of English and American culture, ranging from poetry to popular rock music." In 1896, chronicling the advantage of dying before the glory fades, A. E. Houseman published the poem "To an Athlete Dying Young." The following is a passage from that poem:

Now you will not swell the rout
Of lads that wore their honors out,
Runners whom renown outran
And the name died before the man.

So set, before the echoes fade,
The fleet foot on the sill of shade,
And hold to the low lintel up
The still-defended challenge-cup.

And round that early-laurelled head
Will flock to gaze the strengthless dead,
And find unwithered on its curls
The garland briefer than a girl's.

Houseman's verses extol the eternal glory of those who pass in their prime. Scholars such as Ona Click have noted the recent proliferation of Houseman's theme, citing that "artists such as Neil Young have contemporized this notion with songs such as 'Hey Hey My My.' The song contrasts the fates of two rock stars who ultimately took two very different paths, Elvis Presley and Johnny Rotten of the Sex Pistols; while Presley died in a blaze of glory, Rotten's fleeting stardom waned and dulled the cultural memory of his initial rise to fame." In a related article, she notes this theme traveled into the 1980s as Bruce Springsteen's "Glory Days" recalled the tale of "those who outlive their primes and are forced to reduce their glory to nostalgic reminiscences and fleeting grasps at the past." Though we venerate our heroes, culture notes how their position is tenuous at best.

44f │ SLASHES

Slashes to indicate alternative words

Slashes between two words indicate that a choice between them is to be made. When using slashes for this purpose, do not put a space between the slash and words.

INCORRECT	Maya was such an energetic baby that her exhausted parents wished she had come with an on **/** off switch.
CORRECT	Maya was such an energetic baby that her exhausted parents wished she had come with an on**/**off switch.

The following are common instances of the slash used to indicate alternative words:

either/or   he/she or s/he   player/coach
and/or   actor/director   pass/fail
on/off   win/lose

Writing in the World

Should you use *he/she* or *s/he*?

Using *he* as an indefinite pronoun (a pronoun that refers to a person in general rather than to a specific individual) can seem sexist because it omits women. Some writers use *he/she* or the even shorter *s/he* instead. These solutions are unacceptable to many readers, who consider them ugly. Likewise, many readers consider *he or she* annoying. The best solution is to avoid the *he/she* and *he or she* constructions altogether.

SEXIST	Despite popular lore, a hiker bitten by a snake should never suck out the poison. Instead, **he** should tie a tourniquet above the wound to prevent the poison from circulating to vital organs.
INCLUSIVE BUT CUMBERSOME	Despite popular lore, a hiker bitten by a snake should never suck out the poison. Instead, **s/he** should tie a tourniquet above the wound to prevent the poison from circulating to vital organs.

INCLUSIVE BUT CUMBERSOME	Despite popular lore, a hiker bitten by a snake should never suck out the poison. Instead, **he or she** should tie a tourniquet above the wound to prevent the poison from circulating to vital organs.
BETTER	Despite popular lore, a hiker bitten by a snake should never suck out the poison. Instead, tying a tourniquet above the wound will prevent the poison from circulating to vital organs.

Chapter 30 offers more tips for avoiding sexist language and awkward indefinite pronouns.

Slashes to indicate line breaks in short quotations of verse

Line breaks—where the lines of a poem end—are artistic choices that affect how we understand a poem. Thus it is important to reproduce them accurately when quoting poetry. The task is not difficult in MLA style when the quotation is four or more lines long: Simply indent the quoted lines ten spaces and mimic the line breaks of the original verse. When you quote three or fewer lines of poetry, however, and must integrate the quotation into the paragraph rather than setting it off in a block, use slashes to indicate line breaks. Type a space on either side of the slash.

The concluding lines of T. S. Eliot's "Animula" offer a surprising revision of a common prayer. He writes, "Pray for Floret, by the boarhound slain between the yew trees **/** Pray for us now and at the hour of our birth." Replacing "death," the final word in the prayer, with "birth" at the end of this dark poem connotes an uneasy sense that we find ourselves adrift in a new and unfamiliar world.

Slashes with fractions

Place a slash between the numerator and the denominator in a fraction. Do not put any spaces around the slash.

INCORRECT	3 / 4
CORRECT	3/4

Slashes with dates

In informal writing, slashes divide the month, day, and year in a date. A longer format is appropriate for formal academic and professional writing. Omit the slashes, spell out the month, and place a comma after the day.

INFORMAL   Javy, save 1/14/03 on your calendar; I reserved two tickets for the talent show.

FORMAL   It was a pleasure to meet you during my December 14 interview for Universal Oil's marketing internship. As we discussed, I will not be available for full-time employment until my graduation on **May 12, 2004**. However, I am hopeful that we can work out the part-time arrangement you suggested until that date.

EXERCISE 44.4 Take a look at the way the following paragraph uses all the punctuation marks discussed in this chapter: periods, question marks, exclamation points, brackets, ellipses, and slashes. Some are used correctly, and others are used incorrectly or omitted altogether. Correct any punctuation mistakes that you find, and add any necessary marks that have been omitted.

EXAMPLE   Many ask, "Why have snakes become a symbol of religious devotion?

In 1996 alone, over sixty deaths occurred due to religious snake handling. Mark 16-21 in the King James version of the

Bible states, "They shall take up serpents and if they drink any deadly thing it shall not hurt them . . ."! This passage instigated the formation of a religion which thrives among the Irish and English descendants living in Appalachia. (In the 1990s, over 2000 snake handlers lived in Appalachia alone.)

Snake handling has been investigated by both practitioners of the fine arts (Romulus Linney's "Holy Ghosts" (1971) examines snake handling in the South) and news media. One controversial case examined Rev Glenn Summerford who attempted to kill his wife by forcing her to handle rattlesnakes. The general public often sees snake handling as a frightening act of fundamentalism practiced by congregations (often assumed to be undereducated)

Chapter 45

Capitalization and Italics

Of course you know that you should capitalize the first word of a sentence, but you may not be as familiar with the other functions capital letters perform. Capital letters and italics also assist readers by indicating certain kinds and uses of words. Learning a few guidelines will help you to become confident when to use each.

45a CAPITAL LETTERS

Capitalize the initial letters of proper nouns and proper adjectives

Capitalize the initial letters of proper nouns (nouns that name particular people, places, and things), including the following:

NAMES	Sandra Day O'Connor	Bill Gates
TITLES PRECEDING NAMES	Dr. Martin Luther King	Mrs. Fields
PLACE NAMES	Grand Canyon	Northwest Territories
INSTITUTION NAMES	Department of Labor	Amherst College
ORGANIZATION NAMES	World Trade Organization	American Cancer Society
COMPANY NAMES	Motorola	JoJo's Café and Bakery
RELIGIONS	Protestantism	Islam
LANGUAGES	Chinese	Swahili
MONTHS	November	March
DAYS OF THE WEEK	Monday	Friday
NATIONALITIES	Italian	Puerto Rican

HOLIDAYS	Passover	Thanksgiving
DEPARTMENTS	Chemistry Department	Department of the Interior
HISTORICAL ERAS	Enlightenment	Middle Ages
REGIONS	the South	the Midwest
COURSE NAMES	Eastern Religions	Microbiology
JOB TITLE WHEN USED WITH A PROPER NOUN	President Benjamin Ladner	

Capitalize the initial letters of proper adjectives (adjectives based on the names of people, places, and things).

African American bookstore   Avogadro's number   Irish music

Avoid unnecessary capitalization

Do not capitalize the names of seasons, academic disciplines (unless they are languages), or job titles used without a proper noun.

SEASONS	fall, winter, spring, summer
ACADEMIC DISCIPLINES (EXCEPT LANGUAGES)	chemistry, computer science, psychology, English, French, Japanese
JOB TITLES USED WITHOUT A PROPER NOUN	The vice president is on maternity leave.

Computer Strategies

Capitalization in email

some people never press the shift key when typing email. while there are no rules for informal email, long stretches of text with no capitalization are tiresome to read, even in email sent between close friends.

SIMILARLY, SOME PEOPLE TYPE EMAIL IN ALL CAPS, WHICH LIKEWISE IS ANNOYING TO READ OVER LONG STRETCHES. ALSO, SOME PEOPLE FEEL READING ALL CAPS IS LIKE BEING SHOUTED AT.

Capitalization conventions are familiar to readers and thus help make messages easy to read. Using both uppercase and lowercase letters, even in the most informal writing, is a friendly act.

Capitalize titles of publications

In MLA style when capitalizing titles, capitalize the initial letters of all first and last words and all other words except articles, prepositions, and coordinating conjunctions. Capitalize the initial letter of the first word in the subtitle following a colon.

James and the Giant Peach
The Grapes of Wrath
The Writing on the Wall: An Anthology of Graffiti Art

Common Errors

Capitalizing with colons, parentheses, and quotations

Capitalizing with colons

Except when a colon follows a heading, do not capitalize the first letter after a colon unless the colon links two main clauses (which can stand as complete sentences). If the material following the colon is a quotation, a formal statement, or consists of more than one sentence, capitalize the first letter. In other cases capitalization is optional.

INCORRECT   We are all being integrated into a global economy that never sleeps: An economy determining our personal lives and our relationships with others.

CORRECT   We are all being integrated into a global economy that never sleeps: We can work, shop, bank, and be entertained twenty-four hours a day.

Capitalizing with parentheses

Capitalize the first word of material enclosed in parentheses if the words stand on their own as a complete sentence.

Beginning with Rachel Carson's *Silent Spring* in 1962, we stopped worrying so much about what nature was doing to us and began to worry about what we were doing to nature. (Science and technology that had been viewed as the solution to problems suddenly became viewed as their cause.)

If the material enclosed in parentheses is part of a larger sentence, do not capitalize the first letter enclosed in the parentheses.

Beginning with Rachel Carson's *Silent Spring* (first published in 1962), we stopped worrying so much about what nature was doing to us and began to worry about what we were doing to nature.

Capitalizing with quotations

If the quotation of part of a sentence is smoothly integrated into a sentence, do not capitalize the first word. Smoothly integrated quotations do not require a comma to separate the sentence from the rest of the quotation.

It's no wonder the *Monitor* wrote that Armand's chili was "the best in Georgia, bar none"; he spends whole days in his kitchen experimenting over bubbling pots.

But if the sentence contains an attribution and the quotation can stand as a complete sentence, capitalize the first word. In such sentences a comma should separate the attribution from the quotation.

According to Janet Morris of the *Monitor*, "The chili Armand fusses over for hours in his kitchen is the best in Georgia, bar none."

Remember: For elements following colons or within parentheses or quotation marks, capitalize the first letter only if the group of words can stand as a complete sentence.

 For step-by-step discussion, examples, and practice of this common error, go to **www.ablongman.com/faigley047**.

EXERCISE 45.1 Nothing in the paragraph that follows has been capitalized. Revise it as necessary.

> EXAMPLE   ~~c~~ourses in ~~a~~merican history often disregard the
>   founding of the ~~fbi~~ FBI.

the federal bureau of investigation (fbi) has long been considered an american institution that was fathered by president theodore roosevelt. during the early 1900s, the united states was going through what some referred to as the progressive era. (during this period, the american people believed government intervention was synonymous with a just society.) roosevelt, the president during part of this era, aided in the creation of an organization devoted to federal investigations. prior to 1907, federal investigations were carried out by agents-for-hire employed by the department of justice. on wednesday, may 27, 1908, the u.s. congress passed a law prohibiting the employment of agents-for-hire and enabling the establishment of an official secret service directly affiliated with the department. that spring, attorney general charles bonaparte appointed ten agents who would report to a chief examiner. this action is often considered to be the birth of the fbi.

45b │ ITALICS

Italicize the titles of entire works (books, magazines, newspapers, films), but place the titles of parts of entire works within quotation marks. When italicizing is difficult because you are using a typewriter or writing by hand, underline the titles of entire works instead. Use italics with the following kinds of titles.

BOOKS	*Native Son*
MAGAZINES	*Rolling Stone*
JOURNALS	*Journal of Fish Biology*
NEWSPAPERS	*The Plain Dealer*

FEATURE-LENGTH FILMS	*Star Wars*
LONG POEMS	*The Divine Comedy*
PLAYS, OPERAS, AND BALLETS	*Our Town*
TELEVISION SHOWS	*The Brady Bunch*
RADIO SHOWS AND AUDIO RECORDINGS	*Prairie Home Companion*
PAINTINGS, SCULPTURES, AND	*Starry Night*
OTHER VISUAL WORKS OF ART	
PAMPHLETS AND BULLETINS	*Common Sense*

Also italicize or underline the names of ships and aircraft.

Spirit of St. Louis	*Challenger*
Titanic	*Pequod*

The exceptions. Do not italicize or underline the names of sacred texts.

The text for our Comparative Religions course, *Sacred Texts from Around the World,* contains excerpts from the New English Bible, the Qur'an, the Talmud, the Upanishads, and the Bhagavad Gita.

Italicize unfamiliar foreign words

Italicize foreign words that are not part of common English usage. Do not italicize words that have become a common word or phrase in the English vocabulary. How do you decide which words are common? If a word appears in a standard English dictionary, it can be considered as adopted into English.

INCORRECT	My favorite Italian restaurant serves six kinds of *risotto,* including *risotto al radicchio, risotto nero,* and *risotto ai frutti di mare.*
CORRECT	My favorite Italian restaurant serves six kinds of risotto, including *risotto al radicchio, risotto nero,* and *risotto ai frutti di mare.*

In this example, risotto, a dish made with Italian rice and other ingredients, has become familiar enough to appear in standard English dictionaries. The Italian names of specific kinds of risotto are not common and are not included in standard English dictionaries. They should be italicized.

Use italics to clarify your use of a word, letter, or number

In everyday speech, we often use cues—a pause, a louder or different tone—to communicate how we are using a word. In writing, italics help clarify when you use words in a referential manner, or letters and numbers as letters and numbers.

INCORRECT   Shannon promised to contact Joel by early next week, but it soon became clear that her **early next week** actually meant Thursday or Friday.

CORRECT   Shannon promised to contact Joel by early next week, but it soon became clear that her *early next week* actually meant Thursday or Friday.

INCORRECT   Although Giovanni was only two years old, he already knew how to draw **A** and **G**.

CORRECT   Although Giovanni was only two years old, he already knew how to draw *A* and *G*.

Writing in the World

Italicizing for emphasis

Italicizing a word can show the reader where to place the emphasis, but not all readers find italics appropriate. Use them sparingly. If you often find yourself italicizing words to indicate stresses, try to find stronger words that will do the same work.

NOT EFFECTIVE

"You don't *have* to let me win at chess *just because I'm younger*, Lynne."

"I'm not trying to let you win. *I'm just a bad chess player*."

EFFECTIVE

"You don't have to let me win at chess just because I'm younger, Lynne."

"I'm *not* trying to let you win. I'm just a bad chess player."

INCORRECT   Stephen, who was five years old, did not know how to draw 1 or 2.

CORRECT   Stephen, who was five years old, did not know how to draw *1* or *2*.

EXERCISE 45.2 Underline any words in the following paragraph that should be italicized.

EXAMPLE   Both controversial in their own right, the famed clothing designer Coco Chanel and the painter of *Guernica*, Pablo Picasso, are listed by *Time* magazine as two of the "Most Interesting People of the Twentieth Century."

Many think Coco Chanel is to fashion what the *Bible* is to religion. Consequently, various types of media have been used to try to capture the essence of this innovative designer. Films such as *Tonight* or *Never* preserve Chanel's designs for future generations, while the failed Broadway musical *Coco* attempts to embody her life's work. More recently, print and small screen have attempted to encapsulate the impact of the designer in specials like *A&E Top 10: Fashion Designers* and books such as *Chanel: Her Style and Her Life*. Chanel was as monumental and self-destructive as the *Titanic*. She almost single-handedly redefined women's clothing through the popularization of sportswear and the jersey suit. But she also sympathized with Hitler after the release of his book *Mein Kampf* and the relocation of the Jews, and her image was further tarnished by her wartime romance with a Nazi officer. However, after her initial success waned during World War II, magazines such as *Vogue* and *Life* welcomed her back. She reinvented herself and her clothing line in the 1950s, and today she stands as one of the most influential fashion designers in history.

Chapter 46

Abbreviations, Acronyms, and Numbers

Abbreviations and acronyms are used much less often in writing for general audiences than in scientific and technical writing. The use of numbers also varies considerably from technical to general writing.

46a   ABBREVIATIONS

Abbreviations are shortened forms of words. Because abbreviations vary widely, you will need to look in the dictionary to determine how to abbreviate words on a case-by-case basis. Nonetheless, there are a few patterns that abbreviations follow.

Abbreviate titles before and degrees after full names

Ms. Ella Fitzgerald
Prof. Vijay Aggarwal
Dr. Suzanne Smith
San-qi Li, MD
Driss Ouaouicha, PhD
Marissa Límon, LLD

Write out the professional title when it is used with only a last name.

Professor Chin

Doctor Rodriguez

Reverend Ames

Conventions for using abbreviations with years and times

BCE (before the common era) and CE (common era) are now preferred for indicating years, replacing BC (before Christ) and AD (*anno Domini* ["the year of our Lord"]). Note that all are now used without periods.

479 BCE (or BC)

1610 CE (or AD, but AD is placed before the number)

The preferred written conventions for times are a.m. (*ante meridiem*) and p.m. (*post meridiem*).

9:03 a.m.

3:30 p.m.

An alternative is military time:

The morning meal is served from 0600 to 0815; the evening meal is served from 1730 to 1945.

Conventions for using abbreviations in college writing

Most abbreviations are inappropriate in formal writing except when the reader would be more familiar with the abbreviation than with the words it represents. When your reader is unlikely to be familiar with an abbreviation, spell out the term, followed by the abbreviation in parentheses, the first time you use it in a paper. The reader will then understand what the abbreviation refers to, and you may use the abbreviation in subsequent sentences.

The Office of Civil Rights (OCR) is the agency that enforces Title IX regulations. In 1979, OCR set out three options for schools to comply with Title IX.

Common Errors

Making abbreviations and acronyms plural

Plurals of abbreviations and acronyms are formed by adding *s*, not *'s*.

> Technology is changing so rapidly these days that **PCs** become obsolete husks of circuits and plastic in only a few years.

Use an *'s* only to show possession.

> The **NRA's** position on trigger locks is that the government should advocate, not legislate, their use.

Remember: When making abbreviations and acronyms plural, add s, not 's.

For step-by-step discussion, examples, and practice of this common error, go to **www.ablongman.com/faigley048**.

Writing in the World

Latin abbreviations

Some writers sprinkle Latin abbreviations throughout their writing, apparently thinking that these are a mark of learning. Frequently these abbreviations are used inappropriately. If you use Latin abbreviations, make sure you know what they stand for.

cf.	(*confer*)	compare
e.g.	(*exempli gratia*)	for example
et al.	(*et alia*)	and others
etc.	(*et cetera*)	and so forth
i.e.	(*id est*)	that is
N.B.	(*nota bene*)	note well
viz.	(*videlicet*)	namely

In particular, avoid using *etc.* to fill out a list of items. Use of *etc.* announces that you haven't taken the time to finish a thought.

LAZY	The contents of his grocery cart described his eating habits: a big bag of chips, hot sauce, frozen pizza, etc.
BETTER	The contents of his grocery cart described his eating habits: a big bag of chips, a large jar of hot sauce, two frozen pizzas, a twelve-pack of cola, three Mars bars, and a package of Twinkies.

EXERCISE 46.1 The following is a paragraph from a research paper in which every word is spelled out. Decide which words would be more appropriate as abbreviations and write them correctly. Remember, this is formal academic writing; be sure to follow the conventions for using abbreviations in papers. When you have more than one abbreviation style to choose from, select the one recommended in this section. Note: The term "dense rock equivalent" is abbreviated DRE.

EXAMPLE   Peter Francis, ~~Doctor of Philosophy~~ *PhD,* is among the schol-

ars who have written introductory texts on volcanoes.

The unpredictable, destructive nature of volcanoes has attracted the interest of both scholarly and lay circles. Though it erupted in anno Domini 79, Mount Vesuvius is still famous because of its violent decimation of the city of Pompeii. Second to Vesuvius in destructive power is Mount Pelée, which in 1902 killed nearly thirty thousand people (id est, all but four of the citizens of Saint Pierre). Scholars like Professor George Walker have attempted to quantify and predict the effects of volcanoes. Professor Walker developed a system whereby volcanic eruptions are judged by magnitude, intensity, dispersive power, violence, and destructive potential. Walker began using a measurement called dense rock equivalent to measure unwitnessed eruptions. The actual volume of a volcano is converted into dense rock equivalent, which accounts for spaces in the rocks. Walker et alia have continued to perform research which will aid in the study of volcanoes.

46b | ACRONYMS

Acronyms are abbreviations formed by capitalizing the first letter in each word. Unlike abbreviations, acronyms are pronounced as words.

AIDS for Acquired Immunodeficiency Syndrome

NASA for National Air and Space Administration

NATO for North Atlantic Treaty Alliance

WAC for writing across the curriculum

A subset of acronyms are initial-letter abbreviations that have become so common that we know the organization or thing by its initials.

ACLU for American Civil Liberties Union

HIV for human immunodeficiency virus

MLA for Modern Language Association

rpm for revolutions per minute

WNBA for Women's National Basketball Association

YMCA for Young Men's Christian Association

Familiar acronyms and initial-letter abbreviations such as CBS, CIA, FBI, IQ, and UN are rarely spelled out. In a few cases, such as *radar* (*ra*dio *d*etecting *a*nd *r*anging) and *laser* (*l*ight *a*mplification by *s*timulated *e*mission of *r*adiation), the terms used to create the acronym have been forgotten by almost all who use them.

Unfamiliar acronyms and abbreviations should always be spelled out. Acronyms and abbreviations frequent in particular fields should be spelled out on first use. For example, MMPI (Minnesota Multiphasic Personality Inventory) is a familiar abbreviation in psychology but is unfamiliar to those outside that discipline. Even when acronyms are generally familiar, few readers will object to your giving the terms from which an acronym derives on the first use.

The **National Association for the Advancement of Colored People (NAACP)** is the nation's largest and strongest civil rights organization. The **NAACP** was founded in 1909 by a group of prominent black and white citizens who were outraged by the numerous lynchings of African Americans.

Common Errors

Punctuation of abbreviations and acronyms

The trend now is away from using periods after many abbreviations. In formal writing you can still use periods, with certain exceptions.

Do not use periods with

1. **Acronyms and initial-letter abbreviations:** AFL-CIO, AMA, HMO, NAFTA, NFL, OPEC
2. **Two-letter mailing abbreviations:** AZ (Arizona), FL (Florida), ME (Maine), UT (Utah)
3. **Compass points:** NE (northeast), SW (southwest)
4. **Technical abbreviations:** kph (kilometers per hour), SS (sum of squares), SD (standard deviation)

Remember: Do not use periods with postal abbreviations for states, compass points, technical abbreviations, and established organizations.

 For step-by-step discussion, examples, and practice of this common error, go to **www.ablongman.com/faigley049.**

Computer Strategies

Acronyms and abbreviations in the world of computers

Acronyms and initial-letter abbreviations are as much a part of the world of computers as hard drives, keyboards, and monitors. Some

(continued next page)

acronyms refer to specific kinds of hardware such as PDA (personal digital assistant), LAN (local area network), RAM (random-access memory), and DSL (digital subscriber line). Some refer to key concepts in computing: bps (bits per second), FTP (file transfer protocol), and GUI (graphical user interface). Others refer to computer languages and formats such as HTML (hypertext markup language), JPEG (Joint Photographic Experts Group), and GIF (graphic interchange format). Some refer to companies: AOL (America Online), IBM (International Business Machines), and MSN (Microsoft Network). Still others refer to activities associated with email: CC (carbon copy), BCC (blind carbon copy). And still others are a kind of shorthand: IRL (in real life), IMHO (in my humble opinion), LOL (laughing out loud), and TMOT (trust me on this).

When you write about the digital world, think about your potential readers and how familiar they are with the acronyms of computing.

EXERCISE 46.2 The following paragraph from a research paper uses some abbreviations correctly and some incorrectly. Revise the paragraph, adding abbreviations where needed and spelling out the words where needed. You may also need to add or subtract punctuation marks such as parentheses and periods. Refer to the following list for the relevant abbreviations. Remember to make decisions based on whether or not the general population is familiar with the abbreviation.

- UNDAT—United Nations Declaration Against Torture
- LAPD—Los Angeles Police Department
- KKK—Ku Klux Klan
- DEA—Drug Enforcement Agency
- IRA—Irish Republican Army
- CIA—Central Intelligence Agency
- SERE—Survival, Evasion, Resistance, and Escape
- HRC—Human Rights Campaign
- ACLU—American Civil Liberties Union

EXAMPLE   In 1992, the ~~Los Angeles Police Department~~ *LAPD* was ac-

cused of unduly torturing an African American mo-

torist, Rodney King.

Various organizations define torture in different ways; however, UNDAT officially defines torture as undue pain suffered at
the hands of a public official. Despite the various definitions,
however, the general public knows torture when it sees it. From
Ku Klux Klan lynchings to the torture of American DEA agents
by the Mexican government, torture is alive and well in the
American consciousness. Though we often associate torture with
medieval times or extremist groups such as the I.R.A., America's
Central Intelligence Agency has been accused of using torture as a
method of coercion. Torture is so present in the world that the
U.S. armed forces put their personnel through a special training
program—SERE. SERE theoretically prepares soldiers to survive
torture. Because of the prevalence of torture in what are generally
considered civilized societies, organizations such as HRC and the
ACLU fight to preserve the rights of those who cannot protect
themselves.

46c NUMBERS

In formal writing spell out any number that can be expressed in one or
two words, as well as any number, regardless of length, at the beginning of
a sentence. Also, hyphenate two-word numbers from twenty-one to ninety-
nine.

My office is **twenty-three** blocks from my apartment—too far to
walk but a perfect bike riding distance.

When a sentence begins with a number that requires more than two words,
revise it if possible.

Correct but awkward
Fifteen thousand six hundred runners left the Hopkinton starting line at noon in the Boston Marathon.

Better
At the start of the Boston Marathon, **15,600** runners left Hopkinton at noon.

The exceptions. In scientific reports and some business writing that requires the frequent use of numbers, using numerals more often is appropriate. Most styles do not write out in words a year, a date, an address, a page number, the time of day, decimals, sums of money, phone numbers, rates of speed, or the scene and act of a play. Use numerals instead.

In **2001** only **33%** of respondents said they were satisfied with the City Council's proposals to help the homeless.

The **17** trials were conducted at temperatures **12–14°C** with results ranging from **2.43** to **2.89** mg/dl.

When one number modifies another number, write one out and express the other in numeral form.

In the last year all **four 8th** Street restaurants have begun to donate their leftovers to the soup kitchen.

Only after Meryl had run in **12 fifty**-mile ultramarathons did she finally win first place in her age group.

EXERCISE 46.3 All of the numbers in the following paragraph are spelled out. Decide where it would be more appropriate to use the numerals instead and revise. Remember to add hyphens where necessary.

Example   Caused by the dysfunction of two tiny joints near the ears, a form of temporomandibular joint dysfunction (TMJ) was identified in ~~nineteen hundred thirty four~~ *1934* by Doctor Costen.

Five hundred sixty is the number of times you heard a popping sound resonating from the jaw of the woman sitting next to you on the plane. She may be one of over nine point five million people suffering from TMJ, a condition that often causes symptoms such as popping, swelling, and aching in the jaw. At least one study has shown that women on hormone treatments are seventy seven percent more likely to develop TMJ symptoms. The disorder goes by at least six names, most of which include the initials TM, for temporomandibular: Costen's Syndrome, TMJ, TMD, TMJDD, CMD, and TMPD. Doctors currently prescribe at least forty nine different treatments for the disorder, ranging from one-dollar-and-fifty-cent mouth guards to prevent tooth grinding to a myriad of treatments which could cost thousands of dollars.

If English Is Not Your First Language

10

Chapter 47
Nouns and Articles

Hurdlers in track races try to clear every hurdle, yet it's not unusual to see even the most experienced runners clip one or two—and sometimes several—in a single race. If English is not your native language, you've probably "clipped" some of the rules governing English more than once. Throughout Chapters 47 through 50, you'll see references to a Web site that is designed to help nonnative speakers with some of the more difficult customs of English language usage. There, in addition to explanatory text, you'll find many practice exercises to reinforce the guidelines in Chapters 47–50.

Perhaps the most troublesome conventions for nonnative speakers are those that guide usage of the common articles *the*, *a*, and *an*. To understand how articles work in English, you must first understand how the language uses **nouns**.

47a   KINDS OF NOUNS

There are two basic kinds of nouns. A **proper noun** begins with a capital letter and names a unique person, place, or thing: *George W. Bush, Russia, Eiffel Tower*. In the following list, note that each word refers to someone or something so specific and unique that it bears a name.

PROPER NOUNS

Beethoven	Michael Jordan	South Korea
Concorde	New York Yankees	Springfield
Empire State Building	Picasso	Stockholm
Honda	Queen Elizabeth	United States

The other basic kind of noun is called a **common noun**. Common nouns do not name a unique person, place, or thing: *man, country, tower*. Note that the words in the following list are not names and so are not capitalized.

COMMON NOUNS

airplane	canyon	continent
athlete	car	dog
baseball team	citizen	downtown
building	city	woman

Common nouns can also refer to abstractions, such as *grace, love,* and *power.* Distinguishing proper from common nouns is as simple as remembering that proper nouns are names and are always capitalized, while common nouns are not names and are not capitalized.

EXERCISE 47.1 Underline the common nouns in the following paragraph once and underline the proper nouns twice. Correct any errors in capitalization.

EXAMPLE   In 1903, a fire in ~~c~~hicago led to the new safety ~~L~~aws.

In 1903, Chicago opened the new iroquois theater on West Randolph street. Around christmas, the Theater held a performance of "mr. blue beard" starring eddie Foy. Shortly after the play started, a light sparked causing a curtain to catch on fire. Elvira Pinedo said the crowd panicked after a giant Fireball appeared. This panic led to the deaths of more than six hundred people, many of whom died because bodies were pressed against doors that opened inward. Shortly after the Tragedy, mayor Carter h. Harrison was indicted and new laws demanded Theaters have doors that open outward, toward the lobby.

47b | COUNT AND NONCOUNT NOUNS

Common nouns can be classified as either *count* or *noncount.* A count noun can have a number before it (*two books, three oranges*) and can be made plural, usually by adding *-s* (*finger, fingers*). Noncount nouns cannot be counted directly and cannot take the plural form (*information*, but not *informations*). Noncount nouns can be counted or quantified in only two ways: either by general adjectives that treat the noun as a mass (*much* information, *little* garbage) or by placing another noun between the quantifying word and the noncount noun (two *kinds* of information, three *piles* of garbage).

A few nouns can be either count or noncount, depending on how they're used. *Hair* can refer to either a strand of hair, where it serves as a count noun, or a mass of hair, where it becomes a noncount noun. In the same way, *space* can refer to a particular, quantifiable area (as in *two parking spaces*) or to the heavens. In each case, the meaning of the word changes, depending on its context.

Writing in the World

Noncount nouns in English

In some languages, all nouns can take singular and plural forms. In English, noncount nouns refer to a collective mass that, taken as a whole, does not have a particular or regular shape. Think of the noncount noun as a mass that can be subdivided into smaller parts without losing its identity. Noncount nouns like *information, garbage, bread,* and *sand* can be broken down into smaller units and remain unchanged in essence: *bits* of information, *piles* of garbage, *slices* of bread, *grains* of sand. Count nouns like *train, finger,* and *ocean* cannot be subdivided without becoming something else: a wheel on a train, a knuckle on a finger, but no longer simply a train or a finger.

CORRECT USAGE OF *HAIR* AS COUNT NOUN
I carefully combed my few **hairs** across my mostly bald scalp.

CORRECT USAGE OF *HAIR* AS NONCOUNT NOUN
My roommate spent an hour this morning combing his **hair**.

A small number of conditions determine when and how count and noncount nouns are preceded by articles.

1. *A* or *an* is not used with noncount nouns.

   The crowd hummed with ~~an~~ excitement.

2. *A* or *an* is used with singular count nouns whose particular identity is unknown to the reader or writer.

   The security guard was reading a book.

3. *The* is used with most count and noncount nouns whose particular identity is known to the reader. The noun may be known for one of several reasons:
   a. The noun has already been mentioned.
   b. The noun is accompanied by a superlative such as *highest, lowest, best,* or *worst* that makes its specific identity clear.
   c. The noun has a unique identity, such as *the moon.*
   d. The noun's identity is made clear by its context in the sentence.

4. *The* is not used with noncount nouns meaning "in general."

   INCORRECT The war is hell.

   CORRECT   War is hell.

EXERCISE 47.2 The following sentences include various types of plural nouns: count, noncount, and those that can be either, depending on how they are used. Underline the correct plural form from the choices provided.

EXAMPLE Barry Gordy's Motown Records made much (money/monies) and introduced America to many (entertainer/entertainers) who would have otherwise been silenced because of their race.

1. In the late 1950s, Detroit was one of America's many (city/cities) famous for the production of (numbers of automobile/automobiles).

2. Detroit's sound soon changed from the auto industry's assembly line of heavy (pieces of equipment/equipments) to Motown's assembly line of superstar musical (groups of act/acts).

3. Gordy was famous for his (kinds of method/methods) of production; he tailored images down to the styles of performers' (hair/hairs), dances, and musical numbers.

4. The (positions of employment/employments) were clear; (all of the employee/employees) were allowed to perform only the tasks for which they were specifically hired.

5. Though Gordy's techniques led Motown to (much wealth/wealths), the same techniques sent entertainers packing for labels that would provide them with more (personal satisfaction/personal satisfactions).

47c | SINGULAR AND PLURAL FORMS

Count nouns usually take both singular and plural forms, while noncount nouns usually do not take plural forms and are not counted directly. Quantifying noncount nouns requires either that we either use general adjectives like *much* or *little* or that we insert another noun between the quantifying word and the noncount noun: four *loads* of laundry.

Common Errors

Singular and plural forms of count nouns

Count nouns are simpler to quantify than noncount nouns. But remember that English requires you to state both singular and plural forms of nouns consistently and explicitly. Look at the following sentences.

INCORRECT The three **bicyclist** shaved their **leg** before the big race.

CORRECT The three **bicyclists** shaved their **legs** before the big race.

In the first sentence, readers would understand that the plural form of *bicyclist* is implied by the quantifier *three* and that the plural form of *leg* is implied by the fact that bicyclists have two legs. (If they don't you would hope that the writer would have made that clear already!) Nevertheless, correct form in English is to indicate the singular or plural nature of a count noun explicitly, in every instance.

Remember: English requires you to use plural forms of count nouns even if a plural number is otherwise indicated.

 For more help using count and noncount nouns, see the exercises at www.ablongman.com/faigley050.

EXERCISE 47.3 The following paragraph includes many examples of singular/plural inconsistency. Correct any incorrect versions of nouns.

> EXAMPLE   In the history of fashion, many ~~word~~ *words* have lost their
> original ~~meaning~~ *meanings*.

Every year, thousands of bride and groom don traditional attire while attending their wedding. One garment associated with many of these traditional wedding is the groom's cummerbund or decorative waistband. This garment dates back many century to Persia where grooms would wrap their loin in a tight cotton cloth called a "kamarband" or "loin band." This cloth was meant to hide the genitals from the various bride-to-be. By the time many British settler inhabited the Middle East, the original meaning of the tradition had disappeared, and like a number of garment, it was being worn strictly as decoration.

47d ARTICLES

Once you have a basic understanding of how nouns are made plural in English, you're prepared to understand how and when to use articles. Articles indicate that a noun is about to appear, and they clarify what the noun refers to. There are only two kinds of articles in English, definite and indefinite:

1. **the**   *The* is a **definite article**, meaning that it refers to (1) a specific object already known to the reader, (2) one about to be made known to the reader, or (3) a unique object.

2. **a, an**   The **indefinite articles** *a* and *an* refer to an object whose specific identity is not known to the reader. The only difference between *a* and *an* is that *a* is used before a consonant sound (*man, friend, yellow*), while *an* is used before a vowel sound (*animal, enemy, orange*).

Look at these sentences, identical except for their articles, and imagine that each is taken from a different newspaper story:

Rescue workers lifted **the** man to safety.

Rescue workers lifted **a** man to safety.

By use of the definite article *the*, the first sentence indicates that the reader already knows something about the identity of this man and his needing to be rescued. The news story has already referred to him. The sentence also suggests that this was the only man rescued, at least in this particular part of the story.

The indefinite article *a* in the second sentence indicates that the reader does not know anything about this man. Either this is the first time the news story has referred to him, or there are other men in need of rescue. When deciding whether to use the definite or indefinite article, ask yourself whether the noun refers to something specific or unique, or whether it refers to something general. *The* is used for specific or unique nouns; *a* and *an* are used for nonspecific or general nouns.

Common Errors

Articles with count and noncount nouns

Knowing how to distinguish between count and noncount nouns can help you decide which article to use. Noncount nouns are never used with the indefinite articles *a* or *an*.

INCORRECT   Maria jumped into a water.

CORRECT   Maria jumped into the water.

No articles are used with noncount and plural count nouns when you wish to state something that has a general application.

INCORRECT   The water is a precious natural resource.

CORRECT   Water is a precious natural resource.

INCORRECT   The soccer players tend to be quick and agile.

CORRECT   Soccer players tend to be quick and agile.

Remember:

1. Noncount nouns are never used with *a* and *an*.
2. Noncount and plural nouns used to make general statements do not take articles.

For more help with using articles, see the exercises at
www.ablongman.com/faigley051.

EXERCISE 47.4 Underline the correct definite or indefinite articles for the nouns in the following paragraph.

EXAMPLE   Both (a/an/the) novel and (a/an/the) screenplay have been written about the career of (a/an/the) African American boxer Jack Johnson.

In (a/an/the) early 1900s, boxing films were (a/an/the) extremely popular form of entertainment; (a/an/the) fight would be filmed and shown in movie houses across (a/an/the) country. This practice changed after (a/an) race riot occurred following (a/an) match between (a/an/the) white man, ex-champion Jim Jeffries, and (a/an/the) black man, Jack Johnson. Jeffries had previously refused to fight (a/an) African-American boxer, but after Johnson defeated (a/an/the) current white champion, Jeffries agreed to meet (a/an/the) challenger. After Johnson defeated (a/an/the) ex-champion, a nationwide race riot erupted in large portions of (a/an/the) South, as well as (a/an/the) number of other locales. These riots caused alarm in (a/an/the) United States Congress, and within three weeks, (a/an) bill was passed prohibiting (a/an/the) public screening of such films.

EXERCISE 47.5 The following paragraph includes several examples of properly and improperly used articles. Underline the articles, identify the types of nouns they modify (plural or singular, count or noncount), and correct any improperly chosen articles.

EXAMPLE   Just after <u>an</u> end of American involvement in <u>a</u> un-
singular count ... *singular count*
popular war, one of <u>a</u> most quirky fads of <u>a</u> twenti-
plural count
eth century brought piles of a <u>money</u> to an <u>American</u>
singular count ... *noncount*
advertising agent.
singular count

REWRITTEN   Just after ~~an~~ *the* end of American involvement in ~~a~~ *an* unpopular war, one of ~~a~~ *the* most quirky fads of ~~a~~ *the* twentieth century brought piles of ~~a~~ money to an American
advertising agent.

While Americans recovered from a Vietnam War, Gary Dahl sat in the California restaurant talking with friends. Dahl joked of the inconveniences of the traditional pets owned by his buddies; this conversation produced the brainchild that would bring him much a wealth and satisfaction. His idea was to maintain the fun of the live pet in the form of a unique pet rock: a rock, training manual, and carrying case. By the mid-1970s, buying your girlfriend pieces of a jewelry had been replaced by giving the popular Pet Rock. A curiosity made the news and earned Dahl millions of dollars.

Chapter 48

Verbs

You cannot write a sentence in English without using a verb. As the heart animates the body, verbs animate sentences: Without them, nothing—either real or imagined, past or present—happens. Though both native and nonnative speakers of English encounter problems with verbs, this chapter focuses on the conventions of the verb system that give nonnative speakers particular trouble. See also Chapters 34 and 35.

48a | *BE* VERBS

The verb system in English can be divided between simple verbs like *run, speak,* and *look,* and verb phrases like *may have run, have spoken,* and *will be looking.* In these examples, the words that appear before the main verbs—*may, have, will,* and *be*—are called **auxiliary verbs** (also called **helping verbs**). Helping verbs, as their name suggests, exist to help express something about the action of main verbs: for example, when the action occurs (tense), whether the subject acted or was acted upon (voice), or whether or not an action occurred.

Indicating tense and voice with *be* verbs

Like the other auxiliary verbs *have* and *do, be* changes form to signal tense. In addition to *be* itself, the **be verbs** are *is, am, are, was, were,* and *been.* To show ongoing action, *be* verbs are followed by the present participle, which is a verb with an *-ing* ending:

INCORRECT	I **am** think of all the things I'd rather **be do**.
CORRECT	I **am** thinking of all the things I'd rather **be** doing.
INCORRECT	He **was** run as fast as he could.
CORRECT	He **was** running as fast as he could.

To show that an action is being done to, rather than by, the subject, follow *be* verbs with the past participle (a verb usually ending in *-ed, -en,* or *-t*):

INCORRECT　The movie **was direct** by John Woo.

CORRECT　The movie **was directed** by John Woo.

INCORRECT　The dessert **will be eat** by the guest of honor.

CORRECT　The dessert **will be eaten** by the guest of honor.

Writing in the World

Verbs that express cognitive activity

English, unlike Chinese, Arabic, and several other languages, requires a form of *be* before the present or past participle. As you've probably discovered, however, English has many exceptions to its rules. Verbs that express some form of cognitive activity rather than a direct action are not used as present participles with *be* verbs. Examples of such words include *know, like, see,* and *believe.*

INCORRECT　You **were knowing** that I would be late.

CORRECT　You **knew** that I would be late.

But here's an exception to an exception: A small number of these verbs, such as *considering, thinking,* and *pondering,* can be used as present participles with *be* verbs.

CORRECT　I **am considering** whether to finish my homework first.

EXERCISE 48.1 The following paragraph is filled with *be* verbs. In each case, underline the correct verb form from the choices provided in parentheses.

EXAMPLE　Rosh Hashanah, one of the religious High Holy Days, (is celebrated/is celebrating) during the second day of the seventh month of the Jewish calendar, Tishri.

Though many think it marks only the Jewish New Year, those who celebrate Rosh Hashanah (understand/are understanding) that it represents the New Year, the day of Shofar blowing, the day of remembrance, and the day of judgment. It long (has been consider/has been considered) the only High Holy Day that warrants a two-day celebration; those who (observe/are observing) the holiday consider the two-day period one extended forty-eight-hour day. Families (feast/are feasting) on foods that (are sweetened/are sweetening) with honey, apples, and carrots, symbolizing the sweet year to come. Challah, the bread that (is eating/is eaten) on the Sabbath, is reshaped into a ring, symbolizing the hope that the upcoming year will roll smoothly.

48b | MODAL AUXILIARY VERBS

Modal auxiliary verbs—*will, would, can, could, may, might, shall, must,* and *should*—are helping verbs that express conditions like possibility, permission, speculation, expectation, obligation, and necessity. Unlike the helping verbs *be, have,* and *do,* modal verbs do not change form.

Two basic rules apply to all uses of modal verbs. First, modal verbs are always followed by the simple form of the verb. The simple form is the verb by itself, in the present tense, such as *have,* but not *had, having,* or *to have.*

| INCORRECT | She should **had** walked past the accident. |
| CORRECT | She should **have** walked past the accident. |

The second rule is that you should not use modals consecutively.

| INCORRECT | If you work harder at writing, you **might could** improve. |
| CORRECT | If you work harder at writing, you **might** improve. |

Speculation:	If you had flown, you **would** have arrived yesterday.
Ability:	She **can** run faster than Jennifer.
Necessity:	You **must** know what you want to do.
Intention:	He **will** wash his own clothes.
Permission:	**May** I leave now?
Advice or	You **should** wash behind your ears.
advisability:	I **should** wash behind my ears.
Possibility:	It **might** be possible to go home early.
Assumption:	You **must** have stayed up late last night.
Expectation:	You **should** enjoy the movie.
Order:	You **must** leave the building.

EXERCISE 48.2 The following sentences contain modal auxiliary verbs. Some are used properly and some improperly. Identify the conditions they express (speculation, ability, necessity, and so on) and correct any incorrect modal usage.

EXAMPLE The cause of Karen Silkwood's death might could being one of the great conspiracies of recent American history.

REWRITE The cause of Karen Silkwood's death **might be** one of the great conspiracies of recent American history. (Possibility)

1. In the 1970s, the Kerr-McGee plutonium plant was accused of violations that may shall have endangered workers' lives.
2. After becoming contaminated with airborne plutonium, Karen Silkwood decided she would working harder to effect change.
3. Silkwood believed she had information that should have gone public and would having incriminated the company.
4. On the day she would have shared her information, she died in an automobile accident.
5. Some think her death might have been part of a conspiracy carried out by the company.

48c | VERBS AND INFINITIVES

Several verbs are followed by particular verb forms. An infinitive is *to* plus the simple form of the verb. These are some of the more common verbs that are followed by an infinitive:

afford	expect	promise
agree	fail	refuse
ask	hope	seem
attempt	intend	struggle
claim	learn	tend
consent	need	wait
decide	plan	want
demand	prepare	wish

INCORRECT   **You learn playing** the guitar by practicing.

CORRECT   **You learn to play** the guitar by practicing.

Some verbs require that a noun or pronoun come after the verb and before the infinitive:

advise	instruct	require
cause	order	tell
command	persuade	warn

INCORRECT   I would **advise to watch** where you step.

CORRECT   I would **advise you to watch** where you step.

A few verbs, when followed by a noun or pronoun, take an *unmarked infinitive*, which is an infinitive without *to*.

have	let	make

INCORRECT   I will **let** her **to plan** the vacation.

CORRECT   I will **let** her **plan** the vacation.

EXERCISE 48.3 Complete the following sentences by choosing the proper verb, pronoun, and infinitive combinations from those provided in parentheses. Underline the correct answer.

> **EXAMPLE** Many Slavic myths (to advise you/<u>advise you to</u>) reevaluate the significance of nature.

1. The evil Koshchei the Deathless would attempt (you to hide/to hide) under a giant oak tree.
2. The goddess of death Baba Yaga would (cause to turn victims/cause her victims to turn) into stone.
3. Hiding in corn, field spirits called Poleviks would make drunken farm workers (fear/to fear) for their lives.
4. You can (learn/to learn) from earth goddess Mati-Syra-Zemlya by digging a hole and listening for her advice.
5. Rusalkas, souls of infants or drowned girls, could (order you to die/order to die you) a watery death with their songs.

48d | VERBS AND *–ING* VERBALS

Other verbs are followed by gerunds, which are verbs ending in *-ing* that are used as nouns. Here are some of the more common verbs that are followed by a gerund.

admit	discuss	quit
advise	enjoy	recommend
appreciate	finish	regret
avoid	imagine	risk
consider	practice	suggest

> **INCORRECT** She will **finish to grade** papers by noon.
>
> **CORRECT** She will **finish grading** papers by noon.

A smaller number of verbs can be followed by either gerunds or infinitives.

begin	hate	love
continue	like	start

| WITH GERUND | She **likes** **working** in the music store. |
| WITH INFINITIVE | She **likes** **to work** in the music store. |

For more help using gerunds and infinitives, see the exercises at
www.ablongman.com/faigley052.

EXERCISE 48.4 The following sentences include verbs that should be followed by either gerunds or infinitives. Underline the correct gerund or infinitive from the options provided in parentheses. If both options are correct, underline both.

> EXAMPLE   Some will suggest that (to research/<u>researching</u>) folklore is a difficult task.

1. Historians risk (misidentifying/to misidentify) actual origins when stories have been passed down simply by word of mouth.
2. Though some like (to believe/believing) that Edward O'Reilly found the story of Pecos Bill circulating among American cowboys, it is hard to prove.
3. The story of little Bill, who was raised by coyotes, fails (to go/going) away despite its ambiguous origins.
4. Despite the confusion, stories about Bill's bride Slue-Foot Sue and his horse Widow Maker continue (to spread/spreading) as part of Americana.
5. Because of the debate over authenticity, however, some consider (to call/calling) the story popular culture, rather than folklore.

48e | CONDITIONAL SENTENCES

Conditional sentences express *if-then* relationships: They consist of a subordinate clause beginning with *if, unless,* or *when* that expresses a condition, and a main clause that expresses a result. The tense and mood of the verb in the main clause and the type of conditional sentence determine the tense and mood of the verb in the subordinate clause.

Conditional sentences fall into three categories: **factual, predictive,** and **hypothetical**.

Factual conditionals

Factual conditional sentences express factual relationships: If this happens, that will follow. The tense of the verb in the conditional clause is the same as the tense of the verb in the result clause:

INCORRECT	If commuters use public transportation instead of driving, they would save money.
CORRECT	If commuters use public transportation instead of driving, they save money.

Predictive conditionals

Predictive conditional sentences express predicted consequences from possible conditions. The verb in the conditional clause is present tense, and the verb in the result clause is formed with a modal (*will, would, can, could, may, might, shall, must,* and *should*) plus the base form of the verb.

INCORRECT	If you **take** the long way home, you **enjoy** the ride more.
CORRECT	If you **take** the long way home, you **will enjoy** the ride more.

Hypothetical conditionals

Hypothetical conditional sentences express events that are either not factual or unlikely to happen. For hypothetical events in the past, the conditional clause verb takes the past perfect tense. The main clause verb is formed from *could have, would have,* or *might have* plus the past participle.

INCORRECT	If we **had fed** the dog last night, he **would not run** away.
CORRECT	If we **had fed** the dog last night, he **would not have run away**.

For hypothetical events in the present or future, the conditional clause verb takes the past tense and the main clause verb is formed from *could, would,* or *might* and the base form.

INCORRECT	If we **paid** off our credit cards, we **can** buy a house.
CORRECT	If we **paid** off our credit cards, we **could** buy a house.

For more help using conditionals, see the exercises at
www.ablongman.com/faigley053.

EXERCISE 48.5 Rewrite the following sentences to reflect the conditional category represented in the parentheses following the sentence.

EXAMPLE   If you were to browse through the twentieth-century

culture, you ⌃*would* discover many phrases used to describe

human mating rituals. (Predictive)

1. When a fraternity boy wanted to become engaged to his girlfriend, he pin his fraternity pin on her blouse. (factual)
2. When a turn-of-the-century male wanted to schedule an appointment with his love, he make a "date." (factual)
3. If you had bruised the neck of your partner in the 1920s, you blame the "hickey" on a rope burn or the like. (hypothetical)
4. If you cannot afford to buy your own car and fuel, you find "double dating" more economical. (predictive)
5. If you had been accused of "petting" in the North, you accuse with "necking" in the South. (hypothetical)

48f | PARTICIPIAL ADJECTIVES

Recall that the present participle always ends in *-ing* (*boring, exciting*), while most past participles end in *-ed* (*bored, excited*). Both participle forms can be used as adjectives.

When participles are used as adjectives, they can either precede the nouns they modify or they can come after a connecting verb.

It was a **thrilling** book. (*Thrilling* modifies *book*.)

Stephanie was **thrilled**. (*Thrilled* modifies *Stephanie*.)

Present participles like *thrilling* describe a thing or person causing an experience, while past participles like *thrilled* describe a thing or person receiving the experience.

INCORRECT   Students considered the teacher **entertained**.

CORRECT   Students considered the teacher **entertaining**.

EXERCISE 48.6 The following paragraph includes participial adjectives. Underline each participial adjective once and the word being modified twice.

EXAMPLE   The <u>whirling</u> <u>tornado</u> is often considered one of the world's most <u>damaging</u> natural <u>disasters</u>.

Many tornadoes are created by a special rotating thunderstorm called a supercell. A rising gust of warm wind combines with the raging storm; the warm air begins spinning as the rainfall causes a rushing downdraft. This interaction creates a harrowing twister that is awful for those in its path. The United States is honored to bear the devastating distinction of hosting the world's most tornadoes per year; homeowners in the regions known as "Tornado Alley" and "Dixie Alley" are terrified when they see the funneling tornado heading for their houses.

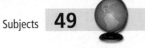

Chapter 49
English Sentence Structure

Performing musicians are not judged by the number of songs they know. Likewise, multilingual speakers understand that a good vocabulary is not enough to communicate effectively. Words derive much of their meaning from context, and the basic contextual unit is the sentence. Your ability to understand and convey information accurately in English depends to a high degree on your understanding of how sentences are put together.

49a | SUBJECTS

Except for imperatives (*Be careful!*), sentences in English always contain a subject and a predicate. A subject names who or what the sentence is about; the predicate contains information about the subject. Many languages allow the writer to omit the subject if it's implied, but English requires that each sentence include a subject, even when the meaning of the sentence would be clear without it. In some cases, you must supply an expletive, *it* or *there*, to stand in for the subject.

INCORRECT	Snowing in Alaska.
CORRECT	**It's** snowing in Alaska.
INCORRECT	**Won't** be enough time to climb that mountain.
CORRECT	**There won't** be enough time to climb that mountain.

Both main and subordinate clauses within sentences require a subject and a predicate. A main clause can stand alone as a sentence, while subordinate clauses can only be understood in the context of the sentence of which they're a part. Still, even subordinate clauses must contain a subject. Look at the underlined subordinate clauses in the following two correct sentences.

We avoided the main highway <u>because **it** had two lanes blocked off.</u>
We avoided the main highway, <u>**which** had two lanes blocked off.</u>

In the first example, the subject of the subordinate clause is *it,* a pronoun representing the highway. In the second sentence, the relative pronoun *which*—also representing the highway—becomes the subject. Once you've stated the subject, however, don't repeat it within the same clause.

INCORRECT   We avoided the highway, which **it** had two lanes blocked off.

In this sentence, *it* repeats the subject *which.*

EXERCISE 49.1 Underline all of the subjects in the following sentences. Some sentences may have more than one subject; some may appear to have none. If the sentence appears to have no subject, supply the needed expletive.

EXAMPLE   Though <u>you</u> may have heard of Lee Harvey Oswald and John Wilkes Booth, many lesser-known <u>individuals</u> have put presidents in harm's way.

1. Though some assassins are widely known, Charles Guiteau and Leon Czolgolsz are relatively obscure.
2. Guiteau shot President James Garfield in 1881, and was little doubt he would be hung for the murder.
3. Twenty years later, Czolgolsz stood face to face with his victim, President William McKinley.
4. History books are littered with the names of would-be assassins such as Giuseppe Zangara, Samuel Byck, and Sarah Jane Moore.
5. You should protect your leaders because is no way to tell what the future will bring.

EXERCISE 49.2 In the following sentences, underline main clauses once and subordinate clauses twice. Circle the subjects in each.

> **EXAMPLE**   When (scientists) explain phenomena such as volcanoes and earthquakes, (they) often use the theory of plate tectonics.

1. Geologists based the theory on an earlier one that had observed that the continents fit together like pieces of a puzzle.
2. In the 1950s and 1960s, scientists found evidence to support the earlier theory, so they were able to confirm its hypothesis regarding continental drift.
3. Although water and earth appear to be distinctly separate, they share a similar underlayer called the asthenosphere.
4. This asthenosphere possesses high temperatures and pressures, and these conditions allow for fluid rock movement.
5. As plates move around, they can create volcanoes or increase and decrease the size of oceans and mountains.

49b ENGLISH WORD ORDER

All languages have their own rules for sentence structure. In English, correct word order often determines whether or not you succeed in saying what you mean.

The basic pattern in English is subject + verb.

Birds fly.

This is the simplest sentence structure in English. If a verb is transitive, it needs a direct object to complete its meaning. The direct object receives the action of the verb. If the verb is intransitive, like *exist*, it does not take a direct object. An intransitive verb does not require any following word or words to complete its meaning. It can, however, take an indirect object, which names the person or thing to whom or for whom the action takes place. A few verbs (*write, learn, read,* and others) can take both direct and indirect objects, depending on how they're used. Most dictionaries indicate whether verbs are transitive or intransitive.

Usually, a direct or indirect object will follow the verb. Here's a sentence with a transitive verb and a direct object.

The goalie blocked the kick.

Kick, the direct object, receives the action described by *blocked.*

In another simple pattern, the transitive verb is replaced by a linking verb that joins its subject to a following description.

The tallest player was the goalie.

Linking verbs like *was, become, sound, look,* and *seem* precede a *subject complement* (in this example, *the goalie*) that refers back to the subject.

At the next level of complexity, a sentence combines a subject with a verb, direct object, and indirect object.

INDIRECT   DIRECT
OBJ   OBJ
The goalie passed her the ball.

Passed is a transitive verb, *ball* is the direct object of the verb, and *her* is the indirect object, the person for whom the action was taken. The same idea can be expressed with a prepositional phrase instead of an indirect object:

DIRECT   PREP
OBJ   PHRASE
The goalie passed the ball to her.

Other sentence patterns are possible in English. (See Chapter 32.) However, it is important to remember that altering the basic subject + verb + object word order often changes the meaning of a sentence. If the meaning survives, the result may still be awkward. As a general rule, try to keep the verb close to its subject, and the direct or indirect object close to its verb.

EXERCISE 49.3 Label the parts of speech in the following sentences: subject (S), transitive or intransitive verb (TV or IV), linking verb (LV), direct object (DO), indirect object (IO), subject complement (SC), and prepositional phrase (PP). Not all sentences will contain all of these parts, but all will contain some.

EXAMPLE   Hinduism includes several gods and heroes in its system of beliefs.

1. Ganesh is the god of good luck.
2. Young Ganesh stood at the doorway to his mother's house.
3. He denied his father entry.
4. His father beheaded him.
5. His mother replaced his head with the head of an elephant.

49c | PLACEMENT OF MODIFIERS

The proximity of a modifier—an adjective or adverb—to the noun or verb it modifies provides an important clue to their relationship. Modifiers, even more than verbs, will be unclear if your reader can't connect them to their associated words. Both native and nonnative speakers of English often have difficulty with misplaced modifiers.

Clarity should be your first goal when using a modifier. Readers usually link modifiers with the nearest word. In the following examples, the highlighted words are adjective clauses that modify nouns.

UNCLEAR	Many pedestrians are killed each year by motorists **not using sidewalks**.
CLEAR	Many pedestrians **not using sidewalks** are killed each year by motorists.
UNCLEAR	He gave an apple to his girlfriend **on a silver platter**.
CLEAR	He gave an apple **on a silver platter** to his girlfriend.

An adverb—a word or group of words that modifies a verb, adjective, or another adverb—should not come between a verb and its direct object.

AWKWARD	The hurricane destroyed **completely** the city's tallest building.
BETTER	The hurricane **completely** destroyed the city's tallest building.

While single-word adverbs can come between a subject and its verb, avoid placing adverbial phrases in this position.

AWKWARD	Galveston, **following the 1900 hurricane that killed thousands**, built a seawall to prevent a future catastrophe.
BETTER	**Following the 1900 hurricane that killed thousands**, Galveston built a seawall to prevent a future catastrophe.

As a general rule, try to avoid placing an adverb between *to* and its verb. This is called a *split infinitive.*

AWKWARD	The water level was predicted **to not rise**.
BETTER	The water level was predicted **not to rise**.

Sometimes, though, a split infinitive will read more naturally than the alternative. Note also how the sentence with the split infinitive is more concise:

WITHOUT SPLIT INFINITIVE	Automobile emissions in the city are expected **to increase by more than two times** over the next five years.
WITH SPLIT INFINITIVE	Automobile emissions in the city are expected **to more than double** over the next five years.

Certain kinds of adverbs have special rules for placement. Adverbs that describe how something is done—called *adverbs of manner*—usually follow the verb.

The student listened **closely** to the lecture.

These adverbs may also be separated from the verb by a direct object:

She threw the ball **well**.

Adverbs of frequency usually are placed at the head of a sentence, before a single verb, or after an auxiliary verb in a verb phrase.

Often, politicians have underestimated the intelligence of voters.

Politicians have **often** underestimated the intelligence of voters.

It's common practice in English to combine two or more nouns to form a compound noun. Where two or more adjectives or nouns are strung together, the main noun is always positioned at the end of the string:

12-speed road **bike**, tall oak **tree**, computer **table**

EXERCISE 49.4 The following sentences include confusing modifiers. Underline the confusing modifiers, identify the broken rule (far away from modified word; adverb between verb and direct object; adverbial phrase between subject and verb; split infinitive), and rewrite the sentence clearly.

> **EXAMPLE**   Japanese film often is defined by the work of Akira Kurosawa <u>worldwide</u>. (Far away from modified word)
>
> **REWRITE**   Japanese film often is defined worldwide by the work of Akira Kurosawa.

1. Kurosawa chose initially painting as his preferred career.
2. Kurosawa, realizing painting would not bring riches, turned to film in 1936.
3. He was able to by 1943 direct his own films.
4. He is remembered for his Samurai films by many.
5. Many of his films, embraced in the West, retold Shakespearean tales.

EXERCISE 49.5 Underline all the adjectives and adverbs in the following sentences. Label adverbs of manner or adverbs of frequency, and correct improper word order where you find it.

> *adverb of frequency*
> **EXAMPLE**   Americans associate <u>often</u> cards and dice with <u>shady</u> gamblers <u>Las Vegas</u>.
>
> **REWRITE**   Often, Americans associate cards and dice with shady Las Vegas gamblers.

1. By the fourteenth century, cards playing were used widely for gambling and predicting the future.
2. The invention of the printing press directly connects to the proliferation of card games standardized.
3. Ancient dice directly can be traced to Tutankhamen's tomb.
4. Gamblers hollowed frequently the center of an illegally rigged die.
5. These classic games have withstood well the test of time.

Common Errors

Dangling modifiers

A dangling modifier does not seem to modify anything in a sentence; it dangles, unconnected to the word or words it presumably is intended to modify. Frequently, it produces some funny results:

When still a girl, my father joined the army.

It sounds like *father* was once a girl. The problem is that the subject, *I,* is missing:

When I was still a girl, my father joined the army.

Dangling modifiers usually occur at the head of a sentence in the form of adjective clauses, with a subject that is implied but never stated.

INCORRECT　　After lifting the heavy piano up the stairs, the apartment door was too small to get it through.

CORRECT　　After lifting the heavy piano up the stairs, **we discovered** the apartment door was too small to get it through.

Whenever you use a modifier, ask yourself whether its relationship to the word it modifies will be clear to your reader. What is clear to you may not be clear to your audience. Writing, like speaking, is an exercise in making your own thoughts explicit. The solution for the dangling modifier is to recast it as a complete clause with its own explicit subject and verb.

Remember: Modifiers should be clearly connected to the words they modify, especially at the beginning of sentences.

For more practice with modifiers as adjective clauses, see the exercises at **www.ablongman.com/faigley054.**

EXERCISE 49.6 The following sentences include dangling modifiers. Rewrite the sentences so that the relationship between subject, verb, and modifier is clear.

> EXAMPLE   In his early thirties, France was dealt a hefty blow by Maximilien Robespierre.

> REWRITE   In his early thirties, Maximilien Robespierre dealt France a hefty blow.

1. His philosophical role model, Robespierre followed the writings of Jean Jacques Rousseau.
2. Elected on the eve of the French Revolution, the people were enthralled by his skillful oratory.
3. Gaining further power in the following years, his influence over domestic affairs was unmistakable.
4. A bloodbath known as the Reign of Terror, Robespierre ordered a rash of executions of members of the aristocracy and his political enemies.
5. After they tired of his aggressive tactics, he was overthrown by his own political party.

Chapter 50
Idiomatic Structures

Imagine a single piece from a jigsaw puzzle. While it makes little or no sense by itself, the surrounding pieces make its contribution to the puzzle clear. Similarly, idioms are phrases whose meaning cannot be determined from the meanings of their component words. From verbal phrases like *drag one's feet* (meaning to delay) and *grab a bite* (get something to eat) to phrases that use prepositions in unpredictable and irregular ways, English is filled with idiomatic expressions. Unfortunately, there are few shortcuts for the nonnative speaker attempting to learn them, but a few general guidelines can save you time and confusion.

50a PREPOSITIONS

Prepositions are positional or directional words like *to, for, from, at, in, on,* and *with.* They are used before nouns and pronouns, but they also combine with adjectives and adverbs. Each preposition has a wide range of possible meanings depending on how it is used, and each must be learned over time in its many contexts.

Some of the most common prepositional phrases describe time and place, and many are idiomatic. Consider the following examples:

INCORRECT	On midnight
CORRECT	At midnight
INCORRECT	In the counter
CORRECT	On the counter
INCORRECT	In Saturday
CORRECT	On Saturday

INCORRECT   On February

CORRECT   In February

Over time, you may notice some patterns that help you determine the appropriate preposition. For example, *at* precedes a particular time, *on* precedes a day of the week, and *in* precedes a month, year, or other period of time.

Common Errors

Misused prepositions

The correct use of prepositions often seems unpredictable to non-native speakers of English. When you are not sure which preposition to use, consult a dictionary.

Of FOR *ABOUT*	The report on flight delays raised criticism ~~of~~ about scheduling of flights.
ON FOR *INTO*	The tennis player went ~~on~~ into a slump after failing to qualify for the French Open.
TO FOR *IN*	Angry over her low seeding in the tournament, Amy resigned her membership ~~to~~ in the chess club.
TO FOR *OF*	The family was ignorant ~~to~~ of the controversial history of the house they purchased.

Remember: When you are uncertain about a preposition, consult a dictionary intended for nonnative speakers of English such as *The Longman Dictionary of American English*.

 At **www.ablongman.com/faigley055,** *you'll find a list of common verbs with the prepositions that follow them. Following the list are exercises that allow you to practice using verb + preposition combinations.*

EXERCISE 50.1 Underline the proper preposition in parentheses in the following paragraph.

EXAMPLE (In, On, At) the 1940s, several dozen pilots died trying to break Mach one, the speed of sound.

(In, On, At) this time, pilots were familiar (with, in, on) the "wall of air" that existed (in, on, at) the speed of sound. Many airplanes shattered (into, onto, from) a million pieces because of this "wall of air." Pilots were especially afraid (for, on, of) a condition called "compressibility," which would make them lose control (in, of, on) the plane. Air Force pilot Chuck Yeager tried to break the sound barrier (from, with, on) *Glamorous Glennis*, a plane named (from, for, to) his wife. (In, On, At) October 14, 1947, Yeager made an attempt to reach Mach one. The ground crew heard a boom (from, at, in) the distance and feared that *Glamorous Glennis* had crashed. They cheered (with, from, in) joy when they heard Yeager (with, in, on) the radio a few moments later saying he had broken the sound barrier.

50b ADJECTIVES WITH PREPOSITIONS

Prepositions also combine with adjectives in specific ways. Prepositions precede nouns and pronouns, but they follow adjectives. Other than that basic guideline, however, you will have to stay alert when you hear and read English if you wish to gain confidence with these idiomatic structures.

Some common adjective-preposition phrases follow.

anxious about	grateful to	proud of
aware of	interested in	scared of
fond of	jealous of	sorry for
full of	nervous about	disgusted with

EXERCISE 50.2 The following paragraph contains adjective-preposition phrases. Choose the correct preposition.

EXAMPLE   The Statue of Liberty was (full for/<u>full of</u>) significance for the millions of immigrants.

The United States remains (grateful to/grateful with) the people of France for the gift of the Statue of Liberty. France supported the colonists during the American Revolution and continues to be (proud for/proud of) its role in creating the United States. Although many Americans today are not (aware of/aware with) the importance of French support in the founding of their country, they are nonetheless (interested in/interested with) French culture and (fond of/fond with) its cuisine.

50c | PHRASAL VERBS

The liveliest and most colorful feature of the English language, its numerous idiomatic verbal phrases, also gives many nonnative speakers the greatest difficulty.

Phrasal verbs consist of a verb and one or two **particles:** either a preposition, an adverb, or both. The verb and particles combine to form a phrase with a particular meaning that is often quite distinct from the meaning of the verb itself. Consider the following sentence:

I need to **go over** the chapter once more before the test.

Here, the meaning of *go over*—a verb and a preposition that, taken together, suggest casual study—is only weakly related to the meaning of either *go* or *over* by itself. English has hundreds of such idiomatic constructions, and the best way to familiarize yourself with them is to listen to and read as much informal English as you can.

Like regular verbs, phrasal verbs can be either transitive (they take a direct object) or intransitive. In the preceding example, *go over* is transitive. *Quiet down*—as in *Please quiet down*—is intransitive. Some phrases, like *wake up,* can be both: *Wake up!* is intransitive, while *Jenny, wake up the children* is transitive.

In some transitive phrasal verbs, the particles can be separated from the verb without affecting the meaning: *I made up a song* is equivalent to *I made a song up.* In others, the particles cannot be separated from the verb.

INCORRECT	You shouldn't **play** with love **around**.
CORRECT	You shouldn't **play around** with love.

Unfortunately, there are no shortcuts for learning which verbal phrases are separable and which are not. As you become increasingly familiar with English, you will grow more confident in your ability to use phrasal verbs.

Writing in the World

Idiomatic phrases every college student should know

To a greater degree than most languages, English is flexible and highly adaptable to different needs of expression. The best evidence of this can be found in its proliferation of idiomatic phrases. English dictionaries must undergo regular revision just to keep pace with the shifting meanings attached to its words.

This flexibility comes at a cost, however, and much of it is borne by those learning the language as adults. Handbooks such as this one will help you learn the conventions of English. But for idioms, there is no shortcut around old-fashioned memorization. While you would be right to think that memorizing the hundreds of idiomatic expressions in English is a *tall order* ("a difficult and time-consuming task"), the most effective way to memorize requires little extra effort. You only need to remain alert to words used in unfamiliar ways. Usually, you can puzzle out their meaning by paying close attention to the sentence they're used in.

Here are a few expressions common on virtually every college campus in the United States.

Idiomatic phrase	Meaning	Sample sentence
bone up on	acquaint oneself with	You should bone up on baseball before you watch a game.
catch up on	do something that was earlier postponed	Let's catch up on what we've missed.
cram for	study intensively, usually at the last minute	He spent the weekend cramming for the zoology test.
get cracking	hurry up	I need to get cracking on this essay.
go over	study quickly	I need to go over my notes once more.
kiss up to	flatter someone for the sake of preferential treatment	He kisses up to his history teacher by always agreeing with him.
lip service	express something in a shallow or insincere way	The commissioner gave lip service to neutrality, but he was clearly biased.
out of the question	impossible	Failing this course is out of the question.
place out	receive credit for a course by earning a high score on a placement test	I placed out of calculus.
to the letter	do precisely	I followed the teacher's instructions to the letter.

EXERCISE 50.3 The following paragraph contains a number of idiomatic phrasal verbs. Underline the phrasal verbs and write a short explanation of the meaning of each.

EXAMPLE   As a poet, scholar, and possibly a traitor, Ezra Pound
                                     to restate the main points
had a history that is difficult <u>to sum up</u>.

During World War II, Ezra Pound became a supporter of Mussolini and railed against Jewish people in a series of radio broadcasts. American officials caught up with him in Pisa and arrested him. They locked him up in an outdoor cage for several weeks. However, because he was declared psychologically unfit, it was out of the question to make him stand trial for treason. Thus, he was packed off to St. Elizabeth's mental hospital in Washington, D.C. While there, Pound carried on with his work as a poet. Even ten years after he was put in St. Elizabeth's his friends refused to give up on freeing him. As a result, he finally got out in 1958 and made a beeline back to Italy, where he hung his hat until his death in 1972.

Writing Essay Examinations

If you are a student who groans at the prospect of an essay exam, take heart. Writing essay exams is a skill you can learn. Your ability will improve with practice and careful preparation.

PREPARING FOR THE EXAM

The key to preparing for an essay exam is to use common sense. Get a good night's sleep. Eat breakfast. Don't wait until the last minute to study. And most of all, be prepared. The following steps will help you prepare for an essay exam.

1. **Learn what to expect.** Ask the instructor to describe the format of the exam. How much time will you have? How many points will each portion of the exam be worth? What qualities is the instructor looking for in an essay? Can you look at any sample questions or old exams? If you need a dictionary, can you bring one?

2. **Study early and often.** Material studied regularly over a period of time has a much better chance of staying in your long-term memory than material crammed in between gulps of coffee the night before the exam. Review your notes and assigned readings for the major concepts and terms being tested. Practice explaining, applying, and analyzing them. Think about how the texts or concepts relate to one another. Form a study group with a few equally serious classmates, divide up the concepts likely to appear on the exam, and practice explaining them to each other.

3. **Anticipate possible questions.** Generate essay questions you think might appear on the exam, then outline possible responses. Almost all essay questions will ask you to prove your ideas about certain concepts using specific examples. In your outline, list examples you might use and note how they illustrate the concept. If you're working with a study group, critique and strengthen each other's questions and outlines.

4. **Make a plan.** You can reduce your anxiety about taking an essay exam if you have a plan for budgeting your time and approaching the questions. Decide in what order you will answer questions. You may want to tackle those worth the most points first to ensure you'll have enough time to do them well. Allow time to plan, pre-write, revise, and proofread in addition to actually writing the essay.

WRITING A SUCCESSFUL EXAM

After *be prepared*, the best piece of advice for writing essay exams is *don't panic*. It's easy to feel pressured as you hear the clock ticking away during an exam. Too often that pressure leads students to rush into an essay, dumping all the information they can remember into a few rambling paragraphs. Although time is limited, don't forsake the writing process when you write an essay exam.

Understand the question

This piece of advice sounds obvious, but you would be surprised how many students botch essays because they don't take the time to read the question carefully. When you read the question, underline important words or phrases. If the question asks you to address more than one issue, number them. Ask the instructor to clarify confusing questions. Be on the lookout for prompting words like the following, which tell you what kind of essay the instructor wants.

ANALYZE

Analyze the social and academic effects of social promotion on high school students.

> Make an original argument that seeks to illuminate some aspect of the issue for the reader. Divide your analysis into logical categories or themes. An analysis offers you leeway to make connections to other similar issues; for instance, you could place social promotion in the same context as the current development of children's sports leagues that don't keep score.

ASSESS OR EVALUATE

The president's long-standing rationale for recommending most-favored nation (MFN) status for trade relations with China is that our openness encourages human rights reforms in China. Assess whether China's MFN status for the past four years has been a success on those grounds.

> A question that asks for assessment or evaluation involves making a judgment based on well-supported reasons. Avoid oversimplified judgments. Instead, weigh the evidence on each side. Rebut the opposition's argument. Support your view with examples.

COMPARE/CONTRAST

Compare Jane Austen's use of free indirect discourse in *Pride and Prejudice* with James Joyce's use of stream of consciousness in *A Portrait of the Artist as a Young Man*.

How does physical anthropology's approach to studying the Incas in Peru contrast with cultural anthropology's approach?

> *Compare/contrast* questions call for arguments about similarities or differences between texts or issues. A compare/contrast essay should not be simply a description of similarities or differences. Also, it should avoid making judgments about which item in the comparison is better. Instead, make an original argument about those similarities or differences. Consider how those similarities or differences work toward the same or different ends and evoke shared themes differently. Consider how they rise out of their historical circumstances.

DESCRIBE

Describe how aphasia can affect sufferers' language skills.

> *Describe* questions ask for a recounting of some course material rather than an original argument. Decide how you will order the paragraphs: chronologically, by theme, or from most to least important. Pay special attention to transitions in order to keep the argument structure clear.

DISCUSS

Discuss Giotto's reputation as a transitional figure between medieval and Renaissance painting.

> *Discuss* questions usually require a student to make an argument. These sorts of questions leave you loads of space in which to work. Thus, your challenge is to pinpoint a specific and manageable original argument. One way to tackle the Giotto essay, for instance, would be to break it down into the three major components the question mentions: medieval painting, Renaissance painting, and Giotto. Since *discuss* can be a vague prompting word, be sure to ask your instructor if you need clarification.

EXPLAIN

Explain why we would die of thirst if we drank only salt water.

> Take on the role of teacher. Your goal in this essay is to make the reader understand a concept. Begin by breaking the subject down into categories or steps. Carefully detail and illustrate those categories or steps. Use the terms covered in the course where appropriate.

EXPLORE

Explore how antitrust laws affected the telecommunications industry in the 1980s.

> Like discussion questions, *explore* questions tend to be vague. Thus, part of your task is to develop a focused argument. Avoid the temptation to respond with an equally vague thesis. (Antitrust laws had a considerable effect on the telecommunications industry during the 1980s.) Decide which key issues and terms you want to address.

Plan

After you read the essay question, breathe deeply and think. Take a few minutes to sketch an outline of your answer. Decide what argument you want to make. Break the argument into manageable chunks, logical steps, or categories. Note the examples you want to analyze in order to illustrate each chunk of the argument.

Write the essay

An essay exam is not the place to be subtle. Highlight your argument clearly at the beginning of the essay and map out the upcoming paragraphs. In the body of the essay write clear transitions that link paragraphs. Relate the point of each paragraph clearly to the larger argument. Offer examples to support your argument, and remember that examples aren't self-explanatory. Analyze your examples to prove that they illustrate the argument. Then write a conclusion that repeats your argument and the steps you took to prove it.

Revise and proofread

While your instructor won't expect essay exam answers to be as polished as other types of writing, your prose still affects your credibility. Reserve time at the end of the exam period to revise your essay, expanding on explanations, adding any examples that strengthen your argument, and clarifying muddled sentences. Then read the essay for errors in spelling, punctuation, and grammar.

Glossary of Grammatical Terms and Usage

The glossary gives the definitions of grammatical terms and items of usage. The grammatical terms are shown in blue. Some of the explanations of usage that follow are not rules, but guidelines to keep in mind for academic and professional writing. In these formal contexts, the safest course is to avoid words that are described as *nonstandard, informal,* or *colloquial.*

a/an   Use *a* before words that begin with a consonant sound (*a train, a house*). Use *an* before words that begin with a vowel sound (*an airplane, an hour*).

a lot/alot   *A lot* is generally regarded as informal; *alot* is nonstandard.

absolute   A phrase that has a subject and modifies an entire sentence (see Section 32d).

The soldiers marched in single file, **their rifles slung over their shoulders.**

accept/except   *Accept* is a verb meaning "receive" or "approve." *Except* is sometimes a verb meaning "leave out," but much more often, it's used as a conjunction or preposition meaning "other than."

She **accepted** her schedule **except** for Biology at 8 a.m.

active   A clause with a transitive verb in which the subject is the doer of the action (see Section 26a). See also **passive**.

adjective   A modifier that qualifies or describes the qualities of a noun or pronoun (see Sections 32b, 37a, and 37b).

adjective clause   A subordinate clause that modifies a noun or pronoun and is usually introduced by a relative pronoun (see Section 32c). Sometimes called a *relative clause.*

adverb   A word that modifies a verb, another modifier, or a clause (see Sections 32b, 37a, and 37c).

adverb clause   A subordinate clause that functions as an adverb by modifying a verb, another modifier, or a clause (see Section 32c).

advice/advise   The noun *advice* means a "suggestion"; the verb *advise* means to "recommend" or "give advice."

affect/effect   Usually, *affect* is a verb (to "influence") and *effect* is a noun (a "result"):

Too many pork chops **affect** one's health.

Too many pork chops have an **effect** on one's health.

Less commonly, *affect* is used as a noun and *effect* as a verb. In the following examples, *affect* means an "emotional state or expression," and *effect* means "to bring about."

The boy's **affect** changed when he saw his father.

The legislators will attempt to **effect** new insurance laws next year.

agreement   The number and person of a subject and verb must match—singular subjects with singular verbs, plural subjects with plural verbs (see Chapter 34). Likewise, the number and gender of a pronoun and its antecedent must match (see Section 36b).

all ready/already   The adjective phrase *all ready* means "completely prepared"; the adverb *already* means "previously."

The tour group was **all ready** to leave, but the train had **already** departed.

all right/alright   *All right*, meaning "acceptable," is the correct spelling. *Alright* is nonstandard.

allude/elude   *Allude* means "refer to indirectly." *Elude* means "evade."

He **alluded** to the fact that he'd **eluded** capture.

allusion/illusion   An *allusion* is an indirect reference; an *illusion* is a false impression.

The painting contains an **allusion** to the *Mona Lisa*.

The painting creates the **illusion** of depth.

among/between   *Between* refers to precisely two people or things; *among* refers to three or more.

The choice is **between** two good alternatives.

The costs were shared **among** the three participating companies.

amount/number   Use *amount* with things that cannot be counted; use *number* with things that can be counted.

A large **amount** of money changed hands.

They gave him a **number** of quarters.

an   See **a/an.**

antecedent   The noun (or pronoun) that a pronoun refers to (see Section 36b). *Jeff* is the antecedent of *his* in the following sentence.

Jeff stopped running when **his** knee began hurting.

anybody/any body; anyone/any one   *Anybody* and *anyone* are indefinite pronouns and have the same meaning; *any body* and *any one* are usually followed by a noun that they modify.

Anybody can learn English, just as anyone can learn to bicycle.

Any body of government should be held accountable for its actions.

anymore/any more   *Anymore* means "now," while *any more* means "no more." Both are used in negative constructions.

No one goes downtown anymore.

The area doesn't have any more stores than it did in 1960.

anyway/anyways   *Anyway* is correct. *Anyways* is nonstandard.

appositive   A word or a phrase placed close to a noun that restates or modifies the noun (see Section 32d).

Dr. Lim, my physics professor, is the best.

articles   The words *a, an,* and *the* (see Sections 32b and 47d).

as/as if/as though/like   Use *as* instead of *like* before dependent clauses (which include a subject and verb). Use *like* before a noun or a pronoun.

Her voice sounds as if she had her head in a barrel.

She sings like her father.

assure/ensure/insure   *Assure* means "promise," *ensure* means "make certain," and *insure* means to "make certain in either a legal or financial sense."

Ralph assured the new client that his company would insure the building at full value, but the client wanted higher approval to ensure Ralph was correct.

auxiliary verb   Forms of *be, do,* and *have* combine with verbs to indicate tense and mood (see Section 32b). The modal verbs *can, could, may, might, must, shall, should, will,* and *would* are a subset of auxiliaries.

bad/badly   Use *bad* only as an adjective. *Badly* is the adverb.

He was a bad dancer.

Everyone agreed that he danced badly.

being as/being that   Both constructions are colloquial and awkward substitutes for *because.* Don't use them in formal writing.

beside/besides   *Beside* means "next to." *Besides* means "in addition to" or "except."

Does anyone, besides your mother, want to sit beside you when you're coughing like that?

between   See **among/between**.

bring/take   *Bring* describes movement from a more distant location to a nearer one. *Take* describes movement away.

Bring me the most recent issue. You can take this one.

can/may   In formal writing, *can* indicates ability or capacity, while *may* indicates permission.

If I may speak with you, we can probably solve this problem.

case   The form of a noun or pronoun that indicates its function. Nouns change case only to show possession: the dog, the dog's bowl (see Section 32b). See pronoun case (Section 36a).

censor/censure   To *censor* is to edit or ban on moral or political grounds. To *censure* is to reprimand publicly.

The Senate censored the details of the budget.

The Senate censured one of its members for misconduct.

cite/sight/site   To *cite* is to "mention specifically"; *sight* as a verb means to "observe" and as a noun refers to "vision"; *site* is most commonly used as a noun that means "location," but is also used as a verb to mean "situate."

He cited as evidence the magazine article he'd read yesterday.

Finally, he sighted the bald eagle. It was a remarkable sight.

The developers sited the houses on a heavily forested site.

clause   A group of words with a subject and a predicate. A main or independent clause can stand as a sentence. A subordinate or dependent clause must be attached to a main clause to form a sentence (see Section 32c).

collective noun   A noun that refers to a group or a plurality, such as *team, army,* or *committee* (see Section 34d).

comma splice   Two independent clauses joined incorrectly by a comma (see Section 33c).

common noun   A noun that names a general group, person, place, or thing (see Sections 32b and 47a). Common nouns are not capitalized unless they begin a sentence.

complement   A word or group of words that completes the predicate (see Section 32c). See also linking verb.

Juanita is my aunt.

complement/compliment   To *complement* something is to complete it or make it perfect; to *compliment* is to flatter.

The chef complemented their salad with a small bowl of soup.

The grateful diners complimented the chef.

complex sentence   A sentence that contains at least one subordinate clause attached to a main clause (see Section 32e).

compound sentence   A sentence that contains at least two main clauses (see Section 32e).

compound-complex sentence   A sentence that contains at least two main clauses and one subordinate clause (see Section 32e).

conjunction   See **coordinating conjunction**; **subordinating conjunction**.

conjunctive adverb   An adverb that often modifies entire clauses and sentences, such as *also, consequently, however, indeed, instead, moreover, nevertheless, otherwise, similarly,* and *therefore* (see Sections 32b and 37c).

continual/continuous   *Continual* refers to a repeated activity; *continuous* refers to an ongoing, unceasing activity.

Tennis elbow is usually caused by continual stress on the joint.

Archaeologists have debated whether Chaco Canyon was inhabited intermittently or continuously.

coordinate   A relationship of equal importance, in terms of either grammar or meaning (see Section 28c).

coordinating conjunction   A word that links two equivalent grammatical elements, such as *and, but, or, yet, nor, for,* and *so* (see Section 32b).

could of   Nonstandard. See **have/of**.

count noun   A noun that names things that can be counted, such as *block, cat,* and *toy* (see Section 47b).

dangling modifier   A modifier that is not clearly attached to what it modifies (see Section 37e).

data   The plural form of *datum*; it takes plural verb forms.

The data **are** overwhelming.

declarative   A sentence that makes a statement (see Section 32a).

Dover is the capital of Delaware.

dependent clause   See **subordinate clause**.

determiners   Words that initiate noun phrases, including possessive nouns (*Pedro's violin*); possessive pronouns (*my, your*); demonstrative pronouns (*this, that*); and indefinite pronouns (*all, both, many*).

differ from/differ with   To *differ from* means to "be unlike"; to *differ with* means to "disagree."

Rock music **differs from** jazz primarily in rhythm.

Miles Davis **differed with** critics who disliked his rock rhythms.

different from/different than   Use *different from* where possible.

Dark French roast is **different from** ordinary coffee.

direct object   A noun, pronoun, or noun clause that names who or what receives the action of a transitive verb (see Section 32c).

Antonio kicked **the ball**.

discreet/discrete   Both are adjectives. *Discreet* means "prudent" or "tactful"; *discrete* means "separate."

What's a **discreet** way of saying "Shut up"?

Over the noise, he could pick up several **discrete** conversations.

disinterested/uninterested   *Disinterested* is often misused to mean *uninterested*. Disinterested means "impartial." A judge can be interested in a case but disinterested in the outcome.

double negative   The incorrect use of two negatives to signal the same negative meaning.

We **don't** have **no** money.

due to the fact that   Avoid this wordy substitute for *because*.

each other/one another   Use *each other* for two; use *one another* for more than two.

effect   See **affect/effect**.

elicit/illicit   The verb *elicit* means to "draw out." The adjective *illicit* means "unlawful."

The teacher tried to **elicit** a discussion about **illicit** drugs.

emigrate from/immigrate to   *Emigrate* means to "leave one's country"; *immigrate* means to "settle in another country."

ensure   See **assure/ensure/insure**.

enthused   Nonstandard in academic and professional writing. Use *enthusiastic* instead.

etc.   Avoid this abbreviation for the Latin *et cetera* in formal writing. Either list all the items or use an English phrase such as *and so forth*.

every body/everybody; every one/everyone   *Everybody* and *everyone* are indefinite pronouns referring to all people under discussion. *Every one* and *every body* are adjective-noun combinations referring to all members of a group.

> Everyone loves a genuine smile.
>
> Every one of the files contained a virus.

except   See **accept/except**.

except for the fact that   Avoid this wordy substitute for *except that*.

expletive   The dummy subjects *it* and *there* used to fill a grammatical slot in a sentence.

> It is raining outside.
>
> There should be a law against it.

explicit/implicit   Both are adjectives; *explicit* means "stated outright," while *implicit* means just the opposite, "unstated."

> Even though we lacked an **explicit** contract, I thought we had an **implicit** understanding.

farther/further   *Farther* refers to physical distance; *further* refers to time or other abstract concepts.

> How much **farther** is your home?
>
> I don't want to talk about this any **further**.

fewer/less   Use *fewer* with what can be counted and *less* with what cannot be counted.

> There are **fewer** canoeists in the summer because there is **less** water in the river.

flunk   In formal writing, avoid this colloquial substitute for *fail*.

fragment   A group of words beginning with a capital letter and ending with a period that looks like a sentence but lacks a subject or a predicate or both (see Section 33a).

further   See **farther/further**.

gerund   An *-ing* form of a verb used as a noun, such as *running, skiing,* or *laughing* (see Section 32b).

good/well   *Good* is an adjective and is not interchangeable with the adverb *well*. The one exception is health. Both she feels *good* and she feels *well* are correct.

> The Yankees are a **good** baseball team. They play the game **well**.

hanged/hung   Use *hanged* to refer only to executions; *hung* is used for all other instances.

have/of   *Have*, not *of*, follows *should, could, would, may, must,* and *might.*

> I should have [not *of*] picked you up earlier.

he/she; s/he   Try to avoid language that appears to exclude either gender (unless this is intended, of course) and awkward compromises such as *he/she* or *s/he.* The best solution is to make pronouns plural (the gender-neutral *they*) wherever possible (see Section 36c).

helping verb   See auxiliary verb.

hopefully   This adverb is commonly used as a sentence modifier, but many readers object to it.

> I am hopeful [not *Hopefully*] we'll have a winning season.

illusion   See allusion/illusion.

immigrate   See emigrate from/immigrate to.

imperative   A sentence that expresses a command (see Section 32a). Usually the subject is implied rather than stated.

> Go away now.

implicit   See explicit/implicit.

imply/infer   *Imply* means to "suggest"; *infer* means to "draw a conclusion."

> The ad implied that the candidate was dishonest; I inferred that the campaign would be one of name calling.

in regards to   Avoid this wordy substitute for *regarding.*

incredible/incredulous   *Incredible* means "unbelievable"; *incredulous* means "not believing."

> Their story about finding a stack of money in a discarded suitcase seemed incredible; I was incredulous.

independent clause   See main clause.

indirect object   A noun, pronoun, or noun clause that names who or what is affected by the action of a transitive verb (see Section 32c).

> Antonio kicked the ball to Mario.

infinitive   The word *to* plus the base verb form: *to believe, to feel, to act.* See also split infinitive.

infinitive phrase   A phrase that uses the infinitive form of a verb (see Section 32d).

> To get some sleep is my goal for the weekend.

interjection   A word expressing feeling that is grammatically unconnected to a sentence, such as *cool, wow, ouch,* or *yikes.*

interrogative   A sentence that asks a question (see Section 32a).

> Where do you want to go?

intransitive verb   A verb that does not take an object, such as *sleep, appear,* or *laugh* (see Sections 32c and 35c).

irregardless   Nonstandard for *regardless.*

irregular verb   A verb that does not use either *-d* or *-ed* to form the past tense and past participle (see Section 35b).

it is my opinion that   Avoid this wordy substitute for *I believe that.*

its/it's   *Its* is the possessive of *it* and does not take an apostrophe; *it's* is the contraction for *it is.*

> *Its* tail is missing. *It's* an unusual animal.

-ize/-wise   The suffix *-ize* changes a noun or adjective into a verb (*harmony, harmonize*). The suffix *-wise* changes a noun or adjective into an adverb (*clock, clockwise*). Some writers are tempted to use these suffixes to convert almost any word into an adverb or verb form. Unless the word appears in a dictionary, don't use it.

kind of/sort of/type of   Avoid using these colloquial expressions if you mean *somewhat* or *rather. It's kind of hot* is nonstandard. Each is permissible, however, when it refers to a classification of an object. Be sure that it agrees in number with the object it is modifying.

> This *type of* engine is very fuel-efficient.
>
> These *kinds of* recordings are rare.

lay/lie   *Lay* means "place" or "put" and generally takes a direct object (see Section 35c). Its main forms are *lay, laid, laid. Lie* means "recline" or "be positioned" and does not take an object. Its main forms are *lie, lay, lain.*

> He *lays* the papers down. He *laid* the papers down.
>
> He *lies* down on the sofa. He *lay* down on the sofa.

less   See **fewer.**

lie   See **lay/lie.**

linking verb   A verb that connects the subject to the complement, such as *appear, be, feel, look, seem,* or *taste* (see Section 32c).

lots/lots of   Nonstandard in formal writing; use *many* or *much* instead.

main clause   A group of words with a subject and a predicate that can stand alone as a sentence (see Section 32c). Also called an *independent clause*.

mankind   This term offends some readers and is outdated. Use *humans, humanity,* or *people* instead.

may/can   See **can/may**.

may be/maybe   *May be* is a verb phrase; *maybe* is an adverb.

> It **may be** time to go.
>
> **Maybe** it's time to go.

media   This is the plural form of the noun *medium* and requires a plural verb.

> The **media** in this city are biased.

might of   See **have/of**.

modal   A kind of auxiliary verb that indicates ability, permission, intention, obligation, or probability, such as *can, could, may, might, must, shall, should, will,* or *would* (see Section 32b).

modifier   A general term for adjectives, adverbs, phrases, and clauses that describe other words (see Chapter 37).

must of   See **have/of**.

noncount noun   A noun that names things that cannot be counted, such as *air, energy,* or *water* (see Section 47b).

nonrestrictive modifier   A modifier that is not essential to the meaning of the word, phrase, or clause it modifies and should be set off by commas or other punctuation (see Section 38c).

noun   The name of a person, place, thing, concept, or action (see Section 32a). See also **common noun** and **proper noun** (see Section 47a).

noun clause   A subordinate clause that functions as a noun (see Section 32c).

> **That the city fails to pick up the garbage** is ridiculous.

number   See **amount/number**.

object   Receiver of the action within the clause or phrase (see Sections 32c and 32d).

OK, O.K., okay   Informal; avoid using in academic and professional writing. Each spelling is accepted in informal usage.

owing to the fact that   Avoid this wordy, colloquial substitute for *because*.

parallelism   The principle of putting similar elements or ideas in similar grammatical form (see Sections 28c, 28d, and 28e).

participle   A form of a verb that uses *-ing* in the present (*laughing, playing*) and usually *-ed* or *-en* in the past (*laughed, played*). See Section 35a. Participles are either part of the verb phrase (*She had played the game before*) or used as adverbs and adjectives (*the laughing girl*).

participial phrase   A phrase formed either by a present participle (for example, *racing*) or by a past participle (for example, *taken*). (See Section 32d.)

parts of speech   The eight classes of words according to their grammatical function: nouns, pronouns, verbs, adjectives, adverbs, prepositions, conjunctions, and interjections (see Section 32b).

passive   A clause with a transitive verb in which the subject is being acted upon (see Section 26a). See also **active**.

people/persons   *People* refers to a general group; *persons* refers to a collection of individuals. Use *people* over *persons* except when you're emphasizing the idea of separate persons within the group.

   "**People** have the power" was the theme of the rally.

   Occupancy by more than 135 **persons** is illegal.

per   Try to use the English equivalent of this Latin word except in technical writing or familiar usages like *miles per gallon*.

   The job paid $20 **an** hour.

   As you requested [not *per your request*], I'll drive up immediately.

phenomena   This is the plural form of *phenomenon* ("observable fact" or "unusual event") and takes plural verbs.

   The astronomical **phenomena** were breathtaking.

phrase   A group of words that does not contain both a subject and predicate.

plenty   In academic and professional writing, avoid this colloquial substitute for *very*.

plus   Do not use *plus* to join clauses or sentences. Use *and, also, moreover, furthermore*, or another conjunctive adverb instead.

   It rained heavily, **and it was also** [not *plus it was*] bitterly cold.

precede/proceed   Both are verbs but they have different meanings: *precede* means "come before," and *proceed* means "go ahead" or "continue."

   In the United States, the national anthem **precedes** every major league baseball game.

   We **proceeded** to the train station.

predicate The part of the clause that expresses the action or tells something about the subject. The predicate includes the verb and all its complements, objects, and modifiers (see Section 32a).

prejudice/prejudiced *Prejudice* is a noun; *prejudiced* is an adjective.

The jury was **prejudiced** against the defendant.

She knew about the town's history of racial **prejudice**.

preposition A class of words that indicate relationships and qualities (see Section 32b, 50a).

prepositional phrase A phrase formed by a preposition and its object, including the modifiers of its object (see Section 32d).

pronoun A word that stands for other nouns or pronouns. Pronouns have several subclasses, including personal pronouns, possessive pronouns, demonstrative pronouns, indefinite pronouns, relative pronouns, interrogative pronouns, reflexive pronouns, and reciprocal pronouns (see Section 32b and Chapter 36).

pronoun case Pronouns that function as the subjects of sentences are in the **subjective** case (*I, you, he, she, it, we, they*). Pronouns that function as direct or indirect objects are in the **objective** case (*me, you, him, her, it, us, them*). Pronouns that indicate ownership are in the **possessive** case (*my, your, his, her, its, our, their*) (see Section 36a).

proper noun A noun that names a particular person, place, thing, or group (see Sections 32b and 47a). Proper nouns are capitalized.

question as to whether/question of whether Avoid these wordy substitutes for *whether*.

raise/rise The verb *raise* means "lift up" and takes a direct object. Its main forms are *raise, raised, raised*. The verb *rise* means "get up" and does not take a direct object. Its main forms are *rise, rose, risen*.

The workers carefully **raised** the piano onto the truck.

The piano slowly **rose** off the ground.

real/really Avoid using *real* as if it were an adverb. *Really* is an adverb; *real* is an adjective.

The singer was **really** good.

What we thought was an illusion turned out to be **real**.

reason is because Omit either *reason is* or *because* when explaining causality.

The **reason** he ran **is that** he thought he was late.

He ran **because** he thought he was late.

reason why   Avoid using this redundant combination.

The reason he's so often late is that he never wears a watch.

relative pronoun   A pronoun that initiates clauses, such as *that, which, what, who, whom,* or *whose* (see Section 32b).

restrictive modifier   A modifier that is essential to the meaning of the word, phrase, or clause it modifies (see Section 38c). Restrictive modifiers are usually not set off by punctuation.

rise/raise   See **raise/rise**.

run-on sentence   Two main clauses fused together without punctuation or a conjunction, appearing as one sentence (see Section 33b).

sentence   A grammatically independent group of words that contains at least one main clause (see Section 32a).

sentence fragment   See **fragment**.

set/sit   *Set* means "put" and takes a direct object (see Section 35c); its main forms are *set, set, set. Sit* means "be seated" and does not take a direct object; its main forms are *sit, sat, sat. Sit* should not be used as a synonym for *set.*

Set the bowl on the table.

Please sit down.

shall/will   *Shall* is used most often in first person questions, while *will* is a future tense helping verb for all persons. British English consistently uses *shall* with first person: *I shall, we shall.*

Shall I bring you some water?

Will they want drinks, too?

should of   See **have/of**.

sit/set   See **set/sit**.

some time/sometime/sometimes   *Some time* means "a span of time," *sometime* means "at some unspecified time," and *sometimes* means "occasionally."

Give me some time to get ready.

Let's meet again sometime soon.

Sometimes, the best-laid plans go wrong.

somebody/some body; someone/some one   *Somebody* and *someone* are indefinite pronouns and have the same meaning. In *some body, body* is a noun modified by *some,* and in *some one, one* is a pronoun or adjective modified by *some.*

Somebody should close that window.

"Some body was found on the beach today," the homicide detective said.

Someone should answer the phone.

It would be best if some one person could represent the group.

sort of See **kind of/sort of/type of.**

split infinitive An infinitive with a word or words between *to* and the base verb form, such as *to boldly go, to better appreciate* (see Section 37d).

stationary/stationery *Stationary* means "motionless"; *stationery* means "writing paper."

subject A noun, pronoun, or noun phrase that identifies what the clause is about and connects with the predicate (see Sections 32a and 32c).

subject–verb agreement See **agreement.**

subordinate A relationship of unequal importance, in terms of either grammar or meaning (see Section 28a).

subordinate clause A clause that cannot stand alone but must be attached to a main clause (see Section 32c). Also called a *dependent clause.*

subordinating conjunction A word that introduces a subordinate clause. Common subordinating conjunctions are *after, although, as, because, before, if, since, that, unless, until, when, where,* and *while* (see Section 32b).

such Avoid using *such* as a synonym for *very.* It should always be followed by *that* and a clause that contains a result.

It was a very [not *such a*] hot August.

sure A colloquial term used as an adverb to mean "certainly." Avoid using it this way in formal writing.

You were certainly [not *sure were*] correct when you said August would be hot.

sure and/sure to; try and/try to *Sure to* and *try to* are correct; do not use *and* after *sure* or *try.*

Be sure to [not *sure and*] take out the trash this morning.

Try to [not *try and*] finish first.

take See **bring/take.**

that/which *That* introduces a restrictive or essential clause. Restrictive clauses describe an object that must be that particular object and no other. Though some writers occasionally use *which* with restrictive clauses, it is most often used to introduce nonrestrictive clauses. These are clauses that contain additional nonessential information about the object.

Let's listen to the CD **that** Clarence bought.

Clarence's favorite music, **which** usually puts me to sleep, is too mellow for me.

transition   A word or phrase that notes movement from one unit of writing to another.

transitive verb   A verb that takes a direct object (see Sections 32c and 35c).

verb   A word that expresses action or characterizes the subject in some way. Verbs can show tense and mood (see Section 32b and Chapter 35).

verbal   A form of a verb used as an adjective, adverb, or noun (see Section 32b). See also **gerund, infinitive, participle**.

well/good   See **good/well**.

which/that   See **that/which**.

who/whom   *Who* and *whom* follow the same rules as other pronouns: *Who* is the subject pronoun; *whom* is the object pronoun (see Section 36a).

Sharon's father, **who** served in the Korean War, died last year.

Sharon's father, **whom** several of my father's friends knew, died last year.

will/shall   See **shall/will**.

-wise/-ize   See **-ize/-wise**.

would of   See **have/of**.

you   Avoid indefinite uses of *you*. It should only be used to mean "you, the reader."

The [not *your*] average life span in the United States has increased consistently over the past 100 years.

your/you're   The two are not interchangeable. *Your* is the possessive form of "you"; *you're* is the contraction of "you are."

Your car can be picked up after 5 p.m.

You're going to need money to live in Manhattan.

Glossary of Computer Terms

absolute link   Full URL address.

AltaVista   Internet portal with powerful search engine at **http://www.altavista.digital.com**.

analog   General term in electronics for signals that vary continuously across a range. Telephones, cassette recorders, radio, and television have all relied on analog signals, which are now being replaced by digital signals.

ASCII   Acronym for American Standard Code for Information Interchange. The plain text format that all computers can read.

bandwidth   The speed at which data can be transmitted, usually listed in bits per second (bps). The bigger the pipe, the faster the flow. Standard telephone modems run at 28,800 bps (28.8 kbps) or 56 kbps (although phone lines often limit the speed). Cable modems offer rates up to 10 mbps (10,000,000 bps).

baud rate   The rate at which a modem's signal changes per second in transmitting data.

bit   The smallest unit of digital data, expressed as a binary value, either 1 or 0.

bookmarks   Netscape file that stores URLs so you can easily return to pages you have looked at on the Web. Called *favorites* on Internet Explorer.

browser   The computer program that finds and displays Web sites. Netscape and Internet Explorer are by far the most popular browsers.

browser-safe colors   See **Web-safe colors**.

cable modem   High-speed modem that uses cable TV lines for Internet connections.

cache   Temporary storage of Web files that allows your browser to reload pages quickly.

CD-ROM   Stands for compact disk-read only memory. The information on the disk can be read or copied but cannot be edited.

compression   Method of reducing the amount of data necessary for recreating a file, thus allowing the file to load faster.

cookie   Small file placed on your computer by the Web server so that it recognizes you the next time you access the site from the same browser.

dial-up modem   Older, slower modems that use phone lines to connect with the Internet.

digital   Binary coding of data into bits, either 1 or 0.

DSL   Stands for digital subscriber line. High-speed connection to the Web via telephone lines.

directory   See **Web directory**.

dpi   Stands for dots per inch. Measurement in print graphics for the resolution of an image.

Electronic media document   A document created by computer software that can be used in a variety of output formats, including print and online.

favorites   Internet Explorer file that stores URLs. Called *bookmarks* on Netscape.

FireWire   Fast connection from a computer to external devices such as a scanner.

fonts   Typeface styles such as bold and italic. A complete set of type of one size and face.

frames   Frames divide a Web page into multiple windows, with each window acting as a nested Web page.

ftp   Stands for file transfer protocol. Programs that allow you to access a computer at remote locations and move files between that computer and your computer.

GIF   Stands for graphic interchange format. Preferred Web format for images with sharp lines, text, and small images.

Google   Powerful search engine at **www.google.com**.

home page   The page you see when you open your browser; or the opening or main page on a Web site.

HTML   Acronym for HyperText Markup Language, the display language used for creating Web pages.

hypertext   Document that allows you to connect to other pages or documents by clicking on links. The Web can be thought of as one huge hypertext.

image editors   Programs that allow you to create and manipulate images.

image map   An image that has been divided into regions and connected to actions, which are usually links. When you click on a particular part of the image, you jump to another Web page.

internal modem   A modem that is built into a personal computer.

ISP   Stands for Internet service provider, a company such as AOL that offers Internet service.

JPEG   Acronym for Joint Photographic Experts Group. Preferred Web format for photographs.

kpbs   Stands for kilobits (1,000 bits) per second. Most dial-up telephone modems run at 28.8 kbps or 56 kbps.

link   Words or images that connect to another Web page or file that can be displayed or downloaded.

mbps   Stands for megabits (1,000,000 bits) per second. Cable modems run up to 10 mbps.

navigation bar   A set of links on a Web page displayed as icons, text, or both, most often at the top of a page.

newsgroups   Usenet discussion groups that allow users to post messages that all users can read.

operating system   The system software, such as Windows, Mac OS, or UNIX, that controls a computer.

PDF   Acronym for portable document format, created by Adobe Systems for use on Adobe's Acrobat Reader.

pixel   A dot on a picture that is the basic unit of images. Images are sized in pixels according to height and width.

platform   Computer hardware and operating system combination such as Wintel, an Intel-based PC running Windows.

plug-in   Helper applications, such as QuickTime movies, that give your browser additional capabilities.

portal   Web site designed to be a starting point for Web users, complete with search tools, news, and other information.

RAM   Acronym for random access memory. The active area of a computer's memory, used for running programs.

relative link   Partial URL for a file on the same Web site.

scanner   Image-capturing device that reproduces an image in digital format.

search engine   A program that searches for information in electronic formats. Web search engines such as Google and AltaVista search through indexes of the entire Web.

server   Host computer for Web files.

source   The HTML file that creates a Web page.

tags   HTML commands enclosed in angle brackets, such as **<P>**.

TCP/IP   Stands for transfer control protocol/Internet protocols. The protocols that allow computers to communicate on the Internet.

UNIX   Operating system used by many Web servers.

URL   Stands for universal resource locator. Addresses on the Web.

USB   Stands for universal serial bus. A newer generation of connections from Mac and Windows to external devices such as digital cameras.

Web directory   Subject guide to Web pages grouped by topic and subtopic.

Web editors   Programs that allow you to compose Web pages.

Web translators   Programs such as Microsoft Word and Excel that include a **Save as HTML** command.

Web-safe colors   Palette of 216 colors that will appear the same on different platforms and most browsers. Also called *browser-safe colors* and *browser-safe palette*.

Windows operating system   System software for IBM/Intel-based computers.

World Wide Web Consortium (W3C)   A group of representatives from universities, Web designers, and software companies who oversee the development of standards and technologies for the Web.

WYSIWYG   Stands for *What you see is what you get*. What you print or see on the Web will look like what's displayed on your monitor.

Yahoo   Popular Web directory at **http://www.yahoo.com**.

zip   Compression format used for transferring and storing files.

zip disk   Removable disk for storing and exchanging files.

Index

838   Index

Credits

AltaVista Subject Browse Web Page. Copyright © AltaVista Company. Reprinted by permission.

Amnesty International Web page on Tunisia, copyright © Amnesty International Publications, http://www.amnesty.org, 1 Easton Street, London WC1X 0DW, United Kingdom. Reprinted by permission of Amnesty International Publications.

Screen shot from the Art Institute of Chicago Web site. Copyright © The Art institute of Chicago. Reprinted by permission.

Baughman, Fred A., Jr. Screen shot entitled "The Fraud of Child Psychiatry, ADD/ ADHD, Attention Deficit Disorder and Ritalin" from outlooki.com, Copyright © Fred. A. Baughman, Jr., M.D., Inc. Reprinted by permission of © Fred A. Baughman, Jr., M.D., Inc.

Bernhardt, Grace. "Secondhand Smoke: the Risk and the Controversy" by Grace Bernhardt. Copyright © by Grace Bernhardt. Reprinted by permission of the author.

Braitman, Keli. "Body Objectification: Relationship with Fashion Magazines and Weight Satisfaction" by Michael Moshenrose and Keli Braitman. Copyright © by Keli Braitman. Reprinted by permission of Keli Braitman.

Excerpt from "Literary Illusion" by Chris Brice from the February 9, 2002 issue of *The Advertiser* © 2002 by *The Advertiser*, reprinted by permission of the publisher.

Citron, Michelle. Excerpt from *Home Movies and Other Necessary Fictions*.

Excerpt from Forest Watch brochure. Copyright © Forest Watch, 10 Langdon Street, Suite 1, Montpelier, Vermont 05602. Reprinted by permission.

Screen shot from EXPANDED ACADEMIC ASAP, by Gale Group, © 2002 Gale Group. Reprinted by permission of The Gale Group.

Excerpts from "Virtual Love" by Tad Friend from the November 26, 2001 edition of *The New Yorker*.

Lupfer, Eric. "Thru-Hiking" by Eric Lupfer. Copyright © Eric Lupfer. Reprinted by permission of the author.

Screen shots from maganda.org. Copyright © by Christine Castro. Reprinted by permission of Christine Castro.

Screen shots from www.metmuseum.org. Copyright © 2000–2002 by The Metropolitan Museum of Art. All rights reserved. Reprinted by permission of The Metropolitan Museum.

Quammen, David. Excerpt from *The Song of the Dodo: Island Biogeography in an Age of Extinctions* (New York: Scribner, 1996).

Screen shot of Biochemistry Web page from The University of Illinois, Urbana-Champaign. Copyright © by The University of Illinois, Urbana-Champaign. Reprinted by permission.

Yahoo! Directory page on Attention Deficit Disorder. Reproduced with permission of Yahoo! Inc. © 2002 by

Yahoo! Inc. YAHOO! And the YA-HOO! Logo are trademarks of Yahoo! Inc.

Yahoo! Issue and Causes Index. Reproduced with permission of Yahoo! Inc. © 2002 by Yahoo! Inc. YAHOO! And the YAHOO! Logo are trademarks of Yahoo! Inc.

Yahoo! Subject browse page on Health. Reproduced with permission of Yahoo! Inc. © 2002 by Yahoo! Inc. YAHOO! And the YAHOO! Logo are trademarks of Yahoo! Inc.

Yahoo! Web page subject directory for "Cookies." Reproduced with permission of Yahoo! Inc. © 2002 by Yahoo! Inc. YAHOO! And the YAHOO! Logo are trademarks of Yahoo! Inc.

Photographs
pp. 4–5: Julia Allen
p. 23 bottom: Denise Schmandt-Besserat
p. 112: Dorothea Lange, Library of Congress
p. 115: Alexander Gardner, Library of Congress
p. 125: Frank Dodd
pp. 129–131: Sylvia Herrera
p. 143: John Hillers, Smithsonian Institution
p. 145: Engraving from *Exploration of the Colorado River of the West and Its Tributaries*, 1875.
Part 4 opener: © Rob Lewine/CORBIS;
Part 5 opener: Courtesy "Ain't It Cool."
Chapter 7 icon: © Bettmann/CORBIS.
All other photographs and line art are from the author.